ECONOMIC INQUIRIES AND STUDIES

The Development of Industrial Society Series

Robert Giffen

ECONOMIC INQUIRIES AND STUDIES

Volume 2

IRISH UNIVERSITY PRESS
Shannon Ireland

First edition London 1904

This I U P reprint is a photolithographic facsimile of the first edition and is unabridged, retaining the original printer's imprint.

ISBN 0 7165 1758 2 Two volumes
ISBN 0 7165 1759 0 Volume 1
ISBN 0 7165 1760 4 Volume 2

T M MacGlinchey Publisher

Irish University Press Shannon Ireland

PRINTED IN THE REPUBLIC OF IRELAND BY
ROBERT HOGG PRINTER TO IRISH UNIVERSITY PRESS

ECONOMIC INQUIRIES AND STUDIES

ECONOMIC INQUIRIES

AND

STUDIES

BY

SIR ROBERT GIFFEN, K.C.B.

VOL. II

LONDON

GEORGE BELL AND SONS

1904

CHISWICK PRESS: CHARLES WHITTINGHAM AND CO.
TOOKS COURT, CHANCERY LANE, LONDON.

CONTENTS

ECONOMIC INQUIRIES AND STUDIES

XIII.

THE UTILITY OF COMMON STATISTICS.[1]

IN commencing our labours for another session, we are painfully reminded that during the past twelve months the Society has sustained two heavy losses, in the death of Mr. Newmarch and Professor Jevons. At a meeting like the present, some tribute is due to the memory of these distinguished members. To some extent a record of Mr. Newmarch's death and services has already been preserved in our proceedings, but something, I feel, ought also to be said at this inaugural meeting, considering his many and diversified statistical labours, and the length of the period during which he was identified with us, first as Secretary and Editor of the "Journal," and afterwards as President. The death of Professor Jevons—all the more to be regretted as a lamentable accident—has occurred since the last meeting of last session, and this is the first opportunity we have had of paying a tribute to his memory.

With regard to Mr. Newmarch, it will be unnecessary to go over the record of his life in detail, or to enumerate his various works; of these a very full account will be found in the March number of the "Journal" of this year. What I should like to do now is to put on record the special consideration in

[1] Inaugural Address as President of the Statistical Society. Delivered on Tuesday, 21st November, 1882.

which he was held here for his knowledge of economic statistics, especially trade and banking statistics, and his skill in using them. He was remarkable not merely as a statistician, but as a man of business and as an economist, and his special *forte* as a statistician was to throw light on problems connected with the theory of business—especially banking—and on the applications of political economy to the real world by means of statistics. In labours of this kind he was among the first in the field. Mr. Tooke, whom he recognized as a master, had preceded him as a pioneer, showing the way to reason out disputed points in the theory of currency and banking by statistical illustrations from actual business experience: his demonstrations on such points as the dependence of prices on credit, and the fact of a rise of prices preceding and not succeeding the expansion of a paper currency, being still among the best examples of the right use of statistics in economic discussions. But Mr. Newmarch followed in the steps of his great master with a command of facts, and a power of analyzing and grouping figures, which in the same field were at that time without example. His most signal achievement was the preparation of the last two volumes of the "History of Prices," a book well known here, though it has been long out of print. The information and comments in those two volumes on the great economic changes about the middle of the present century, including the introduction of free trade, the Bank Charter Act, the Irish famine, the French revolution of 1848-51, the gold discoveries in Russia, California, and Australia, and finally the Crimean war, make them still a most valuable record; while the discussion on many points of banking practice and economic theory, especially on all points relating to the use and abuse of credit, and the periodicity of movements in trade, remains to this day the fullest exposition on these topics to which the student can be referred. There are better books perhaps on single points, such as Mr. Bagehot's "Lombard Street," in which the constituent elements of the money market are described, and the theory of a bank reserve is set forth and illustrated; but the number and variety of topics in Mr. Newmarch's book, and the way in which the various economic movements of the time are grasped and set in one picture, make it of unique value. Whether it is the effect of the gold discoveries in bringing new resources into the money market, and giving a vast impetus to trade, or the effect of a great movement of migration on the trade of old and new countries alike, or the financial consequences of a great war, Mr. Newmarch is at home in the discussion. Apart also from the light it throws on the special questions treated, and as regards which it may be of course superseded by fuller and later statistics, and by wholly new circumstances, the book must long remain of value, I believe, as a specimen of method and of what can be done by the use of statistics. Indirectly, I believe, it has been the beginning of much financial writing, as it is really the parent of a book like M. Neumann-Spallart's "Annual Review of the World's Trade," on the one hand, and of much of that writing on "trade and finance" and those columns of "City notes" which we now see in many newspapers. Mr. Newmarch, in fact, popularized the idea that the daily changes in the movement of business can be generalized and referred to the working of the laws of human nature, and in a thousand ways the idea has been worked out and made useful to the world. That in the end the course of business will be better understood generally, with useful results both to business men and to society, there can be little doubt.

Besides thus recognizing Mr. Newmarch's special place as a statistician, we are bound to say a few words here on his special services to the Society. Among these I would place in the first rank his labours as editor of the "Journal." Looking over the back numbers, it may be perceived that from the time he took the "Journal" in hand there was not only a considerable improvement in the miscellaneous information, which was more particularly in his own care, but an improvement as well in the general character of the papers read at our meetings. One explanation of this improvement must of course have been the steady growth of the Society in numbers and resources, and in the standard of statistical excellence; but the improvement was not altogether a spontaneous growth from below, it was encouraged from above in a variety of ways. I can speak from personal knowledge of Mr. Newmarch's exertions to make the best use of his materials, and to diffuse a genuine love and appreciation of the study he favoured. It was extremely characteristic of him that to the last he was strongly interested in young men. Wherever he could see any talent or liking for economics and statistics in a younger generation than his own, he was the first to applaud. I am proud to acknowledge for myself that I owe the beginning of my close connection with the business of the Society to Mr. Newmarch's kindness, and I have had reason to observe in many other cases his warm interest in youth, and the pains he took to encourage and bring others forward. His services, however, were manifold, and it is only fitting that, as he identified himself so closely with us, we should do honour to his name. The success of the Newmarch Memorial Fund must be to all of us a matter for satisfaction. The memory of the great services he rendered will be perpetuated in an appropriate manner.

In the death of Professor Jevons the Society has also sustained a very great loss. Partly because he was so much junior to Mr. Newmarch, and had probably many years of life left in which to render us distinguished service, and partly because of the engrossing nature of his literary work, which made formal business distasteful to him, Mr. Jevons never took the prominent part in the daily work of the Society for which his eminent gifts and labours as a statistician so well qualified him. He was for some years, however, one of our secretaries, a regular attendant of our meetings, and a frequent contributor to the "Journal." In the proper work of a statistician, moreover, there are few men who have left a better name on our records. I need only refer specially to three of his principal works. Twenty years ago, when he was still comparatively a young man, his book on the depreciation of gold arising from the gold discoveries justly attracted no small attention, both from the completeness of the method employed, and the striking character of the conclusion which he came to—that while there had been depreciation to a moderate extent, there had been no such depreciation as many great economists had anticipated. A few years afterwards his book on the "Coal Supply" drew attention to a problem which is inevitably raised by the limited character of the English coal field, and the rapidly increasing demands upon it. This book had a wide success of notoriety, and it was unfortunate, perhaps, that it was only too popular, the public, which seldom makes nice distinctions, running away with the notion that Mr. Jevons predicted the actual speedy exhaustion of the English coal supply. This, of course, was nonsense. His real conclusion, however, viz., that one of the present conditions of English prosperity was rapidly altering for the worse, was undeniable, and was amply justified by the experience of the coal famine of 1873. Few more interesting books have, perhaps, been written; and there are few better examples of the kind of statistical works which ought now, with the increasing breadth of statistical data, to be more largely written, viz., those dealing with the characteristic social and economic problems of the age. It is to such works statesmen and politicians must look for a right comprehension of their task. Shortly afterwards, in 1868, Mr. Jevons read a paper on the state of our gold coinage, in which the same thoroughness and completeness exhibited in all his statistical works was again conspicuous, and which has since been the model of more than one similar inquiry. Besides these, Mr. Jevons wrote many smaller works, which were all characterized by great completeness of method; but these three larger works are quite sufficient to found his reputation. They all show inventiveness and resource, and a careful attention to every point which can qualify the figures so that the real facts, and not the apparent ones, are brought out. An index number, such as he used in the first paper of all on the gold question, has proved an instrument of great value since in all inquiries on prices; and for this institution of an "index number" we may consider ourselves indebted to Mr. Jevons.[1] In the later years of his life Mr. Jevons became even better known as an economist and a writer on logic than as a statistician, the place he took being a high one; and without discussing his work in that capacity, we must recognize how his qualifications for other departments of literature were no disqualification, but the reverse, for the study and practice of statistics. His statistics would not have been as good as they were if he had not had wider interests, and a remarkable faculty for clear scientific exposition in other branches of science.

Such are the two men we have lost within the short period of twelve months. The loss is a heavy one; but few would have been more ready to recognize than those we have lost that the work remains, whatever becomes of the individual. With Mr. Newmarch this feeling, as I have already hinted, was always present. It was always of good work in statistics and not of his own good work he was thinking. If younger men could be induced to come into the field, he was but too well pleased to give up the task to them, so long as the work was done. His example and spirit will be handed

[1] An index number was used by Mr. J. B. Smith as long ago as 1840 in giving evidence on the Bank Acts. Practically, Mr. Jevons was the first to systematize the use of the method. [See my evidence given to the Gold and Silver Commission for after-acquired information on this point.]

down, I trust, through many generations of labourers at these meetings. In another point also the example and spirit of both Mr. Newmarch and Mr. Jevons, it may be hoped, will be imitated. I have already glanced at the point, but it may be specially emphasized. It is that they were neither of them specialists, but they were both otherwise distinguished—Mr. Newmarch as a man of business and an economist; and Mr. Jevons, as a *littérateur*, a man of science, and a logician. It will be an unfortunate day for us if men of business like Mr. Newmarch, and men of general scientific and literary eminence like Mr. Jevons, do not take an interest in our pursuits. Statistics are related to so many different sciences, and the knowledge of them is so essential to the politician and historian, that there is no study which is more certainly failing to obtain its proper place, if it is not known to and made use of by those who are identified with other pursuits and by men of general culture.

I am sure you will not think I have taken up too much of your time in doing honour to the friends whom we have lost. I pass on with some diffidence to deal with some topic of general interest, such as you have been accustomed to have dealt with in their introductory addresses by my predecessors. In recent years the field has been very fully occupied. You have had such papers, for instance, as that of Mr. Lefevre, on the use and abuse of statistics, covering a great deal of the ground for discussion on the theory of statistics. You have had other papers by experts in particular branches of statistics, such as the addresses by my distinguished immediate predecessor,[1] on the agricultural depression of the country and the probable future of the agricultural industry. The field of new observation has thus been greatly reduced. It has occurred to me, however, that without attempting a new discussion on the theory of statistics, or giving an address on some

[1] Sir James Caird.

particular topic of urgent interest, I may perhaps be able to say something useful, by pointing out some of the uses to society of the more common figures of statistics, especially those figures which assist in modifying or directing the political thought of the time, or in presenting problems for politicians and philosophers to consider, even if they do not much assist in the solution. The greater successes of statistics, and their main uses, though not so well known as they should be, are nevertheless fairly understood. The construction of life insurance tables, for instance; the means of comparing rates of mortality in different places, and between the same places at different times; the constant utility of statistics in political discussion, and their equal utility in daily business—are all matters tolerably well known and admitted. But what seems not to be so well understood is our indebtedness to the common figures of statistics for many wide and far-reaching political ideas, which influence and guide political thought and action and philosophic speculation insensibly. With the systematic collection of statistics continued for many years, there has come to be published a whole library of statistical annuals—whether they are official statistical abstracts or *annuaires*, such as many countries now publish, or unofficial publications like the "Annuaire d'Economie politique," or the "Statesman's Year Book," or M. Neumann-Spallart's "Annual Review of the World's Industry." These books, it seems to me, besides having many practical uses, supply a necessity of political thought at the present time, and are constantly and insensibly guiding political and philosophical speculation. What I propose to discuss to-night, then, are some of the more common figures which lie on the surface of the most accessible books. As with other good and common things, we have become so used to such books that we hardly know what we should miss if they were blotted out,—if public men and writers were without them, as in fact they were without them until about half a century ago. If we attempt to realize what we should do without such books, we shall not fail to see that statistics have many unsuspected uses, and not least are they useful for the knowledge they insensibly diffuse throughout the world.

I shall deal more especially with the most common figures of all, viz., those of population. The utility of the most general notion which we derive from statistics of the distribution of the earth's surface among different races and nations is palpable. We can see at once that a small corner like Europe is closely peopled by the European family of nations, whilst the northern peoples of that family also possess a large new field of territory in North America, Australia, and Northern Asia, and the more southern peoples a large new field of territory in Central and South America. The European family is thus *de facto* in possession of a large tract of the earth's surface for its own habitation, perhaps a half or more of the area available for producing the food of civilized races. Further consideration would show what races in particular, among the nations of Europe, have this inheritance; but the point is, the predominance of the European race in mere extent of territory, coupled with the peculiarity that the bulk of this population is still living on a comparatively narrow tract in Europe. The rest of the world—China, India and Africa—is possessed by races of greatly differing type, on whose territory Europeans do not press as colonists, though they may settle in small numbers as governors, or traders, or both. Granting, on the average, a difference in point of material strength per unit of population between these European and all other races, it is easy to understand at once the idea that the future of civilization belongs to the European group, and that the problem of how the other races are to live in harmony with the European group without being jostled, and in what way they are to be affected by the European civilization, is one of the most curious presented for the solution of modern societies. If the European numbers were less, the problem might well be whether European civilization, in spite of its assumed superiority in type, could maintain itself. The numbers and rate of increase being what they are, it is easy to see that the main problem resulting from the relations of the European and non-European races cannot be whether the European civilization will be able to maintain itself by force, but how it will be affected by its varying relations to the other races.

Confining ourselves again to the European group, and first of all to the nations within European limits, another leading fact in international politics is immediately suggested by the statement of the numbers of the people. This is the existence of five leading powers —Russia, Germany, Austria, France, and the United Kingdom—each greatly stronger than any of the other powers not among the five, except two; each big enough to "take care of itself," though there are, of course, differences of strength between them; and besides these, the two others excepted, viz., Italy and Spain, which come short of a first place, but by a less degree than the minor States. All these relations of the great powers are based largely on the mere enumeration of the peoples. Three out of the five, viz., France, Austria-Hungary, and the United Kingdom, have each about the same population, in round numbers, 35 to 38 millions; one of the others—Germany—has about one-fourth more, and Russia only has a much larger number in Europe, viz., 80 millions. While numbers, therefore, are not everything, or Russia would be preponderant, which is notoriously not the case, and Germany would not, as it does, count for more than in proportion to its numbers, and the United Kingdom would not have a peculiar position among the others, on account of the undeveloped state of its military resources on the one side, and the immensity of its wealth and latent strength on the other side, yet it is obvious that the mere numbers are a most vital element in appreciating the political position of these five powers and the lesser powers around them. Perhaps if statesmen were always wise, and rulers and peoples free from prejudice and passion, the popular knowledge of the figures would be even more serviceable than it is in demonstrating the absolute insanity of offensive war. It is impossible to conceive what object any of these five great powers could gain by the misery and suffering of war with another, adequate to repay that misery and suffering: the very magnitude of the wars forbids the possibility of gain.

The past history and future prospects of the balance of power among these nations are also illustrated by a mere consideration of the numbers. We have only to glance at the population of the different States as at the close of the great wars in 1815 and as they are now, to see that great changes have happened:

	1815.		1880.	
	Population in Millions.	Per Cent. of Total.	Population in Millions.	Per Cent. of Total.
Russia in Europe	48	33	80[1]	34
Germany[2]	21	14½	45	19
Austria-Hungary	28	20	38	16
France	29	20½	37	16
United Kingdom	17	12	35	15
Total	143	100	235	100

Thus in 1815 a compact France possessed several millions more than the population of Germany, nearly

[1] The exact figure by the last census is 84 millions, but I have preferred to be a little under the mark, so as to allow a little for more exact enumeration in the latter censuses. For the present purpose the difference between 80 and 84 is immaterial.

[2] Germany was also much divided in 1815.

twice that of the United Kingdom, and more than half that of Russia. Austria-Hungary also came near, as it now does, to the French numbers. Now the population of Germany considerably exceeds that of France; that of the United Kingdom is nearly equal, and that of Russia is more than double. These facts correspond very closely with the transfer of military preponderance on the Continent from France to Germany, and with the increasing prominence of Russia, which would probably be much more felt but for the simultaneous growth of Germany. They also explain why it is that the United Kingdom, with an economic and social development resembling that of France in many respects, has fallen less behind in the political race; why its relative position among European powers, though not what it was fifty years ago, is less weakened than that of France has been. Fifty years ago it was the leader among powers which were occupied in restraining France, singly a greater power than any. Now it is about equal in numbers to France, although its whole position is changed by the fact that no power, not even Germany, preponderates to the same extent as France once did.

As regards the future again, what the figures suggest clearly is a possible rivalry between Russia and Germany, and the further relative decline of Austria and France—the United Kingdom continuing to grow, but occupying from year to year a different place, as its interest in the so-called balance of power becomes less. Our change towards Europe is, however, affected in part by the growth of our relations beyond seas, which is another of the great facts of population, evident on the surface of the figures, that I shall afterwards have to notice.

Of course these changes have had the effect of raising questions of domestic, as well as of foreign, interest; and here again we are indebted to statistics mainly for the suggestion of the questions. One of these questions is, in the case of France, what are the causes and probable consequences, socially and economically, as well as in its relations in respect of the balance of power to its neighbours, of the stationariness of the population? This is one of the most remarkable facts, both in itself and in comparison with the facts of other countries, which population statistics disclose. The present would not be the place to discuss the answer to the questions raised, or the solution of the problems involved. All I am concerned to point out is that it is to the common figures of statistics, such as did not exist until the present century, that we owe the putting of the questions for answer. But for them it would not have been quite certain whether the population of France was stationary or not. Now the facts are exactly known and even familiar, and discussion goes on. Another question presented is as to the increase of population in countries like Germany and Russia, and the rapid encroachment there has been on the unused agricultural resources of those countries. As the stationariness of the population in France, however beneficial in some social aspects, is not an unmixed good, because it weakens France in its external political relations, so the increase of population in Germany and Russia, while they still remain mainly agricultural, appears to be attended by some mischiefs. The social condition of the rural population of Germany leaves much to be desired, as we may see from the extensive emigration, and from the difficulty of increasing the national revenue. In Russia, again, the threatened difficulties appear most formidable. Until lately Russia has been largely in the condition of a new country, with vast quantities of land over which a growing agricultural population could spread. Now the European area is more or less filled up, and unless the vast territory of Siberia can be largely utilized for settlement, which appears doubtful, the pressure of population on the means of subsistence in Russia may soon become very great. The soil may be capable of supporting with better agriculture a larger population: but this is not the point. The kind of agriculture possible in any country is related to the existing capacity of the population, or to such improvements in that capacity as are in progress, and with the Russian population as it is, there are certainly traces in Russia of an increasing severity in the struggle for existence, which may at any moment become most serious. The change in the conditions of expansion for the population internally as compared with what they were fifty years ago ought at any rate to be recognized at the present day, suggested as they are by the most obvious statistics of Russian population. Italy, it may also be noticed, is fast increasing its population without any increase of new soil or corresponding increase of manufactures.

Last of all, another fact presented by these obvious figures is the dependence of the population of the United Kingdom very largely, and to a less degree of France, Germany, Belgium, and Holland, on the importations of food from abroad. The facts as to the United Kingdom have been much discussed in all their bearings lately, Mr. Bourne, as we know well, having taken a large part in the discussions; but you have only to turn to the pages of the "Statistical Abstract for Foreign Countries," to perceive that the United Kingdom is not quite isolated in the matter. It is much more dependent in degree than any other European country, but in the fact of dependence it is not altogether singular. The fact is, of course, partly due to the increase of population in far greater ratio than the increase of agricultural production, the prediction of Malthus, that the population of England would not be supported on the soil of England if it increased at anything like the rate in his time, having thus been verified, though not exactly as he anticipated; but it is also partly due to an increase in the consuming power of the same population, and the larger consumption of more expensive kinds of food, requiring larger proportionate areas to produce them. France, with a stationary population, increases its imports of food, and the increased consumption per head among our own population of the quantity of such articles as sugar and tea also suggests that articles of home agricultural production are now consumed more largely than they were twenty years ago or more by the same numbers. To these two causes combined then, the increase of population and increase of consuming power per head, coupled with a comparatively stationary agriculture, Europe owes the unique phenomenon of large masses of population supported by imports from foreign and distant countries. The social and political consequences of this new fact must be manifold, and again it is to the common figures of statistics we owe our knowledge of it. This great fact would hardly be known at all if periodic censuses and the system of recording imports and exports had not previously been introduced.

Socially and politically perhaps the phenomenon is not yet sufficiently appreciated, and as compared with what it will be, it is probably only beginning to be important, but it is one which must before long play an important part in international politics and in the economic life of nations. Both the countries which grow the surplus food and the countries which receive it are profoundly concerned.

In another way the internal growth of population in different countries of Europe is also connected with great political changes. In Germany, for instance, it was partly the special growth of the population under the Prussian monarchy which assisted to make United Germany. In Russia, again, the great growth of population outside Poland has, from year to year, and decade to decade, dwarfed the Polish difficulty as a bare question of the balance of power in Russia. But we have even a more striking case of political change from the internal changes of population nearer home. Every one must have been struck, during the last few years, by the calmness of the country generally in presence of Irish agitation, and the evident hopelessness of any insurrection arising out of that agitation. When Mr. Parnell and other Irish Members were arrested in October last year [1881], and the Land League suppressed, there was hardly even a fractional fall in consols. Forty, fifty, eighty years ago, things were entirely different, the Irish difficulty being incessantly spoken of as most menacing, which indeed it was. The present calmness and the former apprehension are obviously due very much to a mere change in population numbers. Ireland, at the beginning of the century, held about one-third of the population of the United Kingdom; as late as 1840 it still held very nearly one-third; now its population is only one-seventh. Apart from all relative changes in the wealth of the populations, these changes in numbers make a vast difference in the Irish difficulty. It becomes easier for us on the one hand to bear the idea of an alien State like Ireland in our close neighbourhood, wholly independent, or possessing Home Rule like the Isle of Man or the Channel Islands: the power of mischief of such a community is less to be feared by a State of England's greatness than was the power of a separate Ireland fifty or eighty years ago, by the England of that time. A separate Ireland then might have been used by France against the very existence of the English Empire and the independence of England itself. Now this would hardly be possible either to France or to any other State. On the other hand, any possible insurrection in Ireland is as nothing to the power of the United Kingdom compared with what it would have been when Ireland held a third of the whole population. Hence the calmness of recent years in comparison with the agitation of a former period, and which is all the more remarkable because the agitated memories survive and colour a good deal of the thought about the Irish difficulty still. A still more careful examination would show, I think, that the difficulty has diminished in intensity—that it is the alien part of Ireland which has most diminished in numbers, while the loyal part—

Ulster—has relatively increased; but here again I wish to confine myself to patent and obvious figures, the lesson of which has more or less sunk into the popular mind.

It is not difficult to perceive, moreover, that these changes in figures must gradually tell more effectively than they have yet done on the Irish difficulty. In 1832 Ireland was endowed with one hundred and five members, its proportion of the population of the United Kingdom being then one-third. If one-third was then considered to entitle it to one hundred and five members, one-seventh, it is clear, would only give it at the present day about forty-five. Of these forty-five, again, one-third would be from Ulster, and almost exclusively among the remaining two-thirds, or thirty in all, if we are to judge from the present appearance, should we find Home Rulers. The parliamentary Home Rule difficulty would thus seem to have largely arisen from the failure to adapt the representation of the country to changes in the population. There is certainly nothing in the increased wealth or vigour of the Irish population, compared with that of the rest of the United Kingdom, to suggest that Ireland should have a larger representation in proportion to its population than it had in 1832; yet if its representation were only to be reduced in proportion, the parliamentary difficulty would largely disappear. Even if no greater change were now to be made than the introduction of equal electoral districts, and assuming that the present changes in population continue, and that Irish representation is adapted to the probable relative population of Ireland and the United Kingdom at the next census, then the representatives of Ireland in Parliament would be reduced from one hundred and five to eighty-three, and of these eighty-three only fifty-five would be sent from those parts of Ireland in which there is disaffection, so that the maximum number of Home Rulers, unless there are great changes of party, which I am not discussing, would apparently be less than fifty-five. Of course I am not discussing the possibility or expediency of any political changes. I am merely pointing out the ideas which the figures on the surface are suggesting for consideration, and which must affect the politics of the next few years. Here again it is the common figures of statistics—those derived from the systematic record of facts commenced within the last century, and only brought to a condition of tolerable advancement within the last fifty years, which are so fertile and suggestive.[1]

Still continuing the use of the most common statistics of population, I propose next to direct attention to one of the most formidable problems which have to be dealt with by our imperial government, and for the knowledge of which we are mainly indebted to statistics. I refer to the growth of the population of our great dependency—India. I have already referred in the most general terms to the peculiar and complicated relations which are likely to grow up between nations of the European family and the races or nations of different types. At no point are these relations more interesting than they are in connection with the supremacy the English race has gained over the subject races of India. The point of interest in these relations for our present purpose lies, however, chiefly in this—that the Roman peace we have established in India appears to be effective in removing many obstacles to the growth of population which formerly existed—what Malthus described as the natural checks—so that under our rule the Indian population is growing in numbers from year to year, and trenching with alarming rapidity on the means of subsistence. I believe I am within the mark in saying that there is no more anxious subject for the consideration of our public men. The late Mr. Bagehot I know was profoundly impressed by the fact, and repeatedly wrote his impressions, though I do not remember whether anything he wrote is collected among his

[1] See *supra*, vol. i., p. 277.

published writings. Others of our leading public men and economists are also deeply impressed by the fact, though it is considered almost too delicate for public discussion. There can be no doubt, however, of the formidable nature of the problem. India has now on its 1,400,000 square miles of territory a population of 240 millions—I am dealing in round figures—or about 170 to the square mile: not an excessive proportion according to formal comparisons with other countries, but in reality leaving the people no margin. It appears, from the most careful studies, that whatever the number of people to the square mile, there is very little new and fertile soil to appropriate; that much soil has been so appropriated during the last century of our rule; and that the population continues to grow fast without any increase of the land revenue, or any other sign that land is being rapidly taken into cultivation—with signs, on the contrary, of exhaustion in the agriculture, and of an approach to the limits of production according to the means at the disposal of the population. So much is more or less accurately known by statistics; and of the cardinal fact—the magnitude and increase of the population—it is statistics from which we learn everything. The broad figures are here not so clear as they might be, because improved methods in taking the censuses have from time to time revealed larger populations than could be accounted for by taking the totals of one previous census and adding the probable or possible increase of population meanwhile; but of the actual fact of increase between two census periods there is no doubt, while the rate of increase, if we are successful in coping with famines, proves to be nearly 1 per cent. per annum. In ten years, therefore, there will be 20 millions more people in India to feed; in twenty years upwards of 40 millions more; and the problem thus brought before the Indian Government is in what way and by what means so to develop the character of the people that their industry may become more efficient upon practically the same soil. Failing any speedy alteration in the character of the people, the prospect seems inevitably to be that in India from decade to decade larger and larger masses of the semi-pauperized or wholly pauperized, the landless classes, as Sir James Caird calls them in the Famine Commission report, will grow up, requiring State subventions to feed them, and threatening all attempts to reform Indian finance, while raising social and political difficulties of the most dangerous kind. It seems certain, then, that India for many years to come will be an increasingly dangerous problem for our statesmen to deal with—the more dangerous perhaps because any change in the character of the people, bringing with it increased energy of production and increased strength of character altogether, will also bring with it a rise in the scale of living, tending to make the masses discontented instead of submissive to their lot. Whatever course events may take, our rule in India must apparently for generations become a problem of increasing difficulty and complexity. The problem is analogous to what seems to lie before a government like that of Russia, with this difference, that the government is in Russia a native institution, whereas in India it is that of an alien nation governing a host of subject races.

I shall be told, perhaps, that if statistics suggest problems like this, they are only making us uncomfortable before the time: the evils apprehended are purely speculative. But in the case of India this cannot be said. The actual creation of a famine fund is a proof that the evil is imminent. The fund is created in order to secure that large numbers of people are kept alive in times of famine, millions being in this way semi-pauperized. The prospect is that before long there may be millions to be kept alive in non-famine and famine years alike, people without land or means of living, and without the possibility of being employed as labourers. Thus the difference between the present condition of things and what seems imminent, unless, as I have stated, there is an unlooked-for change in the character of the people, is one not of kind but of degree. The statistics only bring to light and set out an immediate difficulty. The solution at present devised of a famine fund by which millions of the Indian people are virtually pauperized is certainly not one to be contemplated with any satisfaction. It may be unavoidable, but from the point of view of civilization and progress it is little more than a confession of the hopelessness of the difficulty.

The last broad fact I shall refer to as presented and made familiar to us by these statistics of population is that of the growth of population in the United States—a subject, perhaps, of even greater interest than any I have yet referred to, and complicated also with one or two interesting questions already glanced at, viz., the existence and increase of large European populations which are supported by imports of food from new countries, and mainly from the United States. In this case I may have to make some use in passing, not merely of common and familiar figures, but of a few less generally known; but I shall use none except what are easily accessible, and in all cases the ideas to be presented will be those suggested by what is common and familiar.

The broad fact presented by the United States is that of the doubling of the population in periods of about twenty-five years. There is a little doubt about the exact population at the time of the War of Independence, and down to the first census at the beginning of the present century, but for the present purpose the figures we get are good enough:

	In Milns.		In Milns.
1780	3.0	1840	17.1
'90	4.0	'50	23.2
1800	5.3	'60	31.4
'10	7.2	'70	38.5
'20	9.6	'80	50.1
'30	12.9		

In other words, the population of the United States has multiplied itself by sixteen in the course of the century—this being the result of its doubling itself every twenty-five years for that period. In another twenty-five years, at the same rate of increase, the population will be 100 millions, in fifty years 200 millions, in seventy-five years 400 millions, and at the end of a century 800 millions! Such is the first aspect of the broad fact presented to our consideration by the increase of population in the United States. The rate is such as to be fairly bewildering in its probable consequences. The phenomenon is also without a precedent in history. There has been no such increase of population anywhere on a similar scale, and above all no such increase of a highly civilized and richly fed population. The increase is not only unprecedented in mere numbers, but it is an increase of the most expensively living population that has ever been in the world. For the idea of such an increase we are indebted exclusively to statistics. The United States, among the other new ideas of old civilizations they have had the benefit of, have had the idea of a periodical census, which is even made a part of their constitution, and as the result we have before us, not only in a general way, but with some precision, so that discussion may have an assured basis, this phenomenon of an unprecedented increase of population which is perhaps the greatest political and economic fact of the age.

The fact has altered in the first place the whole idea of the balance of power of the European nations. A century ago the European nations in their political relations thought little but of each other. Now the idea of a new Europe on the other side of the Atlantic affects every speculation, however much the new people keep themselves aloof from European politics. The horizon has been enlarged, as it were, and the mere fact of the United States dwarfs and, I think, restrains the rivalries at home. European Governments can no longer have the notion that they are playing the first part on the stage of the world's political history. And this sense of being dwarfed will probably increase in time. In this country, at any rate, we cannot but feel greatly attracted by the United States. Because of the magnitude of that country, the European continent is less to us—our relations are elsewhere.

It is in connection, however, with our own home problems of population that the increase of the United States is most interesting to us. The increase is partly at our expense, and at that of the other European nations. If the United States or some other new country had not received our emigrants, it is quite clear that our whole history would have been different from what it is. We should either have had in our midst the people who emigrated, and their descendants, straining the resources of our soil and mines and capital, or the pressure upon these resources would have checked in various ways the growth of the population itself, so that probably at this moment, but for the new countries, more people would now be living in the United Kingdom than there are, and larger numbers of the population would be paupers, or on the verge of pauperism. The actual numbers we have lost altogether, and specially to the United States, have been:

	To United States.	Altogether.
Before 1820	50,000	123,000
1820-30	100,000	247,000
'30-40	308,000	703,000
'40-50	1,094,000	1,684,000
'51-52[1].	511,000	704,000
'53-60	805,000	1,312,000
'60-70	1,132,000	1,571,000
'70-80	1,087,000	1,678,000
Total	5,087,000	8,022,000

[1] Previous to this date the figures include foreigners.

Some correction of these figures would be necessary in the earlier years for foreigners included, and in the later years for persons returning home, but the correction in the present view would make no material difference. If these people had not emigrated, and had increased as the rest of the population has done at home, the existing population in the United Kingdom would now be many millions more than it is. The difference made by the emigration to the United States alone must be a good many millions.

The influence of the United States and other new countries has been greater still. On a rough calculation about 12 millions at least of the people of the United Kingdom live on imported food, and a certain part of the populations of Germany, France, Belgium, and Holland also live on imported food—the importations being mainly from the United States. These new countries therefore not only have permitted an increase of population in a century, till it is sixteen times the population at starting, but a much larger increase. To take the United States alone, we cannot estimate its contribution to the support of foreign populations at less than an amount equal to the support of a population of 10 millions, similar in character to that of the United Kingdom. Its exports of bread-stuffs and provisions are now about 90 million pounds annually, at the value as they leave the United States; and at £9 per head, corresponding approximately to a value in the United Kingdom of £11 per head, which is about our consumption of agricultural products per head, this would be equal to the support of 10 million persons. In other words, then, the United States, from supporting 3 millions of people a century ago, are now supporting at least 60 millions—virtually an increase of twenty times the original number. The growth of population thus becomes more astonishing than ever. Altogether there must be about 15 millions of people in Europe supported by the produce of the new countries; and adding together the populations of Canada,

Australia, and the United States to this 15 millions, less a deduction for the population in these countries a century ago, there remains a total of about 70 millions of European population,[1] or about one-fifth of the population now living in Europe, which is supported by the produce of newly opened regions. The history of Europe we may well say would have been entirely different from what it has been during the last century but for the new countries. It is difficult indeed to overestimate the extent to which the existence of a new field for population, such as the United States presents, has dominated the recent economic history of Europe. We are so accustomed to a set of economic circumstances in which population, constantly increasing in numbers and in the capacity for food consumption per head, finds practically unlimited means of expansion, that we can hardly understand economists like Malthus who were oppressed by the only too evident limits which nature, at the time he wrote, had apparently set.

It seems impossible, however, not to see that a period in which the pressure of limits to growth and expansion may again be felt is not far off. The approach of such a period seems to me to be suggested by the figures which are on the surface, and I may perhaps be permitted to anticipate that the idea of such an approach, if it is not now, will soon become a familiar subject for speculation.

The very language in which reference has been made to the increase of population in the United States itself, viz., that the present rate of increase implies twenty-five years hence a population of 100 millions, a hundred years hence a population of 800 millions,

[1] To make these figures quite exact, a correction ought to be made on account of the non-European element in the population of the United States, the coloured population in 1880 being about 6½ millions. The coloured population in the United States, however, is brought into competition with the European, and in some degree Europeanized. It seems unnecessary, therefore, for our present purpose, to make any correction.

indicates that a continuance of this rate of increase may be considered incredible. It implies future changes in the industrial power of the race which we have no warrant to anticipate. The area of the United States, exclusive of Alaska, which does not count, is 3 million square miles, and of this area there are at least 1 million square miles, if not more, which are sterile or rainless, so that cultivation, so far as we can now foresee, is out of the question. There remain then 2 million square miles, and on this area a population of 800 millions would give 400 to the square mile—one-third as much again as the present population per square mile in the United Kingdom, twice as much per square mile as the population of the United Kingdom which is supported by the home agriculture, and more than twice as much per square mile as the present population of France. Allowing for the greater consuming power of people in the United States as compared with that of the French people, this is as much as to say that a rate of increase of population like what has been going on in the United States for a century is impossible in the next century, unless the power of the human race to extract food from the soil is enormously increased. No doubt the United States may lose in each decade that special force of addition to its rate of increase due to immigration. As its own population increases, the proportion of the area from which immigrants are drawn will diminish, and hence there is apparent reason to anticipate that the proportion of the immigration itself will diminish. But at present there is hardly a sign of change in the proportion of the immigration, and for some time to come at least no material difference seems likely from this cause in the rate of increase of the United States population. The increase of population between 1870 and 1880 was almost at as great a rate as any that has occurred. Besides, it does not follow that the diminution of the area from which immigrants are drawn should diminish the immigration itself. Other things being equal, a larger and larger share of the increasing population of older countries will emigrate, and if they do not emigrate they will have to be supported by the inport of food from new countries, which comes to the same thing. Moreover, a much smaller increase in the United States than we have supposed, say to 400 millions only in a century, would presuppose practically so violent a change in existing economic conditions, that the difference between it and the more violent change which an increase of population to the larger figure would require need not be considered.

The bare statement of such figures appears to me quite enough to indicate that the present economic circumstances of the European family of nations, including the United States as an offshoot and part of the family, are not likely to continue for more than a generation or two. We are within measurable distance of very great changes. No doubt there are other new lands—in Australia, in Canada, at the Cape, and elsewhere—which will be more or less available in the future; but, singly, the United States is so much the larger field, that the influence of these other new lands need not be considered. Assuming the United States to possess only half the area of new country available for the European races, a single doubling of the population, after the United States has been filled up—the work of a generation or two—would absorb all these other new lands; their existence only postpones the date when they will all be in the position calculated for America alone at the end of a century by thirty years or so. In the course of a century, then, we may affirm that the present economic circumstances of the European races which make possible an indefinite expansion of the numbers of the people, coupled with an increase of their consuming power, will have entirely changed.

The facts appear to me so interesting, that I ask leave to add something more, though the figures I have now to give you, while easily accessible, are not quite so much on the surface, and have not been popularized.

These figures relate to the actual appropriation of land for settlement, and the actual growth of population in the new and old States respectively. What I wish to bring out is that a much larger portion of the available area of the United States has been "taken for settlement" than is commonly imagined; that in fact not only the thirteen original States and their three subsections have been so taken for settlement, but what are known as the Western States, exclusive of the Pacific territories, have also been taken for settlement; that the growth of rural population in this second group of States has now brought them nearly to the level of the rural population in the older States; that there is no longer much room for growth by taking up new lands in all these portions of the States; that the remaining available area is so small as to render inevitable its being taken for settlement before very long; and that from this point, probably within twenty or thirty years, the new economic circumstances I have been referring to must begin to make themselves felt.

The total area of the United States, according to the last census, exclusive of Alaska, is given as 3,025,600 square miles, of which there is a land surface of 2,970,000 square miles. Of this the portion belonging to each of the three groups named, with the quantities of each respectively taken for settlement, is as follows, the figures being worked out from the data of area and population as given by the last census:

Area of United States and Area taken for Settlement, in Three Groups.

	Total Area.	Area taken for Settlement.
GROUP I.	Square miles.	Square miles.
Thirteen to sixteen original States	393,000	362,000
GROUP II.		
Twelve Western and Southern States[1]	605,000	560,000
GROUP III.		
Remaining States and Territories—		
a. Six Far West States[2]	620,000	370,000
b. Pacific States and Territories[3] .	1,407,000	277,000
Total of Group III. . .	2,027,000	647,000
Grand Total	3,025,000	1,569,000

Thus out of the total area of 3 million odd square miles, rather more than one-half is the area taken for settlement; and the area not for settlement is almost exclusively in the last group of all. This group I have subdivided in two sections, the first comprising States like Iowa and Minnesota, more or less completely settled, and the second comprising the Pacific States and Territories; and of the first subsection, it will be observed, more than half is already included in the area taken for settlement. The question then arises—How much of the unsettled portion is available for settlement? and to this the answer must be, little. When I mention that Mr. Porter, a well-known American statistician, and one of the Tariff Commission now sitting, in his book on "The West," estimates that there are

[1] Viz., Kentucky, Tennessee, Ohio, Indiana, Illinois, Michigan, Missouri, Arkansas, Louisiana, Mississippi, Alabama, and Florida.

[2] Viz., Iowa, Wisconsin, Minnesota, Kansas, Nebraska, and Texas.

[3] Viz., California, Oregon, Dakota, Colorado, Nevada, Arizona, Idaho, Montana, Wyoming, Utah, New Mexico, Washington.

1,400,000 square miles of territory in the West, of which only a tithe will ever be available for cultivation, it will be seen that the wholly unoccupied portion of the available territory must now be reduced to very small dimensions.

The next point to which I wish to draw attention is the actual population of the first two groups, exclusive of the town population, and the proportion to the square mile. This figure I work out from the tables at pp. 26-31 of the Introduction to the Population Statistics of the United States Census:

Net Rural Population of the United States, exclusive of the Town Population, in different Groups of States, with the Numbers per Square Mile.

	Total Population.	Town Population.	Net Rural Population.	Number per Square Mile of Rural Population.
Group I. . . .	21,835,111	7,939,334	13,895,777	35
" II. . . .	19,656,666	3,614,835	16,041,831	26½
" III. *a* . . .	6,761,132	847,282	5,913,850	9½
" III. *b* . . .	1,902,874	534,659	1,368,215	1
Total of III. .	8,664,006	1,381,941	7,282,065	—
Grand Total .	50,155,783	12,936,110	37,219,673	12½

Thus while the rural population in the thirteen original States is 35 per square mile, it amounts to no less than 26½ per square mile in twelve other States which we are accustomed to speak of as more or less unoccupied. This is clearly not the case. An addition of 8½ per square mile, or of little more than 5 millions in all, would make them as populous as the rural parts of the original States. Group III.*a*, though it has a larger area to fill up, would nevertheless become as populous per square mile rurally as the older group of

States by an addition of about 15 millions of population. It appears, however, that a large part of this area belongs to the rainless region; so that probably less than two-thirds of this 15 millions would fill up the available area to the limit of the thirteen original States. There remains only the last division of all; but it would seem that the available area here cannot be put at more than 400,000 square miles, on which the present rural population would be about 3 per square mile; so that if the population grows to the limit of the older States, the addition to the population necessary would be about 10 to 12 millions only. Altogether an addition of about 20 to 25 millions to the rural population of the United States[1] would seem all that is required to occupy the available area in the same way that the oldest and most settled part is now occupied. When that point is reached, the present conditions of expansion must begin to change.

How long will it be till the point is reached? Some idea of this may be formed from a comparison of the increase of the total population with the increase of the city population. This is shown in a table at p. 29 of the Introduction to the Population Statistics of the Census, already referred to, from which it appears that the total population increased nearly 12 millions in the last census period, and the urban population nearly $3\frac{1}{2}$ millions, so that the rural population increased $8\frac{1}{2}$ millions.[2] Of course it may be urged that the rural population may have increased in the older parts of the country as well as the new, but it is interesting to observe how much of the absolute increase of population is in the second and third groups, and not in the first. This is shown in the table on the next page, extracted from the "Introduction to the United States Census."

[1] Viz., 5 millions to second group, 10 millions to Group III.*a*, and 10 millions to Group III.*b*.

[2] The following is a copy of the figures here referred to, the urban population here accounted for, however, being somewhat less than

Population and Number of Inhabitants per Square Mile in each of Three Groups in the United States at the Date of each Census.[1]

Date.	First Group.		Second Group.		Third Group.	
	Population.	Average Density (Persons to a Square Mile).	Population.	Average Density (Persons to a Square Mile).	Population.	Average Density (Persons to a Square Mile).
1790. .	3,819,846	17.0	109,368	7.2	—	—
1800. .	4,922,070	18.5	386,413	9.8	—	—
'10. .	6,161,566	20.6	1,078,315	9.8	—	—
'20. .	7,417,432	23.8	2,216,390	11.3	—	—
'30. .	9,158,721	26.3	3,707,299	13.1	—	—
'40. .	10,638,004	30.1	6,357,392	14.5	74,057	4.7
'50. .	13,218,496	36.7	9,078,288	18.4	895,092	7.1
'60. .	15,818,547	43.8	12,637,882	24.3	2,968,892	9.5
'70. .	17,964,592	50.1	15,594,721	29.5	4,999,058	12.9
'80. .	21,835,111	60.3	19,656,666	35.1	8,664,006	13.4

Thus in the last decade about 4 millions of the total increase of population is in the second group, and 3,700,000 in the last group. At this rate, clearly, the increase of population in the second group in ten years from 1880, if all agricultural, would be such as nearly

above stated, which includes towns of a smaller size than are reckoned in this comparative table:

Number of Total Population of United States at each Census, and Number of Urban Population, with the Proportion of the Urban to the Total.

Date.	Population of United States.	Population of Cities.	Inhabitants of Cities to each Hundred of Total Population.
1790	3,929,214	131,472	3.3
1800	5,308,483	210,873	3.9
'10	7,239,881	356,920	4.9
'20	9,633,822	475,135	4.9
'30	12,866,020	864,509	6.7
'40	17,069,453	1,453,994	8.5
'50	23,191,876	2,897,586	12.5
'60	31,443,321	5,072,256	16.1
'70	38,558,371	8,071,875	20.7
'80	50,155,783	11,318,547	22.5

[1] To prevent misunderstanding, it should be noted that the figures per square mile in this table refer to the whole population, whereas in the table on p. 30 the figures relate to the rural population only.

to fill up the country with a rural population to the level of the older States, while the same increase would go a very long way towards filling up the last group in the same way. But the speed with which the vacuum will be filled will probably be even greater. The population in the new regions grows at an increasing rate as regards amounts. In 1840 the population in the third group was about 74,000 only; in 1850 it had increased by rather more than 800,000; by 1860 there had been a further increase of 2 millions; by 1870 there had been another addition of 2 millions; and between 1870 and 1880 there is an addition of nearly 4 millions. Thus only in one decennial period, viz., between 1860 and 1870, is the increase less than about double what it had been in the previous decennial period. The increase of population in this new region at the past rate would therefore be, not 4 millions, but 8 millions, or about half what is required to fill up the region with a rural population to the level of the thirteen original States. By 1890, therefore, not only will the second group of States very probably be filled up to the level of the thirteen original States, but the work of filling up the last group of all will have advanced very nearly towards completion. In another ten years, that is by 1900, assuming the same progressive rate of increase, the addition to the population in the last group of all would be 16 millions, which would be far more than sufficient to fill up the vacuum.

There is still another way of looking at the matter. During the decennial period 1870-80, the increase of population in the United States was about equally distributed between the three groups—about 4 millions to each, the increase in the first group being, however, mainly in the cities. Assuming an equal division of the 50 millions additional population which will be on the territory of the United States in twenty-five years —and it is more likely that the Western States will have a larger proportionate share—this would give 16 millions more to the second group, or 11 millions more than is necessary to fill up the rural districts to the level of the Eastern States, and 16 millions to the third group, which would suffice to fill the rural districts to the Eastern level. Even looking at the matter in this way, then, the prospect is that the available area in the United States will be peopled up to the level of the thirteen original States, as regards the rural population, in the course of twenty-five years. But the distribution of the increase between the groups, as I have said, is likely to be unequal, and the West will probably be filled up with even greater rapidity. To look at the matter in yet another aspect: of the 50 millions additional population, assuming an increase of the town population like what has been going on in the past, about 12 millions will be a town population, leaving 38 millions as the rural increase. But unless rural population is to increase in the original States, and is also to increase in the second group to more than the present level of the original States, the whole of this 38 millions, except the 5 millions required for the growth of rural population in the second group to the level of the original States, will be left for the occupation of the available area in the third group, or double what is required. Whatever way we look at the matter then, it seems certain that in twenty-five years' time, and probably before that date, the limitation of area in the United States will be felt. There will be no longer vast tracts of virgin land for the settler. The whole available area will be peopled agriculturally, as the Eastern States are now peopled.[1]

[1] These various calculations may be put more shortly still. Assuming the available area for settlement to be altogether 2 million square miles—and it seems not quite so much—this would absorb altogether, at 35 per square mile, a rural population of 70 millions. With that number the entire available area of the United States would have as thickly settled a rural population as the thirteen original States now have. But the present rural population being over 37 millions, only 33 millions more at the outside are needed to fill up the available area to the level of the Eastern States, or less than the

All this must involve a great change in the conditions of the growth of population and the general economic conditions of the country. It confirms in the most ample manner what was to be surmised from the bare statement of the geometric increase of population itself, pointing as it did to a population of 800 millions at the end of a century from this time. Long before that it is plain, and I think quite certainly within twenty-five years, the conditions of the expansion of population must be substantially different from what they are now.

It will be urged that it is notorious the United States can support enormous masses of population. Its available agricultural area in round figures is twelve or thirteen times that of the United Kingdom, and eight times that of France. Considering what the population of the United Kingdom or that of France is, and the superior fertility of many tracts of the United States, it appears safe enough to assume that the United States can support an indefinite increase of population, and that there is room for great expansion of population within the settled area. But assuming all this to be the case, what we may observe is that it is not quite to the present point. This is not a question of supporting a large population anyhow; *how* they are to be supported is here all-important. The moment there is little new land to occupy, the conditions of expansion must change; every year must bring nearer the date when the fruits of the soil will be extracted with increasing difficulty. The agriculture must become different from what it is now. What has been already said, moreover, as to the United Kingdom and France not supporting all their own population, and as to what the position in the United States would be, even as compared with the United Kingdom and France, if the geometric increase in the United States should continue no more than a century,

estimated addition to the rural population at the present rate of increase in the next twenty-five years.

may show that there is, after all, no room for an indefinite expansion of population within the settled area in the United States. I should like to go further, and suggest that the limits of such expansion, without a very great and almost inconceivable change in the agriculture itself, must be very narrow. Comparisons with European States on this head seem very apt to mislead. But the figure of 35 per square mile as the rural population of the older parts of the United States is, after all, one-fourth of the agricultural population of France per square mile; and there are two important differences between the agriculture of France and the United States: 1. The consuming power of the United States population is much greater, perhaps double that of the French population, so that the soil cannot be expected to support the same number of Americans as French. 2. The western farmer in the United States grows for export, not merely to the towns of the country, but abroad. A rural population one-fourth that of France may thus be quite sufficient to settle up the country. We must not come to the subject with European ideas as to the scale of living.

It would be foreign to my purpose to indulge in speculation as to what will be the consequences of this approach to a complete settlement of the United States, coupled with the fact that population, whether in the United Kingdom, or in Germany, or in the United States, shows no sign of abatement in the rate of increase. It is sufficient for my purpose to point out that as the existence of vast tracts of virgin soil in the United States has permitted, during the last hundred years, an expansion of the European population without a precedent in history, has made the economic history of Europe in that period entirely different from what it would otherwise have been, so now the approach to a complete settlement must profoundly affect the world. The conditions of economic growth will be fundamentally altered. Possibly there may be chemical or other inventions rendering possible great improvements in agriculture, which will have practically the same effect as an increase of the quantity of new land available. Possibly we may have the rate of growth of population itself checked. But with the change of one condition others must change, if the masses of European people are to remain at their present level of prosperity. If there is no change, the nature of the difficulties that will arise is obvious: the masses of labourers will have to contend under increasing difficulties[1] against a fall in the scale of living.

But while I refrain from indulging in general speculation, I may, perhaps, be allowed to point out some of the more immediate consequences which are likely to follow from an approach to complete settlement in the United States, of which we seem to be within a measurable distance. First of all there will probably be a diversion of a larger part of the stream of emigration from Europe and the Eastern States of the American Union to the north-west provinces of Canada. Here there are probably about 400,000 square miles of territory available for settlement, equal in quality to the best land in the United States West. As there is no such field in the United States itself, the stream must apparently be to the new land.[2] The second immediate consequence I should look for would be an increase of manufactures and of town population in the United States. The agricultural outlet becoming less tempting, and agricultural wages tending to fall, the population will inevitably be more and more largely drawn into manufacturing.[2] And a third consequence will probably be a check to the tide of emigration from older countries, a greater demand upon the agriculture of those countries, or at least a mitigation of the extreme competition it now sustains from virgin soils,

[1] See "Some Leading Principles of Political Economy Newly Expounded." By J. E. Cairnes, M.A. Macmillan and Co., 1874. Pp. 332-334.

[2] These anticipations are now being fulfilled [1903-4].

and possibly a reversal of the present tendency for rents to fall. Such changes may hardly be apparent for a few years, with the exception, perhaps, of the diversion of the stream of emigration to the north-west of Canada, which has begun; but it seems hardly possible to doubt that they must begin to be felt before very long—perhaps in the course of ten, and almost certainly in the course of twenty years.[1]

To sum up this long review. These easy figures of population evidently go to the heart of much of our politics and political economy. To quote only the illustrations I have given, we may say, first, they give some idea of the mass of the European populations in the world, and consequently of the overwhelming strength of European civilization. Next, as we have seen, they help to explain the existence of five leading powers in Europe, and the changes in the balance of power which have occurred in the last fifty or sixty years. They equally help to explain domestic changes in each country, such as the diminished intensity of the Irish difficulty in the United Kingdom, or the growth of social difficulties in a country like Russia through the population increasing with no other opening but a restricted agriculture, or such external difficulties as we have brought on ourselves by the conquest of India and the Roman peace we have established. Finally, they set before us in a clear light the great economic phenomenon of our time, the creation of the United States of America, and the provision by this and similar agencies for a growth of population, not only in the United States, but in Europe, which is entirely without precedent. I have endeavoured to supplement the last figures with a few others designed to throw light on the question of the continuance of this portentous

[1] As a matter of fact the second and third of these consequences have followed very much as stated in the text, while the first—the influx of population into the Canadian north-west—is now (1903) attracting no small attention.

growth, and the probability of a check to it; but the figures here used are also easily accessible. I trust you will agree with me that we may conclude from all this review, that the easy figures of statistics which we are all more or less familiar with are fruitful. How impossible it would be even to conceive some of the problems which are now raised for discussion if there were no statistics, and how inexplicable many of the facts of the present day and of history would become if statistics did not explain them.

If time permitted, it would not be difficult to show how other familiar figures in statistics also supply problems for discussion, and colour all our political thought. Let me only add, however, that the fact of these easy figures being so useful should encourage the development of the study of statistics. Familiar as are some of the things we have been discussing, it is often too evident that they are not sufficiently appreciated—that hazy ideas are widely held which a clear knowledge of statistics would disperse. Still more, not only should the accessible and easy figures be more studied, but it is most desirable to digest other masses of figures and increase the field of what can be readily understood. The difficulties in the way in some branches, as in the case of many trade figures, the figures of national income, and the like, are enormous, in consequence of the varying aspects of the data and the difficulty of impressing on the public mind some of the most elementary conceptions of the statistician, such as the propriety of using figures of trade on an imperfect basis to show progress or the reverse for a series of years, because the basis, though imperfect, is throughout the same. There is no doubt, however, that with time and attention, order can be educed of what is now chaotic to the public mind, and many facts of some complexity brought to the general knowledge. We have likewise to remember that time is working with us. The influence of simple population statistics upon political thought, and in suggesting ideas which colour literature and philosophy, which has been our theme to-night, is the result of a systematic collection of statistics, which commenced only eighty years ago, and which is still extremely deficient. We may reasonably hope for more light from statistics as time passes by, and as it becomes possible to draw out comparisons over longer periods. The statisticians of the present day labour for the future, and we need not be discouraged if in many departments we have yet to wait for results. [1882.]

XIV.

ON INTERNATIONAL STATISTICAL COMPARISONS.[1]

AN old jest runs to the effect that there are three degrees of comparison among liars. There are liars, there are outrageous liars, and there are scientific experts. This has lately been adapted to throw dirt upon statistics. There are three degrees of comparison, it is said, in lying. There are lies, there are outrageous lies, and there are statistics. Statisticians can afford to laugh at and profit by jests at their expense. There is so much knowledge which is unattainable except by statistics, especially the knowledge of the condition and growth of communities in the mass, that, even if the blunders in using statistics were greater and more frequent than they are, the study would still be indispensable. But just because we can afford to laugh at such jests we should be ready to turn them to account, and it is not difficult to discover one of the principal occasions for the jest I have quoted, and profit by the lesson.

Statistics are easily mishandled, for the simple reason, amongst others, that people like short cuts, and they are apt to take different figures and compare them with each other, because the things represented by them are called by the same names, without any consideration of the question how the figures are obtained, and whether the things compared are throughout of a like kind. Thus two states will be compared with each other as regards their revenue for Imperial purposes,

[1] Paper read at the meeting of the Australasian Association for the Advancement of Science at Hobart, January, 1892. Reprinted in "Economic Journal" for that year.

without any consideration of the fact that in the one certain expenses of government are borne on the Imperial budget, which in the other are borne on the local budget, or perhaps left to private agency; or without any consideration of such a fact as the inclusion in the one budget of loans or the proceeds of the sales of public property as revenue, which in the other are excluded altogether, or specially dealt with. The statistics, however, are not lies in themselves; it is only in the handling of them that the lying takes place. I have thought it would be of interest, therefore, in a meeting like this, to raise explicitly for discussion some of the principal dangers in the handling of statistics to which the inexpert, and some of us perhaps, who think we are expert, are exposed, through the too ready comparison with each other of figures which apparently are applied to facts of a like kind, but which really cover dissimilar facts. Such a discussion becomes more and more indispensable, I think, on account of one of the most important causes of the increased diffusion of statistical knowledge in recent years—the extensive development of statistical abstracts, hand-books, year-books, manuals, dictionaries, statistical atlases, and such like works of reference. Accustomed to see quantities, which are really dissimilar in kind, placed together under the same heading, which is done primarily for the mere purpose of reference, we come to neglect the dissimilarity in our speech, and, by and by, in thought. The numbers of different communities are compared as if numbers alone were something in themselves, without any thought of the different qualities of the units: production, imports and exports, and money wages in different communities are spoken of as if they in all cases meant the same things, and without any preliminary discussion of what the figures really do mean. All this is essentially mischievous, and is contrary to the most elementary lessons in the study of statistics. It is the part of the student to re-act against the temptation to which he is exposed to use works which are only good for reference in this haphazard fashion.

Population Statistics.

At the risk of being commonplace through enforcing considerations which no one will dispute, I propose to begin with the foundation statistics of all—those of population. It is obvious at the first sight, when the statement is made, that for very few purposes can the populations of different countries be placed together as if the units were the same. The peoples of Europe and the United States are as a rule units of a very different value from the units of population in Hindoo, Chinese, negro, and aboriginal communities. Even among European peoples themselves there are enormous differences.

It follows, then, that many questions of first importance for which statistics of population are used, cannot be discussed at all without reference to the quality of the units. The fact has only to be stated to be admitted. Among such questions, for instance, is the question of the population that a given area will support. The plain of Bengal, say, supports some seventy million Hindoos—the population, in numbers, of the United States. But if the consuming power of the Hindoo were at all like that of the average man of the United States, how many could Bengal support? The same, *mutatis mutandis*, comparing even a French or German with a United States population. The units in the different cases are entirely different. The area of the United States might suffice with the same total value of production that it now has for the support of perhaps twice as many French or Germans as it could support of people of the actual type of those now planted on the soil of the United States. The question may be turned about another way. Along with the increased capacity of consumption there may, or may not, be an increased capacity of production. If there is such an increase of the capacity of production, or even a greater proportionate increase than there is of consumption, it might well be that on the area of Bengal there could be planted an even larger population than there now is, yet with the average consuming power of the people of the United States, and not merely the average consuming power of the Hindoo. So greatly different may be the varying units of population which we are so ready to speak of as alike.

Among other questions of the same kind is that of the strength of dfferent populations for war and industry. The differences between peoples are really almost infinite, and are not always coincident as regards war and industry. The Hindoo population, for instance, appears to be differentiated from a European race in respect of fighting force to a much greater extent than it is differentiated in respect of industrial force. The Chinese population, on the other hand, though it is weaker at present than European populations in fighting power, as well as industrial power, is, perhaps, not so much differentiated as the Hindoo is, and presents altogether a more difficult problem for their possible or probable antagonists. Negro populations, again, are differentiated in a different way, having a capacity for great exertion in some directions, but not in others. Such differences among peoples are so obvious that no one will dispute them when stated.

Even if units of population were generally alike instead of varying greatly, and in all sorts of directions, another question arises with reference to frequent comparisons of population and areas. The number of inhabitants per square mile is often quoted as denoting conditions adverse or favourable to the populations concerned. But of course there are areas and areas, originally and as modified by the qualities of the people dwelling upon them. In order to make a comparison of the number of inhabitants per square mile of any practical value at all, the nature of the areas, and of the qualities of the inhabitants, must be studied, and the facts must also be adapted to the discussion of particular questions, such as the relation of area to conditions of health, and the like. To say, for instance, that Belgium has so many inhabitants to the square mile, and France so many fewer, does not mean anything, because the size of the communities compared is entirely different, and in point of fact there may be areas included in France more thickly peopled than Belgium. It is the same in the comparison of a European country with the United States. The conditions are entirely different; while not a few of the comparisons so readily made would be upset by the consideration that one-third of the area of the United States, excluding Alaska, is desert, and is, properly speaking, not inhabitable at all. A similar remark would also apply to the countries of Australasia treated as a unit. The facts are all useful enough for reference; that is not disputed; but the moment they come to be discussed, the nature of the quantities must be studied, and strict attention given to the point of the comparison attempted.

Connected with this last is another question of the same kind. What is the area which really supports a given population? If people on a given spot are able to carry on industries which enable them to buy from the rest of the world what they want, are they supported by that area, or are they not? In a sense they are supported, for they live by the industries which they carry on there. In another sense they are not, because they are not self-contained. Foreign trade is the breath of their life. But this description is applicable not merely to countries like the United Kingdom, which manufacture largely, and carry goods largely for all the world: it is equally applicable to a country like the United States, which exports food, raw cotton, and other raw materials, wherewith to buy the things of which it stands in need; or to countries like Australasia, which export wool, the precious metals and other metals, to an extent without example in history.

All these considerations are so obvious that I have

to apologize for introducing them. No one, it will be urged, can make the blunder of overlooking them. But in point of fact, and this is my justification, the grossest blunders are constantly made. We know, for instance, in regard to the question of the population which a given area will support, that nothing is so common in books of travel or geographies, with reference to unoccupied or partially occupied areas, than statements that a given area will support so many million inhabitants. Nothing is said as to what kind of inhabitants. But clearly the sort of inhabitants will make all the difference. The idea of boundlessness of area so common in new countries, and which is to some extent an illusion, if I may venture the remark, is also due to neglect of the fact of quality of population. The area of a given country in a sense may be practically boundless, but it may be equally true that the full occupation of the country would imply a continual re-adaptation of the people to new economic conditions—that there is by no means boundless room for the same sort of people carrying on the same sort of industries. To the same effect, the idea of narrowness of area so common in old countries, where there is constant wonder as to what is to be done with the growing population, is based largely on the vague assumption that there must be some proportion between area and population, whereas, as we have seen, and as experience proves, populations of indefinite magnitude may be supported on narrow territory. Every city is an illustration in disproof of the supposed connection between population and area in the sense stated. Area is no doubt necessary to a wholly self-contained people, if such a people can be conceived of, short of one which occupies the whole habitable territory of the globe; but, as no nation is self-contained, there is equally no means of settling *a priori* the maximum limit of inhabitants per square mile which a community may occupy; and that a nation reaches a high maximum is no proof of its being in an unfavourable economic condition, or the reverse.

Other illustrations may be given of an underlying confusion of thought in these matters, which occasionally comes to the surface. I have seen, for instance, at home an attempt made to show that the English Empire is more aggressive than that of Russia, because in a given period it had annexed a larger area and a larger population than Russia had done, the truth being that the area annexed by either country in the period in question was largely desert, so that it hardly counted one way or the other, and that the populations annexed were of most various quality. The point of real aggressiveness or not was studiously overlooked in this ingenious statistical comparison. Constantly at home, also, there are continual discussions on the balance of power, in which the numbers of the populations and the armies they can put in the field are simply counted; whereas the whole question turns largely upon the quality of the respective populations and the state of their warlike preparations, and not so much upon mere numbers. The question of quality of population arises in a different way in those political questions which are settled by numbers at the ballot-box in democratic communities, and I am not sure but that some of the underlying assumptions of politics are based on the refusal to recognize the essential differences of different peoples, as, for instance, in the concession at home to the people of Ireland of an equality and, really, far more than an equality, of voting power and representation in the Imperial Parliament, whereas, in some qualities, such as wealth, they cannot be regarded as equal, although they may be equal, or superior, in other qualities. Commonplace, therefore, as it seems, to say that, when we see columns of comparative figures of population, we must not assume the units to be alike, the applications of the doctrine are not really commonplace. We are all subject to the influence of unexpressed and underlying assumptions, and I have only given a few out of many possible illustrations of the dangers that may arise in using these verv ordinary figures without constantly thinking of what they mean.

I come finally to less debatable ground in one way, but where there is practical mischief from the misuse of figures. Nothing is more common than to compare populations which may be assumed to be racially very nearly alike, or approximating in certain qualities, but which really differ greatly from each other in regard to the distribution of the population according to age. France and Germany, for instance, are continually spoken of as if the difference of their numbers made a corresponding difference in their force. In fact the population of Germany contains a much larger percentage of children than that of France does, and the numbers of adults in the two countries do not differ so much in proportion as their total numbers do.

To show what differences there may be in the relative proportions according to ages in different communities, I have brought together certain figures extracted from the last census, in each case showing the total numbers, the total male population, the males above the age of 20, and the males between 20 and 40, in France, Germany, and the United Kingdom, respectively. (See Table A annexed.) From this it will be seen that France, with a population of close on 38 millions, has 11,828,000 males above 20; and Germany, with a population of just under 47 million inhabitants, or upwards of 20 per cent. more than that of France, has 12,435,000 males above the age of 20, or only 5 per cent. more of this class of the population than France has. The proportion of males above 20 is in the one case 31 per cent., and in the other 26½ per cent. only. In the United Kingdom, where the total numbers, by the last census available for me in preparing this paper, are less than in either France or Germany, the proportion of males above 20 to the total population is 25½ per cent. only. On the other hand, the number of males between 20 and 40 is proportioned more equally in each case to the total numbers of the population, being about a seventh. Consequently France, although it has a total male population approximating to that of Germany, in spite of its smaller numbers, has only 5,376,000 males between 20 and 40, as compared with 6,577,000 in Germany; while the United Kingdom, with its smaller population than France, had in 1881 very nearly the French numbers of males between 20 and 40. No doubt in 1891 the figures would show a still greater superiority on the part of Germany to France in this particular, while the United Kingdom would be nearly on an equality, but without the very latest figures these are good enough for illustration. France has undoubtedly a much greater mass of old lives to support in proportion to its population than either Germany or the United Kingdom. As they all have, however, the same proportion of males between 20 and 40, it follows that in Germany and the United Kingdom there is a much heavier burden of children than in France. These are material differences in the constitution of the respective populations. At present the burden on the vigorous in each case is much the same, though heaviest, perhaps, in the case of France, as the old lives may be assumed to be more costly than the young, but natural growth must inevitably make an enormous difference in a few generations. Every ten years Germany and the United Kingdom, with the same proportion of non-effectives to support that France has, add greatly to their total numbers, and increase their preponderance over France in numbers alone.

The point is not without interest in comparisons between young and old countries. There are many comparisons in which, owing to the different composition of the population in a new country from what it is in an old country, the apparent superiority of the new country is to be explained, not by any superior quality, but by the mere fact that there is a less percentage of the people at ages above 40, and a larger percentage in the prime of life, than there is in an old country. For this reason in part there may be less mortality, less sickness, and larger consumption of certain necessaries and luxuries, in a new country than there is in an old country measured *per head.* But so far as this explanation holds, there is no superiority in the race of the new country over the old. As far as rates of mortality are concerned, statisticians in Australasia are familiar with the fact, and quote rates not upon the actual population, but upon a standard population in which the totals are redistributed according to age, but the correction is required in many other directions as well.

Moreover, although statisticians are usually correct when they deal with such figures, the point is not without practical importance. I have seen arguments at home, for instance, in which the attempt has been made to prove the superiority of Australians to the people of the United Kingdom in respect of health by means of statistics of the general rate of mortality among the two populations, no account being taken of the different distribution of the populations according to age. The comparisons I have in my mind failed on another point, being based upon a hypothesis as to the connection between mortality rates and the sickness of a population which had not been proved to be true generally; but even if the hypothesis had been generally true, the neglect of the point of distribution according to age made it entirely misleading.

Mortality Statistics.

I pass on to other statistics. Reference has already been made to mortality statistics in connection with the special point of the constitution of populations according to age, but there are many other traps in using such statistics for a comparison between nations. The mere question of how the deaths are recorded, and along with that the births, as far as many inferences from the mortality statistics are concerned, here becomes important. Before the statistics of two countries can be compared there must be a certainty that the registration process as to numbers is effective and complete in each. This is not the case in all countries, and it is an especially important matter in historical investigations even in the same country; the registration of births and deaths in England, for instance, being notoriously deficient until a comparatively modern period. Even a great country like the United States is still most deficient in this vital particular; there is no such thing as a good birth and death rate for that great country. In Philadelphia some years ago a local report of the registrar of births, deaths, and marriages was put into my hands, from which it appeared that the deaths exceeded the births. I learnt on inquiry that the explanation of a fact which would have been somewhat startling if true was simply the neglect of the laws or administration in the matter of the registration of births. I do not know whether there has been improvement since in this particular city of the United States, but that there is still a lack of a uniform and effective system of registration throughout the country is most certain. It is necessary then to reiterate again and again the necessity for the utmost caution in the use of such common figures as birth and death rates. Always when a writer would make a comparison, let him see that his facts are really comparable. He must not be content to take them from a dictionary without inquiring.

These remarks hold good of other comparisons sometimes made, particularly as to the prevalence of certain kinds of disease. I need not say to an audience of experts what difficulties arise in the definition of disease, and how doctors, apart from mistakes as to what the disease really is of which a man dies, may honestly vary in their statement of the fact from the number of causes themselves, one doctor giving a proximate and another an ultimate cause. Before statistical comparisons can be made, something must be ascertained as to whether definitions and method of registration are substantially the same in the two countries compared. In historical investigations, even in the same country, the precaution is equally indispensable.

Statistics as to Character of Population.

I proceed next to statistics, from which inferences are commonly drawn as to the qualities of a population—I mean statistics on such subjects as education, crime, sexual morality, drunkenness, insolvency, and thrift. On all these points different countries have statistics, which may have a meaning when they are properly used, but which it is most difficult to use properly.

To begin with education. Which is the most fortunate population of the world as regards the general education of the people? One often hears of the United States in this connection—of the numbers of children of school age and the numbers attending school as compared with less fortunate populations. But let me take the following passage from a memorandum by Mr. (afterwards Sir Joshua) Fitch, one of Her Majesty's chief inspectors of training colleges, on the working of the Free School system in the United States, France, and Belgium:

"In England and Wales the calculations of average attendance are made on the assumption that every school is open at least 400 times or 200 days in the year. It is on this basis that the annual returns in the official report of the Education Department state the average attendance of scholars in infant schools and departments to be 68 per cent., and that in schools for older children to be 82.2 per cent. But in the United States there is no uniform or generally accepted rule respecting the length of the school year. In the principal cities, especially in the East and West, the schools are open ten months out of twelve, and in these the statistics of attendance may be fairly compared with our own. But taking the country through, the average number of days in which the public schools are open is 129 in the year, and this fact implies that in the country places, especially in the South Atlantic and South Central States, the number of school days falls much below that average. In Alabama and in Georgia the schools are open only three months in the year, the teachers are paid by the month, and hold no permanent appointment. In Louisiana and Missouri the small sum appropriated to education by the State barely suffices to keep the schools at work more than four months in the year. In Nebraska the returns for 5,407 schools show 3,904 to be kept open for six months and upwards, 529 for more than four but less than six months, and 974 for less than four months. In New Hampshire the average length of the school term is 22.9 weeks; in North Carolina it is twelve weeks; in South Carolina, three and a half months. In Texas the towns give an average of eight months, and the country districts five months. On the other hand, in some of the Atlantic States the rate is much higher. In Pennsylvania, exclusive of Philadelphia, in which the school year includes ten months, the average is 7.17 months; in Rhode Island, nine months eleven days; and in New Jersey, nine months ten days. It is manifest, therefore, that the figures representing the regularity of attendance require material correction and reduction before they can be properly compared with the statistics of European countries in which schools are, as a rule, kept open during nearly the whole of every year."

From this it is quite clear that one has the greatest difficulty in discussing such a question as the education of a people. You can hardly get to know to what extent children of school age are attending schools of some kind. There are other difficulties behind, as the report from which I have quoted shows, such as the difference of surroundings in which children find themselves when they leave school, the United States, from the general vigour and energy of the whole population, being much more favourable to the development of general intelligence and mental cultivation among its people than countries which may be more fortunate as regards primary school education. There is also the difficulty caused by the kind and character of secondary education, and the extent to which it is diffused. Simple at first sight as the problem seems, then, there is nothing more difficult than to compare some countries with each other as regards the degree of their education.

The second subject I have named in this connection is crime, and in thinking of it I confess I have had in mind certain comparisons which have been made in England by visitors returned from Australia to the disadvantage of Australia. There is twice the crime in Australian colonies per head of population, we have been told, that there is in England. But, as we all know who have to handle statistics, there are few statistics so difficult to handle as those of crime. A distinction has to be made between mere police and administrative offences, which vary largely according to the things which Legislatures in their wisdom subject to fine or not, and the more serious offences, such as robbery and murder, which are what we think of when we talk of crime. But in hardly any two countries that I know of is the distinction drawn on exactly the same lines. You are almost never quite sure, therefore, what you are doing, unless you are specially careful, when you compare two countries as regards crime. Further, even if the distinctions were much the same, another difference is made by the police. You may have fewer trials and convictions in one country than in another, simply because the police for various reasons is less efficient, not because there is less crime. When comparisons, therefore, are made between the criminal statistics of two countries without attention to vital considerations like these to show that the subject has been really studied, it is safe to dismiss them without further thought.

But admitting that exact comparisons can be made, that statistics of crime in two countries are reduced to common denominators, I should like to point out that the logic of using them as indicative in any way of the general superiority of one population over another may be at fault. So far as can be judged, the so-called crime statistics of a country are not necessarily significant very much of the general quality of a population, but they may be significant only of the existence of a criminal element, which is like a disease from which a community suffers, but a disease of a superficial, and not of a vital character. One population may thus have more crime in it than another, even much more crime, but substantially the two peoples may be almost alike, the extent of the criminality in both being quite immaterial. Say, for instance, that the criminal population by which almost all the crime is done in one country is 1 in 500, or $\frac{1}{5}$ of 1 per cent., and in another population it is 1 in 250, or $\frac{2}{5}$ of 1 per cent., is not the criminal element in either so small as to tell you nothing of the general constitution of the people? Not only, therefore, must criminal statistics be used with care as far as the mere data are concerned, but the difficulty of using them as indicative of the general qualities of a population is overwhelming. They can only be used, if used at all, in conjunction with much other information and statistics.

The statistics bearing on sexual morality are equally difficult to handle. The test here that is most commonly used is that of illegitimacy; but the truth is that illegitimacy by itself tells little, for the simple reason that in a town community there may be prostitution without illegitimate births, whereas in a rural community there may be even less profligacy than in the town, but with a larger number of illegitimate births, in consequence of there being no prostitution. In one country also the births may be registered as legitimate, through the children being born in wedlock; but this may go along with a general laxity of morals of a remarkable kind. Sexual immorality is also like crime itself, even when it can be measured on the same basis in two different communities, more or less a thing apart, and it may or may not be significant of the general *morale* of the population. I suppose it is true, for instance, that the rural population of Ireland stands better, as far as statistics of illegitimacy are concerned, than that of Scotland, but it would be a rash inference that in general *morale* the rural population of Ireland is superior to the Scotch. For certain purposes the statistics are good enough, but they must not be pushed to conclusions they do not bear.

Statistics as to drunkenness also require a good deal of careful handling. In fact, I see no way myself of establishing statistically that one population is more or less drunken than another. Apart from the difficulty already referred to, arising from the different distribution of two populations according to age, so that one population has proportionately more adults than another, and consequently has a larger proportion of convictions for drunkenness and a larger proportionate consumption of alcoholic liquors—the two tests usually applied in such comparisons—it has to be considered that the tests themselves are not very good. The convictions for drunkenness, it is plain, like convictions for crime generally, may be very largely a matter of definition and of police administration. Before comparisons can be made, the state of legislation and of police administration in the countries compared must be considered. As regards the consumption of alcoholic liquors, again, I have never seen any statistics satisfactorily connecting a relatively large consumption of alcoholic liquors with drunkenness. On the contrary, the consumption in every community is probably at all times much more largely the consumption of sober people than that of people who drink to excess, and you may have much drunkenness among a people who, like the Americans, are generally total abstainers, and little among a people like the populations of the Southern States of Europe, who are generally moderate drinkers. Thus the question of drunkenness, or the reverse, in a population is not to be easily treated by statistics.

The statistics of bankruptcy or insolvency again are often quoted as a test of the comparative excellence of commercial communities. Here again I have had in my mind some recent comparisons at home between certain of the Australian colonies and England as regards insolvency. These colonies, we have been told, have twice as many failures per head of population as England, or some such proportion. But the traps in dealing with bankruptcy statistics are innumerable. Even in England it is not easy to compare one period with another, owing to difference of legislation making the conditions and record of official insolvency different at one time from what they are at another. The law at one time makes whitewashing so easy that debtors readily avail themselves of the courts to make themselves officially insolvent, and so you have a large number of bankruptcies in the official statistics. At another time the law is so stringent that debtors evade the courts, while creditors do not make them bankrupt because it is not worth while to do so, and so the official bankruptcies diminish. At one time, also, non-traders may be made bankrupt, at another time they may not be; and so the record varies. Unless, therefore, the whole basis of the bankruptcy law in each case is studied, no comparison is possible either between period and period in the same country or between different countries. Further difficulties would arise in any comparison, owing to the length of the commercial cycle which renders it most dangerous to take the figures of one year only or even of two or three years for comparison. We can imagine, then, what wild work is made by amateurs when they compare the insolvency of Australia and England. Apart from these differences there are others which are due to fundamental differences of economic condition. I believe, for instance, that in England a larger proportion of the business done is carried on by Joint Stock Companies than is the case in Australia. This may or may not be the case. But, supposing it to be the case, how can the failures of England be compared at all with those of Australia, without taking account of the liquidations of Joint Stock Companies, and to how many units of individual failures is that of a Joint Stock Company to be considered equal? I would not go so far as to say that no useful comparison could be drawn from existing data by those who go carefully into the subject and study all the conditions. What I am contending for is, that it is utterly impossible for writers in a hurry to make anything of the first figures that come to hand, and assume that the official record of failures in one country at one time means the same thing as the official record of failures in a totally different country at the same or another time.

Here, too, I would also demur to the test of bankruptcy itself as indicative of the general commercial character of a people, even if figures for comparison could be correctly ascertained. More bankruptcy in the one case than in the other may simply mean greater enterprise making more opportunity for failure, and not an excess of dishonesty in one compared with another. It may also mean that the industries carried on in one country, and which are suitable to be carried on in it, are essentially more fluctuating at a given period than the different industries of another country. Farming is often the most fluctuating of all industries. A country dependent on farming may suffer more from bankruptcy at a given date than a country less dependent. In turn, a manufacturing or commercial country may suffer more from catastrophes like war or invasion than an agricultural country would suffer. Perhaps even these difficulties could be overcome or evaded, and bankruptcy statistics be handled so as to indicate differences of character between two peoples; but the labour of the comparison would be very considerable indeed if anything is to be made of it at all.

I come finally to the last branch of statistics referred to as being often used to compare the character of two peoples, viz., the statistics of thrift or the diffusion of property among the masses. Here the temptation is to take some one form of saving, such as savings banks, or the holding of land, or investment in Government stocks, and roughly judge one people by their habits as to this one form of saving. So far as I have observed, the usual comparisons in detail, even as to the one branch of saving selected for comparison, are most erroneous. Thus, I have seen the number of separate inscriptions of French *rentes* in the books of the French Ministry of Finance treated as the number of separate holders. The truth is that the question of the number of inscriptions of *rentes*, the inscriptions being anonymous, is purely a formal matter, depending upon the subdivisions which are most convenient for dealing. One individual may, and as a rule does, hold many inscriptions. When the French issued new loans in 1871 and 1872 to pay the war indemnity to Germany, and in subsequent years to re-equip their army and extend their railways, the number of inscriptions in the books of the Ministry of Finance enormously increased, but it did not follow that the number of separate holders of French *rentes* increased in the same degree, or even increased at all. The same with the holding of land. A broad distinction has to be drawn between the number of separate occupiers and the number of separate occupations, the latter (as in Ireland) being often far more numerous than the former. But, admitting that the figures as to one branch only can be got hold of, it is plain that, unless saving habits in all directions can be compared, no useful comparison can be made at all. What is done by friendly societies, building societies, insurance companies and the like, must all be taken into account as well as the savings banks, which are most often quoted, or the holdings of the Government debt, or the holdings of land, which are the favourite investments of the masses in some countries. But I do not know of any comparison of the kind in which these conditions are complied with. French peasants and working men are often assumed to be much more saving than the corresponding classes of England, but the statistical proof seems to be wanting, and I am not sure that if the accumulations of English unions, friendly societies, and co-operative societies, were properly taken account of, as well as savings banks, holdings of Government debt, and investments in land, that the English working classes would come so very badly out of the comparison. At any rate, the comparison is more difficult than is often thought.

Even if comparisons could be made, there would remain the question of the comparison of character. A working population which feeds and clothes itself well and makes itself in all ways efficient, provided it saves enough for security, may really be making more of life than a population which starves itself in the present through fear that it may starve in the future. The proper proportion of saving for a working class community is itself a subject which requires some study.

These points are of special interest in new communities where the working classes have large means. No good is done by using unsound arguments even for so excellent an object as the promotion of thrift. If examples are to be taken from other countries such as France, the so-called example should first of all be adequately explained, and a true comparison made, and then an inquiry made as to whether and how far the French example is sound and worthy of imitation. The fact already brought out as to the larger proportion of old life in France than there is in either Germany or the United Kingdom may also render saving a greater necessity there in order that as much may be got out of life as in the neighbouring countries. The requirements as to saving may thus be essentially different.

To sum up this branch of the discussion: what we may say is that the rough comparison of communities as regards moral characteristics based on statistics of education, crime, insolvency, and the like, is entirely useless and mischievous because the figures are of such a kind that values can only be assigned to them by the most careful study. To take them haphazard from statistical abstracts and dictionaries, and assume that figures called by the same names in different countries have exactly the same values, is either foolish or dishonest. Dictionaries are for reference, and are not intended to give all the materials for discussion; and when they are used for purposes for which they are not intended, all who are interested in the subjects under discussion must look out. Some dictionaries, however, might be made more useful than they are by the addition of a few notes to the figures, referring to such points as the nature of the legislation applied to the subjects of the figures, the mode of collecting the latter, and other vital qualifications of the figures themselves. I may claim the credit of privately stifling many an argument which inquirers were going to use by taking figures from books as they found them, because I pointed out to them what different values the figures might have. But the dictionaries themselves could often put inquirers on their guard.

Industrial Statistics.

I pass on next to a class of statistics which are still more frequently used for international comparison, viz., the statistics of production, industry, and trade. There is money in the comparisons here. There are competing policies whose merits are supposed to be capable of judgment by statistics. Or a country may wish to advertise its resources so as to attract immigrants or capital. There is also the patriotic bias or sentiment to be gratified or stimulated, or the anti-patriotic bias, which is really an inverted form of the patriotic bias itself.

The leading statistics thus used may be classed under the heads of agricultural production, manufacturing production, imports and exports including shipping, wages, and, finally, accumulated wealth. The division is not a logical one, but it appears convenient for the present purpose, which is to explain the principal dangers into which the unwary in dealing with the vast branches of statistics included in this department are apt to fall.

As regards agricultural production, then, the initial difficulty of all the statistics is that which we have already had in dealing with population itself—the different value of the units which go by the same name. The wheat, oats, and barley of one country, though called by the same names, are not the same as the wheat, oats, and barley of another country. There are the very greatest differences in quality, as any price list of London or other market, where grain from every part of the world is sold, would show. Yet nothing is so common as comparisons of the world's production of wheat, for instance, in which this difference of quality is ignored, and fine reasonings are indulged in where this difference of quality might seriously affect the result. What is true of grain is as true, if not more true, of live stock. There are sheep and sheep, cattle and cattle, horses and horses; in truth the agricultural live stock of any two countries, instead of being susceptible of ready comparison, can hardly be compared directly at all. The point is notoriously of great importance in historical investigations. In comparing England of the present day with the England of previous centuries the difference of the average weight and quality of the live stock called by the same names has always to be considered. In nothing in recent years, as I understand, have some continental countries such as France made more remarkable improvement than in the quality of their live stock, so that with no increase in numbers, or little increase, there has been an enormous advance in real production. But the point is of equal importance in international comparisons. If Australia is to reckon with competitors in wool production, like the Argentine Republic, the average clip per sheep in the respective countries is obviously a necessary coefficient in the calculation, and it becomes of great importance to study in what countries the average is increasing or diminishing, and so on. Officials at the head of the agricultural department in France have been greatly impressed by considerations like these, and have endeavoured to substitute a count of cattle by weight for the mere count of heads, but even a correction like this would by no means be sufficient, as there might still be serious differences of quality. The comparisons, then, of agricultural production which one often sees, in which unlike units are taken as equal without more ado, and reasoned upon as if there were no qualifications, are most misleading. Rectification to any exact degree might not in many comparisons be possible, but the consideration of the point would usually make it possible to turn the figures to support some useful conclusion.

In connection with these comparisons, it should also be noticed that many of the deductions per head and per acre, into which it is usual to convert the figures of agricultural production, are calculated to mislead, even when the units themselves are comparable, because the comparisons are with the total acreage and total population of a country, and not with the special acreage and agricultural population. What could be more useless, for instance, than to compare two countries like England and the United States as regards their production of wheat or any other agricultural product per head of the whole population, the one population living on its own wheat and other products, and the other not? All such comparisons to be of any value should be made from the purely agricultural point of view—to illustrate differences in the style of agriculture carried on, or in the fertility of any two countries. But they are often made with lingering notions that all States can, to some extent, be dealt with as agricultural units, which is far from being the case.

Coming to statistics of manufacturing production—and this to some extent applies to agricultural and mining production—what we find is that, save as to some particular industry in detail, and for the purposes of discussions of that industry by itself, there is really no common denominator between countries, except in so far as the production of their respective industries can be represented in money. The coal and iron of one country are not the same as the coal and iron of another; the wool is not the same; the cotton, woollen, and linen manufactures of the one cannot be expressed in the same units of quantity as the similar manufactures of the other; the same with manufactures of metals, leather, and wood, and with machines of all kinds. Even if there is a general likeness in industrial characteristics between any two countries such as England and France, yet the different distributions of the leading industries makes any real comparison between the two as a rule impossible, except so far as it can be done in money. To make the comparison in money, again, presents new difficulties. The value of different kinds of production cannot well be reckoned up. A country like England, with the machinery of its income tax, has special facilities for reckoning up its income as far as possessed by individuals above a certain minimum; but it has little official knowledge, by comparison, of incomes below that limit. France, again, has a special knowledge of its agricultural wealth, by means of the cadastre, and the system of registration and taxation of transfers of property, but it has not equal means of estimating its income from manufacturing. Money also is itself variable in value from time to time, as measured by the average of the commodities or services it is used to exchange, and in comparing two countries, as regards their production measured in money, no little care would be needed. I have seen few attempts to do so in which attention has been paid to the necessary conditions and difficulties, or in which the existence of such dangers and difficulties has even been recognized. The Americans in their census have attempted a great deal in this direction, but the least that can be said is that the result has not been encouraging.

Coming next to imports and exports, the point I would urge first is the initial difficulty of a bare comparison of the figures themselves. Imports and exports, instead of giving us easy statistics for many of the purposes for which they are used, are really very difficult. I refer especially to the values. Imports are stated in one country at the value of the goods as at the place of shipment; in another, as at the place of arrival. In one country the basis of the statement is a declaration of the value by the importer, checked by the Customs authorities; in another there is an efficient commission of values, which takes note of market prices, and fixes official prices for everything at more or less frequent intervals. The same with the exports. The denominators are hardly ever the same in any two countries. The result is, that there are continual misstatements by amateurs on such questions as a comparison of two countries in respect of the progress of their foreign trade, or in respect of what is called the balance of trade. The falling off of the foreign trade of one country is contrasted with the growth of the foreign trade of another country at the same time, the truth being that in the one case, owing to the system of valuing by merchants' declarations, the volume of the foreign trade expressed in money responds instantly to variations in market price, while, in the other, owing to the system of official prices fixed at intervals, the volume of trade does not respond at once to variations in market price. In one country, again, what is called an adverse balance of trade appears to be larger in proportion than it is in another country, largely because the imports are valued as at the place of arrival, including freight and other charges to that place; while in the country with which comparison is made, the value is taken at the place of shipment, and does not include such additions. In the latter case, therefore, the exports form a total more nearly approximating to that of the imports than in the former. All this confusion is due simply to the fact that the units of the imports and exports are not, in fact, the same. The record is not made in the same way.

Assuming, however, that the record is made in the same way formally, there remain some essential differences in the foreign trade of different countries, which make comparisons between them most difficult, and it is mainly to one or two of these essential differences I would now desire to call attention.

First of all, there are the differences which I discussed at length in a paper I wrote long ago on "The Use of Import and Export Statistics,"[1] due to the facts that a nation may be largely engaged in the business

[1] See *supra*, vol. i., pp. 282 *et seq.*

of carrying goods for others, or may have made large investments abroad, on which it is entitled to dividends or interest, while another nation may have its goods carried for it, or may owe large dividends and interest. In the former case, a large amount of imports is required to set off the balance due to the nation concerned, quite apart from what is required to set off the exports officially recorded as such. In the latter case a large amount of exportation is required to set off the balance of indebtedness with which the nation, as it were, begins its import and export account. The character of the foreign trade of the two classes of nations is essentially differentiated all the way through for those reasons. It may be found afterwards that, in fact, a nation in the first class exports as much, or nearly so, as the official record of its imports; or that a nation in the second class imports as much, or nearly so, as the official record of its exports. But the inferences would be very different as to the economic conditions implied. In the first case the near balance of imports and exports would imply that the nation in question is at the time lending largely to other communities. In the latter case the inference would be that the nation in question is borrowing largely, for useful or useless purposes as the case may be. Before the statistics can be handled at all, in short, so as to throw light on the economic conditions, the standard of equilibrium has to be adjusted to allow for the other elements described.

England, I need hardly add, is a conspicuous example of a nation in the first class, its freight-carrying and its investments abroad being both enormous. But France, Belgium, Holland, Germany, and the Northern nations of Europe are all more or less in the same category. On the other hand the United States of America, India, Australasia, the South American countries, and many more are all nations in the second category, having their carrying trade done for them, and having dividends and interest to pay to nations in the first category. But there is much discussion on relative import and export statistics in which these essential differences are lost sight of, and imports and exports are treated as if in all cases they were the same.

The next point I would urge is that the imports and exports of what I would call an *entrepôt* country are not of the same species as the imports and exports of a country which has a direct import and export trade only: that is, which exports its own home produce on the one side, and imports articles for final consumption on the other side. A country which largely receives either raw produce or produce in different degrees of advancement towards the form in which it is finally consumed, and then, after manipulating that produce to a greater or less extent, re-exports it, has obviously a very different kind of foreign trade from a country which manipulates nothing or hardly anything it receives, and does not re-export. The imports and exports in the respective cases have not the same relation to the general economic conditions of the countries concerned. To compare the *entrepôt* country with a country which has only direct foreign trade, so as to show the volume of imports and exports in respect of what is received for final consumption and what is exported of the labour of the country, it would be necessary to deduct from both sides of the account of the *entrepôt* country the value of the produce imported and afterwards re-exported in a manipulated form. In this way, I am sure, the imports and exports of the United Kingdom would be largely reduced from what they appear to be, and the United Kingdom would not appear to import so much more than some others for final consumption, or to export so much more than some others with which to obtain purchasing power abroad. Reckoning in this manner, I am not sure but that Australasia would appear even more at the head of exporting countries than it now does, the labour per head represented in its exports being truly enormous. Some countries, such as Belgium and Holland, again, would have their tale of imports and exports reduced even more than that of the United Kingdom, as their business is so very much a business of transit only. In any case these are points obviously requiring consideration, when the imports and exports of different countries are compared or contrasted. They ought not to be put together at all in any discussion till they are reduced to common denominators.

Another point I would urge is the importance of the question of size and general similarity in conditions in comparing the volume of the foreign trade of any two countries. If the United Kingdom were to be split up, and Ireland, say, were to have separate customs, the foreign trade of Great Britain would be enhanced by the addition to the account of the imports from Ireland on one side, and the exports to it on the other, which would then become foreign trade, deducting, however, the present imports into Ireland from foreign countries, and the exports from it to foreign countries which are now included in the foreign trade of the whole United Kingdom. If Holland, again, were to be united with Germany, and Belgium with France, it is doubtful whether the foreign trade of both Germany and France would be increased very much, and might not even be diminished, so much of the foreign trade of Germany and France being now with Holland and Belgium; while the aggregate foreign trade of the world would be diminished by the elimination of the two countries named as separate countries, and they would no longer appear as having the largest amount of imports and exports per head. In the same way the formation of the Australasian countries into a federation with a single Customs frontier would greatly diminish the volume of imports and exports as now stated. According to Table B appended, the imports of the Australasian colonies added together, for the year 1889, amounted to about £69,043,000, and the exports to £62,706,000; but if we separate what each colony imports from and exports to the rest of the world, excluding what it imports from and exports to its neighbours, the total would be

£40,481,000 only for imports, and £35,902,000 for exports. These would be the proper figures to use in a comparison with other countries, such as Canada or the Argentine Republic, in more or less similar economic conditions. Compared with either of these two states, and assuming for the present that the figures are made up in much the same way, as I believe is the case, the foreign trade of Australasia comes out at about double that of either of the countries named. Its exporting power is so much greater than theirs. This is a true comparison. But a comparison in which the intercolonial trade is not eliminated would give an altogether untrue notion. Australasian foreign trade would appear about thrice or four times that of Canada, instead of about double only; and this would be a false comparison. The truth is favourable enough to Australasia.

Generally, however, I should like to add that the selection of foreign trade, as specially a test of the welfare of nations, does not seem to be in any way justified. Whether the foreign trade of a given country is large or small in proportion to its whole production is an affair to a large extent of size or of historical evolution, and nothing can be made of comparisons unless attention is given to the point I have already suggested—that of size and general similarity of conditions. But it is quite conceivable that nations might approximate to each other in many respects, and the one have a large foreign trade and the other not, yet both be in much the same condition of individual prosperity. Accident might determine that the one should be more self-contained than the other, so that its exchanges with other countries should bear a less proportion to its total industry. France and England are very good illustrations of essential differences of this sort, England having much more manufacturing, shipping, and foreign trade than France, but France being certainly a highly prosperous nation, with home industries of different kinds which England either has not at all or not to the same degree, and the products of which are only or largely obtained in England by exporting something else. All these general comparisons between nations in which the foreign trade is spoken of or assumed to be representative of the total trade are, therefore, very much to be deprecated. Import and export statistics, apart from the special danger of using them, which I have described, cannot be properly used for such comparisons.

I come next to international statistical comparisons in respect to wages, which present some curious difficulties of which most of those who make such comparisons seem totally unaware. In the primary use of records of wages, viz., their use by the labourer or workman, who has no employment, or small wages, in one place, and finds he can better himself by going to another, these difficulties do not arise. If the facts recorded are true, the labourer or workman has something on which to act, and he can attend to all the points and qualifications necessary. But when the same records are used, or an attempt is made to use them, for more general purposes, difficulties begin. Length of working day, continuity of employment, and other points must all be recorded when a general statistical account of the wages-earning classes of a people has to be built up. So little have such matters been studied, however, that I doubt the existence of any comparison of wages in different countries which is even formally complete. No country has, as yet, a tolerably complete account of its own wages in which attention is given to all these points; much less is there any possibility of international comparisons.[1]

As the primary records are, however, sometimes used for such comparisons, and we get such statements based on them as that wages are 50 or 100 per cent. higher in the United States, say, than in England, special attention may be drawn to the failure of the comparison in point of logic. In the absence of any account of length of the working day and continuity of employ-

[1] Since this was written wages statistics have been greatly improved, but international comparisons continue to be most difficult (1903-4).

ment, no proper comparison can be made. This applies specially to a comparison between wages in out-of-door trades in a country like the United States, with a severe climate, and wages in the same trades in England. Wages in the former country may well be higher per nominal day or week of actual work, and yet the difference not be so great when the earnings and hours of labour of the whole year in England are reckoned.

What I would most desire to direct attention to, however, is the statistical importance of a somewhat different point. This is the distribution of the population according to remuneration. It is quite conceivable that in one of two countries the earnings, and still more the nominal wages, may be higher than in the other in every single employment which can be enumerated and compared, and yet the average earnings of the average wages-earning man may be higher in the latter country than the former, the reason being the different distribution of the people according to earnings. This can be shown very clearly in a theoretical comparison. Take first a community of 1,000 wages-earners, with the people distributed according to earnings, in the following classes—A, B, C, D, and E—as follows:

First Community.

Class.		Per Annum.	Nos.	Total.
A.	Earnings . .	£50	500	£25,000
B.	" . .	60	200	12,000
C.	" . .	70	100	7,000
D.	" . .	80	100	8,000
E.	" . .	90	100	9,000
	Total		1,000	£61,000

Average per head, £61.

And compare this with another community of equal numbers, in which there are also five grades, each remunerated at a lower rate than the corresponding grade in the first community, but in which the average of the whole is higher because of the different distribution of the people among the grades:

Second Community.

Class.		Per Annum.	Nos.	Total.
A.	Earnings . .	£40	100	£4,000
B.	,, . .	50	100	5,000
C.	,, . .	60	100	6,000
D.	,, . .	70	200	14,000
E.	,, . .	80	500	40,000
	Total		1,000	£69,000

Average per head, £69.

In a comparison of rates of wages merely according to the nature of the employment, the wages in the first community would obviously appear higher than in the second, and this would be strictly true in a sense: but the inference would be untrue that the average earnings of the wages-earning classes in the first community, striking a true average, would be higher.

The principle of this theoretical comparison, I believe, helps to explain the actual facts as between an agricultural new country like the United States or Australasia and an old country like England. In the former agricultural wages are higher than in England, and almost every sort of employment, subject, however, to some qualifications, such as length of day and continuity of employment, is better paid than in England; but it is a *non sequitur*, not at first apparent, that the average earnings all round are also higher, the truth being that owing to the larger proportion of artisan classes in England the average earnings of the working classes may be as high or higher in England than in the United States, or at any rate not very far short. The mode of comparing wages in two countries is thus a most critical question. I have been often puzzled myself to explain how it is that we arrive in England at comparatively high figures for the aggregate income of the nation when most of the rates of wages are apparently so much lower—employment for employment—than they are in the United States or Australasia, and to a large extent I believe the solution I have now suggested is the true one. It is not enough, then, to compare employment with employment, but mass must be compared with mass.

Other dangers in these international statistical comparisons, such as differences in the purchasing power of money in different places, may be suggested. But I should not be disposed to lay so much stress on any other point as upon that of the relative importance of different employments in different countries. In these days of cheap freights and rapid transit, the equalization of prices in all countries has been carried very far indeed, the most important differences that remain being, I believe, artificial, arising from the protection of food products in countries like Germany and France, and the like causes. The different distribution of populations according to employments remains, however, an enduring cause of differences in their relative aggregate earnings and average earnings per head.

Wealth Statistics.

Finally I have some remarks to make on the dangers of comparisons between nations as to their aggregate wealth.

Apart from all other difficulties that of the data themselves is here very great. It is hardly possible to obtain an account of the wealth of any country on any basis that can give a minutely accurate result, and it is the more difficult to obtain such accounts for any two nations made up in exactly the same way. If one country, therefore, is made out to have an aggregate wealth of about £250 per head, and another of £300 per head, it may well be that, owing to the necessary want of exactness in the calculation itself for any country and the differences of method employed in each case, the facts represented by these figures may either be much the same, or the country whose wealth is computed at the smaller figure may really be the richer of the two. Before any comparisons can be made at all, then, the methods observed in each case must be carefully followed, and particularly it must be observed whether they are likely to give a rack valuation or not. My own impression is that, except where the differences are enormous by almost any method of calculation, but little can be made of differences between country and country. Figures that are within sight of each other as much as are £250 and £300 per head, provided much the same methods have been followed, are practically much the same thing.

The comparison, also, is of little value unless accompanied by statistics of relative income, statistics of the sources of the wealth or income, and the like information. Accumulated wealth is only one element of economic strength.

A special point of great difficulty is how to deal with the wealth of a community which includes individuals having large investments abroad, and with the wealth of another community which is indebted to persons resident abroad in its public capacity, and whose individual members are also indebted to members of other communities. To a certain extent the foreign investments of a community in the first case are not available resources. Suppose the investments to be made in a foreign country with which it goes to war, the whole resources which are counted part of its wealth would really count on the other side. In the same way a country which has borrowed largely has the whole wealth really available for many purposes without any deduction for what it has borrowed. In war with a community from which it had borrowed this would at once be apparent, but in other contingencies, also, the indebtedness is not a real deduction, the wealth belonging to the foreign non-resident being really taxable as if he were resident. I have thought it expedient in my own calculations of the wealth of the United Kingdom to include the foreign investments of the members of the community at home as far as possible, and similarly I would make a deduction in the case of an indebted community equal to the amount of its indebtedness. All this, however, would be on the assumption of a continuation of peace, and subject to the qualification that in certain circumstances a different calculation would practically require to be made.

There is one point in addition to be noticed in regard to the method of these calculations. Where property in two countries appears to be subject to a tax like probate duty or income tax on apparently much the same basis, the temptation is very strong to apply the calculated amount of such property per head to each nation respectively, but nothing could be more dangerous owing to the difficulty of the data. The laws and their administration in the respective countries compared would need careful examination before any such short cut could be used, and even then one ought not to be too sure of any single method. Unless some detail could be given, no such method should be employed except as a check on a more detailed method. Such a method is also specially dangerous when the wealth of a community is arrived at without any items being given; by such a method, for instance, as that of dividing the average wealth subject to probate duty in a year by the numbers dying in a year, assuming the wealth per head thus arrived at to be the average wealth per head of the community, and then multiplying the numbers of the community by that figure so as to arrive at the aggregate wealth. The method may yield useful results if care be taken to establish *aliunde* what is the relation between the wealth per head of those members of a community who die within a year, and the wealth per head of the members of a community as a whole, but when no such care is taken, and communities are compared whose probate and income-tax laws are not really the same, the result of the comparisons may be the merest chance.

Conclusion.

The conclusion of this long review may be very shortly stated. All the leading branches of statistics without exception, when examined, give numerous illustrations of the dangers of taking the figures relating to them from dictionaries or works of reference at haphazard for international comparison, as if the figures called by the same names in different countries meant the same things, or the units had the same values. On the contrary, from the simplest figures as to population and area, through the more complex figures as to the moral qualities of communities indicated by statistics like those relating to education and crime, down to the still more complex figures relating to production, trade and wealth, the same tale is told as to the necessity for constant watchfulness lest things that are really unlike be put together as if they were like. The moral is what was stated at the outset, that the figures as such may be right enough, though there are many difficulties as to the data themselves to be faced in statistics, but the exact meaning of the figures called by the same name, when place and circumstances are different, may require a great deal of elucidation. Perhaps some may think that the difficulties are so great as to make it hopeless to handle most statistics in such a way as to reach any conclusion. This is, however, by no means the case. When care is taken true conclusions begin to appear, and a picture is obtained of the general conditions of communities in the mass which would otherwise be unattainable. The negative results which are the effect of the criticism applied to the rough and ready methods of amateur statisticians are also valuable and important. There are so many errors about respecting the condition of most communities, partly derived from, and partly nursed by, the rash use of statistics with a more or less conscious bias towards a desired conclusion, that it clears the air to have a demonstration of the impossibility of these errors being proved to be true. When one knows, for instance, how intrinsically difficult it is to prove statistically the greater prosperity of one country than another when the differences between them are not very great, it is not difficult to estimate at its due weight any argument in which the difficulties are ignored and statistics are dealt with by short cuts when they seem to support the side on which the arguer has ranged himself. If we help by this discussion to strengthen the wholesome attitude of doubt, and to discredit the short cuts of the amateur partisan, the discussion, it may be hoped, will not have been wholly in vain.

TABLE A.—*Total Population, and Total Male Population above age of twenty, in the Undermentioned Countries (according to the latest information available).*

	France. (Census, 1886.)	Germany. (Census, 1885.)	United Kingdom. (Census, 1881.)
Total Population . .	37,930,759	40,855,704	34,884,848
Total Male Population	18,900,312	22,933,664	16,972,654
Total Male Population above age twenty .	11,828,363	12,435,796	8,898,529
Total Male Population between twenty and forty	5,376,254	6,577,383	4,838,585

TABLE B.—*Statement showing the value of Imports and Exports into and from each of the Australasian Colonies during the year 1889 from and into (1) the remaining Australasian Colonies and (2) all other Countries.*

Colonies.	Imports.		
	From Australasian Colonies.	From other Countries.	Total.
	£	£	£
New South Wales . .	10,647,312	12,215,745	22,863,057
Victoria	8,539,854	15,862,906	24,402,760
South Australia . . .	4,045,691	2,758,760	6,804,451
Port Darwin, N.T. . .	132,054	62,290	194,344
Western Australia . .	334,969	483,158	818,127
Tasmania	1,037,078	573,957	1,611,035
New Zealand . . .	1,107,132	5,189,965	6,297,097
Queensland	2,717,671	3,334,891	6,052,562
Total	28,561,761	40,481,672	69,043,433

Colonies.	Exports.		
	To Australasian Colonies.	To other Countries.	Total.
	£	£	£
New South Wales . .	10,741,045	12,553,889	23,294,934
Victoria	4,022,054	8,712,680	12,734,734
South Australia . . .	3,283,734	3,975,631	7,259,365
Port Darwin, N.T. . .	87,836	32,380	120,216
Western Australia . .	147,557	613,835	761,392
Tasmania	1,208,006	251,851	1,459,857
New Zealand . . .	2,145,671	7,193,594	9,339,265
Queensland	5,167,790	2,568,519	7,736,309
Total	26,803,693	35,902,379	62,706,072

XV.

THE GROSS AND THE NET GAIN OF RISING WAGES.[1]

IN the discussions to which former papers of mine on working-class progress have given rise, there are some criticisms which have interested me very much. They are made by members of the working class themselves, who are slow enough to admit the average increase of their money earnings in the last fifty years, which the figures demonstrate. But, admitting some increase of money, they go on to say, and admitting, too, the low prices, the improvement after all is not without drawbacks, or, as I have suggested in the above title, it is mainly in the gross. There are drawbacks which take away much of the apparent advantage. A general statement like this, apart from particular allegations to support it, could not but excite my attention, although I have avoided hitherto any discussion of it. It is a good rule to do one thing at a time. An improvement of money earnings and no increase of prices appeared to be two points worth establishing, whatever the drawbacks of a less apparent kind, and which the working classes could themselves best appreciate, might be. But while avoiding the discussion hitherto, I have been none the less observant, for the simple reason that each class knows its own grievances as no others can, and that such complaints, though easy enough to prove unfounded, are apt to cover facts which will reward investigation—which will throw light, when properly understood, not only on the particular problems in hand, but on larger problems. I propose

[1] From the "Contemporary Review" of 1889.

in the present paper to communicate some reflections which I have made. The alleged drawbacks, when considered, do, in fact, suggest for consideration questions of a weighty nature, which go to the root of ideas of progress, and affect the most general views of the prospects of modern civilization.

The alleged drawbacks of which I speak are mainly the following: First, it is said, working men in many cases have more to pay for rent than they would have to pay when earning less money under different conditions, or they have to pay railway or 'bus fares or similar charges for conveyance to and from their work, which are in the nature of an increase of rent. Consequently, although the money wage is more, the workman is not so much better off than he was, because a large part of that money wage has to be paid as a fine, practically, to enable the working man to be in a position to earn it. In other words, the gross sum is more, but the net sum is not so much more. It is easy to perceive also that this principle may have a much wider application than may at first be surmised. The case usually thought of is that of rent, or an equivalent fine on a workman, which he pays in order to be in a certain place where the money wage can be earned. Suppose the climate in which he has to live in order to earn a larger money wage than he can get elsewhere is so exhausting as to compel a larger consumption of food in order that the money may be earned? The question of gross and net is thus of a wide-sweeping kind.

Next, it is maintained that along with a great increase in production which has undoubtedly taken place, there has come an increase in the severity of the labour, and that the workman's remuneration has not risen in proportion. It seems to be suggested at times that the increase in the labour is itself an evil, even if it were proportionately remunerated, but the complaint rather is that the severer toil is not adequately compensated: the workman has a severer call made on his energies, and he is not so much better off. To be able to earn more money, it is sometimes urged, he must, in fact, spend more money on food and other things than he formerly did. Here, again, is a question of gross and net, and it will be observed how the last complaint raises in a different form the question already suggested under the first head by a consideration of the effects of climate. A distinction is made between the gross earning and the net surplus, the difference being something which the working man has to pay as a fine to enable him to earn the net sum which he wishes to spend.

Last of all, it is maintained that on all sides the scale of living has become more expensive. The working man has to get more food, clothing, and shelter for his family than he would formerly have had to get; more is expected of him; and he has to pay for such things as the education of his children to a much greater extent than he would formerly have had to pay. In this way the strain upon the working man has increased. As I understand the complaint, he is no more a free man than before. His energies are mortgaged in advance, and he has all the old difficulty to keep his footing in the world.

Now, whether these complaints are right or wrong, well or ill founded, it is clear that they involve problems of a most vital kind as to the general effect upon the working classes of the conditions of modern civilization. To take the first head of complaint. If it be the case that a rise of rent or the charge for travelling between the place of living and the place of work or similar expenditure is sufficient to deprive working men of the advantage of increased money wages, then the congregation of men in cities or in certain parts of cities, where higher money wages are to be obtained than elsewhere, which appear to be the conditions of modern industrial life, would be fatal to improvement. It would be the same with the necessity for working in an exhausting climate. The problem, as stated, is certainly of the gravest kind. The questions raised by the second head of complaint are just as important. If increase of toil, not proportionately remunerated—for which, perhaps, there can be no proportionate remuneration—comes with the increase of productive capacity and the greater call thus made on the nervous and mental energy of the workman, what is the working man the better off for all the civilization? Finally, as regards the increased cost of living through a rise in the scale, may it not be the case that such a rise in the scale of living is to some extent what is meant by progress, though the drawback of the slavery of the workers, which some working men appear to feel so keenly, remains? How far is the "slavery" itself avoidable, so long as human nature is what it is, unless at the risk of all civilization perishing? Such problems are obviously of the deepest interest. The desire for leisure, for an ease to a severe strain, in all these complaints, is itself very striking, and may, perhaps, be held of itself to indicate a change of working-class conditions, as compared with a time when the masses simply endured, or were content to drag on a dull existence, with little colour in it, and without hope of change. The whole subject, at any rate, should be well worth considering. What are the facts, and what should be the conclusions regarding them?

Dealing with the first head of complaint, which is perhaps the simplest and most easily dealt with, we must allow it to be obvious on the surface that there is a real point for discussion. Under the essential conditions of modern life, principally the concentration of huge masses on narrow room, competition among labourers undoubtedly produces monopoly rent, the payment of which is a simple deduction from the gross money wages which workmen receive. If workmen, to avoid paying more than they can help, live at a distance from their work, they only escape the evil partially, because charges for conveyance to and from their work have to be paid. Clearly workmen under such conditions, as compared with conditions under which no monopoly rent or its equivalent has to be paid, are at a disadvantage. To show their real position for the purpose of comparison, the monopoly portion of the rent must be deducted. It is quite obvious, also, on the merest superficial aspect of the question, that as regards many workmen, at least, the disadvantage may easily be so serious as to compensate, and more than compensate all the difference between the money wage of the country, where there is no monopoly rent, and the money wage of the town. Take the case of a west Highland peasant fifty years ago, living on a scanty wage of a few shillings a week, or the produce of a poor croft eked out by kelp-gathering or fishing, and his descendant at the present time in the slums of a great city, earning perhaps 15*s.* a week, but disbursing 4*s.* or 5*s.* for rent. The improvement in money earnings may be immense, perhaps 100 per cent., and as regards prices of commodities there may be no drawback in the change, but the rent takes a monstrous cantle out of the margin. Comparing all the conditions, it may certainly be doubted whether the peasant, in the case supposed, in exchanging the hard life of the country, which still had the advantage of being in the open, for the hard life of the city, has made any real advance. Take a case higher in the scale. A doctor, to earn a living, resides in a city rather than in the country, pays a huge monopoly rent to begin with, and incurs many other analogous expenses, so that altogether he has a large leeway to make up before he can reckon that net income which can properly enter into comparison with that of his country colleague. The difference may easily be so great, I believe, that in many cases a professional man in a small country town with £300 or £400 a year may have a larger net income for the real objects of life, dealing with the question in a wise philosophic spirit, than a professional man in London with £1,000 or £1,200 a year. There are differences even between London and smaller provincial cities. Thus the question between gross and net, which working men have raised in these discussions, apropos of monopoly rent or the equivalent, is a real question. It is a new form of the old theorem, that people may buy gold too dear.

I have already, in part, dealt with the question practically as far as working men are concerned, by pointing out the really narrow limits of monopoly rent,[1] and practically the final conclusion must be reached by the statistical method, and in the way I have already used. But I wish to avoid statistics for the present, and to indicate merely the general conditions of the problem to be solved, which appear to minimize the possible extent of the alleged drawback.

It is clear, first of all, on general grounds that the concentration of men in cities is due to the fact that cities, on the whole, weigh in the balance against the country. There is more and better employment there than in the country, all deductions made, in the opinion of those interested, and that seems a conclusive answer to the question as to whether, on the whole, there is not a net as well as a gross improvement in wages as far as this drawback is concerned.

Next, it is plain that as a great part of the improvement of the last fifty years has consisted in the substitution of artisan and other highly-paid labour for merely rude labour, the additional monopoly rent payable in the cities can only be, in most cases, a comparatively trifling drawback. It may be the case, that if we compare the former peasant of the country with the rude labourer of the city, and especially of the Metropolis, the latter has hardly gained; but if we compare the former peasant of the country with the town artisan of the present time, although the latter has to pay monopoly rent or an equivalent charge for conveyance, there is still an enormous gain in the latter's position. It is the same with the professional classes. If the latter were stationary in number, or increasing only *pari passu* with the increase of population, then

[1] See *supra*, vol. i., pp. 397-398.

the larger gross income on the average earned by the masses of professional men in cities, as compared with the professional incomes earned in the country formerly, might show little *net* improvement; but allowance has to be made for the fact that the number of such incomes has enormously increased, and that the earners largely compare with the earners of wholly inferior incomes in former times, whether in town or country. As the increase of these classes could not have taken place without the growth of cities, there must be a large net as well as gross gain to be reckoned when the comparison is properly made.

To bring the matter to a point, what I have to urge is, that the very growth of cities implies the existence of conditions under which workmen of higher grades take the place of workmen of lower grades, so that, although class for class a workman passing from country to town does not seem to gain so very much, on account of the difference between gross and net, yet, man for man, on the average there is an enormous gain. Illusion is produced because the proper terms of the comparison are lost sight of. The point is especially important, as regards what is known as the residuum. Nothing can appear so deplorable or so hopeless as the conditions of the floating mass of rude labour in large cities. Monopoly rents in this case appear to sweep away all possible advantage which may result from higher money wage, comparing the labourer of the town with the labourer of the country. In many cases, even, it must be admitted, the "residuary" of the city is on a lower level than the "residuary" of the country. His "net" earnings are less. But the question, after all, is one of proportion. The absolute magnitude of the city residuum must not blind us to the fact that it may be, not an increasing, but a diminishing, element with reference to the population generally. I believe it is a diminishing element, but this would hardly be the place to discuss the point, and I am content for the present to call attention to its importance in the discussion.

The assumption so often made, that the residuum is increasing relatively, is one which requires proof, and I have never seen any attempt at proof, while there are some broad facts, such as the diminution of serious crime and of pauperism, against it.

The question of the way in which the net value of an increase of money wages may be affected by the necessity of living in a more exhausting, or in some way more expensive, climate, or by the specially exhausting character of a highly paid occupation, such as puddling, is one of the same kind. There is clearly a point in the matter for consideration and discussion. I am disposed to believe, for instance, that the exhausting climate of the United States, compelling the consumption of more food to enable the same work to be done, is a distinct drawback to the American working man as compared with his competitor in Western Europe, and especially in Great Britain. I am not sure but that living in the South of England, owing to climate, is more expensive than in the North and in Scotland. The point has hardly been expressly considered, the working man practically having been right to go where he gets the highest money wage, but it is one that may become of increasing practical interest now that charges for conveyance are so low throughout the world as to make it quite unnecessary for men to live near the places where their food and raw materials are produced. I shall be well content for the present if the remarks here made induce some working men to elaborate it from their practical experiences. Of course, in any discussion it would also have to be considered that the greater expense of living may not be a pure drawback. The ability to consume and produce more, to bear exhausting climate or occupation, in fact, may be a good thing, and bring its own compensation, although the net gain, taking matters strictly, may hardly be appreciable.

The next head of complaint is the increase in the

severity of labour and the want of any proportionate remuneration.

On this head it may be admitted, to begin with, that there is apparent foundation for some of the complaints. Workmen in particular employments do not get a reward at all in proportion to the increase of production in those employments. The illustration of a cotton mill is familiar. A single attendant on a number of machines will "produce" as much in an hour as formerly in a year or two, but his wages are only double—or perhaps not quite double—what they were when the production was so much less. A great steamship supplies another illustration. The ship does many times the work which could have been performed by the sailing ship it has displaced, and with much fewer men in proportion to the tonnage conveyed. But the wages of the average member of the crew are again only double, or not quite double, what they were when the conveyance done was so much less. In these and similar cases, who gets the benefit of all the increase of production? The workmen in the particular employments concerned receiving only a fraction of the gain may be excused for suspecting that there is something inexplicable in those social and economic arrangements by which the benefit is spirited away from them.

But, however natural the question, it is not difficult to point out that there is a good reason why workmen in some given employments should only receive a fraction of the benefit from the increased productiveness of those employments, and that this fact is quite consistent with an improvement in the position of workmen all round in proportion to the generally increased productiveness of labour, which is the real question we are now investigating, for the purpose of comparing this increase of productiveness with the increase of the severity of labour throughout society. The short explanation is that the employments in which there is a great increase of production, being mainly the employments in which there are great mechanical improvements from time to time, constitute only a part of the whole employment for labour, and that by a natural law labour in each employment finds its level, the increase of the return arising from an invention in a particular employment resulting in a gain, not to the particular labourers concerned, but to the whole community of labourers. That the gain may be general, it is, in fact, essential that labourers generally should gain as consumers rather than as producers, which implies that in a given employment wages should increase, not in proportion to the increased productiveness of that employment by itself, but in proportion to the increased productiveness of labour generally. Hence, it may well be that while the productive power of machines may enormously increase, yet the general increase of productive power may be much less than would at first be thought, owing to the comparatively small proportion of labourers after all who use machinery of great capacity largely in their employments. Looking at the number of domestic servants, of clerks, of professional men and women, of unskilled labourers of every kind, of skilled labourers, such as painters, who do not use machines, I should doubt very much whether one-fourth of the labourers, even in a society like that of England, the most manufacturing in the world, use machinery of great capacity in their employments. It is easily to be accounted for, therefore, why in a given employment there should be a great increase of production without a corresponding increase of remuneration to those engaged in that particular employment. The gain has to be diffused through society, and the increase of production generally is not so great, and not nearly so great, as in a few special cases.

Another observation must be made. There may be a considerable improvement in the quality of production in employments of a non-mechanical kind, which it is difficult or even impossible to note by quantities, but where the labour competes with all other labour for remuneration. Where the increased remuneration should go to, when machines improve, is thus not so easy to determine *à priori*.

It is also obvious that even in an advancing community the remuneration of certain kinds of labourers, whose numbers continue disproportionate, may either not increase at all, or increase very little, the whole gain from increased productiveness being for the benefit of the labourers whose own labour improves in quality, apart from the fact that it is employed on more productive machines. Strictly speaking, unless there is a rise in the scale of living, accompanied by an improvement in quality all round, there is no reason why, in modern times, a man who can only drive a spade into the ground, or wheel a barrow, or carry bricks up a ladder, should receive any higher reward than similar labourers in former ages. The fact that such labourers are little better off is not inconsistent with the fact that workmen generally receive a larger reward than in any former period.

The way is thus cleared for answering the question as to whether the remuneration of labour has increased generally in proportion to the increased severity of labour.

It cannot be denied, first of all, that there is a great increase of the productiveness of labour itself, as well as a great increase of the absolute amount of remuneration. This is admitted on all sides. The increase of production is the very fact which is assumed. Nor is the increase of remuneration denied—the only question is of the proportionate remuneration. Before passing from this point, however, I should like to dwell a little on the fact already referred to, of an improvement in the quality of non-mechanical labour, because, as this labour is largely the subject of direct exchange without much intervention of capital, the mere fact of improvement implies almost a proportionate increase of remuneration. At any rate, the labourers concerned get almost the whole benefit, because they exchange with each other. I refer to such employments as those of teaching, medical attendance, nursing, domestic service, dressmaking, and the like among the upper and middle classes. The increase of remuneration here may not be in proportion to the improvement of quality; the game may not be worth the candle; but, at any rate, the exchanges are direct. Now, as to the fact of great improvement, I believe there is no doubt. Nursing, for instance, is said to be an entirely different thing in hospitals from what it was only fifteen or twenty years ago. Domestic service, as regards cooking, waiting, and other points, is also, on the whole, better, notwithstanding manifold complaints, just because of the general improvement in education and intelligence. The same with dressmaking. More intelligence and skill are everywhere applied, and in direct exchanges, without much intervention of machines or of capital.

Next, it has to be considered, as regards the question of proportionate remuneration, that by the very mode of here stating the question, it appears that it is not so much a question of increase in the severity of labour generally, as of a change in the character of the labour. If the quality of labour has altered and improved in many directions, there is, in truth, no proper term for comparison between the present and former times. The improvement of the quality of the labour, which is another name for the increased intelligence and energy of society, may not be proportionately remunerated; but there is no means of telling. People would not go back to the conditions of a former society, where less intelligence and energy were required for a lower scale of living, even if they had the choice. The new advantages, with all their drawbacks, are accepted as part of a higher state. The complaints are to some extent a sign of the perpetual unrest of human life, and of the fact of improvement itself.

There can equally be no doubt, looking at the matter in this way, that in certain directions there may be a very poignant and not unjustifiable feeling as to an increase in the severity of labour. This appears to be the case as regards employments which involve the watching of machines, the very employments where there is apparently the greatest increase of production and the least proportionate increase of the remuneration of labour. The strain upon the nervous system, through the combined monotony of the employment and the constant vigilance required, are no doubt very often most severe, and are perhaps felt the more because the present generation is comparatively untrained. But the increased severity of toil, without proportionate remuneration, might be admitted in those special employments without altering the fact that remuneration has increased generally. What seems to have happened in these cases is, that the development of society imposes a heavy burden on a special class, involving rapid change in the quality of its labour, to which it is hardly equal, but that the improvement in quality is part of the general improvement in society. The nervous power to stand monotony and supply the necessary vigilance and other moral qualities necessary for the supervision of machines may exist in greater abundance in the next generation, along with a continued improvement in the quality of labour in non-mechanical employments.

It will, perhaps, be urged that the workman does not get a proportionate remuneration because the capitalist obtains for himself the increased product—the socialist argument. But the facts are all against this explanation. One of the most remarkable facts of recent years is the general decline in the return to capital. Capitalists from year to year have been willing to invest for a smaller and smaller return. We must assume, then, that if they have gained at all it has only been by the immense cheapening of commodities, and labour has gained more than in proportion. This would appear to be the case: only the labourers who have gained, as we have seen, are not specially those who are occupied about machines. The gain is generally diffused, and is received by labourers generally in proportion to the relative values of their work. Apparently the greatest gain has been among the higher artisan and lower professional classes—the very classes, it may be remarked, by whom the strain of modern life is felt the most intensely.

The conclusion, then, is, that if the return to labour generally is not proportionate to the increase of the severity of toil itself, the reason must be that people are working for inadequate objects. The game, in one sense, may not be worth the candle. The problem is another form of the very same problem that has been considered with reference to the payment of monopoly rents. On the whole, notwithstanding all the drawbacks of city life, there is some improvement which makes the payment of monopoly rents worth while. People would not change back to the former conditions. So, on the whole, notwithstanding all the drawbacks of really severer toil, and the inadequacy of the additional remuneration, people would not change back. What has happened is really a revolution in the quality of labour and the general conditions of life. The net gain, in one view, is less than the apparent gross improvement, looking at the matter strictly; in another view, the gain is so great as to make the present condition of workmen on the average incommensurable with their former condition. The two things are not on the same plane, and can hardly be compared.

An important corollary seems to be suggested by these considerations. If there is so much doubt about the adequacy of the reward for the additional labour thrown on workmen by the conditions of modern society, is not that reward really a minimum reward? In other words, may not the amount of production itself be conditioned by the energy of the workman, which is in turn a function of the food and other things on which he expends his wages, so that the quality of labour by which modern society is carried on would not itself exist if the remuneration were less than it is? The complaint we are dealing with is that of the severity of modern toil, and implies that the workman is tasked to his full capacity, and can just do the work, so that the remuneration cannot be reduced. And that this is really the case in many employments may be easily enough illustrated. It is quite certain that the driver of an express engine could not go through the very formidable labours he undergoes if he only had the food of the rude labourer of a former time, and only lived in the way that such a labourer used to live. He would not, under such conditions, have the energy or brain power for the work to be done. It is the same with workmen in a factory who have to attend to many machines. The constant strain simply could not be endured if the workman had to live as the factory worker of a former time had to live. The present worker is really cheaper than the former worker, because he does more in proportion; but dear as he is, yet, in another respect, he may perhaps be viewed, according to a suggestion already made, as really engaged at a minimum wage—without which he could not do the work at all. This is not a question merely of a rise in the scale of living, though that question is intermixed with it. It is a question of the actual necessity on the part of the workman that certain things should be put into him, or supplied to him, as a condition of his doing the work which he actually performs. What is true of the workman specially referred to is of course still more true of the higher kinds of work involving artistic or other skill.

It may also be added, that the suggestion already made as to the reason for the non-increase of remuneration in certain directions being that the work done has not itself improved in quality, is fully confirmed by the general view thus stated. If the work which has improved in quality is itself only so remunerated as to make it doubtful whether the remuneration is adequate, whether the game is worth the candle, and is, in fact, at the point of minimum, so as to enable the work to be done at all, out of what fund is the remuneration of the work that has not improved in quality to come? In the midst of plenty, apparently, such workmen, by comparison, must starve, because, notwithstanding all the plenty, those who really do the hard work of modern society are only just paid, and no more. It is easy for such workmen and their so-called friends to point to the capitalists as living on *their* labour; and no doubt if it were possible to divide the earnings of capitalists amongst society generally, according to numbers, these particular workmen might be much better off. But it is not from the labour of such workmen that capitalists mainly derive their income, while those who do work, as we have seen, have so large a remuneration that they can have no quarrel with the capitalist. The suggested division would therefore only be for the benefit of a special class whose existence is itself a danger to society, and which should rather be discouraged than encouraged, the whole efforts of society being rather directed to their transformation by education and similar agencies into a higher class, than to securing an increased payment for their work under present conditions. The curse of the very poor, in more senses than one, is their poverty—poverty in strength, in mental capacity, in moral qualities. They are poor because they cannot earn more. If they were stronger they would have the earnings, and would have no quarrel with the capitalists. To improve their condition they must be made stronger, and not merely given more to spend, which would be a curse to them instead of a blessing, as it is to the merely idle capitalist whose luxury they envy, whose existence is a danger to society also, and whose obliteration, or rather transformation into a different class, is equally to be sought for.

The next head of complaint is that a workman has more expenses now, in consequence of the rise in the scale of living. Not only himself, but his family, must live better. They must have better and more food, be better clothed and sheltered, be better educated, and so on. The workman himself, on whom the burden falls, has no more surplus than before. He is not a freer man.

This head of complaint, however, demands very little remark. The statement of complaint is, in truth, one of the best evidences of progress. Of course there has been a rise in the scale of living. Such a rise was quite certain to come with an improvement in the earnings of workmen. The fact that it has come, is itself one of the proofs of improvement. No doubt there is a continued absence of a free surplus. I suspect, however, that at no time have many people, in this country at least, had philosophy enough to be thrifty and careful, and to do without some things that appear to be necessary for their sphere in life, so as to have what is meant by a surplus. Its absence is certainly no proof that the condition of those who make the complaint has not improved. The scale of living has risen, and this rise, beyond all question, imposes a strain upon many workmen which only the greatest care and philosophy can mitigate. It involves of necessity severer toil on the part of the bread-winner, with no apparent surplus for himself.

It is apparent, however, that to some extent what is called a rise in the scale of living is, in reality, an improvement in the mode of living, which is absolutely necessitated by the work itself, without which, in fact, the work could not be done. Where moral qualities are to be displayed, and great vigour, punctuality, and energy are required, they are not to be expected except from workmen of a certain class, whose scale of living has, in fact, risen to the standard necessary, and whose "medium" and "atmosphere," of which the condition of wife and children or relations is a part, is altogether different from what it was. Before human beings can display the qualities and exert the energies required, they must have certain tastes and wants to gratify, or there would be no motive to exhibit those qualities and energies. Hence a rise in the scale of living is only another mode of describing the improvement in the character of the workman, which is essential to the performance of the work to be done.

The conclusions of this long argument may now be very shortly restated. In certain cases the increase of net earnings by the advance of the last fifty years cannot be so great as the increase of gross earnings, because some classes of workmen have to submit to an increased charge for rent and railway fares, and similar expenditure, which really amount to a reduction from the gross earnings which they receive. But on the whole, the classes of workmen affected in this way must, from the nature of things, be comparatively small, while the general conditions are such that the deduction from gross earnings, as a rule, still leaves an enormous net gain. Next, the allegation as to the increased severity of labour, and as to workmen not getting a sufficiently adequate remuneration or a sufficient share of the increased gross produce, is met by the admission generally of an increase in the severity of labour, which, however, is found to be more properly described as a revolution in the quality of the labour, and to be connected with the fact of improvement generally, and to be evidence of improvement in the workman's condition. The character of labour generally has so changed that it cannot really be measured in comparison with the labour of a former time. Some workmen engaged about machines may appear to get comparatively little of the increased production for themselves, but the reason is that the improvement in machines is for the benefit of society as a whole, and not specially for that of the particular workmen engaged upon them, who only participate in the improvement as consumers, and not as producers. Substantially, however, there is more severe toil all round, and whether the additional remuneration is adequate or not, the change in the quality of the labour is necessary to the production, the labourer gets all the possible remuneration, and the labour itself could not be carried on without the remuneration obtained. It is the same with the complaint as to the rise in the scale of living. The rise in the scale is at once a proof of the improvement in the workman's condition, and of the necessity for an improvement in his living to enable him to do the new work. The two things are inextricably connected. On the whole, the complaint of workmen as to the difference between gross and net is not unjustified, but it points to changes in their condition of a remarkable kind, which are in every way deserving of farther study. To show fully what these changes are, statistics would be needed, but the necessary conditions of the problem are apparent without statistics. The complaints here dealt with could not exist without that improvement in society and the condition of the masses which the complaints seem to call in question.

A further conclusion may be drawn. The conditions of life thus indicated seem favourable, on the whole, to a continuous improvement in society, so long as science and art make progress, and heavier and heavier calls are made on the intelligence and energy of workmen, along with an increase of their capacities on the one side and their wants on the other. The whole structure of modern society is such as to require greater and greater knowledge, greater and greater energy and moral power, greater and greater capacity of every kind, so as to make sure that machines and inventions are maintained and improved, and that artistic capacities and the arts of living are developed to correspond. The continuous improvement implies a continuous improvement, on the average, of the human being who really belongs to the new society. So long as society, therefore, continues to progress—that is, for our present purpose, so long as the average workman continues to produce more quantity or better quality—there must be continuous improvement and progress in the quality of workmen themselves, and the conditions of their existence, although we should not expect that complaints would cease as to the greater severity of toil and as to particular classes of workmen not getting for themselves the full benefit of the increased production. Still, the improvement is there, and the complaints, when analyzed, are, in truth, signs of the improvement.

The one doubtful sign, it appears to me, as regards the future, is pointed at by the qualification implied in the words—the human being *who really belongs to the new society.* It may possibly happen that there will be an increase, or at least non-diminution, of what may be called the social wreckage. A class may continue to exist and even increase in the midst of our civilization, possibly not a large class in proportion, but still a considerable class, who are out of the improvement altogether, who are capable of nothing but the rudest labour, and who have neither the moral nor the mental qualities fitted for the strain of the work of modern society. On the other side, as already hinted, the existence of what may be called a barbarian class among the capitalist classes, living in idle luxury, and not bearing the burden of society in any way, seems also a danger. But speculations of this sort would perhaps take us too far at present. Substantially, as yet there seems to be no reason to doubt the steadiness of the improvement in recent years among the working classes, both those practically so called and those who may be included when we use the language in its widest—that is, the strictly economic—sense, and that this improvement goes on from year to year, and from generation to generation, and must, in the nature of things, go on, in consequence of the improvements and inventions of the modern world, and the general spread of education, so long as nothing happens to prevent a continuous improvement in the efficiency of human labour and the average return it can obtain from the forces with which it works.

XVI.

THE RECENT RATE OF MATERIAL PROGRESS IN ENGLAND.[1]

IN coming before you on this occasion it has occurred to me that a suitable topic in the commercial capital of England, and at a time when there are many reasons for looking around us and taking stock of what is going on in the industrial world, will be whether there has been in recent years a change in the rate of material progress in the country as compared with the period just before. Some such question is constantly being put by individuals with regard to their own business. It is often put in political discussions as regards the country generally, with some vague idea among politicians that prosperity and adversity, good harvests and bad, in the most general sense, depend on politics. And it must always be of perennial interest. Of late years it has become specially interesting, and it still is so, because many contend that not only are we not progressing, but that we are absolutely going back in the world, while there are evident signs that it is not so easy to read in the usual statistics the evidence of undoubted growth as it was just before 1870-73. The general idea, in my mind, I have to add, is not quite new. I gave a hint of it in Staffordshire last winter, and privately I have done something to propagate it so as to lead people to think on what is really a most important subject. What I propose now to do is to discuss the topic

[1] Address as President of Section F at British Association meeting, Manchester, 1887.

formally and fully, and claim the widest attention for it that I possibly can.

I.

There is much *primâ facie* evidence, then, to begin with, that the rate of the accumulation of wealth and the rate of increase of material prosperity may not have been so great of late years, say during the last ten years, as in the twenty or thirty years just before that. Our fair-trade friends have all along made a tactical mistake in their arguments. What they have attempted to prove is that England lately has not been prosperous at all, that we have been going backwards instead of advancing, and so on; statements which the simplest appeal to statistics was sufficient to disprove. But if they had been more moderate in their contentions, and limited themselves to showing that the rate of advance, though there was still advance, was different from and less than what it was, I for one should have been prepared to admit that there was a good deal of statistical evidence which seemed to point to that conclusion, as soon as a sufficient interval had elapsed to show that the statistics themselves could not be misinterpreted. There has now been ample time to allow for minor variations and fluctuations, and the statistics can be fairly construed.

I have to begin by introducing a short table dealing with some of the principal statistical facts which are usually appealed to as signs of general progress and the reverse, and I propose to go over briefly the items in that table, and to discuss along with them a few broad and notorious facts which cannot conveniently be put in the same form. (See p. 101.)

The first figures are those of the income tax assessments. What we find is that if we go back thirty years and compare the amount of income tax assessments in the United Kingdom at ten years' intervals, there appears to be an immense progress from 1855 to 1875,

Statement as to production or consumption of staple articles in the United Kingdom in the undermentioned years, with the rate of increase in different periods compared.

	1855.	1865.	1875.	1885.	Ratio of Increase per cent. 1855-65.	1865-75.	1875-85.
Income Tax assessments, million £	308	396	571	631	28	44	10
Production of coal, million tons	64	98	132	159	53	35	20
" pig iron "	3.2	4.8	6.4	7.4	50	33	16
Receipts from railway: goods traffic per head of population	—	11s.[1]	18s.[1]	21s. 2d.[1]	—	63	18
Clearances of shipping in foreign trade, million tons	10	15	24	32	50	60	33
Consumption of tea per head, lbs.	2.3	3.3	4.4	5.0	43	33	13½
" " sugar " "	30.6	39.8	62.7	74.3	30	58	19

[1] These figures are for 1860-64, 1870-74, and 1880-84.

the first twenty years, and since 1875 a much less progress. The total amount of the assessments themselves, stated in millions, was as follows:

	Millions.		Millions.
1855	£308	1875	£571
1865	396	1885	631

and the rate of growth in the ten yearly periods which these figures show is—between 1855 and 1865, 28 per cent.; between 1865 and 1875, 44 per cent.; and between 1875 and 1885, 10 per cent. only.

Making all allowance for changes in the mode of assessment by which the lower limit of the tax has been raised, for the apparent increase before 1875 which may have been due to a gradual increase of the severity of the collection, and for the like disturbing influences, I believe there is no doubt that these income tax assessments correspond fairly well to the change in the money value of income and property in the interval. How great the change in the rate of increase is, is shown by the simple consideration that if the rate of increase in the last ten years, instead of being 10 per cent. only, had been 44 per cent., as in the ten years just before, the total of the income tax assessments in 1885, which is actually 631 millions, would have been 882 millions! Something then has clearly happened in the interval to change the rate of increase.

These figures being those of money values, an obvious explanation is suggested which would account in great part for the phenomenon of a diminished rate of increase in such values without supposing a reduction of the rate of increase of real wealth, of the things represented by the money values, to correspond. This is the fall of prices of which we have heard so much of late years, and about which in some form or another we shall no doubt hear something at our present meeting. It is quite clear that if prices fall then income tax assessments must also be affected. The produce of a given area of land, for instance, sells for less than it would otherwise sell; there is less gross produce, and in proportion there is even less net produce, that is, less rent; consequently the net income appearing in the Income Tax Schedules is either less than it was or does not increase as it did before. The same with mines, with railways, and with all sorts of business under Schedule D. The things themselves may increase as they did before, but as the money values do not increase but diminish, the income tax assessments cannot swell at the former rate. It is the same with salaries and other incomes not dependent so directly in appearance on the fall in prices. Salaries and incomes are of course related to a given range of prices of commodities, and a fall in the prices of commodities implies that the range of salaries and incomes is itself lower than it would otherwise be, assuming the real relation between the commodities and incomes to be the same after the fall in prices as it would have been if there had been no fall in prices. Hence the income tax assessments by themselves are not a perfectly good test in a question like the present. The change implied may be nominal only, so far as the aggregate wealth and prosperity of the community are concerned, though of course there can be no great and general fall of prices without a considerable redistribution of wealth which must have many important consequences.

This criticism, however, does not apply to the remaining figures in the short table submitted, and to various other well-known facts, which we shall now proceed to discuss.

The production of coal, then, is found to have progressed in the last thirty years as the income tax assessments have done. The figures in millions of tons at ten years' intervals are as follows:

	Million Tons.		Million Tons.
1855	64	1875	132
1865	98	1885	159

And the rate of growth in the ten yearly periods which

these figures show is between 1855 and 1865, 53 per cent.; between 1865 and 1875, 35 per cent.; and between 1875 and 1885, 20 per cent. only. The rate of growth in the last ten years is much less than in the twenty years just before. The percentages here, it will be observed, are higher than in the case of the income tax assessments. The increase in the last ten years in particular is 20 per cent. as compared with an increase of 10 per cent. only in the income tax assessments. But the direction of the movement is in both cases the same.

I need hardly say, moreover, that coal production has usually been considered a good test of general prosperity. Coal is specially an instrumental article, the fuel of the machines by which our production is carried on. Whatever the explanation may be, we have now, therefore, to take account of the fact that the rate of increase of the production of coal has been less in the last ten years than in the twenty years just before.

Then with regard to pig-iron, which is also an instrumental article, the raw material of that iron which goes to the making of the machines of industry, the table shows the following particulars of production:

	Million Tons.		Million Tons.
1855	3.2	1875	6.4
1865	4.8	1885	7.4

And the rate of growth which these figures show is between 1855 and 1865, 50 per cent.; between 1865 and 1875, 33 per cent.; and between 1875 and 1885, 16 per cent. only. Whatever the explanation may be, we have thus to take account of a diminution of the rate of increase in the production of pig-iron, much resembling the diminution in the rate of increase of the production of coal.

At the same time the miscellaneous mineral production of the United Kingdom has mostly diminished absolutely. On this head, not to weary you with figures, I have not thought it necessary to insert anything in the above short table; but I may refer you to the tables put in by the Board of Trade before the Royal Commission on Trade Depression. Let me only state very briefly that while the average annual amount of copper produced from British ores amounted in 1855 to over 20,000 tons, in 1865 the amount was about 12,000 tons only, in 1875 under 5,000 tons, and in 1885 under 3,000 tons. As regards lead again, while the production about 1855 was 65,000 tons, and in 1865 about 67,000 tons, the amount in 1875 had been reduced to 58,000 tons, and in 1885 to less than 40,000 tons. In white tin there is an improvement up to 1865, but no improvement since, and the only set-off, a very partial one, is in zinc, which rises steadily from about 3,500 tons in 1858, the earliest date for which particulars are given, to about 10,000 tons in 1885, considerably higher figures having been touched in 1881-83. There is nothing, then, in these figures as to miscellaneous mineral production to mitigate the impression of the diminution in the rate of increase in the great staples, iron and coal, in recent years.

Agricultural production, it is also notorious, has been at any rate no better, or not much better, than stationary for some years past, although down to a comparatively recent period a steady improvement seemed to be going on. Making all allowance for the change in the character of the cultivation, by which the gross produce is diminished, although the net profit is not affected to the same extent, and which might be held to argue no real decline in the rate of general growth if the population, diverted from agriculture, were more profitably employed, yet the facts, broadly looked at, taken in connection with the other facts stated as to diminished rate of increase in other leading industries, seem to confirm the supposition that there may have been some diminution in the rate of increase generally.

It is, unfortunately, impossible to state in a simple manner the progress at different dates in the great textile industries of the country. Everything as regards these industries is thrown out by the disturbance consequent on the American War. It does not appear, however, that what has happened as regards the main textile industries, cotton and wool, would alter sensibly the conclusions above stated, drawn from the facts as to other main industries of the country. If we take the consumption of raw materials as the test, it would appear that the growth in the cotton manufacture is from a consumption of 28 lbs. per head in 1855 to about 38 lbs. per head in 1875, while in 1885 the consumption is nearly 42 lbs. per head, an increase of 4 lbs. per head in the last ten years, against 10 lbs. per head in the previous twenty. The percentage of increase in the last twenty years must therefore, on the whole, have been less than in the previous twenty, although in these twenty years the great interruption due to the American Civil War occurred. Of course the amount of raw material consumed is not here an absolute test. There may be more spinning and weaving now in proportion to the same quantity of raw material than was formerly the case. But the indications are at least not so certain and direct as when the consumption of raw material could be confidently appealed to. As regards wool, the comparison is unfortunately very incomplete, owing to the lack of some data for the earlier years: but what we find is that the amount of wool consumed per head of the population of the United Kingdom has in the last ten years rather declined than otherwise, from nearly 11 lbs. per head in the five years 1870-74 to 10 lbs. per head only in the five years 1880-84. Here, again, the explanation suggested as to cotton—viz., that there may be more spinning and weaving now in proportion to the same quantity of raw material than was formerly the case—applies. But the answer is also the same, that at any rate the indications of progress are no longer as simple as they were. The reality of the former rate of advance is not so clearly manifest.

Of course I need hardly add that in the case of another great textile, silk, there has been no progress, but the reverse, for some years; that this is also true of linen; and that the increase in the allied manufacture, jute, can only be a partial set-off.

In the textiles, then, as in other staple industries of the country, the rate of advance in the last ten years, measuring by things, and not merely by values, has been less than in the twenty years immediately before.

We pass on, then, to another set of figures included in the short table above submitted. We may look not only at leading industries of production directly, but at the broad figures of certain industries which are usually held to reflect, as in a mirror, the progress of the country generally. I refer to the railway traffics as regards the home industries of the country, and the entries and clearances of shipping in the foreign trade as regards our foreign business.

As regards railways, what we find is, if we take the receipts from the goods traffic in the form in which they were summarized for the Royal Commission on Trade Depression, viz., reduced to so much per head of the population on the average of quinquennial periods, that in the five years 1860-64, which is as far back as the figures can be carried, the receipts per head were 11*s.*; ten years later, viz., in 1870-74, the receipts per head were 18*s.*; and ten years later, viz., 1880-84, the receipts per head were 21*s.* 2*d.* The rate of growth shown in the first ten years' interval is 63 per cent.; in the second ten years' interval it is only 18 per cent.; and in the last year or two, I may add, there has been no further improvement. Here the question of the value of money comes in again, but this would only modify partially the apparent change. There is also a question as to railway extension having been greater in the earlier than in the later period, so that growth took place in the earlier period because there were railways in many districts where they had not been before, and there was no room for a similar expansion in the later period. But the difference in the rate of growth it will be observed is very great indeed, and this explanation seems hardly adequate to account for all the difference. At any rate, to repeat a remark already made, the indications are no longer so simple as they were. There is something to be explained.

The figures as to the number of tons of goods carried are not in the above table; nor are such figures very good, so long as they are not reduced to show the number of tons conveyed one mile. But, *quantum valeant*, they may be quoted from the Board of Trade tables already referred to. The increase, then, in minerals conveyed between 1855 and 1865 is from about 40 million to nearly 80 million tons, or 100 per cent.; between 1865 and 1875 it is from 80 to about 140 million tons, or 75 per cent.; and in the last ten years it is from 140 to 190 million tons only, if quite so much, or about 36 per cent. only. As regards general merchandise, again, the progression in the three ten yearly periods is in the first from about 24 to 37 million tons, or rather more than 50 per cent.; in the second from 37 to 63 million tons, or 70 per cent.; and in the third from 63 to 73 million tons, or 16 per cent. only. As far as they go there is certainly nothing in these figures to oppose the indications of a falling-off in the rate of increase of general business already cited.

Coming to the movement of shipping in the foreign trade, the series of figures we obtain is the following, which relate to clearances only, those relating to entries being of course little more than duplicate, so that they need not be repeated: 1855, 10 million tons; 1865, 15 million tons; 1875, 24 million tons; 1885, 32 million tons. And the rate of growth thus shown is between 1855 and 1865 no less than 50 per cent.; between 1865 and 1875 no less than 60 per cent.; and between 1875 and 1885 about 33 per cent. only—again a less rate of increase in the last ten years than in the period just before. Here, too, it is to be noticed, what is unusual in shipping industry, that in the last few years the entries and clearances in the foreign trade have been practically stationary. The explanation no doubt is in part the great multiplication of lines of steamers up to a comparatively recent period, causing a remarkable growth of the movement while the multiplication of lines was itself in progress, and leaving room for less growth afterwards because a new framework had been provided within which traffic could grow. But here again it is to be remarked that the whole change can hardly, perhaps, be explained in this manner, while the remark already made again applies, that the fact of explanation being required is itself significant.

The figures of imports and exports might be treated in a similar manner, as they necessarily follow the course of the leading articles of production and the movements of shipping. But we should only by so doing get the figures we have been dealing with in another form, and repetition is of course to be avoided.

The short table contains only another set of figures, viz., those of the consumption of tea and sugar, which are again commonly appealed to as significant of general material progress. What we find as regards tea is that the consumption per head rises between 1855 and 1865 from 2.3 to 3.3 lbs., or 43 per cent.; between 1865 and 1875 from 3.3 to 4.4 lbs., or 33 per cent.; and between 1875 and 1885 from 4.4 to 5 lbs., or 13½ per cent. In sugar the progression is in the first period from 30.6 to 39.8 lbs. per head, or 30 per cent.; in the second period from 39.8 to 62.7 lbs., or 58 per cent.; and in the third period from 62.7 to 74.3 lbs., or 19 per cent. only. In the last ten years in both cases the rate of increase is less than in the twenty years before.

These facts, I need hardly say, would be strengthened by a reference to the consumption of spirits and beer, the decline in the former being especially notorious. In tobacco again in the last ten years there has been no increase of the consumption per head; which contrasts with a rapid increase in the period just before—viz., from about 1.31 lbs. per head in 1865 to 1.46 lbs. per head in 1875.

No doubt the observation here applies that the utmost prosperity would obviously be consistent with a slower rate of increase per head from period to period in the consumption of these articles, and with, in the end, a cessation of the rate of increase altogether. The consumption of some articles may attain a comparatively stationary state, the increased resources of the community being devoted to new articles. But here, again, we have to observe the necessity for explanation. The indications are no longer so sure and obvious in all directions as they were.

It is difficult, indeed, to resist the impression made when we put all the facts together, leaving out of sight for a moment those of values only. We are able to affirm positively—(*a*) That the production of coal, iron, and other staple articles has been at a less rate in the last ten years than formerly; (*b*) that this has taken place when agricultural production has been notoriously stationary, and when the production of other articles such as copper, lead, etc., has positively diminished; (*c*) that there has been a similar falling-off in the rate of advance in the great textile industries; (*d*) that the receipts from railway traffic and the figures of shipping in the foreign trade show a corresponding slackening in the rate of increase in the business movement; and (*e*) that the figures as to consumption of leading articles, such as tea, sugar, spirits, and tobacco, in showing a similar decline in the rate of increase, and, in some cases, a diminution, are at least not in contradiction with the other facts stated, although it may be allowed that there was no antecedent reason to expect an indefinite continuance of a former rate of increase.

From these facts, however we may qualify them, and many qualifications have already been suggested, while others could be added, it seems tolerably safe to draw the conclusion that there has probably been a falling-off in the rate of material increase generally. The income tax assessment figures, though they could not be taken by themselves in such a question, are, at least, not in contradiction, and there is nothing the other way when we deal with these main figures only. I should not put the conclusion, however, as more than highly probable. Some general explanation of the facts may be possible on the hypothesis that there is no real decline in the rate of growth generally at all; that the usual signs for various reasons have become more difficult to read; that owing to the advance already made, the real growth of the country and, to some extent, of other countries, has taken a new direction; and that the utmost caution must be used in forming final conclusions on the subject. But the conclusion of a check having occurred to the former rate of growth may be assumed meanwhile for the purposes of discussion. The attempted explanation of the causes of change, on the hypothesis that there is a real change, may help to throw light on the question of the reality of the change itself.

II.

Various explanations are suggested, then, not only for a decline in the rate of our progress, but for actual retrogression. Let us look at the principal of these explanations in their order and see whether they can account for the facts; either for actual retrogression, or for a decline in the general rate of material growth equal to what some of the particular facts above cited if they were significant of a general change in the rate of growth imply—a decline, say, from a rate of growth amounting to 40 per cent. in ten years to one of 20 per cent. only in the same period.

One of the most common explanations, as we all

know, is foreign competition. The explanation has been discredited because of the exaggeration of the alleged evil to be explained; but it may possibly be a good enough explanation of the actual facts when they are looked at in a proper way. In this light, then, the assertion as to foreign competition would be found to mean that foreigners are taking away from us some business we should otherwise have had, and that, consequently, although our business on the whole increases from year to year, it does not increase so fast as when foreign competition was less. Those who talk most about foreign competition have actually in their mind the unfair element in that competition, the stimulus which the Governments of some foreign countries give or attempt to give to particular industries by means on the one hand of high tariffs keeping out the goods we should otherwise send to such countries, and giving their home industry of the same kind a monopoly which sometimes enables them to produce a surplus they can sell ruinously cheap abroad, and by means on the other hand of direct bounties which enable certain industries to compete in the home market of the United Kingdom itself as well as in foreign markets. But there is a natural foreign competition as well as a stimulated foreign competition to be considered, and it may be the more formidable of the two.

Dealing first with the stimulated competition, the most obvious criticism on this alleged explanation of the recent decline in the rate of increase of our material progress is that the stimulus given by foreign Governments in recent years has not been increasing, or, at any rate, not materially increasing, so as to account for the change in question. People forget very quickly; otherwise it would not be lost sight of that after 1860, as far as European nations are concerned, there was a great reduction of tariff duties—a change, therefore, in the contrary direction to that stimulus which is alleged to have lately caused a change in the rate of our own development. Since about five or six years ago the movement on the Continent seems again to have been in the direction of higher tariffs. France, Italy, Austria, Germany, and Russia have all shown protectionist leanings of a more or less pronounced kind. Some of our colonies, especially Canada, have moved in the same direction. But, on the whole, these causes as yet have been too newly in operation to affect our industry on a large scale. As a matter of fact, with one exception to be presently noticed, the period from 1860 to 1880 was one in which the effect of the operation of foreign Governments in regard to their tariffs could not be to stimulate additional competition of an injurious kind with us in the way above described, but to take away, if anything, from the stimulus previously given. The changes quite lately brought into operation, if big enough, and if really having the effects supposed, might stimulate foreign competition in the way described in the period now commencing; but, as an explanation of the past facts, it is impossible to urge that foreign competition had recently been more stimulated by additions to tariffs than before, and that in consequence of this stimulus our own rate of advance had been checked.

The one exception to notice is the United States. Immediately after 1860 the civil war in that country broke out, and that war brought with it the adoption of a very high tariff. Curiously enough, however, that tariff operated most against us in the very years—that is, the years before 1875—in which our rate of advance was greater to all appearance than it has lately been. In 1883 there was a great revision of the tariff, having for its general result a slight lowering, and not an enhancement of the tariff, and it is with this reduction—that is, with a diminution of the alleged adverse stimulus—that the diminution in our own rate of advance has occurred.

Of course the explanation may be that, although Governments have not themselves been active till quite lately in adding to their tariffs, yet circumstances have occurred to make the former tariffs more injurious in recent years than they were down to 1875. For instance, it may be said that owing to the fall of prices in recent years the burden of specific duties has become higher than it was. The duty is nominally unchanged, but by the fall of prices its proportion to the value of the article has become higher. This is no doubt the case to a large extent. On the other hand, *ad valorem* duties have been lowered in precisely the same way. The fall of prices has brought with it a reduction of duty, and especially on articles of English manufacture, where the raw material is obtained from abroad, the reduction of duty, being applicable to the whole price, must certainly have had for effect to render more effective than before the competition of the English manufacturer. Whether on the whole the reduction of *ad valorem* duties consequent on the fall of prices has been sufficient throughout the range of our foreign trade to compensate the virtual increase of the weight of specific duties from the same cause seems to be a nice question. This being the case, it must be very difficult indeed to show that on the whole the weight of foreign tariffs, apart from the action of foreign Governments, has been increased in recent years so as to affect our own growth injuriously.

Foreign tariffs, it may be said, have become more effective for another reason. Manufacturing industry having itself developed abroad, the same amount of protection given to the foreign industry becomes more efficient than it was. But this, of course, raises the question of the effect of natural foreign competition, which will presently be discussed.

So much for the stimulus to foreign competition due to high tariffs. With regard to bounties very little need be said. They have been the subject of much discussion and agitation for various reasons, and in what I have to say I propose not to touch on the practical question whether these bounties are injurious, and the nature of the political remedies that may or may not be possible. I limit myself strictly to the point, how far any effect which such bounties can have had would account for a diminution in the rate of material growth of the country generally in the last ten years as compared with the ten years just before. Dealing with the question in this strictly limited fashion, what I have to observe first is that hitherto very few bounties have been complained of except those on sugar production and refining; and next, that the whole industries of sugar production and refining, important as they are in themselves, hardly count in a question of the general industry of the United Kingdom. Even if we refined all the sugar consumed in the United Kingdom, and the maximum amount we have ever exported, the whole income from this source, the whole margin, would not exceed about £2,000,000 annually, not one-six-hundredth part of the income of the people of the United Kingdom; and of this £2,000,000 at the worst we only lose a portion by foreign competition, while all that is really lost, it must be remembered, is not the whole income which would have been gained if a certain portion of our labour and capital had been employed in sugar refining, but only the difference between that income and the income obtained by the employment of the same labour and capital in other directions. The loss to the empire may be greater because our colonies are concerned in sugar production to the extent at present prices of £5,000,000 to £6,000,000 annually, which would probably be somewhat larger but for foreign competition. But it does not seem at all certain that this figure would be increased if foreign bounties were taken away, while in any case the amounts involved are too small to raise any question of foreign bounties having checked the rate of growth of the general industry of the country.

Per contra, of course, the extra cheapness of sugar, alleged to be due to the bounties, must have been so great an advantage to the people of the United Kingdom, saving them perhaps £2,000,000 to £3,000,000 per annum, that the stimulus thereby given to other industries must apparently have far more than compensated any loss caused by the stimulus of foreign bounties to sugar production and refining abroad. But to enlarge on this point would involve the introduction of controversial matter, which I am anxious to avoid. I am content to show that nothing that can have resulted from sugar bounties could have affected seriously the general rate of material growth in the country.

Mutatis mutandis, the same remarks apply to other foreign bounties, of which indeed the only ones that have been at all heard of are those on shipping. But as yet, at least, the increase of foreign shipping has not been such as to come into comparison with our own increase, while the portion of the increase that can be connected with the operation of bounties is very small. It would be useless to enter into figures on so small a point; but few figures are so well known or accessible as those relating to shipping.

In neither way, then, does there appear to be anything in the assertion that the protectionist action of foreign Governments in recent years can have caused the check alleged to the rate of growth in our industry generally, assuming such a check to have occurred. I may be dispensed, therefore, from entering on the theoretical argument, which I only notice in passing, that in the nature of things no enhancement of foreign tariffs and no grants of foreign bounties could really check our own rate of growth, except by checking foreign growth still more, which is not the case we are considering, because the allegation is that foreign competition is increasing at our expense. That I do not insist on this argument is not to be considered as a sign that it is dropped, or that I am not fully sensible of its logical completeness. It seems enough, at present, to fortify it by considerations from actual practical facts which no one can dispute.

The question of an increase of foreign competition from natural causes is more difficult. It is beyond all question, as I have pointed out elsewhere, that foreign competition in every direction from natural causes must continue to increase, and that it has increased greatly in recent years. But when the facts are examined, it does not appear that this competition has been the cause of a check to our own rate of growth. One of the facts most commonly dwelt upon in this connection is the great increase of the imports of foreign manufactured articles into the United Kingdom. But the increase in the last ten years is not more than about £18,000,000, taking the facts as recorded in what is known as Mr. Ritchie's return, viz., from about £37,000,000 in the quinquennial period 1870-74 to £55,000,000 in the quinquennial period 1880-84, or about 50 per cent.[1] Out of £18,000,000 increased imports of such articles it is fair to allow that at least one-half, if not more, is the value of raw material which we should have had to import in any case; so that only £9,000,000 represents the value of English labour displaced by these increased imports. Even the whole of this £9,000,000 of course is not lost, only the difference between it and the sum which the capital and labour "displaced" earns in some other employment, which may possibly even be a *plus* and not a *minus* difference. If we add articles "partly manufactured" no difference would be made, for the increase here is only from £26,000,000 to £28,000,000 in the ten years. Such differences, it need not be said, hardly count in the general total of the industry of the country. Further, the rate of increase of these imports was just as great in the period when our own rate of growth was greater as in the last ten years, the increase in manufactured articles between 1860-64 and 1870-74 being £19,000,000, viz., from £18,000,000 to £37,000,000, or over 100 per cent. as compared with 50 per cent. only in the last ten years, and in articles partly manufactured from £17,000,000 to £26,000,000, an in-

[1] See Appendix to "First Report of Royal Commission on Trade Depression," p. 130.

crease of £9,000,000 as compared with an increase of £2,000,000 only in the last ten years. Making all allowance for the fall in prices in recent years, these figures still show a greater relative increase of imports of manufactured articles before 1875 than afterwards. It cannot, therefore, be the increased import of foreign manufactures which has caused the check to our own growth in the last ten years.

But foreigners, it is said, exclude us from their own markets and compete with us in foreign markets. Here again, however, we find that any check which may have occurred to our foreign export trade is itself so small that its effect on the general growth of the country would be almost *nil*. Take it that the check is as great as the diminution in the rate of increase in the movements of shipping, viz., from an increase of about 55 per cent. to one of 33 per cent. only, that is, broadly speaking, a diminution of one-third in the rate of increase of our foreign trade, whatever that rate may have been. Assuming that rate to have been the same as the rate of increase in the movements of shipping itself, the change would be from a rate of increase equal to one-half in ten years to a rate of increase equal to about one-third only. Applying these proportions to the exports of British and Irish produce and manufactures, which represent the productive energy of the country devoted to working for foreign exchange, and assuming that ten years ago the value of British labour and industry in the produce and manufactures we exported, due deduction being made for the raw material previously imported, was about £140,000,000,[1] then it would appear that if the same range of values had continued, the check to the growth of this trade would have been that at the end of ten years the British labour represented in it instead of having increased 50 per cent., viz., from £140,000,000 to £210,000,000, would have increased one-third only,

[1] See *supra*, vol. i., p. 426.

or from £140,000,000 to about £187,000,000. The annual difference to the energy of the country developing itself in the foreign trade would on this showing be about £23,000,000 only; an insignificant sum compared with the aggregate income of the people of the country, while the country, it must be remembered, does not lose the whole of this sum, but only the difference between it and the sum earned in those employments to which those concerned have resorted, which again may be a *plus* and not a *minus* difference. Even therefore if foreign competition is the cause of a check to our general growth, yet the figures we are dealing with in our foreign trade are such that any visible check to that trade which can have occurred must have been insufficient to cause that apparent diminution in the rate of our material growth generally which has to be explained.

It has to be remembered, moreover, that when the figures are studied and the fall of prices allowed for it is not in our foreign trade that any check worth mentioning seems to have occurred at all. The diminution in the rate of increase in the movements of shipping is very largely to be accounted for in the way already explained, viz., by the fact that the increase just before 1875 was largely owing to the multiplication of lines of steamers, and that a framework had then been provided up to which the traffic has since grown. Even an increase of one-third in the movements in the last ten years may thus show as great an increase in real business as an increase of 50 or 60 per cent. in the movements in the twenty years before. Foreign competition, even from natural causes, is thus insufficient to account for the diminution in the rate of increase of our material growth in the last ten years.

These figures may be put directly another way. The increase of our foreign exports per head between 1860-64 and 1870-74 was from £4 14*s.* 11*d.* to £7 7*s.* 5*d.*, or about 55 per cent., and allowing for an average rise of prices between the two dates may be put as having been at the extreme about 50 per cent. Between 1870-74 and 1880-84 instead of an increase there is a decrease, viz., from £7 7*s.* 5*d.* to £6 12*s.* 9*d.*, but deducting about one-third from the former figure for the fall in prices, the real increase in the last ten years would appear to be as from £4 16*s.* 3*d.* to £6 12*s.* 9*d.*, or over 35 per cent. The difference in the rate of increase in the last ten years compared with the previous ten is thus the difference between 35 and 50 per cent. only, equal to about £21,000,000 annually on the amount of £140,000,000, assumed to represent the value of British industry in our foreign exports, deduction being made for the value of raw material included. A deduction of this sort from the annual income of the country is too small to account for such a check to the rate of our growth generally as that we are now discussing as probable, especially when we recollect that the labour is only diverted, and it is not the whole £21,000,000 that is lost, but only the difference between that sum and what is otherwise earned, which may even be a *plus* and not a *minus* difference.

To bring the matter to a point, an increase of 40 per cent. in the income of the country in ten years would on an assumed income of 1,000 millions only in 1875, —and the figure must then have been more,—have brought the income up to 1,400 millions; an increase of 20 per cent. would have brought it up to 1,200 millions only, a difference of 200 millions, which must have arisen from the alleged difference in the rate of our material growth in question if it had occurred. Clearly nothing can have happened in our foreign trade to account for anything more than the smallest fraction of such a difference. The figures are altogether too small. We may repeat again then that it is not the check to our foreign trade which foreign competition may have caused to which we can ascribe the recent check to our general rate of growth.

I need hardly add that in point of theory foreign competition was not likely to have the effect stated.

I have set forth elsewhere in an elaborate essay[1] the reasons for holding this opinion; why it is, in fact, that as foreign nations grow richer we should be better off absolutely than if they were to remain poor, though relatively they might advance more than we do. But, whatever theory may say, in point of fact the check to the rate of our material growth cannot, for the reasons stated, have been due to anything which has happened to our foreign trade.

Another explanation which has been suggested, and to which I have myself been inclined to attach considerable weight as being plainly, as far as it goes, a *vera causa*, is the extent to which the hours of labour have been reduced in many employments in consequence of the improvement in the condition of the working classes in the last half-century, and the growth of a disposition to take things easier, which has been the result of the general prosperity of the country. Such causes when they exist, and when they are brought into operation, must tend to diminish the rate of material growth in a country as compared with a period just before when they were not in operation. If we could suppose them brought into operation suddenly, all other things, such as the progress and development of invention, remaining the same, such a reduction of hours of labour and growth of a disposition to take things easy, must produce a check to the former rate of growth.

After some consideration, however, although there is no doubt of the general tendency of the causes referred to, I begin to doubt whether they would explain adequately such a check to the rate of material growth generally throughout the country as is assumed to have occurred. As regards the shortening of the hours of labour, which is the more definite fact to be dealt with, it cannot but be observed that the shortening has by no means been universal. It has been conspicuous

[1] See my "Essays in Finance," 2nd series, "Foreign Manufactures and English Trade," p. 240.

among certain trades organized into trades unions; but the unions, after all, only include about a tenth part of the labour of the country. There has been no such conspicuous shortening of the hours of labour among professional men, clerks, domestic servants, and many others whose labour is an essential part of the general sum total. Next—and this is perhaps even more important—the shortening of the hours of labour is not coincident with the beginning of the last ten years, though it has been in full operation for the whole of that period, but rather with the beginning or middle of the previous ten years, viz., 1865-75; so that it should have been fully in operation upon the production of 1875; and the check to our rate of growth if due to this cause should thus have been felt between 1865 and 1875, rather than between the latter date and the present time. The same with the general disposition to take things easy. This disposition did not spring up in a day in 1875, but was probably as effective as a cause of change in the earlier, as in the later, period. It must count for something as a cause of the annual production of the country being less at a given moment than it would otherwise be; but in comparing two periods, what we have to consider is whether the growth of this disposition has been greater in one period than in another; and there are no data to support such a conclusion as regards the last ten years compared with the previous ten.

We must apparently, therefore, reject this explanation also. It is not adequate to account for the apparent change that has occurred in the rate of our growth from the year 1875 as compared with the period just before. Our progress in periods previous to 1875 took place in spite of the operation of causes of a similar kind which were then in operation, and there is no proof at all that the shortening of the hours of labour and the growth of a disposition to take things easy have been greater since 1875 as compared with the period just before than they were between 1865 and 1875 as compared with the period just before that. What is wanted is a new cause beginning to operate in or about 1875, and the shortening of the hours of labour and the growth of a disposition to take things easy do not answer that description sufficiently. Something of the apparent change may be due to an acceleration in recent years of the growth of a disposition to take things easy, but on the whole the explanation halts when we make a strict comparison.

Another cause which may properly be assigned as a *vera causa* of a check to the rate of material growth in the country is the unfavourable weather to agriculture and the generally unprofitable conditions of that industry in recent years. *Pro tanto* such influences would make agricultural production less to-day than it would otherwise be. Employment in that industry would also be diminished comparatively, and perhaps absolutely, and a check to production generally would take place while labour was seeking new fields. But the check arising in this manner, as far as the general growth is concerned, has obviously not been very great. More land in proportion has been turned into permanent pasture, but very little land has gone out of cultivation altogether, and even the amount under the plough has not much diminished. Agricultural labour, in somewhat greater proportion than before, has been obliged to seek other employments; the flow of population from country to town has been increased somewhat; but nothing new has happened to diminish production generally to a serious extent, and it is a new cause, it must be remembered, for which we are seeking. As far as unfavourable weather is concerned, again, that is only a temporary evil. One year with another, the weather is not worse now than at any former time; the remarkably unfavourable weather which lasted from 1874 to 1880 has passed. The other conditions unfavourable to agriculture, especially foreign competition, are more enduring; but these seem much more unfavourable to rent than to production itself, which is the point now under consideration; and we do not know that they will be permanent at all when prices and wages are fully adjusted.

The disturbance to industry by the fall of prices generally is also a *vera causa* of a check to the rate of material growth. But the effect of such a cause seems to be confined within narrow limits, and it is not a new cause. It occurs in every time of depression due to discredit, being partly the effect and partly the cause of the depression itself. All that is new recently is the extreme degree of the fall, and I must express the greatest doubt whether a mere difference of degree aggravates materially the periodical disturbance of industry, tending to check production, which a fall of prices from a high to a low level causes. So far as past experience has gone, at any rate, no such cause has been known to check production to any material extent. If any such cause tended to have a serious effect we should witness the results every time there is a shrinkage of values owing to the contraction and appreciation of an inconvertible paper currency, and I am not aware of any such contraction having had the effect described on production, though the effect in producing a feeling of depression is beyond all question. The facts as to the great contraction in this country between 1815 and 1820 are on record, while the experience of the United States after the civil war is also fresh in everyone's recollection. Contraction of currency and fall of prices, though they are painful things, do not stop production materially.

Another explanation suggested is that there is in fact no antecedent reason for supposing that the rate of material growth in a community should always be at the same rate—that a community may, as it were, get "to the top" as regards its development under given conditions, and then its advance should be either less rapid than it had been or it should even become stationary. The defect of this explanation is that it assumes the very thing which would have to be proved.

Is there any other sign except the alleged check to the rate of our material growth itself that in or about the year 1875 this country got "to the top"? It has, moreover, to be considered that on *à priori* grounds it is most unlikely a community would get to the top *per saltum*, and then so great a change should occur as the apparent change we are considering. The persistence of internal conditions in a given mass of humanity is a thing we may safely assume, and if these conditions are consistent with a given rate of development in one period of ten years, it is most unlikely that, save for an alteration of external conditions, there would be another rate of development in the succeeding ten years. Human nature and capacities do not change like that. Scientific opinion, I believe, is also to the effect that the progress of invention and of the practical working of inventions, which have been the main cause of our material growth in the past, have been going on in the last ten years, are still going on, and are likely to go on in the near future, at as great a rate as at any time in the last fifty years. Except, as already said, the apparent check to the rate of our material growth itself, there is no sign anywhere of our having got to the top, so that a stationary condition economically, or a condition nearly approaching it, has been reached.

Last of all, it is urged that the diminution in the rate of material growth, which is in question, must be due to the fact that we are losing the natural advantages of coal and iron which we formerly had in comparison with the rest of the world. This is perhaps only another way of saying that we have got to the top by comparison, though the community of nations generally has not got to the top, and another way of saying also that foreign competition affects us more than it formerly did; an argument already dealt with. But the question whether coal and iron at home are really so indispensable to our material growth as is sometimes assumed appears itself so important that I may be excused for specially discussing the question, notwithstanding that it has virtually been disposed of, as far as any explanation of past facts is concerned, by what has been already said.

The argument proceeds on the supposition—which is no doubt well founded in the abstract and as far as the past experience of mankind is concerned—that in addition to natural capacities of its own a community requires for its prosperity certain natural advantages, fertility of soil, rich and easily worked mines, a genial climate in which labour may conveniently be carried on, and so forth. A community possessing all these things, or the like things, will flourish, but as it ceases to lose any of them its prosperity must become precarious, and population must flow to the places where they can be secured. Of course climate is not a thing which changes, as far as any practical experience is concerned; but relatively the advantage of a fertile soil may be lost, as England has lately lost it in comparison with the United States and other new countries, its soil having become inadequate for the whole population; and still more the advantage of mines, especially mines of coal and iron, on which the miscellaneous industries of a manufacturing country depend, may be lost. Hence it is said the check to our rate of growth in recent years. We have long since lost our agricultural advantages by comparison. Now we are also beginning to lose the special advantages which coal and iron have given. Our mines are becoming less rich than those of foreign countries, and the balance is turning against us. Why should not population relatively flow from England to the United States and other countries as it has passed within the limits of the United Kingdom itself from Cornwall and Sussex to Staffordshire, Lancashire, Yorkshire, and the north? In this view the coal famine of 1873 was the sign of a check such as Mr. Jevons anticipated. What has happened since is only a sequence of the like causes.

I need not repeat in opposition to this view what has already been said as to the inadequacy of any actual decline in our foreign trade to account for such a check to our general growth as is supposed to have occurred. If the loss of our natural advantages of coal and iron in addition to agriculture is having the effects supposed, we ought to witness them in our foreign trade, and in fact we do not witness them to the extent required for the production of the phenomenon in question.

What I wish now specially to urge is that, in consequence of the progress of invention and the practical application of inventions in modern times, the theory itself has begun to be less true generally than it has been. It is no longer so necessary, as it once was, as in fact it always has been until very lately, that people should live where their food and raw materials are grown. The industry of the world having become more and more manufacturing and, if one may say so, artistic, and less agricultural and extractive, the natural advantages of a fertile soil and rich mines are less important to a manufacturing community than they were at any former period of the world's history, because of the new cheapness of conveyance. Under the new conditions, I believe it is impossible to doubt, climate, accumulated wealth, acquired manufacturing skill, concentration of population become more important factors than mere juxtaposition to the natural advantages of fertile soil and rich mines. The facts seem at any rate worth investigating, judging by what has happened in England and other old countries in the last half-century and by what is still happening there.

Take first the question of food. Wheat is now conveyed from the American Far West to Liverpool and London and any other ports in the Old World for something like five shillings per quarter—equal to about half a farthing on the pound of bread, or a halfpenny on the quartern loaf. The difference between the towns of a country with fertile soil, therefore, and the towns of a country with inadequate soil is represented by this small difference in the price of bread. At about fivepence the quartern loaf the staff of life may be about

10 per cent. cheaper in the fertile country than it is in a country which does not grow its own food at all, and which may be thousands of miles away. As the staff of life only enters into the expenditure of the artisan to the extent of 20 per cent. at the outside, and into the expenditure of richer classes to a smaller extent, the difference on the whole income of a community made by their living where the staff of life would be cheaper would be less than 2 per cent.—too small to tell against other advantages which may be credited to them. What is true of wheat is even more true of meat and other more valuable articles of food where the cost of conveyance makes a less difference in the proportionate value of the food *in situ* and its value at a distant point. The same more and more with raw materials. Cotton and such articles cost so little to transport that the manufacturing may as well go on in Lancashire or any other part of the Old World as *in situ* or nearly *in situ*; and even as regards metals or minerals, except coal and perhaps iron, the same rule applies, the cost of conveyance being as nothing in proportion to the value of the raw material itself. As regards coal and iron, moreover, there are many places where they are not in absolute juxtaposition, and if they have to be conveyed at all they may as well be conveyed to a common centre. Iron ore and iron at any rate are beginning to be articles of import into the old countries of Europe, to which the cost, in fact, offers very little difficulty. The additional cost to the miscellaneous manufacturing of a country through its having to bring iron and coal from a distance may thus be quite inconsiderable, and apparently is becoming more and more inconsiderable. As regards raw materials generally it has also to be considered that, owing to their immense variety, there is an undoubted convenience in a common manufacturing centre to which they can be brought. Hitherto they may have come to England and other old countries of Europe in part because coal and iron were abundant there in

juxtaposition; but the habit once set up, there seems no reason why they should not concentrate themselves on the old manufacturing centres. The ruder parts of the coal and iron industry may be attracted to other places, but the higher branches of manufacturing will be at no disadvantage if carried on at the old centres.

On the other hand, the old centres will retain the advantages, which are obviously very great, of climate, accumulated wealth, acquired skill, and concentration of population. That population under the new conditions is to go from them merely because they do not grow food which can be transported to them at the cost of a mere fraction of the aggregate income, and because they have not coal and iron in abundance and in juxtaposition, that abundance and juxtaposition, owing again to the diminished cost of conveyance, being no longer so indispensable as it was to the higher branches of manufacturing, appears certainly to be a large order. What I have to suggest most strongly at any rate is that the advantages I have spoken of as possessed by old manufacturing centres are not unlikely to tell more and more under the new conditions, and that the indispensability of coal and iron is no longer to be spoken of as what it has been in the last century, during which apparently England owed so much of its precedence in manufacturing power to these causes.

To the same effect we may urge the specially great increase of the efficiency of coal in recent years. Cheap coal *in situ* cannot be relatively so important as it was in days when five or ten tons of coal were required to do the work which can now be done by one.

The truth is that the whole change that has been occurring is only a continuation of much larger historical changes. There has almost always in English history been some one industry that was supposed to be king. In the middle ages it was the growth and export of raw wool; last century it was the woollen manufacture itself; early in this century and down to a very late date cotton was king; more lately, since the beginning of the railway and steamship era, it has been coal and iron. How do we know, how can we know, that coal and iron are to reign indefinitely, any more than wool, or the woollen manufacture, or cotton themselves have done? Changes are always going on, and for that reason I believe we should attach the more importance to the increasing signs that it is no longer necessary or indispensable for prosperous communities to live where their food and raw materials are grown—that there may be advantages of climate, of accumulated wealth, of acquired skill, of concentration of population which are now, under the new conditions, overwhelmingly more important. It would be absurd to dogmatize in such a matter. I hope, however, I have said enough to those who care to reflect to satisfy them that the indispensability even of coal and iron to the continuance of our material growth is no longer to be assumed, that there are wholly new conditions to be considered.

To come back to the practical point in all this discussion. Not only is there no sign in anything that has yet happened that the apparent check to our former rate of material growth is due to the loss of natural advantages which we once possessed, but the theory of natural advantages itself requires to be revised. Equally in this way as in the other ways that have been discussed, it is impossible to account for the apparent check to the former rate of our material growth which has been observed.

III.

Having carried matters so far, however, and having found the insufficiency of the various causes which have been assigned for the check to our former rate of material growth, because they have not produced the sort of effect in detail which they ought to have produced so as to lead to the general effect alleged, or because they existed quite as much when the rate of growth was great as in recent years when a diminution has apparently been observed, it would seem expedient to inquire whether, in spite of the accumulation of signs to that effect, the apparent check to our rate of growth may, after all, not be a real one. To some extent I think we must conclude that this is the case. There are other facts which are inconsistent with a real and permanent check such as has been in question, and a general explanation of the special phenomena of arrest seems possible without supposing any such real check.

The first broad fact that does not seem quite reconcilable with the fact of a real diminution of the kind alleged in the rate of material growth generally is the real as distinguished from the apparent growth of the income tax assessments when allowance is made for the fall of prices which affect, as we have seen, all aggregate values. Assuming the fall of prices to be about 20 per cent., then we must add one-fourth to the assessments in 1885 to get the proper figure for comparison with 1875. The total of 631 millions for 1885 would thus become 787 millions, which is a falling-off of 35 millions, or 4 per cent. only, from the figure of 822 millions, which should have been reached if the rate of growth had been the same between 1875 and 1885 as between 1865 and 1875. Allowing for the raising of the lower limit of the income tax in the interval, this is really no decrease at all.

Of course this comparison may be thrown out if we are to assume the difference made by the fall of prices on the income tax assessments to be 15 or 10 per cent. only, instead of 20 per cent. But a point like this would involve a most elaborate discussion, for which this address would hardly be the occasion. I hope to find a better opportunity shortly in a continuation of my essay of ten years ago on the Accumulations of Capital in the United Kingdom.[1] There is no doubt, however, that an allowance must be made for the difference of prices, and when any such allowance is made

[1] See "The Growth of Capital," G. Bell and Sons, 1889.

the rate of material growth would not appear to be so very much less between 1875 and 1885 than in the period just before, as it does in the above figures.

Another broad fact not easily reconcilable with the fact of a great diminution in the real rate of material growth in the last ten years is the steadiness of the increase of population and the absence of any sign, such as an increase in the proportion of pauperism, indicating that the people are less fully employed than they were. The increasing numbers must either be employed or unemployed, and if there is an increase in the proportion of the unemployed the fact should be revealed in the returns of pauperism somehow. The existence of trade unions, no doubt, prevents many workmen coming on the rates who might formerly have done so, but there are large masses of workmen, the most likely to feel the brunt of want of employment, to whom this explanation would not apply.

What we find, however, is that population has increased as follows: between 1855 and 1865 from 27,800,000 to 29,900,000, or 7½ per cent.; between 1865 and 1875 from 29,900,000 to 32,800,000, or nearly 10 per cent.; and between 1875 and 1885 from 32,800,000 to 36,300,000, or over 10 per cent. If it is considered that the figures are not fairly comparable for the early period, owing to the specially large emigration from Ireland, which took away from the apparent numbers of the United Kingdom as a whole, but still allowed of as great an increase in the manufacturing parts of the country as there has been later, then we may take the figures for England only, and what we find is—between 1855 and 1865 an increase from 18,800,000 to 21,100,000, or 12½ per cent.; between 1865 and 1875 from 21,100,000 to 24,000,000, or nearly 14 per cent.; and between 1875 and 1885 from 24,000,000 to 27,500,000, or 14½ per cent. Whether, therefore, we take the figures for the United Kingdom or for England only, what we find is a greater increase of population in the last ten years than in either of the previous decades when the rate of material growth seemed so much greater. If there had been such real diminution in the rate of material growth, ought there not to have been some increase in the want of employment and in pauperism to correspond?

It is one of the most notorious facts of the case, however, that there has been no increase, but instead a very steady decrease of pauperism, excepting in Ireland; which is so small as not to affect the general result. As regards England, the figures are very striking indeed. The average number of paupers and proportion to population have been as follows in quinquennial periods in England since 1855:

	Number of Paupers.	Proportion to Population per cent.
1855-59	895,000	4.7
1860-64	948,000	4.7
1865-69	962,000	4.5
1870-74	952,000	4.2
1875-79	753,000	3.1
1880-84	787,000	3.0

Thus there has been a steady diminution in the proportion to the population all through, accompanied by a diminution in the absolute numbers between 1865-69 and 1875-79, though there has since been a slight increase. In spite of all that can be urged as to a more stringent poor-law administration having made all the difference, it is difficult to believe that a real falling-off of a serious kind in the rate of our material growth in late years as compared with the period just before should not have led to some real increase of pauperism. Change of administration may do much, but it cannot alter the effect of any serious increase in the want of employment in a country.

The corresponding figures as to Scotland are much the same:

	Number of Paupers.	Proportion to Population per cent.
1855-59	123,000	4.2
1860-64	125,000	4.2
1865-69	131,000	4.3

	Number of Paupers.	Proportion to Population per cent.
1870-74	123,000	3.7
1875-79	103,000	2.9
1880-84	100,000	2.7

Here there is the same steady diminution in the proportion of pauperism to population all through as we have seen in the case of England, accompanied in this case by a steady diminution of the absolute number of paupers since 1865-69. The Scotch administration has been totally independent of the English, but the same results are produced.

In Ireland, as already hinted, the history has been different. There has been an increase in the pauperism accompanied by a decline of population. But Ireland is too small to affect the general result.

We are thus confronted by the fact that if there had been a real check of a serious kind to the rate of our material growth in the last ten years as compared with the ten years just before, there ought to have been some increase in the want of employment and in pauperism, but instead of there being such an increase there is a decline. The population apparently, while increasing even more rapidly in the last ten years than before, has been more fully employed than before. To make these facts consistent with a check to the rate of our material growth, we must contrive some such hypothesis as that employment has been more diffused as regards numbers, but the aggregate amount of it has fallen off; another form of the hypothesis as to the effect of shorter hours of labour already discussed. But a little reflection will show that any such hypothesis is hardly admissible. It is difficult to imagine any change in the conditions of employment in so short a time which would make it possible for larger numbers to be employed along with a diminution in the aggregate amount of employment itself.

Another fact corresponding to this decrease of pauperism is the steady increase of savings bank deposits and depositors. These deposits are not, of course, the deposits of working classes only, technically so called. They include the smaller class of tradesmen and the lower middle classes generally. But, *quantum valeant*, the facts as to a growth of deposits and depositors should reflect the condition of the country generally in much the same way as the returns of pauperism. What we find then is, as regards deposits, that the increase between 1855 and 1865 was £34,300,000 to £45,300,000, or about one-third; between 1865 and 1875 from £45,300,000 to £67,600,000, or about one-half; and between 1875 and 1885 from £67,600,000 to £94,053,000, or just about 40 per cent.—a less increase than in the previous ten years, but not really less, perhaps, if allowance is made for the fall of prices in the interval, and in any case a very large increase. Then, as regards depositors, what we find is an increase between 1855 and 1865 from 1,304,000 to 2,079,000, or 59 per cent.; between 1865 and 1875 from 2,079,000 to 3,256,000, or 56 per cent.; and between 1875 and 1885 from 3,256,000 to over 5,000,000, or over 50 per cent. Whatever special explanations there may be, facts like these are at least not inconsistent with a fuller employment of the population in the last ten years than in the previous ten.

Yet another fact tending to the same conclusion may be referred to. The stationariness or slow growth of the income tax assessments in general in the last ten years, as compared with the rapid increase in the ten years just before, has already been referred to as one of the signs indicating a check to the rate of advance in our material growth. But when the returns are examined in detail, there is one class of assessments, more significant, perhaps, than any, of the general condition of the nation, viz., houses, which is found to exhibit as great an increase in the last ten years as in the previous decade. Between 1865 and 1875 the increase in the item of houses in the income tax assessments in the United Kingdom was from

£68,800,000 to £94,600,000, or just about 37 per cent. In the following ten years the increase was from £94,600,000 to £128,500,000, or just about 36 per cent. In "houses," then, as yet there is no sign of any check to the general rate of the material growth of the country. Allowing, in fact, for the great fall in prices in the last ten years, the real increase in houses would seem to have been more in the last ten years than in the ten years just before.

Other facts, such as the increase of Post Office business, may be referred to as tending to the same conclusion. But there is no need to multiply facts. If no hypothesis is to be accepted except one that reconciles all the facts, then these facts as to the increase of population, diminution of pauperism, increase of savings bank deposits and depositors, increase of houses must all be taken into account, as well as those signs as regards production and other factors, which have usually been most dwelt upon in discussing the question of the accumulation of wealth and the material growth of the people. If the signs of a check to production in some directions can be reconciled with the fact of an unchecked continuance of the former rate of growth generally, then the later facts cited as to increase of population, diminution of pauperism, and the like, may be allowed to have their natural interpretation and to be conclusive on the point.

Such a general explanation, then, of the facts as to production in leading industries and the like, referred to in the earlier part of this address, consistent with the fact that there is no serious falling-off in the rate of our material growth generally, is to be found in the supposition that industry by a natural law is becoming more and more miscellaneous, and that as populations develop, the disproportionate growth of the numbers employed in such miscellaneous industries, and in what may be called incorporeal functions, that is, as teachers, artists, and the like, prevents the increase of staple products continuing at the former rate. This supposition, it will be found, has a good deal to support it in the actual facts as to industry and population in recent years.

The foreign trade shows some sign of the change that is going on. Looking through the list of export articles, some remarkable developments are to be noticed. The annexed short table (see p. 138) speaks for itself.

Thus there are not a few articles, of which jute is a conspicuous example, in which there has been an entirely new industry established within a comparatively short period; and though the percentage of increase may not in all be so great in the last ten years as in the previous ten just because the industry is so wholly new, yet the amount of the increase is as great or greater. In other articles, such as soap and British spirits, there is a new start in the last ten years after a decline in the previous periods. Such cases as oil and floor cloth, paper other than hangings, and plate glass are also specially noticeable as practically new trades. The list I am satisfied could be considerably extended, but I am giving it mainly by way of illustration. Finally, there is the item of other articles not separately specified—an item which is always changing in the statistical abstract because every few years one or more articles grow into sufficient importance to require separate mention, so that any extended comparison of this item for a long series of years is impossible. Still it is ever growing, and what we find in the last ten years is that, in spite of the fall of prices, the growth is from £9,700,000 to £10,600,000, or nearly 10 per cent. Many of the articles referred to, it is plain, cannot run into much money, but the indications of a tendency are none the less clear. What is happening in the foreign trade is happening, we may be sure, in the home trade as well, of which in another way the increase in the imports of foreign manufactures, already referred to in another connection, is really a sign, as it implies the growth of miscellaneous wants among the consumers.

The census figures as to occupations tend, I believe,

Exports of the undermentioned Articles in the Years stated, with the Rates of Increase in 1855-65, 1865-75, and 1875-85 compared.

	Quantities Exported.				Increase per cent.		
	1855.	1865.	1875.	1885.	1855-65.	1865-75.	1875-85.
Candles, million lbs.	4	4	5.3	7.8	nil	33	47
Cordage and twine, thousand cwts.	110	168	111	177	53	- 34	59
Plate glass, million sq. ft.	0.3	0.6	1.6	3.9	100	166	143
Jute yarn, million lbs.	not stated	4.9	15.9	30.7	—	224	93
Jute manufacture, million yds.	,,	15.4	102.1	215	—	563	110
Iron hoops, sheets, etc., thousand tons	,,	116	204	331	—	76	62
Tinned plates, thousand tons	,,	63	138	298	—	119	116
Other wrought iron, thousand tons	,,	214	239	348	—	12	45
Oil and floor cloth, million sq. yds.	0.5	2.4	6.3	11.3	380	162	79
Paper other than hangings, thousand cwts.	106[1]	145	319	733	37	120	130
Dressed skins and furs, millions	not stated	not stated	0.37	3.45	—	—	832
Soap, thousand cwts.	205	140	251	402	- 32[2]	79	60
Spirits, million gals.	3.8	2.0	1.0	2.7	- 47[2]	- 50[2]	170
Unenumerated, values millions	—	—	£9.7	£10.6	—	—	10

[1] 1858 not separately stated before.
[2] Decrease.

to confirm this observation as to the special growth of miscellaneous industries, but the discussion of the figures would require more preparation than I have had time for, and perhaps more space than can well be spared.

As to the growth of incorporeal functions, which is another fact significant of the supposed change in the direction of the employments of the people, I propose to appeal to the testimony of the census figures. I need refer on this head only to the paper read some time ago to the Statistical Society by Mr. Booth. Among those classes of population whose numbers in England and Wales in the last ten years have shown a disproportionate growth are the following:

Numbers and Percentage of Self-supporting Population employed.

	Numbers.		Percentage.	
	1871.	1881.	1871.	1881.
Transport	524,000	654,000	4.9	5.6
Commercial Class . .	119,000	225,000	1.1	1.9
Art and Amusement .	38,000	47,000	0.3	0.4
Literature and Science	7,000	9,000	—	0.1
Education	135,000	183,000	1.3	1.6
Indefinite	124,000	269,000	1.2	2.3
Total . . .	947,000	1,387,000	8.8	11.9

Following the indication of these figures, whatever qualification they may be subject to, we are apparently justified in saying that an increasing part of the population has been lately applied to the creation of incorporeal products. Their employment is industrial all the same. The products are consumed as they are produced, but the production is none the less real. If a nation chooses to produce more largely in this form as it becomes more prosperous, so that there is less development than was formerly the case in what were known as staple industries, it need not be becoming poorer for that reason; all that is happening is that its wealth and income are taking a different shape.

It is quite conceivable, then, and is in truth not improbable, that a check to the former rate of material growth in certain directions may have taken place of late years without any corresponding check to the rate of material growth generally, which would seem to be inconsistent with such facts as the growth of population, diminution of pauperism, increase of houses, and the like. The truth would seem to be that with the growth of staple industries, such as cotton, wool, coal, and iron, up to a point, there being reasons for the remarkably quick development of each for many years up to 1875, there comes a growth of new wants, the satisfaction of which drafts a portion of the national energy in new directions. Just because certain staples developed themselves greatly between 1855 and 1875 the time was likely to arrive when they would grow not quite so fast. For the same reason the rapid increase for a certain period in the consumption per head of articles like sugar and tea was likely to be followed by a less rapid increase, the wants of consumers taking a new direction. Probably owing to the more and more miscellaneous character of modern industry, it will become more and more difficult to follow its development by dealing with staple articles only, while changes in aggregate values are untrustworthy as indications of real changes owing to changes in prices. Already there seems to be no doubt the staple articles are no longer a sufficient indication.

A supplementary explanation may be added which helps to explain another difficulty in the matter by which people are puzzled. I can imagine them saying that it is all very well to pooh-pooh the non-increase or slower increase of the production of staple articles, and to assume that industry is becoming more and more miscellaneous; but other countries go on increasing their production of these same staple articles.

The increase of the manufactures of cotton, wool, coal, and iron in Germany and the United States, they will say, has in recent years been greater in proportion than in England, which is undoubtedly true. The explanation I have to suggest, however, is that the competition with the leading manufacturing country, which England still is, is naturally in the staple articles where manufacturing has been reduced to a system, the newer and more difficult manufactures and the newer developments of industry generally falling as a rule to the older country. Even in foreign countries, however, there are signs of slower growth of recent years in the staple articles as compared with the period just before. In Germany, for instance, the production of coal increased between 1860 and 1866 (I take the years which I find available in Dr. Neumann Spallart's "Uebersichten") from 12,300,000 tons to 28,200,000, or nearly 129 per cent.; between 1866 and 1876 the increase was from the figure stated to about 50,000,000, or about 77 per cent. only; between 1876 and 1885, another period of ten years, from the figure stated to 74,000,000 tons, or less than 50 per cent.—a rapidly diminishing rate of increase. In the United States of America the corresponding figures for coal are 15, 22, 50, and 103 million tons, showing a greater increase than in Germany, but still a rather less rate of increase since 1876 than in the ten years before. The experience as to the iron production would seem to be different, the increase in the United States and Germany having been enormously rapid in the last ten years; but I have not been able here to carry the figures far enough back for comparison. Still the facts as to coal in Germany are enough to show how rapidly the rate of increase of growth may fall off when a point is reached, and that the experience of the United Kingdom is by no means exceptional. As the staple articles develop abroad the rate of increase in such articles will diminish too, and foreign industry in turn will become more and more miscellaneous.

The conclusion would thus be that there is nothing unaccountable in the course of industry in the United Kingdom in the last ten years. In certain staple industries the rate of increase has been less than it was in the ten years just before, but there would seem to have been no increase or little increase in the want of employment generally, while there is reason to believe that certain miscellaneous industries have grown at a greater rate than the staple industries, or have grown into wholly new being, and that there has also been some diversion of industry in directions where the products are incorporeal. These facts also correspond with what is going on abroad, a tendency to decline in the rate of increase of staple articles of production being general, and industry everywhere following the law of becoming more miscellaneous. Abroad also, we may be sure, as nations increase in wealth the diversion of industry in directions where the products are incorporeal will also take place. What the whole facts seem to bring out, therefore, is a change in the direction of industry of a most interesting kind. If we are to believe that the progress of invention and of the application of invention to human wants continues and increases, no other explanation seems possible of the apparent check to the rate of material growth which seems to be so nearly demonstrated by some of the statistics most commonly appealed to in such questions.

At the same time I must apply the remark which I applied at the earlier stage to the opposite conclusion, that there had been a real check to the rate of increase in our material growth. When the main statistics bearing on a particular point all indicate the same conclusion, it is not difficult to reason from them and to convince all who study them; but when the indications are apparently in mutual conflict it would be folly to dogmatize. I have indicated frankly my own opinion, but I, for one, should like the subject to be more fully thrashed out. It is a very obvious suggestion, moreover, that one may prove too much by such figures—

that it is an outrage on common sense to talk of there being no check to the rate of growth in the country when times are notoriously bad and everybody is talking of want of profit. What I should suggest finally, by way of a hypothesis reconciling all the facts, would be that probably there is some check to the rate of material growth in the last ten years, though not of the serious character implied by the first set of figures discussed; that this check may even be too small to be measured by general statistics, though it is sufficient to account for no small amount of *malaise*; and that the *malaise* itself is largely accounted for, as I have suggested on a former occasion, by the mere fall of prices, whatever the cause, as it involves a great redistribution of wealth and income, and makes very many people feel poorer, including many who are not really poorer, but only seem so, and many who are really richer if they only allowed properly for the increased purchasing power of their wealth. All these facts are quite consistent with the fact of a very slight real diminution in the rate of our material growth generally, and with that change in the direction of the national industry, significant of a general change beginning throughout the world, which would seem to have occurred.

To some extent also it ought to be allowed that the tendency in the very latest years seems unsatisfactory, and that the developments of the next few years should be carefully watched. Up to now there is nothing really alarming in the statistics when they are analyzed and compared. It may be the case, though I do not think it is the case, that causes are in operation to produce that great check and retrogression which have not as yet occurred, though many have talked as if they had occurred. The exact limits of the discussion should be carefully kept in mind.

Fortunately, however, there is no doubt what some of the conclusions on practical points should be. If it be the case that the hold of an old country like England on certain staple industries of the world is less firm than it was, and, as I believe, must be less and less firm from period to period, owing to the natural development of foreign countries and the room there is among ourselves for development in new directions, then we should make assurance doubly sure that the country is really developing in new directions. If our dependence must be on the new advantages that have been described, such as acquired manufacturing skill, concentration of population, and the like, then we must make sure of the skill and of the best conditions of existence for the concentrated population. If, in point of fact, shorter hours of labour and taking things easy have contributed to check our rate of progress slightly, there is all the more reason for improving the human agent in industry, so as to make work in the shorter hours more efficient. Looking at the stir there now is about technical education and such matters, and the hereditary character of our population, I see no cause to doubt that the future will be even more prosperous than in the past. The national life seems as fresh and vigorous as ever. The unrest and complaints of the last few years are not bad signs. But the new conditions must be fully recognized. The utmost energy, mobility, and resource must be applied in every direction if we are only to hold our own.

XVII.

PROTECTION FOR MANUFACTURES IN NEW COUNTRIES.[1]

SO many questions in political economy being questions mainly of degree it may be wondered that appeal is not made more frequently to statistics to help in their solution. These are questions in which no one doubts the main theory, or where for practical discussion the main theory is admitted. We may instance the equality of taxation. In whatever way equality is considered to be established as between classes and individuals, whether by equal taxes *pro rata* upon all or by taxes at progressively higher rates upon the larger incomes, yet equality is allowed to be the thing to be aimed at. In practice, however, there must obviously be degrees of inequality. By the nature of the case the State cannot make a very nice adjustment; it must think of classes and not individuals; while there are many doubts as to the real and ultimate incidence of a great many taxes. If, then, taking the principal taxes in any comparison that may be made, we find inequalities arising through deviations from an average taxation of 5 per cent. on the community, making the percentage $7\frac{1}{2}$ on some and only $2\frac{1}{2}$ on others, with of course intermediate rates, it is quite possible that this state of things may be one which it would be a greater evil to attempt to remedy than to let alone. On the other hand, a deviation from the 5 per cent. average amounting to a proportion of 20 per cent. on some classes of the taxpayers would probably be thought so serious by those affected, that a remedy at all hazards, in a free and self-governing community, would have to

[1] From the "Economic Journal" of 1898.

be found. But clearly what is true of the one mischief may not be true of the other mischief, and may not compel to the same action.

A similar illustration would be furnished by the well-known case of the shilling duty on corn. Import duties on articles of food to protect the home-grower are, of course, bad economically; but given a very small duty of long standing, may not the disadvantages of removing it, necessitating an addition to a disproportionate income tax, be greater on the whole than those of letting it remain? It is the question of degree, as in the previous case of inequality of taxation, which is here the material question.

I have often thought that the principle might be usefully applied in the discussion of Mill's famous exception to the universal applicability of free trade principles, viz.: that import duties for protective purposes might be permissible in new countries in order to begin industries naturally suitable, an idea which has been applied by other writers to manufacturing industries generally, the alleged object being to give variety to the economic *régime* of such countries and promote the increase of a town population. I need not say here that Mill has been very much misrepresented. His exception was a very limited one, and was no more than a statement that there might be cases for protection in the way he mentioned, whereas his statement has been used as an authority for every sort of protectionist mischief, in old as well as new countries. But taking it in its more exact and limited meaning, what seems to me worthy of examination from a statistical view is whether, in fact, manufacturing industries can be promoted to any material extent in really new countries, so as to give that variety to their economic *régime* which protectionists contend for. In other words, how much variety can so be given to the industries of a new country?

Let us begin by quoting the exact words from Mill, in which he gives a little countenance to protection for new countries. First he states (Book V., chap. x., sec. 1):

"The only case in which, on mere principles of political economy, protecting duties can be defensible, is when they are imposed temporarily (especially in a young and rising nation) in hopes of naturalizing a foreign industry, in itself perfectly suitable to the circumstances of the country. The superiority of one country over another in a branch of production often arises only from having begun it sooner. There may be no inherent advantage on one part, or disadvantage on the other, but only a present superiority of acquired skill and experience. A country which has this skill and experience yet to acquire, may in other respects be better adapted to the production than those which were earlier in the field; and besides it is a just remark of Mr. Rae, that nothing has a greater tendency to promote improvements in any branch of production than its trial under a new set of conditions. But it cannot be expected that individuals should, at their own risk, or rather to their certain loss, introduce a new manufacture and bear the burthen of carrying it on until the producers have been educated up to the level of those with whom the processes are traditional. A protecting duty, continued for a reasonable time, will sometimes be the least inconvenient mode in which the nation can tax itself for the support of such an experiment. But the protection should be confined to cases in which there is good ground of assurance that the industry which it fosters will after a time be able to dispense with it; nor should the domestic producers ever be allowed to expect that it will be continued to them beyond the time necessary for a fair trial of what they are capable of accomplishing."

Next (Book V., chap. x., sec. 2) it is remarked, speaking of American protectionists:

"It is an injustice to them to suppose that their protectionist creed rests upon nothing superior to an economic blunder; many of them have been led to it much more by consideration for the higher interests of humanity, than by purely economic reasons. They, and Mr. Carey at their head, deem it a necessary condition of human improvement, that towns should abound; that men should combine their labour, by means of interchange with near neighbours, with people of pursuits, capacities, and mental cultivation different from their own, sufficiently close at hand for mutual sharpening of wits and enlarging of ideas, rather than with people on the opposite side of the globe. They believe that a nation all engaged in the same, or nearly the same pursuit—a nation all agricultural—cannot attain a high state of civilization and culture. And for this there is a great foundation of reason."

And then Mill proceeds to argue, amongst other things, that in the case of America protective import duties would not set up towns in Ohio and Michigan, but would merely favour New England as against Old England. He does not dispute, however, that in a really new country protective import duties would have the effect contended for by American protectionists. He rather assumes that the effect will be produced.

At any rate, whatever was Mill's precise view, there is no doubt that protectionists like Carey profess to aim at a larger settlement of population in a new country, so that the agriculturist may have a local market, and so on. Even in Mill, however, one can see that he has in view a large economic change that may be effected by means of protective import duties in new countries—that the question in his mind is a big one and not a little one.

If I were to discuss these passages generally, I should have a good deal to say upon them. It is not a sufficient reason to employ protective duties to set up a new industry in a country that the industry is believed to be suitable for it. Proof is also required that after paying the expense of the operation people will be better off in any way than they would otherwise have been. But I am not discussing the passage generally. I confine myself to the point whether manufactures—what is popularly known as manufactures—can be set up to any material extent in a new country in the way described.

The suggestion I would now make is that, in the nature of things, as far as manufactures are concerned, the possible variation in economic conditions in a new country by means of so-called protective duties to set up manufactures must be quite insignificant. The maximum of the manufactures that are capable of being affected by protective duties is so small, that a new country even if it could get all the manufactures conceivably possible, would practically remain as before without the variety desiderated and without adding sensibly to its population and resources.

The first point I have to make is to note that the primary supposition of all in the above extracts, viz., that an agricultural population is all agricultural, or almost all agricultural, is itself erroneous. If any one follows the distribution of population throughout the world generally, it will be found that a common model of distribution in an agricultural country to which the United States conformed lately, and to which such dissimilar countries as Ireland and India still conform, gives 60 per cent. of the population to agriculture and 40 per cent. to other pursuits, including building, tailoring and millinery, transportation, distribution, and the professions.[1] In some of the Australasian colonies the agricultural proportion is even less, the rural population being only 45 per cent. of the total. The idea that in an agricultural population the people are almost all agricultural is thus, to begin with, entirely wrong, for only about half are agricultural, and if manufactures are to be set up so as to diminish the importation of manufactured articles the problem will be to divert so much of this half as is already producing for export wherewith to buy manufactures into manufacturing for home consumption. But this again is a small proportion. In every country the exports are very largely not for the purpose of buying manufactures, but for the purchase of tea, coffee, sugar, salt, coal, or other articles which are not produced at home. This is conspicuously the case in America and our Australian colonies.

The rule may be made even more general. The predominant industry in any community only employs about half the people. I have been informed by military friends that if a town is permitted to grow up beside a fortress its population may be expected to equal and exceed that of the garrison itself. There is thus,

[1] At the last census the proportion in the United States of the agricultural population was even less than here stated (1904).

by the nature of things, a natural variety of occupation everywhere. Greater variety may be desirable if a country is to be among the most advanced, but it is not true that there may not be great variety without.

The next point is, that in the nature of things there are many manufactures in every country which are either not factory manufactures or are necessarily local. Among the former are the local blacksmith, wheelwright, and saddler, and many more, where even if there is much in proportion that can be imported from abroad there is necessarily a good deal that is always local, because repairs are incessant, and for repairing shops must be at hand. Among the latter are the factories required in newspaper printing for instance, for a newspaper is necessarily local; in the making and planning of windows, floor cloth, carpets, curtains, and other articles in connection with building and furnishing; in the manufacture of mineral waters which are costly to transport; in saw mills in a district with natural timber; to which must now be added refrigerating machinery, where the exports consist in part of chilled or frozen meat, or butter and cheese. Consequently there is not only variety of industry even in an agricultural country, but there are natural manufactures also which it cannot be without. The only manufactures which are in question, therefore, when we speak of protective import duties to set them up, are manufactures of a certain kind, the leading manufactures of the world, which, owing to the great production and other causes, need not be local in their character; and these manufactures, it is clear, can only be a small part of the industry of any country where they are for the home market alone.

My next remark is that we may derive from the experience of England itself, a manufacturing country *par excellence*, a clear indication that the manufactures which are not in the nature of the case local, and which are to be brought into existence by protective duties, must be very small, at best, in a new country. The

United Kingdom is the workshop of the world, but, notwithstanding this, the proportion of the occupied population engaged in manufacturing, including many manufactures that are local in their nature, does not appear to be more than about 20 per cent. The figures are a little difficult, but if we refer to that useful publication, "The Abstract of Labour Statistics," pp. 170-190, we find the total factory population[1] given as $3\frac{1}{2}$ millions, as compared with a total occupied population of $16\frac{1}{2}$ millions, or about one-fifth. Certain deductions, however, must be made for manufactures that are necessarily local, and probably if that were done we should arrive at a proportion of less than a fifth of the population of the United Kingdom occupied in those manufactures which are suitable for exportation, and which new countries would seek to establish by means of protective import duties. To what proportion would that fifth sink if the English manufacturers had only the home market? Answering this question I may say that I doubt extremely if more than 5 to $7\frac{1}{2}$ per cent. of the population would be employed, although the home market of England, owing to the great accumulation of wealth in the country, is no doubt much larger in proportion to population than that of any other country. There is no means of giving an exact answer, but the proportion must certainly be much less than a tenth. Comparing the exports themselves with the above figures of occupied population it appears that about two-thirds of those engaged in manufactures are making for export and one-third for the home market, which would give the proportion above stated; and whatever the real proportion may be, it cannot at any rate be much higher.

My next point is, that if we look at the import statistics of new countries themselves, and compare the manufactures they import with their population and re-

[1] This does not include a workshop population of half a million where the industries, however, are almost purely of a local nature for local consumption.

sources, we shall find that these manufactures, if all done at home, would not employ more than the proportion stated of the population, viz., 5 to 7½ per cent.

One or two illustrations may be given. We find that in New South Wales, out of about £16,000,000 of imports in a recent year, as given in the statistical abstract, the woollen, cotton, and textile manufactures, and all other manufactures identifiable, inclusive of beer and spirits, amount to about £6,000,000 only. The principal items are:

Imports of Principal Manufactures into New South Wales.

	£
Apparel and slops	1,004,000
Boots and shoes	307,000
General drapery	1,880,000
Iron and steel	577,000
Hardware	200,000
Machinery	271,000
Agricultural implements	35,000
Bags and sacks	148,000
Beer and ale	234,000
Spirits	318,000
Paper	182,000
Musical instruments	47,000
Books	123,000
Earthenware and china	57,000
Drugs and medicines	138,000
Furniture	55,000
Stationery (except paper)	94,000

This is apparently the maximum consumption of manufactures in New South Wales, for which home manufactures could be substituted, even if New South Wales ceased to import any at all, which is inconceivable. The sum cannot be more than 10 per cent. of the total production of New South Wales, and excluding what for climatic and other reasons could not be made in New South Wales at all, we are left with a smaller proportion, say 5 per cent. as the maximum, to which the process of substitution could by any possibility apply.

The corresponding figure for Victoria would be about £4,000,000, the smaller figure here than in New South Wales being partly accounted for perhaps by Victoria having one or two industries, like boots and shoes, where she is an exporting country, and naturally supplies the home market also, and partly by Victoria, though having much the same population, not being quite so prosperous as New South Wales. Still in Victoria we have £4,000,000 only as the maximum of new manufactures that could be set up or much less than 10 per cent. of the total production. The principal items are:

Imports of Principal Manufactures into Victoria.

	£
Apparel and slops	172,000
Bags and sacks	112,000
Beer and spirits	257,000
Books	163,000
Boots and shoes	35,000
Chinaware, etc.	50,000
Drugs and chemicals	83,000
Cotton piece goods	927,000
Furniture and upholstery	12,000
Glass and glassware	40,000
Haberdashery	248,000
Hardware and ironmongery	86,000
Hats, caps, and bonnets	57,000
Hosiery and Gloves	193,000
Galvanized sheet	107,000
Wire	63,000
Leather goods (except saddlery and harness)	91,000
Linen piece goods	27,000
Machinery	121,000
Patent medicines	40,000
Musical instruments	40,000
Printing paper	124,000
Silk and manufactures	214,000
Stationery (except paper)	42,000
Woollen and woollen piece goods	496,000

A similar figure for New Zealand, which has a smaller population than either Victoria or New South Wales, would be about £3,000,000, again much less than 10 per cent. of the total production.

It would be needless to multiply instances, though there are some even more striking because the new countries are smaller. In Tasmania we should have about £400,000 only of manufactures imported of every kind, and here the smallness of the amount, apart from any question of proportion to total production, is important. The least sense of the scale of modern manufacturing production makes it obvious that no manufactures to any great extent, such as will create towns and promote improvement, can be set up in a new country like Tasmania by protective import duties or any other protectionist device.

The next stage of the argument is that, by the nature of the case, many, if not most, of the manufactures which are not local in a new country cannot be established there at all because the market is not large enough. I should define a new country to be where a population of not more than 1 to 1½ millions is spread over a territory the size of England or more. Such a population is quite able to occupy a country agriculturally, and it is a population of this sort that is to be found in our Australian colonies, in many parts of the United States, in Canada, and in the Argentine Republic. And no such community of a million or so spread over a territory like England, and *a fortiori* spread over a larger territory, can have more than a few descriptions of factory manufactures if there is only to be a home market. It is easy to speak of cotton, or woollen, or linen, or silk, or iron, or leather manufactures. But each of these designations in reality includes many manufactures, and for each one of these there may be no adequate market in a population of a million. Therefore, such manufactures cannot be locally established in a new country however much you try. Take shipping. Suppose by some monopoly the colony of Victoria were to endeavour by means of import duties to obtain ships of its own, equal to doing one-half of its foreign shipping business, for on protective principles no country could expect more than half. The total entries and clearances in Victoria in the foreign trade are $4\frac{1}{2}$ millions in round figures, or $2\frac{1}{4}$ millions one way. Many of the voyages to and from Victoria are to the adjacent colonies and consequently very short, but allowing ten round voyages in the year on the average, we should still have only 200,000 tons of shipping required for all the foreign trade of Victoria, one half of which is 100,000 tons. Accordingly 100,000 tons of shipping would be the ship-owning Victoria could have a monopoly of, which would give twenty-five liners of 4,000 tons each. How much shipbuilding would be necessary to keep going a fleet of 100,000 tons? Perhaps one ship of 4,000 tons per annum with repairs of an equivalent amount. How can Victoria then have a real shipbuilding industry of its own, for the home market alone, which is not more than a plaything? Take the iron trade again. The home consumption of iron in England is about 4,000,000 tons per annum, or about 100,000 tons for every 1,000,000 of the population. This would be the production of pig-iron required in a new country if its wants were on the same scale. How, then, could a new country have a pig-iron industry? The minimum which a single modern blast furnace can produce, without which production cannot be economical, is about 100,000 tons a year, and a country does not require one kind of pig-iron only, but many. The same principle applies to all the stages of the iron manufacture, to rolling mills, the making of bar and hoop iron, and bolt and angle iron, not to speak of the subsequent manufacture of machinery. A new country may make small machinery, perhaps, but the miscellaneous products of the iron industry are plainly not for it. Take again the earthenware and china manufacture, of the products of which home and imported we consume about £4,000,000 annually. On the same scale a new country of 1,000,000 inhabitants would consume about £100,000 worth. A single earthenware and china factory producing only £100,000 worth would not be a very large one, and of course it has to be remembered that pottery is most various, that several factories are wanted if there is to be variety at all—in fact that hardly any one country, not even England, can provide all the variety required. How then can there be important earthenware and china factories in really new countries, if the market is only to be a home market? We might go through the list of cotton, woollen, silk, and other manufactures. Some small manufactures may be set up where there is a combination of a large local demand for some article, coupled with the possibility of meeting it by moderate sized factories, but as a rule the new country is not "in it" in the nature of things, because there is not a large enough market for the minimum production consistent with economy.

My next point is the actual experience of Australasia. One has heard much of the relative advantages of Free Trade and Protection as exemplified by Victoria and New South Wales. But, as a matter of fact, neither country has factory manufactures—not of a local character—to any sensible extent. Take Victoria. According to the Year Book of Victoria for 1895, the latest in my possession, the hands employed in factories, workshops, etc., in 1894 were just about 40,000,[1] the total population of the colony being about 1,200,000, and the occupied population, it may be assumed, being about 500,000. In other words, the manufacturing population, so called, is less than 10 per cent. of the whole number of "bread-winners." The chief constituents of these 40,000 again are:

[1] See pp. 768-772.

	Numbers employed.
Printing and stationery	4,481
Iron foundries and engineering establishments	4,175
Agricultural implements	946
Carriage and harness	2,126
Furniture	889
Boot manufactories	3,307
Clothing manufactories	4,239
Hat and cap manufactories	530
Biscuits, confectionery, flour, milk, and jam	2,230
Drinks and stimulants	3,135
Tanneries	1,564
Boiling establishments, etc.	848
Sawmills	2,404
Gas and electric works	1,124
Brickyards and potteries	897
	32,895
Miscellaneous	6,578
Total	39,473

This is the analysis of the factory population of the colony of Victoria, of whose Protectionist policy we have heard so much. It is obvious that the great textile manufactures—cotton, woollen, silk, linen—are conspicuous by their absence; and, equally, the great metal manufactures, with hardware, small wares, earthenware, and leather manufactures. The only manufactures, properly speaking, appear to be boots and shoes and clothing (I believe, mainly, apparel and slops), both of which are articles which Victoria exports to neighbouring colonies. Another exception may, perhaps, be made for ironfoundry and engineering. But the remainder are mostly only so-called manufactures, as the word is popularly understood, and are, besides, obviously local in their nature, such as tanneries, sawmills, brickyards, boiling establishments, and, I believe, printing establishments, which are no doubt largely newspapers.

I should add that the last census of Victoria shows larger figures, partly because 1894 was a year of depression compared with 1891, but also in part, according to the explanation in the Year Book, because in the census every individual blacksmith, or carpenter, or harness maker is put down as engaged in manufacture. The factory population, however, is all included in the above figures, which show quite plainly that Victoria, being a new country with a Protectionist tariff, has not acquired the variety of manufacturing industry which the tariff, according to the academic arguments for Protection, was designed to give it.

New South Wales has not been steadily a Protectionist country, and is not now Protectionist; but, as far as manufactures are concerned, it is in much the same economic condition as we should expect it to be if the thesis here supported is true. According to Mr. Coghlan's book on "The Wealth and Progress of New South Wales" (p. 539), the hands employed in factories in 1894 numbered 42,751, out of a total population much the same as that of Victoria, viz., about 1,200,000. The composition was also much the same, Mr. Coghlan's analysis being as follows (p. 541):

	Numbers employed.
Treating raw material, the production of pastoral pursuits	4,020
Preparing materials used as food or drink	7,254
Clothing and textile industries	5,394
Manufacture of building materials	6,176
Metal and machinery works	7,373
Shipbuilding and repairing, etc.	1,505
Furniture and bedding works	794
Paper printing, binding, and engraving	4,284
Vehicles, harness, and saddlery	1,548
Light and heat	1,683
Miscellaneous	2,720
Total	42,751

Thus the Free Trade country, being in like economic conditions, has much the same factory manufactures as the so-called Protectionist country. And in neither case are the manufactures of a description other than those naturally suitable to a new country, which are independent of a Protective tariff. I do not consider exceptions the cases where the colonies in question happen to manufacture for export, this being also a natural development.

The experience of New South Wales and Victoria is therefore in accordance with what a common sense consideration of the question would teach us. The tariff of one is bad, but the bad tariff and the good alike fail to set up the factory manufactures. This cannot be done at all, owing to the want of a market.

We may sum up, then, by repeating that the whole foundation of the idea in Mill is based on a misunderstanding. There is natural variety of industry, even in an agricultural country, to a much greater extent than is commonly supposed. There are also natural manufactures, employing 5 to 10 per cent. of the population, for which Protective duties are wholly unnecessary. Factory manufactures of other kinds, again, have no such place in the economy of a self-contained country as is often assumed. Even in a manufacturing country for export, like England, they are smaller than commonly supposed; and we can well believe that in no country can the factory manufactures, for home consumption only, ever occupy much more than 5 per cent. of the working population. But for such manufactures, as a rule, a new country has not a large enough market. We can see, then, that before Protectionists can discuss their theory as to the benefit of import duties in setting up manufactures so as to give variety of industry, they should discuss the preliminary question as to whether substantial variety can be given that way at all. If, instead of using general language, the Protectionists to whom Mill appears to give assent had said that possibly, but not probably, by means of import duties 1 or 2 per cent. of the population that would not otherwise be occupied in manufacturing might come to be so occupied, the practical look of the remark would have been entirely different from what it is. If Mill, in commenting on it, had introduced the question of quantity and degree of effect, his assent would probably have been much less appreciated by Protectionists than it has been.

The question will naturally arise—How about new countries, or countries with a large new area, and larger populations than we have been dealing with? To this the answer is, that there is more room in such countries for promoting manufactures by means of import duties, or by any other method. There is a larger market, and if you can give a monopoly to any manufacturer within the ring fence, you may establish him in such a country, though you cannot establish manufactures in a new country of the ordinary type. There is more possibility of such Protection in Canada, for instance, than there is in an Australasian colony; and when the Australasian colonies are confederated there will be more possibility of Protection in the united colonies than there is now in the separate ones. This was, in fact, Mill's answer to the American Protectionists. They could advance New England by giving it a monopoly, he pointed out. But the manufactures so to be set up, it should be understood with Mill, are not manufactures complying with the conditions in view. They will not be local manufactures spread over the new country, but manufactures in one or two corners of a large territory, of as little importance in the economic *régime* of a really new area as manufactures in a corner of England. United States Protectionists had thus no excuse at any time for quoting Mill. To set up manufactures in New England instead of Old England, thousands of miles from the new areas, was not setting up manufactures in the new areas themselves.

It would take me away from the present subject to discuss whether manufacturing can be promoted to any good purpose in a country like the United States or Canada, or like what Australasia is going to be, by means of Protective import duties. This involves the direct issue between Free Trade and Protection, and I do not mean to go into that at present. We are discussing the new countries question at present only. But, apart from all theory, we may observe that the intermediate countries between purely new countries and the old ones are at best in a transition stage; that a growth of manufacturing in such countries is inevitable; and that the conditions are also such as to make them so like those of complete Free Trade that the transition to complete Free Trade itself becomes no more than a step. I pointed this out in a recent address in North Staffordshire in another connection,[1] but it is useful to recollect it in the present connection also.

The general case as between Free Trade and Protectionist policy, reviewing the different groups of countries, stands thus. In new countries you cannot promote new manufactures, for reasons in the nature of things, by means of protective duties; in old manufacturing countries you cannot, because such countries, if they are to make way at all, must manufacture for export; in intermediate countries between old and new, matters are in a transition stage, and they are fast approaching the conditions of the older countries. Protectionist policy is thus opposed by the force of circumstances, and another generation or two will probably see the last Protectionist politician, not only in England, but throughout the world. The breed, I am confident, is very nearly extinct, because the modern atmosphere and conditions, not theory, are making the policy next to impossible.

[1] See *postea*, p. 178.

XVIII.

NOTE ON THE GRESHAM LAW.

THERE is a good deal of misunderstanding of the real law as to bad money "driving out" good, and an overrated metal in a bimetallic system "driving out" the underrated metal, which is commonly spoken of as the Gresham Law. It is assumed that the money driven out must be physically driven out of the country, *i.e.*, exported, and this export is regarded as a fundamental part of the Gresham Law.

In point of fact Sir Thomas Gresham is only responsible for the suggestion that bad coins, *i.e.*, worn and deteriorated coins, drive good ones of the *same metal* out of circulation. Export is, no doubt, specially referred to as the usual effect of such driving out, as it was no doubt the usual consequence in circumstances such as those Sir Thomas Gresham dealt with. But the "law" was only an observation that it is difficult, if not impossible, for good and bad coins of the same metal to circulate together, and the good coins are selected for exportation when a demand for exportation arises. The export is not a necessary part of the "law."

In point of fact, also, good and bad coins will circulate together in a given country as if they were all good when the circulation itself is not in excess of the demand for it. We have many good and bad sovereigns circulating together now in England.

Sir Thomas Gresham made no reference at all to what happens in a bimetallic system or in the analogous case of inconvertible paper when the paper drives the metal out of circulation. Nor are these last cases quite on all fours with those Sir Thomas Gresham referred to. In the case where bad coins drive out good coins of the same metal, the good and bad coins are both doing the same work; so the good are driven out of circulation when there is a surplus because they are more useful for other purposes than the bad, containing more of the metal. When it is a question, however, between two different metals, the coins of the different metals may be performing quite different work. The "driving out" process in this last case must consequently be a different one, when it takes place, from what it is in the case of bad *versus* good coins of the same metal. The same with inconvertible paper *versus* metal. The metal and the paper may be required for *different* purposes, and, so far as that is the case, the paper does not drive out the metal from the same cause or in the same way, or proportions, as bad coins drive out good coins of the same metal. Gold is actually used less or more in currency in every country whether gold or silver is the standard, or whether there is a bimetallic standard with silver as the overrated metal; and gold, and sometimes silver, is also used in inconvertible paper countries in the same way, although the paper is the standard money.

What is true is that the overrated metal and the inconvertible paper in the cases supposed drive the metal they compete with, the underrated metal, out of circulation *as standard money*. As there can only be one standard, the overrated metal or the inconvertible paper, as the case may be, becomes the sole standard. But the underrated metal is not thereby physically driven out of the country at all. It depends upon circumstances whether it is exported or not and how much the export is. Three things happen (besides export, or the chance of it).

1. The underrated metal may be hoarded. This is largely the case, I believe, in almost all cases of inconvertible paper. There were, no doubt, hoards of gold in this country in the inconvertible paper period at the beginning of the century, in the United States during

the inconvertible paper *régime* which began in the civil war, and more recently in Italy, when it had inconvertible paper; and there are hoards of gold at the present day in Austria, Russia, and the Argentine Republic, which are inconvertible paper countries.

2. The underrated metal may be used in actual circulation at a market ratio different from the legal ratio. Locke's proposal was that, as there would always be a market ratio different from the legal ratio, a legal ratio was superfluous or worse. Harris proposed that a legal ratio should be fixed, but changed from time to time as found convenient, the market being followed. But practically in a bimetallic system, although the proceeding is encumbered and inconvenient, the underrated metal can be, and is, commonly used to some extent at a ratio different from the legal ratio.

Gold was always used in circulation in France as a monetary merchandise, when silver was the overrated metal, without any difficulty, but at a premium, not at the legal ratio.

3. Coins of the underrated metal may circulate as a species of token money, either because there has been a heavy seignorage on them, or because they have become worn and deteriorated, so that they occupy the same place, and do the same work, as token coinage of a different metal than the standard does in a monometallic system. This was notably the case in England with the silver coinage during last century. Silver was underrated, and gold had become the standard; but a silver coinage of a very bad description remained, which was used exactly as the silver-token coinage is now used.

In these three ways, then, coins of an underrated metal in a bimetallic system, and coins of different metals in an inconvertible paper country, may remain physically in a country when they go out of use as standard money, without being actually exported.

When export does, in fact, take place, it arises from the formation of a surplus of the underrated metal, through changes of circumstances as regards the use of it in the various ways specified.

For instance, the habit as to hoarding itself, or as to the use of a particular metal for hoarding, may change. From either cause less of the underrated metal may be hoarded than would otherwise be the case, and a surplus may thus come into existence which will be exported if no other use can be found for it. Much also would depend upon the price. The offer of a higher price might draw from the hoards what would not otherwise be drawn.

The demand for full-weighted coins of the underrated metal for use within the country may also vary from time to time. The different range of transactions, change of custom as to the use of cheques and bank-notes, and the like causes may make a difierence. Here again price may also make a difference, though this is not so likely, perhaps, as with regard to hoarding.

As regards worn and deteriorated coins circulating as token money, a surplus may arise through considerable changes in habits as to the use of token money. But probably considerable changes would be necessary to cause the stock of such coins to be drawn on for export, as the price of the underrated metal would have to rise to a point sufficient to make the coins worth more as metal than as coins, before a question of their export could arise.

XIX.

FANCY MONETARY STANDARDS.[1]

IT may be of some service to the study of questions of "money" if I take the opportunity furnished by Mr. Aneurin Williams's paper on "A Value of Bullion Standard" in the last issue of the "Economic Journal," to refer students to a paper by Mr. Bagehot on what is substantially the same topic published in the "Economist" of November 20, 1875. The article in question is entitled "A New Standard of Value," and is a criticism of Mr. Jevons's suggestion of a "multiple standard" in his book on "Money," in the International Scientific series which had just then appeared. Mr. Bagehot's article is anonymous, but of course it is well known that he was then the editor of the "Economist," and I am in a position to state that the article was in fact his own writing. The subject is one in which he took a good deal of interest, as the article itself shows.

Mr. Williams's proposal of a "Value of Bullion Standard" and Mr. Jevons's of a "Multiple Standard" are not in all respects identical. Mr. Williams's proposal, as I understand it, is to provide for an issue of paper which is to consist of promises to pay a varying quantity of bullion, the variation to be made according to the average variation in the price of leading commodities arranged by an "index number." Thc paper thus issued is to constitute the "pounds" of the new system. Mr. Jevons's suggestion was that, while pounds are still to be so much bullion, the number of pounds payable for a debt was to be varied according to the variations of the "index number." In substance, it

[1] From the "Economic Journal" of September, 1892.

seems to me, the two proposals are so far identical. A promise to pay a varying quantity of bullion, the promise being regarded as the pound, and a promise to pay a varying number of sovereigns, which are still to be called pounds, appear to be much the same things. Mr. Bagehot's criticism applies alike to both proposals.

If the editor of this "Journal" would adopt the suggestion, it would perhaps be a good thing to reprint Mr. Bagehot's article in full, so that students can refer to it easily.[1]

Mr. Bagehot's objections to this multiple standard or value of bullion standard are four in number, and are of the most serious kind.

First.—The adoption of such a standard in this country would endanger our foreign trade. The foreigner draws bills on London and makes bills payable in London, and so business is attracted to us, because both parties are sure of the medium in which they will pay or be paid, and that medium is gold. Mr. Williams would no doubt say that if his standard were generally adopted, this objection would fail, but clearly, until it is generally adopted, a country like England, with an immense foreign trade as well as foreign investments, cannot have such a standard.

The *second* objection is that banking would be impossible with such a standard. The customers of a bank, the mass of plain people who have debts to receive and pay, would not understand the variations in the amounts of gold paid for the same nominal debt according to the date at which that debt happened to be contracted.

The *third* objection is that it would not be quite so easy as those who propose such standards seem to think to settle and define the units of all the different commodities that were to enter into the "index number." This statement has been most fully confirmed, I

[1] This suggestion has been adopted, and Mr. Bagehot's article is reprinted in the present number. See next article.—*Editor of "Economic Journal."*

may add, by the consideration which the recent Committee of the British Association gave to the subject, and which found the practical difficulties to be such that we may wait a long time for the adoption of an official "index number" which can be used even for the more limited purpose of determining the amount of deferred annuities—an attainable object, I believe, but a very different thing from a monetary standard to be in daily use.

The *fourth* and final objection is that it is necessary to a good monetary standard that the thing which is the standard should itself be the medium in which payments are made, or that the medium should consist of currency readily convertible into the thing which is standard, whereas the proposed standard, consisting really of quantities of a great many articles, could never be seen or handled.

For these reasons Mr. Bagehot came to the conclusion that such standards could not be of any use in practice.

This criticism appears to be altogether so destructive as to make it unnecessary to go farther, but for practical purposes I venture to add a few comments of my own, mainly to enforce one or two elementary lessons about money which are apt to be lost sight of by students unacquainted with money market conditions.

First.—Money is not a subject which can be discussed to much profit from the academical point of view alone. Matters of theory must of course be academically considered, but when proposals are made for practice, the main points which must be thought of in practice require to be discussed. Mr. Williams, to speak plainly, does not, from this point of view, discuss the subject at all.

No change in a monetary standard, if it is a tolerably good one, ought to be proposed or considered unless upon grounds of overwhelming necessity. For a good money is so very difficult a thing to get, and Governments, when they meddle with money, are so apt to make blunders (and have, in fact, made such blunders without end in the past, of which we have had so many illustrations lately in the experience of the United States, the Argentine Republic, Russia, and other countries), that a nation which has a good money should beware of its being tampered with, and especially should beware of any change in the foundation —the standard for money. Locke, and other older economists, went further, and maintained that a change of standard should *never* be made, because every change involves injustice. But without going so far as this, we may recognize that there are various practical reasons for not changing lightly or readily—that is, for not changing for any other reasons than those of overwhelming necessity.

These considerations apply especially to the standard for money in a country like England, where the standard is the foundation of a fabric of credit, whose extension and delicacy make the slightest jar apt to produce the most formidable effects. In their recent arguments against bimetallists some of my friends have dwelt very strongly on the importance to us of maintaining our gold standard, because the standard has appreciated when measured by commodities, and there is a great deal due to us as a community in gold. But I should not put the argument that way. What impresses me is that, with our enormous liabilities and credits, with transactions of all kinds, the ramifications of which no man can follow out, all based on a gold standard, we can never tell, when we touch that standard, what confusion and mischief we may be introducing.

Now, Mr. Williams, if he will forgive my saying so, does not show in his paper any sense of the gravity of a change such as he proposes, and he does not even try to adduce reasons of overwhelming necessity. All that he has to say is that the new standard would probably be a more steady unit of purchasing power than the present one of gold. I do not agree with him even on this point, for reasons to be afterwards stated;

but admitting his contention, where is the overwhelming necessity for considering a change in our monetary standard? It would serve the purposes for which it is used very well, with even greater fluctuations in purchasing power than there have been.

The *second* point I wish to observe upon, is the way in which Mr. Williams talks of "suppressing paper" when bullion falls in price, *i.e.*, when prices rise, because then the notes cover a greater quantity of bullion than before, and the notes are only to be issued against bullion the Government holds; and of "increasing paper" when bullion rises in price, *i.e.*, when prices fall, because then more notes can be issued against the same quantity of bullion, the assumption being that the suppression of paper will make bullion rise again, *i.e.*, will make prices fall, and that the increase of paper will make bullion fall again, *i.e.*, will make prices rise. In this way, he thinks, fluctuations of prices will be automatically corrected.

This is a manner of speaking about paper which I do not understand. How is an issuing institution to "suppress paper" or "increase paper" at will, unless it be inconvertible and managed paper? There is no will in the matter, unless it be that of the customers of the institution, whose demands for paper may vary indefinitely according to customs and habits of every sort and kind, and whose demands must be complied with automatically in any credit system, if frequent shocks to credit are to be avoided. Sometimes much paper will be wanted, as happened, for instance, after the City of Glasgow Bank failure in 1878, and the demand must be met at any cost. No automatic regulation by an issuing body is possible. At other times less paper will be wanted, and, equally, no issuing body can force it, though the attempt at forcing may produce disastrous results.

No doubt it may be said for Mr. Williams's idea that there is much in the language of the authors of the Bank Charter Act, notwithstanding their general soundness on currency, to favour the notion that by putting out or drawing in paper prices could be affected. Lord Overstone and others favoured an idea like this; but surely they were too absolute on this point, and there has been a great deal of experience since the Act of 1844.

Certainly, if paper such as Mr. Williams suggests is to be made a kind of standard, and is only to be issued for the amount of bullion held at the time, it will be necessary to provide that representative paper may be issued containing promises to pay in the standard paper of the Government, so as to prevent the mischiefs of a cast-iron and rigid Government issue. A combination of banks to pledge their mutual credit, such as the New York banks entered into in 1873 when the standard was inconvertible paper incapable of increase, would have much the same mitigating effect. But room for mitigation there must be, and if there is mitigation, how is the anticipated effect on prices to be produced?

I need hardly repeat what I have said elsewhere, as to the complexity of the relations between the quantity of money and prices and the different senses in which the word "money" may be used; and how far apart from reality are speculations like those here indulged in as to the way in which prices may be regulated.

It would facilitate farther the study of the subject, if, in the case of so novel a proposal, those who make it, instead of writing of "paper" in the abstract, would give a specimen of one of their notes, so that one may see what is promised, who makes the promise, and so on. I cannot help thinking that the writing of a specimen note in this case would have brought out some of the difficulties of the undertaking.

A *third* matter, on which I desire to make a remark, is the difficulty of obtaining prices for the "index number," which Mr. Bagehot makes so much of, but which Mr. Williams treats so lightly that he imagines it will be quite a simple matter for a government to make up its index number *daily*. Surely this is not a thing to be taken for granted; but Mr. Williams and any authors of like proposals should give us their idea of what prices are to be got, what guarantees there are to be for them, and why it is thought they can be got daily, or weekly, or monthly, or whatever may be the period fixed for changing the index number.

The only practical index number that has yet been tried, I think, is that of the Corn Returns, on which the tithe average is fixed, and the corresponding fiars prices in Scotland. Here the prices are derived from returns of actual transactions on an extensive scale, and, for fixing the tithe average in England, the prices are the average of the sales of a year over the whole country. To get rid of all inequalities this immense labour is undergone. Finally, while the price for each year is fixed in this way, a farther attempt to get rid of inequality is made by arranging for the payment of the tithe on a septennial average—the average in each year of the prices of the seven years previous. In Scotland the fiars prices are settled by a kind of judicial investigation in each county annually. Now, what is to be the procedure when an official index number is published, embracing perhaps fifty or a hundred commodities, and when the index number is to be varied not annually as in the case of the tithe, but monthly as Jevons proposed, and daily as Mr. Williams proposes? Are the prices to be the average of actual sales, or what; and what basis is to be considered sufficient?

In considering the question of a measure for deferred payments, along with the Committee of the British Association, I suggested a procedure resembling that followed in the case of the Corn Returns and the tithe average, giving the department power to obtain returns of actual sales, and having in view an extensive mass of transactions, and an index number to be varied only at long intervals, such as a year. Even to provide an index number for such a purpose was difficult enough in my judgment, but at the notion of a daily index number I stand aghast.

In a daily index number, either the prices would not be those of actual sales, for often there would be no transactions, or the basis would be so narrow as to give speculators an opportunity of making profit by sales and purchases *ad hoc*, a practical danger of a very serious kind, and which was felt practically when the Corn Returns were made the basis of the sliding scale of corn duties, even upon a six weeks' average.

And if the prices are not to be the average of actual sales, what are they to be? The quotations of dealers in the market of the rates at which they are willing to do business; or what? Such quotations under present conditions are often good enough for statistical purposes when judiciously handled; but an official index number on which transactions are to be based, and on which a great deal of money will depend, is a very different thing. Before talking of a daily or weekly, or even monthly index number, Mr. Williams should give some thought to the construction of index numbers in their practical aspect. If an index number, such as he contemplates, is impossible in practice, as I believe it to be, there is clearly no use in discussing "a value of bullion standard" as a substitute for our present gold standard in the daily business of the country. The construction of the index number is the first step.

Fourth.—A "value of bullion standard," though it might have some effect in mitigating the fluctuations in the unit of purchasing power as measured by commodities, might not really be so stable a standard *for all purposes*, as that which we now have in gold alone. The reason is that in using a monetary standard we have to measure "incomes" as well as commodities.

It is just as important for many purposes that the average money incomes of a community per head, and still more the average-money wages of the wages-earning part of the community per head, should not fluctuate greatly over short periods, as it is that the average prices of commodities should not fluctuate.

But as real incomes and real wages are liable to increase, and happily increase greatly, in a comparatively short period of years, in these days of continual progress in science and the applications of science, it follows that if the standard for money is kept steady with reference to the average of commodities, then it must be unsteady with reference to incomes. Money incomes and money wages must increase greatly on the average, when real incomes and wages are increasing, if the standard for money is at the same time kept even with the average of commodities, that is, if prices are prevented from falling. I do not see that this will be at all a good thing. The rise of real wages between 1850 and 1870 was a good thing; but it would have been better, had it taken the shape of stationary money wages with a fall in prices.

Worse still, Mr. Williams contemplates a daily change in his index number. And as there are always great oscillations, this means that rates of wages would have to be moved up and down continually, so as to give the workman the benefit which he now obtains by a fall of prices without any change in his nominal rate of wages.

I cannot help thinking that our standard for money in the last twenty years has answered social necessities generally much better than a standard which would have varied with the average of commodities. There has been some rise in money incomes and wages in the interval, but not a great rise, and the community generally and workmen particularly have got the benefit of the appreciation of the standard measured by commodities quietly and almost unconsciously, without the excitement which would probably have accompanied a great rise of money wages, such as would have been necessary with "a value of bullion standard" to enable them to receive the advantage of the rise in real wages that they have enjoyed.

In this view, then, the mere statement that "a value of bullion standard" will probably diminish fluctuations in the prices of commodities is not the same thing as a proof, even if the statement were true, that "a value of bullion standard" will be more stable for all the purposes for which a monetary standard is required than a bullion standard itself. Admitting that such a proof could be given, we should still have to inquire whether, all things considered, a bullion standard is not the best, and whether, in particular as regards England, a case can be made out for incurring the risk and inconvenience of changing the bullion standard we have already got; but, even on the score of the superior stability claimed theoretically for "a value of bullion standard," there is no case made out.

These various objections all go to show that "a value of bullion standard" is not a thing which can be put forward as a practical scheme. There must be a great deal of discussion on many points which its author does not refer to before it can even be entertained. Mr. Bagehot might have stated many more objections than he did, and I am sure, if the matter were gone into, there are many more objections behind.

I shall probably be told, as I have been told, that to object to currency proposals in this way is to raise up a *non possumus* sort of barrier to all currency improvement, and that this is to be too conservative. The answer is, that the objection is to such proposals as matters of practice, and that there would not be the same objection to them if they were put forward as merely theoretical proposals, with some acknowledgement of the practical conditions which make their acceptance in any real world, and especially in the real world of England at the present day, out of the question. Put forward in this manner, they could be discussed freely, and there are many theoretical points about money which would probably reward discussion, to which for one I should by no means be averse. It is conceivable, for instance, that in an ideal world an improvement could be made on any existing monetary system by leaving the issue of paper entirely free to everybody, on the distinct understanding that notes are credit instruments only, payable on demand by the issuers. I believe that, if in the past such a plan had been fairly tried, we should now in England have a better monetary system than we have, excellent and nearly perfect as I believe that system to be for all the great ends of a monetary system; and we should be free of a great deal of the dismal discussion that has arisen in consequence of paper being made legal tender and being supposed to be money in some peculiar sense that cheques and the like credit instruments are not. Our whole banking system would also have been better than it is, because more naturally arranged. It is conceivable, again, that in an ideal world one pound notes would be advantageous, especially if the system of issuing them had grown up naturally. But I should not dream of suggesting or defending any of these theoretical improvements practically. They are not great enough to excuse a disturbance of the existing system. The use of discussing them at all is that experts may be prepared for emergencies and for dealing with monetary systems in disorder, when reasons of overwhelming necessity can be given for change. Always, however, in the discussion of such points, if it is to be profitable at all, its necessarily theoretical character should be kept in mind; and the very different points that must be considered in dealing with a practical proposal, such as I have explained above, should be equally remembered. If a monetary system is of such a character that it can hardly be meddled with at all, even for the best objects, without great risks and inconvenience, then the advantages to be gained must always be weighed against such risks, or apprehended risks, whenever we come to business, and this question of relative advantage, supposing the theoretical case for improvement to be made out, is very often the main matter in the practical discussion. I hardly think that of late years the enormous practical dangers of meddling with a settled monetary system, which hardly any theoretical gain would compensate, have been sufficiently realized by our younger economists, fresh from the universities and but little acquainted with the conditions of money and business, and I trust that what has been said here will be of some use as a caution.

XX.

PROTECTIONIST VICTORIES AND FREE TRADE SUCCESSES.

DURING the American Civil War a friend of mine, who was a careful student of the military operations, used often to remark that the war was one in which the South had all the victories, and the North all the substantial successes.

I am often reminded of this when I hear the common talk of the victories of Protection.

Free Trade, we are often told, is going back in the world. Every country except England has a Protectionist policy. Every day we hear of Protectionist measures being introduced in this country or the other. In other words, Protectionists are having many victories. They have not quite so many as they seem to have. On the other side we have to count such a victory as the last one of the Free Traders in New South Wales, or the recent stroke of Sir Wilfrid Laurier and his colleagues in Canada.

But we may grant to the Protectionists that they do score many victories, or so-called victories. What I wish to point out is the continual and substantial success of Free Trade throughout the world.

Free Trade, in my view—*i.e.*, the practice of Free Trade—is really spreading and growing while Protectionist politicians are talking of their victories, and making a tremendous fuss over this and that petty interference with trade—over an autonomous tariff, perhaps, or over the stoppage of the importation of prison-

[1] Speech delivered at the annual dinner of the North Staffordshire Chamber of Commerce, at Stoke, December 15th, 1897.

made mats and brushes, or over the imposition of countervailing duties on sugar.

The real extent of Free Trade.

The demonstration that the real success is all the while with Free Trade is easy enough.

Let me begin first of all by showing that the bulk of the industry of the world—nine-tenths, or ninety-nine hundredths, or perhaps even more—is already carried on under Free Trade, and not under Protectionist conditions.

Take the fact to begin with, that the British Empire is, on the whole, with one or two exceptions, unimportant by comparison, a Free Trade Empire. What does this mean?

The answer is that the Protection of every other country—grant that the rest of the world is Protectionist—is modified by the existence of this great Free-Trading community.

Protectionist countries may erect barriers against trading with us, but so long as we erect none the net hindrance to trade is very much less than if we were to follow their example.

Do not suppose that we are only one of several approximately equal nations in this matter. The British Empire is a very large part of the world, commercially speaking. I do not wish to bore you with figures, but if we take the aggregate imports and exports of the world, omitting some places like Gibraltar, Malta, and Holland, which are places mainly of transit trade, we might reckon that out of a total of three thousand millions or thereabouts the British Empire alone counts for one thousand millions. If we include with it various minor countries—such as China, for instance—which are really not Protectionist in their foreign trade, we may say broadly that a third to half the world is Free-Trading.

Hence, Protection is far less mischievous even to

Protectionist countries than it would otherwise be, and the world as a whole suffers less from Protection than it certainly would do, if the British Empire, like some of its neighbours, were to engage in the game of erecting barriers to trade.

This is not all. The greater part of the world is now formed into large States, and within the ring-fence of each there is complete Free Trade.

We have now at the top of the world six great States—the British Empire, the United States, Russia, Germany, Austria-Hungary, and France, to which Italy might, perhaps, be added as a very considerable State. The bulk of the foreign trade of the world is carried on between these States themselves, and if they are all, excepting ourselves, Protectionist in their policy in their external relations, they are as certainly Free-Trading internally, each within its own borders.

The only exceptions, not important ones, are some of our own self-governing colonies.

The British Empire, no doubt, is also not within a single ring-fence. For geographical reasons it cannot have a Zollverein. But trade is practically free inside the Empire all the same, with exceptions which are of no real importance.

All this means that the great countries of the world have so much Free Trade at home that the conditions of each individual industry at home are assimilated or approximate to those which would exist if there were unrestricted competition with all the world.

It is quite obvious that the larger and more varied in geographical conditions the area of a State is—the more that it is an image of the whole world—the more like the conditions of trade inside it must be to those of the world generally.

Protectionists, however, notwithstanding all their boasting, have not the courage of their convictions. They will not set up Customs lines with Protective tariffs inside a particular political area, however large, although all the economic conditions are present which they plead as excusing such tariffs. We must not be surprised, therefore, if some of the mischiefs of "Protection" which theory and experience make us expect do not make themselves much felt in the real modern world. Even the most Protectionist country is far from having unadulterated Protection.

We may go a little further. Protectionist countries, even as regards their foreign tariffs, are far from giving much Protection. They have mostly very extensive lists of free imports. Half the imports into some of them, I should say, are either admitted free of duty or at very low rates of duty not calculated to be of a Protective character.

Again, of the remaining duties there are a large number that are really not Protective.

There is often some confusion on this head. A high Customs tariff is often spoken of as if it were a Protective tariff. But this is a *non sequitur*. A high Customs tariff is usually a bad thing, apart from its Protective effect, but we must not call it Protective unless there is a home industry whose products escape the duties that are charged on the like articles imported from abroad. In this sense many of the duties imposed in so-called Protectionist countries are not Protective at all. There is no home industry in existence to be Protected. The high duties are thus revenue duties, often bad duties of their kind, but they are not Protective in the proper sense of the word.

I was greatly struck during a visit to Australia some years ago by the ineffectiveness of the tariffs of the Australian colonies, even those that were most Protectionist in their policy, for any purpose of Protection, because the industries to be protected did not exist. The whole manufacturing population of a colony like Victoria, with a total population of 1¼ millions, is not more than 50,000 or 60,000, and a large part are engaged in the manufacture of mineral waters and in other manufactures, which would, in any case, be local, whatever the tariff.[1] Even with countries more advanced in manufacturing, like France, the United States, and Germany, there are many specialties where there is no home industry to compete with the imports. To take the United States; it is doubtful whether even 5 per cent. of the producers receive any Protection from the tariff of any sort or kind. Thus, in spite of all that Protectionist policy may do, even the most Protectionist country nowadays conducts the greater part of its business under Free Trade conditions.

I believe it cannot help doing so; but, theory apart, there is no doubt of the fact.

Successes on the side of Free Trade.

I come, then, to the proof of the proposition with which I started—that the substantial successes in matters of commercial policy have been for a long time past, and still are, on the side of Free Trade, and not on the side of Protection.

Not only is there far more Free Trade in the world than people sometimes think, but much of it is of very recent growth.

(1) The great success of Free Trade in England half a century ago was itself so gigantic that it amounted to a conversion of the world for good to the practice of Free Trade. From being almost all Protectionist the world at a jump became half Free Trade. It was the decisive step which cannot be undone.

I believe this all the more because I am quite satisfied that the step was not taken out of any love for the abstract theory of Free Trade. It arose out of necessary conditions which were felt in the daily life of the nation, because the great industries of the country had no need of Protection at home, and because cheap food and raw materials were essential to the welfare of the masses and to the prosperity of the export trade.

The like conditions must make the leading coun-

[1] See *supra*, vol. ii., p. 145.

tries of the world Free-Trading in time, whatever their theories of policy may be. Free Trade in England has, in any case, come to stay.

(2) The next great Free-Trading measure, the Cobden Treaty of 1860, has never been really reversed. There is much talk as if it had been. We have heard a great deal of the revival of Protection in France and elsewhere. I believe, also, that the policy of commercial treaties is antiquated. But practically the tariffs of the leading countries of the world still show the marks of the Great Revolution of 1860. They have not gone back to the astonishing perversities and absurdities of the pre-Cobden period.

(3) The great growth of large communities in ring fences, which are of more or less recent establishment, has itself been a continuous triumph of Free Trade during a century or more. Little more than a century ago Europe outside Russia was carved into almost innumerable States, while within the boundaries of countries like France and the United Kingdom, more or less united, there was more than one Customs line. At the same time, there was no Indian Empire; Russia was comparatively a small State; and the United States were only just beginning to be.

Look at the changes that have been made. The Customs lines inside France were abolished with the Revolution. Inside the United Kingdom they came to an end early in the century. Instead of the innumerable German States, a Zollverein was created in 1857, followed by the creation of the German Empire in 1871. Instead of the many Italian States, a united Italy was formed in 1862. Instead of a small Russia, we have an enormous empire in population as well as area within a ring fence, while the closer political union established with Poland and other dependent States has also diminished Customs barriers in that empire.

Looking further afield, we find an Indian Empire also created; and last of all, but certainly not least, we have the United States, created by its Constitution a

Free Trade State within its own domain, and the growth of population during this century being absolutely without precedent in the world's history.

All this huge consolidation of States and growth of large communities, each with Free Trade in its own borders, is virtually a triumph of Free Trade. They make quite certain that the bulk of the industry of the world will henceforth be carried on under conditions assimilated to those of absolute Free Trade. From this condition of things to the most absolute Free Trade itself is not a large step.

Without speculating on the future we may also notice, I think, that very considerable movements in the same direction are now in progress. The Confederation of Canada twenty-five years ago was a step in this direction, the importance of which will appear more clearly with the great growth of the Canadian population which is now at hand.

The completion of the Australian Confederation will be another step of the same kind.

The extension of the South African Customs Union, which we must all look forward to, will be a third step of the same kind.

(4) Next, we must claim on behalf of Free Trade all those scientific inventions of the century—the steam-engine, the locomotive, the iron and steel ship, the electric wire, and submarine cable, and many more—which have facilitated communication between different parts of the world, or which have diminished the cost of production.

The true enemy of a Protectionist policy is the man of science. The man of science makes it possible to bring a particular commodity to Europe at a half or a third of the cost at which it could formerly be brought. When trade is quite free, Europe is so much the richer. The Protectionist steps in and says, "Nothing of the kind, Europe must continue to use the old machinery and old processes, and not be any the richer at all."

In this duel between Protectionist politicians and

men of science, however, we must put our money, I believe, on the man of science.

Somehow or other, the world will be the richer for all these inventions, and the Mrs. Partingtons of politics, however great and highly placed they may seem for a time to be, will only make themselves ridiculous by striving to sweep away the inrushing ocean.

(5) Last of all we must notice, as making for Free Trade, the rapid growth of conditions in the leading countries of the world, especially in Germany and the United States, such as those which existed in this country when it became Free-Trading, and which, in fact, compelled it to be Free-Trading.

The modern nations are all becoming great manufacturing States, where the manufacturing is partly for export, and where, by this very condition, it is generally able to hold its own at home and abroad in face of the unrestricted competition of the world. Such countries have need of cheap food and raw materials, which must consequently be made free imports, and there is nothing else that needs to be or can be Protected.

The time is at hand, then, when our great rivals *nolens volens* will be forced into the Free-Trade camp. I am quite aware of the reluctance of Germany, France, and Austria-Hungary to accept the inevitable. They fight against cheap food and cheap raw materials, essential to their prosperity, by duties for the Protection of their agriculturists. But the game is plainly a losing one, as they are finding out (what we found out long ago) that protection of this sort does not protect. We may confidently await the issue.

The Future of the United States.

As far as the United States is concerned the position is even clearer, because there is no question there of Protection to agriculture. I cannot do better than quote some remarks from a distinguished American economist, Mr. Taussig, which I find in the last number of the American "Quarterly Journal of Economics":

"With the wide diffusion of a high degree of mechanical ingenuity, of enterprise, of intelligence and education, it is certain that the United States will be, and will remain, a great manufacturing country. The Protective system will be of less and less consequence. The deep-working causes which underlie the international division of labour will indeed still operate, and the United States will still find her advantages greater in some directions than in others. The ingenuity of legislators will still find opportunity to direct manufacturing industry into channels which would not otherwise be sought. Witness some of the minor duties, complicated in form and weighty in effects, under the Acts of 1890 and 1897. But the absolute effect, still more the proportional effect, of such legislation on the industrial development of the country will diminish. The division of labour within the country will become more and more important, while international trade will be confined more and more to what may be called specialties in manufactured commodities, and articles whose site of production is determined mainly by climate. Not only sugar (for the present), tea, coffee, and the like, but wool also belong to the class last mentioned, as to which climatic causes dominate; and the duties on wool, with those on woollen in their train, are thus the most potent in bringing a substantial interference with the course of international trade. But, on the whole, Protective duties, however important they may be in this detail or that, cannot seriously affect the general course of industrial growth, and will affect it less and less as time goes on. Some indications of this trend are already to be seen in the eagerness with which a fresh opportunity for applying the Protective system is welcomed, and even sought, by the party now dominant. And an important consequence is that this question can hardly avail much longer as a great issue in politics. As the great industries of the community become more and more indifferent to legislative bolstering, the public will become more and more indifferent to the Protective controversy."

All this, I believe you will agree with me, is most interesting. Protection is played out in the United States, because the economic conditions are now such that there is nothing substantially to protect.

Some Protectionists will perhaps say that this is the result of their policy, America having got its manufactures by means of Protection in the past—a proposition in which I cannot follow them. But, whatever the past history may have been, the present position is clear. The United States *nolens volens* must very soon become a country of international Free Trade.

The Facts on the Side of Free Trade.

To sum up, then, you have the actual facts on the side of Free Trade, not only of the great success of Free-Trade policy, first in the conversion of the British Empire and next of a very general extension of its policy by means of the Cobden Treaties, but you have on the same side the consolidation of States and the growth of great communities each with internal Free Trade; you have also the constant tendency of science to cheapen the cost of production and means of communication; and you have, finally, the growth of conditions in the most important countries of the world such as heralded complete Free Trade in this country itself, causes which must produce the like results.

The old order is changing rapidly, and Protectionist commercial policy is fast dying, if it is not as good as dead.

The average man and politician, therefore, who talk glibly of their Protectionist policy, are the Rip van Winkles of the modern world. The world is moving on in spite of them, and their petty interferences are too ridiculous for serious discussion. Is it possible to suppose that the people who propose M'Kinley tariffs on the other side of the Atlantic, or the people who here propose countervailing duties and other old-world apparatus of Protection, are not going to be found out, when all the actual conditions of business are against them?

I have given you, I fear, a long sermon, but my application will be short. I am not in any case one of those people who profess to instruct business men what to do in their own business. If people in business do not bestir themselves to do their very best in order to make a living, they will hardly be moved by lectures in consular reports or in newspaper articles as to their remissness in seeking foreign markets and catering for their customers. Business men, however, are sometimes found to rely on some hoped-for Protection from Government, and in this way I hope it will do some good, especially to the younger generation, if it is made clear, and yet again clear, that the time is past for Protection, and that no industry can live anywhere which is not able to face the most unrestricted competition.

A better living, I believe, can now be made by every one who is willing to work than could have been made at any previous time of the world's history; but work there must be in the bracing and tonic air of competition; no reposing in quiet corners with comfortable monopolies or under the protection of a paternal Government which takes care of people who do not care for themselves.

XXI.

CONSOLS IN A GREAT WAR.[1]

How far is the present price of Consols due to special and transitory causes, irrespective of the Government credit, and at what price could a large amount of the stock be issued if a great emergency should arise?

A QUESTION like what is here proposed is obviously rather a speculative one. No one can tell beforehand what the circumstances of a great emergency, in which new borrowing by the English Government may become necessary, will be. We can conceive of a possibility such as the sudden outbreak of war with a great military power and the defeat of the English fleet by such power. In the case of such an emergency there will perhaps be no price or regular market for securities at all. We have also to consider that the general level of the rates of interest changes from time to time; and possibly in the next few years the general level for first-class securities, instead of being at a point for $2\frac{1}{2}$ per cent. stocks between 90 and 100, exclusive of Consols themselves, which are about 110, might be such that the general level of even 3 per cent. stocks would be under what $2\frac{1}{2}$'s now are. It is conceived, however, that the discussion of a question like the above can proceed upon two assumptions—the first, that there is a great emergency, but stopping short of a great calamity and disaster such as one that would threaten the very existence of the British Empire

[1] This paper was prepared for the purpose of a discussion on the question stated early in June, 1899. How far the price of Consols has since changed in accordance with the anticipations of the paper it will be for the reader to judge.

itself; and second, that the rate of interest before the emergency comes about has not changed from the present level, apart from the usual oscillations between times of good and bad credit. Such a discussion may bring up interesting points as to the conditions of national credit, and the use of a sinking fund for the redemption of debt, or for the provision in some other way of a reserve against emergencies, by a Government in the position of that of the United Kingdom.

The high price of Consols at the present time naturally suggests that in time of stress the rate at which new loans could be raised would be correspondingly high. The rate would be less of course than the present, because any new issue tends to lower the price for the time of existing issues, and still more a new issue in circumstances like those suggested, but the rate would still be high. It is the assumption that the rate would be *correspondingly* high, which I propose to dispute. On the contrary, the market for Consols for some years has been an artificial one. When it becomes a natural market again, as it must do when large new issues take place, and when practically a new market would have to be found, the price would be considerably lower than it is now.

Passing over for the moment the fact of the artificial character of the market for Consols at the present time, there are plenty of precedents to show that if the market were natural the price will probably not fall very much at first in the circumstances described. In the Franco-German war in 1870 the drop in French 3 per cents. on the declaration of war was from 73 to 66. A fortnight before the declaration of war in this case everything was peaceful, and there was no sign whatsoever of any such outbreak being at hand. Consequently, the price after the declaration of war and the price a fortnight before measure the difference caused by the war itself, and by the apprehensions immediately excited as to what new issues would be.

The event was not discounted beforehand. This difference, then, was from 73 to 66, or about 10 per cent. In the case of Germany the fall in Government stocks was even greater; but that is hardly a good precedent, on account of the small amount of the stocks themselves, and the absence of a first-class market for securities at that time in Germany. The fall in other stocks at the same time, especially the fall in the weaker foreign stocks, such as Italian, was much greater than what has been stated, partly owing to the suddenness of the panic which broke out on the Paris Bourse and on the London Stock Exchange; but in such emergencies, for obvious reasons, the change in the value of Stock Exchange securities may be greatest, not in the securities of the Governments themselves who are directly concerned, but in those securities in which at the time there happens to be most speculation and which happen to be weakly held. In the first-class securities of the Governments themselves, the change is much less, and the case of what happened in France when the war of 1870 broke out is accordingly very much to the point. Similarly at the time of the Penjdeh incident, when there was great apprehension of an immediate war between this country and Russia, the drop in Consols in one day was about five points, or more than 5 per cent. At the time of the recent Fashoda incident, threatening as matters looked for a few days, the drop in Consols was even less, and was very quickly recovered.

There is no reason in substance, if we think of the matter, why the fall in such a case should be very great, assuming all the present prices to be natural prices. Apart from panic the appearance of great States as borrowers for a few hundred millions is not calculated really to disturb the markets very much, as these issues to a large extent would do no more than absorb new savings which now go into all sorts of other new issues. I should say, however, that in the event of an actual outbreak of war between this country and one or two great powers such as France, Germany, and Russia, the commotion at first would probably be somewhat greater than anything that was indicated even by what happened in France at the time of the Franco-German war. At that time all the markets were steadied by the neutrality of England, in which lay far and away the biggest market for securities at the time. A war in which England would itself be engaged would be one in which the same equanimity could not prevail in the general markets for securities, because it is the country of the chief market which would be concerned.

I should be inclined to assume, then, following the precedent of 1870, that the outbreak of a great war in which England itself would be engaged, would depress the price of first-class securities even more than the 10 per cent. which was the measure of the difference to France at the beginning of its war with Germany. The difference perhaps would be not less than about 15 per cent.

In support of the latter view it may be pointed out that as the war between France and Germany progressed, and indicated a greater danger for France than had been at first anticipated, the 3 per cents. quickly fell to the price of 53, which was the price just after Sedan and the beginning of the Siege of Paris. Just for the reason that there would be no outside market to support prices, such as there was in England in 1870 when the Franco-German War broke out, any great calamity happening to England must have a greater effect on the market for English stocks than the calamities which happened to France in 1870 had upon French stocks.

On the outbreak of war, then, between England and other countries, there is fair reason to expect in this view that the price of first-class securities all round would fall something like 15 per cent.; and my special contention now is that in English Government securities in particular, owing to the market at the present time being artificial, the fall would probably be greater. The artificial premium in fact would disappear, and then the English Government securities would share in the general fall which the outbreak of war occasions.

Before showing in detail the reasons for thinking that at present the price of English Government securities is artificial, it will be expedient to discuss generally what are the conditions of a natural market for securities of the best kind; that is, a first-rate market.

These conditions appear to be as follows: (1) There must be a large quantity of the security itself; the security, in fact, must be large enough for many people to be interested in it, and for large dealings to take place. (2) There must also be a large quantity of the security relatively to the general business of the market. It is a help to such a security if it is the leading security in the market, because in that character it attracts a great deal of speculative interest, and speculative dealings take place accordingly in that security almost to the exclusion of others. It was noticed at the time when English Government securities were divided into two large classes, one Consols and the other New and Reduced, that although these two stocks were identical in every respect in their conditions, yet the fact of the speculative dealings being in Consols permanently raised the price about a half to 1 per cent. above that of the New and Reduced stock, which was identical in every respect except that of being called by the same name. (3) There must be a large quantity of the security in the hands of dealers and other holders about the market who study the security and are always ready to buy and sell. This last condition almost follows of necessity from the other two; in the case of the leading security in any market, it could not be leading unless a considerable amount of it was held from time to time by dealers, both those persons known as dealers in the market itself and others who are about the market, and are technically not known as dealers, but who are, in fact, frequently ready to buy and to sell. It is necessary, however, to state the point separately when large masses of securities have come to be in existence without any speculative dealing taking place in them. It may be possible to use the average prices of such securities from time to time to show the general level of interest which prevails; but experience has shown that no such average, however ascertained, can be taken as a real test of market price in the same way that the price of a security fulfulling all the conditions above stated can be taken. In the latter case the market price is a safe guide; in no other case can it be taken as a complete guide, especially as regards any particular stock, when a considerable change is about to occur in the quantity of the stock itself or in the general conditions of the market. Without such a guide, an enormous addition to the supply of any stock implies, in fact, the making of a new market, for which new customers and operators have to be found.

Formerly, and until quite recent years, the above were especially the conditions of the market for Consols. English Government securities in the early years of the century were of very great amount—£900,000,000 sterling after the close of the great war in 1815. They were also almost the whole market for securities at the time, occupying, at any rate, not merely a pre-eminent but a predominant position. The funds were then something *sui generis*, spoken of in contrast with land, houses, and other investments not on the Stock Exchange. Even a quarter of a century ago Consols still occupied a leading place. The debt was then still £800,000,000, and the funded debt alone about £740,000,000. No doubt even then Consols were beginning to be thrust aside by other great markets,—the English railway market, the market for American Government and other securities, the market for various foreign loans (Turkish, Egyptian, Italian, Russian, and others, including for a time French Government securities), and other miscellaneous markets gradually growing in importance. Still, Consols occupied a pre-eminent if not a predominant position, and they were the leading market. They still complied with all the conditions of a first-class market.

But in the last quarter of a century, and especially within the last few years, the position has been entirely changed.

1. The Debt is still large, being now about £630,000,000, or £670,000,000 if we include a stock which has been separated, called the Local Loans Stock; but the debts of other Governments have come to exceed or to approach the English amount. The Government Debt of France, for instance, is £1,100,000,000, a sum greatly in excess of the present English Debt. Then we have an Austro-Hungarian Debt of nearly £600,000,000; Italian, £520,000,000; Russian, £700,000,000; while there are Debts of £100,000,000 and £200,000,000 owing by quite a number of States, for the most part incurred in comparatively recent years. The English Debt accordingly does not hold the place it did in the general markets for securities, and the amount of foreign issues quoted on the London Stock Exchange alone amounts to about £2,000,000,000.

2. The proportion of the Debt itself to the total securities dealt in has enormously diminished, partly, as has been seen, by the redemption of the Debt, though this redemption, while important with reference to the amount of the Debt, does not seem to be of importance as compared with the growth of other securities, which is the main cause of the change in proportion between the English Debt and those other securities. This change in proportion has already been indicated by the facts stated as to foreign Government Debts and issues. But a fuller statement may be useful. Whereas sixty or seventy years ago the English

Debt amounted to about one-third or one-fourth of the whole capital of the community, it is now perhaps no more than one-twentieth. Whereas formerly it was almost the sole Stock Exchange security, it is now less than one-tenth of the securities quoted on the London Stock Exchange alone. The exact figure of such stocks quoted in the official list of the London Stock Exchange at 31st December, 1898, is stated to be £7,609,000,000, of which, as already mentioned, about £2,000,000,000 are foreign Government issues. In addition, the markets for securities all over the world (in the United States, in Germany, in France, in Austria, in Italy, in Russia, and in our Australian Colonies and South Africa) have increased in even greater proportion; and as they all form practically one market, the relative importance of Consols has greatly diminished. Many securities are dealt in in more markets than one, especially Government securities; but making all deductions for such double entries, one can hardly be wrong in estimating that the figure above stated for issues dealt in on the London Stock Exchange would at least have to be doubled if we were to include the issues upon all the different markets throughout the world. Of this vast mass, English Government securities are clearly a very small percentage indeed.

3. While the mass of the English Government Debt with reference to other securities has thus been diminishing, it is also to be noticed that the amount in the hands of the public has diminished even more than the amount of the Debt itself, and this diminution has been very marked in recent years. This is chiefly the consequence of the investment of savings bank money in Government stocks. The total amount of such savings bank money is now about £180,000,000, all of which must be invested in the English Government Debt, while other amounts of stock are held by other departments of the Government. It would seem that admitting the amount of the English Government

Debt to be £630,000,000 or £670,000,000 including the Local Loans Stock, nearly the whole of it in excess of £400,000,000 is held by the National Debt Commissioners for the savings banks or by other Government departments. The small amount which can be dealt in is shown in another way. The amount of the leading stock, Consols, actually quoted in the Stock Exchange official list is £522,000,000; and if we allow that some part of this amount is held by the savings banks and other Government departments, though their holdings, of course, are not exclusively in Consols, we can easily see that the amount of Consols themselves in the hands of the public is probably not much more than £400,000,000.[1] When it is considered, moreover, that the greater part of this sum is locked up, being held by trustees and other holders who are not in a position to sell, or by banks who are not so limited, but who prefer for various reasons to invest in Consols or keep a portion of the reserve in Consols, and who never sell, it can be quite well understood that the amount of the stock available for actual market purposes is so small as to take from it not merely the predominance but the pre-eminence it once had among securities dealt in on the Stock Exchange.

4. What is equally undoubted is that the stock in the hands of dealers, technically or practically so, has so greatly diminished that now the markets for Consols cannot properly be called a great leading market at all. There is no longer a class of large holders interested in the security constantly ready to buy and sell, and consequently in Consols there is no longer that sort of market which has been described above as a free and natural first-rate market on the Stock Exchange. I am assured that as a matter of fact the number of capitalists constituting the Consol market, and able to engage in large business, has con-

[1] This is quite confirmed by the last returns as to the holding of Government securities by the different departments of the Government.

spicuously diminished in the last twenty years, till now it is quite obvious that the market is insignificant, to a degree, compared with other markets on the Stock Exchange.

5. The increase of savings bank money has taken place very largely since 1895, when the annual addition to the deposits in the savings banks from being about £4,000,000 to £5,000,000 suddenly went up to over £10,000,000. And this change is coincident with a change in the relative prices of Consols and the leading debenture stocks of railways, apparently indicating that Consols during the last two or three years have been subject to especial influences. A few years ago the 3 per cent. Debenture Stock of the London and North-Western Railway stood at 124, while Consols were at 114. Now the 3 per cent. Debenture Stocks of the London and North-Western Railway are at 111, showing a loss of 13 points, while Consols are about 110, showing a loss of four points only. Consols have thus been sustained by a cause not applicable to first-rate securities generally, and the explanation, no doubt, is the application of the savings bank money to investment in Consols.

As the whole result, we may say that Consols during the last quarter of a century, and especially during the last few years, have lost the characteristics of a first-rate market for securities. They are of less amount in themselves than they were; for various reasons the whole amount is not upon the market at all; and now the market is so small that there is no free dealing in them, such as is necessary for a first-class market. There is, in fact, what one may call a corner in Consols, and as in all corners, the present price is not a real indication of what the market would be when natural conditions are restored.

In the circumstances we may expect, then, that if there are large new issues, this will so alter the general condition of Consols that the premium due to what we may call the present corner must disappear. That premium would seem to be from 5 to 10 per cent. in amount, which may be considered an extra premium not indicating any special credit which the English Government has, but merely the special conditions which have made Consols scarce; when the stocks become abundant again all this premium will disappear, and the price of large new issues will be determined by the circumstances of the issue and the general state of credit. The English Government will still hold a premier position, but it would not be more than a shade better than other first-class borrowers. In the event of a first-class war, in fact, English Government securities stand to lose not merely the 15 per cent. which is likely to occur in all first-class securities, but the extra premium of 5 or 10 per cent. which has come about in consequence of the corner in Consols.

This being the position, what may be considered, apart from Consols, the general level of credit at the present time? I have to submit the following short table, showing the prices of the leading first-class securities:

	Price.
French 3 per cents.	101
German ,,	90
United States 4 per cents.	130, equal to 3 per cent. at 98
Russian ,,	100, equal to 3 per cent. at 75
New South Wales 3 per cents.	101
Indian Government $2\frac{1}{2}$ per cents. (gold)	94
Canadian $2\frac{1}{2}$ per cents.	91
Metropolitan ,,	97
London County Council $2\frac{1}{2}$ per cents.	95
London and North-Western Railway 3 per cent. Debenture Stock	111, equal to $2\frac{1}{2}$ per cent. at $92\frac{1}{2}$
Great Western $2\frac{1}{2}$ per cent. Debenture Stock	92

From these figures we may consider that the general level of credit at the present time is represented by the price of the best $2\frac{1}{2}$ per cent. Railway Debenture Stocks, viz., 92, or, at most, something intermediate between that and the $2\frac{1}{2}$ per cent. stocks of the London County Council, or of the Indian Government, viz., 94 or 95. An easy calculation would thus show that the probable price of the best new issues at $2\frac{1}{2}$ per cent. in the event of a great war, allowing for a 15 per cent. fall, will be something a little over 80, or, say, 85; the corresponding price of the 3 per cent. issue would be over par, but there would, of course, be special difficulties in connection with an issue of stock over par. These would also be about the prices, I believe, at which the English Government could borrow, assuming that the present extra premium on Consols due to artificial causes is 5 or 10 per cent. A reduction of 10 per cent. from the present price of Consols would bring them down to about par, and from that a fall of 15 per cent. would give the price of 85. A good deal will, of course, depend upon the exact amount of the present artificial premium on Consols. But whatever we take it to be, *some* allowance must be made practically for the existence of such a premium when business comes to be done.

It is of little use quoting expert authority in such matters, for experts are not unlikely to differ; but a few weeks ago I happened to obtain the opinion of a gentleman, since deceased, who would be universally recognized in the City as one of the best authorities upon such a point. As it happened, he had also considered the matter very fully. His opinion was that in the event of a great war and of large issues of Consols by the English Government at $2\frac{1}{2}$ per cent., the price would probably be about 80, and the price for three per cents. would be a little over 90. Other authorities seem inclined to think that the prices in the case supposed would be higher than these; but I do not know of any authority who was quite so well qualified as the friend to whom I have referred, or who had so fully entered into all the *pros* and *cons* of the subject.

Of course, these calculations do not carry us beyond the actual beginning of a war and the beginning of large issues consequent upon it. What would happen as the indirect result of all the commotion and excitement attendant upon a war, and the great efforts which might have to be made to carry it on, is a little beyond even the slight prevision which may be considered possible on the assumption with which we started. The great point is that we must not assume too hastily that there is not going to be a great fall in Consols, quite disproportionate to what there may be in other first-class securities.

I might stop at this point, having answered the question put; but there is a practical issue on which the facts stated appear to have some bearing, viz., the question of the use of a sinking fund for the redemption of debt or for the accumulation of a reserve against emergencies by a Government like our own. The bearing of the facts stated seems to be that the credit of the Government for purposes of business is not improved by the redemption of the debt or by the accumulation of a reserve fund against emergencies, because its credit is already of the highest possible quality, and its borrowing power will be regulated accordingly by the general conditions of credit, and not by the increase or decrease of the debt by a few millions annually. The Government is one of many first-class borrowers, and a little redemption of its own debt does not seem to matter as far as its credit is concerned, one way or the other. This may seem a hard saying; but when we perceive the credit of a country like Russia increasing from year to year, notwithstanding increasing debt, and the credit of a country like France increasing the same way, we have surely cause to doubt what precise part is played by the redemption of debt on our own credit. Formerly this debt redemption was undoubtedly an important factor. When our debt was so large as to amount to one-third of the property in the country, and when it was also almost the sole Stock Exchange security, its redemption of course affected credit generally. But now, in comparison with the great forces in the market, the redemption does not seem specially important to the security upon which it is exercised. The redemption is, in fact, for the benefit of all high-class stocks, not specially for the benefit of English Government stocks; and upon this large mass it does not seem to exercise a very great influence.

The gain to us, therefore, from the reduction of debt must apparently be limited to the direct gain; the indirect gain from the effect upon credit generally, or from the effect upon the special credit of the Government not being material. As regards this direct gain, assuming all the payment made for the redemption of debt to be an additional saving of the community which would not otherwise be made, then the country gains about £25,000 annually for every million applied to the payment of debt. The application of a hundred millions would accordingly save to the country annually £2,500,000, which is hardly a perceptible item in the aggregate income of the country. It is about equal to the annual present which sugar bounty countries are alleged to give to our sugar consumers by means of the bounty.

But if the payment is not an additional saving at all, but a transfer from one holder to another, as appears to be the case while so much of the income of the Government is derived from taxes on capital, the question may well arise whether the redemption of debt in present conditions is of any use to the State. The direct gain in the last case is absolutely *nil*. What the Government gains, the community as a whole loses; and so the resources of the State are actually unchanged by the process.

The general effect of this argument is accordingly to show that there is no necessity at the present time for our reducing debt or for accumulating a reserve against emergencies. We seem to gain nothing by the process, because it is one which is not required for its effect upon credit, and the direct gain is quite inappreciable; and it is perhaps doubtful, looking to the nature of our taxation, whether there is any direct gain at all. My own opinion is that it would now be the wisest thing for us to give up any attempt at the reduction of debt, so long at least as the means for paying the debt are really derived from taxes on capital.

I do not, however, put forward the present argument as fully covering the whole question. All that is here claimed is that the usual arguments for the reduction of debt are not what they are supposed to be, and that the whole question requires a great deal of consideration. I hope to return to this subject on an early occasion.

XXII.

SOME ECONOMIC ASPECTS OF THE SOUTH AFRICAN WAR.[1]

THE war in South Africa appears to furnish a good opportunity for studying some of those questions which arise in connection with such disturbances of the economic equilibrium. It stops far short of being one of those great disturbances which sometimes occur, such as the war between North and South in the United States, thirty-five to forty years ago, or such as the war between France and Germany in 1870, when millions of people were involved on both sides, and there was in consequence great stoppage and diversion of industry, continued in the case of the war between North and South for nearly four years. On the other hand, the war is not one of those little wars which are incident to the existence of the British Empire, being unavoidable on the doctrine of chances with an Empire so widely extended as our own, and on so small a scale with reference to the resources of the Empire generally that they pass almost unnoticed in the economic life of the nation. Without being a war of the first kind, involving a great and obvious disturbance of the whole industry of the people, the present war is still on a large enough scale to produce some visible and palpable effects which are the result of war, and it can by no means be spoken of as war with limited liability.

The war then may be looked at from several points of view in its economic relations. First, and not the least important, the circumstances of South Africa itself have to be considered. The war may not be a first-rate affair economically, as far as the British Empire is

[1] Written in 1900.

concerned, but yet it may be of transcendent importance in that respect for the communities of South Africa who are directly involved. Second, the precise effects, as far as the United Kingdom and the Empire are concerned, have to be studied. What is, in fact, the interruption to trade, and what are the temporary and permanent losses sustained? In connection with this, what is the tendency of the war on account of political and other changes that may result in relation to the industry of the country? Third, special consideration has to be given to the finance of the war, and the illustrations supplied by it as to the method of raising loans and new taxes in similar emergencies.

Taking these problems in their order, we have to begin by noticing the extent of the disturbance of industry in South Africa itself. The war has perhaps brought about, as far as the local communities are concerned, a more extensive stoppage of industry in proportion to the whole business done than almost any war on record. The chief industry of the Transvaal was that of gold mining. The gross produce of this industry when the war actually broke out amounted to £20,000,000 sterling per annum, many times the gross produce of all the other industries of the country. This big industry sustained a large community in Johannesburg and on the Rand, comprising a white population of about 60,000 and a black population whose numbers I find difficult to estimate, but probably of at least equal magnitude. The industry again, besides supporting all this population, supplied the means for the expenditure of the Transvaal Government itself, besides large dividends for shareholders, not merely in South Africa and in London, but all over the world. All at once, four-fifths, if not five-sixths, of this industry have been put an end to for the time. Half the white community by which it was carried on have been displaced, and obliged to leave as fugitives the country where they were settled, and to subsist, many of them, upon charity in Natal and the Cape Colony. In proportion to the area affected, then, there could not be a greater disturbance. The war has spelt temporary ruin to many thousands of people, including the most advanced and civilized portion of the population of the Transvaal. There has also been some destruction of capital which will have to be renewed after the war, but not representing any large sum in comparison with the annual product of the industry.

This disturbance, perhaps, has not been an inevitable incident of the war. It was quite possible for the Transvaal Government to permit the Uitlander to live and work in peace, although war was going on. As a matter of fact, however, contrary to their own interest, the governing classes of the Transvaal have not permitted the industry to go on, because they have expelled the only people by whom it could in fact be managed. In any case there would have been some disturbance through the fear of the Uitlander, who distrusted the Transvaal Government in time of peace, and was naturally ten times more apprehensive when war approached, but the Uitlander has not in fact been left to his own fears. He has been forcibly deprived of the means of living by the act of the Government of the Transvaal.

In other respects, in the Transvaal itself, and elsewhere throughout South Africa, there has been no great stoppage of industry. At Kimberley, where the great diamond mining industry is carried on, even the siege did not altogether stop the industry itself, while the usual employment throughout the region, that of pastoral farming, is not one of a kind which war seriously interrupts. The farms lose something by the absence of the farmers themselves who have been called away to the field to fight, but not a great deal in proportion. To these interruptions must be added the interruption of coal mining in Natal and the Cape Colony, and the interruption to business generally in those parts of Cape Colony, Natal, and the Orange Free State, which have been the actual theatre of the war. None of these interruptions, however, can be considered of great importance in themselves. The coal mining of Natal and Cape Colony, everything reckoned, has occupied a few hundreds of people only, and the districts of Cape Colony and Natal, as well as the Orange Free State, which have been the seat of war, are very sparsely populated. The losses sustained in these ways are not to be compared with the suspension of so much of the chief industry in the Transvaal itself, which has to be reckoned as the one great economic loss of the war, as far as South Africa is concerned.

Indirectly, some of these stoppages may have been important. The interruption of coal mining, for instance, may have helped to aggravate the coal famine. But it would take us too far here to follow out such indirect consequences. We are speaking now from the point of view of the communities directly affected by the war.

On the other hand, large numbers of the communities of South Africa have probably gained a great deal directly and indirectly through the war. Viewed economically, from the standpoint of the people of South Africa, the conduct of the war has in fact been equivalent to the establishment of a new industry in the region, providing a good market for the produce of the country and giving large employment to labour, and all this being done by means of new money coming into the country from abroad. There is no doubt waste and loss somewhere in connection with the war, but the waste and loss do not fall upon the people of South Africa generally. The losers have been the people of Johannesburg and the Rand, who have been driven from their homes and prevented from carrying on their usual industry; but the farmers and towns-people of Cape Colony and Natal generally, and the farmers and towns-people of that portion of the Orange Free State occupied by our troops, are all clearly gainers *pro tanto* by the war expenditure. Farmers everywhere throughout those districts have a better market for their produce, and every local industry is stimulated. This result is no new thing in war experience. At the points where opposing armies are in actual contact, the circumstances are inconvenient and injurious to the people in the neighbourhood; but in those other districts forming the base of operations it is not a bad thing for a country to be the seat of war where the troops concerned come from a distance and bring with them a great deal of money to be expended in the country. The position in the Transvaal is not quite the same. In this case there is no introduction of money from abroad to be spent in the country. The people here must be using up their capital and resources generally. But they are probably not much worse off for the present than they were in time of peace, excepting so far as they are affected by the diminution of their share of the income from the gold mines. The male white population is mostly fighting in the army; but even if they had been at home they would not have been adding much to the product of the industry of the country, which goes on very much independently of them—at any rate for a time.

Thus, the war is very far from having been an unmixed loss in an economic sense to the communities of South Africa. The temporary interruption of the gold mining industry of the Transvaal and the minor interruptions of industry elsewhere are made up for very largely to the local communities by the new industry of carrying on the war itself, bringing with it in Cape Colony and Natal a large expenditure by what is really an immigration from abroad. The loss and waste of the war have thus not fallen upon the communities of South Africa as they have fallen elsewhere.[1]

We come *secondly* then to the question of the precise effects of the war as far as the United Kingdom and the Empire are concerned. And the point here is, that while a considerable interruption to trade has to be taken note of, an interruption which would be very

[1] This was written in 1900, before the extensive interruption to the agricultural industry by the guerilla warfare occurred

serious in its magnitude if measured against the business of South Africa only, yet because of the magnitude of the United Kingdom and the British Empire, against which the interruption has really to be measured, it is hardly sensible. What it comes to, as far as the United Kingdom is concerned, is mainly the stoppage of the labour of the reservists and volunteers who have been called out and who have left the country for service in South Africa. There is no industrial loss, additional to what was going on in time of peace, as far as the services of those soldiers who were with the colours when war broke out are concerned. They are maintained by the country in time of war just as they were maintained in time of peace. The case, however, is different with the reservists and those who have volunteered, numbering about 120,000. They represent so much labour diverted from its usual occupation. Estimating the product of the labour of 120,000 men as worth on the average to themselves and to the community about £80 each per annum, we have a sum of about £10,000,000 sterling annually lost to the community by the diversion of industry which the war occasions. This is not all. It is a fair calculation that for every person actually in the fighting rank, another person in civil occupation is employed in manufacturing implements of war, clothing, saddlery and harness, and other requisites for the field army; and as our field army is altogether about 200,000 men, we must assume that there are 200,000 men in civil employments in this country practically as much engaged in working for the war as if they were in the field army itself. In other words, besides the £10,000,000 which we lose through the abstraction of the people from industrial pursuits to engage in the fighting line itself, we must lose from £16,000,000 to £20,000,000 annually by the abstraction of people from ordinary civil occupations into the business of making things for those who are engaged in the fighting line.

This is the economic loss of the war properly so

called. What the Government pays is a different thing. What it pays is a payment really from some members of the community to others, many of whom make large profits; and the net loss to the community as a whole must be measured in some such way as has now been applied.

What the final loss will be, then, depends on the length of the war. A year of it will apparently involve a loss of about £30,000,000 to the community, that is a net loss; and if the war continues longer the loss will be much more.

From the point of view of the Government, the position is perhaps more serious. They estimate an expenditure of £60,000,000 for the past and the present financial years, and it is probable that this sum will be exceeded. Very likely the charge may be even £100,000,000 before the present financial year expires, as we have not merely to beat the enemy, but to occupy the country inch by inch. In any case the outlay by the Government must be enormous. It must not be confused with the net loss to the community; but, looked at by itself and from the point of view of the national finances, it seems a formidable figure.

Large as the sum is, however, it cannot be said to be a very formidable one when compared with the resources of the United Kingdom itself. £100,000,000 is about a seventeenth part only of the aggregate annual income of the people of the United Kingdom, and almost an infinitesimal amount compared with the fifteen or sixteen thousand millions at which the wealth of the country is estimated. It is no matter for surprise therefore that the burden of the war seems to be hardly felt at all. Important as the war is for the loss of life it has occasioned, and in other aspects, it is in reality a little war as far as our resources in men and money are concerned.

It seems unnecessary to say anything as to the loss of the war to other parts of the British Empire. The other parts of the Empire outside the United Kingdom and South Africa appear to have supplied about 10,000 soldiers altogether, and they have spent some money in fitting out and equipping these soldiers. The maintenance of these soldiers in the field, however, and the supply of arms and other requisites have substantially fallen upon the United Kingdom, and it may be doubted whether the war has cost anything to the Colonies which have helped us. We are, in fact, providing a fairly good occupation for about 10,000 colonists outside those belonging to South Africa itself, and the Colonies so far really benefit by the war expenditure in the same way that the communities of South Africa benefit by it.

It is, no doubt, in contemplation that South Africa is to furnish an indemnity towards the outlay which we incur by carrying on the war. In this way it may be said the cost of the war, which is incurred in the first instance by the home Government, will be transferred to the communities of South Africa. As a matter of fact, however, the Transvaal indemnity will never be directly paid. When it comes to be settled the money will be supplied by a borrowing operation, and the loss, when it falls ultimately on the communities of South Africa in the shape of the interest payments on the loan, will fall largely on a different people from the present, while the repayments will go to our successors, and not to the generation which has suffered the loss. In this aspect what the Government pays for the war may be said to be an investment of capital which will directly come back to us in time along with all the profits which we shall receive as the result of the peace and prosperity to be established by means of the war.

Some will, perhaps, be surprised at the burden of the war being thus in appearance whittled down. To minimize the evils of war in any fashion may even be regarded as almost criminal. It is necessary, however, to state facts precisely if we are to have clear ideas at all, and if we do so it is beyond question that the economic evils of the war as far as we have gone are not of a very serious kind. The broad reason is, that notwithstanding the importance of the war in many aspects, the burden of it is really small compared with the immense resources of the United Kingdom, while the burden on the South African communities, where the disturbance of industry has been very great, is mitigated in the various ways we have described. As far as the United Kingdom is concerned, the injury may be described as equivalent to what would be caused by a big strike such as we have had in recent years in the coal mining industry and in the engineering industry. In the coal mining strike several years ago, about 200,000 to 300,000 people were engaged, and the industry to that extent was suspended. In the engineering strike, not quite 100,000 engineers struck work, but the numbers really involved and put out of employment directly were considerably greater. We know, however, in how small a degree the product of the general industry of the country was diminished by these events when accounts came to be made up at the end of the year. Similarly now the abstraction of 200,000 to 300,000 people from their usual occupations into direct and indirect military service appears to be lost in the general volume of the national activities. The numbers, large as they are, are not big enough to be missed, and the effect in proportion to the numbers is, perhaps, less than it was in the case of the big strikes referred to, because in these strikes, especially the coal strike, other employments were almost immediately affected through the deficient supply of raw material to work with, whereas in the present case workmen are taken in proportion from great varieties of employments, and there is no stoppage in consequence of the failure of some particular industry to supply its quota of raw material for the others. Apparently, also, the abstraction of workers from active industry is not equal in numerical amount to the numbers of reservists and volunteers who have gone to the front, because there are included in the latter considerable numbers who were more or less unemployed, and they did not therefore form a part of the army of labour proportionate to their numbers.

There remains, however, the final question under this head as to the tendency of the war on account of political and other changes in relation to the industry of the country. A large field of speculation is here opened up. It is quite plain to begin with that the revelation of the country's want of preparation for any considerable military undertaking will lead to the very greatest changes in our military and naval departments at home. The country has been thoroughly alarmed at the necessity which has been imposed upon us of sending all available troops to a distant field like South Africa, so that no reserve is left for any other contingency which may befall. Even greater alarm has been produced by the apparent ignorance of the art of war in high quarters throughout the British army, and the consequent necessity for improvising everything which is necessary to create an army as distinguished from a mob of armed men. In particular, the lack of the best provision in the way of weapons and ammunition and the shortness of supplies of every kind have made a most painful impression. It is therefore undoubted that at the end of the war great reforms must be taken in hand; the numbers of the regular army greatly increased, and everything done which has been so long neglected to make the framework of the army complete and efficient, so that operations can be undertaken at any moment without danger of a breakdown. At the same time measures have obviously become necessary to render more efficient every kind of auxiliary force at home, so that in an emergency the country may not be left without a reserve force for a second unfortunate contingency when we are already deeply engaged. All this means a very considerable addition to the outlay for the army and navy in the next few years of a more or less permanent kind. Estimates vary as to what the addition should be; but I am inclined to think that a very high estimate will not be short of the mark, for two reasons: 1. The necessity for increasing the permanent standing army by 100,000 to 150,000 men, which is rendered unavoidable in part by the state of affairs in South Africa, and in part by the necessity for strengthening our garrisons in Egypt and other places which the defects of our want of preparation in South Africa have made manifest. 2. The evident necessity which has arisen for increasing sensibly the pay of the army all round. At present about 150,000 is the number of the regular establishment, exclusive of India. An addition of £10 per head to the pay of this force alone would come to £1,500,000 per annum; but the additional pay must be given not to 150,000 merely, but probably to 250,000 or 300,000 men at the very time also that preparations are being made for improving the auxiliary forces at home, and that reserves of stores, guns, and ammunition are being prepared on a scale that has not hitherto been thought of. It is hard to see, then, in what way the doubling of the Army Estimates, which just before the war had mounted up to £20,000,000 sterling, can be avoided.

The indirect teaching of the war goes further. It has brought the country face to face with new and unwonted political dangers. The hostility to us of almost every continental people has been revealed, and the nation has felt that in its fight in South Africa it has been fighting not merely the Boers, but the continent of Europe. No continental Government has actually menaced us with intervention; but the will has been there, and our success in South Africa will be bitterly resented. The feeling evidently is in France, in Germany, and in Russia, that England has too much of the world, and that its dominion should be curtailed. Germany and France, moreover, are each of them covetous of some of our possessions for themselves, and Russia at least finds us very much in the way of its own enterprises. The other great world-power, the United States, has also given some encouragement to the idea of intervention on the sentimental ground of sympathy with republican states. As the result, we have to consider that the position of the British Empire in the world is challenged in a way that has not been the case at any time in its previous history, and that at any time we may be called upon to fight for mere existence by one or other of these great powers, or by a coalition. This is the permanent condition; and, considering what some of these powers are, and the immensity of their military and naval preparations, we are bound to recognize that the British Empire in turn must arm itself on similar principles to those of Russia, and Germany, and France, if we are to be secure. In this view even the doubling of the Army Estimates will not be sufficient. We should not be surprised before long to find the Army and Navy Estimates of the United Kingdom amounting together annually to £70,000,000 or £80,000,000 sterling, along with a great development of the defensive forces at home and throughout the English-speaking portions of the Empire. Looking at the growing wealth and numbers of the people, so great an addition to our expenditure would not be beyond our powers, but the whole change in our finances will raise new and difficult problems for the public men and economists of the future. The organization of the British Empire for necessary defence, in the face of the military powers which are beside it, will be a Herculean task indeed.

With regard to the *third* branch of the inquiry, namely, the finance methods which have been used in the war, there is not a great deal to be said. The war as yet has perhaps lasted too short a time to give occasion for expert financial management. The Transvaal and Orange Free State on the one side have been using up resources which were accumulated before the war, while on the other side the efforts of the war, as we have seen, have been on too small a scale to test the capacity of our power. One or two points, however, may be noticed.

As regards the Transvaal and the Orange Free State the problem they have had before them has been how to keep in the field an army of from 50,000 to 60,000 men, which they have had to do along with the simultaneous stoppage as we have seen of four-fifths or five-sixths of the chief industry of the country, namely, gold mining. To put such a force in the field anyhow, and at any rate with the completeness of equipment which the Transvaal Government especially appears to have possessed, must have required a considerable financial effort. This may be said, although we are absolutely without information upon one essential point, namely, whether the Transvaal Government gives any pay to the troops, so many of whom have been commandeered. No accounts that I have seen make the smallest reference to this vital point, except one by an ex-banker from Pretoria, dealing in an interesting manner with the economics of the war in the Transvaal; and this gentleman confesses, that as to this point which he had considered, he is unable to say anything. I think we may assume, however, that the Transvaal Government and the Orange Free State Government pay their men who are in the field something in money, besides finding their food and other necessaries. One reason for this opinion is, that a certain proportion of the Transvaal and Orange Free State armies consists of foreign mercenaries and other volunteers who could not be obtained without pay; while it would be clearly difficult, if not impossible, to have some men in the armies paid, and others not paid, especially when those others consist of "burghers" jealous of their rights and privileges, and rather apt to look down upon the mercenaries associated with them. Mention is also made in the reports as to some positions we have captured of the existence of canteens and stores in the Boer camps at which purchases could be made, and of course as purchases cannot be made without money, money must have been in circulation in those camps. In any case, in whatever way the cost is reckoned, the South

African Republic, in order to keep 50,000 to 60,000 men in the field, must be spending at least £100 per man, or say at the rate of £5,000,000 to £6,000,000 sterling per annum. This cannot be done out of the actual revenue of the State, because the gross produce of the one-fifth or one-sixth of the gold mining industry which has been carried on cannot exceed £4,000,000 sterling, and not more than half of this sum would be net profit. Practically there is no other source of revenue available for the Government. And as the Transvaal Government has been unable to borrow, clearly the money which it is spending must be derived in part from the accumulations of previous years and in part from the funds which it has commandeered at and since the outbreak of the war, commandeering being really only another name for forced loans. As the money commandeered at the beginning of the war was not much more than about £1,000,000 sterling, and the net sum gained from working the mines since cannot be much more than another million, it would seem that the money resources of the South African Republics must be approaching exhaustion. It does not follow that these Governments are unable to carry on war, as long at least as they have reserves of ammunition and other stores accumulated before the outbreak; but the approach of exhaustion is certainly a point to be considered. The industrial equipment of the Transvaal and the Orange Free State Republics is not adapted for the maintenance of armies during a long war, and they have not the means with which they can make purchases abroad, even if the things purchased could be readily introduced into the country.

Comparatively little attention has been paid to the financial arrangements of Cape Colony, Natal, and Rhodesia, although these must all be affected by the war. As far as may be necessary these States will of course be financed from home, and an adjustment of liabilities made at the end of the war. The chief change that has been noticed appears to be that the revenue of both Cape Colony and Natal has suffered greatly during the war, as might have been expected. The receipts from import duties have diminished greatly, and the net income from the railways, as far as the general public is concerned, has also diminished, although it remains to be seen whether in the end, when an account is stated, the sums due from the Imperial Government for the use of the railways for war purposes will not more than make good the loss of income to the Colonial Governments from the general use of the railways being diminished.

We come last of all then to the finance of the Imperial Government, as to which one or two questions have arisen, although not of first-rate importance. The war is estimated to cost the Government, as we have seen, rather more than £60,000,000 sterling, this being the addition to the Army and Navy Estimates for the past and the current financial years in excess of charges for the ordinary establishments of army and navy, including some charges which have been incurred in consequence of defects in our equipment which the war has revealed, but the filling up of which is not put down as a war charge. Of this amount it has been arranged to borrow £30,000,000; while the remainder, with the exception of £14,000,000 of additional taxation, has been made good by means of suspending the sinking fund, providing a sum of about £10,000,000 altogether for the two years, and by means of the enormous increase of revenue in excess of budget estimates which has taken place during the last two years. The marvellous ease with which the cost of the war has been borne is thus very striking. More than half the cost is being met out of current revenue, but not half of that half has to be supplied by new taxation.

With regard to the borrowing itself there was much discussion by anticipation as to the best method of borrowing; whether more Consols should be issued, or whether the amount should be obtained by Treasury Bills, or whether a loan repayable at a short date should be tried. The choice has been for the latter expedient, and a loan of £30,000,000 bearing $2\frac{3}{4}$ per cent. interest, repayable in ten years' time, and issued at $98\frac{1}{2}$, has been the definite outcome of all the discussions. The issue was also very successful, the loan from the first being quoted at about 2 premium, and that price having been maintained for some time, though lately there has been some weakness. The circumstances were such however that almost any method would have been successful, and nothing turns upon small variations in what is substantially an easy task. It may be said also that in spite of the success of the loan and the general favour with which it was received exception may well be taken to the plan of making the whole amount repayable upon a definite date in the future. To fix such a date seems to be rather a departure from sound principle, as no one can tell whether the bill may not come due when it is inconvenient to pay. To have retained the option of repayment from and after ten years would perhaps have been a preferable course. The point, however, is not important to our finances, which are generally so prosperous.

The new taxation has consisted of an addition of 4*d.* in the £ to the income tax, making the rate 1*s.* per £, and also of small additions to the spirits, beer, tobacco, and tea duties. The addition to the income tax is estimated to yield about £8,000,000 sterling annually, or more nearly £9,000,000, the total yield of this tax at a shilling being now upwards of £27,000,000 sterling. The additions to the indirect taxes named again are estimated to yield about £6,000,000, and those two sums of £8,000,000 from direct taxation, and £6,000,000 from indirect, make up £14,000,000, which have been contributed by new taxation to the cost of the war. The money comes in easily enough; but the weak point of the arrangement undoubtedly is that recourse has been had to direct taxation to an excessive extent, and that the additions to indirect taxation, while yielding so little money, have placed the particular duties from which the amount is derived at too high a point. The obvious criticism is that the *cadres* of our indirect taxation are much too limited, and that in a time of real stress our entire fiscal system must be revised, while the issue has been raised as to the necessity of revising the system even in time of peace. In this connection, however, we can only note the question and pass on. The discussion of different systems of taxation can hardly be made incidentally in the course of an article on the economics of the war. If, however, the opinion is well founded that the war must lead to a complete revision of our military and naval methods for defence of the Empire these questions as to the methods of taxation can only be postponed.

There remains finally a question as to the indemnity to be paid by the South African Republics when the war is finished, as we assume it will be, by the complete success of the British arms. What should the indemnity be, and how will it be raised? We have already pointed out that inevitably the financial arrangements for the South African Republics at the close of the war must involve large borrowing, and this will be the case whether the indemnity is large or small. In order to be put upon their legs again the communities of South Africa must borrow largely, not merely to pay an indemnity, but for the purposes of adding the necessary machinery for the mines, permanent way and plant for railways, and other expenditures which are necessary to re-establish and develop their economic position. Their financial circumstances must also be considered with reference to the extent of the military occupation which will be for some time necessary. But these are all questions for the future, and can hardly perhaps be discussed until it is seen in what way the final settlement will shape itself.

To sum up. Our broad conclusions thus are that although the war has caused a great disturbance of local industry, greater in proportion to the industry of the localities which are the seat of war than any similar disturbance upon record, yet the war altogether has not caused any great economic disturbance because it has really been small in proportion to the resources of the British Empire. The disturbance of the local industries again has been compensated, except to the Uitlanders expelled from the Transvaal, by the benefits which the local communities have derived from the expenditure on the war itself in their midst, that expenditure taking place not at their own expense but at the expense of an outside power. The whole circumstances are such as to bring to light and emphasize the enormous strength of modern communities. We are writing thus of a war which involves a contest between from 50,000 to 60,000 men on one side, probably the best militia which has ever appeared in the field for defensive purposes, and about 200,000 men on the other side, by far the largest army which England at any time has put into the field. Our operations in Wellington's Peninsula campaigns, the largest military operations ever before undertaken by a British army, employed not more than from 30,000 to 40,000 English troops, and at Waterloo itself these troops were not more than about 30,000. Both in the Crimea and in India at the Mutiny we had not much more than these numbers of English troops engaged. The present scale of operations is thus beyond precedent in our history; yet we cannot but write as to the expense in the way we have done. All things considered the war is really a small one as far as the resources of the mother-country and the Empire are concerned. The question of questions for the future must undoubtedly be that of our position with reference to the more serious possibilities of defence which the development of other great powers of an essentially military disposition may force upon us before long.

XXIII.

THE RELATIVE GROWTH OF THE COMPONENT PARTS OF THE EMPIRE.[1]

THE object of the present paper is to call attention to the growth of the Empire in detail—to compare the progress in one part with the progress in another, and to make a few comments on the ideas thus suggested. The growth of the Empire in the mass is a familiar idea, but the nature of the growth will be better understood if we also take the different parts by themselves.

For this purpose a few tables have been prepared, and are put in the Appendix. These deal with the area, population, revenue, imports and exports, and other particulars of the main divisions of the Empire in a recent year—1897, where possible—compared with 1871. A still shorter period would have been preferable, as the object is to throw light upon the sort of progress in the Empire that is actually going on; but 1871 to some extent marks a new era, coinciding with the Franco-German War and other events about that time, which have altered greatly all international relations. It is also a census year, and there is no very good date, subsequently, which could have been the starting-point for a comparison. It may be remarked parenthetically that although statistics are made use of, this is not a paper of statistical research. Well-known figures only are used, extracted from such every-day publications as the "Statistical Abstracts for the

[1] Read at a meeting of the Royal Colonial Institute, February, 1899. For Appendix see Journal of the Institute of that date.

United Kingdom and the Colonies," the "Colonial Office List," and the "Statesman's Year-book." The ordinary figures are simply rearranged under divisions to bring out the main features of the Empire as they appear in a general survey, and to show where, and of what nature, the increase has been.

The Empire, as thus viewed, is a territory of 11,500,000 square miles, or 13,000,000, if we include Egypt and the Soudan, which have been added *pour mémoire* to the Tables; and in this territory there is a population of about 407,000,000, which would be increased to over 420,000,000 if Egypt and the Soudan were included—a population about one-fourth of the whole population of the earth. Of this population again, about 50,000,000 are of English speech and race, the ruling race—in the United Kingdom, in British North America and in Australasia; and the remaining 350,000,000 to 370,000,000 are the various subject races, for the most part in India and Africa, the proportion of the governing to the subject races being thus about one-eighth. (South Africa is an exception, being self-governing, with a white minority in power, but with the black subjects greatly predominating in numbers.)

The increase in area and population in this Empire, again, excluding Egypt and the Soudan, amounts, since 1871, to 2,854,000 square miles of area, or more than one-fourth of the whole, and to 125,000,000 of population, which is also more than one-fourth of the whole. The increase of the ruling race included in this population amounts to about 12,500,000, or about one-fourth of the number in 1897; and the increase in the subject races is 112,000,000, or nearly one-third the numbers in 1897. The increase in these subject races is largely, but by no means exclusively, due to annexation.

The present revenue of the different parts of this Empire added together amounts to £257,653,000, and the imports and exports to £1,375,000,000, not to mention other particulars of an economic nature. The increase since 1871 also amounts to £115,143,000 for revenue, or more than 40 per cent. of the present total, while the increase in imports and exports amounts to £428,000,000, or about one-third of the present total. The latter increase is perhaps greater in appearance than it really is, as all the figures are not reduced to a gold valuation, those for India for instance being in tens of rupees; but it has also to be considered that the gold valuation itself, owing to the increase in the purchasing power of gold since 1871, prevents the real growth of almost any economic factor being fairly shown by values only. The import and export figures are also subject to the observation that the trade of each part of the Empire is largely with other parts of the Empire, so that for some purposes they ought not to be added together. I refer here especially to Australasia, where the totals would be less if the intercolonial trade were to be omitted. But this observation does not affect our present comparisons. The revenue of the self-governing English portions of the Empire also amounts to £145,000,000, having increased £60,000,000 since 1871, and the imports and exports of the same portions to £1,036,000,000, having increased £247,000,000 since 1871. The revenue of the states of subject races also amounts to £112,000,000, having increased £55,000,000 since 1871, and the imports and exports to £338,000,000, having increased £181,000,000 since 1871. What has been said above as to the difference between nominal and real increase applies, however, specially to this separation between the self-governing parts of the Empire and the other portions. The increase in the non-self-governing portions of the Empire would be less by comparison if the gold valuation were uniformly followed.

Such is a very summary account of the tables which thus bring out the proportion of the British race in the Empire to the subject races and states, and the relative rate of increase, which is on the whole, on account largely of recent annexations, rather greater among the subject races and states than in the English portions. There are, however, many other points to be noticed, including the different rates of growth of the different portions of the white and the subject races respectively.

The division of the tables, it will be observed, is into seven groups. The first three are the United Kingdom, British North America, and Australasia, which constitute the English-speaking self-governing portions of the Empire. Next comes (4) Southern Africa in a group by itself, which is generally placed along with the portions of the Empire consisting of subject races, but which is really of a mixed character, being self-governing politically but peopled for the most part by coloured races among whom the white population is only a small minority. Next we have (5) the other portions of the main land of Africa belonging to the Empire, (6) India, and (7) the miscellaneous possessions of the Empire, which are further classed in seven subdivisions, according to their geographical situation, and which, with the exception of one or two detached positions, comprise a coloured population. The effect of this arrangement is that the Empire appears to consist mainly of three English-speaking portions—the United Kingdom, British North America, and Australasia; of one mixed portion, as yet small in population, the Colonies and territories in South Africa; and of three other portions where we have subject races to deal with and only a small white population, the Empire in Africa, the Empire in India, and the various miscellaneous possessions all over the world. We begin with an account of the relative rate of progress in the English-speaking portions of the Empire.

As to population in these English-speaking portions we have the following comparison, there having been no change here in the area since 1871:

Population of United Kingdom, British North America, and Australasia in 1871 and 1897 compared.

[In millions.]

	1871.	1897.	Increase.	
			Amount.	Per cent.
United Kingdom	31.85	40.20	8.35	26
British North America	3.84	5.40	1.56	41
Australasia	1.98	4.48	2.50	126
Totals	37.67	50.08	12.41	33

The percentage increase in the United Kingdom is thus much smaller than in the two great groups of English-speaking Colonies. It is only 26 per cent., whereas in North America it is 41 per cent., and in Australasia it is no less than 126 per cent. in little more than a quarter of a century. It is Australasia, therefore, which has been going ahead among the English portions of the Empire. In amount, however, the increase of population is still much larger in the United Kingdom than in the other two parts of the Empire, the numbers added there being 8,350,000 as compared with 1,560,000 only in British North America and 2,500,000 in Australasia. Relatively also the United Kingdom remains predominant, the numbers of the people there being 40,000,000 out of a total of 50,000,000.

A similar comparison as to revenue gives the following results:

Revenue of United Kingdom, British North America, and Australasia in 1871 and 1897 compared.

[In millions sterling.]

	1871.	1897.	Increase.	
			Amount.	Per cent.
United Kingdom	69.9	106.6	36.7	52
British North America	4.4	8.1	3.7	86
Australasia	11.7	30.9	19.2	165
Totals	86.0	145.6	59.6	69

The increase of revenue is thus in all cases greater than the increase of population, but the same relative position is maintained by the three different portions of the Empire. The percentage increase is again greater in British North America and Australasia than in the United Kingdom, but the amount of the increase is much the largest in the United Kingdom. The comparison is subject to the observations that new taxes may have been imposed in the interval in different degrees, and that on a very strict comparison changes in the form of the accounts may have to be allowed for, the figures on the surface thus requiring rectification. But these are niceties which can hardly be followed up in so general a comparison: the broad conclusions do not seem to be affected.

Next we have a comparison of imports and exports:

Imports and exports of United Kingdom, British North America, and Australasia in 1871 and 1897 compared.

[In millions sterling.]

	1871.	1897.	Increase.	
			Amount.	Per cent.
United Kingdom . . .	686	843	157	23
British North America . .	38	55	17	45
Australasia	65	138	73	112
Totals	789	1,036	247	31

Here again the increase is larger in percentage in British North America and Australasia than in the United Kingdom, but the amount of the increase is much the largest in the United Kingdom, while the aggregate foreign trade of the United Kingdom is four-fifths of the total. The percentage increase is also largest in Australasia, corresponding to the increase of population.

It is unnecessary to carry the comparison through the other factors mentioned in the tables, although it would be of obvious interest to contrast the reduction of debt in the United Kingdom with the increase in the Colonies, and to bring out similar points. The general character of the growth is sufficiently indicated by the facts stated. The Colonies progress at a greater rate than the Mother Country, as their increase of population is greater, this increase being specially manifest in Australasia; but the growth in the United Kingdom in amount is still much the largest, and, in such a matter as the increase or reduction of debt, the comparison is rather to the advantage of the Mother Country, though there need be no question of the necessity and usefulness of the borrowing itself.

A similar set of tables for the subject states of the Empire, including South Africa for the sake of convenience, would give the following results:

Population in subject states in the British Empire in 1871 and 1897 compared.

[In millions.]

	1871.	1897.	Increase.	
			Amount.	Per cent.
South Africa	1.0	3.75	2.75	275
Other parts of Africa . .	0.54	33.69	33.15	—
India	238.60	311.50	72.90	31
Miscellaneous Possessions	4.64	8.39	3.75	81
Totals	244.78	357.33	112.55	46

Revenue of subject states in British Empire in 1871 and 1897 compared.

[In millions sterling.]

	1871.	1897.	Increase.	
			Amount.	Per cent.
South Africa	0.9	9.7	8.7	910
Other parts of Africa . .	0.2	0.8	0.6	370
India	51.4	94.1	42.7	83
Miscellaneous Possessions	3.9	7.2	3.3	84
Totals	56.4	111.8	55.3	98

Imports and exports of subject states in British Empire in 1871 and 1897 compared.

[In millions sterling.]

	1871.	1897.	Increase.	
			Amount.	Per cent.
South Africa	7.7	47.2	39.5	513
Other parts of Africa . .	2.5	10.8	8.3	332
India	97.5	198.9	101.4	104
Miscellaneous Possessions	49.5	81.2	31.7	64
Totals	157.2	338.1	180.9	115

The broad facts here are that the increases, with the exception of the "miscellaneous possessions," are greater than in the English-speaking portions of the Empire. The percentages and amounts of increase are both very large, and speak for themselves. This is no doubt explained, as already mentioned, by the increase of the Empire through annexation; but some other changes are also significant. Attention may be drawn to the following points:

1. The great increase in South Africa. The increase in population shows a very large percentage, but the numbers are still small, about 3,000,000 only. In this portion of the Empire, however, although the population is only mixed, the increase of revenue and of imports and exports is larger in proportion than anywhere else, and the totals are significant. The revenue from being less than a million in 1871 is now about £10,000,000, an increase of over 900 per cent., and the imports and exports, including bullion and specie, from being just under £8,000,000 in 1871 are now £47,000,000. Of course, we must beware of putting too much stress upon such figures when we compare them with others. The imports and exports, we may suppose, are swollen in part by a portion of what is really transit trade of the Orange Free State and the

Transvaal. But, making all deductions, large figures would still be left. Economically, also, the Orange Free State and the Transvaal are a part of South Africa, developed largely by British capital and enterprise, and British settlers. We should get still larger figures of revenue and of imports and exports if we were to include them, and not much larger figures of population. This great advance of South Africa is one of the main features which are shown by the general comparison we have been making.

2. The remarkable growth of India. The figures here comprise the whole population of India, including the native states, as to all intents and purposes they form part of the Empire. The magnitude of the increase of population will not fail to strike the most inattentive. There are now more than 300,000,000 of people for whose government we are responsible in India; and of these, 73,000,000 have been added, mainly by the ordinary growth of population, since 1871. One is almost staggered by such figures, especially when it is remembered that the resources hardly grow in proportion, and that there are many millions in this vast multitude in a state of the extremest poverty.

At first sight the figures of the growth of revenue and growth of imports and exports in India appear to signify a growth of resources in much larger proportion than population; but unfortunately this conclusion cannot be accepted, owing to the explanation already given as to the figures not being reduced to a gold valuation. Were the gold valuation applied to the later years the apparent increase both of revenue and of imports and exports would be less than it is. What better figure could be substituted it is not so easy to say. The increase in other parts of the Empire may be less than would have been the case if they had not had the gold valuation. Without going into such niceties, it may be sufficient to note that the apparent growth in the revenue, and in the imports and exports of India, is not to be taken literally, especially in a comparison with other parts of the Empire.

3. The comparative smallness of our miscellaneous possessions, the scattered possessions we hold all over the world exclusive of the main divisions already described, and the want of progress shown in some of them by comparison. All told, the long list of small possessions enumerated in group 7 only gives a population of not quite 8,500,000, and if we were to exclude Ceylon, which ought perhaps to be included with India, the population would be almost exactly 5,000,000, or about an eightieth part only of the whole Empire. Although in the group generally there is remarkable increase since 1871—81 per cent. in population, 84 per cent. in revenue, and 64 per cent. in imports and exports—we have to consider that we are here dealing with small amounts only, and not with the large figures of other parts of the Empire. The figures of the imports and exports would, however, be larger than they are if the imports and exports of such places as Hong Kong, Gibraltar, and Malta, whose trade is a depôt and transit trade, could be properly dealt with for such a comparison as the present.

In spite of the general increase in the group also, we have to note one or two unfavourable symptoms among the older Colonies. I refer especially to the subdivision (*c*) of group 7, and principally the West Indian Islands and British Guiana. In this group there is a large percentage increase of population amounting to 45 per cent.; the revenue also shows an increase amounting to 56 per cent.; but when we turn to the imports and exports we find the increase in the imports to be 7 per cent. only, and that there is an actual decrease in the exports of 14 per cent. In British Guiana there is a decrease of 32 per cent. in the imports and of 35 per cent. in the exports. These figures tell their own tale, which is confirmed by the figures as to growth of debt and other particulars. This is almost the one unfavourable feature in the picture of general progress in the British Empire which the statistics present to us.

4. The addition of an African Empire. In most of the figures to-night we have had to deal mainly with the progress of population on the same area or with small additions to the area. In the English-speaking portions of the Empire this is conspicuously the case. It is also for the most part the same in India and other parts of the Empire, with the single exception of the African Continent. Here, on the contrary, whether in South Africa, or Central and North Africa or West Africa, or Egypt and the Soudan, we have to deal for the most part with new areas added to our responsibilities, the whole constituting already an area of about 3,000,000 square miles, with an estimated population of 34,000,000 if we exclude Egypt and the Soudan, and an area of over 4,000,000 square miles with a population of 50,000,000 if we include the latter. The African Empire thus begun is no small rival to the Indian Empire itself. The India we possessed at the beginning of the century was not much greater in population, I think, than the population we already govern in Africa, while the conditions are such that the growth of population in our African dominions, considering what the population has been in former times in the Soudan, is likely to be extremely rapid. The nucleus of this Empire in revenue and trade, looking at Egypt on the one side, and South Africa on the other, as well as at West Africa, is also considerable. When the events of the present generation pass into history the magnitude of the achievement will become even more evident than it is now. We can hardly realize as yet the responsibilities and possibilities involved, or how much the change affects our general position in the world.

This general survey of progress in the last quarter of a century leaves no doubt on one point at least—the interest and picturesqueness of the progress of the

Empire. Whether we look at the varying developments in the purely English parts of the Empire, the magnitude of the growth at home, the increase at a greater rate in British North America, or the increase at a greater rate still in Australasia; or at such a phenomenon as the rapid development of South Africa where the white races are actual colonists in association with the subject races; or at the vast growth of India; or at the beginning of a new Empire in Africa; or at the special incidents not so favourable which are happening to our older possessions in the West Indies; to which we may add the latest development of all in the Klondike, of which we had so striking an account from Miss Shaw a fortnight ago, but which is so new a development that the figures for British North America are not yet affected as those of South Africa have been —we find ourselves in possession of an Empire in which a great deal is happening, and with which the fortunes of the human race itself are very largely concerned. In whatever way such an Empire has come to exist, the influence it must have on the various peoples, and especially on those who have anything to do with the government or with the administration of large affairs must be enormous; and on the whole, we must assume, beneficial, clearing the mind of prejudices and narrow bias of every sort, and proving to all how much such an Empire must be self-developing because no single mind could pretend to mould so vast an organism. It is an education of itself to belong to such an Empire, and to help, in however small a degree, in carrying out the common work.

One or two special questions cannot but be suggested. The first of all is involved in the division between the English parts of the Empire and the states of subject race on which I have insisted. Is the central force of the Empire, the power to hold it together, increasing as rapidly as the Empire generally? The question of force is unavoidable in dealing with such a problem, and it would be a serious matter if the Empire were to be increasing beyond the force of the race by which it is held together.

The figures we have had to-night, however, supply the answer. The increase of the Empire in population altogether has been 44 per cent., and would be a little more if we included Egypt and the Soudan; and the increase in the English parts of the Empire is 33 per cent. Numerically this implies a growth of the subject populations generally in excess of the growth of the governing race. On the other side, however, has to be reckoned the enormous growth of the governing race in resources. The increase of revenue and of business, apart from annexations, is most remarkable, in reality, in the English portions of the Empire; and if we were to go more into detail, and include such elements as the growth of the shipping fleet of the Empire, this relative growth of the English portions of the Empire would be still more remarkable. Apart also from the special additions to the Empire by way of annexation, the growth of the governing race appears to keep pace with that of the subject races. Large as is the growth of population in India, the most important part of our subject Empire, the percentage increase is only 31 per cent., which includes a certain amount of annexation, while the percentage increase in the governing races without any annexation is 33 per cent. Looking at all the probabilities we may consider it fairly certain that this relative growth will continue. The proportion of the governing race to the subject races, barring annexations, will rather increase than diminish.

The serious fact in this question of force to hold the Empire together is, however, not the internal position, but the position of the Empire with reference to other nations, on which, perhaps, one may be allowed to say a word. Very great changes have been occurring in the world outside our Empire, as well as within the Empire itself, and our position may be thereby affected, although we are stronger internally than before.

In one respect we are clearly better off than before. The great competitor we had at the beginning of the century and have had until recent years is France. At the beginning of the century, apart from the additions made to it by the Napoleonic wars, France was a State of about 26,000,000 of people, occupying the most fertile territory in Europe, and well advanced in arts and manufactures. This was our rival at a time when we had virtually a population of 11,000,000 only, that being the population of Great Britain when Ireland was still a serious burden and in no way a help. Now the population in France is very much the same as the population of the United Kingdom, and we have all the white population in other parts of the Empire to the good. Thus, from being a state of less than half the population of France we have become a state very much superior in the numbers of population.

The development of our resources has also been much more rapid than that of France, so that altogether the change in our relative positions, materially speaking, is something enormous. As far as rivalry with France is concerned, therefore, our position in the world is much better for holding a Colonial Empire than it was in the past times of our history.

The changes that are going on from day to day and from year to year are also to our advantage. While France has very much the same white population now that it had twenty or twenty-five years ago, there has been in the same time an addition, as we have seen, of nearly 12,000,000, or more than one-fourth of the population of France itself, to the white population of our Empire. The next twenty or twenty-five years in all probability will witness a similar difference in our favour.

France at the same time has not strengthened but weakened itself by the addition of a vast Empire of subject races, especially in Africa, without a good self-governing or self-supporting possession amongst them. With a stationary white population she takes on herself the burden of a large Empire.

But, while our position relatively to France appears to have thus changed enormously to our advantage, we have further to consider that whereas at the beginning of the century, and even as late as twenty-five years ago, we had no rivals in the business of colonizing or of over-sea Empire, the position is now altogether changed. One of the greatest changes is made by the rise of the German Empire and its recent disposition to go into the business of colonizing and holding possessions abroad. Germany, from being an aggregate of divided states with a population of less than 20,000,000 at the beginning of the century and with no prospects of colonial ambitions, has now become a united empire with a population of between 50,000,000 and 60,000,000, nearly one-third of which population has been added to it by the natural increase arising from the excess of births over deaths during the last twenty-five years. If, then, we have gone ahead of France, it is to find at the end of the term that a new power has arisen with which we may have to deal, and a power more formidable than France.

Russia, in the same way, which was almost out of the reckoning as a world-power at the beginning of the century, and which, even twenty-five years ago, was hardly in a position to interfere with us in any part of the world, has developed very rapidly by means of its railway extensions and otherwise, and is now a great power with a growing population touching the British Empire in India and touching our interests in China and elsewhere. This power also has a population of 130,000,000, mainly a white population, and the addition to the numbers since 1870 appears, from the official statistics, to be close on 60,000,000, an enormous increase if we consider it to arise mainly from the natural increase of population and not from annexation. Possibly part of the increase is apparent, being explained by the improvement in the method of taking the census; but there is no doubt as to a huge increase. I should not consider the growth of

Russia to be of so serious a nature in many respects as the growth of Germany, because Germany is much more advanced educationally and otherwise than Russia; but the people of Russia have of late years gone largely into industrial and manufacturing pursuits, and, if this internal development goes on, as it seems likely to do, a rapid increase in the material force of Russia and in its mobility for purposes of external action is to be looked for.

Lastly, we have to consider the United States, where the increase of population has been so remarkable for more than a century, and where the development of industrial and manufacturing power internally has also been greater than any similar development that has ever been witnessed. This state too has just within the past year definitely adopted a policy which brings it into action as a colonizing power. The population of the United States, mainly a population of the same character as the white population of the British Empire itself, is, moreover, between 70,000,000 and 80,000,000, or much greater than the white population of the British Empire, increasing also at rather a more rapid rate.

The general effect, then, is that while we held our Colonial Empire in former times with no other rival than that of France capable of challenging our possessions, we have now France in a position of inferiority as compared with what it was, but at the same time we have three other powers—Germany, Russia, and the United States—who may also have to be reckoned with. Externally, then, our position is somewhat different from what it has been in former times.

As the net result I do not believe that, for the present at least, the British Empire is in any real danger. Each power with whom we have to deal has its own difficulties, and a coalition of powers seems unlikely in the last degree, their interests being so entirely different. At the same time, all of them, excepting perhaps Germany, have for the present a large amount of internal organization to undertake. The Colonial Empire of France, for instance, is by comparison almost entirely undeveloped. Russia has still an enormous amount of work to do to fill up decently the huge vacant places within its ring-fence, and which are capable of being filled by white population. The United States, again, are just beginning their colonial policy, and have a serious work before them to adapt their Constitution to the new conditions imposed by such a policy. Still the condition of our Empire, looking at the existence of all these powers, is seriously different from what it has been, and the next two or three generations will have much to do in adjusting our relations with co-ordinate powers.

Another question suggested by a review of the Empire is the economic one presented by a state like India, which has an enormous growth of population mainly dependent on agriculture, and where there are some signs of an excessive growth of multitudes who have barely the means for the scanty subsistence which is aimed at and who are always on the verge of starvation. Amidst our great success in the development of population and wealth throughout the Empire, in which there is so much cause for pride and rejoicing, the reverse of the shield which we find to exist in the growth at the same time of a vast population on the verge of starvation ought also to be looked at. It appears to be the one great economic difficulty which the governing races will have to deal with, and which is beginning to embarrass them. In assuming an Empire like that we have taken upon ourselves in Africa we do not know whether we may not have enormously added to such embarrassments, which consist at bottom in the fact that it is comparatively easy to produce a *Pax Britannica* in the regions we undertake to govern, and thereby promote a huge growth of population by the removal of what Malthus called the preventive checks; but it is quite another thing to secure a more rapid increase of the means of subsistence than the increase of the population itself such as has been secured in the English portions of the Empire. The moral is that our position as a governing race remains not altogether satisfactory so long as we have not created such life and energy in the subject races that an improvement in quality and power of production per head may accompany the increase of numbers. In India such an improvement has taken place among many classes of the native community. But it is not quite universal, and it does not go deep enough down among the lower classes. Something more is wanted, and we should not despair of that something more being added, if the governing races have it made clear to them how vital and urgent the problem may become for the general welfare of the Empire. A natural flow of capital to India and other parts of the Empire for purposes of internal development, and the cultivation of a capacity to use capital among the native races themselves, are, in fact, indispensable if the Empire is to prosper. As yet on this head the progress we have made is far from what it should be.

The constitutional changes which the growth of the Empire must render necessary, make another question suggested by such a review as we have taken to-night. Although force is not wanting to keep the Empire together, the drain upon the energies of the Parliament and Cabinet at Westminster increases with all the vast growth of population and resources. Already we have two ministers, the Secretary of State for India and the Secretary of State for the Colonies, occupied with the affairs of our possessions abroad, and the departments which these ministers attend to have long been increasing. The Foreign Minister has also been entangled in Egypt and elsewhere with what is in fact Colonial administration. It is quite on the cards, I should say, that before long we may have a separate Secretary of State for Africa, or for a part of it like South Africa, so urgent and absorbing may become the administration of what is really another India. All this will also make an additional claim on the energies of an overworked Parliament. Some considerable change must accordingly take place in order to relieve the central Government, the business of administration being reduced to a system, and the review of Parliament being applied in a more systematic way. With this is connected the more general problem of the federation of the Empire, by which the self-governing Colonies would share the responsibilities of Empire with the Mother Country—a problem, however, which is now so familiar that it need only be mentioned in passing as clearly suggested by the review we have had before us. The announcement just made of the success achieved in promoting the Federation of the Australian Colonies is of good omen for the larger Confederation of the Empire to which we must look forward.

The practical issue to which these considerations lead is the necessity for all agreeing to make the most of the Empire in the way of development and organization. I speak as one having so great a sense of the difficulties and dangers of a great Empire that if there had been free choice in the matter at any time I should have deprecated the conquest of India and other conquests which have made the Empire what it is. But the choice has not been quite free, and especially it is not open to us to give up any part of the Empire at will without making so great an alteration of our position in the world that our freedom and independence at home would be endangered. As the worst thing possible is to halt between two opinions, we must accordingly, even if we dislike Empire, make the best of our position. We are in for this great Empire, and there is an end of the matter. On all sides then, on little Englanders as well as great Englanders, the main idea of policy should now be to knit the different parts of the Empire together so that they should support each other and support the whole. There must be a common scheme of defence; there must be a provision of adequate force in each part of the Empire according to that scheme; communications must be rapidly improved. It would be out of place for me to suggest or discuss any detailed scheme, but perhaps the study of the composition of the Empire in the most general way, and of what the growth has been, may assist the public comprehension of the plans which those who are responsible produce.

[NOTE.—Since this paper was written the Empire has been enlarged by the annexation of the Transvaal and the Orange River colonies; but important as these acquisitions are the total figures would not consequently require much change. The resulting addition to the population, especially the white population, of the Empire, forms but a small percentage of the totals here dealt with; while the import and export figures are mostly included in those of Natal and Cape of Good Hope, through which the trade passed as above explained. We are still waiting for an Imperial scheme of defence as suggested at the close of the paper.—1904.]

XXIV.

THE STANDARD OF STRENGTH FOR OUR ARMY; A BUSINESS ESTIMATE.[1]

ONE of the difficulties of the discussions on Army Reform is how to make a bridge between the experts and the public whose support is invited by reformers. As regards the Navy, the public have been impressed by the idea that our Navy must equal in apparent magnitude the navies of any other two Powers. This idea is of course imperfect, as it may be necessary to have a navy equal to those of any other three or four Powers, and as it is also obvious that apparent may be a very different thing from real magnitude, and the public are not good judges on the point. The idea serves, nevertheless, as a pivot of discussion, and gives the public something tangible to go for. As regards the Army, however, there is nothing analogous. Should we have an army equal to a third or a fourth or any other proportion of the army of any one of the great military Powers; and if so, which? or should we have an army on the scale of one of the military Powers themselves? or should we have the magnitude of our Army fixed in some totally different way? There is the farther difficulty as to the magnitude of the army required on a peace footing and on a war footing respectively. This difficulty does not seem to exist as regards the great military Powers which are free from little wars, and whose armies are always potentially convertible from a peace to a war footing in so short

[1] From the "Nineteenth Century" of 1901.

an interval as to make the war footing the only one of real importance to be considered. But it is an unavoidable difficulty as regards the English Army, whose peace duties include little wars which are almost annual in their occurrence, and a constant state of preparedness for such wars. In what way, then, is a standard for the English Army to be arrived at, first on a peace footing, and next on a partial or full war footing, and what is the interval of time to be contemplated in arriving at the latter condition either in part or fully? It is to further an understanding on some of these points between the experts and the public that the present paper is written.

The starting-point of the discussion must, of course, be the preponderance of the Navy. The condition of the British Empire without command of the sea is hardly conceivable. We should then be at the mercy of any Power which had such command. Our communications could not be maintained. We should be liable to blockade at home and to the ruin of our foreign commerce, nor could we keep India or any other dependency by force. We should be no worse off perhaps than Holland, which is in no condition to defend its independence or its empire against neighbouring States; but the condition of Holland is obviously, for many reasons, not a desirable one, while it may be doubted whether small States like Holland would be so numerous and prosperous as they are if there were not Powers like England capable of maintaining public international law against freebooting Powers. We start, then, with the idea of an army to be used in conjunction with a preponderant navy. What are the purposes for which such an army is required, and what numbers are needed first on a peace and then on a war footing?

The *first* use of an army is for purposes of defence against internal commotion. This statement may surprise some people who think of police only when questions of internal order are concerned and have not for many years witnessed the soldier in evidence in civil commotion or insurrection. But we shall have no true idea of what armies exist for unless we begin with this, perhaps in importance the highest, function of an army. The ultimate guarantee of civil order is, in fact, the soldier. The unarmed policeman is nothing without him, and no one can foresee how necessary the soldier may at any moment become. We have a standing illustration in the case of Ireland, where a police force is maintained which is really a military force, and with a large number of Regular soldiers behind it. Another illustration is just being given in South Africa, where the new police force is really being armed and organized as a military body with Regular forces behind it. An illustration of a different kind was afforded by the great civil war in America. If the United States had been able to dispose at the beginning of the war of a Regular army of 100,000 or even 50,000 men, there would have been no civil war. The losses and miseries of four years' civil strife, with its enormous waste of human lives, would have been entirely prevented. It is not cheap for a nation, therefore, even on the score of internal policy, to be without an irresistible army for all purposes of home defence. I put down, then, as the first object of an army, the maintenance of civil order in the State.

There is a special reason for mentioning this, as it is not unconnected with the problem or ideal of a general disarmament, of which one hears so much. The problem is quite insoluble, for the simple reason, among others, that internal conditions are everywhere different. Having regard to their own home conditions, the most orderly and law-abiding peoples might perhaps disarm completely, or nearly so, though the danger of so doing, as we have seen, was only too strongly illustrated in the United States. But if they disarm they are immediately at a disadvantage internationally in dealing with States which are obliged by internal necessities to maintain large armies—States like France, or Austria-Hungary, or Russia, and many others. Thus the existence of

States liable to internal disorder and which must maintain large armies initiates a competition in arming internationally which there is no means of getting rid of. We are saved from the international competition, or think we are saved, by a preponderant Navy; but we must not deplore the fact itself as if it were altogether preventible. I doubt if we can say that the expense of the additional armaments undertaken by some Governments beyond what is necessary for internal defence is in actual conditions a great or serious burden.

The *second* object of an army in an empire like that of England appears to be the garrisoning of the mother country so as to prevent raids upon fortified positions or depôts or commercial centres, or even raids of a wider range, at the outbreak of a war, and in the interval which may elapse before our preponderance at sea is converted into overwhelming superiority in fact by the defeat and destruction of the enemy's fleets. What kind of raid we should be prepared against, assuming our actual preponderance at sea, is of course a question of detail; but judging by the experience of history, and allowing for the greater mobility now given by steam as compared with the facility of movement formerly, I should say that we ought always to have in view in a great war with a naval Power the possibility of a descent of 20,000 or 30,000 men upon Ireland—in a war, for instance, between us and a Power like France, which has numberless soldiers and a considerable fleet at its disposal. Up to the limit stated, the launching against us of an expeditionary force which is prepared to face the prospect of being cut off or blockaded, for the sake of striking a serious blow and shaking the nerve of the English Government, seems always possible by way of surprise even without command of the sea by our enemy. Perhaps twenty large ships altogether, perhaps ten only, would suffice for the whole expedition, which might save bulky transport, for instance, by relying for a beginning of success on assistance in the shape of transport to be obtained in Ireland itself.[1] A similar expedition might suffice to punish any weakness of which we might be guilty in leaving places like Woolwich or Chatham or Portsmouth or any other of our stations insufficiently protected by land. The expeditionary force would know it was only sent on a forlorn hope, with almost the certainty of its being cut off; but that would not weigh, probably, with the Government sending it, if great destruction and loss were meanwhile effected. The calculation might also be that our preponderance at sea would not, in fact, be converted into overwhelming superiority—everything is doubtful in war until actual experiment is made—and then an expedition of this sort, properly aimed, might assist the enemy largely in the main contest itself. The army at home, as wars may break out suddenly, must therefore always be prepared to meet raids of considerable magnitude, and not merely to defeat them in the end, but to make them so difficult that they will not even begin to succeed.

The *third* object for which an army is required is the garrisoning of the positions necessary to the Empire abroad, the garrisoning of places like Malta, Gibraltar, and Aden, necessary as fortified naval depôts and coaling stations, and the garrisoning of dependencies like India, Egypt, and South Africa both against internal tumults and raids from the outside. We are responsible for defending our Empire abroad as well as for home defence; and although we are here assisted by various local resources the organizing of Imperial defence generally rests with the mother country, which must also very largely supply white troops from home, if it does not always pay for them. The remarks applicable to the possibility of a raid upon our home defences appear to be applicable here. Vital coaling stations may be assailed by small expeditionary forces landed for the purpose, as well as attacked by sea, with the

[1] Some of the transports in the South African war carried 3,000 men each over ten times the distance which would have to be traversed by a French expedition to Ireland.

additional temptation, hardly present in the case of an expedition to the United Kingdom itself, that the force may be able to get away safely after performing its work of destruction. The ambition of foreign Powers may fly at even higher game. If an expeditionary force, notwithstanding our preponderant Navy, may effect a landing by surprise in Ireland or even in Great Britain itself, a similar force apparently might be landed in Egypt or South Africa, or some other vulnerable part of our wide Empire, by a Power like France or Germany. The threat of a number of attempts may withdraw the fleet and ships we could oppose from the quarter where the real surprise may be tried. Curiously enough, history itself supplies the record of a landing by surprise on the part of the French in Egypt at a time when the English fleet was preponderant in the Mediterranean and when Nelson was on the look-out for the French expedition. What has happened before may happen again, and the change made since Nelson's time by the substitution of steamers for sailing ships appears all in favour of the possibility of surprise. A foreign surprise of this sort may appear even more tempting to an enemy than a raid upon Ireland or Great Britain. The temporary possession of Egypt by an enemy would upset all our arrangements for Imperial defence generally, and the calculation would be that much might happen before we were in a position to send another expedition to Egypt to restore our power. It was nearly two years after the French landed in Egypt in 1799 before we were able to land a force to dispossess them. But whether in Egypt or elsewhere, our widely scattered Empire is clearly liable to surprise at some point, and the surprise may be serious if we have not at all necessary points suitable and adequate garrisons. The provision of such garrisons, then, is one of the main duties of an English army in time of peace.

I have spoken only of the possibility of raids by sea, as that is the main matter, having regard to the position of the great military Powers who may be our enemies. But of course there is a possibility of raids by land as well, as our Indian experience tells us. Happily, the enemies who may raid us by land at any point are mostly insignificant, but the possibilities are not to be altogether overlooked. They reinforce *pro tanto* the necessity for strong garrisons at all vulnerable points in time of peace.

The *fourth* object for which an army is required appears to be to repel a possible invasion at home—not a mere raid only, but a serious invasion. The opinion is sometimes expressed, and there is a great deal of force in it, that we have hardly to concern ourselves with a serious invasion, as the loss of command of the sea which would render invasion possible would mean our complete destruction as a Power, without the necessity of invasion at all. We should then be liable to blockade, and a strict blockade would mean our ruin. After much consideration, I have come to the conclusion that a condition of things might arise in which a strict blockade would not follow the defeat of our battle fleets at sea, and invasion might be resorted to instead by the successful enemy. The reason is that even after our battle fleets were defeated, supposing that to happen, the blockade of the English coasts by hostile fleets would be a tedious and difficult matter, requiring many ships of a miscellaneous character as well as battleships, which we could probably make a fight against, with our natural maritime superiority, for months and even years, until we were able to challenge once more the enemy's battleships. It might be the case of our fighting an Armada over again. But, while blockade would be difficult or impossible for an enemy, it is not inconceivable that if they had overcome our battle fleets they would be able to command the narrow seas sufficiently to convoy transports bringing enormous forces for the invasion of the country. We might thus be brought in contact on our own soil with the legions of continental Powers. What operations would be possible for an enemy in such circumstances need not be discussed in detail, but the possibility of even two or three hundred thousand men being thrown on our shores in a short time, and kept reinforced, appears not altogether outrageous in the conditions stated. If we are to recover, then, we must be able to defend our home citadel by land, pending the preparation of new fleets.

The *fifth* object we have to keep in view is the possibility of a formidable attack on some part of our Empire by land, which we shall have to meet with large military force. We think of India mostly in such a connection, and of Russia as a possible assailant, as we must always remember that the India we are bound to defend practically includes Afghanistan, with which Russia in Central Asia is conterminous. But there are other possibilities also, of which the recent invasion of our territory in South Africa is an illustration. I cannot help thinking that we are less secure against land attack at other points than we are often assumed to be. When the Fashoda incident occurred, there was no little amusement at the talk in French newspapers of making a land attack on Egypt from Algeria. There was good cause for amusement, as no such attack could be improvised. But, great as the distance is from Algeria to Egypt, is it so certain that, in conditions which are not inconceivable, an attack of this sort, long foreseen and arranged, would be altogether without chances of success such as would encourage adventurous generals and officers? Another possibility is that Turkey in alliance with other Powers might attack Egypt from Asia Minor, as Egypt has so often been attacked in historical times, and our defence might not be so easy. These are only illustrations. An empire with land frontiers like those of the British Empire cannot but need land defence, and those who have charge of the military forces of the Crown must consider all the chances.

A *sixth* object was suggested by Mr. Brodrick in his speech on Army Reform. The Army, it is said, may have to take part in continental warfare by assisting an ally, in which case two or three army corps would be required for a respectable appearance on the scene. With combatants nearly balanced, a force of this sort thrown into the scale by England would possibly have the kind of effect which resulted from the appearance of English troops in the Peninsula in the great war with France; but the use of the English Army in this fashion would arise from diplomatic and military incidents of a peculiar kind, and does not appear a special object to provide for. As the greater includes the less, provision for the other objects stated will secure that we can participate, when required, in a European war.

Having stated the problem in this way, I come to the question of numbers—how many on a peace, how many on a war footing?

It will be obvious from the description above given of the objects of our Army that the peace footing should adequately provide for the first three of these objects, viz., defence against civil commotion; defence against raids by sea on the mother country at the outbreak of war and until our general naval preponderance is converted in fact into unquestioned and overwhelming superiority over the particular enemy engaged against us; and the similar defence of our dependencies and coaling stations and depôts abroad. The essence of security against civil commotion is the provision of a force adequate to prevent any riot becoming a rebellion; and the use of garrisons is to prevent surprise, so that they should be always ready. On the outbreak of war it will be too late to raise new levies and reinforce stations that are inadequately protected. The Army on a peace footing, then, must be equal to the duties described. In addition, the peace army must be a nucleus of force, and must contain an organization enabling it to expand on a war footing for the other purposes contemplated—defence against possible invasion at home in contingencies that are not impossible, defence against serious invasion by land of any part of our extended Empire, and offensive action in certain contingencies against other Powers.

What force, then, is needed on a peace footing to meet these various objects?

I should say, to begin with, that about 30,000 men appear to be necessary, at least, for garrisoning our fortified depôts and fortified commercial centres at home. Portsmouth, Plymouth, Chatham, the Thames, the Mersey, the Tyne, the Clyde, Queenstown, and other places must all have fortifications sufficient to protect them against stray cruisers, and even against stronger attempts by sea, which may become possible by the successful evasion of our fleets. How this can be done with less than 30,000 men, if it can be done with even that number, it is difficult to imagine. Fortifications swallow up men. The Garrison Artillery on the home establishment appears to amount to about 10,000 men, and with Engineers and other troops to supplement them a figure of 30,000 is very soon arrived at. These are all required, let it be repeated, on the peace establishment. Should war break out, the garrisons may perhaps be increased or set free for other work by mobilizing Militia and Volunteers; but the brunt of the outbreak, the defence at the most critical moment, must be borne by the effective garrison actually in existence.

In addition, there should always be a field force at home of 80,000 trained soldiers at least, to guarantee civil order and to meet a descent upon Ireland or a large raid of that description. Half the 80,000, or nearly that number, will apparently be required in Ireland itself, about 30,000 to prevent the scandal that would be caused by any civil commotion, and the remainder being added to make sure that no expeditionary force can effect a successful landing. Many years ago, when I referred to the actual and indispensable garrison of Ireland as being about 30,000, military authorities challenged the statement, holding that although 30,000 soldiers were kept in Ireland, yet this was largely for reasons of convenience, and a garrison of 10,000, it was held, would suffice. I ascertained, however, that in the opinion of the highest civil authorities in Ireland nothing less than 30,000 was considered sufficient, the object being not merely to hold the country with a firm military grip, but to prevent even the beginning of a rising. In putting down 40,000, therefore, as the needful force to be stationed in Ireland for all objects in time of peace, including the stoppage of raids at the outbreak of war, I believe I am not so wide of the mark.[1] The estimate, again, of other 40,000 troops at home, in addition to garrisons, does not seem extravagant. We must be ready in Great Britain against raids at the outbreak of war on at least as great a scale as we are ready in Ireland, and even the chances of civil commotion are not wholly to be overlooked.

Along with the garrisons of fortified places, therefore, we should on this estimate always require at home on a peace footing about 110,000 trained soldiers —30,000 for garrisons, and a field force of 80,000. If we had such a field force it is obvious that incidentally an emergency like the late South African war could be met. The field force could be sent away and reserves of some kind called out to take their place. But equally the force must be there on a peace footing before such a use could be found for it.

I have to call special attention to the phrase "trained soldiers" which I have used. There is a great deal of confusion in these matters, from the way in which, for certain purposes, the numbers on the home establishment of the Regular Army are spoken of. These numbers, by the last estimate, are 155,000, which is 45,000 in excess of the number of trained soldiers required. Unfortunately the 155,000 comprise a vast number of raw recruits and immature youths who cannot be considered fit for service, to the number of perhaps 90,000 altogether. Deducting this 90,000 from

[1] See also the references in the debate on Mr. Brodrick's Resolutions to Mr. Childers's letters at the time of the Majuba business.

the 155,000, we get no more than 65,000, in place of the 110,000 which is the minimum number we ought to have according to the above estimate. But this by the way. I am only calling attention for the moment to a cardinal ambiguity in the Army statistics which is apt to confuse the amateur when politicians are handling the figures, not for the purpose of enlightenment, but in order to throw dust in his eyes.

Next, what should be the peace footing of the Army outside the United Kingdom? Here again it must be remembered that, for the ordinary objects in view, peace footing and war footing are identical expressions, as at the outbreak of war there will be no time, and there may not be time for a certain period afterwards, to call out new forces and send them to the threatened points.

Answering this question, what we find is that, voluntarily or involuntarily, many parts of the Empire are capable of a great deal of self-defence, and do in fact raise forces which can be useful not only on their own territories but elsewhere. Canada and Australia are especially useful in this respect; but there are local defence forces in some of our Crown Colonies as well, while even settlements like Hong Kong and Singapore provide in part for their own defence. The strength already added to the Empire in this way is enormous, and with proper organization would be incalculable. It renders secure, with little or no Imperial effort, a great many commercial centres, depôts, and coaling stations throughout the Empire, and in a serious struggle, while we are preponderant at sea, gives us a large area from which to draw men and supplies. But the Imperial Government itself must contribute to the defence. The garrisons are a very serious matter. Apart from India, we maintain during peace about 55,000 troops in our dependencies, including the garrisons of Gibraltar, Malta, Hong Kong, Capetown and Simon's Bay, etc., etc., and no one can say the numbers are too many. About 40,000 of these garrisons also are English soldiers, notwithstanding all that has been done to replace them in part by troops belonging to tropical races. In India we have or ought to have in normal times an English garrison of 70,000 men in addition to about 125,000 native troops: again another illustration of the local resources which the Empire can draw upon. Assuming for the present that the garrisons of such places as Gibraltar, Malta, Hong Kong, etc., etc., and of the great dependency of India, are generally sufficient on a peace footing—I should be very sorry to believe the contrary—yet there are one or two points in this business of garrisoning the Empire where the normal provision with which our rulers have hitherto been content is apparently inadequate. I would refer especially to South Africa and Egypt. In South Africa in 1899 we had no more than 15,000 troops, and according to the latest War Estimates this is apparently the normal garrison contemplated in future. I cannot help thinking, after the experiences we have had, that this is not business. No doubt South Africa is properly expected to provide largely for its own defence. Hence we are to have such forces as Baden-Powell's police. But a larger garrison of our own would appear to be necessary to make sure that we shall not have to fight another South African war. Instead of 15,000 we ought to have 50,000 men in South Africa for a few years at least, perhaps 100,000, mostly mounted men. There is the more reason for suggesting this as South Africa will obviously be an excellent training ground for the Army, giving plenty of room for manœuvres; while troops there, if they happen to be in excess, will be placed conveniently for transport to the East, or even home, if any emergency should arise. As regards Egypt, what I have said already will have indicated the nature of my apprehension. We have an English garrison in Egypt of 5,000 men only; and it may well be asked, What is this to meet a surprise and a raid by 20,000 men or more, which seems not altogether impossible? Of course there are native Egyptian forces, but precisely one of the dangers to be feared is the nerve of such troops when pitted against a European force, and possibly the existence of treachery at a critical moment. To those who urge the impossibility of even a surprise on Egypt while we are preponderant at sea, it may also be pointed out that the Suez Canal is theoretically neutralised, and foreign troops are continually passing through it; so that at the outbreak of war, in addition to the raiders by force, we might suddenly have upon our hands a few thousand enemy's troops passing through the Canal ostensibly on legitimate business, but suddenly diverted to an attack upon the English position in Egypt. Here, again, is a case for making sure. An addition of 15,000 men to the permanent garrison is apparently required.

Let us see, then, how we stand as regards our Army on a peace footing. The numbers required, exclusive of recruits and exclusive of the native troops used in India and elsewhere, appear to be as follows:

Home—Garrisons of forts, etc.	30,000
„ Field Army	80,000
India	70,000
Other garrisons abroad—actual	40,000
Addition required in South Africa	35,000
Addition required in Egypt	15,000
Total	270,000

To these numbers, moreover, must be added the number of recruits and young soldiers in training required to feed the effective army with drafts. These recruits and young soldiers are untrained or otherwise unfit for active service, but they have to be paid for from the time they enlist. The numbers required with our present system of recruiting must, however, be about 90,000,[1] making the total numbers on our peace estab-

[1] This was practically unquestioned in the recent debates on Mr. Brodrick's Resolutions.

lishment 360,000. This is 90,000 more than are now provided for in the Estimates and on the India establishment; but can it be said that the proposed numbers are at any point excessive? Recollecting what happened in the United States for want of an army, and what happened to ourselves in South Africa two years ago, we can all see how much cheaper it is to maintain a proper force than to run any risks such as we are now doing. Whatever nice calculations we make, we should conform in this matter to the practice of engineers in estimating for works, and add a large percentage for under-estimates and the unforeseen.

We come then to the second question as regards the Army, viz., the numbers on a war footing. Here we have in view the last three objects above mentioned as those for which an English army is maintained, viz., the provision against invasion at home on a large scale, or against a great war abroad on a land frontier, or in support of a European ally. Those who deny the possibility of an invasion of the mother country will at least admit the chance of more serious war elsewhere, so that the practical conclusion is very much the same. No doubt if we retain command of the sea we shall have some time after the outbreak of war to prepare forces for such eventualities, but we shall save much by having a good organization meanwhile, and trained forces in reserve which can be called out in a short time—the quicker the better.

What I should like to see would be first of all a reserve of Regular trained soldiers equal in quality to the 270,000 trained soldiers, exclusive of recruits, who are to constitute, according to the above sketch, the peace army. The numbers of this reserve should also be considerable, at least equal, I should say, to the home field army *plus* half the force we maintain abroad—that is, to about 160,000 men in all. One half of these reserves would replace the field army at home when it was called away for foreign service, and the remainder would not be too many for drafts to maintain the fighting line for a certain time until recruits were sufficiently trained to come to the rescue. Here there is an enormous hiatus in our arrangements. In the current year's Estimates the reserve of the Regular Army appears as 90,000 only, which, according to the testimony of all experts, is far too small. The numbers in the first line, if serious war is contemplated, should be equalled by the numbers behind them who can be called on with certainty and without delay. How we are to get a reserve of trained soldiers may be even a more difficult question than how we are to get an army of trained soldiers on a peace footing to begin with; but we must of course state the problem if it is to be solved at all.

On a complete war footing we may want still larger numbers of Regular soldiers, although the numbers stated, it will be observed, would provide a considerable force either for defence against a great invasion at home or defence against invasion by one of our land frontiers. We should have 80,000 of the field army at home *in esse*, and to that might be added at once another 80,000 drawn from the reserve, still leaving a reserve of 80,000 men behind. An effective field army of 160,000 men with 80,000 behind, apart from recruits and volunteers, would be able to defend a line of over a hundred miles, and thus neutralize a very large invading force, which could only have a narrow space to deploy in, looking to the conditions of harbours which have to be secured as a base of operations. If employed abroad, in India for instance, the 160,000 would bring up the local army, exclusive of native troops, to 230,000, which would again be a considerable force, looking at the line or lines of attack which must necessarily be followed by a land invader. Still we may want more numbers. We may be defeated at sea, and invasion thus rendered possible, while a large part of our field army is locked up in India or elsewhere. The training and discipline of forces beyond the numbers stated appear accordingly to be suggested. And such forces must either form part of the one Regular Army and be trained and disciplined as such, or must be auxiliary forces such as the Militia, Volunteers, and Yeomanry now are, not so fully trained as the Regular soldiers and only to be called out on emergency, but still sufficiently trained to form part of the fighting line.

What should be the numbers of such forces? On this head I should be disposed to accept the promise of Mr. Brodrick that he aims at about 150,000 of Militia and Militia Reserve, 250,000 Volunteers, and 50,000 Yeomanry, giving a force in all of 450,000, or say, making deductions for recruits and youths as in the case of Regulars, 350,000. This would give in all an army on full war strength, not including recruits or men unfit for service, as follows:

Regular Army, including garrisons . . .	270,000
Regular Army Reserve	160,000
Auxiliary forces	350,000
	780,000

Deducting the garrisons at home and abroad the numbers would be 620,000, and would suffice, perhaps, to raise the army in the field for any specific purpose from the figure of 160,000 above stated to one of about 400,000, which the numbers in reserve would suffice to replenish for a considerable time.

Looking at the matter in detail we cannot say, I believe, that the figures stated for the Army on a peace and on a war footing are too high. The total of the Army on a full war footing is obviously somewhat speculative. As the contingency cannot occur without our having some time and warning to develop all the force required, the question has not perhaps the urgency of other Army questions; but, with this exception, all the various questions are most urgent indeed, especially the question of the peace establishment of the Army. The work it may be called on to do is mostly of a kind that it has always to be ready for in peace, and the larger army which events may compel us to raise will only become a possibility if we have an effective Regular Army to begin with. The practical point to keep before the public is the need for numbers. Our forces all told, excluding colonial forces and the native armies of India and other possessions, must be over 600,000 on a full war footing; and in time of peace we must not have fewer than 360,000 men, including about 90,000 recruits and young soldiers, under arms in the Regular Army, including India, with 160,000 men of the Regular Reserve behind them, ready to be called on without delay.

As to the composition of the force, the proportions of the different arms, the organization into army corps and otherwise, the provision of reserves of guns, ammunition, and equipment, these are all matters for experts where the public can hardly expect to follow. The experience of the late war showed that the man in the street was frequently sounder in his judgment even on technical matters than the War Office expert. He "spotted" the necessity for more mounted men and for reserves of ammunition while the War Office remained densely ignorant. But it is none the less impossible for the outsider to follow the details of technical discussion. He may be right at one time and wrong at a dozen other times. On these points experts must be left to watch each other, and the opinion of the Army itself is the only means to keep the authorities straight. When the War Office fails to command the assent of the Army on such points, there is sure to be something wrong.

Two points, however, remain on which public opinion has to form a judgment. How are the requisite numbers to be obtained? And what are the resources of the country to pay the bill?

As to the numbers of the Regular Army, I am sorry to say, from all the study I have been able to make of the subject, that all the discussions hitherto have been in the air, because the authorities will not face the dilemma in which they are placed—the one horn being that of paying the Army properly so as to ensure a supply of men, and the other that of conscription so as to obtain by force a service that is not given in sufficient abundance by those who are competent to perform it. This is the crux of the whole question of Army Reform. Men are wanted, and men are not got under present conditions and at the present rates of payment. As my military friends are never weary of repeating, the position is that the pay of the Army is quite insufficient to attract young men old enough and intelligent enough to go into the fighting line after a few months' training, and with constitutions sound enough to stand the wear and tear of service. Instead, we have lads who are many of them rather stupid, who take a year or two to train, and who take a year or two, perhaps two or three years, to grow old enough for the work. The result is a formidable wastage. One-third of the recruits, I am told, never become soldiers at all, but have to be discharged, and the time of drill-instructors and officers is wasted in trying to convert intractable material into fighting men. In such conditions it is a miracle that so much good material is obtained, but unfortunately there is not enough. The official establishments are not only fixed too low, but they are not maintained. As to the remedy, I have myself no doubt. We must, like other employers, pay the wages needed to attract the service, if we can afford the money, as I have no doubt we can. What the addition to the Army pay should be is, of course, a difficulty. It would be folly to offer too much. It would be equal folly to offer too little and fail. But, as far as I can form an opinion, the sum to offer the private is an effective 2*s*. a day or thereabouts and all found, as compared with the present offer of 1*s*. a day subject to stoppages and without everything being found. Two shillings a day would come to about £40 a year; and everything found, including clothing, would add about £25 a year to the sum, thus bringing the soldier up to the level of the average wage receiver in the country, instead of leaving him far below it as he now is. Other ranks would, of course, have to be raised in proportion; and the officers also, especially as more is to be exacted from them in future, must have their pay increased. But whether the present suggestion is sufficient or not, there must be no hesitation in the matter. The question is one of terms, and we must bid as high as necessary for the article required if we adopt the alternative of paying for it instead of obtaining it by force.

As to the alternative of conscription or force, I have no objection to it in principle. We must have men for the service of the country, and force may have to be used in the last resort. What I doubt, however, is the economy of the proceeding. If we force people into the ranks of the Army who are able to earn outside the equivalent of 2*s*. a day with everything found and upwards, and we pay them substantially less, we may be quite sure of a discontent so great as to be intractable. It is not in human nature for large masses of people to submit to such odious exaction, and we cannot have the instrument of maintaining social order, on which the cohesion of society depends, in the hands of the discontented and mutinous. We save all such risks by having a volunteer army, and by raising the terms to the necessary amount. If there are practically no terms which will bring volunteers in the requisite number, then conscription there must be; but equally we must pay the conscript army the equivalent of the average wages they would receive outside.

Of course, so great an addition as that of 1*s*. a day to the pay of men in the Army, with other equivalent additions, would add greatly to the cost. On the present establishment of 155,000 men at home, and 55,000[1]

[1] These include about 15,000 men of tropical races (see above); but this is a minor detail and may be passed over.

men in the colonies, whose cost is chargeable to the English Budget, the addition of 1*s.* a day per man would come to £3,832,000, or say £4,000,000 per annum. If at the same time the numbers of the Army are considerably increased, we can perceive at once how formidable is the question of an increase of the pay of the Army to the English Treasury and to the House of Commons. All that can be said is that the question, however disagreeable, must be faced. There is no use pretending to have an adequate Army if we shrink from the necessary outlay. In my own judgment, this shrinking would be most unworthy of a great nation and excessively foolish. The profit to be derived from an adequate Army, in the security of social order and freedom from international disturbance, is so overwhelmingly great that it is worth the price and more.

It would be a mistake, further, to suppose that there will be no compensating economies. On the contrary, we may set against the increase of pay the saving to be effected by a diminution of the number of boys and other incapables with whom the recruiting sergeant now fills the ranks. Suppose, instead of including on the home establishment 90,000, or about two years', recruits, we were able to reckon as immature and untrained only 40,000, we should save the whole cost of 50,000 men whom we now pay for and who are unfit for duty—a number almost as great as the addition proposed to be made to bring up the garrisons of Egypt and South Africa to the proper strength. In other ways the saving would also be considerable. We should have a larger army than we now have, and a good army all through, instead of an army spoilt by gross defects, and this of itself would facilitate other economies.

Regarding the auxiliary forces, there is not quite the same difficulty that there is with the Regular Army as to obtaining the numbers wanted. Very large numbers on paper are now obtained, probably sufficient for all practical purposes if a portion only can be trained so as to form an effective part of the fighting line, which it is the opinion apparently of the military authorities they can become. At the least, the training of the auxiliary forces advances the individuals so far that at need the Regular Army has a certain amount of raw material to draw upon which can be licked into shape more quickly than the ordinary recruits. One suggestion I have to make on this head would be that to a certain extent the Militia and Yeomanry as paid forces must be paid in proportion to the Regular Army according to the work they have to do, and this may be a serious matter if even a moderate standard of efficiency is insisted upon. The great danger of such auxiliary forces is that they may exist on paper only. Another suggestion is that conscription, while it may be found inapplicable to the Regular Army, may be used both to strengthen the auxiliary forces in numbers and to make them genuinely efficient. It is not unfair in the State to require that all young men as they come to the age of twenty-two should have qualified themselves to perform military service if they are medically fit, and that if found not so qualified they should be compelled to train in the Militia or Yeomanry for one or two years so as to become qualified. Such an obligation would stimulate volunteering or enlistment in the Militia or Yeomanry, while giving the military authorities a firmer hold over the Volunteers by their being able to define effectively the qualification to perform military service. It would certainly be of great advantage to the State to possess the large numbers of trained men which such regulations would give them, and to have Militia and Volunteers so far trained that the entire Regular Army and Reserves could be spared at need in some form or other for foreign service.

The conclusion, then, is that for the purpose of obtaining sufficient numbers the pay of the Regular Army must be sensibly increased, and that the pay of Militia and Yeomanry may also have to be increased in proportion; but that the numbers of the auxiliary forces generally may be increased by a modified form of compulsory service, to which I believe there could be no objection. The difficulty when faced is thus not a real one. It may be said, and many no doubt think, that it would be far simpler to have nothing but a Regular Army, and to leave the auxiliary forces out of the reckoning. The money spent on the latter, it is urged, would bring in a better return if it were used to make an addition to the Regular Army. But there is a great advantage, it seems to me, in having both a Regular Army, if it is sufficient for all the miscellaneous duties of the English Army in time of peace, and auxiliary forces along with it. We cannot tell how much the nation may be called on in great emergencies, and when these come we shall be all the better prepared if military training and skill in shooting are widely diffused among the population. It will be an advantage to the State also to have the whole population thus educated in the elementary duties of citizenship and the meaning of Imperial privileges and burdens.

There remains the question of ways and means. Already we have Army Estimates of £30,000,000 per annum, apart from the South African war, as compared with £20,000,000 two or three years ago. If the pay of the Regular Army is increased as proposed, this will add directly about £4,000,000 to the Estimates, and a further large sum will be required on the score of additions to the numbers of the Regular Army, about 50,000 net as compared with present establishments, allowing for the substitution of effective men for ineffectives. This would cost another £5,000,000 or thereabouts. Other outlays are also in view, such as the provision of improved barrack accommodation, the increase of reserves of ammunition and equipment, the multiplication of officers so as to secure the training of reserves and auxiliary forces, the increase of the proportion of mounted men in the Service, the increase of artillery, and so on. It is quite certain, practically, that with all the economy possible we shall have Army Estimates of £40,000,000 and upwards in peace times before very long. We were living in a fool's paradise before the South African war, and are now awaking to the realities of life. I would point out, however, that, although the figures sound large, people forget how large has been the increase of wealth in the country for many years past. With Army Estimates of £40,000,000 and Navy Estimates of equal amount, we shall be paying no more in proportion than other countries do, and less than we have paid in former times, and less than we have paid even in this South African war for a couple of years when money has been made to flow like water, and numberless lives have been lost, all because we were so unprepared. The country can well afford to meet such outlays, and the sacrifice should be willingly made.

I have written at greater length than I intended when I began, but perhaps a summary of a few principal points may be allowed, so as to familiarize the reader with the essential ideas, in my judgment, which should be kept in mind in these discussions:

(1) The Regular Army is required primarily, as all other armies are required, for the maintenance of internal order; and for this reason alone—that is, to garrison Ireland and to keep order in Great Britain—a considerable force must be kept.

(2) The Regular Army is required, further, for defence of fortified ports and centres at home, and for the defence of the whole country against raids by foreign Powers either at the outbreak of war or in the interval which must elapse before our general preponderance at sea is converted into overwhelming superiority in fact over the particular enemy engaged.

(3) For these two purposes alone we appear to require about 110,000 trained soldiers altogether, exclusive of recruits and immature men, viz., 30,000 for garrisons and 80,000 as a mobile force.

(4) There is much confusion in these matters, from the War Office habit of counting recruits and immature men as part of the home establishment; so that with the present establishment of 155,000 there are not in fact more than 65,000 trained and mature men, instead of the 110,000 actually required both for garrisons and field force. The three army corps of 120,000 Regulars supposed to be ready for foreign service according to Mr. Brodrick's scheme cannot in fact exist, because there are only 65,000 available for all purposes, including garrisons; and deducting 30,000 for garrisons, there are only 35,000 available instead of 120,000.

(5) The Regular Army is further required for garrisoning India, South Africa, Egypt, Malta, Gibraltar, and other possessions and fortified places abroad, and it appears on this head that considerable additions ought to be made, both South Africa and Egypt in particular being insufficiently provided for. The numbers we require in all for these garrisons appear to be 160,000, instead of 110,000 as stated in the Army Estimates. It seems unnecessary to labour this point while about 140,000 of the Regular Army, besides irregular forces, are in South Africa alone, engaged in garrisoning the country, and not in actual war. We must make up our minds to have larger figures to deal with for garrisoning the Empire than the Government put forward as their peace estimate.

(6) Altogether, including the Indian force, we require a Regular Army of 270,000 men, besides 90,000 recruits and immature men on the present system of recruiting, or a total of 360,000 in all.

(7) In addition, we require about 160,000 reserves for the Regular Army, besides help from the auxiliary forces, so as to provide for the possibility of serious invasion by sea when invasion, though not strict blockade, may be possible to a momentarily superior enemy, and so as to provide also for serious wars abroad.

(8) To get the numbers required an increase of pay for the Regular Army is absolutely necessary; and the

increased pay, coupled with the necessary additions to the trained men in the Army, after allowing for the substitution of effectives for ineffectives by means of higher pay, would probably add about £10,000,000 to the existing peace Estimates of £30,000,000, making £40,000,000 in all.

(9) We must remember, however, that there has been an enormous increase of wealth in the country for many years past, and that we are only awaking to the realities of existence as far as military and naval preparation is concerned. Even if we had to pay £40,000,000 apiece for Army and Navy we should still be less burdened than other nations and should not be paying more than we can well afford.

(10) Conscription appears to be unnecessary for the Regular Army, as to which we must trust to higher pay, but it may be useful in connection with the auxiliary forces, qualification for military service being required from all young men on reaching a certain age, failing which they must be enrolled in the Militia. It is desirable, for many reasons, that military training should be widely diffused.

(11) Organization is specially for the military experts, but nothing can be done without numbers, and the numbers I have stated are the minimum of what is now required, looking to all our commitments in India, South Africa, Egypt, and elsewhere, and on the assumption, which is a matter to be seen to, that our Navy is really preponderant.

XXV.

THE STATISTICAL CENTURY.[1]

THE present meeting takes place at an interesting date. We are within a few weeks of the close of a century which is, historically speaking, the statistical century *par excellence*. There were statistics, of course, before the Nineteenth Century. People made statistical statements and compiled statistics long before they were called statisticians. The business of rulers could not, in fact, have gone on at any time without statistical knowledge, and statistical statements are to be found accordingly in the records of Egypt, Assyria, and Babylonia thousands of years ago, just as they are to be found in old European chronicles and histories long before last century. But while people for a long time, like the Frenchman in the play who talked prose, have thus been statisticians without knowing it, it is towards the end of the Eighteenth Century, and at the beginning of the century now expiring, that statistics began to be formally recognized as a distinct branch of knowledge. From that time attention has been explicitly and increasingly given by governments to the collection of statistics. Statistical offices have been established for births, marriages, and deaths, for statistics of foreign trade and movements of shipping, for agricultural statistics, and for many more subjects, as well as central offices for statistics generally. Last, but not least, with the commencement of the century, we had the institution of the census in this country, following the ex-

[1] Address at the Annual Dinner of the Manchester Statistical Society, October 17th, 1900.

ample of the United States a little while before, and other experiments, chiefly in the Scandinavian countries, in the Eighteenth Century. Decennial and frequently quinquennial censuses have already become almost universal throughout the civilized world. To all this must be added a wide cultivation of statistical methods apart from government. Associations like your own have been formed to promote the study. Professorships of statistics have likewise been set up in the universities, though fewer, much fewer, in this country than in Germany, France, and the United States. Men of business have also been giving their minds to the subject till almost every sort of business and administration—financial, banking, railway, insurance, etc., etc.—has each its own statistics, while business and economic journals, all dealing largely with statistics, are to be counted by scores and hundreds.

All this makes the expiring period characteristically a statistical century. What is gained, then, it may be asked at a gathering like the present, by all this figuring and adding up, which hardly existed in the world by comparison before last century began? To answer this question would be to engage in a discussion on the utility of statistics which would be commonplace in a statistical society. The question also answers itself, for statistics would have been abolished by common consent long ago if people in business, for instance, had not felt the convenience of following the statistical position of their different trades, and if public men had not found it equally necessary and convenient to acquaint themselves with the facts of trade and social conditions which the census and the records of the Registrar-General's and other public offices give them.

Without attempting to answer the question fully, however, it may be of some use and interest, I hope, to draw attention to one or two leading statistical ideas which the statistics of the first statistical century, when a general survey is made, cannot but suggest. This is not a new topic with me, as it is the subject of addresses to the Royal Statistical Society of London about eighteen years ago. The lapse of time since then, however, makes the figures even more decisive and impressive than they were, just as the close of the century gives us a more definite period. I trust I shall be excused, then, for returning to the topic. When your invitation was received there was a chance that we should by this time have the exact figures of the American census for this year, so that it might be possible to compare actual progress since 1880 with the rate of progress before that, but the chance unfortunately has not come off. Still there are materials for the discussion proposed, as the results of the census within limits are no way in doubt.

A leading idea, then, which the census figures of civilized countries supply is the prodigious rate at which the civilized world—the community of European nations and nations of European origin—is growing. The population of Europe and of nations of European origin, like the United States, may now be put at something over 500 millions. The United States themselves may be put at nearly 80 millions; Russia, in its recent census, shows a population which must already have grown to about 135 millions; Germany, about 55 millions; the United Kingdom, with the self-governing Colonies of Canada and Australasia, and the white population of South Africa, 55 millions; Austria-Hungary, 45 millions; France, 40 millions; Italy, 32 millions; Spain and Portugal, 25 millions; Scandinavian countries, 10 millions; Holland and Belgium, 10 millions; and other European countries 20 millions. These are all round figures, of course, and if they are not exact at the moment they will certainly be exceeded in a year or two, so that they are safe round figures to take as the total numbers of the peoples concerned at the end of the century. We are quite within the mark, then, in saying that the total population of Europe and of nations of European origin, excluding the subject peoples of the English Empire, exceeds 500 millions.

A century ago, however, the corresponding figure to this 500 millions would not have been more than about 170 millions. A French statistician, M. Moreau de Jonnés, whom I quoted in 1885, gave the figure in 1788 for Europe alone, excluding the United States, as a little less than 150 millions, and making one or two corrections and allowing for some growth in the interval from 1788 to 1800, we cannot arrive at more than 170 millions a century ago for comparison with the 500 millions of the present time. The United States which now counts for nearly 80 millions was only about 5 millions at the beginning of the century; Russia did not count for more than, perhaps, 40 millions at the outside; the United Kingdom, which had then hardly any Australia or Canada, 15; Germany, 20; France, 25; Austria-Hungary, 20; Spain and Portugal, 15; Italy, 15; Scandinavia, 5; other European states, 10—total about 170. In the century, therefore, Europe and nations of European origin have grown to three times their former numbers; and this without counting the population of Mexico and South America, amounting now to 45 millions, which ought, perhaps, to be included as Europeanized, though not wholly European in race. When I wrote formerly, dealing with the figures up to 1880, the populations in question numbered less than 400 millions. More than one-fifth of the 500 millions is an addition of the last twenty years!

Not only is the century interesting, therefore, as a characteristically statistical century, but the statistics themselves are in the highest degree surprising. For generations and centuries the growth of Europe must have been slow, owing to war and pestilence and the other checks to population of which Malthus wrote, and then all at once in a single century we have this sudden multiplication of numbers. In my former addresses I discussed some of the causes of this change —the growth of large states, the profound peace existing as compared with former times, and the occupation of new lands in America and elsewhere—but it would occupy too much of our time now to resume the discussion, and I can only note its importance in passing, especially the importance of the transitory nature of one of the causes, the occupation of new lands, which has given Europe a breathing time for a few generations, but for a few generations only.

The economic development of the people, I need hardly say, is even more marvellous. Agriculture has extended indefinitely over the new territory, and there have been vast improvements in new and old territory alike; the figures of trade have been multiplied ten times and more; the wealth of the peoples all told, which would probably not have been reckoned at more than five thousand millions sterling at the beginning of the century, must be reckoned now by tens of thousands of millions. It would probably not be far short of the mark to say that while the millions of the advanced portion of the human race have increased in numbers as described, each unit on the average is two or three times better off than the corresponding unit at the beginning of the period.

Again, the development is for the most part not uniform among the European populations; it is most marked in the Anglo-American section. The increase here is from a population of not more than about 20 millions, which was the population of the United States and the United Kingdom together a hundred years ago, to a population of not less than 130 millions at the present time. Russia and Germany also show remarkable increases, but nothing like this; while the other nations of Europe are by comparison nowhere as regards this increase, France especially being nearly stationary. The Anglo-American section shows an even more significant economic development, which it is needless to enlarge upon. It is the United States especially, again, which has been advancing the most rapidly of all. One explanation, of course, is that to some extent the overflow from Europe, including Russia and Germany, has gone to the United States, which is a reason for taking all the countries together in a general survey; but, none the less, the gain is to the United States which absorbs the immigrants and transmutes them into Americans—part of the foremost nation of the time, and not members of the nationalities from which they sprang.

This astonishing growth of population means a great change in the relative position of the European nations in the world—their relative weight in international politics. Practically, the non-European races of the world have all the time been stationary, except in India, where the *pax britannica* has permitted the native population to expand. They have been living in the same places and under the same conditions as they have done for centuries, peopled up to the limits of subsistence under those conditions, and, therefore, incapable of expansion. The result is that the forces of civilization as against those of the black and yellow races have become practically irresistible. The numbers are relatively far greater than ever they were before and the economic force is indefinitely greater.

A great change in the distribution of political power among European nations themselves is also indicated. The existence alone of the United States implies an immense change. If we consider that an empire like that of Britain has its strength rather diminished than increased by the possession of territories like India, then the United States, having a larger European population than that of the British Empire, may be considered the most powerful state in the world, as far as population and resources are concerned. The white population is over 70 millions as compared with 55 in the British Empire and an equal number in Germany, and much smaller numbers in any other state except Russia. No doubt, Russia has much larger numbers, but the inferiority of the units is so great that the pre-eminence of the United States is not in question. And this is the position of a new state which had birth a little more than a hundred years ago. At the same time, Germany, Russia, and the United Kingdom have all grown, while France and Austria have, by comparison, remained stationary; so that now the great world powers are four only—the United States, Britain, Russia, and Germany, with France a doubtful fifth. The extent of the revolution that has taken place in a century is evident and obviously accounts for much that is going on in international politics.

There is yet another aspect of the statistics which we cannot leave out of sight. The changes which have occurred in the past century are still going on. The statistics are those of growing forces, and as the rest of the world is stationary, while there is unequal growth among the European nations themselves, the international position cannot but be modified at some near date in the future. An absolutely definite statement cannot be made as to what lies before us, because tumults and revolutions from which history has never been free may change so much. We may recognize, however, that if the forces now in existence continue to operate as they have done in the past century for only a few more generations, the close of the coming century must witness a farther transformation, whose beginnings will be apparent in the lifetime of some amongst us. It is a reasonable probability that unless some great internal change should take place in the ideas and conduct of the European races themselves, the population of 500 millions will, in another century, become one of 1,500 to 2,000 millions. The black and yellow races still remaining, as far as one can see, comparatively stationary, this will make a greatly changed world. The yellow peril, for instance, of which we hear so much, will have vanished, because the yellow races themselves will be so outnumbered. What will be the 400 millions of China compared with 1,500 or 2,000 millions of European race? Farther progress must also be made in the re-distribution of power among European nations. The next century will not be far advanced before the United States, which is already in reality the most powerful single state in the world, will be generally recognized as such. By 1930 its population will, probably enough, be 150 millions, as compared with about 90 millions of European race in the British Empire, with about 80 millions in Germany, and with the numbers not so much increased, compared with the present, in other countries of Europe. Russia may then, perhaps, have a population close upon 180 millions, but the units unequal to those of the United States. As the century advances, moreover, Russia will probably be surpassed even in population, and the pre-eminence of the United States will be unquestioned. Other nations like France will have fallen still more into the background, and international politics will be more and more limited to the affairs of what are already the four great powers—the United States, United Kingdom, Germany, and Russia.

In all this let it be repeated there is no attempt at prophecy. It is merely a bare statement of what must be, assuming the continuance for a generation or two only of the present conditions as to the growth of population and wealth in the countries referred to. Should the assumption fail, however, this will of itself imply other changes of a remarkable kind. Population cannot stop growing at the prodigious rate of last century or something approaching it, without a great deal besides happening of an astonishing nature. Looking at past experience, however, the probabilities are entirely against a speedy check to this growth.

The most serious problem will, of course, be whether the dilemma stated by Malthus, and which has been rather put aside for a century in consequence of the occupation of new lands by the growing European populations, will, at length, become an urgently practical question. Sir W. Crookes's paper at the British Association two years ago, though it was not without defects, may be taken as evidence that the idea cannot be easily got rid of. It is simply impossible not to wonder which of the two forces—the growth of population and the increase of the needs of the growing population on the one side, and the growth of invention and mechanical power in supplying human wants on the other side—will gain as time goes on. It is hardly possible that there can always be equilibrium, or that the conditions of the Nineteenth Century, in which the growing population has always been provided for, will continue indefinitely. A turn may come at any moment in the opposite direction. Possibly the force of the dilemma may be first felt in our dealings with those black and yellow populations which are subject to civilized rule, and which begin to increase under that rule without any proportionate increase of their resources; but the conditions of the dilemma are always there, and the statesman of the future must certainly look out for difficulties of a formidable kind. It is not merely a question of food we must remember. As Professor Cairnes long ago pointed out, it is a question of everything necessary to supply human wants; the metals presenting as much, or even more, difficulty than food.

To turn from these topics I should like to advert for a moment to yet one more conclusion, which seems to be suggested by the statistics, and which may not be without practical value in economic discussion. Many people are puzzled by what they speak of as the necessity of finding new markets, with competition on all sides increasing around us. For this reason they are anxious to obtain possession of the territory occupied by black or yellow races, or to prevent the exclusive occupation of such territory by rival powers. The same idea has obviously dominated the politics of Germany and France, and it has not been without some influence perhaps even in the United States, which is now to be included among the countries manufacturing for export. But the figures we have been dealing with point to quite another source of new markets, within the control of the very peoples for whom there is so much anxiety. Surely, there can be no lack of new customers if the 500 millions of the advanced races themselves are to be doubled in 30 to 50 years, and trebled or quadrupled in a century. With such a growth of population there must be growing markets, each nation having its own share, apart from any possible improvement among the black and yellow races, though such improvement as a source of new trade is not to be ignored or despised.

In this view, then, the statistics as to the actual growth of population in the world are reassuring. We have the same certainty of growth that people would have had a hundred years ago, if they had foreseen the discovery and occupation of region upon region inhabited by uncivilized tribes which has been one of the features of last century's progress. To create a new population comes to the same end as finding a population already existing. The latter can no longer be hoped for as the world is being explored and occupied; but the former remains, and it is the more important factor in the progress of trade.

In conclusion, may we not entertain the hope that the coming century, like the one which is passing away, will be characteristically a statistical century? We have had satisfactory experience so far of the uses of statistics, and the problems before the world where statistics can help are likely to be not less, but more, difficult and anxious than they have been. Politics must be more and more governed by true ideas drawn from statistical information, and as time goes on the statistician should be more and more recognized as preceding the "statist" and economist. Associations like yours must also prove of increasing interest and importance, and for this final reason I have the greater pleasure in proposing the toast intrusted to me — the Manchester Statistical Society.

XXVI.

ARE WE LIVING ON CAPITAL?[1]

THERE has been much talk lately of the waste or expenditure of National Capital in different ways. One of these ways is the expenditure upon armaments and preparation for war. Nations, it is alleged, are engaged in a competition where all must lose, spending more than they can afford in preparation for the evil days of a war which may never come, and piling up heavy debts which they can ill bear, so that their whole industry is crippled in consequence. While they are not alone in the matter, American statisticians and economists, as well as American public men generally, have a good deal to say on this head to the disadvantage of European nations compared with America. The greater welfare of the American people, and the superior productiveness of their industry, are asserted to be the result of the freedom of America as compared with Europe from such wasteful expenditure. Another kind of discussion which has taken place is with reference to the position of this country in its international trade. The allegation is made that, in the course of this trade, we are living upon our capital, parting with valuable property in order to obtain food and other things which we import from abroad, in excess of the goods which we are able to export. Metaphorically speaking, it is said that, as a nation, we shall, before long, be in the poor-house, or what answers internationally to the poor-house. It may be useful, there-

[1] Read before the Institute of Bankers on Wednesday, May 22nd, 1901.

fore, to examine, in a general way, the meaning of the expressions used, and inquire to what extent, and in what manner nations may waste or expend their capital. In doing so I may refer with some frequency to actual concrete cases presented to us by history or recent experience, and especially to one or two of the cases now forming the subjects of criticism and discussion.

There appears to be a good deal of confusion of mind in these discussions and in the use of phrases as to expending or wasting national capital and a nation living on its capital, which is really due to a false analogy, the analogy of an individual who wastes his capital or lives upon his capital, and, in consequence, comes to poverty. We are all familiar with such individual cases. There is the well-known case of the young spendthrift, who comes into a fortune, and who then, as it is said, "goes the pace" and parts with one bit of property after another in order to obtain the commodities and services which he consumes or gives away. Then we have the business man who draws out of the concern in which his capital is invested more than his profits and lives at a greater rate than he can afford, who does in a quiet way, in short, what is done by the spendthrift and wastrel recognized as such, and, substantially, in the same form, that is, by parting with one bit of property after another. Then we have the business man who makes bad speculations, buying repeatedly at a high price and selling at a low one until at last his own money or capital disappears, or who makes bad debts, which is really another form of the same disease, the low price at which he sells being, sometimes, merely an irrecoverable debt. In these different ways an individual may waste or expend his capital, and so, it is assumed in common speech, a nation gets through its capital when it engages in a process of wasting or expending or living upon its capital.

What I should like to point out, however—and this

is the substance of much that I propose to say—is, that the individual analogy fails in the case of a community or a nation. It is of the essence of the individual process of waste in most cases that the property of the spendthrift or wastrel should be sold or transferred to some other person or persons in the community, either for no consideration or in exchange for goods or services forming part of the accruing income of the community, and which the spendthrift consumes. The spendthrift parts with property, with things which constitute capital, and receives, in exchange, other things which are really income, and not capital, and which he consumes, that is, if he receives any actual equivalent at all. The final result is that he and his capital are parted; but the capital itself, the money, the estate, or the house, of which it consisted, remains, having passed into the hands of others, sometimes without any real equivalent, but, at other times, in exchange for part of the accruing income in the hands of the people to whom the spendthrift has transferred his property, and whose share in the transaction is really the investment of an amount equal to that which the spendthrift has parted with. There is waste of capital, accordingly, as respects the individual, but there need be no waste, and usually, I should say, there is no waste, or very little waste indeed, as far as the community is concerned. But when we come to the case of a community or a nation expending its capital there is, plainly, not the same room as in the case of an individual for the process of selling or transferring property, either for no consideration, or for commodities and services that are immediately consumed, which makes the waste of capital so easy to the individual. There are some questions, perhaps, as to transfers of securities from one nation to another, but, broadly speaking, a community cannot waste capital in the same way that an individual may do by selling property and consuming what is obtained from the sale. A community cannot sell or transfer to itself. When a community or nation, therefore, expends or wastes capital, or lives upon its capital, what is meant is, either that the nation does not properly repair and renew machines, houses, and other property of a fixed kind, or that some of the more perishable property, such as the flocks and herds of an agricultural community is actually consumed, so that at the end of a given period there are fewer things in existence constituting the capital and wealth of the community than there were at the beginning. In these ways, and no other, can a community or nation waste its capital or live on its capital. As far as individuals are concerned, A may be poorer and all the other letters of the alphabet richer, the aggregate property remaining the same, but when we deal with a community as a whole, there must be an actual diminution of the aggregate wealth or property to constitute a waste of capital.

To be quite accurate, we must allow, of course, for the changing population of a community. If the numbers of a community are constantly increasing, and the capital remains the same without any actual diminution, then at the end of a given period there is less capital per head of the community than there was at the beginning. In other words, a community which is constantly adding to its numbers must be constantly adding to its capital, if things are to remain in equilibrium. If the addition of capital again is not equal to the addition of numbers, there may still be some diminution of capital per head, although not so great as in the case where no addition is made whatsoever to the capital. While noticing these refinements, however, we must recognize that the broad fact to be kept in mind is the necessity of an actual diminution or deterioration of the things which constitute capital relatively to the numbers of the population in order to establish a waste of national capital in a particular case.

There is no doubt the exceptional case which has been referred to of a nation parting with securities or properties it possesses to other nations, in exchange for consumable commodities, which are, in fact, consumed.

Where and to what extent this may be done are, of course, questions of fact. It is important to observe, however, that even such a transfer, though it may take place, would not of itself show a nation engaged in the transfer to be living on its capital. If a nation, at the moment of parting with some of its property or capital to individuals of another nation, should at the same time be investing an equal amount at home, clearly there would be no reduction of that nation's capital in the aggregate. It would merely be substituting an investment at home for an investment abroad, an economic circumstance of some importance, but not the same thing as a nation living on its capital.

When we come, then, to examine specific cases of nations wasting or spending their capital, what we have to look for are signs of the national estate or property deteriorating for want of repairs, or signs of its stocks of useful things diminishing in the aggregate. All must be put together and an increase in one direction set against a decrease in another direction. For this purpose, it will, probably, be found convenient to apply values to each kind of property, so as to be furnished with a common denominator for measuring loss in one direction and gain in another. But it must not be inferred or assumed in any way that a diminution of capital in some specific direction involves an equivalent loss, on balance, to the community. It might happen, for instance, that stocks of some of the goods diminish because of an acceleration of business methods which make a smaller stock sufficient for the work to be done. If, against the smaller stock of some goods, there could be set some increase of other goods, or an increase of fixed property of equal value, then such diminution of stocks would clearly imply no impoverishment in any way. The effect is that the valuation of the whole property of a nation, at frequent intervals, appears to be the best way to bring to book the question of expenditure or waste of the property itself. Whatever may be the precise method followed, there must be a balancing of loss and gain, so as to draw out the net result to the community as a whole.

With these preliminary observations I propose to deal, first, with the question of a nation living on its capital in consequence of the nature and results of its international trade. The case is quite different from that of a nation losing its capital in consequence of excessive expenditure on armaments, although the one thing may, of course, to some extent be the cause of the other. A nation which is extravagant on armaments may have to part with its capital to provide for the extravagance, just as it would part with its capital in order to provide for any other extravagance. It is not suggested, however, that extravagance on armaments has been the main part of that general extravagance which has created the excess of imports over exports that gives concern to so many people as the final and complete proof of our commercial decay.

The allegation, generally, is that we are living on our capital because there is an excess of about £180,000,000 in imports over exports. In the year just passed the excess is almost exactly £170,000,000 sterling. The imports in that year were £524,000,000, and the exports, including British and Irish produce and Foreign and Colonial merchandise, were £354,000,000, leaving the difference stated. And, as such like excesses have been going on for many years, and increasing from period to period, it is argued that the waste of capital in the United Kingdom must really have been enormous, and that we must be getting poorer and poorer in our relations with foreign countries. It is further urged in proof, I believe, that as a matter of fact, we have lately been parting, in our international dealings, with certain kinds of securities, especially American securities, and that, to some extent, our foreign neighbours have been lenders and depositors in the Short Loan Market of Lombard Street to a greater extent than at any former period. In other words, then, it is said there can be no doubt we have been living upon our capital, as we have been sending abroad the securities which we once possessed, and have been becoming indebted to foreign countries, results corresponding, in fact, to the excess of imports over exports shown in our trade returns.

Such is the allegation, and the question is how we are to deal with it in a particular case according to the principles laid down at the beginning of this paper.

I would notice then, first of all, that the statements are not even formally complete for the purpose of proving the point to which they are addressed. That we are parting with our securities and becoming, on balance, less of a creditor nation than we were before, is not a fact, even if it were true, which would prove that we are living on our capital. In stating the matter theoretically, I drew attention to the possibility that a diminution of investment abroad might be accompanied by an increase of investment at home, and that, before we could infer from a diminution of our investments abroad that we were living on capital, we must go further, and demonstrate that there had been no equivalent increase of our capital at home. I must add, further, that this is no mere theoretical and argumentative point. Somewhat more than thirty years ago, when I was assisting Mr. Bagehot in the editorship of the "Economist," the question of an excess of imports being treated as a proof that we were, as a nation, living on our capital even then arose, and Mr. Bagehot's first idea on the subject was, that it was quite possible for the country to be parting with some of its foreign investments, and yet not to be diminishing its capital. The very things we were importing, he said, the food and the raw materials, were the articles required by labourers who would be employed in building the houses and factories, and making the railways, and executing other works which would constitute investment at home. The diminution of our investments abroad, and the consequent increase, for the time, of an excess of imports over exports, even if these things do take place, are thus no proof whatsoever that a nation is living on its capital. The test is whether, on the whole, we are diminishing our investments or not.

Tried by this test, then, we have simply to look, as far as this country is concerned, at the return of the assessments to the Income Tax. The assessments are, of course, assessments of the amount of income yielded, and not assessments of capital value, but the result is much the same. The bulk of the income, although some of it is personal, is really from property, and the value of property, of late years, as we know, has risen rather more in proportion than the increase of income. In former years I have, at different times, drawn out an estimate of the value of property in the country, based upon these returns of Income Tax, and may do so again, but it is unnecessary for the present discussion to go quite so far. We can deal directly with the returns. We find, then, that in the last ten years the increase of the annual assessments to the Income Tax has been from £631,000,000 sterling[1] to £759,000,000 sterling,[2] or an increase of £128,000,000 altogether, and of 20 per cent. in ten years. In some way or other, then, even if we have been diminishing our investments abroad in this period, we have not been expending our capital as a whole. On the contrary, if there has been a diminution of our investments abroad, there must have been a far more than equivalent increase of our investments at home. In other words, we must have at home far more houses, factories, machinery, railway and other roads, and stocks of furniture and

[1] The actual figure of the assessments in 1890 was £669,000,000, but this included about £38,000,000 of income under Schedule B. which is not included according to the method now followed, and this amount has accordingly to be deducted in order to obtain a figure for comparison with the present time.

[2] This is the figure for 1899 only, not quite a ten years' period. The latest figure since published is £867,000,000 sterling.

other articles, one thing or the other, at any rate, than we had ten years ago, and we must have more in the aggregate, including securities both at home and abroad, than we had at the beginning of the period.

It is especially to be observed that the increase of 20 per cent. is at a much greater rate than the increase of population in the period, which could not have been more than about 10 per cent. There is, consequently, an increase of the total capital per head as well as an absolute increase of the amount of capital, not considering the increase of the numbers of the people.

The Income Tax returns are not in such a form as to show separately the whole income derived from foreign investments, but I believe, if inquiry were made, and the whole income from foreign investments could be stated separately, it would not appear that the foreign capital itself has actually been diminished. The inquiry, however, would require a greal deal of elaboration. What we can say with certainty is, that there is nothing on the face of the figures to indicate any material diminution of our foreign investments such as would be implied if there were any diminution in amount to correspond to the excess of imports over exports.

The matter might be left at this point, but, of course, there are further observations to be made, as a wrong idea of this nature when once it gets into people's minds is not easily eradicated. It is, therefore, expedient once more to point out that the excess of imports itself, as a real expression of the balance of our trading transactions with other countries, is not correct, and that, in any case, a certain large excess is to be expected as the expression of the payment of interest on previous investments that we have made abroad. As regards the first point, that the excess of imports is not the same thing as the balance of our trading transactions with foreign countries, I need only refer to what I have urged before as to the exports not including the freight and other charges which become due to us in the course of our trade as ship-owners and commission merchants, yet these being charges with which we are as much entitled to debit foreign countries in the course of our foreign trade as we are to debit them with the so-called exports themselves. In order, therefore, to deduce from the excess of imports a notion of the balance actually due upon our trading transactions, we must add to the exports the value of the freight and other charges which we are entitled to bring into account, by which the apparent excess of imports over exports treated as a balance of trade would have to be enormously reduced, perhaps about one half. The remainder would correspond roughly to the amount of interest which we are entitled to receive upon our capital invested abroad. In reality, then, when analyzed, the excess of imports about which so many people are concerned does not at all imply that we are diminishing our capital abroad. It merely shows that our charges to foreign countries which the imports are sent us to meet are much greater than the so-called exports which appear in our trade returns, and that, in addition we have an amount of interest to receive without sending a commercial equivalent abroad. The facts which we find in studying the Income Tax returns showing no diminution of our capital, but, on the contrary, a very large increase, are thus in accordance with a correct interpretation of the import and export returns themselves. There is no question in any of them of the nation living upon its capital, but they all show, on the contrary, that our capital is steadily increasing, and they are all consistent with each other.

With regard to the increase of foreign banking money, or short loan money belonging to foreigners in London, it might be useful, in this connection, to point out the necessary limitations of any such foreign investments in this country. The amount of short loan money held by foreigners in London is necessarily conditioned by the limited nature of the short loan market itself. If the amount of money people want to borrow at call or at very short terms is itself limited by the nature of the transactions in which such money is useful, then the share of that short money held by foreign bankers and foreign merchants at any time, must equally be limited. Clearly they cannot be holders of all the short money in the market, because home bankers and others find it equally necessary and convenient to hold such money. At the most, then, foreign bankers and merchants can have but a share. Whatever, then, may be the amount of the short money borrowed and lent at a given time in the London market, say, perhaps, £200,000,000 to £300,000,000 sterling, foreign bankers and merchants at the outside can only be holders of a part, considering the magnitude of English banking money and the necessarily large proportion of that money which bankers must hold at call or short notice. My own impression is, that a sum of about £50,000,000 sterling held by foreign bankers and merchants in London and liable to be called at short notice would probably be a maximum amount, but on this head, of course, the audience before me will have better means of forming an opinion from time to time than I can possibly have. But whatever the amount may be, even if it should be such a maximum as £100,000,000 sterling, which seems far over any possible mark, the point to be observed is that any change in the amount of a fund of this nature from time to time can have little to do with the question of the nation living on its capital. The whole capital of the nation at the present time is probably not far short of £15,000,000,000 sterling, while the annual increase in ordinary times must at least be between £200,000,000 and £300,000,000 sterling.[1] A difference of a few millions, therefore, say, ten or twenty millions in the

[1] I have not made any recent calculations on the subject since the publication of my book on the "Growth of Capital," which dealt with the figures down to 1885, but, from the increase of Income Tax Returns, it is evident that there has been an enormous growth since then, justifying some such figure as that here suggested.

aggregate funds of the Short Loan Market or in the aggregate share of those funds held by foreigners, which does not exceed, probably, a total of £50,000,000 sterling, is a comparative trifle. Such changes may be very important in connection with the conditions of the money market at certain times, but they are not important in connection with a question like this as to a nation living on its capital. Were we, as a nation, to be living on our capital, the signs of it would be very different, and of a much more portentous character.

A different question seems to be raised by the investments on behalf of foreigners in the war loans lately issued, which would appear to indicate, especially in connection with the re-purchases of their own securities by foreigners, especially re-purchases of this sort lately made by Americans, that, in certain directions, English investment abroad is partly diminishing, and partly being set off by foreign investment in England. To the extent that such a process is going on, England would, of course, be diminishing its foreign investments on balance, though not its capital as a whole, and this would, *pro tanto*, be an explanation of an excess of imports. The amounts parted with in this way must, however, be very small in proportion to our whole capital, and looking at the ordinary processes of the Stock Exchange and the money market, I am of opinion that, on balance, we are still year by year increasing, and not diminishing, our investments abroad. We must not be guided in such matters by one or two symptoms only, or the phenomena of one or two years only, as there are great fluctuations to be noted. Whether there would be any means of giving a strict account seems, to me, very doubtful. There has lately appeared a remarkable and interesting statement by an American economist, Mr. Bacon, as to the position of America in recent years, during which its indebtedness abroad has been diminishing, and some of our younger economists would do well, perhaps, to make a similar investigation respecting the increase or decrease of English investments abroad, and the increase or decrease of foreign investments in England, which is another side of the same economic processes.

For our present purpose, however, nothing that is likely to be found in such investigations can affect the main conclusion that, as a nation, we are not living on our capital, which is established directly by the evidence of the increase of the national property, and of the increase of such property per head which we find in the Income Tax returns.

I propose next to deal with the question of nations wasting capital on war and armaments, perhaps the more practical of the two questions at the present time. What I have to say first of all on this head is to point out some conspicuous cases on record of the expenditure of vast sums for those purposes without capital being diminished, with capital, on the contrary, increasing all the time. Such cases do not show, of course, that capital may not be wasted in this way, but they raise a presumption that ordinary expenditure in time of peace, great as it may be, may not involve an actual diminution of the capital of the nations concerned, however mischievous some of the effects may be. There may, in fact, be a loss of means for the moment, for no one can eat his cake and have it, but momentary loss of means, however serious, is not the same thing as a diminution of capital, and must not be confounded with it.

The first illustration I have to give is that of the experience of England during the great war with France, at the end of the eighteenth and the beginning of the nineteenth century. During the latter part of the war especially, enormous sums were expended. The annual amount for some years towards the close of the war, including what was raised by loans as well as what was raised by taxation, amounted to about £100,000,000 sterling,[1] or not far short of that sum, and this was estimated to be equal to one-third of the aggregate annual income of the individuals constituting the nation at that time. We find, however, when we examine the records, especially the records of the Income Tax, that the amount of property in the country must have increased very rapidly during the entire period that this expenditure was going on. A few years after the beginning of the century, viz., in 1802-3, the average annual value of real property, according to the Income Tax returns, amounted only to about £35,000,000 sterling. In 1814, or thereabouts, the amount was £53,500,000 sterling. In other words, in about ten years' time the property of the nation, so far as it was derived from real property, increased about 50 per cent., and we may assume that there was an equal increase in the property itself.[2] All this, it must be remembered, was taking place during the strain of a great war, when the expenditure on armaments was at its maximum in this country. Of course, capital might have increased still more if there had been no war. The useful production of the nation might also have been much greater than it was if the labour of soldiers and sailors and those preparing clothing, food, and ammunition for them had been available for other occupations. The strain was undoubtedly very great. The facts stated in Porter's "Progress of the Nation" as to the non-increase of the yield of taxes in proportion to the increase of population between 1801 and 1821 are significant (see Porter, p. 496 *et seq.*). Still, in actual fact, the capital of the nation does not appear to have been encroached upon, and the resources of the

[1] The actual figures were:

1811	£84,000,000
1812	89,000,000
1813	106,000,000
1814	107,000,000
1815	92,000,000

[2] See Mr. Goschen's "Report on Local Taxation," p. 69, No. 470, Session 1870.

nation must have been increasing all through this period. Great as the armaments were, the nation was by no means living upon its capital.

The next case I have to mention is that of the great civil war in the United States in the early 'sixties. In this case there were four years of war which must have cost the country very nearly £1,000,000,000 sterling. The actual gross outlay of the central government in the years of war and in the two years 1867-8, following the war, when war debts were, no doubt, still in course of payment, were:

1862	$566,000,000
1863	900,000,000
1864	1,295,000,000
1865	1,906,000,000
1866	1,139,000,000
1867	1,093,000,000
1868	1,069,000,000
Total . .	$7,968,000,000

This is equal to about £1,600,000,000; and, making deductions for the normal outlay, as it stood before the war, about £17,000,000 sterling annually, or about £120,000,000 in all, we should still have a sum of not far short of £1,500,000,000 as the apparent cost of the war to the Government. But these figures, apparently, include expenditures in repayment of debt already charged to the war, and the net outlay of the Government, not including such repayments, is, apparently, about the figure named.

Between 1860 and 1870, however, we find that according to the estimates made at each census in the United States, the aggregate property in the country increased from $16,000,000,000 to $30,000,000,000, or, say, from £3,200,000,000 sterling to £6,000,000,000 sterling, an increase in the whole period of £2,800,000,000 sterling. If, therefore, there had been waste of capital during the American Civil War, it must have been more than made good during the five years after the close of the war down to 1870, and the nation must in addition have created new capital to the extent of £2,800,000,000 sterling.[1] My conviction is, however, that at no time during the civil war itself could the capital of the nation have been diminished. Great expenditures were being incurred to carry on the war, and there was a great diversion of labour from other pursuits to carry it on, but the expenditure, great as it was, must have been borne out of the income of the country, and did not prevent the investment of new capital in houses, in factories, in railway construction, and in other public works.

The increase of capital here referred to, it must also be remembered, is an increase that took place after allowing for any diminution that may have occurred in the Southern States of the Union which were defeated, and were, no doubt, in a state of great exhaustion at the end of the war. Whatever diminution may have been due to this cause, the figures stated allow for it, the Southern as well as the Northern States of the Union being comprised in the return. Probably enough, the exhaustion of the south may have been exaggerated from the present point of view. The capital of the south was not, in fact, destroyed by the war any more than the capital of the north, because it consisted so largely of land and property which could not run away, and what was injured was really the fringe of the capital, and not the main capital itself. The moment peace was restored means were found to resume industry almost as if there had been no war.

The next illustration I propose to give is that of the Franco-German war, which involved an enormous outlay during the short period it lasted and, probably, cost France, according to a calculation which I made

[1] Some deduction ought perhaps to be made from the latter sum on account of the depreciation of paper money, which was the money of the country in 1870, but after all allowances the increase would still be enormous.

many years ago, shortly after the war itself, about £700,000,000 sterling.[1] This includes every kind of loss, direct and indirect, as far as I could calculate, which France sustained. But the whole of this amount was not a loss of capital to France, the net loss on that head being about £600,000,000 sterling, including the payment of the indemnity and the cession of territory, about £264,000,000 altogether, which were the result of the war. The case of France, however, was a very special case of loss of capital. The experience of Germany was quite different, the calculation being that Germany, instead of losing by the war, gained about £150,000,000 sterling, and gained in capital even more than that, about £174,000,000 sterling. If we state the gain of Germany against the loss by France, the total loss of capital even by the Franco-German War to the two nations concerned was probably not over £400,000,000 sterling, or about £200,000,000 apiece. Much of the burden of the expenditure was, in fact, borne at the time out of the income, and the loss of capital, in whatever way it may be calculated, was not nearly so great.

We may say, perhaps, that the loss of capital in the great Franco-German War amounted to no more than a few years' ordinary accumulation of capital in the countries concerned, and it was in fact made good more quickly than was commonly anticipated in 1872. The recovery in France, especially, was prodigiously quick.

When we get such figures in connection with great wars it is, perhaps, unnecessary to refer to the kind of loss which occurs in the little wars which this country has had to carry on at different times. Wars in India, apart from the fact that they have mostly been paid for out of the Indian Exchequer, a war like the Abyssinian War, or West African Expeditions, or Chinese entanglements, have, obviously, occasioned the expendi-

[1] See *supra*, vol. i., "The Cost of the Franco-German War."

ture of sums which are quite insignificant compared with those which have been mentioned. If the great wars did not involve loss of capital or waste of capital, clearly the little wars need hardly enter into consideration. The South African War, from which we are now emerging, has called for a more serious effort. The war estimates for two years in succession have been close upon £90,000,000 sterling annually, as compared with £20,000,000, which was the figure before the war. The whole of the difference is not due to the war, but we are dealing here with the question of armaments in the most general fashion; and the fact of £90,000,000 sterling for Army estimates, added to about £30,000,000 more for the Navy at the same time, makes a total expenditure on armaments for two years of about £120,000,000 a year. This is even a larger figure than the amount that was spent annually about a hundred years ago, in the great war with France. We have seen, however, that even the great war with France, notwithstanding the much smaller resources of the country at that time, compared with the present, did not, in fact, result in any waste of capital, but the reverse, the accumulation of capital going on in the country the whole time. It is not surprising, therefore, to find that the recent expenditure on the South African War hardly seems to have disturbed the ordinary course of business in the country. Whatever the exact proportion of the outlay to the resources of the country may be, we have evidently been paying for it out of income, and not out of capital. Of course, it is quite true that the Government as a Government has been borrowing largely in order to meet the expenditure. The borrowings, apparently, amount to something over £100,000,000 altogether in about two years. But, although the Government borrows, it may none the less be quite true that, as far as the whole community is concerned, the entire outlay is defrayed out of income. Those who provide the Government with the money provide it out of income, and not out of capital, and there are no doubt large additional savings and investments going on at the same time.

We come finally to the question of the expenditure upon armaments in time of peace, which are the subject of those remarks by American and other critics referred to at the beginning of this paper, to the effect that European nations are at a disadvantage, economically, as compared with America, in consequence of these peace armaments. What has been said as to the expenditure in time of war itself, and the possibility of capital accumulating notwithstanding, obviously suggests that, perhaps, the nature and effects of expenditure upon armaments in peace time have not been fully considered by some of the economists and statisticians who have made such remarks. But we may look at the facts directly. To take four of the great European nations, we find that the outlay of these four nations, England, France, Germany, and Russia, for military and naval armaments in time of peace, may be stated something as follows:

	Army.	Navy.	Total.
England[1] . . .	£30,000,000	£30,000,000	£60,000,000
France	27,000,000	12,000,000	39,000,000
Germany . . .	32,000,000	7,000,000	39,000,000
Russia	30,000,000	7,000,000	37,000,000

These are the figures taken from the latest Budget statements of the respective Governments. I fear that they are under-statements to some extent, as it is somewhat difficult in these matters to get the "true truth" out of the official documents. But even if we add to them a considerable margin for error, or in consequence of the very latest figures of actual expenditure not being available, say, if we add altogether 10 or 20 per cent., we should still have figures that are quite inconsiderable, I believe, compared with the aggregate income and capital of the nations concerned.

In our own case the comparison would be with an

[1] Excluding India and the Colonies.

aggregate income of not less than £1,500,000,000 sterling, Germany with an aggregate income of about £1,000,000,000, if not more, France with an aggregate income, also, of £1,000,000,000, and Russia with an aggregate income that must also now be closely approaching, if not exceeding, £1,000,000,000.[1] The question is whether it can be said that the expenditure of such sums is likely to trench in any way upon the capital of nations which enjoy such large incomes. Clearly, we may say, in our own case, that an expenditure of £60,000,000 or even £80,000,000 sterling out of about £1,500,000,000, that is, an expenditure of 4 or 5 per cent., is an outlay which can well be met out of income. No doubt there are all kinds of other outlays connected with the Government of a great country, but many of these outlays, especially those connected with local government and those connected with Post Office administration, are really outlays of a reproductive character, and hardly involve even the question of burden upon the community affected. The really serious burden for a State is always Army and Navy expenditure. But in the case of England, the burden, in time of peace, after all, amounts to no more than has been stated, and all the consequences of the mischief of bloated armaments and the rest, in time of peace, as far as this country is concerned, must arise from the expenditure of about 4 or 5 per cent. of our income only. With Germany and France, it will be seen, the position is much the same, although, in their case, it has to be considered that, probably, the taxable margin in proportion to the aggregate income of the people is smaller than it is in our own case.

[1] I do not support these figures by detailed calculations, which appear unnecessary for the present purpose. I may refer to the calculations of Mr. Bowley as justifying the figure stated for the United Kingdom, justified as they are by the previous calculations of Dudley, Baxter and others, and by considerations of the numbers of the people, the income assessed to Income Tax, and the average earnings of the working classes; while similar calculations can be made for other countries.

A great deal is made, in the discussions on these subjects, of the fact that in France and Germany, owing to conscription, the outlay stated in the Budget is much smaller than the real burden on the people, because the soldiers are obtained at less than cost price, and although the Government does not pay the money, the nation sustains the loss of the withdrawal of so many hands from employments where they would be paid more than they receive in the Army. I cannot find, however, that any addition to be made to the expense of Army and Navy in Germany and France, on this head, would really be very material for the purpose before us, while it is also maintained, in Germany especially, as you are no doubt aware, that the training in the Army is economically beneficial to the recruits who are conscripted, and that, finally, there is no loss at all to themselves or to the nation in connection with the conscription. With regard to Russia, the case is, perhaps, more serious, because here the margin for taxation, in proportion to the gross income of the people, is, probably, much less than it is in the case of the three other nations referred to. As far as I can judge, the margin of taxation in Russia must be very small indeed. Still, even here, there is, apparently, no question as to the expenditure on armaments trenching on the *capital* of the country. There is no reason why the whole amount should not come out of the annual income.

These statements might be followed in detail by an examination as to the growth of indebtedness in the different countries, no matter what the cause may be; but I am anxious to concentrate attention on the main point, and the question of debt brings in so much the question of financial management that it would encumber a paper like this to discuss it in detail. There has obviously, however, been no such increase of debt lately as to involve any formidable addition to the annual burdens on any of the people concerned. Of our own debt I need say nothing. The French debt was added to immensely by the Franco-German war; afterwards there was a great addition in consequence of the schemes of public works, but of late years the additions have been inconsiderable. Ten years ago the annual interest on the funded debt in France was about £34,000,000. Now it is about £32,000,000 only, showing no increase of annual burden at all. In Germany the whole Imperial Debt, after thirty years of existence, was still about £120,000,000 only until the present year, and the annual charge inconsiderable. In Russia the annual charge ten years ago was about £26,000,000, and is still only about £27,000,000. One reason, no doubt, is the fall in the rate of interest of late years, a reason which comes close home to a banking audience; but whatever the cause, we have here to do with the fact that leading nations have not sensibly been adding to their annual burdens in the shape of interest on their debts.

In conclusion, then, I must dissent, in the strongest way, from a great deal of the criticism to which the expenditure upon military armaments in time of peace has been subjected on the score of their diminishing the national capital. A good deal of the criticism is the reflection, I believe, of ideas which were formed in times of great stress, such as those which existed at the beginning of last century. Armaments are still talked of in a way which was justified at a time when great burdens were imposed upon the people, and almost as much was taken by the tax collector out of their pockets as possibly could be taken. The point, however, is that the burden of armaments in time of peace, as happens even with the much greater burden which has to be borne in time of war, may fall exclusively on the income of the people at the time, especially when the charge is so moderate, as it is in our own case, as not to be more than 4 or 5 per cent. of that income, and there is no question whatsoever as to national capital itself being expended or wasted. There is also an error in what seems to be a common supposition on the matter. I have heard it said that an additional saving, equal to 4 per cent., or even less than 4 per cent., of the aggregate income of the nation would be an enormous addition to the annual savings of the country, and would, in the course of a few years, have a great cumulative effect. What I must point out, however, is that there is no ground for believing that a cessation of the expenditure on armaments or the cessation of Government expenditure of any kind defrayed out of taxes would bring with it the saving and investment of an equivalent amount as capital. On the contrary, people not paying the taxes would be able to spend the amount on something else, and it does not at all follow that the whole amount would be saved and invested, although a certain small proportion, bearing the same proportion to the taxation remitted as the present savings bear to the total income of the country, might be so saved and invested. As a matter of fact also, it is common knowledge that neither Germany nor France has been fettered in any way for many years past by the lack of capital to develop their industries. The alleged effect of the expenditure on armaments is thus not merely contrary to theory, but is contradicted by the actual experience of many years.

It would be natural to complete this statement by entering into the statistics of the actual growth of capital in each of the countries concerned. I have already had occasion to deal with this matter, however, as far as this country is concerned, in connection with the question of our living upon our capital as the result of the excess of our imports over our exports in international trade, and it would take us too far afield, perhaps, to enter into a statistical inquiry with regard to the other countries I have named where statistics are not so easily available bearing upon this particular point of the growth of capital. The importance of studying the question of the growth of capital, however, is never to be lost sight of in these discussions. The onus of proof that expenditure on armaments in time of peace, to the extent of the actual expenditure of different nations that we see, tends to a waste of national capital, lies upon those who dwell upon the mischief of the armaments themselves. I have never yet seen, however, any attempt to show that the capital of any great military countries such as Germany, France, or Russia, has been diminished, or even the growth of capital greatly checked, by such expenditure. There is a constant assumption that great expenditure on armaments must mean such a diminution of capital, or check to its growth, and there is no attempt to prove the case by actual experience.

The final conclusion on the whole matter is, that the facts, when examined, hardly support the common talk as to this country living on its capital in its transactions with foreign countries, and as to nations wasting and expending their capital by means of excessive armaments. As to the former point, we have found that the whole talk on this subject which we have been criticising is sheer nonsense. The phenomena, when examined, do not even suggest that we are living upon our capital at all. As to the second point, the conclusion is that nations in their armaments may go very far indeed without trenching on their capital, and, in particular, they may go very much further at the present time than any nation is now doing. In former times countries have gone through great wars and great catastrophes, and have been found a few years after to be in possession of much more capital than at the beginning of the catastrophic period. At the present moment nations are expending 4, 5, and, perhaps, in some cases, 10 per cent. of their income upon armaments, but such expenditures, however serious, do not involve necessarily any waste of capital, because they can be borne out of income. In some cases, in past times, particularly in the case of this country during the great war with France, the strain upon income was undoubtedly prodigious. The loss and suffering entailed were enormous, and people would have been much better off if they had had no war to pay for. What I have endeavoured to show, however, is that the question of loss and suffering is one thing, and the question of waste or diminution of capital quite another thing.

Having stated this conclusion, I desire to add one or two practical comments. I have rather avoided comment in the course of the paper, believing it to be essential to arrive at the facts, whatever the commentary may be, but comment itself may be useful in order to avoid misapprehension. It ought not to be inferred from anything that has been said that the question of large military preparations is a matter of indifference to any country, but the inference may be drawn all the same, however erroneously, from an argument intended to cut down some of the usual statements on the subject and to show that some of the alleged mischiefs of these armaments do not, in fact, exist. It may be useful, therefore, to state some of the practical lessons of the facts, as ascertained.

I fear, then, we must conclude that there is no practical advantage in arguing against the continuance of bloated armaments by the great military powers, or against the necessity of corresponding armaments by more peaceful powers like England. The military powers have no idea on the subject but that of developing their military strength to the utmost practical limit, and to show that the margin of their resources is yet unexhausted is to show that they may continue the game. It would be a different matter if the nations they represent were exhausting their capital, so that their taxpaying power was diminishing; but the contrary is the case. The Governments are quite aware that their subjects would have more to spend if taxation were to be diminished, but they consider expenditure on armaments necessary to the State and, for them, that is the end of the question. So long, therefore, as the yield of the taxes is maintained, the military powers are practically certain to go on maintaining and adding to their armaments. This entails corresponding outlay on the part of other powers more disposed to peace, especially on the part of a power like England, which has a foot in every continent, and depends on predominance at sea for its very existence as a State. Whether other powers like it or not, in fact, the great military powers, in this matter, set the pace. Unless they are to be at the mercy of the military powers, which would obviously be a dangerous position, the industrial and peaceful powers must be prepared to show fight.

The second inference I would draw is that in the game of preparation the more economic and peaceful powers ought to be able to keep pace while straining their resources less than the military powers themselves. It is easy to see that, in spite of the great increase of our Navy in recent years, and the increase in the Army, apart from the war in South Africa, the expenditure burdens the United Kingdom much less in proportion than the expenditure for the same objects burdens our military neighbours. We could add greatly to that expenditure and still be no more burdened in proportion. It will be unpleasant to spend the money. There is so much else to be done with the amount if it were available. But if the expenditure is judged necessary it can be met by present sacrifice and without trenching on capital.

A third inference is that, as the expenditure is unavoidable, the best should be made of the necessity, and if, as is alleged, part of the sacrifice called for may be repaid by the benefits which extensive military training ought to confer on the population of the country, then an attempt ought to be made so to arrange matters as to procure the largest indirect return for the inevitable outlay. The value of athletic exercises to the population in universally recognized.

Military training, however, according to the common belief in Germany, is also valuable; and the development by a nation of its Army and Navy need not, consequently, be a pure loss in an economic sense. At any rate a people which is called on to devote a part of its energies to making an Army and a Navy may be asked to consider, before grudging the expenditure, whether the things that would practically be obtained if the amount spent were free for other objects would be so much more valuable to the individuals than the military training and preparation itself when properly organized.

Last of all, it is a set-off, so far, to the cost of great armaments in time of peace that they are an undoubted insurance against war, with the wholesale expenditure and loss of life and disease which a state of war brings. When various great powers are strongly armed, and none can hope for a speedy victory by surprise, such as Germany achieved over France in 1870, then peace is far more likely than if ambition were to be encouraged by tempting opportunities. In this way we may affirm that the almost unbroken peace in Europe since 1870 is due to the very armaments in time of peace which have been so freely condemned. It would be better, of course, to have an out-and-out peace instead of an armed peace which, in some respects, is little better than a truce, but if a choice must be made, then an armed peace is better than war, and Europe has been well repaid for its armaments for many years by the possession of actual peace.

What the final upshot will be of all these warlike preparations it would be useless to speculate. One Government after another may not improbably grow weary, and the competition will become less keen, equality and not superiority being aimed at by each power. On the other hand, it is within the range of possibility that competition will become so excessive as to bring out the very mischief of waste of capital alleged of the system as it actually exists. But these are guesses for the future. We have to deal with an actual situation in which a less severe call is made on our energies, and where we may consider what our preparations ought to be without running any risk of outlays beyond what may well be borne.

XXVII.

A FINANCIAL RETROSPECT, 1861-1901.[1]

Introductory.

IN consequence of certain letters of mine which appeared lately in "The Times," on the "Financial Outlook,"[2] some of my friends on the Council of this Society were good enough to suggest that a short statistical paper, resuming the figures for the last forty years—the past period covered by the letters,—would be useful to the Society by way of record, and would allow of Members discussing from the financial point of view the topics of economic development and national progress, which have so frequently been the subject of debate at our meetings. In a moment of weakness, I fear, the suggestion was accepted, and the present paper is the result. Accidentally as the suggestion has been made, there is a good reason of substance for making 1861 the starting point of such a retrospect. In that year the Free Trade work of Sir R. Peel and Mr. Gladstone had been practically completed. The last great clearance of the tariff, consequent on the Cobden Treaty of 1860, had just been made; the great struggle respecting the paper duty had just been finished; and our tax system was free of any duties for the purpose of protection, if we except a small timber duty, and the registration duty of a shilling per quarter on the import of corn, which were exceptions of a formal, and not of a material, kind. The disturbance of our financial arrangements caused by the Crimean

[1] Read before the Royal Statistical Society, 18th March, 1902.
[2] See the "Times" of 7th, 9th, and 10th January, 1902.

war had also ceased to leave its mark, or nearly so, by 1861. What we have to observe then is the development actually taken by our finance under a Free Trade *régime* all through, and in general circumstances of great material prosperity.

The tables which have been prepared, it will be found, are extremely simple in form. Nothing more has been done than to put together, from the Statistical Abstract mainly, the figures of actual revenue and expenditure and other financial data for a particular year, at intervals of ten years, since the beginning of the period, adding in some cases the estimate for 1901-02, so as to make the comparison more up to date. In a more elaborate study the figures for each year should have been inserted, and averages for groups of years stated; but the present arrangement is simpler and less confusing, while if error arises occasionally, in consequence of the single year in some cases not corresponding with the average at the period to which it belongs, a reference to the very familiar Statistical Abstract can easily be made. But no great error, I believe, arises in this way, although in one case, 1871, the figure of expenditure is rather understated, the total being lower than it would have been if any other one of several years before and after had been selected. The changes, however, between the earlier and the later years are so great that not much turns on the excess or diminution of any particular year compared with the average. In addition to the financial tables proper, supplementary tables are added for convenience of reference, dealing with the factors of population, production and consumption, which are obviously matters requiring consideration in any study of financial questions. It is not proposed, however, to give a formal account of these tables as is done for the financial tables themselves.

The General Growth of Expenditure.

Taking the tables in their order, I begin by noticing Tables I. to IV., dealing first with the revenue and expenditure of the Imperial Government of the United Kingdom, in the gross, and then specially with the expenditure. The lesson of the first table is striking. Expenditure increases from 72.8 million £ in 1861 and 69.5 million £ in 1871, to 80.9 million £ in 1881, 87.7 million £ in 1891, and then in 1901 to 183.6 million £, which is exceeded by the estimates of the current year. Revenue increases in much the same way, lagging a little behind in the last period of all. The figures are 70 million £ in each of the years 1861 and 1871, 82 million £ in 1881, 89.5 million £ in 1891, and 130.4 million £ in 1901, and finally 142.5 million £, estimated in the current financial year. The change from the earlier period is most striking, and practically it has come with a rush in the latest period of all, that is since 1891. The explanation on the surface is that the recent growth is mainly due to the war in South Africa. The sum of nearly 70 million £ is put down for war expenditure in South Africa and in China in 1901, only a small part being for China. But in a general retrospect such as the present, too great stress must not be laid on such explanations. The present period is obviously different from the past, whatever may be the cause. Possibly it may be found after a few years that the figure of 180 to 190 million £ exceeds the normal expenditure of the period into which we have come; but as prudent men we must accept the warning for the present, and not fix upon a much less figure than what has actually lasted for nearly three years, say a less figure than 150 million £, until there is experience of the reduction.

This is not the whole account of the growth of expenditure. Appended to Table I. is an account of the revenue received by the Imperial Government, and handed over by them to the local authorities of the country without appearing in the ordinary budget at all. This was an arrangement commencing about 1887, when some services hitherto charged on the Imperial Budget were handed over to the local authorities along with certain revenues. Clearly in a fair comparison with a former period the expenditure on such services ought still to be shown. The total money thus collected for the local authorities and handed over to them now amounts however to close upon 10 million £, which the Imperial Government really pays, although it is not seen in the ordinary budget. In putting the current expenditure at a very high figure, therefore, compared with 1861 and 1871, and disregarding a good deal the special explanation of war, we are acting safely. There must be a very high figure when normal conditions are established.

Before analysing the growth of expenditure and revenue in detail, we may inquire generally as to the relation of the new burden to the resources of the country. The first table shows that the aggregate expenditure per head of population, after falling from £2 10*s.* 8*d.* in 1861 to £2 4*s.* 3*d.* in 1871, and then rising slightly to £2 6*s.* 4*d.* and £2 6*s.* 6*d.* in 1881 and 1891, has all at once jumped up to £4 8*s.* 6*d.* and £4 12*s.* 2*d.* per head, not including the extra 10 million £ of expenditure which has dropped out of the Imperial Budget. A natural presumption from these figures would seem to be that the national resources are more severely drawn on than they were, as is undoubtedly the case when we make comparison with a recent date, such as 1891. The matter will be discussed more fully afterwards; but it may be useful to point out, even at this early stage, that the maintenance of a low figure of expenditure per head for so long a period as from 1861 to 1891 itself implies an enormous reduction of the burden of Government in proportion to the resources of the people. The period, as we all know, was one of great and continuous prosperity, the wealth of the community increasing fast. It is quite possible, therefore, that with £2 6*s*. 6*d*. per head in 1891, the people were much less burdened than with £2 10*s*. 8*d*. per head in 1861, and that they would be no more burdened now than they were formerly, even if there should be a considerable increase in the expenditure per head. The point is one for investigation and not for assumption on any side. That there has been an enormous increase of wealth is however obvious from two sets of facts, which are corroborated by many others. First, there has been an enormous increase in the consumption of such articles as tea and sugar,—in the former case from 2.69 lbs. per head in 1861 to 6.11 lbs. per head in 1900, and in the latter from 35½ lbs. to 88 lbs. per head (see supplementary tables), increases which would have been impossible without a material improvement in the well-being of the masses. Next there has been an enormous increase of the yield of a penny of the income tax, from £1,100,000 in 1861 to £2,400,000 at the present time (see Table IX.), although in the interval the lower limit of the tax has been raised from £100 to £160, and the limit up to which abatements are given has been raised from £150 to £700. It cannot be assumed then that the country is now burdened more in proportion to its resources by the expenditure of the present time than it was by the expenditure of 70 million £ in 1861. Both sides of the account have to be looked at, and not one only.

The growth of expenditure about 1861, it may be interesting to note, was discussed at the time just as the expenditure of the present day is being discussed in some quarters. On 3rd June, 1862, Mr. Stansfeld moved a resolution of protest against growing expenditure, and was strongly supported, Mr. Disraeli dwelling on "bloated armaments," while Cobden and other authorities joined in the onslaught. There was, however, no real discussion of what the expenditure of the State should be and for what purposes, and of what could really be borne by the community, any more than there is now or ever has been at any time in my recollection. The nearest approach to comparisons of that kind was made by Mr. Stansfeld, who described the expenditure of 70 million £ as equal to a tax of 6*s.* in the £ on the income tax income of the country, and who said that this, at £1 per week per family, would be equal to the maintenance of seven million persons of the working classes for a year. Six shillings per £ on the income tax at £2,400,000 per penny, the present rate of yield, would give an expenditure of no less than 173 million £, which approaches the figure of the present time, while the proportion of the working classes that could be maintained for that sum, owing to the increased income of the class, now far more on the average than £1 per week per family, would be diminished and not increased. Such comparisons, however, are hardly to be encouraged, as the expenditure for Government is necessarily the first charge upon the resources of every community, and if it has to be met, no help is given in its proper administration by showing that, as with Mrs. Caudle's £5, something else could be done with the money.

Analysis of Increased Expenditure and Revenue.

Analysing the expenditure in detail, we may notice the following points:

1. The annual charge for the debt (Table II.) appears to have considerably diminished. The figure is 26.3 million £ in the budget of 1861, and in the estimate for 1902 it is 21.6 million £. This is subject to the observation, of course, that the annual charge in 1861 included a considerable sum for the reduction of debt, while the annual charge at the present time does not, but there is clearly no question that the annual charge, apart from repayment of debt, has rather diminished. The capital has diminished, there has been some reduction of interest by conversion, and there will shortly be a further reduction of interest of the same kind to

be set against the actual increase of debt during the last few years.

2. The Civil Service expenditure of a miscellaneous kind accounts for very little of the large growth of expenditure with which we have been dealing (Table IV.). The Financial Abstract now shows in a line the whole of the expenditure for civil government, including the Civil Service estimates and the charges on the Consolidated Fund, apart from the debt charge, but excluding the charges for the collection of revenue and for the Post Office. The figure of this expenditure last year was £24,854,000, and if we carry it back, we find that the corresponding figure in 1861 was £9,659,000. This is a considerable increase, nearly £15,000,000, but on further analysis we find that the increase in the education charge alone was from £1,097,000 to £12,662,000, or nearly 12 million £ of the total, and that the miscellaneous Civil Service expenditure—the general charge for the civil government of the country—has only increased from £6,266,000 to £10,623,000, or, including Consolidated Fund charges, from £8,562,000 to £12,192,000, or about 3½ million £. This is again subject to the observation above made as to services transferred to local authorities, and to some doubts as to the manipulation of the estimates, by which the expenditure is partly concealed; but, making all allowance for such observations, the facts appear to show that a common impression as to the formidable growth of Civil Service expenditure, on which about fifteen years ago Lord Randolph Churchill thought he could save 10 million £, is hardly well founded. Lord Randolph Churchill, in fact, sacrificed his career for a pure blunder.

3. The growth of education expenditure in particular, to which attention has been drawn, is an undoubted makeweight in the present position.

4. The charge for collection of the revenue, apart from the Post Office, like the Civil Service expenditure generally, has remained comparatively stationary, being

£2,834,000 now, as compared with £2,569,000 in 1861. In other words, Customs and Inland Revenue, though we collect double the revenue, cost hardly more now than they did in 1861.

5. The largest increase in civil expenditure, besides education, is in the Post Office department, where the expenditure has risen from about 3 million £ in 1861, to 13½ million £ in 1901. This is expenditure, as is well known, which is accompanied by a corresponding growth of revenue, and implies a corresponding increase of services rendered to the country. Even if it grows, therefore, out of proportion to the growth of population and income, it is a beneficial expenditure, and need be viewed without concern, although it may involve an increase of the charge per head of population.

6. We come finally to the real question involved in the growth of expenditure, viz., the growth of charges for Army and Navy. It is these charges, including the charges for actual war, which account mainly for the whole growth between 1861 and 1901. The increase in Army and Navy (see Table III.) is in fact 90 million £, if we compare 1861 with the present time, viz., from just over 31 million £ to just over 121 million £, and it is no less than 100 million £ if we compare 1871 with the present time, viz., from 22½ million £ to just over 121 million £. There appears indeed to have been a decided falling off in the charge for the Navy, especially between 1861 and 1871, so that 1871, as already mentioned, becomes an exceptionally low year to start from. What will surprise some of us is that Army and Navy were kept under, as they appear to have been, down to as late a date as 1891, so that then as compared with 1871 they show no greater an increase than about 10 million £.

There is, unfortunately, no doubt about the increase of 100 million £, or thereabouts, since 1871. We are spending over 121 million £, where we spent just over 22 million £ in 1871. Of this increase, as already suggested regarding the growth of expenditure generally, a large part must be really permanent, but the point should be specially considered, as a certain part of the general growth of expenditure, viz., the expenditure for education, and for Post Office, which is also in all probability permanent, is in an entirely different category from expenditure on armaments. We should disregard then, I believe, the classification of 70 million £ of this army and navy expenditure as being for "war," and impliedly, therefore, temporary. The question is one of opinion, and I should deprecate a very full discussion here, as involving questions of politics; but the overruling facts appear to be that a war expenditure for two years amounting to about 70 million £ a year, followed by an estimate of 40 million £ for the next year, must be held to indicate a situation of a chronic character, implying expenditure of a similar nature for some years to come. The expenditure, in fact, is not so much for war as for the more or less permanent occupation of a difficult country, which unavoidable circumstances, I for one should admit, compel us to occupy, where there are good reasons also for believing the burden will diminish, and diminish greatly, in time, but where improvement is conditional on our facing the evil at its worst. What we have really to face then on account of South Africa is a costly army of occupation, with corresponding charges for an army at home to send reliefs to it as we now send reliefs to India and our other colonial possessions. As to Army and Navy generally, also, the international position appears to be such that for some years to come the British Empire must exhibit a great and unwonted development of force. The reason is that we are surrounded as we never were before by great military powers who possess powerful and increasing navies; that we have extensive land frontiers in all parts of the globe, with active enemies near them, especially in Asia and Africa, such as we never had before; and that our staying power, if we are checked, owing to our absolute dependence on sea communications for needful raw material as well as food, and for the sale of the productions by which our people live, may be unexpectedly curtailed. Hence we must make preparations for eventualities, not only as if we were one of the unfortunate continental States who are perpetually in terror of the spectre of invasion, and whose case we have been accustomed to lament from our superior position as girt by the inviolate sea; but we must prepare as if we were exposed to even greater dangers than any continental neighbour. Our whole position has been revolutionised internationally, and as like causes produce like effects, we must go through the experience in the way of military preparation which our continental neighbours have gone through.

The only question is as to the exact figure at which the permanent increase of Army and Navy expenditure should be put. It will probably be something less than the 121 million £ at which it now stands, comprising one-half for ordinary Army and Navy expenditure and one-half for so-called war. The estimates for next year provide for about 100 million £ only. But take it as a rough guide that every 100,000 men of regular army and navy, allowing for increased pay, must cost about 13 million £ a year, and that new ships and repairs, merely to keep our fleet going, must cost about 15 million £ annually, we can easily calculate what large sums must be spent. Mr. Brodrick estimates the regular army, including India, at 250,000 men, but this omits South Africa, and with South Africa the numbers will certainly not be less than 300,000, omitting India altogether. At the rate of 13 million £ for each 100,000 men, this will mean an expenditure for army alone of nearly 40 million £, apart from charges for auxiliary forces and the like. The navy, again, has nearly 130,000 men, involving at the above rate a charge for the *personnel* of about 17 million £, besides 15 million £ for repairs and renewals of the *matériel*, and charges for fortified coal depôts, etc., let alone an increase of the fleet to keep pace with foreign fleets—total over 40 million £. As I have often insisted, therefore, I see no way by which, in fact, charges of 40 million £ each for Army and Navy are to be avoided in future, and practically we may consider ourselves fortunate if the charge should ever again be less than about 100 million £ in all.

These are very different figures indeed from the 20 to 30 millions which were the occasion of the lively debates of forty years ago. But we have travelled far from that time, and that is all that can be said.

Analysis of Growth of Revenue.

Analysing the growth of revenue in detail, we may notice the following points:

1. No part of the increase of revenue since 1861 can be ascribed to the imposition of new taxes or the increase of existing taxes. The increase in all, comparing 1901 with 1861, is from 70 million £ to 130 million £; but the whole of this extra 60 million £ is due exclusively to the larger yield of existing taxation, and not to any new burdens. This appears clearly from Table XIII. in the appendix, summarizing the well-known table in the Statistical Abstract, which gives the taxes repealed or reduced, and imposed or increased in each year, with the estimated loss or gain to the exchequer in a complete year, and other particulars. There have been many ups and downs in the tax list in the interval, but finally the reductions all told amount to 71 million £, and the increases to 62.6 million £, leaving a net reduction of 8.4 £, which ought to be added to the increase of revenue above stated to show what the real growth has been. The growth must have been even larger. A reduction or increase of the same rate of tax, when revenue is growing rapidly, is necessarily represented by a smaller amount of taxation in an earlier than in a later period. When reductions take place, therefore, in the earlier part of the period over

which the comparison extends, and increases in the latter part, the comparison of the amounts of taxation affected does not quite show the real reduction that has taken place, but it shows a figure that may be a good deal less. In the last ten years there is an increase of taxation of no less than £19,500,000 on balance, but the same changes of taxes in the first ten years of the period would have come to a good deal less money, and it is this amount which should be compared with the early reductions, so as to show what the real growth of revenue has been.

If we made the comparison with the estimates of the current year the result would be much the same. We should have to add about 11 million £ for the increased taxes in last budget, thereby showing a small increase of taxation on balance to be deducted from the apparent growth of revenue from 70 million £ in 1861 to 142½ million £ in the current year. But this apparent increase, according to the explanation above given, would be far more than the real increase, and on balance there would be no such increase. We are quite within the mark in saying that the doubling of the revenue since 1861 has been effected without any increase of taxes on balance, but rather along with a decrease.[1]

2. The second point which is obvious on the surface of the tables is the fact of a great change in the relative importance of different branches of the revenue in the total product. A glance at Table V. shows that, while Customs in forty years have increased from 23.3 million £ to 26.3 million £, or about 15 per cent.; Excise from 19.4 million £ to 33.1 million £, or 70 per cent.; and Stamps (excluding death duties) from 4.9 million £ to 7.8 million £, or 57 per cent.; we find income tax increasing from 10.9 million £ to 26.9 million £, or nearly 150 per cent.; death duties from

[1] No difference would be made in this conclusion by including the revenues handed over to local authorities. The net reduction of taxation shown would be so much less, but the growth of revenue would be so much greater.

3.4 million £ to 13 million £, or 286 per cent.; and Post Office charges from 3.4 million £ to 17.3 million £, or over 400 per cent. If the current year were taken into account these contrasts would be still as marked. Certain additions have been made to Customs and Excise, so that they exhibit a larger percentage of increase than was the case a year ago; but income tax has also been added to, and the comparison shows up much the same. Leaving aside the Post Office, where the charges stand by themselves as being largely charges for services rendered, and not bare taxation, we may say broadly that, during the last forty years, income tax and death duties have largely increased in relative importance among the different branches of revenue, and Customs and Excise and Stamps have declined.

The comparison would be still more significant if we started from 1871 instead of 1861. Here we find the contrast in the growth of the branches of revenue mentioned to have been as follows:

First Group.

	1871.	1901.	Increase.	
			Amount.	Per Cent.
Customs	20.1	26.3	6.2	31
Excise	22.8	33.1	10.3	45
Stamps	3.6	7.8	4.2	116
	43.5	67.2	20.7	44

Second Group.

Income tax . .	6.4	26.9	20.5	320
Death duties . .	4.8	13.0	8.2	170
Post Office . .	5.3	17.3	12.0	226
	16.5	57.2	40.7	247

Thus, while an addition of about 21 million £ has

been made to the first three branches of revenue in thirty years, an increase of less than 50 per cent., the addition in the case of the second group is almost exactly double, or 41 million £, and has been at the rate of 250 per cent. Here, again, the effect of the contrast would hardly be mitigated by including the additional taxes imposed a year ago. The additional weight thrown on income tax and death duties "leaps to the eyes."

3. The next point must be that this change in relative position among different branches of the revenue has not occurred automatically in any way, that is by some taxes in course of time, through a natural development, becoming more productive than others. It has occurred, on the contrary, at least very largely, as the result of legislative and other changes. If we analyse, in fact, the list of taxes repealed or reduced, and taxes imposed or increased, to which reference has already been made, we find that the reductions in the early period are largely reductions of duties of Customs and Excise, and the increases in the later period are largely increases of income tax and death duties. On this head the list of rates of duty on principal heads of Customs (Table X.) appears instructive. There is a slight increase in the charge for spirits; a slight increase on tobacco generally, but a decrease in the rates for cigars and snuff; a great decrease in tea, from 1*s.* 5*d.* to 6*d.* per lb.; a great reduction in sugar, from 18*s.* 4*d.*, or 2*d.* per lb. on refined, in 1861, to about ½*d.* per lb., in 1871, while after that the heading disappears altogether, only to be restored very partially in the current year; corn, which was 1*s.* a quarter in 1861, had disappeared from the list in 1871, though only just before that year; and timber and various other articles which were dutiable in 1861, have likewise vanished. The reductions, except sugar and tea, were not generally important in amount, but the changes on balance have been all one way. In Excise there have been fewer or hardly any reductions, if we except the transfers made between

1881 and 1891 to local authorities, but the amount yielded by Excise has increased more than Customs, and the two of course should be taken together. On the other side, it will be seen that income tax, after beginning at 10*d.* per £ in 1861, and being as low as 4*d.* in 1871, has since been raised to 1*s.* in 1901, and now stands, as all of us know, at 1*s.* 2*d.* in the £. No doubt another change in the way of reduction has taken place in the income tax as already mentioned, viz., the increase of the lower limit of the tax and the increase of the limit up to which abatements are made (see Table VII.); but this does not alter the fact of the increase of the rate of the tax as far as incomes above £700 are concerned. With regard to death duties it would be tedious to make an arithmetical comparison, but two or three changes of obvious effect have been made, viz., the subjection of real property to the same rates and mode of charging as personal property, an increase of the duties generally, and a special increase of the rate of duty in proportion to the increase of the size of properties. The marvellous increase of the death duties is thus in no way surprising.

The net result of the whole change is the substitution of income tax and death duties in our tax system for duties of Customs and Excise, especially for duties on tea and sugar, on which we relied largely in 1861, and still relied to some extent as late as 1871. They also take the place, of course, of the minor Customs duties on corn and timber, etc., which existed without any feeling against them as involving a breach of Free Trade, because in fact they yielded some useful money to the exchequer without inconvenience to business.

4. To show the exact proportion of certain branches of revenue to the total revenue at different times, a separate table (Table XII.) has been added in the appendix. This table speaks for itself. It confirms fully what has already been said as to the change in our tax system which has occurred. Income tax and death duties, which supplied 20 per cent., or one-fifth of the revenue

in 1861, and 16 per cent. only in 1871, supplied in 1901 no less than 31 per cent. of the total. Customs and Excise, on the other hand, which supplied 61 per cent. in 1861, and 63 per cent. in 1871, now supply 45 per cent. only.

Summing up this analysis of revenue, and comparing the results with the corresponding facts as to the growth of expenditure already dealt with, we may conclude, I believe, that the showing in some respects is not unsatisfactory. It is unpleasant to have to spend so much as we do on armaments, and to recognise that this expenditure, or at least a large part of it, is of a permanent character, and is not coming to an end with a definite closing of the South African war. It is nevertheless satisfactory so far that we can meet a high expenditure—double and more than double the figures of forty and even thirty years ago—as easily in reality as the expenditure of those years was met. A Rip Van Winkle of the early sixties, if he were to come back to life now, would not find his imperial burdens any greater. If he were a total abstainer and his income were below the income tax level, he would find his burdens even less than they were. A great change has been made in the interval in the substitution of some taxes for others; but we have only to do with substitution and not with an increase of burdens. Opinions will of course differ as to how far the substitution has been wise, and whether the pressure of income tax and death duties on the community as a whole, is not more severe than the pressure of the sugar and tea duties, which contributed a great deal, and the corn, timber, and other duties which contributed a little, to the revenue of thirty and forty years ago; but this is the only point of dispute raised by the present retrospect. As to the changes themselves and the causes, and our ability to meet the increased expenditure of the present time, with no real increase of burden as compared with a recent date, there is absolutely no dispute.

II.

The Growth of Wealth.

The income tax tables and the supplementary tables generally contain further information as to the growth of the resources of the country upon which the expansion of the revenue depends. Though it is not really necessary to show the growth of the country's ability to meet the largely increased expenditure of recent years —and I shall probably have an opportunity after 1905, if the Society will permit me, of continuing those studies on the income tax returns which were commenced before you in 1878—still I may be allowed to add a few more remarks bearing directly on this question.

What I should like to notice first of all, then, is that the doubling of our wealth and of our ability to bear increased burdens does not depend on any astonishing change in the productiveness of the industry of the country. It depends mainly on two factors: (1), the growth of population, and (2), a very moderate increase in the wealth of the population per head. If the population had doubled, the wealth per head remaining the same, there would be no doubt of the country having twice its former ability to bear taxation. But short of doubling, the population may increase so greatly in a given time that a very moderate addition to the wealth per head may produce the same result. Now the increase of population is obscured for this purpose by dealing with the United Kingdom as a whole, which causes the decrease of population in Ireland to set off in part the increase in Great Britain, although the two peoples are not homogeneous. If we put the two together the increase is from 28.9 millions in 1861 to 41.5 millions in 1901, or 43½ per cent., which would require an increase of nearly 40 per cent. in the wealth per head in the interval to account for the doubling of the resources of the country. But if we take Great Britain only, the progressive part of the country, we find the increase of numbers is from 23.1 to 37 millions, or 60 per cent., which would suffice for the doubling of the resources of the country with an increase of 25 per cent. only in individual wealth per head, by no means so astonishing an increase as that which must be allowed for with a smaller increase of population. Against such an increase the deduction of a portion of the poorer population would be a very small set-off.

What the actual increase per head is since 1861 has been already glanced at. It cannot, in any view, be less than 25 per cent., in face of the figures showing the growth of income tax assessments between 1861 and 1901 from 335½ million £ to 788 million £, or over 130 per cent., as compared with a growth of population, reckoning Great Britain only, of 60 per cent. This would imply an increase of 40 to 50 per cent. per head, and would certainly more than justify the assumption of an increase of 25 per cent. only, which is necessary to the doubling of the resources of the country. Reckoning, moreover, the changes in the income tax returns by which the gross amount is understated as compared with what was the case formerly, that is adding nearly 40 million £ to the above figure of 788 million £, the increase then would be no less than 140 per cent. as compared with an increase of 60 per cent. in population, and would imply an increase of wealth per head of over 50 per cent.

Comparing 1871 with 1901, we have an increase from 465.5 million £ in the income tax assessments to the above figure of 788 million £, or, rather, 828 million £, or at the rate of about 80 per cent. as compared with an increase of 54 per cent. in the population of Great Britain only. This would be equal to an increase of 16 per cent. per head, and, although not quite doubling the whole wealth of the country in thirty years, comes very near to doing so.

If it were in my power to go more into detail with the income tax figures than has been found possible at short notice, these conclusions would be strongly supported. The large growth of "houses" for instance, nearly 200 per cent. (see Table XI.), cannot but attract observation.

The great increase of the consumption of tea and sugar has already been adverted to, but the figures as to consumption of meat and other articles in the supplementary tables are equally instructive, and it is unnecessary to repeat them in detail. The evidence is, moreover, cumulative, the facts as to revenue supporting the other evidence as to the growth of wealth, and being themselves explained by that growth as they could not otherwise be explained. Nor is another fact apparent on the face of the supplementary tables and of the income tax returns, viz., the fact of a decline or stationary condition of agriculture and of some other industries, inconsistent with this conclusion. There is always an up and down in every sort of industry. New industries are continually starting up, and no one can foresee from year to year in what new directions we are to advance and where it is inevitable we should recede. The point is to have an increase of wealth and income on balance, and not set too much store on special changes.

Summary and Conclusion.

This paper has extended, I fear, beyond the modest limits intended by my friends. Let me hasten therefore to summarize what has been said, and add a word or two of comment, if not exhortation.

1. The expenditure of the Imperial Government of the United Kingdom has increased since the completion of Free Trade reform in 1861, and mostly since 1891, from an initial figure of about 70 million £ to the present total of 180 million £ or thereabouts, of which about 150 to 160 million £ may be considered of a permanent character.

2. No part of this increase is due to the increase of the debt charge, which has rather diminished.

3. Further, the increase is only due in small degree

to Civil Service expenditure, which has increased a few millions only, apart from education, while the expenditure of Customs and Excise has hardly increased at all. The increase for education, however, is nearly 12 million £.

4. A large part of the increase is due to the Post Office department, the outlay for which has risen from 3 to 13½ million £, in consequence, it is obvious, of the additional services which the department conducts for the benefit of the public as compared with what it formerly managed, and in consequence of the extensive growth of the older services themselves.

5. The main increase of expenditure is, however, due to Army and Navy, on which we spent in 1900-01 over 121 million £ as compared with little more than 30 million £ in 1861, and about 22 million £ only in 1871. Although 70 million £ of this increase is set down in the budget as for war, the ordinary growth of Army and Navy being set down as no more than about 30 million £, reasons are given for the opinion that the expenditure for armaments is not permanently reducible by so large a figure as the amount set down for war. A total permanent outlay of at least 150 million £ is considered to be highly probable, of which 80 million £ or over will be for Army and Navy.

6. The revenue has also increased greatly since 1861, viz., from about 70 to 130 million £ in 1900-01, and to an estimated figure of 142½ million £ in the current year.

7. It is considered, however, that notwithstanding the increase of burden, the country is as well able to bear this load as it was to bear the smaller sum of 70 million £ levied in 1861 and 1871. It is pointed out that the population of Great Britain has increased 60 per cent. since 1861, and that with a very small increase of wealth per head, so large an increase of the progressive part of the population implies the doubling, and more than doubling, of the resources of the country.

8. A table is also given, compiled from the official returns, as to taxes repealed or reduced, and imposed or increased since 1861, showing that on balance the taxes have not been increased, but have rather been diminished in the interval. The diminutions amount to 71 million £, and the additions to 62.6 million £, making a net reduction of 8.4 million £. Reasons are given for the opinion that the real reduction is even greater, but the fact is placed beyond question that the larger revenue now raised is not due in any way to new taxation as compared with 1861 and even 1871, but is exclusively an automatic growth, due to the increased productiveness of the former scale of taxation.

9. While taxation generally has not increased, great changes have occurred among the taxes themselves. While income tax and death duties have been increased enormously, indirect taxes have been struck off, particularly duties on tea and sugar, besides minor duties on corn, timber, and other articles, all of which, it is pointed out, were in existence at a time when Free Trade had been completely established, so that there is no question of Free Trade involved in the substitution in question.

It is submitted, then, in conclusion, without going into all the arguments *pro* and *con*, that the time has now come for reviewing the question of national expenditure in a business way with reference to the international position and duties of the country, and without any concern as to the ability of the country to meet what is required. The time would also appear to have come for inquiring into the reasons for substituting income tax and death duties for certain indirect taxes. It can hardly be contended that the change has been deliberately made, seeing that the reductions of indirect imposts were made in the buoyant days, when prosperity was advancing by leaps and bounds, and we were drinking ourselves out of the "Alabama" claims, while the increase of income tax and death duties has taken place quite recently as a ready means of getting money, and without any inquiry as to the actual duties that had been last got rid of. No question as to Free Trade, it may be again repeated, is involved, as the nation was never more free trading than it was in the sixties. One or two duties, such as the corn duty, may be technically a breach of Free Trade, but the mischief resulting from such a breach, as it was considered in the days of Cobden, is much less than the mischief of a high income tax which is now the substitute. It is not proposed, however, to argue out the question here, but only to show that it is inevitably raised for discussion.

[NOTE.—I desire specially to express my thanks to Dr. Ginsburg, Secretary, and Mr. Mackenzie, Chief Clerk of the Royal Statistical Society, for the preparation of the annexed tables. I have only been able to revise them partially, but I am sure they are completely trustworthy. I have also to add (1904) that while a little difference would be made in some of the figures by taking the latest financial year, following on the close of the war, the results yielded by the retrospect generally would not vary substantially from those here stated. The Appendix following does not include the supplementary Tables in the original paper, which will be found in the Statistical Society's Journal for 1902. —R. G.]

APPENDIX I.

TABLE I.—*Revenue and Expenditure of the Imperial Government of the United Kingdom.*

Years ending 31st March.	Revenue.	Expenditure.	Population of United Kingdom.	Expenditure per Head of Population.
	Mln. £.	Mln. £.		£ *s.* *d.*
1861	70.3[1]	72.8[1]	28.9	2 10 8
'71	69.9[1]	69.5[1]	31.5	2 4 3
'81	81.9	80.9	34.9	2 6 4
'91	89.5	87.7	37.7	2 6 6
1901	130.4	183.6[2]	41.5	4 8 6
Estimate for 1901-02 .	142.5	191.3	41.5	4 12 2

TABLE IA.—*Revenue received by Imperial Government, and paid over to Local Authorities, and Government subventions as acknowledged by Local Authorities.*

[Mln. £'s.]

	Amount Received and Handed Over to Local Authorities.	Subventions as Acknowledged by Local Authorities.
1861	—	—[3]
'71	—	—[3]
'81	—	3.4
'91	7.1	8.6
1901	9.6	14.2

Note.—The amounts in column 1 do not appear in the ordinary accounts of Imperial revenue and expenditure. The amounts in the second column include the amounts in the first column as well as in the grants.

[1] These figures include Army and Navy extra receipts and contributions by India for military charges, and are not strictly comparable with the later years. Excluding these amounts, the figures for 1871 would read, revenue 68.2 million £, expenditure 67.8 million £.

[2] Including 68.6 million £ for war expenditure.

[3] There were Government grants in 1861 and 1871, as well as in later years; but the summary of the local taxation accounts in the "Statistical Abstract," from which the figures in this column were taken, does not go so far back as 1861, and the exact sums for comparison could only be ascertained with difficulty. They would be less, and not more, than in 1881.

TABLE II.—*Amount of the National Debt, and Charge for Interest.*

[Mln. £'s.]

Years ending 5th April.	Total Debt, excluding Local Loans Stock after 1881.	Annual Charge for Interest and Sinking Fund in Budget.
1861	824.6	26.3
'71	789.2	26.8
'81	770.8	29.6
'91	686.0	25.2
1901	705.7	19.8
'02 (estimated) . .	—	21.6

Note.—The annual charge includes the amount of the whole instalment for annuities as well as interest on the permanent funded debt, and also includes other appropriations for repayment of debt, varying in different years. After 1881 a separate issue was made of local loans stock, and the amount of this stock is not now included as part of the national debt, there being corresponding assets on the other side, and the receipts and payment of interest being outside the budget. To make a proper comparison, the amounts for the earlier years, 1861, 1871, and 1881, should be reduced somewhat. The local loans about 1887, when the change was made, amounted to 36 million £.

TABLE III.—*Army and Navy Expenditure, excluding Amounts Charged to Capital.*

[Mln. £'s.]

Years.	Army.	Navy.	Total.
1861	15.0	13.3	31.3[1]
'71	13.5[2]	9.0	22.5
'81	14.7	10.5	25.8[3]
'91	17.9	15.5	33.5
1901	91.9	29.5	121.4[4]
'02 (estimate) . .	90.0	30.9	120.9[5]

[1] Including 3 mln. £ for Chinese war.
[2] Including 1.4 mln. £ vote of credit, war in Europe.
[3] Including £500,000 grant for Afghan war, etc.
[4] Including 68.6 mln. £ for war expenditure.
[5] The figure has been changed several times, and this is the nearest I can give.

TABLE IV.—*Civil Service and Post Office Expenditure.*

[Thousand £'s.]

1	2	3	4	5	6	7
Years ending 31st March,	Consolidated Fund Charges, exclusive of Debt Charges.	Education.	Other Civil Service Expenditure.	Total.	Revenue Collection, Excise and Customs.	Post Office Telegraphs and Packet Service.
1861 . .	2,296,	1,097,	6,266,	9,659,	2,569,	2,999,[1]
'71 . .	2,113,	1,859,	7,991,	11,963,	2,573,	3,949,
'81 . .	1,670,	4,281,	11,405,	17,356,	2,850,	5,372,
'91 . .	2,068,	6,114,	9,551,	17,733,	2,643,	8,661,
1901 . .	1,569,	12,662,	10,623,	24,854,	2,834,	13,471,

Note.—The figures in column 4 are obtained by subtracting the totals of columns 2 and 3 from column 5.

[1] Post Office and packet service only.

TABLE V.—*Principal Branches of Revenue.*

[Mln. £'s.]

	1861.	1871.	1881.	1891.	1901.
Total Imperial expenditure . .	72,8 [1]	67,8	80,9	87,7	183,6
Total Imperial revenue:					
Customs	23,3	20,1	19,2	19,5	26,3
Excise	19,4	22,8	25,3	24,8	33,1
Stamps (excluding death duties)	4,9	3,6	4,5	5,9	7,8
Income tax	10,9	6,4	10,7	13,3	26,9
Land tax [2] . . . . . } House duty . . . . . }	3,1	2,7	1,0	1,0	8
			1,7	1,6	1,7
Death duties	3,4	4,8	6,6	7,5	13,0
Post Office and telegraphs .	3,4	5,3	8,3	12,3	17,3
Miscellaneous (including interest on advances for local works and Government Suez Canal shares, etc.)	1,9	2,5	4,6	3,6	3,6
Total	70,4	68,2	81,9	89,5	130,4
Revenue [3] received and paid to local authorities:					
Customs	—	—	—	2	2
Excise	—	—	—	1,1	1,4
,, licences	—	—	—	3,4	3,9
Death duties	—	—	—	2,4	4,1
Total	—	—	—	7,1	9,6

[1] Including Army and Navy extra receipts, and the contributions by India for military charges, formerly brought to account as revenue, and thus causing a corresponding increase in expenditure.

[2] These figures were not given separately in the "Statistical Abstract" in 1861 and 1871.

[3] These receipts formerly formed part of the Imperial revenue; since 1888-89 they have been paid to the local authorities in relief of local burdens.

TABLE VI.—*Net Receipts from Principal Heads of Customs.*

[Thousand £'s.]

	1861.	1871.	1881.	1891.	1901.
Customs:					
Spirits (foreign and colonial) .	2,624,	4,419,	4,444,	4,493,	4,770,
Tobacco and snuff	5,606,	6,614,	8,659,	9,534,	12,839,
Tea	5,420,	3,235,	3,866,	3,412,	6,265,
Sugar and molasses	6,067,	3,219,	—	—	—
Coffee	439,	416,	200,	182,	190,
Cocoa	—	32,[1]	53,[1]	105,	242,
Currants, raisins, and dried fruits	219,[1]	463,	491,	324,	349,
Wine	1,145,	1,584,	1,376,	1,318,	1,488,
Corn, meal, and flour . . .	869,	—	—	—	—
Timber	237,[1]	—	—	—	—
Other imported articles . .	395,	127,	88,	80,	90,
Miscellaneous receipts . . .	258,	129,	34,	32,	39,
Total	23,278,	20,239,	19,210,	19,479,	26,271,

TABLE VII.—*Income Tax Assessments, Schedules A—E, Gross Amounts, Years ending 5th April.*

[Mln. £'s.]

Divisions.	1861.	1871.	1881.	1891.	1900.
England	282,2	398,4	493,6	597,3	678,7
Scotland	30,4	41,0	55,5	63,4	75,8
Great Britain	312,6	439,4	549,1	660,7	754,5
Ireland	23,0	26,1	36,1	37,8	33,5
United Kingdom	335,6	465,5	585,2	698,4	788,0

Year . .	1861.	1871.	1881.	1891.	1900.
General rate to tax . .	10*d.*	4*d.*	6*d.*	6*d.*	1*s.*
Lowest income without abatement . . .	£150	£200	£400	£400	£700
Lowest income taxed . .	£100	£100	£150	£150	£160
Abatements:					
On income under . .	£150	£200	£400	£400	(*a.*) £400 (*b.*) £500 (*c.*) £600 (*d.*) £700
Amount of abatement .	Pay 7*d.* rate only	£60	£120	£120	(*a.*) £100 (*b.*) £150 (*c.*) £120 (*d.*) £70

[1] Gross receipts.

TABLE VIII.—*Net Receipts from Principal Heads of Excise.*

[Thousand £'s.]

	1861.	1871.	1881.	1891.	1901.
Excise:					
Spirits	9,226,	11,464,	14,394,	14,771,	19,207,
Malt	6,209,	6,978,	2,676,	—	—
Beer	—	—	3,482,	9,390,	13,491,
Sugar used in brewing	—	95,	502,	—	—
Chicory	—	} 17,	{ 1,	2,	1,
Coffee mixture labels	—		—	3,	2,
Railways	—	506,	748,	324,	331,
Licences	1,493,	3,729,	3,568,	230,	250,
Other receipts	2,621,	45,	—	4,	5,
Total	19,548,	22,834,	25,372,	24,724,	33,287,

Net Receipts of Duties Collected for Local Authorities by Imperial Officers.

Additional beer and spirit duties { Customs	—	—	—	206,	219,
Additional beer and spirit duties { Excise	—	—	—	1,095,	1,367,
Excise licences	—	—	—	3,360,	3,886,

TABLE IX.—*Yield of a Penny on the Income Tax at different Periods.*

	Figures from the Budget Speech.	Figures from Inland Revenue Returns.
	£	£
In 1901 a penny produced	2,400,000	2,426,000
,, 1891 a penny produced	2,300,000	2,215,856
,, '81 a penny produced	1,943,000	—
,, '71 a penny produced	1,525,000	—
,, '61 a penny produced	1,100,000	—

TABLE X.—*Rates of Duty on Principal Heads of Customs.*

Articles.		1861.	1871.	1881.	1891.	1900-01.
Spirits, foreign and colonial	*per gall.*	10*s.* 2*d.* to 10*s.* 5*d.*	10*s.* 2*d.* to 10*s.* 5*d.*	10*s.* 4*d.*	10*s.* 4*d.* and 6*d.* for local taxation	11*s.* 4*d.*
[1] Tobacco and cigars: Unmanufactured	*per lb.*	3*s.*	3*s.* to 3*s.* 6*d.* and 5 per cent. add.	3*s.* 6*d.* to 3*s.* 10*d.*	3*s.* 2*d.* to 3*s.* 6*d.*	3*s.* to 3*s.* 4*d.*
Tobacco and cigars: Manufactured and cigars	,,	9*s.*	4*s.* 6*d.* to 5*s.*	4*s.* 4*d.* to 5*s.* 6*d.*	4*s.* to 5*s.*	3*s.* 10*d.* to 5*s.* 6*d.*
Tobacco, snuff	,,	6*s.*	3*s.* 9*d.*	4*s.* 1*d.* to 4*s.* 10*d.*	3*s.* 9*d.* to 4*s.* 6*d.*	3*s.* 7*d.* to 4*s.* 4*d.*
Tea	,,	1*s.* 5*d.*	6*d.*	6*d.*	4*d.*	6*d.*
Sugar and molasses, *per cwt.*: Raw		12*s.* 8*d.* to 16*s.*	4*s.* to 5*s.* 8*d.*	—	—	—
Sugar and molasses, *per cwt.*: Refined		18*s.* 4*d.*	6*s.*	—	—	—
Coffee: Kiln dried	*per lb.*	—	—	2*d.*	2*d.*	2*d.*
Coffee: Raw	,,	4*d.*	4*d.*	—	—	—
Coffee: ,,	*per cwt.*	—	—	14*s.*	14*s.*	14*s.*
Cocoa	*per lb.*	1*d.*	1*d.*	1*d.*	1*d.*	1*d.*
,, chocolate and paste	,,	2*d.*	2*d.*	and prep	ared cocoa	imported
				2*d.*	2*d.*	2*d.*
,, butter	,,	—	—	—	—	1*d.*
,, in husk	*per cwt.*	2*s.*	2*s.*	2*s.*	2*s.*	2*s.*
Currants	,,	7*s.*	7*s.*	7*s.*	2*s.*	2*s.*
Raisins, figs, etc.	,,				2*s.* 7*s.*	2*s.* 7*s.*
Wine (not in bottles)	*per gall.*	1*s.* to 2*s.* 11*d.*	1*s.* to 2*s.* 6*d.* and	1*s.* to 2*s.* 6*d.* 3*d.* a degr	1*s.* to 2*s.* 6*d.* ee over 42	1*s.* 3*d.* to 3*s.* proof
Corn: Wheat	*per qr.*	1*s.*	—	—	—	—
Corn: Meal, etc.	*per cwt.*	4½*d.*	—	—	—	—
Timber: Hewn	*per load*	1*s.*	—	—	—	—
Timber: Sawn, etc.	,,	2*s.*	—	—	—	—
Timber: Teak, for ships	,,	1*s.*	—	—	—	—
Beer: Mum and spruce	*per 36 gall.*	£1	£1 1*s.* to £1 4*s.*	£1 6*s.* to £1 10*s* 6*d.*	£1 6*s.* to £1 10*s.* 6*d.*	£1 12*s.* to £1 17*s.* 6*d.*
Beer: Other sorts	,,	£1	8*s.* to 16*s.*	6*s.* 6*d.*	6*s.* 6*d.*	8*s.*
Hops	*per cwt.*	£1	—	—	—	—
Malt	*per qr.*	£1 5*s.*	£1 4*s.* To 1st April, 1871, £1 5*s.*	—	—	—
Cards, playing	*per doz. packs*	15*s.*	3*s.* 9*d.*	3*s.* 9*d.*	3*s.* 9*d.*	3*s.* 9*d.*
Corks, ready made	*per lb.*	3*d.*	(Free from	1st April,	1861)	
Dice	*per pair*	£1 1*s.*	—	—	—	—
Hats or bonnets	*per lb.*	£1 3*s.*	(Free from	1st April,	1861)	
Paper: Paper and books	*per cwt.*	15*s.* to 16*s.*				
Paper: Printed, painted or stained paper hangings	,,	14*s.*	(Free fro	m 1st Octo	ber, 1861)	
Plate: Gold	*per oz.*	17*s.*	17*s.*	17*s.*	—	—
Plate: Silver	,,	1*s.* 6*d.*	1*s.* 6*d.*	1*s.* 6*d.*	—	—
Ships: foreign, built of wood. On the registration thereof as British ships, for *every ton* of gross registered tonnage, without any deduction in respect of engine room or otherwise		1*s.*	—	—	—	—
Varnish, containing any quantity of spirit or alcohol	*per gall.*	12*s.*	12*s.*	—	—	—
Vinegar	,,	3*d.*	3*d.*	—	—	—
,, pickles, preserved in vinegar	,,	1*d.*	1*d.*	—	—	—

[1] Tobacco. In 1871 and 1881, higher duty charged when containing less than 10 per cent. of moisture.
In 1891, higher duty charged when containing less than 13 per cent. of moisture.
,, 1900-01 . ,, ,, 10 ,,

TABLE XI.—*Gross Assessments to Income Tax of Lands, Houses, and Railways (United Kingdom). Years ending 5th April.*

[Million £'s.]

	Lands.	Houses.	Railways (United Kingdom).
1862	60.3	61.9	14.8
'71	65.4	86.3	22.0
'81	69.3	117.5	29.1
'91	57.7	140.6	36.4
1900	52.8	174.4	39.4

TABLE XII.—*Proportion of certain Branches of Revenue to Total Revenue (Exchequer Receipts). Years ended 31st March.*

Branch of Revenue.	1861.		1871.		1881.		1891.		1901.	
	Mln. £	Per cent. of total.	Mln. £	Per cent. of total.	Mln. £	Per cent. of total.	Mln. £	Per cent. of total.	Mln. £	Per cent. of total.
a. Property and income tax	10.9	15	6.4	9	10.7	13	13.3	15	26.9	21
b. Death duties	3.5	5	4.8	7	6.7	8	7.4	8	13.0	10
c. House duty and land tax	3.1	4	2.7	4	2.7	4	2.6	3	2.5	2
Total	17.5	24	13.9	20	20.1	25	23.3	26	42.4	33
d. Customs and excise	42.7	61	42.9	63	44.5	54	44.3	49	59.4	45
e. Stamps	5.0[1]	7	3.6[1]	5	4.4[1]	5	6.0[1]	7	7.8	6
f. Post office and telegraph service	3.4	5	5.3	8	8.3	10	12.3	14	17.3	13
Miscellaneous	1.8	3	2.5	4	4.6	6	3.6	4	3.5	3
Total revenue	70.4	100	68.2	100	81.9	100	89.5	100	130.4	100

[1] Excluding death duties.

TABLE XIII.—*Statement of Taxes Imposed or Increased, and Repealed or Reduced, in the Years 1861-1901, showing the Estimated Gain or Loss in a complete Year.*

[In million £'s.]

Years ended 31st March,	Period 1861-71.		Years ended 31st March,	Period 1881-91.	
	Imposed or Increased.	Repealed or Reduced.		Imposed or Increased.	Repealed or Reduced.
1862 . .	0.1	2.7	1882 . .	0.7	2.6
'63 . .	0.3	0.4	'83 . .	2.8	—
'64 . .	—	4.6	'84 . .	—	3.3
'65 . .	0.1	3.4	'85 . .	2.0	—
'66 . .	—	5.3	'86 . .	4.3	—
'67 . .	—	0.6	'87 . .	—	—
'68 . .	1.6	0.3	'88 . .	0.1	2.6
'69 . .	1.5	—	'89 . .	0.9	3.5
1870 . .	1.1	4.8	1890 . .	1.4	3.7
'71 . .	0.1	4.6	'91 . .	—	3.1
	4.8	26.7		12.2	18.8
Years ended 31st March,	Period 1871-81.		Years ended 31st March,	Period 1891-1901.	
	Imposed or Increased.	Repealed or Reduced.		Imposed or Increased.	Repealed or Reduced.
1872 . .	3.1	—	1892 . .	—	—
'73 . .	—	3.9	'93 . .	—	—
'74 . .	—	3.2	'94 . .	2.2	—
'75 . .	—	4.3	'95 . .	7.2	1.6
'76 . .	—	—	'96 . .	—	—
'77 . .	1.8	0.4	'97 . .	—	2.3
'78 . .	—	—	'98 . .	—	—
'79 . .	4.5	0.1	'99 . .	—	1.3
1880 . .	—	—	1900 . .	1.0	—
'81 . .	11.6	8.4	'01 . .	14.2	—
	21.0	20.3		24.6	5.2

Summary.

Period.	Imposed or Increased.	Repealed or Reduced.
1861-71	4.8	26.7
'71-81	21.0	20.3
'81-91	12.2	18.8
'91-1901	24.6	5.2
	62.6	71.0
Deduct taxes imposed or increased	—	62.6
Net reduction	—	8.4

XXVIII.

THE IMPORTANCE OF GENERAL STATISTICAL IDEAS.[1]

I TRUST you will excuse me, on an occasion like the present, for returning to a topic which I have discussed more than once—the utility of common statistics. While we are indebted for much of our statistical knowledge to elaborate special inquiries such as were made by Mr. Jevons on prices and the currency, or have lately been made by Mr. Booth into the condition of the London poor, we are indebted for other knowledge to continuous official and unofficial records, which keep us posted up to date as to certain facts of current life and business, without which public men and men of business, in the daily concerns of life, would be very much at a loss. What seems to me always most desirable to understand is the importance of some of the ideas to be derived from the most common statistics of the latter kind—the regular records of statistical facts which modern societies have instituted, especially the records of the census, which have now existed for a century in most European countries and among peoples of European origin. Political ideas and speculation are necessarily coloured by ideas originating in such records, and political action, internationally and otherwise, would be all the wiser if the records were more carefully observed than they are, and the lessons to be derived widely appreciated and understood.

I propose now to refer briefly to one or two of these ideas which were taken up and discussed on former occasions, and to illustrate the matter farther by a re-

[1] Address as President of the Economic Science and Statistics Section of the British Association, held at Glasgow, 1901.

ference to one or two additional topics suggested in the same manner, and more particularly by the results of the last census investigations, which complete in this respect the record of what may be called the statistical century *par excellence*—the century which has just closed.

Increase of European Population during last Century.

The first broad fact then of this kind, which I have discussed on former occasions, is the enormous increase of the population of European countries and of peoples of European origin during the century just passed, especially the increase of the English people and of the United States, along with the comparative stationariness of the population of one or two of the countries, particularly France, at the same time. The growth all round is from about 170 millions at the beginning of the century to about 510 millions (excluding South American countries and Mexico); while the growth of the United States alone is from a little over 5 to nearly 80 millions, and of the English population of the British Empire from about 15 to 55 millions. Germany and Russia also show remarkable growth—from 20 to 55 millions in the one case, and from 40 to 135 millions in the other—partly due to annexation; but the growth of France is no more than from 25 to 40 millions. Without discussing it, we may understand that the economic growth is equally if not more remarkable. The effect necessarily is to assure the preponderance of European peoples among the races of the world—to put aside completely, for instance, the nightmares of yellow or black perils arising from the supposed overwhelming mass of yellow or black races, these races by comparison being stationary or nearly so. The increase of population being continuous, unless some startling change occurs before long, each year only makes European preponderance more secure. Equally it follows that the relative position of the English Empire, the United

States, Russia, and Germany has become such as to make them exclusively the great world powers, although France, for economic reasons, notwithstanding the stationariness of its population, may still be classed amongst them. When one thinks what international politics were only a hundred years ago—how supreme France then appeared; how important were Austria, Italy, Spain, and even countries like Holland, Denmark, and Sweden—we may surely recognize that with a comparatively new United States on the stage, and with powers like Russia and Germany come to the front, the world is all changed politically as well as economically, and that new passions and new rivalries have to be considered.

The figures also suggest that for some time at least the movements going on must accentuate the change that has occurred. According to the latest figures, there is no sign that either in France or any other European country which has been comparatively stationary, has any growth of population commenced which will reverse the change, while a large increase of population goes on in the leading countries named. This increase, it is alleged, is going on at a diminishing rate—a point to be discussed afterwards—but in the next generation or two there is practically no doubt that the United States will be a larger international factor than it is, both absolutely and relatively, and that Russia, Germany, and the English people of the British Empire will also grow, though not in such a way, apparently, as to prevent the greater relative growth of the United States, and notwithstanding perhaps some relative changes of a minor character amongst themselves.

The foreign nations then with which the British Empire is likely to be concerned in the near future are Russia, Germany, and the United States; and other powers, even France, must more and more occupy a second place, although France, for the moment, partly in consequence of its relations with Russia, occupies a special place.

Special Position of British Empire.

Another idea which follows from a consideration of the same facts, is the necessity laid upon the British Empire to consolidate and organize itself in view of the large additions of subject races made to it in the last century, and especially in the last twenty years of the century. In a paper which I read before the Royal Colonial Institute two years ago, an attempt was made to show that the burden imposed on the white races of the Empire by these recent acquisitions was not excessive as far as the prospect of internal tumults was concerned. Relatively to some other powers, especially France, we had also been gaining internationally in strength and resources. But whether we had gained internationally on the whole, looking at the growth of powers like the United States, Russia, and Germany, and their greater activity in world-politics, was a different question. The problem thus stated remains. It would be foreign to the scope of an address like this, which must avoid actual politics, to examine how far light has been thrown on it by the South African war. No one can question at least that the organization of the Empire must be governed by considerations which the international statistics suggest, and that no step can be taken safely and properly unless our public men fully appreciate the ideas of international strength and resources as well as other considerations which are germane to the subject.

Europe and Foreign Food Supplies.

Another idea to which attention may be drawn, appears to be the increasing dependence of European nations upon supplies of food and raw material obtained from abroad. We are familiar with a conception of this kind as regards the United Kingdom. For years past we have drawn increasing supplies from abroad, not merely in proportion to the growth of population, but in larger proportion. The position here obviously is that, with the industries of agriculture and the extraction of raw material (except as regards the one article, coal) practically incapable of expansion, and with a population which not only increases in numbers, but which becomes year by year increasingly richer per head, the consuming power of the population increases with enormous rapidity, and must be satisfied, if at all, by foreign imports of food and raw materials; there is no other means of satisfaction. But what is true of the United Kingdom is true in a greater or less degree of certain European countries—France, the Low Countries, the Scandinavian countries, Austria-Hungary, Italy, and Germany. Especially is it true in a remarkable degree of Germany, which is becoming increasingly industrial and manufacturing, and where the room for expansion in agriculture is now very limited. Those interested in the subject may be referred to an excellent paper by Mr. Crawford, read at the Royal Statistical Society of London about two years ago. What I am now desirous to point out is the governing nature of the idea, which necessarily follows from the conception of a European population living on a limited area, with the agricultural and extractive possibilities long since nearly exhausted, and the population all the time increasing in numbers and wealth. Such a population must import more and more year by year, and must be increasingly dependent on foreign supplies.

I shall not attempt to do over again what is done in Mr. Crawford's paper, but a few figures may serve to illustrate what is meant. In the "Statistical Abstract" for the principal and other foreign countries, I find tables for certain European countries classifying the imports for a series of years into articles of food, raw and semi-manufactured articles, etc. From these I extract the following particulars for all the countries which have tables in this form:

Imports of Articles of Food and Raw Materials and Semi-Manufactured Articles into the undermentioned Countries in 1888 *and* 1898 *compared.*

ARTICLES OF FOOD, ETC.

		1888.	1898.	Increase.	
				Amount.	Per Cent.
Russia	1,000 roubles	78,975	105,391	27,416	35
German Empire	mln. marks	907	1,819	912	100
France . . .	1,000 francs	1,503,000	1,505,000	Nil	Nil
Switzerland . .	,,	238,000	332,000	94,000	40
Italy	1,000 lire	274,480	391,600	117,120	42
Austria-Hungary	1,000 gulden	(1891) 108,441	191,919	92,478	85

RAW AND SEMI-MANUFACTURED MATERIALS.

Russia	1,000 roubles	241,497	313,629	71,132	29
German Empire	mln. marks	1,507	2,247	740	49
France . . .	1,000 francs	2,014	2,348	334	16
Switzerland . .	,,	308,110	390,111	82,001	27
Italy	1,000 lire	398,330	509,418	111,088	28
Austria-Hungary	1,000 gulden	231,000	293,000	62,000	27

The drawback to this table is that it is one of values. Consequently the increase of values in the later years may in part be one of values only without corresponding increase of quantities. But the general course of prices in the period in question was not such as to cause a great change of values apart from a change in quantities. The inference seems undeniable then, that the continental countries named, especially Germany, have largely increased their imports of food and raw materials of recent years—that is, have become increasingly dependent on foreign and over-sea supplies. The position of Germany, with its enormous increase of food imports —from 907 to 1,819 million marks, or from 45 to over 90 million sterling, and its corresponding increase of raw material imports—from 1,507 to 2,247 million marks, or from 75 to 112 million sterling—is especially remarkable.

An examination in detail of the quantities imported

of particular articles would fully confirm the impression given by the summary figures. But it may be enough to refer to the "Statistical Abstract" from which I have been quoting, as well as to Mr. Crawford's paper. The figures are not out of the way in any respect, and it is the idea we have now to get hold of.

The inference is that the difference between the United Kingdom and continental countries, especially Germany, as regards dependence on foreign supplies of food and raw materials, is only one of degree, and that as regards Germany at least the conditions are already remarkably like those of the United Kingdom, while the more rapidly Germany increases its manufacturing and industrial population, the more like it will become to this country. In other words, in the future there will be two great countries, and not one only, dependent largely for their food and raw materials on supplies from abroad. What their position is to be economically and otherwise relatively to the United States, which is at once the main source of supply, and a competitor with European countries in manufactures, is obviously a matter of no little interest. As a believer in free trade, I am sure that nothing but good will come to all the countries concerned if trade is interfered with as little as possible by tariffs and government regulations. I believe, moreover, that the practice of free trade, whatever their theories may be, will unavoidably be accepted by all three countries before long. Obviously, however, as the new tariff in Germany indicates, there is to be a great struggle in that country before the situation is accepted, and if some people in this country had their way, notwithstanding our long experience of free trade and its blessings, we should even have a struggle here.

There is another point of view from which the facts should be studied. We are accustomed, and rightly so, I think, to consider naval preponderance indispensable to the safety of the Empire, and especially indispensable to the safety of the country from blockade, and from the interruption of its commerce, which would be our ruin. But our position in this respect is apparently not quite exceptional. Less or more our continental neighbours, and especially Germany, are in the same boat. In the event of war, if they could not make up the loss by traffic over their land frontiers, they would be just as liable to suffer from blockade and interrupted commerce as we are. It is conceivable, moreover, that in certain wars some of the countries might not be able to make up by traffic over their land frontiers for blockade or interruption of commerce by sea. We may apprehend, for instance, that Germany, if it were victorious by sea in a war with France, would insist upon Belgium and Holland on one side, and Italy and Spain on the other side, not supplying by land to France what had been cut off by sea. One or more of these countries might be allies with Germany from the first. Contrariwise France and Russia, if at war with Germany and the Triple Alliance, might practically seal up Germany if they were successful at sea, insisting that the Scandinavian countries and Holland should not make up to Germany by land what had been cut off by sea. Germany in this view, apart from any possibility of rupture with this country, has a case for a powerful fleet. It is not quite so much liable to a blockade as we are, but there is a liability of the same kind. The question of naval preponderance among rival powers may thus become rather a serious one. If preponderance is to be nearly as essential to Germany as it is to this country, who is to preponderate? What our practical action ought to be in the premises is a question that might easily lead us too far on an occasion like this, but the facts should be ever present to the minds of our public men. We may be quite certain that they are quite well known and understood in the councils of the Russian, German, French, and other continental governments.

New Population and New Markets.

Another idea suggested by the facts appears to be an answer to the question as to how new markets are to be found for the products of an increasing population—a question which vexes the mind of many who see in nothing but foreign trade an outlet for new energies. The point was mentioned in my address at Manchester a year ago, but it deserves perhaps a more elaborate treatment than it was possible then to give it. What we see then is that not only in this country, but in Germany and other continental countries, millions of new people are, in fact, provided for in every ten years, although the resources of the country in food and raw materials are generally used to the full extent, and not capable of farther expansion, so that increasing supplies of food and raw material have to be imported from abroad. How is the thing done? Obviously the main provision for the wants of the new people is effected by themselves. They exchange services with each other, and so procure the major part of the comforts and luxuries of life which they require. The butcher, the baker, the tailor, the dressmaker, the milliner, the shoemaker, the builder, the teacher, the doctor, the lawyer, and so on, are all working for each other the most part of their lives, and the proportion of exchanges with foreign countries necessary to procure some things required in the general economy may be very small. These exchanges may also very largely take the form of a remittance of goods by foreign countries in payment of interest on debts which they owe, so that the communities in question obtain much of what they want from abroad by levying a kind of rent or annuity which the foreigner has to pay. If more is required, it may be obtained by special means, as for instance by the working of coal for export, which gives employment in this country to about 200,000 miners, by the employment of shipping in the carrying trade, by the manufacture of special lines of goods, and so on. But the main exchanges of any country are, and must be as a rule, at home, and the foreign trade, however important, will always remain within limits, and bearing some proportion to the total exchanges of the country. Hence, when additions to the population, and how they are to live are considered, the answer is that the additions will fill up proportionately the framework of the various industries already in existence, or the ever-changing new industries for home consumption which are always starting into being. These are the primary outlets for new population even in old countries like the United Kingdom and Germany. Of course active traders and manufacturers, each in his own way, are not to take things for granted. They must strive to spread their activities over foreign as well as over home markets. But looking at the matter from the outside, and scientifically, it is the home and not the foreign market which is always the most important.

The same may be said of a country in a somewhat different economic condition from England and Germany, viz., the United States. I can only refer to it, however, in passing, as the facts here are not so clearly on the surface. Contrary to England and Germany, which have no food resources and resources of raw material capable of indefinite expansion, the United States is still to a large extent a virgin country. Its increasing population is therefore provided for in a different way for the most part from the increase in England and Germany. But even in the United States it has been noticeable at each of the last census returns that the increasing population finds an outlet more and more largely, not in agriculture and the extraction of raw materials, but in the miscellaneous pursuits of industry and manufacture. The town population increases disproportionately. In the last census especially it was found that the overflow of population over the far Western States seemed to have been checked, the increase of population being mainly in the older States and the towns and cities of the older States. The phenomena in England and Germany and in other continental countries are accordingly not singular. The older countries, and the older parts even of a new country like the United States, are becoming more and more the centres where populations live and grow, because they are the most convenient places for the general exchange of services with each other among the component parts of a large population, which constitutes production and consumption. A small expenditure of effort in proportion enables such communities to obtain from a distance the food and raw materials which they require. Migration is no longer the necessity that it was.

Decline in Rate of Growth of Population.

I come now to another idea appearing on the surface of the census returns when they are compared for a long time past, and the connected returns of births, marriages, and deaths, which have now been kept in most civilized communities for generations. Great as the increase of population is with which we have been dealing, there are indications that the rate of growth in the most recent census periods is less in many quarters than it formerly was, while there has been a corresponding decline in the birth-rates; and to some extent, though not to the same extent, in the rate of the excess of births over deaths, which is the critical rate of course in a question of the increase of population. These facts have suggested to some a question as to how far the increase of population which has been so marked in the past century is likely to continue, and speculations have been indulged in as to whether there is a real decline in the fecundity of population among the peoples in question resembling the decline in France, both in its nature and consequences. I do not propose to discuss all these various questions, but rather to indicate the way in which the problem is suggested by the statistics, and the importance of the questions thus raised for discussion, as a proof of the value of the continuous statistical records themselves.

The United States naturally claims first attention in a matter like this, both on account of the magnitude of the increase of population there, and the evidence that recent growth has not been quite the same as it was earlier in the century. Continuing a table which was printed in my address as President of the Statistical Society, in 1882, above referred to, we find that the growth of population in the United States since 1800 has been as follows in each census period:

Population in the United States, and Increase in each Census Period of the Nineteenth Century.

	Population.	Increase since previous Census.	
		Amount.	Per Cent.
	Mlns.	Mlns.	
1800	5·3	—	—
'10	7.2	1.9	36
'20	9.6	2.4	33
'30	12.9	3·3	34
'40	17.1	4.2	33
'50	23.2	6.1	36
'60	31.4	8.2	36
'70	38.5	7.1	23
'80	50.1	11.6	30
'90	62.6	12.5	25
1900	75·7 [1]	13.1	21

Thus it is quite plain that something has happened in the United States to diminish the rate of increase of population after 1860. Up to that time the growth in each census period from 1800 downwards had ranged between 33 and 36 per cent. Since then the highest rates have been 30 per cent. between 1870 and 1880, and 25 per cent. between 1880 and 1890. There is a certainty moreover that, owing to errors in the census of 1870, which were corrected in 1880, and which have been officially acknowledged by the United States census authorities, the increase between 1870 and 1880

[1] This does not include population of Indian reservations, etc., now included in the official census for the first time.

was not quite so high as stated. There is accordingly a somewhat steep decline from a growth in each ten years prior to 1860, ranging between 33 and 36 per cent., to a growth first of about 25 per cent., and finally of 21 per cent. only. The Civil War of the early sixties naturally occurs to one as the explanation of the break immediately after 1860, but the effects could hardly have continued to the present time, and a more general explanation is suggested.

Other special explanations have occurred to me as partly accounting for the change. One is that, prior to 1860, the United States at different times increased its territory and population partly by purchase and partly by annexation. But I cannot make out that either the purchase of Louisiana early in the century, or the subsequent annexations following the Mexican War, would make a material difference. There is a considerable increase certainly after the Mexican War, but it would be difficult indeed to estimate how much of the population of Texas and New Mexico which was then added to the Union had previously swarmed over from the Union, and had thus been from the first economically, if not politically, part of the United States. Another obvious suggestion is that possibly immigration into the United States has fallen off as compared with what it formerly was. But this explanation also fails, as far as the official figures carry us. The proportion of immigration to the total increase of population in each census period since 1820, previous to which I have not been able to obtain figures, has been as follows:

Proportion of Immigration to Total Increase of Population in the undermentioned Periods in the United States.

	Per Cent.		Per Cent.
1820-30 . . .	4.7	1860-70 . . .	35.0
'30-40 . . .	14.2	'70-80 . . .	24.2
'40-50 . . .	27.9	'80-90 . . .	42.1
'50-60 . . .	31.5	'90-1900 . . .	29.4

Immigration, according to these figures, has thus in late years played as important a part as it formerly did in the increase of population in the United States. Possibly the official figures of immigration of late years are a little exaggerated, as the United States Government does not show a balance between immigration and emigration; but whatever corrections may be made on this account, the recent figures of immigration are too large to permit the supposition that the failure of immigrants accounts in the main for the diminished rate of increase of the population generally. The ten years' percentage of increase without immigrants, I may say, varied before 1860 between 24 and 32 per cent., and has since fallen to 14 and 15 per cent. Even if the latter figures should be increased a little to allow for the over-estimate of immigration, the change would be enormous.

Passing from the United States, we meet with similar phenomena in Australasia. Indeed, what has happened in Australasia of late has been attracting a good deal of attention. The following short table, which is extracted from the statistics of Mr. Coghlan, the able statistician of the Government of New South Wales, gives an idea of what has occurred:

Population of Australasia at different Dates, with the Annual Increase per Cent. in each Period.

	Population.	Annual Increase per Cent. since previous Date.
	Thousands.	
1788	1.0	—
1801	6.5	15.13
'11	11.5	11.94
'21	35.6	5.88
'31	79.3	8.34
'41	211.1	10.28
'51	430.6	7.36
'61	1,253.0	11.30
'71	1,924.8	4.39
'81	2,742.5	3.60
'91	3,809.9	3.34
'99	4,483.0	2.1

Supplementary Table of Rate per Cent. of Increase since 1890.

	Per Cent.		Per Cent.
1891	3.34	1896	1.84
'92	2.10	'97	1.86
'93	1.96	'98	1.40
'94	1.95	'99	1.44
'95	1.88		

The decline in the rate of increase is so great and palpable as to need no comment.

Here the perturbations due to immigration have obviously been greater than in the case of the United States. The country was in fact settled mainly between 1850 and 1870, without previously having had a population to speak of. But deducting immigration, the increase would appear to have been as follows in each decade:

Rate of Increase per Cent. of Population in Australasia, Deducting Immigration, in the undermentioned Periods.

	Per Cent.		Per Cent.
1851-60 . . .	48.5	1880-90 . . .	24.5
'60-70 . . .	30.0	'90-99 . . .	16.0
'70-80 . . .	25.0		

Of course, so long as immigration continues, the effect is to swell indirectly the natural increase of population, so that the large increases here shown between 1851 and 1870, and even down to 1890, may be accounted for in part as the indirect result of the large immigration that was going on. But whatever the cause, the fact is unmistakable that the rate of increase, apart from the direct immigration, has declined just as it has done in the United States.

There has been a similar though not nearly so marked a decrease in England, at any rate if we carry the comparison back to the period before 1850. The population at each census period since 1800 in England, with the percentage increase between each census period, has been as follows:

Population of England at the Date of each Census since 1800, with Percentage of Increase between each Census.

	Population.	Increase per Cent. since previous Census.
	Mlns.	
1800	8.9	—
'10	10.2	14.0
'20	12.0	18.1
'30	13.9	15.8
'40	15.9	14.5
'50	17.9	12.9
'60	20.1	11.9
'70	22.7	13.2
'80	26.0	14.4
'90	29.0	11.6
1900	32.3	12.2

Thus the increase between recent census periods has been sensibly less than it was before 1850; and the slight recovery between 1860 and 1880 has not been maintained. We are thus in presence of much the same kind of change as has been shown in the United States and in Australasia.

It should be noted, however, in order that we may not strain any fact, that when the United Kingdom is viewed as a whole, Scotland and Ireland, as well as the senior partner being taken into account, it cannot be said that there is any falling off in the rate of growth of the population since 1850. For several decades after that, in fact, the rate of growth of the United Kingdom as a whole was diminished enormously by the emigration from Ireland, and the growth since 1860 has been at a greater rate than in the thirty years before. There may be new causes at work which will again diminish the rate of growth, but in a broad view they do not make themselves visible owing to the disturbance caused by the Irish emigration. Still the facts as to the United Kingdom as a whole ought not to prevent us from considering the facts respecting England only along with the similar facts respecting the United States and Australasia.

These diminutions in the rate of growth of large populations, as I have indicated, are corroborated by a study of the birth-rates, and of the rate of the excess of births over deaths.

The United States unfortunately is without birth or death-rates, owing to the want of a general system of registration over the whole country. This is a most serious defect in the statistical arrangements of that great country, which it may be hoped will be remedied in time. In the absence of the necessary records, I have made some calculations so as to obtain a figure which may be provisionally substituted for a proper rate of the excess of births over deaths, which I submit for what it may be worth as an approximation and an approximation only. In these calculations one-tenth of the increase of population between two census periods, apart from immigration, is compared with the mean of the population at the two census dates themselves, with the following results:

Approximate Rate of Excess of Births over Deaths in the United States, calculated from a Comparison of One-Tenth the Increase of Population between the Census Periods, Deducting Immigrants, with the Mean of the Numbers of the Population at the Two Census Dates.

Year.	1 Population.	2 Mean of Population between Two Censuses.	3 One-Tenth of Increase since previous Census, less Immigrants.	4 Calculated Excess of Births over Deaths per 1,000, proportion of Col. 3 to Col. 2.
	Mlns.	Mlns.	Thousands.	
1800 . . .	5.3	—	—	—
'10 . . .	7.2	6.2	—	—
'20 . . .	9.6	8.4	—	—
'30 . . .	12.9	11.2	308	28
40 . . .	17.1	15.0	360	24
'50 . . .	23.2	20.1	441	22
'60 . . .	31.4	27.3	565	21
'70 . . .	38.5	35.0	462	13
'80 . . .	50.2	44.4	878	20[1]
'90 . . .	62.6	56.4	722	13
1900 . . .	75.7	69.2	923	13

[1] See remarks on pp. 348-349 on errors in Census of 1870.

Thus, while the excess rate was as high as 21 to 28 per 1,000 before 1860, it has since fallen to one of 13 only, or about one-half. Whatever validity may attach to the method of calculation, the real facts would no doubt show a change in the direction of the table—a decline in the rate of the excess of births over deaths from period to period. The decline in the growth of population is thus not merely the direct effect of a change in immigration, but is connected with the birth and death-rates themselves, although these rates are of course indirectly affected by the amount and proportion of immigration. It would be most important to know what the decline in the birth-rate is by itself, and how far its effects on the growth of population have been mitigated or intensified by changes in the death-rate; but United States records generally give no help on this head.

Dealing with Australasia in the same way, we have the advantage of a direct comparison of both birth and death-rates and the rate of the excess of births over deaths. This is done in the following table:

Birth-Rate and Death-Rate and Rate of Excess of Births over Deaths in Australasia for undermentioned Years.

[From Mr. Coghlan's statistics.]

	Birth-Rate.	Death-Rate.	Excess of Births over Deaths.
1861-65 . .	41.92	16.75	25.17
'66-70 . .	39.84	15.62	24.22
'71-75 . .	37.34	15.26	22.08
'76-80 . .	36.38	15.04	21.34
'81-85 . .	35.21	14.79	20.42
'86-90 . .	34.43	13.95	20.48
'91-95 . .	31.52	12.74	18.78
'96-99 . .	27.35	12.39	14.96

Thus from a high birth-rate forty years ago, Australasia has certainly gone down to very ordinary birth-rates, lower than in the United Kingdom and in continental countries, and Australasia certainly has had heavy declines in the rate of excess of births over deaths, viz., from 25.17 in 1861-65, to 15 in 1896-99, which is to be compared with the decline in the United States, as above stated approximately, from 28 in 1820-30, and 21 as late as 1860, to 13 in the last twenty years.

A similar table for England only gives the following results:

Birth-Rate and Death-Rate and Rate of Excess of Births over Deaths in England for undermentioned Years.

	Birth-Rate per 1,000.	Death-Rate per 1,000.	Excess of Birth-Rate over Death-Rate.
1851 . . .	34.2	22.0	12.2
'61 . . .	34.6	21.6	13.0
'71 . . .	35.0	22.6	12.4
'81 . . .	33.9	18.9	15.0
'91 . . .	31.4	20.2	11.2
'99 . . .	29.3	18.3	11.0

Note.—Highest birth-rate in 1876, 36.3.

Here the birth-rates, to begin with, are not so high as in Australasia, and, presumably, in the United States, and the excess of births over deaths, though it has declined a good deal since 1871-81, when it was highest, has been by comparison fairly well maintained, being still 11 per 1,000, as compared with 12.2 in 1851.

We have thus on one side a manifest decline in the rate of growth of population in three large groups of population, coupled with a large decline of birth-rates in England and Australasia where the facts are known, and a smaller decline in the rate of the excess of births over deaths, this decline in England as yet being comparatively small. Such facts cannot but excite inquiry, and it is an excellent result of the use of continuous statistical records that the questions involved can be so definitely raised.

As I have stated, it would be foreign to the object of this paper to discuss fully the various questions thus brought up for discussion, but one or two observations may be made, having regard to some inferences which are somewhat hastily drawn.

1. The rate of growth of population of the communities may still be very considerable, even if it is no higher than it has been in the last few years. A growth of 16, 15, or even 12 per cent. in ten years, owing to the excess of births over deaths, is a very considerable growth, though it is much less than the larger figures which existed in some parts forty or fifty years ago. What has happened in the United Kingdom is well worth observing in this connection. Since 1840 the population of the United Kingdom as a whole has increased nearly 60 per cent., although the increase in most of the decades hardly ever exceeded 8 per cent., and in 1840-50 was no more than 2½ per cent. The increase, it must be remembered, goes on at a compound ratio, and in a few decades an enormous change is apparent. The increase from about 170 to 510 millions in the course of the last century among European people generally, though it includes the enormous growth of the United States in those decades, when the rate of growth was at the highest, also includes the slower growth of other periods, and the slower growths of other countries. An addition of even 10 per cent. only as the average every ten years would far more than double the 500 millions in a century, and an increase to at least 1,500 millions during the century now beginning, unless some great change should occur, would accordingly appear not improbable.

2. Some of the rates of growth of population from which there has been a falling off of late years were obviously quite abnormal. I refer especially to the growth in Australasia between 1850 and 1880, and the

growth in the United States prior to 1860. They were largely due to the indirect effect of immigration which has been already referred to.

The population to which immigrants are largely added in a few years, owing to the composition of the population, has its birth-rates momentarily increased and its death-rates diminished, the birth-rates because there are more people relatively at the child-producing ages, and the death-rates because the whole population is younger, than in older countries. It appears quite unnecessary to elaborate this point. The rates of the excess of births over deaths in a country which is receiving a large immigration must be quite abnormal compared with a country in a more normal condition, while a country from which there is a large emigration, such as Ireland, must tend to show a lower excess than is consistent with a normal condition. This explanation, it may be said, does not apply to England, since it is a country which has not been receiving a large immigration or sending out, except occasionally, a large emigration. England, however, must have been affected both ways by movements of this character. It received undoubtedly a large Irish immigration in the early part of last century, and in more recent periods the emigration in some decades, particularly between 1880 and 1890, appears to have been large enough to have a sensible effect on both the birth-rate and the rate of the excess of births over deaths. This effect would be continued down into the following decade, and the consideration is therefore one to be taken note of as accounting in part for the recent decline in birth-rates in England.

In addition, however, it is not improbable that there was an abnormal increase of population in the early part of last century, due to the sudden multiplication of resources for the benefit of a poor population which had previously tended to grow at a very rapid rate, and would have grown at that rate but for the checks of war, pestilence, and famine, on which Malthus enlarges. The sudden withdrawal of the checks in this view would thus be the immediate cause of the singularly rapid growth of population in the early part of last century. It is quite in accordance with this fact that a generation or two of prosperity, raising the scale of living, would diminish the rate of growth as compared with this abnormal development, without affecting in any degree the permanent reproductive energy of the people.

3. It is also obvious that one explanation of the decline in birth-rate, and of the rate of the excess of births over deaths, may in part be the greater vitality of the populations concerned, so that the composition of the population is altered by an increase of the relative numbers of people not in the prime of life, thus altering the proportion of the people at the child-producing ages to the total. This would be too complex a subject for me to treat in the course of a discursive address. Nor would it explain the whole facts, which include, for instance, an almost stationary annual number of births in the United Kingdom for more than ten years past, notwithstanding the largely increased population. But the case may be one where a great many partial explanations contribute to elucidate the phenomena, so that this particular explanation cannot be overlooked.

4. There remains, however, the question which many people have rushed in to discuss, viz., whether the reproductive power of the populations in question is quite as great as it was fifty or sixty years ago. We have already heard in some quarters, not merely that the reproductive energy has diminished, but suggestions that the populations in question are following the example of the French, where the rate of increase of the population has almost come to an end. Apart, however, from the suggestions above made as to the abnormality of the increase fifty or sixty years ago, so that some decline now is rather to be expected than not, I would point out that the subject is about as full of

pitfalls as any statistical problem can be, for the simple reason that it can only be approached indirectly, as there have been no statistical records over a long series of years showing the proportion of births to married women at the child-producing ages, distinguishing the ages, and showing at the same time the proportion of the married women to the total at those ages. Unless there are some such statistics, direct comparisons are impossible, and a good many of the indirect methods of approaching the subject which I have studied a little appear, to say the least, to leave much to be desired. We find for instance that a comparison has been made in Australasia between the number of marriages in a given year or years and the number of births in the five or six years following, which show, it is said, a remarkable decline in the proportion of births to marriages in recent years as compared with twenty or thirty years ago. It is forgotten, however, that at the earlier dates in Australasia, when a large immigration was taking place, a good many of the children born were the children of parents who had been married before they entered the country, while there are hardly any children of such parents at a time when immigration has almost ceased. The answer to such questions is in truth not to be rushed, and the question with statisticians should rather be how the statistics are to be improved in future, so that although the past cannot be fully explained, the regular statistics themselves will in future give a ready answer.

5. One more remark may perhaps be allowed to me on account of the delicacy and interest of the subject. To a certain extent the causes of a decline in reproductive energy may be part and parcel of the improved condition of the population, which leads in turn to an increase of the age at marriage, and an increase of celibacy generally through the indisposition of individual members of the community to run any risk of sinking in the scale of living which they may run by premature marriage. These causes, however, may

operate to a great extent upon the birth-rate itself without diminishing the growth of population, because the children though born in smaller proportion are better cared for, and the rate of excess of births over deaths consequently remains considerable although the birth-rate itself is low. The serious fact would be a decline of the rate of the excess of births over deaths through the death-rate remaining comparatively high while the birth-rate falls. It is in this conjunction that the gravity of the stationariness of population in France appears to lie. While the birth-rate in France is undoubtedly a low one, 21.9 per 1,000 in 1899, according to the latest figures before me, still this would have been quite sufficient to ensure a considerable excess rate of births over deaths, and a considerable increase of population every ten years if the death-rate had been as low as in the United Kingdom, viz., 18.3 per 1,000. A difference of 3.6 per 1,000 upon a population of about 40 millions comes to about 150,000 per annum or 1,500,000 and rather more every ten years. In France, however, the death-rate was 21.1 per 1,000 instead of 18.3 as in the United Kingdom, and it is this comparatively high death-rate which really makes the population stationary. The speculations indulged in in some quarters, therefore, though they may be justified in future, are hardly yet justified by the general statistical facts. The subject is one of profound interest, and must be carefully studied, but the conclusions I have referred to must be regarded as premature until the study has been made.

Conclusion.

Such are a few illustrations of the importance of the ideas which are suggested by the most common statistics—those of the regular records which civilized societies have instituted. It is indeed self-evident how important it is to know such facts as the growing weight of countries of European civilization in comparison with others; the relative growth of the British Empire, Russia, Germany, and United States, in comparison with other nations of Europe or of European origin; the dependence of other European countries, as well as the United Kingdom, upon imports of food and raw materials; the ability of old countries and of old centres in new countries to maintain large and increasing populations; and the evidence which is now accumulating of changes in the rate of growth of European nations, with suggestions as to the causes of the changes.

It would be easy indeed to write whole chapters on some of these topics, instead of making a remark or two only to bring out their value a little. It would also be very easy to add to the list.

There was a strong temptation to include in it a reference to the relative growth of England, Scotland, and Ireland, which has now become the text of so much discussion, regarding the practical question of diminishing the relative representation of Ireland in Parliament, and increasing that of England and Scotland. It is expedient, however, in an address like this to avoid anything which verges on party politics, and I shall only notice that while the topic has lately become of keen interest to politicians, it is not new to statisticians, who were able long ago to foresee what is now so much remarked on. This very topic was discussed at length in one of the addresses of 1882, to which reference has been made; and even before that, in 1876, it received attention.[1] Another topic which might have been added is that of the economic growth of the different countries, which was discussed in the address in 1883, and such topics as the increase of population in a country like India, under the peace imposed by its European conquerors, by which the stationariness of the country in numbers and wealth, under purely native conditions, has been changed, and something like European progress has been begun.

[1] See *supra*, vol. i., p. 277; and *supra*, vol. ii., p. 1.

Enough has been said, however, it may be hoped, to justify this mode of looking at statistics and the ideas suggested by them.

May I once more then express the hope, as I have done on former occasions, that, as time goes on, more and more attention will be given to these common statistics and the ideas derived from them. The domination of the ideas suggested by these common figures of population statistics, in international politics and in social and economic relations is obvious; and although the decline in the rate of growth of population in recent years, the last of the topics now touched on, suggests a great many points which the statistics themselves are as yet unfit to solve—what *can* be done with a great country like the United States, absolutely devoid of bare records of births, marriages, and deaths?—still the facts of the decline as far as recorded throw a great deal of light on the social and economic history of the past century, prepare the way for discussing the further topics which require a more elaborate treatment, and enforce the necessity for more and better records. We may emphasise the appeal, then, for the better statistical and economic education of our public men, and for the more careful study by all concerned of such familiar publications as the "Statistical Abstracts," the "Statesman's Yearbook," and the like. The material transformations which are going on throughout the world can be substantially followed without any difficulty in such publications by those who have eyes to see; and to follow such transformations, so as to be ready for the practical questions constantly raised, is at least one of the main uses of statistical knowledge.

XXIX.

THE WEALTH OF THE EMPIRE, AND HOW IT SHOULD BE USED.[1]

IN view of the present meeting of the British Association the suggestion was made to me by your President that a discussion might profitably take place on the wealth of the British Empire, and the uses to which it can be put. We are apt to think in such matters of the mother country only, or even of the separate units of the mother country itself, for the simple reason that the statistics are not uniform. But as the idea of imperial unity takes hold there must come the habit of realising the empire as a whole, and discussing certain problems from an imperial, and not merely a national or local point of view. Among these the question of the use of our imperial wealth ought surely to find a place.

This is not a statistical paper, but it is necessary to start with some idea of what the wealth of the empire really is. We are more or less familiar with ideas of the wealth of the United Kingdom, based mainly on such data as the income tax and death duty returns, whether the expression of that wealth takes the form of an aggregation of individual incomes, or the aggregate of the capitalised value of incomes derived from capital, plus wealth in other forms. For certain purposes, notwithstanding the looseness of all such estimates, it is convenient to have them to our hand, as they check the vagueness of discussions where

[1] Read before the Economics and Statistics Section of the British Association, held at Southport, September, 1903.

quantities and relative proportions, as well as qualitative considerations only, require to be taken into account.

If I were to make the statement, then, that the aggregate of the individual incomes of the people of the United Kingdom is at the present moment somewhere about 1,750 million £, and that the aggregate wealth of the people expressed in a capitalised form may be put at about 15,000 million £ in round figures, if not more, I do not apprehend that there would be much real dispute. The figure as to income is not a great enhancement of the total arrived at by Mr. Bowley in 1895 for the year 1891, and it is very little in excess of the rule of thumb method of stating the aggregate income of the people which has been followed since Dudley Baxter's investigations in 1868, viz.: twice the gross assessment to the income tax, amounting for 1901-02 to 867 million £. The figure as to capital again allows for an addition of 50 per cent. to the total of 10,000 million £ at which I arrived for the year 1885 in my investigations on the growth of capital,[1] since which time there has been an increase of about that amount in the gross assessments to the income tax, which are the principal basis of the calculations as to capital.

But when we come to deal with the rest of the empire there is no such familiarity with data for estimating the income and capital of its various component parts. I believe, however, that if we make calculations as to the aggregate income of the main portions of the empire, based on known data as to production and checking them by data as to imports and exports, yield of revenue and the like as well as by comparison with the figures for the United Kingdom, using also official figures for Australasia, we may arrive at figures which can be provisionally accepted for the purpose of the present discussion. Canada I should put at 270 million £ sterling in round figures, equal to about £48 per

[1] See "The Growth of Capital." George Bell and Sons, 1889.

head of the population, as compared with £42 which is the figure for the United Kingdom. The Australian Colonies and New Zealand, with a population of 4,600,000, as compared with 5,600,000 in Canada, are put at 210 million £ in round figures, giving practically the same total per head as Canada. There is no doubt, it seems to me, of the larger income per head in these self-governing colonies than there is in the United Kingdom, partly because a larger proportion of their populations is in the prime of life. The figures are at any rate more than supported by colonial estimates of the production of their mines, agriculture, fisheries, and manufactures. India I would put down at 600 million £, which is certainly not a large amount for 300 millions of people; but where the adult ordinary labourer works for about 7 rupees a month, if so much, or little over £5 per annum, that is £1 per head, assuming a family of five persons, it would hardly be safe to reckon that the aggregate income of the people is more than equal to twice the amount per head earned among the labouring classes who constitute the mass of the people. The South African colonies I put at 100 million £, equal to nearly £125 per head of the white population, which is vastly outnumbered by the native, whose labour, of course, contributes to the total. I trust the guess does not err greatly by excess or defect, but the data are of course imperfect in the still unsettled state of the country after the late war. With a few years of peace the totals should be much larger. I have not gone into detail with the other parts of the empire, which are rounded off with a total of 200 million £, but these other parts include such rich depôts as Hong Kong and the Straits Settlements, our West Indian and South American colonies, the Mauritius, and our whole remaining territories in Africa, which are no doubt of great actual as well as potential value. I have been anxious not to exaggerate.

Putting all the figures together we get the following estimates of aggregate income for the British Empire:

Aggregate Income.

	Mln. £.
United Kingdom	1,750
Canada	270
Australasia	210
India	600
South Africa	100
Remainder of Empire	200
Total	3,130

The capital or wealth corresponding to this income, allowing it, in the case of other parts of the empire, to be about five or six times the income, which is a smaller proportion than that for the United Kingdom, but where a portion of the capital is already included in the figure for the United Kingdom as a creditor country, would be as follows:

Capital or Wealth.

	Mln. £.
United Kingdom	15,000
Canada	1,350
Australasia	1,100
India	3,000
South Africa	600
Remainder of Empire	1,200
Total	22,250

It will be understood, of course, that these figures as to capital are not figures built up from a multitude of data, but calculations for want of better based on a few data so as to give an approximate basis for the discussion—What should be done with our wealth? As far as the United Kingdom is concerned, I hope before very long to continue the calculations made in former years, but I must leave to younger statisticians to take up the work in detail for the whole empire, for which data will not be wanting.

It must be admitted at the outset that the figures

are enormous, and no such economic force has ever been in the possession of a single state or empire. An income of nearly 3,200 million £ sterling and an accumulated wealth of over 22,000 million £ are overwhelming and unimaginable. France and Germany have each probably not more than a third or a half of these figures. Although they approach the United Kingdom alone very closely, they have neither states of their own kith and kin beyond the seas to be added to their home strength, nor an empire like that of India, with many valuable possessions besides. They have the beginnings of oversea empire, but as yet, in comparison with the United Kingdom, beginnings only. Russia is another state which will no doubt be thought of with its population of over 130 millions, exclusive of Manchuria, but its economic development is too primitive to make it come into the comparison notwithstanding its great population. The United States alone, of all modern states, is comparable to the British Empire. Its aggregate income, at about £35 per head only (and it is probably more, though we must allow for the United States average being brought down by the black population and the large immigration of late years from Eastern Europe and Italy), would not be far short of 3,000 million £, while its capital or wealth appears to be reckoned officially at 18,000 million £. It has the additional advantage that, exclusive of the recent oversea additions, it is all within a ring fence. It would not be going too far to say, I believe, comparing broadly the British Empire and the United States with the leading powers next to them,—Russia, Germany, France, Austria-Hungary, Italy, and Japan—that the two Anglo-Saxon states or empires more than outweigh in economic force the whole of the rest of the world. In what way, then, are such forces to be used?

It will not surprise economists, who have of late years given some attention to family budgets, to be told that the income must be primarily used for maintenance

—for food, for shelter, for clothing, for defence against internal and foreign enemies; and that only a small surplus, comparatively, remains for the higher ends of life—for education, for assisting in religious culture, for amusement, for literature, for art, and the miscellaneous objects of civilized existence. But to show how the matter looks on a large scale, I may be permitted to refer to the method and the figures employed in reports to the British Association twenty to twenty-two years ago by a special committee comprising Mr. Jevons, Mr. Leone Levi, Mr. Stephen Bourne, and other distinguished authorities, Mr. Leone Levi being the reporter of the committee.[1] This committee then found that out of a total estimated expenditure by the people of the United Kingdom, amounting to 878 million £, no less than £500,400,000, or 56.9 per cent., was spent on food and drink; £147,800,000, or 16.8 per cent., on dress; £121,700,000 on "house," including house rent, furniture, coal, gas, and water, while, among other items, there were 1.5 per cent. spent on tobacco, 1.3 per cent. on education (less than on tobacco), 1.4 per cent. on church (also less than on tobacco), 0.8 per cent. on literature, 0.6 per cent. on newspapers, and 0.7 per cent. each on "theatres and music halls" and other amusements. This statement, I believe, was obviously incomplete, and defects were pointed out in it at the time, as, for instance, its omission of locomotion and its failure to deal sufficiently with the expense of government, while a farther distinction was drawn between gross and net expenditure and figures differing from the above given for the net expenditure, the total being about 200 million £ less; but the calculations, as far as they go, are most carefully done, and leave no doubt as to what are the main purposes to which the aggregate income of the people is devoted.

Applying and adapting the figures thus given to the present time, I have drawn up a table (see Appendix A)

[1] See "Proceedings" of meetings at Southampton and Southport in 1881 and 1882.

showing an aggregate expenditure (1,386 million £), at the present time for the following objects:

	Millions.	Per Cent. of Total.
	£	
1. Food and drink	468	34
2. Dress	182	13
3. House	223	16
4. National services (exclusive of education	183	13
5. Miscellaneous[1]	130	9
6. Cost of distribution	200	15
Total	1,386	100

According to this, the proportion of the food and drink bill is much less than in the report of the Committee of twenty years ago, which is largely due to the difference in the mode of arranging the figures. If the last item of all—the cost of distribution—were spread proportionally over the earlier of the above items, and the taxes on tea, sugar, beer and other articles were also included with them, the food and drink bill would be more nearly 600 than between 400 and 500 millions. Another cause of the change, however, is undoubtedly the fall of prices since 1880. The community now obtains a larger quantity of commodities for less money than it did. Another point which will attract attention is the large increase of expenditure for the house, largely due to the doubling of the item of house rent in the course of about twenty years. But I do not propose a minute comparison. In any mode of stating the figures the food and drink bill is still much the highest of the various branches of the national expenditure, and the other items follow the order stated twenty years ago.

Of course, a similar table for the whole empire would alter the proportions somewhat. A poor community like India must spend a larger proportion of its resources

[1] Including 30 million £ for education, 25 million £ for Church, 30 million £ for pleasure, locomotion, etc. See table in Appendix.

in food, while our self-governing colonies are exempt from the defence items which constitute so large a part of the expenditure for national services. But it would take us too long, and would be unsatisfactory without fuller detail, to present any comparisons in a tabular form.

Such being the present distribution of national expenditure, in what way does it vary from an ideal, and on what lines should the governing authorities of the empire, and men of light and leading, in private as well as public capacities, direct their efforts, so as, if necessary, to diminish outlay in some directions and increase it in others?

The *first* point which occurs to me relates to the expenditure on food and drink. The total is enormous, and the question may well arise whether in some directions there is not a possibility of retrenchment, with great advantage to the community. If, as some suppose, there is too much consumption of meat and alcohol among the artisan and wealthier classes for the proper maintenance of health and strength, what we have before us in this enormous consumption of food and drink is in part economic waste. *Per contra*, the question will arise, having regard to recent discussions, whether, in spite of the magnitude of the expenditure generally, there are not large numbers of the people insufficiently fed. The recent investigations of Mr. Rowntree and Mr. Booth would seem to point to a conclusion of this sort, though, for one, I must confess myself unconvinced. The dietary of prisons and workhouses, which is found quite sufficient for health, and, with no great additions, would be found sufficient for full work, is not so very expensive. The question is more a medical one than one to be settled in any way by statistics or general comparisons. There is no doubt that the waste in certain directions, if it could be repaired—I refer especially to the drink expenditure—would go far to provide the expenditure on food required for the proper nourishment of some of the children and families who are now insufficiently fed.

The same may be said of our self-governing colonies. They are food-producing countries, they are richer per head than we are, and there can be no general insufficiency of food, though there may be failure in certain directions, in part, at least, owing to causes which are quite remediable.

The general survey of the empire suggests, however, another aspect of the food question. How vast must be the economic gulf separating the people of the United Kingdom and the self-governing colonies from India and like parts of the empire occupied by subject races, when we find that 42 millions of people in the United Kingdom consume in food and drink alone, if we take the expenditure at the retail point (*after* distribution, and not before as in the annexed table), an amount equal to the whole income of 300 millions of people in India! There is no doubt, I believe, that, whatever may be the physiological and climatic reasons explanatory of the condition of the people of India, the degree of poverty of large masses there is a permanent and formidable difficulty of the British Empire, to which more thought must be given by our public men the more the idea of imperial unity becomes a working force. We cannot safely leave those vast populations, for whom we are responsible, in a condition of semi-starvation, and the palliative of famine relief, highly as we must praise the Indian administration for what it does to save life, is not enough. Nothing short of a revolution in Indian agriculture, and a great development of manufacturing for export, will suffice for the diseased condition we have to face; and how such changes are to be brought about, involving as they do a new education of the Indian agriculturist and an enormous influx of capital into India, it is not easy to perceive. But the public at home must understand that until some work like this is undertaken the Indian problem and difficulty remain substantially untouched.

A *second* point arising upon these figures is that of the expenditure upon housing. The sum is very large, and probably in various directions, by individuals and classes, perhaps so much is spent that there is considerable economic waste; but for the mass of the people, as we all know, the housing arrangements are not sufficient for civilized life, or even for good health. Great as the increase in this item has been since the report of twenty years ago—the expenditure being about double what it was, with an increase of less than one-fourth in the population—we must look for further outlay in this direction as the wealth of the people increases. I fear it must be added that the increase of accommodation has probably not been quite proportionate to the increase of expense. While our food bill has been lightened by the fall in prices, the expense of housing has been greatly increased, among other causes by the rise of rent in the neighbourhood of large towns through the steady growth of population, and the monopoly value thus given to areas suitable for building. The expense of building has also been increased, it is said, by the advance of wages in the building trades; but whether this advance is not largely balanced by a fall in materials, or the substitution of different materials, is not quite so clear. At any rate, there seems to be no doubt about the rise in rent, and the permanent causes of that rise, which certainly add to the complexity of the problem of the housing of the people.

A *third* point which arises is in connection with the item of national services. The total, 183 millions, exclusive of education, is certainly a large one, though smaller than either the food and drink or the housing bill. Is economy here possible or desirable, or the reverse, and on what details can there be economy?

As far as civil and local government is concerned, the sum spent on civil government in the United Kingdom, always exclusive of education, appears to be 113 millions, including about 14 millions the expenditure of the post office and telegraph department. Some deduction ought to be made from the latter department for expenditure that is really part of the general cost of production, letters, telegrams, packets, and parcels being all employed in productive business as well as in the processes of consumption, and the same remark applying to postal and money order business. But in any case the amount does not seem enormous for the postal work of so huge a state as the United Kingdom. The remaining expenditure for civil government comes to about 100 millions, one-fourth by the central government and three-fourths by the local authorities. This is all that is paid for judges and law courts, for prisons, for the collection of revenue, for Foreign Office, Treasury, Home Office, and the other offices of central government; and for the miscellaneous work of local government, including sanitation, the management of roads and markets, police, and the thousand and one odds and ends, excluding always education, which is separately dealt with in this analysis, and one or two items such as harbours, where the expenditure is really a charge on business, or like gas and water, where these happen to be municipally managed, as these are dealt with under the general headings of Gas and Water. In spite of all that is said about municipal extravagance, with much justice as I should admit, still on a general survey no great economy on this expenditure seems possible. The remark was made to me long ago by Mr. Walter Bagehot that to some extent the expenditure by local authorities in a state is a test of relative civilization. The more advanced a community is, the more it requires of its local authorities, which constitute the real and effective government in matters that pertain to the daily life of the people, and where the people come into contact with the government. The central government in its foreign business, in managing army and navy, and in supervising administration generally, does not come in contact with the masses in their daily life as the local authorities do. If, then, we find our local government costing a great deal, we may accept the fact as a proof of the advanced condition of the community. As we get richer, should that be our fortune, more will be spent in all probability in this direction, as new wants are certain to arise. After all, 100 millions for internal government—for that is what the figures come to, if we except the post office, where the expenditure is largely productive—is not an enormous amount for a community with an income of 1,750 millions, being little more than 6 per cent.

There remains the sum of 70 millions for army and navy, for military defence. This matter was discussed so fully two years ago in a paper which I read at the London Bankers' Institute,[1] that it seems permissible not to dwell on it now. The principal points may, however, be repeated. Army and navy being defence expenditure, the question of the amount to be spent is for the most part hardly optional. Defences of a certain quality and extent have to be found if the community is not to go under, and the question how much these should cost is really one for experts. Nor does a sum of 70 millions appear overwhelmingly burdensome for a community with an income and capital so great as has been described, the proportion of 70 millions to the aggregate annual income of the people being about 4 per cent., and to the accumulated wealth, on the calculation above made, about 0.47 per cent.—not a heavy rate of insurance. A comparison of the expenditure of the great military nations—Russia, Germany and France—also shows that we spend less and not more in proportion to means. For these and the like reasons, the conclusion seems unavoidable that there is no real prospect of economy in armaments, and that an increase beyond the present amount is not improbable. Always, however, let me repeat, the question is not one about which there is any real choice. The nature of our government tends to cause neglect of these matters. At a given moment we are more likely to be under-armed than over-armed. But no matter what the government, the pressure to arm and prepare for emergencies

[1] See *supra*, vol. ii., pp. 278-305.

is always being felt, and must be yielded to with good or bad grace by every government.

An imperial survey leads to much the same conclusion, and suggests considerations of very grave import indeed. When we go beyond the United Kingdom and inquire as to military and naval preparation in the rest of the empire, we find that India alone makes a substantial addition to the insurance fund, its military expenditure being about 18 million £. Beyond that, it is doubtful whether so much as 5 million £ is spent by the rest of the empire for military defence, although the wealth of the self-governing colonies is so enormously greater per head than of India. The result is that when we make a comparison for the whole empire, we find that the aggregate income as above stated is no less than about £3,200,000,000, and the aggregate capital over £22,000,000,000; and the military and naval expenditure—the insurance premium of this great and rich empire—is no more than 95 million £, viz., 70 millions for the United Kingdom, 18 for India, and 5 for the rest of the empire, that is, a proportion of about 3 per cent. to the income and 0.4 per cent. to the capital. This hardly seems "good business" for a great and widely scattered empire, liable to be attacked on so many points, and to be sundered into numerous fragments, for a time at least, by a bold and enterprising enemy. One of the worst features of the matter is that the contribution by India, whose poverty we have had to lament, is out of sight much greater, in proportion to its taxable capacity, than that of the rest of the empire, although the Indian army is freely used for imperial and general purposes, and is not employed exclusively for local defence.

The remedy is not specially for the people of the United Kingdom to consider, but it is our business to show the way. Apparently our public men of late years have gone the wrong way to work, as they have tried the method of a joint purse, as it were, to which the different colonies have been invited to contribute, at least for naval purposes. But little success seems to have attended this method, which has arrayed against it the optimism of the colonies themselves, more or less removed as they are from the causes of strife to which other parts of the empire are exposed, and their unwillingness to pay a kind of tribute, as the proposed contribution looks like, to be administered by a distant authority. The colonial plan in this matter appears to be much better. Let each part of the empire provide what defence is expedient according to its local conditions, and be encouraged to do its best both on land and water, without any idea of contributions to a distant centre. A great deal has to be done, and both Canada and Australasia, I maintain, are likely to produce better land and naval forces which can be used in time of war, if they are encouraged to do the work for themselves, than if they are to become contributors to our army and navy departments. India remains a difficulty. It is certainly overcharged as compared with any other part of the Empire. But India might gradually be relieved as the local defences of the whole empire are developed and it is really made unassailable at every point.

A *fourth* and last point on which observations occur to me is with reference to education, included in the miscellaneous category. On the face of the figures it is evident that the aggregate expenditure is not sufficiently directed to the higher ends of life, which are included under the heading "miscellaneous." Literature so called and newspapers, as well as theatres and other amusements, with "locomotion" for pleasure, which may be reckoned among "amusements" in a general sense, are estimated to have spent on them about 75 million £ altogether, and although this expenditure includes a great deal which promotes the higher ends of life, the whole amount cannot certainly be so treated. Of the remainder the item of 25 million £ for church may here be passed over with such reflections as may occur to some respecting the smallness of the amount devoted by the people generally to "saving their souls" compared with the vast sums for food, raiment, shelter, and other purposes. This would hardly be the place to discuss what is meant by religion, and whether any special expenditure for "church" is quite the same thing as expenditure to advance or practice "religion." We are on common and surer ground, I believe, respecting education, on which apparently about 30 million £ is the expenditure; that is less than 2 per cent. of the great income with which we have been dealing. Is such an expenditure quite creditable to a wealthy community, especially when it is considered that, apart from primary education, which is no more than the foundation and beginning of the real education of the community, the sums appropriated are quite insignificant? When we extend our view to the empire as a whole, the question becomes more urgent. Considerable sums are spent in the self-governing colonies on primary education of a kind, but the means for secondary and university education are small by comparison. When we come to India, the situation is still more appalling. Beyond a sum of about 2 million £ appearing in the Indian budget for education, Government does nothing for elevating and training the 300 millions under its care, and it is quite impossible that the poor people of India can spare much for private expenditure.

What, then, should be the measure of national and imperial expenditure on education, including in the latter the scientific training of a higher kind and the laboratory investigations of which your President has shown the necessity? One is almost prevented from suggesting large sums at once, for no other reason than the absence of adequate numbers of trained teachers and investigators, which is due to our past neglect; but as soon as possible, I have no hesitation in saying, the country should be spending 100 millions where it now spends 30, or about 5 per cent. of an aggregate income which is likely to exceed before long the total of 2,000 millions, a total, as we have seen, already exceeded in the United States. Of course, there should be a proportionate expenditure in other self-governing parts of the empire, and the condition of India and other parts where there are subject races ought not to be overlooked. Such sums are not really extravagant. Extensive diffusion of education and scientific knowledge and training are not only essential to the greater efficiency of labour and capital by which the means of living are provided, but they are equally needed for the conduct of life itself, for the health and comfort of the workers, their freedom from debasing superstitions and prejudices, their capacity to enjoy the higher pleasures, and their ability to manage all common affairs.

It will be asked, perhaps, how are the necessary sums to be obtained, as few suggestions seem practicable, on a broad survey of national expenditure, for economy in other directions. When it is doubtful whether large numbers of the people are adequately fed and housed, it seems premature to suggest expenditure on other ends which have not to the popular mind so pressing a claim. The answer is partly that the claim for education and scientific training is really more pressing than any other, because it is the means to the end of properly feeding and housing the great masses of the people, and qualifying them as members of an educated community. Another answer is that if we go to work rightly the expenditure will be quickly remunerative. More efficient workers will produce more, and in that way supply the funds for extending and increasing the educational means of improvement. There is yet another answer. One fault of the present time is that people have been taking things too easily. The means for educational improvement must be found, if need be, by longer hours, harder work, and an increase of the national output with the existing methods and machinery. Our populations, in short, have, to some extent, begun to play too soon, and they are not playing in the right way. They are giving to football and cricketing some of the time that should be given to severer employments, among which educational improvement comes first, and the additional labour necessary to find the means for that improvement. The next generation, it may be hoped, will be more laborious, more energetic, more studious, and less athletic than the present, though neglecting in no way physical exercise and amusement so far as expedient for health under the conditions of life of a highly civilized community. It must not be said, however, that what has been suggested is beyond the means of the community. We are rich enough for anything that is really required, whether for defence or for the ends of education, and if there is any lack it can be made good by a slightly greater effort if we only make up our minds to put it forth.

The case of India and of other subject races under the British Empire requires special consideration, owing to the very poverty of the people who have to be instructed and developed. There are obvious objections to grants from imperial funds on an extensive scale, even if such grants were easily practicable. But some grants ought not to be grudged by way of a beginning, as an increase of industrial force among these subject races is essential to the due development of the British Empire itself. We may trust also, as in our own case at home, to the recuperativeness of the expenditure. Increasing industrial power and an increase of means for their further education will accrue to these subject races at once, so that their finances can be organised on a stronger basis. But education is the watchword, and should be the first thought in all our minds.

Having thus fulfilled my promise to your President to initiate a discussion on the objects of the expenditure of national income, may I express the hope, that some attention will be given at future meetings of the Association to the investigation from time to time of the facts as to actual expenditure and the proportions of the total amount appropriated to each object—to the continuation, in short, of the investigations of the Committee of 1881, of whose report I have made such large use? On some points, for some purposes, minute investigations are hardly needed, because certain broad figures are good enough for practical discussion, and there is no greater waste of time than the elaboration of figures where elaboration is not really required. But a more elaborate investigation than anything attempted in 1881, much more elaborate than anything I have now ventured on, would also supply the bases of many useful comparisons. An investigation in detail, for instance, of the "cost of distribution" among different classes of the community for different commodities would yield some interesting and instructive results. The investigations might be carried further, and comparisons made with other countries, so as to exhibit how variously the problems of living are solved. At the same time the difficulties are endless, as expenditure for one purpose overlaps that of another, and there are curious puzzles as to what are "independent" incomes and what are not, and in what way the direct use of commodities and services by the producer, without being the subject of exchange, is to be treated. Some of our younger statisticians and economists, it may be hoped, will be induced to have a "look in" on this topic.

APPENDIX A.

TABLE *showing the Estimated Wholesale Cost of Various Articles Consumed, and of Services Rendered, in the United Kingdom in* 1902. (See Notes appended.)

I.—FOOD AND DRINK.

	Mln. £.
BREAD.—30,000,000 qrs. of wheat, including 23,000,000 qrs. imported at average price of 29*s.* per qr. plus $1\frac{1}{4}$*d.* per 4 lbs. for manufacture into bread, warehousing, etc. . .	60
POTATOES.—4,500,000 tons, including 287,000 tons imported at value of 1.6 million £	23
VEGETABLES, other than potatoes (including fruit of home production).	25
MEAT, including poultry and game (imports, 48 million £; home production estimated, 82 million £—total 130 million £)	130
FISH.—(Imports less re-exports, 3.5 million £; home production, less exports, 6 million £—total, 9.5 million £).	9.5
BUTTER, CHEESE, AND MILK.—(Imports, 35.3 million £; home production, estimated, 35.3 million £—total, 70.6 million £)	70.6
EGGS.—(Imports, 6.2 million £; home production, estimated, 6.7 million £—total, 12.9 million £)	12.9
	331.0

FRUIT, imported (including fruit, 10.2 million £; rice, 2.5 million £; spices, 0.9 million £; and confectionery, [?])	14
SUGAR.[1]—(Imports, less re-exports, 33,000,000 cwts., valued at 15.5 million £, but deduct 10 per cent. for quantity used in brewing and distilling, and add allowance for refining at home)	16
TEA.[1]—(Imports, less re-exports, 7 million £, plus $\frac{1}{7}$th for landing and warehousing)	8
COFFEE AND COCOA.[1]—(Imports, less re-exports, 3.5 million £, plus $\frac{1}{7}$ for landing and warehousing)	4
	42

[1] See note as to beer.

	Mln. £.
Beer.[1]—(36,000,000 barrels at about £2 per barrel)	70
Spirits.[1]—(45,000,000 gallons at about 4*s.* per gallon)	9
Wine.[1]—(Imports, less re-exports, 4.5 million £, plus ⅓ for landing and warehousing)	6
Tobacco.[1]—(Imports, less re-exports, 5.4 million £, plus allowance for landing, manufacturing, and warehousing)	10
	95
Total of food and drink	468

II.—Dress.

Cotton manufactures (including 5.7 million £ imported)	42
Woollen manufactures (including 13 million £ imported)	75
Linen (including 3 million £ jute and linen imported)	10
Silk (including 13½ million £ imported)	15
Leather: boots and shoes, gloves, etc. (including 10.5 million £ leather manufactures imported)	30
Silver plate and jewellery	10
Total "Dress"	182

III.—House.

House rent (from House Duty Returns)	145
Furniture	22
Coal (25,000,000 tons at 20*s.* per ton)	25
Gas (from official gas returns, 140,400,000,000 cubic feet of gas, estimated average price 3*s.* per 1,000 cubic feet)	21[2]
Water	10[2]
Total "House"	223

IV.—National Services.

Army and Navy	70
Post Office	14
Civil List and Civil Administration (less education)	24
Local Government services (less education, gas, water, and other items)	75
Total National Services	183

[1] See note as to beer.

[2] See note as to gas and water.

V.—Miscellaneous.

	Mln. £.
Education (including 11 million £ Parliamentary grants and 14 million £ School Board rates)	30
Literature	10
Newspapers	15
Church (including 14 million £ for revenues of Church of England, with estimates for Scotland and Ireland, and for dissent)	25
Locomotion (tramways, 6 million £; half receipts from railway passengers, 24 million £). Total, 30 million £	30
Theatres and Amusements	20
Total miscellaneous	130

VI.—Cost of Distribution.

Cost of distribution (estimate of British Association Committee in 1881, 155 million £, plus about 30 per cent. for increase of population and wealth since 1881)	200
Grand total	1,386

Summary.

	Mln. £.
1. Food and drink	468
2. Dress	182
3. House	223
4. National services (exclusive of education, etc.)	183
5. Miscellaneous	130
6. Cost of distribution	200
Grand total	1,386
Add:	
Professional and domestic services, not comprised in other items (*say*)	100
Amount spent on services resulting in permanent works (*investments*) (*say*)	264
Total, equalling estimated aggregate income	1,750

Notes to Table.

In adapting the figures, and to some extent the methods, of the Committee of 1881 to the present time, I have thought it more convenient in showing expenditure on commodities to include only the wholesale cost of commodities consumed, less any allowance for cost of distribution and less taxes, and to show the cost of distribution and the expense of national services as separate items. The final result is, of course, the same as that followed in 1881; but it is important to realize that, taking the community in mass, when a man buys a pound of tea, for instance, or a gallon of spirits, he pays only part of the sum he gives for the tea or the spirits, and that the remainder is paid either for government services or for the expense of bringing it from the wholesale dealer who receives it from the producer, or from the producer himself when there is no intermediary, to the door of the consumer.

It will be observed that two items are added in italics in order to show a correspondence between the aggregate income and aggregate expenditure. But this is merely to "round off," and there is no pretence at exact statement. The question of how professional and domestic services should be dealt with is, of course, a controversial one, but as they are included in the income, an equal sum should appear in the expenditure, less amounts paid for such services included in the cost of production and distribution. The services, as for builders and others, which result in permanent works, really represent an investment of capital, to which the services of a certain portion of the community have been appropriated. They have created so much which is not consumed. The increase of capital since 1885 having been about 5,000 million £, or 277 million £ per annum, the figure of 264 million £ here shown as the annual investment at the present time is fairly justified. Probably the figure is lower than it ought to be, and a higher estimate of income should have been worked up to.

With regard to particular items, I have to make the following observations supplementary to the information contained in the table itself:

Bread.—The value of wheat and wheat flour imported in 1902 was 36 million £ sterling, the quantity being 81,000,000 cwts. of wheat and 19½ million cwts. of flour, or about 108,000,000 cwts. in equivalent cwts. of wheat alone, giving a price of 6*s.* 8*d.* per cwt., and about 29*s.* per quarter. The home produce, estimated at 7,000,000 quarters, gives a sum at the same price of about 10 million £—total, 46 million £, making, with the addition for manufacture, etc., a total of about 60 million £ as here stated. It is an omission, perhaps, as it was in the Report of 1881, that nothing is put down for oats and other grains used as food, but the omission seems immaterial for the present purpose, especially as we should have to make a deduction, if the matter was gone into minutely, for home wheat consumed by cattle and not used as human food. The heading "bread" of course includes biscuits and other manufactures from wheat.

Potatoes.—Imports, about £5 10*s.* per ton, 1.6 million £. Home production for household use at 2 cwts. per head of population, 4,200,000 tons at, say, £5 per ton—total 23 million £. The estimate of 2 cwts. per head of population was given by Mr. Turnbull before the Commission on Depression in Agriculture (see "Minutes of Evidence," vol. iv., p. 546 *et seq.*). His average price was £2 12*s.* 6*d.* only, but I retain a figure more closely approximating the Report of 1881.

Vegetables.—Mr. Turnbull's figure for 1892-93 for home vegetables and fruit was 21 million £ (see vol. iv., p. 543 of "Minutes of Evidence" above referred to). Adding 2½ million £ for import of vegetables other than potatoes, and an allowance for vegetables and fruit grown at home apart from "farming," the figure stated does not appear excessive.

Meat.—The imports for 1902 are as stated. Mr. Turnbull's figure for meat produced at home in 1892-93 was 72 million £, and allowing for poultry and game in addition, the figure of 82 million £ cannot be far wrong. An exact comparison cannot be made, as he includes poultry with eggs, and makes no allowance for game. The quantities are about 21,000,000 cwts. foreign, and 27,000,000 cwts. home, the home proportion being that given by Mr. Crawford in his paper at the Statistical Society in 1899, which does not, however, include poultry and game.

Butter, Cheese, and Milk.—According to Mr. Crawford in the above paper, the home production and foreign imports of dairy produce appear to be about equal. Mr. Turnbull's figure for home dairy produce in 1892-93 was 32½ million £.

Beer.—The Report of 1881 gave a figure of 75 million £, allowing for much the same consumption per head as at the present time. The proportionate figure now would be 90 million £, but this includes a large allowance for cost of distribution, which appears to be as much as 46 million £ on the total of 75 million £ in the Report. This appears rather excessive, and I believe the figure here assumed will represent a better average wholesale price. It will, of course, be observed that taxation here is not included.

Spirits, Wine, Tobacco.—These are all lower figures than those in the Report of 1881, for the reason given above as to beer.

Nothing has been included for "mineral waters" specially, as their cost is partly accounted for under the heading of sugar and other items, and cannot be a large figure wholesale.

Cotton.—The figure in the Report for 1881 was 31 million £, which included 20 per cent. for cost of distribution; but since then the home consumption of cotton, according to the circular of Messrs. Ellison, has risen from 184,000,000 lbs. to 300,000,000 lbs., or 60 per cent. at much the same price. The estimate in the Report for home cotton in 1881, exclusive of cost of distribution, was £22,800,000, which would now be increased to 36½ million £ in proportion to the increase of raw cotton used. Adding to this £5,700,000 imported, and not adding anything for cost of distribution, we get the total of 42 million in round figures.

Wool.—The amount of wool taken for home consumption according to the circular of Messrs. Helmuth Schwarz and Co., appears to have been about 525 million lbs. per annum in the last five years. The exports of manufactured goods have not increased since 1881, when the report was presented to the British Association, and as the quantity taken for home consumption was then 390 million lbs. on the average, giving a production of home manufactures amounting to about 56 million £, there seems reason to believe that a proportionate increase would give us the figures of 75 million £ as the value of home manufactures at the present time. Adding 12 million £ for woollen goods imported, the total is 87 million £. Deduction, however, must be made for woollen manufactures not for dress, about 20 per cent. apparently, according to the Report of 1881, which leaves a net figure of about 70 million £. This figure ought, however, to be increased to allow for a diminution in the consumption of wool for export manufacture, giving a larger amount for home consumption, and I have put it at 75 million £.

Leather, Silver Plate, etc.—No detailed computation here, but an addition allowed for increased consumption since 1881.

House Rent.—The figure is for residential housing only, all other "houses" being deducted. It is double the figure for 1881.

Furniture.—Double the estimate for 1881, corresponding to great increase of house values.

Gas and Water.—The figures as to gas and water have been compared with the Local Taxation Returns, the return "Municipal Corporations' Reproductive Undertakings" (No. 398, Session 1902), and the return as to "London Water Companies" (No. 286, Session 1902). There are some discrepancies in these returns, and no special estimate has been made for electricity and oil, as gas and electricity are used for power as well as light; oil is also used for enriching gas. The gross figure for gas alone is thus allowed to stand for the "group."

National Services.—The figures here are necessarily taken from the budget and local taxation accounts, with some adjustments in respect of education and other items. There is no figure put down for payment of debt interest, as that is not payment for a "current" service, but a mere transfer from A to B among the various members of the community.

Miscellaneous.—The figures of 1881 have in most cases been doubled, increases having taken place in all directions; and for "locomotion" there is a still larger estimate, that being an item omitted at first in the estimates for 1881. There are hardly data for a thorough statement under this head, except after a most elaborate treatment.

XXX.

THE DREAM OF A BRITISH ZOLLVEREIN.[1]

THE federation or closer political union of the British Empire is obviously so important that proposals to stimulate or accelerate it by means of commercial union appear specially attractive. They are much in the air at the present time. It is to be feared, however, that public opinion to some extent is taking a wrong direction, in which the end aimed at may be missed and great mischief follow.

The expediency of political federation itself may be assumed. It does not receive quite the general assent which it ought to command. There are not only "Little Englanders" who would like to see the Empire broken up; but not a few besides, whose love for the State and regard for the Empire are beyond doubt, lament the tone of Imperialistic feeling which prevails and the accompanying ideas of policy, as contrary to the traditional feeling for liberty characteristic of our race and history. These doubters dislike the new atmosphere, and are discouraged by the burdens which Imperial policy seems to entail as well as by the attacks on Free Trade and other parts of the general policy of freedom in which some of the most forward Imperialists love to indulge. But while appreciating the state of mind of this minority I cannot share their doubts. The necessity for Imperial Federation is so great and overwhelming that all good citizens should join in promoting it. The broad reasons are the sentiment of national unity which makes a British subject settled anywhere under the common flag regard his colony as one with the mother country; and with this the instinct of self-preservation which makes it

[1] From the "Nineteenth Century" of May, 1902.

obvious that in these days of great military and naval empires the lives and liberties, and possessions, of English people throughout the world are nowhere safe from military aggression unless the whole are united for common defence. South Africa would probably be German or Dutch-German at the present moment if our fellow-subjects there had not had the help of the whole empire. Australia would be exposed to similar risks from French and German ambition without a great Empire with it and behind it. Our own position in Europe would certainly be most insecure if we were Great Britain and Ireland only, and could not call upon our kith and kin beyond the seas or exercise the force of Empire in distant lands. In spite, then, of many faults of logic and argument among advocates of Imperial Federation, the policy, in my view, should command universal assent. It is unwise and unpatriotic to stand aloof.

It is with this opinion about Imperial Federation itself that I propose to criticise some of the suggestions as to commercial union which are put forward as means to the end. Federation is to be reached mainly, I believe, by political changes, assisted, where this can properly be done, by commercial arrangements, but not by the commercial arrangements which are most discussed and most in people's minds, such as an Imperial Zollverein, or what are called "preferential" arrangements between the mother country and the colonies.

As with many other subjects, a historical retrospect may help to show us where we are. The idea that commercial union inevitably tends to political union, and is the only or best way to arrive at such union, has a slender enough foundation historically.

In older political unions there was little question of mutual commercial advantages. The different provinces of France, for instance, were politically united long before Customs barriers ceased to exist between them. The political union of England and Scotland, again, began to take effect in 1603 by the union of the crowns, but separate Customs continued not only till the formal legislative union a century later but long after. Ireland, though subordinate to the crown of England (and afterwards of Great Britain), was commercially separate till the union of 1800 and even later. One of the Irish grievances is, in fact, the commercial legislation first of England and then of Great Britain directed against Irish industries. In the same way commercial union with colonies was the last thing thought of until modern times, the exploitation of colonies by and for the mother country being the ideal. The distinction between the idea of political union and that of mutual commercial advantages has thus been complete in past times.

There are cases, moreover, in modern times at least, of commercial unions between politically separate entities, which were not intended to lead up in any way to political union. For many years, as is well known, a Reciprocity Treaty existed between the United States and Canada, in spite of their political separation. In the same way, in South Africa before the war, there was a Customs union between Cape Colony, Natal, and the Orange Free State, although the latter was an independent republic. To the same order of arrangements belong, I think, the special regulations between Austria-Hungary and Roumania and other Danubian States for trans-frontier trade; and similar arrangements between France and China as respects the frontier trade between Tonquin and Southern China. There is no question of political union in the matter, but there are arrangements for frontier trade more or less resembling a Customs union.

In this way the precedents are complete for treating political association and commercial association as different things, and as not necessarily involving and implying each other. The assumption that political union follows commercial union is, theoretically at least, incorrect. It appears to be largely due, in reality, to the frequency with which undoubtedly commercial union has followed the political union of separate States, and to one important instance in which a Customs union, that of the German Zollverein, has contributed to the consolidation of an empire; but the cases of the former description are not to the point, while the single instance of the German Zollverein is not enough to prove that Customs unions always conduce to a closer union of a political kind. According to former experience, the commercial union of the British Empire—in time—will follow the political union; but how far mutual commercial arrangements will assist such an object will depend on special circumstances and the nature of the arrangements themselves, which are all matters for investigation.

Looking at the problem in this way, we cannot but recognise that the commercial union of the British Empire, meaning thereby a real Zollverein, or such a union for commercial purposes as exists between the different states of the United States, or the different provinces of the German Empire, in which the same commercial laws prevail, the same money exists for all purposes, and, above all, there is a single Customs barrier against the rest of the world with all internal barriers abolished, must in the nature of things be somewhat difficult. The number of separate legislatures necessitates so many separate commercial codes, which can only be fused into one by common agreement, or by the invention of devices like those of the American Constitution, by which certain subjects are reserved for a central congress. The same remark applies to money which is reserved for the central Government by the Constitutions of both the German Empire and the United States, but has not yet been reserved in the British Constitution, while there would be special difficulties in having a common money in the existence of places like Canada, which happens to lie within the radius of the United States banking system, or Gibraltar, which cannot avoid having Spanish money for common use, or India, which has the rupee for monetary unit and cannot get quit of that unit, or Egypt, which is technically a part of the Turkish Empire and not even a British State. The remark is even more applicable to the subject of a Customs union. This subject is not reserved for a central body by a political constitution as it is in Germany and the United States, while there are obvious practical difficulties which do not exist in those countries, and which would make the establishment of a Customs union impossible even if the central Government had power to deal with the matter. The difficulties are as follows:

(*a*) The physical separation of the different parts of the Empire. The sea, it is said, unites and does not separate, which is true in a sense, but is not true for the purpose of a Zollverein. That purpose is the abolition of Customs barriers where they are most irksome to trade—that is, between adjacent places. This irksomeness, as we have seen, is so great that it has led in some cases to such arrangements as those existing on the Austrian and Southern Chinese frontiers, or such an arrangement as the former Reciprocity Treaty between Canada and the United States. There is a real practical evil which a Customs union deals with in the most effective manner, and, although the sea unites the separate parts of the British Empire, it does not unite them in such a way that the inconvenience of Customs barriers is felt as it was in the trade between the different states of the American Union, or between the different provinces of Germany, or is felt now between any countries having a long land frontier between them. On the contrary, the longer the voyage the less important are the Customs barriers relatively as an obstruction to trade. The long voyage itself and the transhipment, which cannot be got rid of, are the real evils caused by distance in over-sea communication, and not the intervention of the Customs, serious as the latter intervention may be on a land frontier across which there is trade at many points. A Zollverein, therefore, comprising states or provinces separated by great breadths of sea, could not give them the special advantages obtained by a Zollverein between contiguous places. Customs regulations, moreover, must still continue to exist at the ports, as they do even in coasting trade, so that, as far as they are an evil, inter-Imperial trade would still be affected by them.

(*b*) The variety of race and business which makes it expedient for different parts of the Empire to have each its own tariff, even against other parts, if it is to raise revenue by indirect taxes, which all must do. The Indian Empire is obviously so constituted that its inhabitants cannot be brought into line as consumers with the European populations of the British Empire. These populations provide indirect revenue mainly by the consumption of spirits, beer, tobacco, sugar, and tea; and sugar alone among these articles is extensively consumed in India. The people of India, again, are subject to a tax on salt not usually imposed on populations of English race. Still worse, although the Indian people consume sugar, the article with them is also an important article of widespread agricultural production, which would bring the tax-gatherer into close and unwelcome contact with masses of the people if a duty on sugar were imposed. On the other hand, India is a producer of the tea and coffee which are not worth taxing in India, but are a stand-by for finance Ministers in other parts of the Empire.

The self-governing colonies, again, in contrast with the United Kingdom, naturally desire to impose duties for purposes of revenue on the manufactures which they import mainly from Great Britain; while in Great Britain, among the articles most suitable for taxation are to be found the tobacco, tea, coffee, and sugar, which are largely produced in the colonies.

Unless each part of the Empire, therefore, is to arrange its own tariff, it will be extremely difficult for it, if not impossible, to raise suitable revenue by means of indirect taxes.

(*c*) This last difficulty is enhanced by the consideration of the "pooling" arrangements among the different

States which are the indispensable adjunct of a Customs union. The idea is that no province of the union is to have a Customs barrier against another part. Duties are to be levied in common. There must be a common purse, accordingly, not only for the Customs duties which are to be imposed on articles imported from the rest of the world, but on similar commodities produced at home. In other words, the Customs and Excise revenue of each part of the union is to be dependent on the vigilance of the revenue authorities in every other part. In such a union for the British Empire, our spirit revenue, for instance, would depend on the vigilance of authorities in Australia and South Africa. And then out of the common purse each State of the Empire would receive its share. In what way the shares are to be fixed, with heterogeneous populations like India concerned, will be no easy matter, and it will be still more difficult to provide the automatic re-adjustments, according to the changes in population at each census, which existed in the German Zollverein.

(*d*) Difficulties arising from the uncertain political status of States or Provinces which form a portion of the Empire as far as the burden of defence is concerned, and which are popularly reckoned as within the Empire, but which are either not internationally recognised as part of the Empire at all or are subject to special arrangements by political treaties, as, for instance, our West African Protectorates. The doubtful position of Egypt has already been referred to in connection with the question of common money, but in the question of a Zollverein the status of that country would be still more embarrassing. Egypt is legally a part of the Turkish Empire, and it is bound by various international stipulations of that Empire as well as stipulations special to itself as regards shipping and navigation. To make it part of a British Zollverein would involve prolonged negotiations with European Powers that would almost certainly fail, or a rupture of treaties in time of peace involving a risk of war and the equally formidable mischief, perhaps, of throwing doubts on English good faith in carrying out treaties, however disagreeable sometimes their stipulations may be. The Soudan, which we hold in common with Egypt, could perhaps be included in a Zollverein more easily; but how odd a Zollverein of the Empire would look with large parts of it outside the union, and especially a part like Egypt, the strategical centre of the Empire itself.

Such difficulties existing, however, they should be carefully thought out by those who talk of a Zollverein or Customs union for the British Empire before we can even get to business in the discussion. I confess for one my inability to imagine how they are to be overcome. There appears to be no help to a solution in any proposals put forward, as far as I have yet observed.

Passing from this question of a Zollverein, we come to the proposal of "preferential arrangements" in the matter of tariffs between the mother country and the other parts of the Empire. Such arrangements, it is supposed, will effect the same objects as a Zollverein—viz., a closer commercial union, which will also have the same political results as are expected from a Zollverein itself. Such is the abuse of language, that many people when they hear of an Imperial Zollverein are really thinking of a Customs barrier set up in the Empire against foreign countries, leaving the barriers inside the Empire intact, and are not really thinking of a proper Customs union at all.

All such proposals have a common character, so that it would be a waste of time to go into detail. To state their nature is surely to show their ineptitude. What is proposed in effect is a commercial treaty between the colonies and the mother country on a reciprocity basis, each colony consenting to tax differentially certain articles it receives from foreign countries in competition with similar articles received from the mother country or the rest of the Empire, and the mother country in turn taxing differentially certain articles received from foreign countries in competition with articles imported from the colonies. The business is to be arranged on the *Do ut des* principle, and the effect is to be the increased mutual dependence of the different parts of the Empire and their increased joint and several independence of foreign countries.

Such suggestions involve the certainty of injury to both the colonies and the mother country if they are tried, and the uncertainty of any advantage whatsoever. Each part of the Empire is to divert a portion of its trade from the channels in which it naturally flows, a procedure necessarily involving loss, and it is to have the same trade afterwards inside the Empire, only at greater expense. Political advantage may conceivably ensue in the end from the different parts of the Empire sticking closer together even in this way, though it appears unlikely; but there is no commercial advantage at any time. But as to the political advantage, where there is no commercial advantage, may there not also be doubts? One or the other party must be exposed to extreme deception. If the colonies get a better price in the mother country for their raw materials and articles of food than they would otherwise do, some people in the mother country will have to pay more, and it will have to be very clear indeed that they got a *quid pro quo* either in higher prices in the colonies for what they sell or increased profits from large trade with them. At the time of the famous Hofmeyr suggestion that the colonies and the mother country should impose a special tax of 2 per cent. *ad valorem* on all imports from foreign countries, a duty calculated to yield about £7,000,000, which could be appropriated to purposes of mutual defence, I recollect making a calculation, (1) that the portion of the £7,000,000 paid by the United Kingdom would be nearly the whole, (2) that the price of the commodities imported into the United Kingdom from the colonies as well as from foreign countries would be raised by a larger sum, and (3) that the colonies contributing a small part of the amount would be more than compensated by the higher prices obtained for their produce in the United Kingdom, while the mother country in turn would obtain no such compensation from higher prices in the colonies on its exports to them, owing to the small proportion of such exports with which foreign countries really competed. Disillusionment must thus follow any reciprocity arrangement of this sort. Instead of tending to political union, it will almost certainly have the reverse effect.

Quite as serious is the prospect of bad blood with foreign countries, especially with the United States, if we make any arrangement with the colonies which in fact leads to a serious diminution of our trade with foreign countries—the means by which the arrangement is to achieve its end. Could we view without alarm the discontent that might be produced in the United States, with which we desire to promote the most friendly relations, if we differentiated against their wheat, meat, cotton, copper, and other articles for the sake of what we hope our colonies will give us? The mere attempt, even if it should fail, would tend to exasperate. It is quite true, of course, that the United States—and our leading foreign competitors—would technically have no cause to complain. Their own tariffs are as great a discouragement to trade with the United Kingdom as they can be, and have been so for many years. But as a matter of fact we cannot hope to export to them much more largely than we do, even if their tariffs were now as free as our own, so that we lose little by their discourtesy, while we should certainly lose by an increase of political animosity, if we imitate their example, and possibly better their instruction.[1]

It is a supreme interest with us, again, to promote foreign trade, not only that food may be cheap but that we may have the necessary raw materials for our

[1] See the statements in the "Times" of the 16th of April quoted from the "New York Times" as to American retaliation on Canada if it receives preferential treatment in the United Kingdom.

industries. There is no prospect in reality that the colonies, from which we import about £110,000,000 annually and to which we export about £102,000,000 annually, could really for generations take the place in our trade of foreign countries from which we import £413,000,000 annually and to which we export £252,000,000 annually.[1] How are the colonies to do it? Even to take the place of foreign countries to a very partial extent would involve a complete revolution in the conditions of their industry, and an enormous increase in their population which is quite inconceivable.

Apart from the quantity of our purely foreign trade, there is another difficulty in the way of a proposal to substitute colonial trade for it. No country or empire in the world produces every kind of thing it wants; and the British Empire is no exception. However united the Empire may be, the United Kingdom must still go outside for many things—to Spain for iron ore, to the Dutch East Indies for tin, to the United States and Spain for copper, to the United States for raw cotton, and so on. Either foreign countries are the sole producers of such articles or the only producers in quantities necessary for business. It would be no light matter, therefore, to penalise our foreign customers, and make access to their markets more difficult than they make it themselves.

Reciprocal or preferential arrangements between the mother country and the colonies are accordingly most dangerous, economically and politically. It is a complete misconception that they are of the same nature as a Zollverein, which is a measure of pure free trade, but happens not to be possible for the British Empire as a whole.

While the advocates of commercial union as a means to Imperial Federation have thus mistaken their way,

[1] Excluding in both cases the transhipment trade and imports and exports of gold and silver.

and suggested measures that are either impossible or will defeat the object aimed at, the advocacy itself has been hardly less mischievous. The cause of federation of the Empire has come to be identified with a policy of Protection until adherents of a Free-trade policy are almost under compulsion to choose between the abandonment of their ideas and the promotion of Imperial Federation itself. This is not a desirable result. Whether the commercial policy of the federated Empire is to be Protectionist or Free-trading, federation itself is a good thing for sound political reasons. For those who desire it, therefore, to put in the forefront of their arguments a commercial policy which arrays against them large masses of the very people whose co-operation they desire, is a mistake of no small magnitude. It lays them open to the charge from which I fear some of our colonial friends could not easily clear themselves—that it is Protection they seek by means of federation and not federation itself. I recollect first coming in contact with this idea twenty years ago at a dinner in the club at Montreal, when I was obliged to listen to a very heated argument by leading citizens in favour of a preferential duty of 2*s*. 6*d*. per quarter in England on grain from the United States as compared with grain from Canada, an argument so heated that a modest speaker could hardly get in a word edgeways on the other side. Such heat is still observable in colonial arguments for a "preference." They want a "pull," an advantage of some kind out of the mother country, not for the sake of federating the Empire, but because they want Protection so much. They offer hardly any *quid pro quo* which will stand discussion; but even if they did it is surely most lamentable that colonial appeals to the mother country to federate should be mixed up with bargaining on the lowest level of any commercial transaction.

As I write additional evidence is furnished us as to the anxiety in the colonies for Protection. Only the other day Mr. Seddon was reported to have said that the attachment of New Zealand to the mother country was not sentimental, but was based on *£ s. d.* The mother country bought New Zealand mutton, and that was the reason why. No one would attach too much importance to a casual expression in conversation, even if true, but that it should be reported when Mr. Seddon is coming home to advocate his ideas of preference is not quite pleasant reading for friends of Imperial Federation on patriotic grounds. At the same time, we hear from Canada that Sir Wilfrid Laurier has refused an invitation to an Imperial Conference to discuss the subject of defence—surely the main problem of federation—though he was willing to discuss the subject of commercial relations. The Opposition in the Canadian Parliament in turn have complained of the Prime Minister (in long debates), that, if he had acted differently, Canada might have received exemption from the new corn duty, with more of like favours to come. Thus it is always Protection that is being argued for, and not so much the federation which is professedly the excuse. Not only, then, is the cause of Imperial Federation being sought by means of preferential arrangements which will tend to frustrate the object, but the argument is all in the wrong key, and tends very strongly to set against the cause some powerful influences that should be wholly in its favour.

How is federation to be promoted, and what sort of commercial arrangements, if any, will really assist? While rejecting the notion of a Zollverein because it is impossible in the peculiar circumstances of the British Empire, and while rejecting most strenuously the notion of preferential arrangements as economically and politically dangerous, and deprecating the line of argument by which the latter policy is supported as additionally fatal to the prospects of success in promoting federation by means of commercial union, I believe that in various ways such a union may be promoted with mutual advantage to all parts of the Empire, including the further advantage of accelerating a closer political union. We ought to see, at any rate, what can really be done, and walk warily, avoiding above all any obsolete fiscal ideas such as are involved in Protection.

The initial step should be, I think, the recognition by the colonies of the immense aid that has been given to commercial union throughout the Empire by the Free-trade policy of the mother country itself. Just as our Free-trade policy has undoubtedly benefited the whole world because trade with the British Empire is the main part of the foreign trade of every country, and, however Protectionist other countries may be, their foreign trade on one side at least has been carried on under conditions of freedom; so we may contend that the colonies of the United Kingdom which do so much of their business with the mother country have specially gained. The most natural channels for their business have not been interrupted in any way by the policy of the mother country, but mutual trade has been facilitated in the highest possible degree. Colonists may think that the mother country in addition should have given them some bonus or premium to trade more with them, but at least they have not done badly. There is no colonising country in the world, as they must admit, with which they would have done half so well.

From this to the further admission that Free Trade must inevitably be the policy of the British Empire ought not to be a long step. If the United Kingdom is for Free Trade, surely it is a great mistake for self-governing colonies, having only a fifth of the population of the United Kingdom, to try to force the mother country into their way, and drag the rest of the Empire with them. Whatever else may be said for Free Trade, it is at least a uniting force. It does not promote political by means of commercial disunion. It may not promote peace and harmony to the extent Cobden anticipated, but it does help towards these ends. As the hope of the world must still be in peace, therefore, the colonies of a Free-trade Empire can hardly complain that the mother country is attached to a policy which tends to the breaking down of barriers between nations as well as between the separate parts of some nations. As their views of policy enlarge they ought to perceive that many things have to be considered between States besides momentary advantages of the market which may bulk very largely in the eyes of small communities. Larger horizons and larger ideas belong to the politics of Empire.

One of the first points to be determined when the colonies and the mother country are in council cannot but be this question of Free Trade or Protection as the policy of the Empire; and it is the colonies and not the mother country that should give way. Their so doing will be the first step to Imperial Federation, which will hardly be possible on any other footing.

I would next suggest as a help towards commercial union, and as being, in fact, a union of that nature as far as it goes, the formation of an intimate postal, telegraph, and *communication* union, independent of, though not opposing, postal and telegraph agreements with foreign countries. The means of communication between different parts of the Empire should not only be promoted in common, but as much as possible the general direction should be the same. As far as postal and telegraph communication is concerned, it may be assumed, all will be agreed, but the question embraces much more than merely posts and telegraphs. Railways in certain directions, as for example between South and North Australia, or the Cape to Cairo Railway, or the Canadian Pacific Railways, are of interest to the whole Empire. In the same way, I believe it is an Imperial concern that shipping communication between the different parts of the Empire, not only for mails but for the conveyance of goods and passengers, should not be left mainly to chance—as is now practically the case. Steam-shipping subsidies are too exclusively settled as mail subsidies from the departmental view of the Post Office, whereas there are other considerations of a vital kind for the Empire that should not be overlooked. If we are to be a united Empire, the whole body should be knit together by lines of steamers under the Imperial flag which omit no port of consequence, present or prospective, in their visits—direct lines of steamers, for instance, between *East* and South Africa and the mother country, or between East and South Africa and India, Australia, and Canada. In this matter we must add, after the evidence laid before the Shipping Subsidies Committee, that the Imperial authorities, hitherto, have been remiss. "Unconsidered trifles" of trade between British ports have been left for our German friends to pick up, and the employment of British shipping, essential to the life of the Empire, has been correspondingly diminished or checked. This ought not to be. Adequate shipping facilities under the British flag should be provided between all parts of the Empire as a matter of the common business of all. A special union for such an end, besides the immediate good it would do, would clearly help towards a more general federation.

Monetary union, again, should be promoted as far as practicable, and the subject, at any rate, should be studied in common. A complete union for this purpose, at any rate for a long time, for the reasons already given, appears to be out of the question. But the money of the mother country is already the money of South Africa and Australia, and there are some points in which these portions of the Empire are mutually interested with us, such as the division of the profit on token coinage and the arrangements as to the intrinsic value of such coins, which ought not to be left, as they now are, to the decision of the mother country alone, or to be matters of direct correspondence and bargain with each colony. A complete monetary union is also more likely to come about all the sooner if it is a subject of regular official discussion.

Similarly, there could be unions within the Empire for identical legislation in each part as to the various subjects of commercial law—bills of exchange, marine insurance, shipping law generally, bankruptcy, copyright, patents, trade marks, and so on. The business could only be promoted by mutual agreement; but even internationally agreements on some of these matters have been made, and with a decided impulse towards unity in the Empire they should receive a great extension, pending the establishment of an Imperial constitution which would give to a central council some direct legislative power.

Another step that might be taken would be the common negotiation of all commercial treaties, so that no treaty could be made that did not bind the whole Empire on the one side, and did not bind each foreign Government to the whole Empire on the other side. In other words, the unit in all negotiations should be the Empire as one State, so that foreign Governments should not have the chance of recognising different States as existing within its bounds. Everybody was shocked the other day by the reappearance in the Brussels Sugar Convention of a clause binding the mother country to levy the same duties on colonial sugar as on sugar from foreign countries—the same sort of clause that had been the object of adverse criticism in the Belgian and German treaties and had led to the denunciation of those treaties. Against all such possibilities in future the Empire should be prepared, which can only be done effectually by our diplomatists insisting on Imperial unity. It would clearly follow from this arrangement also that the Foreign Secretary should be continually advised, not only by his own permanent officials but by representatives from all parts of the Empire. The misfortune is that some States which are really portions of the Empire, like Egypt, would have to be left out. This exception is rather a serious one, as we have seen, in forming a Zollverein. But it would not be fatal to a union as far as it goes for different purposes between all those parts of the Empire which are internationally recognised as such.

In these different ways, then, I believe, a beginning could be made with an effective commercial union which would tend to unite the Empire and not to dissolve it, and would prepare the way for a formal federation. The condition of most of these arrangements, it need hardly be pointed out, would be the formation of a Council of the Empire, which would consider among other things the whole question of Imperial communications, monetary union, assimilation of commercial law, and finally the negotiation of commercial treaties for the Empire as a unit. At this point we touch upon the more political side of federation. A council of the Empire is as obviously required for purposes of common defence, and for promoting the general welfare of the whole body, as it is for commercial union. By suggesting a variety of matters, therefore, for consideration and treatment, we bring the idea of a council more and more within the sphere of practical politics and with it the question of Imperial Federation itself. Preferential arrangements, as many people are so much attached to them, especially our fellow-citizens in the colonies, would probably enough come up for discussion in such a council; but the existence and usefulness of such a body would be quite independent of that subject, while the discussion might even be of advantage by compelling every side to face the difficulties and to make sacrifices all round for the sake of the common Empire. [1902.]

XXXI.

THE PRESENT ECONOMIC CONDITIONS AND OUTLOOK FOR THE UNITED KINGDOM.

WHAT is the economic outlook for the United Kingdom at the beginning of a new century, following on a century of astonishing material development and several centuries of steady advance? Is the country "played out," as many seem disposed to believe; or are the general conditions still favourable to economic advance and prosperity? The inquiry, apart from political issues, may perhaps not be uninteresting as necessitating some discussion of the conditions of prosperity among industrial communities.

In entering on such a discussion I wish to make clear, what is hardly recognised popularly, but what is really of the essence of any consideration of the general welfare of a country, that the bulk of the exchanges in every community, with rare exceptions, is, and must be, not between the community and the outside world, but among the members of the community themselves. The main quantity of business is in fact always local. The members of the community mainly work for each other and exchange services with each other. The butcher, the baker, the tailor, the dressmaker, the builder, the house decorator and furnisher, the makers of gas and electricity, the doctors, the lawyers, the clergymen, the staffs of newspapers and periodicals, the public entertainers, the postmen, the railway and tramway servants, the hairdressers, the laundry women, and many more servants of the community, whatever raw materials and implements they use, do in fact work on which a great deal, if not the greater part, of the comfort and enjoyment of life depends.[1] Yet all this work is necessarily local; and this characteristic equally belongs to such industries as agriculture, mining and fishing, so far as a community possesses lands and mines and fisheries of its own. It follows from this that the prosperity of every community, if it has the means of obtaining *ab extra* certain essential commodities for use in other production, or which are considered indispensable in consumption according to the scale of living suitable to the degree of civilisation arrived at, depends solely on the mutual industry of the members of the community itself. There is nothing mysterious about the matter. If the butchers, the bakers, the tailors, the dressmakers and all the others are each competent and industrious in their own calling, the whole community will reap the benefit, no one to say them nay. Whatever foreign tariffs and foreign bounties may be, the community itself has its own affairs and its own prosperity substantially in its own hands.

The condition laid down is no doubt important and is of varying degrees of importance in different communities. It is conceivable theoretically that a given community might have so much difficulty in producing things necessary for it to obtain *ab extra* what is indispensable to its existence that no course is open to it but emigration from the unfavourable spot; but in practice there are no such communities of any real importance.[2] The distribution of natural resources and hereditary skill and expertness is such that no important communities exist which do not possess or produce something useful to others, and by which the things it wants *ab extra* can be more or less readily obtained.

Objection will be made by some that this mode of

[1] The proportion of the working population in England engaged in manufacturing for export, or in home manufactures where foreign competition is possible, does not probably exceed 20 per cent. See *supra*, vol. ii., p. 151.

[2] Mr. Balfour's reference to the island of St. Vincent, which can grow nothing but sugar, was a mere academical illustration.

surveying industry is too sweeping, because it lumps together primary and secondary industries, productive and unproductive, productive and distributive, independent and dependent, and so on; whereas the industries of a community are not in fact all on an equal footing, and those that are "primary," "productive," and "independent" come before the others. If an industrial community has not a sufficient share of these, it is said and thought, it cannot exist at all. I must maintain, however, in agreement, I believe, with the best economic authorities, that these distinctions have no foundation in the nature of things economically considered. The one condition necessary to separate existence is the ability to obtain abroad certain things which are in fact required by a given community. Thus a garrison town exists with a population three or four times that of the garrison itself, and whose expenditure, out of means brought to it *ab extra*, enables the whole town to procure the foreign things it wants. In the same way such "pleasure" towns as Brighton, Bournemouth, Hastings, Eastbourne, Southport and Scarborough, and a large district of country like England south of the Thames, with hardly any "primary" industries, subsist by means of wealthy residents who procure from outside not only the means of employing the local population, but the means of giving to that population all that it wants *ab extra*. Populations like those of Klondyke and other mining districts are even more instructive in their character. A single primary industry enables such a community to obtain from abroad what it requires, including a great deal with which it might and would supply itself but for the very productiveness of the primary industry itself. Of course a great state requires much more to be politically as well as industrially independent; it is so far unlike a small community which is only concerned with its economic independence; but the principle is the same as far as the economics of the question are concerned. The things we have to see to in dealing with the prosperity of a given community are the industry of the community itself in all those callings which are essentially local, and the means it has of obtaining *ab extra* what it wants.

Applying these principles, then, to the case of the United Kingdom, the main practical question to be considered is (1) the amount and proportion to the whole industry of the community of the *ab extra* things which the community requires; and (2) the facilities and conditions under which these *ab extra* things are obtained. If the proportion required is not unusually large, and if it is well within the resources of the community, then the conditions for maintaining that community's independence and prosperity, given a climate suitable for carrying on industry and for residence, are also not unfavourable. Everything, as already stated, practically depends on the mutual industry of the people themselves.

A *third* point for inquiry will, of course, be the disposition and equipment of the community for carrying on the home services and exchanges. It may almost be assumed, in the case of an old country, that in this respect there can be no lack, a long-established community having necessarily brought much to perfection which facilitates industry in every form and makes the objects of civilised existence more easily attainable than elsewhere. But the point nevertheless ought perhaps to be formally dealt with.

We begin then by inquiring as to the amount of the things required from abroad in the United Kingdom, and the proportion to the whole income of the people, from capital as well as labour, and from investments abroad as well as at home. These requirements, according to the last Annual Statement of Trade (for 1902[1]), are valued in the gross as follows:

[1] There are later figures for 1903, but it is more convenient to take 1902 as that to which the last Annual Statement relates. I should think also 1902 is on the whole a better average year than 1903.

	Mln. £'s.	Mln. £'s.
General Imports		529
Add—		
Excess of imports of gold and silver over exports		5
		534
Deduct—		
Re-exports	66	
" contained in manufactures exported, estimated	70	
		136
Net imports for home consumption . .		398

Thus we have to obtain from abroad for our home consumption, in round figures, about £400,000,000 worth a year.

The figures show how this sum is arrived at with sufficient clearness, I hope, for those who are accustomed to handle import and export statistics; but as the sum is a little unusual it may be expedient to give a short explanation on one point. This is with regard to the "Re-exports." Everybody is agreed that in order to show what we import for our own consumption the exports of foreign and colonial produce—otherwise the re-exports—ought to be deducted from the imports themselves. So far there is nothing unusual in the above table. The deduction of £66,000,000 for re-exports will be universally allowed. It appears necessary, however, to go a step further and make another deduction of £70,000,000 as above shown. The reason is that the exports of British and Irish produce themselves also contain a mixture of re-exports. When we send away cotton or woollen manufactures to other countries, we send not merely the produce of British labour and capital, but much raw material previously imported from other countries to which our industry has only been applied. Such raw material is manifestly a "re-export" in another form, and ought to be deducted, therefore, from the imports, along with the re-exports so-called, in order to show how much we import for home consumption. The sum at which this additional re-export is here estimated is £70,000,000, a point to be afterwards referred to, but much or little the sum beyond all question should be taken into account.

Estimating, then, at £400,000,000 the amount which we import from abroad for home consumption, we have next to inquire as to its proportion to the total income of the people. Is it a large sum in proportion to our total income or not?

As far as can be judged it is by no means an excessive or unusual amount, looking at the experience of other countries. It is about one-fourth to one-fifth of the total income of the country, which cannot be less than £1,750,000,000, and is almost certainly more.[1] But cases where communities export a fifth, a fourth, or even a third of their income in order to maintain their economic independence are not uncommon. It would probably be found that almost all newly-settled countries have to export some such proportion. Canada, Australia, India, Egypt, for instance, all export so much as to show that the proportion to their income must be very large. Among the great states such as Germany, France, and the United Kingdom, the proportion of the United Kingdom appears the highest, which is no doubt owing specially, I should say, to the necessity of importing food articles from which the United States at least is exempt, and where Germany and France, though partially under the same necessity, are not so yet in the same degree that we are, though they are both, but especially Germany, tending that way. In any case, whatever the proportion is, and however it compares with other countries, our resources for obtaining the £398,000,000 annually without strain seem more than sufficient, and this is the next point for examination.

[1] Statement by Mr. Bowley at Southport meeting of the British Association for Advancement of Science, 1903.

What we find, in fact, on making this examination is that we obtain from abroad what we want in three ways: (1) by means of an income from capital invested and employed abroad, including the salaries and remuneration of subjects of the United Kingdom employed abroad; (2) by means of the exports of the net produce of British capital and labour,—what are commonly known as our exports,—deducting, however, for the reasons above given, the raw material contained in these exports which had been previously imported; and (3) by means of the earnings of our ships employed in the foreign trade, less any part of such earnings that may be spent abroad; also the earnings of our merchants and bankers in the large commission business which is carried on in the City and elsewhere. In the minute study of the subject various minor questions as to the balance of trade would have to be considered. Some of our imports, for instance, really balance the expenditure of American and other tourists and settlers in our midst, so that even the £398,000,000 above stated may be in excess of the real figure we have now to deal with. Contrariwise, a portion of our exports is required to balance the expenditure of Englishmen abroad. There are also times when we are investing abroad, so that part of our foreign income on balance does not in fact come home. But any such questions may be put aside for the present. Substantially what we import from abroad, as above described, consists of things required by the community at home, and the amount must be set off either by our income from property or services abroad; or by our "exports"; or by the earnings of our ships and our commissions as bankers and merchants. In no respect, however, does an examination of these different ways of setting off our imports suggest any strain.

Let us turn *first* to the income from our foreign investments as the easiest mode of obtaining our imports from abroad. Like the wealthy residents of a purely residential town such as Southport, Eastbourne, or Bournemouth, where none but local industries are carried on and there is substantially no export, the United Kingdom obtains so far what it wants from abroad because it is the owner of property abroad. It is quite conceivable theoretically that a particular country might obtain all its foreign supplies in this way, and produce nothing at all for export, and there is no doubt, at any rate, of the existence of several countries which are more or less in this favourable position—Holland, Belgium, France, and Germany being all countries of this description, to which perhaps the Scandinavian countries should be added.

In the case of the United Kingdom the income from foreign investments is an enormous sum. At least about £90,000,000 of the £398,000,000 that we import from abroad for consumption is obtainable in this manner. This was the estimate of the Chancellor of the Exchequer a few years ago, and the figure is probably more. The Inland Revenue Department knows of over £60,000,000 derived from foreign securities on which income tax is expressly paid, and there are other large sums, consisting of the profits of individuals and firms having estates or doing business abroad, where the income tax is otherwise paid, and not expressly as on foreign income.[1] The sum of £90,000,000 is thus very easily arrived at.

It need not be argued how valuable an asset this foreign income is as a means of enabling the community of the United Kingdom to obtain supplies from abroad. The community begins each year with an annual foreign credit of at least £90,000,000, and so far gets what it requires without giving an equivalent at all. I have seen it argued, indeed, that this large annual credit on the foreigner is a misfortune for us. But for it, we are told, people would have to work in some way to obtain the needful foreign supplies, and it is assumed that

[1] See Forty-sixth Report of Inland Revenue Department (section Income Tax, p. 173).

way would be manufacture, which would be good for the manufacturing industries! Those who argue, however, that our wealth is a misfortune may be left to argue. Such misfortunes are only too easily borne.

Nothing need be said in detail as to the way in which this foreign income from property is supplemented by the remuneration of subjects of the United Kingdom employed abroad, *e.g.*, in India, South Africa, and other parts of the world, though the amount is no doubt very large—much larger than any amount for which the United Kingdom is a debtor in respect of foreigners there employed. When our income from abroad is referred to, however, and an attempt made to narrow it in every possible way, the variety of its sources should be kept in mind. It is convenient to deal with the main and obvious items, but not so easy to get hold of every sum which ought to come into the account.

The *second* item of set-off we have to examine is the exports. How much do we export, and what?

Answering the question of how much, we find the gross export so-called of British and Irish produce and manufactures to amount to £284,000,000; but rectifying this amount by deducting the above sum of £70,000,000 for raw material previously imported, and re-exported in a manufactured form, we arrive at a sum of £214,000,000 as the sum of exports of the net produce of our labour and capital which goes away in order to obtain from abroad the things which we require for home consumption. In other words, we get about half the foreign things we require (£398,000,000 altogether) by means of our "export" trade.

The main items of this sum are set out in the accompanying table, which is also so arranged as to exhibit in detail the estimated deductions from the official figures of exports of British and Irish produce on account of the raw material contained in them which had been previously imported:—

Exports of British and Irish Produce and Manufactures in 1902, *less value of Raw Materials previously imported contained in the manufactures exported.*

[In 1000's.]

	Total.	Less Raw Material Imported.	Net Total.
	£	£	£
1. Living animals	824		
2. Articles of food and drink[1] . . .	16,440		17,264
3. Raw materials—			
(*a*) Coal, £27,581; (*b*) Raw hides, £370; (*c*) Wool, £931; (*d*) Other articles, £2,289 . .			31,171
4. Yarns and textile fabrics—			
(*a*) Cotton	65,040	33	
(*b*) Other textiles	38,300	19	
	103,340	52	51,340
5. Metals and manufactures from metals including machinery and ships	67,256	10	57,256
6. Miscellaneous: including Classes IV., E, F, and G, in monthly Board of Trade Returns, and H, Parcel Post	64,511	8	56,511
Total	233,542	70[2]	213,542

Summing up this table, what we find is that of the £214,000,000 of net exports, the sum of £17,264,000, or 8 per cent., consists of "living animals" and "articles of food"; there is another sum of £31,171,000, or 15 per cent., for raw materials, chiefly coal, exported;

[1] These include articles like refined sugar, which are strictly speaking manufactures, and in which raw material previously imported is used; but the amounts are not large enough to make a deduction for the present purpose necessary.

[2] Of course the estimates in this column are exceedingly rough, though giving some idea of the problem. It may be hoped that the subject will be farther investigated.

while the remainder, £165,000,000, or 77 per cent., consists of "manufactures" divided into three groups of nearly equal amount, viz.: textiles, £51,340,000; metals and manufactures thereof, £57,256,000; and miscellaneous manufactures, £56,511,000. Much has been said lately as to the growing importance of coal and raw materials in our exports, and the diminishing importance of our manufactures, but it can hardly be said, I think, that a proportion of 23 per cent. only for food and raw materials among the exports of a manufacturing country is a very high one or alters in any way the impression that our exports are chiefly of manufactures. The relative proportion of the different groups of manufactures themselves appears to suggest something more deserving of remark. There is a common impression that the exports of textile manufactures are by far the most important to us. This was undoubtedly the case many years ago. But when the figures are rectified, so as to compare with each other in respect of the net produce of labour and capital they contain, it is found that the exports of textile manufactures constitute only one of three groups into which these exports of manufactures may be divided, and that the headings of "metals" and "miscellaneous" each rather exceed in importance the textile group. It has long been noted by English economists who are also men of business that this miscellaneous group was increasing in importance. This was especially a constant theme of Mr. Newmarch in his last papers read to the Statistical Society. It suggests, obviously, the magnitude of changes in the course of business which are constantly going on. It may well be that a leading cause of our textile exports declining relatively in importance is largely due to the growth of human wants in all directions which are forcing business into new channels, and that the smaller place of textiles in our exports is a sign of progress and not of retrogression.

As far as the present question is concerned, it may be pointed out that while the appearance of articles of food and raw materials as accounting for 23 per cent. of our exports does not take away in any degree from our quality as a nation manufacturing for export, yet the fact of our having so much to export of articles of this sort indicates that we obtain easily much of what we want from abroad. We are not labouring exclusively in things where we compete under difficulties with all the world, but we have something to sell, coal, which is in the nature of a monopoly, and for which all nations now come to us. This proceeding may raise all sorts of questions as to our parting with capital and so on, which are no doubt most important from the point of view first discussed by Mr. Jevons, but, for the present at least, and in an economic view, the community of the United Kingdom appears to occupy a most advantageous position in relation to other communities. With regard to the other groups of our exports also, the "manufactures," it may also be pointed out that we have to do here not simply with the net produce of "manufacturing," after deducting foreign raw material imported; but that the amounts must include coal and other raw material obtained at home and used up in the articles we export, so that not even the total of £165,000,000 constitutes our "manufacturing" for export. In other words, out of the aggregate income of the community estimated at more than £1,750,000,000, we are only dependent on manufacturing for export to the extent of less than £165,000,000, or at the outside about 8 per cent. of the whole. We obtain the remainder by exporting something more easily procured of which we have a practical monopoly.

It must not be considered, moreover, that the whole of our net manufacturing for export is produced with "difficulty," so that we are maintaining an uphill fight for our economic independence. On the contrary, there are lines of manufactures where skill and experience and previous possession of markets give a practical monopoly, and where the high duties imposed by foreign countries are not in the nature of a tariff wall protecting their home manufacturers, for there are no corresponding home manufactures to protect, but are really revenue duties like our own duties on tea, wine, tobacco and spirits, which are very high *ad valorem*, but are in no way protective in their operation.

We come, then, to the third item in our list of the means by which this country obtains *ab extra* what it requires, viz.: the earnings of our ships employed in the foreign trade less any portion of such earnings spent abroad; plus the commissions to which we are entitled as merchants and bankers doing certain work for foreign trade all over the world. This is a source of importing power which is not an export so-called, but which is strictly speaking analogous to that of the exports themselves. Many years ago I called it an invisible export,[1] and the name has remained. The reason for claiming credit for this business is surely not open to doubt. If we run ships to carry goods all over the world, or if we do commission and agency business for people in every country, this is not for nothing, but we are to be paid for our services. Whatever these cost we must charge, plus a reasonable profit, one year with another, in addition; and this charge is to our credit in international dealing as much as the piece goods, or machinery, or coal, which we put on board ship for export so-called. The payment likewise must come in the form of imports, cash or something else, unless an equivalent amount is invested abroad, which would swell yet more the total foreign investments yielding an income which is the first item on our list. Freight may be paid abroad sometimes, though London is the usual place, but the receiver of the freight abroad immediately buys bills on London with the proceeds, less any expense abroad which the foreigner has to meet, and this he can only do by sending goods to London. Thus, whether freight is paid abroad or in London, the result is the same, the remittance of goods to pay what

[1] See *supra*, "The Use of Import and Export Statistics," vol. i., p. 283 *et seq*.

has been earned by our shipping and agency business, which forms a charge against the foreigner.

The amount coming to our credit annually in these ways cannot but be enormous. As far as shipping is concerned, we are the owners of no less than 10,000,000 net registered tons of shipping, including over 8,000,000 tons of steam shipping. Our annual earnings, therefore, cannot be less than £80,000,000, which is little more than £8 per ton on the average. I need not go into detail, as the matter has been so much discussed, but may refer to my former essays.[1] The main point to insist upon is that the data are mostly on the surface and can be easily checked. Freights in different trades and the amount of shipping employed are well known to many. So are the chief items of expense—the wages and provisioning of crews, the coal used, the dock and harbour dues, the repairs and renewals, the insurance, and so on. Wrong estimates are possible, but those who consider the subject are bound to investigate, and cannot ignore the item when there is so much to put them on inquiry.

The commissions and brokerages of our merchant and banking business for foreign customers appear likewise to be moderately estimated at £20,000,000. A usual charge by a merchant banker for "accepting" is 1 per cent., which would come to about £5,000,000 on the amount of our imports alone, while there are other charges for discount, brokerages on sales of goods consigned, and commissions on goods in transit, which have all to be paid by the foreigner who sends the goods to our markets. The matter is one for estimate, mainly by City men, but the estimate of £20,000,000 has not, I believe, been thought excessive.

Under these two sub-heads, then, the earnings of our ships, and the earnings of our commission and foreign banking business, there is an invisible export of about

[1] See *supra*, "The Use of Import and Export Statistics," vol. i., p. 283; also "The Excess of Imports," Statistical Society's Journal, March, 1898.

£100,000,000, so that in fact our shipping and commission business equals in importance the income from our foreign investments. It counts in this matter for about half only of our export business so-called which amounts to £214,000,000, but if we reckon only our manufacturing for export it is much more than a half, being in the proportion of one to one and a half. Our manufacturing for export *eo nomine* thus holds a smaller place in the economy of our international trade than is commonly supposed, although of course our earnings of freight are really exports in another form, and give similar employment to our metal industries, for instance, as the exports so-called do.

The question with which we set out is thus answered as far as the United Kingdom is concerned. Having to obtain £398,000,000 annually for our consumption from abroad, we have the following credits:

	Mln. £'s.	Mln. £'s.
1. Income from foreign investments, etc. (*under-estimated*)		90
2. Raw materials and articles of food and drink exported		48
3. Net manufacturing produce exported, including some raw material of home production		165
4. "Invisible exports"—		
a. Earnings of ships	80	
b. Commissions and brokerage	20	
	—	100
Total		403

A consideration of the items suggests that so far from its being difficult for the United Kingdom to procure its necessary imports, the balance in some years, owing to its commanding position, must be very much in its favour. Its assets for purchase are so enormous that if a strict account could be taken it would be found that continuous investment abroad is still going on one year with another, increasing our purchasing power in the future, and diminishing still farther the effort needed to obtain what we require abroad.

The final point for our inquiry according to the programme above laid down is the suitability of the United Kingdom as a place of residence and industry, assuming that what is required from abroad can be obtained easily. As already stated, a favourable answer on this head may be taken for granted in the case of an old country like the United Kingdom; but a more formal treatment is proposed, as the wonderful combination of circumstances in our favour is inadequately realised.

Climate is a condition on which much might be written, but the historical opinion that England is a country where you can be out of doors more days than in any other sums up generally the climatic conditions in our favour. Temperateness is the characteristic which our climate possesses in greater degree than that of any of our western European neighbours that come nearest to us in the matter. That other communities, like the United States and Canada, find a drawback in climatic conditions to many industrial advantages they possess appears undoubted. They are countries of extremes, where it costs more for food, shelter and clothing to permit of the same work to be done than it costs in the United Kingdom; and this difference of cost is a considerable advantage to us. Our place of residence has been improved, moreover, by generations of workers, who have executed drainage and sanitary improvements, built roads, streets, walls and fences; created parks, gardens and lawns; and generally increased the amenities of life for a huge town population, such as a population must be that brings its food and raw materials mainly from a distance.

The next advantage we possess in addition to climate and the artificial amenity of the land for residence is compactness of situation. All the different parts of the country are close together, well connected by railways, road and sea, while the sea, of course, affords perfect access to the rest of the world. The United Kingdom is more like a single huge city than a country of districts and towns separated by wide intervals. This is no small advantage for local industry, as it places consumers and producers side by side, just as if they were in a small village with its own neighbourhood, complete in itself.

The equipment of machinery and buildings for the local industries to be carried on has likewise every facility. There is, perhaps, a temptation to carelessness in obtaining the newest and best equipment, as so much can be done with less, owing to our favourable conditions; but it is entirely our own fault if the best is not always done. Hereditary skill and training are likewise consequences of the past which we must long retain, and along with this a perfection of subsidiary industries which facilitates the great industries themselves, as those who attempt to set up manufactures in new countries will understand. There are many daily wants of great manufactures which are supplied by subsidiary industries in all our large manufacturing centres, and these are not brought into existence in a day.

A fourth advantage we possess in following our own home industries is the large importation of raw materials to be used up in our export trade. This helps to make a better market here for all similar materials used in the home trade itself. The one market helps the other, with the result that if there is abundance and variety anywhere it is here. We always get the first offer. This applies, it should be understood, not merely to the raw material we obtain for the manufactures for export so-called; but to the raw materials we import in order to carry on such industries as coal mining, and those other industries, such as shipowning and shipbuilding, which enable us to make invisible exports. Because we have this enormous importation we are in a better position to practise to the fullest advantage all those industries where we work and exchange amongst ourselves.

The fifth advantage is of the same kind, though it requires special mention. This is, that the United Kingdom is a country of free imports, not merely as regards raw material, but as regards articles of food and manufactured articles of all kinds. "Free imports" may not be the same thing as "free trade," as we are frequently told; but it is of no small advantage in some ways to be a "free port." A free port means abundance and variety of everything at the lowest market price. However some individuals may suffer at times, the compensating advantage to the community as a whole, in which the sufferers participate, is immense, and ought not to be lightly regarded. In passing, however, I must say that I for one do not believe that many individuals have suffered by free imports who did not deserve to do so by reason of their own indolence and lack of foresight and intelligence.

Finally, we have an immense advantage in the United Kingdom in the development of our free banking system, and the bankers' tradition of assisting trade by advances to manufacturers and tradesmen. Our banks are full of money which comes to them from all parts of the earth, and every man who has anything to attempt in trade, if he has any property of his own, or can persuade people with property to trust him, may have ready money lent him by the bank. The tales I have heard of a different condition of things elsewhere are simply astonishing to business people in the United Kingdom, who do not know what it is to go without money to carry on their business because the banks themselves have got none to lend. Yet what is unknown here is frequent in the Far West of the United States and in all new countries, and is not unknown on the Continent, ready as Continental banks are to do financial business with which the prudent trader is not concerned.

These are all assets to the good which facilitate every form of home industry, so that the United Kingdom, if it is not so well placed as other nations for the primary industries of agriculture and mining, has yet advantages of its own as a place of residence and for carrying on all other industries, in which no other community excels it.

In all respects, then, the conditions for the industrial future of the country into which we have been inquiring are satisfactory. The amount and proportion of the things we require to import from abroad are not exceptionally large, and we are not in fact put to any exceptional strain in obtaining them. By means of our foreign investments; our exports of certain raw materials of which we have a monopoly; our exports of manufactures *eo nomine*; and the earnings of our ships and other earnings—our invisible exports, as they are called—we do obtain easily enough all that we require, and the conditions up to the latest date remain unchanged. Finally, the United Kingdom is exceptionally favoured by its climate and in other ways as a place of residence and for carrying on all kinds of miscellaneous industries, while it has special advantages as a free and large market, due largely to its system of free imports, and enjoys unequalled banking facilities. If we do not succeed, therefore, in the future as in the past, it must be our own fault. Although we have many defects, there is yet no sign of want of success.

The discussion might be left at this point, but it may be convenient to refer to one or two notions of a misleading kind which have been at the basis of a great deal of the recent fiscal agitation, and which are based in turn on a fundamental misconception of the relative proportion of different functions of the economic organism. They are the fair-trade ideas which have been cropping up at intervals during the last thirty years, long before the full-blown development which has now taken place at Mr. Chamberlain's signal; full of fallacies which the average fair-trader is quite unable to shake off.

One of these misleading notions is that great as our

prosperity is, it is "undermined." Our primary industries, it is said, are decaying; our agriculture, our iron mining, other industries of a primary manufacturing kind, such as the making of pig-iron and steel, of iron and steel bars, and so on. In the same way, it is said, we are not getting on with our leading manufactures for export—our cotton and woollen manufactures, not to speak of such "lost" industries as the silk manufacture, tin-plate making, glass manufacture and so on. Farther, even our home manufactures, or rather our manufactures for home consumption, are being attacked, and have been attacked for many years, by the imports of foreign manufactures, so that the production in these particular industries does not increase as it should, and they are no longer so profitable as they were. We are prosperous generally, it is admitted, but the indications for the future are bad. This "case" is sadly defective in detail when analysed. In many respects we hold our own better than is supposed in regard to those industries where decay is alleged, while foreign competition mostly supplements, and by no means supplants, the home industries with which it is engaged. Nor is foreign competition, as far as it is effective, the consequence of the protectionist measures of foreign countries which we can possibly counteract. But leaving aside this obvious criticism, what I desire to point out is that the ideas themselves assume the desirability and possibility of a community choosing deliberately, and by means of its legislature, a different economic development from that which the natural play of economic forces gives it. The free play of those forces in the United Kingdom has led to an unexampled development of secondary and what we may call tertiary industries, the whole of an increasing population being as a final result, fully employed; but it would have been better, we are told, if the development had taken a different form. As Mr. Chamberlain put it in one of his speeches, he could conceive of a prosperous community without primary industries and depending largely on the prosperity of residents who derived an income from foreign investments; but prosperity of this sort was not desirable for a great state. The "form" of economic development is thus regarded as important, and there is much, it is assumed, which is unsatisfactory in ours. To this whole conception I demur. Economic conditions like those which have come to exist in England display themselves when the time comes, and it is best to let the community adapt itself to the changes in its own way. That modifications may be introduced by legislation for political reasons is, no doubt, theoretically admissible; but practically the limits of any such political action must be circumscribed if a nation is to possess real economic independence.

How important a natural development is we can see, as regards the primary industries themselves, agriculture and mining. Surely no one supposes for a moment that a population of 42,000,000 in the United Kingdom could be supported by its own agriculture or can derive from that agriculture what it wants for its miscellaneous industries. To do so there should be 12,000,000 acres under wheat,[1] double the acreage that has ever been so cultivated; with a similar increase, as compared with the present, of barley, oats, and other crops; along with an enormous increase of cattle, sheep and pigs. The change in our agriculture, to make us self-supporting as regards food, is accordingly inconceivable. Even so we should still not be self-supporting in other respects as regards agricultural products. We should still be wanting in wool unless our sheep were multiplied three or four times or more; while of course we should remain as dependent as ever for cotton, jute, silk, sugar, and other agricultural products, which the United Kingdom is not adapted to produce. Substantially, then, our agriculture must have taken the

[1] The average yield per acre of wheat would of course diminish with the increase of area, and this allows for three quarters per acre as against an average of $3\frac{1}{2}$ for many years.

course it has taken. Always we must be dependent on foreign imports, in whatever degree we increase the home supply by giving it an artificial price.

It is the same with mining. For a long time, about thirty years, we have been importing iron ore in increasing quantities, and this follows on a gradual substitution of foreign supplies for home in the case of copper, white tin, zinc and lead.[1] Resort to foreign countries has become essential by the exhaustion of our own mines, just as it has been essential for centuries as regards gold and silver themselves, and is so for many other metals and minerals not produced at all, or not produced in any quantity, in the United Kingdom. In coal mining we are still among the leading communities, and coal mining, as we all know, has even developed wonderfully of late, while other mining industries have been decaying; but the general circumstances also point to a change in the future as regards our coal mining, from circumstances quite beyond our control.

In regard to our primary industries, then, I should say that the complaints of fair-traders, as far as they correctly describe what has occurred, merely refer to changes which have been quite inevitable in our economic development, and which no foresight and no action could prevent. However protectionist we might have been we should have arrived at the same result if we had had an increasing population. Probably under protection population would not have increased as it has done, but our general prosperity in that case would have been less than it has been.

Much the same may be said of those manufacturing industries by which we obtain in part the things we require from abroad. Some of the leading manufactures have not developed as they did in former years, and this is a serious matter, we are told, for a country which must obtain so much from abroad. Here the fair-trade

[1] See *supra*, "The Recent Rate of Material Progress in England," vol. ii., p. 105.

case specially requires examination in detail. But apart from that, what is immediately obvious is the actual occupation of a growing community on the one side, and its ability, on the other side, to obtain what it wants by exporting "something" abroad, either in the shape of manufactures so-called, or of those invisible exports which have been above described.[1] If the population is not occupied in one way, it is occupied in another; and the result is surely the best decision of the question of the relative merits of the employments. We may assume without any question that it is in the growing employments that wages are highest; and that in the older manufactures, which grow at a less rate, or perhaps diminish a little, the real difficulty is to obtain labour at a profitable rate when there is so good a demand for it in other directions. Along with the new developments the more profitable parts of the older groups of manufactures remain, and it is the weaker parts, which the workmen leave to find better employment, that shrink. Change of employment is, of course, a serious matter for workmen who have been trained to do certain things, but new machinery and new growths, indirect as well as direct, involve such changes, which workmen, like all others, must make the best of. Much prejudice has been imported into the discussion by assertions that the dice have been loaded by foreign protectionist governments, whose high tariffs prevent the importation of British manufactures while our markets are free, and so on. As a matter of fact, however, the real difficulty in the way of our exporting to what are called protective manufacturing countries with high tariffs, apart from the want of demand owing to changes of fashion and the like, is the ability of those countries to compete with us even in neutral markets, and our own home markets, without any tariff protection at all. The supposition that they do so only by the various processes of "dumping" or by having

[1] See *supra*, vol. ii., pp. 417, 418 *et seq.*

a larger market than our manufacturers have, because they have their own and ours as well, is too absurd for serious argument. In any case, the main point surely is that our people are fully employed, whatever barriers are shut against us, and that no hard and fast rule can be laid down as to certain particular employments being always indispensable, although without them we are fully employed and can easily obtain from abroad all that we require.

As regards our manufactures for home consumption which are also invaded by the foreigner, the same may again be said. The people who feel the stress of competition are naturally alarmed and cry out. The foreigner, with his smaller wages, sends in his goods and "takes the bread out of their mouths." This often means when analysed that in certain employments there is a difficulty in maintaining the high current rate of wage which has been established in similar employments here; but after a time employment is found elsewhere, and the complaints cease. There can be no case of a growing army of unemployed. If there were such, the rates of wages generally could not be maintained.[1]

The signs that our whole industrial position is undermined, as fair-traders contend, in consequence of changes in the general character of employment throughout the country, are thus entirely wanting. On the contrary, the country has developed on natural lines, undergoing the changes necessitated by the inevitable decay and loss of primary industries with the minimum of friction, and equally meeting the changes from one employment to another necessitated by the advance of society itself. Why should not the same process of adaptation continue?

[1] See also the above essay on "The Recent Rate of Material Progress in England," vol. ii., p. 89 *et seq.*, for a discussion of these and other points connected with our present economic position. See also the above essay on "Protection for Manufactures in New Countries," vol. ii., p. 151, for a statement as to the small proportion of population in any country engaged in manufacturing for export, or in home manufactures where foreign competition is possible.

We may fairly expect our miscellaneous exports, invisible as well as visible, and our miscellaneous manufactures for home consumption to grow, though it is quite impossible to anticipate where the growth will be or where there may be relative and even actual decay. A hundred years ago canals and roads occupied the place now held by railways and tramways. As yet gas was not, the electric light had not been so much as imagined, and petroleum was equally unthought of; still less were the improvements in steam and navigation in any way anticipated. We cannot tell whether equally revolutionary inventions may not be at hand, changing the uses and powers of the metals and of innumerable agricultural products, and giving an entirely new direction to different industries and different groups. To stereotype the present conditions by using artificial means to maintain industries which appear to our short-sighted ideas indispensable, but which may be the least fitted to survive, cannot but be the extremest folly. Even if we knew more exactly than is possible what is coming, we should have no power to prevent the substantial changes, but we cannot even look forward for a single generation. The members of the community acting individually will adapt themselves to the new circumstances almost without knowing, the time their legislatures and governments would be plunging widely if they took the matter in hand.

There is nothing accordingly in the fair-trade ideas and suggestions to alter the view we have taken of the economic outlook. They are quite irrelevant in reality to the question of economic development. There is no reason consequently why we should not look forward cheerfully, basing our anticipations on the continuation of a natural evolution to which there appears as yet no sign of a check. Possibly disturbance may come if by any chance our governments should be foolish enough to let fair-trade nostrums have a trial. But there is really little fear, I imagine, that fair-trade will ever get so far, while it is also possible that if it did, its power for mischief would be limited by the smallness of the measures as yet suggested, of which the ineffectual colonial preferences Mr. Chamberlain has talked of are specimens. The dose of protection would of course be of a poisonous nature, but a small dose, after all, might leave our substantial business comparatively untouched. Big doses of protection are in truth impossible under modern conditions.[1] There is more serious danger perhaps to our commercial prosperity, as to that of other nations, in the chances of war among the great civilised powers. But these we may forbear to discuss. They are on the knees of the gods. Still, it is impossible not to think of wars and what may come of them in the midst of the Russo-Japanese debates and the strained preparations of all the leading powers. War may thus alter the entire economic development of the century, as it affected beyond a doubt at the very beginning the developments of the century which has just come to an end.

[1] See *supra*, vol. ii., p. 159.

THE END.

INDEX

CHISWICK PRESS: CHARLES WHITTINGHAM AND CO.
TOOKS COURT, CHANCERY LANE, LONDON.

Gen. 2 vols

£

£40

Facsimile reprint

2 vols

£85 –

390380

ECONOMIC INQUIRIES AND STUDIES

The Development of Industrial Society Series

Robert Giffen

ECONOMIC INQUIRIES AND STUDIES

Volume 1

IRISH UNIVERSITY PRESS
Shannon Ireland

First edition London 1904

This I U P reprint is a photolithographic facsimile of the first edition and is unabridged, retaining the original printer's imprint.

ISBN 0 7165 1758 2 Two volumes

ISBN 0 7165 1759 0 Volume 1

ISBN 0 7165 1760 4 Volume 2

T M MacGlinchey Publisher

Irish University Press Shannon Ireland

PRINTED IN THE REPUBLIC OF IRELAND BY
ROBERT HOGG PRINTER TO IRISH UNIVERSITY PRESS

The Development of Industrial Society Series

This series comprises reprints of contemporary documents and commentaries on the social, political and economic upheavals in nineteenth-century England.

England, as the first industrial nation, was also the first country to experience the tremendous social and cultural impact consequent on the alienation of people in industrialized countries from their rural ancestry. The Industrial Revolution which had begun to intensify in the mid-eighteenth century, spread swiftly from England to Europe and America. Its effects have been far-reaching: the growth of cities with their urgent social and physical problems; greater social mobility; mass education; increasingly complex administration requirements in both local and central government; the growth of democracy and the development of new theories in economics; agricultural reform and the transformation of a way of life.

While it would be pretentious to claim for a series such as this an in-depth coverage of all these aspects of the new society, the works selected range in content from *The Hungry Forties* (1904), a collection of letters by ordinary working people describing their living conditions and the effects of mechanization on their day-to-day lives, to such analytical studies as Leone Levi's *History of British Commerce* (1880) and *Wages and Earnings of the Working Classes* (1885); M. T. Sadler's *The Law of Population* (1830); John Wade's radical documentation of government corruption, *The Extraordinary Black Book* (1831); C. Edward Lester's trenchant social investigation, *The Glory and Shame of England* (1866); and many other influential books and pamphlets.

The editor's intention has been to make available important contemporary accounts, studies and records, written or compiled by men and women of integrity and scholarship whose reactions to the growth of a new kind of society are valid touchstones for today's reader. Each title (and the particular edition used) has been chosen on a twofold basis (1) its intrinsic worth as a record or commentary, and (2) its contribution to the development of an industrial society. It is hoped that this collection will help to increase our understanding of a people and an epoch.

The Editor
Irish University Press

ECONOMIC INQUIRIES AND STUDIES

ECONOMIC INQUIRIES

AND

STUDIES

BY

SIR ROBERT GIFFEN, K.C.B.

VOL. I

LONDON

GEORGE BELL AND SONS

1904

CHISWICK PRESS: CHARLES WHITTINGHAM AND CO.
TOOKS COURT, CHANCERY LANE, LONDON.

PREFACE

THE essays here selected for re-publication were written at intervals during a period of more than thirty years. Accordingly they do not all speak from the same time, and that time the present. It is considered best, however, to print them substantially as they were written in the first instance, with the indications they contain of different circumstances, and a different atmosphere, from those now existing. They do not suffer, I trust, from a comparison between the ideas and anticipations they contain, and those which would now be expressed when new developments have taken place, and fuller information on some points is obtainable. Apart from other reasons for this course, it so happens that one or two of the essays belong to the history of the discussion of the subjects of which they treat. I would refer especially among such essays to those on the fall of prices in the first volume (Nos. II., IV. and V.); to the essay in the same volume on "The Use of Import and Export Statistics" (No. IX.), in which the subject of "invisible exports" was first discussed; and to the essay, also in the first volume, on "The Economic Value of Ireland to Great Britain" (No. XII.), which occasioned a considerable amount of controversy and contributed eventually to the appointment of Mr. Childers's Commission on Financial

Relations. If such essays are to be reprinted at all, therefore, it will be convenient to the reader that he should have the original text before him. This may be the place to state that I have been frequently asked to reprint several of the essays, particularly the last of the series on the fall of prices (No. V. of the first volume—"Recent Changes in Prices and Incomes Compared"), and the above essay on "The Economic Value of Ireland to Great Britain."

Several of the essays, it will be observed, have already formed part of the two volumes of "Essays in Finance," which have been out of print for a good many years. The present issue, indeed, is in part owing to suggestions made to me that a new edition of these "Essays in Finance" is called for. The occasion of some of these older essays is, however, so long past that I hesitate to put them before a new generation, especially as they can be referred to by students, although out of print; while some of them are also superseded by later essays, where the argument is enlarged and completed. The bulk of the essays have not, however, been published before in a collected form. The concluding essay in Volume II., on "The Present Economic Conditions and Outlook for the United Kingdom," has not before been published.

In arranging the order of the essays I have been guided mainly, but not exclusively, by the chronology. In all cases care has been taken to indicate the year of publication or of writing at the beginning of the essay, and sometimes at the end as well. A conspicuous deviation from the chronological order is in the case of the essay on "Recent Changes of Prices and Incomes Compared," which was not written till 1888, but is now reprinted in immediate succession to the essay on "The Fall of Prices" in 1873-79. This juxtaposition appeared obviously expedient to complete the series, and especially to bring together the anticipations of the earlier essays, the first of them, "The Depreciation of Gold since 1848," written in 1872, before the fall of prices began, for comparison with the results ascertained by 1888.

It would be out of place to go over in a preface the discussions contained in the essays themselves, however tempting it may be to do so in view of the fiscal controversy which has been so incessant during the last few months. It may be permissible, however, to notice that several of the essays have a bearing on this discussion, though it has always been my object to avoid controversy. The essays in particular on "Foreign Competition" (No. XI., Vol. I.); on "The Recent Rate of Material Progress in England" (No. XVI., Vol. II.); and the last essay of all, touch upon points that have been raised in recent controversies, though the subjects are treated non-controversially; while the essay on "The Use of Import and Export Statistics," though that was not its purpose, clearly touches on many points which our protectionist or fair-trade friends have put in issue. It is the same with the essay on "Protectionist Victories and Free Trade Successes" (No. XX. in Vol. II.), and the essay "Are we living on Capital?" (No. XXVI. in Vol. II.). I have always avoided discussing the direct issue between free trade and protection, but not from any doubts on the subject. The argument for free trade generally, as expounded by the great authorities from Adam Smith downwards, appears to me complete both theoretically and experimentally, while our own experience under free trade is surely a demonstration that a state which says "Hands off" to its government in matters of business does better for itself than by letting government intermeddle. But every man to his own task, and in this matter the proper *rôle* for myself has hitherto been, I conceive, to explain the character of the statistical arguments which our fair-trade friends have adduced. Looking over the accompanying pages, as they go to press, I am interested to find how old are the complaints of foreign competition, dumping, excess of imports, and all the rest of the fair-trade stock of complaints. The essay on "Foreign Competition" was written in 1877, and that on "The Use of Import and Export Statistics," dealing with excess of imports, in 1882. So old are fair-trade heresies; and they are older still, I believe, for I find that I was writing anonymously as long ago as 1869 about "Revivers of British Industry." There were heretics of an older date still. The well-known author of "The Progress of the Nation," Mr. Porter, was afflicted by them long before, and when he was pressed by them about the ruination of the excess of imports, was wont to remark, I am told, that it was a very pleasant way of being ruined. The same may be said now. If we had believed the fair-traders, we should have gone back to protection thirty years ago and more. If we have been ruined through not following their advice, everybody must admit that so far the way of ruin has been a pleasant one indeed.

My thanks are due to the Editors of the "Economic Journal," the "Contemporary Review," and other editors, for permission to reprint essays which have appeared in their pages. My acknowledgements are specially due to Sir James Knowles for his permission to reprint from the "Nineteenth Century" the essays on "The Economic Value of Ireland to Great Britain," "The Standard of Strength for the Army," and "The Dream of a British Zollverein."

R. GIFFEN.

CHANCTONBURY,
HAYWARD'S HEATH,
January, 1904.

CONTENTS

VOL. I

VOL. II

ECONOMIC INQUIRIES AND STUDIES

I.

THE COST OF THE FRANCO-GERMAN WAR OF 1870-71.

IN the following pages an attempt will be made to answer various questions in relation to the cost of the Franco-German War.

The *first* question is the amount of the actual cost of the war, both direct and indirect. The object will be to reply to this question generally—that is, with as little reference as possible to the distribution of the burden. France and Germany have borne that burden most unequally, and neutral countries perhaps have not wholly escaped a share of the losses; but it will be interesting to ascertain first of all how much the world is really poorer. This will be the more necessary because it is considered that the question of the distribution of the burden raises new problems and requires separate discussion. The burden has not only been distributed unequally, but one country has been made to bear more than the whole cost of carrying on the war.

It is expedient, perhaps, to explain what is meant by the direct and the indirect cost. In the former will be included the outlay of the belligerent Governments, the losses by the destruction of property in warlike operations, the requisitions levied in the invaded districts, and the like. The object, in short, will be to include whatever direct outlay the operations of the war have occasioned and the visible destruction they have caused. The indirect expenses will include every sort of material loss which is fairly traceable to the war—the loss of income to the communities whose pursuits are disturbed, the displacement of capital, the destruction of valuable lives, and the like.

The *second* question is the loss of capital to the world in consequence of the charge of the war. The first and second questions, it is conceived, are entirely distinct from each other. A war may easily cost a great deal more to the communities which engage in it than the permanent loss of capital which it involves. The expenditure may be defrayed as well by the temporary privation of the community as by abstracting capital from individual and national resources. In part the expense of a war is always so defrayed, and it is by not attending to the distinction that people are astonished at the recovery of nations from a war which has cost overwhelming amounts.

The *third* question is the distribution of the burden of the loss among the different communities affected by the war. It is conceived that the peculiar arrangements at the close of the late war, by which an enormous war indemnity was imposed on the diminished area and population of one of the belligerents, are worthy of separate treatment. How much has France been made to bear and what additional loss has been inflicted on the world by so great a burden being thrust on a single nation? How much has Germany gained by the receipt of a war indemnity far exceeding, it will be seen, the expense which it had incurred?

The *fourth* question will be the effect on the money markets of the world, and especially of England, of the financial arrangements made to meet these expenses and losses.

I.—The Direct Expenses.

It is too early yet to state any precise figures as to the actual amount even of the direct war expenditure by the respective Governments. According to the continental plan of dealing with budgets, an effort is made in closing the accounts to throw upon each year every burden properly *incurred* in it, and include every receipt which belongs to it, according to the budgetary laws. The accounts are therefore kept open till the exact destination of each item is properly ascertained, and it is not for two or three years after that we have a closed account. There is likely to be an unusual delay in making up the accounts of the war years in France. The confusion of war creates accounts which it would be difficult in any circumstances to adjust, and the burning of the Hotel of the Ministry of Finance by the Communists will make the difficulty in the present case much greater than usual. The Budget Estimates, however, as revised to the latest date, are probably exact enough for the purposes of the present Memorandum, which need not go much into detail.

To deal with the case of France first. The first item in the direct expenditure is that of the Central Government. The amount under this head will probably be about £100,000,000, viz.:

Extra War Credits to Sept. 4, 1870[1]	£28,000,000
" " " from Sept. 4, to Dec. 31, 1870[1]	38,520,000
" " " in Rectified Budget in 1871 .	26,058,000
Estimated expense of maintaining German troops in France in 1871[2]	9,025,000
	£101,603,000

In addition we should include the expense of maintaining the German troops in France subsequent to

[1] Speech of M. Thiers, June 20, 1871. Rapport sur l'ensemble de la Situation Financière de la France, par M. de la Bouillerie, au nom de la Commission au Budget. It appears that £3,680,000 of the credits opened in 1870 were carried over to 1871, but the amount is apparently not included in the estimates set down for 1871. In any case it will be safe to retain the original figure, to provide against under-estimates.

[2] Rectified Budget of 1871, p. xxv. The actual expense would not be so great as this, as the evacuation was accelerated, but how much

1871, viz., for two years and a quarter; the cost of rebuilding fortresses, re-equipping troops, and the like, which are all to be carried to a special account for liquidation of the cost of "repairing the misfortunes of the war." [1] M. Thiers estimated the probable amount of this liquidation in his Message of 7th December last at £16,000,000, but no proper details have yet been presented, and subsequent unofficial statements represent it as already £20,000,000. In any case, if we carry the above figure of £101,000,000 up to £120,000,000, we shall probably be about the mark as far as concerns the direct cost of the war to the French Government.

Some doubt may be entertained as to whether the expense of rebuilding fortresses and re-supplying the army with war material should be included among the direct war expenses, but it is believed the proper course is to include these sums. A certain supply of fortresses and war material being considered necessary in peace to provide against the chances of war in general, any deduction from the stock in a particular war is a part of the direct cost of that war. And the value of this deduction is best represented by the cost of making up the deficiency. In the present case, the cost to France of the captured fortresses is probably greater than the expense to be incurred for providing makeshifts; but what France has lost Germany has gained, and we shall only have to deal with this point when we try to make an estimate of the burden on France alone.

It will be remarked, perhaps, that the deficits of France for 1870 and 1871 and subsequent years are or will be greater than the above figures, taken in connection with the payments for the indemnity, would imply, but a part of these deficits arises from the failure of revenue, which must be dealt with in a different manner. The Germans, as we shall see, get some of it, and, otherwise, what the Government lost by the

less there is no means of computing. Any excess will be a set-off against under-estimates, which are almost certain to be very large.

[1] M. Thiers' Message, December 7, 1871.

non-payment of taxes the French people, individually considered, gained. It is a set-off against the individual losses we shall afterwards have to reckon.

So much then for the direct cost of the war incurred by the Central Government. There remains to add the amount of requisitions levied by the invading army, the expenditure incurred locally, and generally the direct destruction of property in the war, so far as not provided for in the above items charged on the Central Government. These matters can only be roughly dealt with. The pages of the "Journal Officiel" for many months have been largely filled with *Projets de Loi* giving the Communes borrowing powers to cover their war expenditure. Years must elapse, probably, before the account on these heads can be complete.

Some facts, however, can be ascertained. In September last the Minister of the Interior, in a report to the President, stated the extent of the losses of the kind referred to, according to documents collected by cantonal commissions appointed *ad hoc*. It appears that the amount of the *claims* in the thirty-four departments invaded, excluding Paris, is £32,844,000, composed as follows:

War contributions	£1,562,000
Taxes levied by the Germans	1,965,000
Requisitions	13,113,000
Destruction of property by fire and other causes	5,640,000
Securities, articles of furniture, and other objects carried off without requisition	10,564,000
Total	£32,844,000

To this total, however—assuming the items for the present to be correct—we must add the following items: (1.) One-tenth additional for the losses sustained by the inhabitants of Alsace and Lorraine. These provinces were the seat of war quite as much as the other occupied territory of France which was not annexed to Germany. They were not perhaps the seat of military operations for so long a period, since they were treated as virtually annexed after the fall of Metz, but they had to bear the brunt of much of the active part of the war, including the siege of Strasburg. No account of the individual losses appears to have been drawn up, such as the French Government has compiled for the territory which remained to it; but the German Government has been obliged to vote considerable amounts for indemnity to the inhabitants who have suffered, and doubtless much will remain which will never be compensated by the Government. As the population of the annexed territory is about 1,600,000, and that of the remaining departments of France invaded about 18,000,000, it is plain that about one-tenth of the expenses incurred by the latter is not too small an amount to assign to the former.

(2.) We must add the war contribution levied in Paris at the conclusion of the armistice, and the war expenses and other losses which Paris had to endure. According to the report of M. Leon Say proposing the new loan for Paris last August, the municipality was altogether about £16,000,000 the worse for the siege and insurrection.

The war contribution was	£8,000,000
The loss of revenue was	4,000,000 [1]
The miscellaneous additional expenses were . .	4,000,000
Total	£16,000,000

Deducting from the above amount the item of £4,000,000 for loss of revenue which falls to be dealt with differently, like the loss of the State revenue, we obtain a total of £12,000,000 as the Paris losses by the events of the war, exclusive of its share in the direct national expenditure. According to M. Say's report the above

[1] The revenue of Paris is about £6,000,000 a year, and the city was besieged or in insurrection about seven months, while for other two months communications were much interrupted.

sum does not include the cost which must be incurred in rebuilding the Hôtel de Ville, so that £12,000,000 is rather under than above the mark.

We have thus to add to the above total of £120,000,000, which represents the direct expenditure of the French Government on the war and its consequences, a sum of about £50,000,000, viz.:

Requisitions and other losses in the 34 invaded departments, as above	£32,844,000
Estimated losses of similar nature in Alsace and Lorraine	3,284,000
War contributions on Paris, and other expenses .	12,000,000
Total direct losses and expenditure by local authorities and individuals in France	48,128,000
Less amount voted by French Government on 6th September last and included in above estimates of national expenditure .	4,040,000
Net total	£44,088,000

One or two remarks may be made in explanation of these items. One is, that the item of £10,564,000 for securities and articles carried away by the Germans "without requisition" is in all probability excessive. This is the sort of claim which is apt to be exaggerated greatly, because disproof will be very difficult, and the claimants will be tempted to make the most of the existing prejudice in France against the Germans. The value of the articles for which regular requisition-papers were given by the German authorities is also, in all probability, exaggerated. It will be of little use, however, making any estimate of what the exaggeration amounts to, and deducting the sum from the total above set out. An error of this sort may fairly be set against the extreme probability of under-estimates in other directions which will not appear till the accounts are finally closed.

Another doubt which will be suggested relates to the apparent smallness of the items for the levies of the German armies during the war. Exclusive of the fine on Paris, it will be seen that the total amount received by the German armies from the occupied provinces was not more than between £16,000,000 and £17,000,000, viz.:

War contributions	£1,562,000
Taxes levied by Germans	1,965,000
Requisitions	13,113,000
Total	£16,640,000

And it is not quite certain that the total is so large, for the value of the requisitions, as we have already explained, is doubtful. Even if we add something for the plunder on account of which the French have sent in claims to their Government for £10,000,000, and allow also for the levies in Alsace and Lorraine, the money value to the German Government of the privilege of living on the enemy during the war would probably not be more than £20,000,000 or £25,000,000—only a fourth or a fifth of the war credits of the French Government itself. The expense of maintaining an invading army, according to this view, is not the most formidable item in the bill of war losses which a nation has to sustain. Nor is the fact to be wondered at, though contrary to the popular impression. After all, the invaders, unless they occupy large and wealthy cities—and this was not the case in France—can hardly impose on the country they invade more than the expense of their living. Clothing and munitions of war must all be secured beforehand or at home, and it is difficult to impose money fines which could be immediately useful when credit is suspended, however wealthy a country may be. The great bulk of the wealth is fixed in objects which cannot be carried away at all, or in objects which cannot be carried away quickly and sold, so as to be converted to the invader's use. He must take therefore, even for his own convenience, only what he can consume at once. A prolonged occupation, with military operations suspended in the occupied districts, would enable the conqueror to impose heavier tributes, but such an occupation is only occasionally possible during a war.

Besides all this, there was a considerable local expenditure throughout France in departments not occupied by the enemy in mobilising the National Guard. But the amounts have been reimbursed by the State, and are included in the above war credits.

There are two heads of loss, however, about which, perhaps, there may be some doubt. The first of these is the damage caused to roads and bridges throughout the invaded departments. According to an official report made by a Commission of the Assembly, dated May 21, 1871, these losses appear to have been:

Damage to Communal roads	£400,000
" Departmental roads	360,000
" Imperial roads	366,000
Total	£1,126,000

These losses, however, are probably included in the figures already submitted—the account for liquidating the cost of the war including large votes to the communes and departments, and the budgets including additional votes to the Ministry of Public Works for urgent repairs. The total amount is too small to make any material difference in the estimate of the total cost of the war.

The second doubtful item is the damage done to the railways, but it is not likely to have exceeded in amount the damage to the roads, the *length* of the railways endangered being much less than that of the roads. As a matter of fact, the railways were not much cut up, but were freely used by the Germans through the war. The rolling stock was injured or carried away by the Germans, but the rolling stock of all the railways in France can hardly be worth £20,000,000, and even if it was damaged 5 per cent.—a most liberal allowance

—the loss would be under a million. The omission of any estimate for this head of loss, therefore, should it prove not to be included in the above figures, will not alter materially the totals with which we shall have to deal.

We may put the direct losses in France therefore at about £164,000,000, viz., £120,000,000 directly expended by the Government, and £44,088,000 expended or lost by destruction of property in the provinces. It remains to inquire what expense was incurred by Germany of a similar nature.

And first as to the Government expenditure. The amount, it is believed, cannot exceed between £40,000,000 and £50,000,000. We have been unable to obtain any exact figures, but a few considerations may satisfy us that £50,000,000 will be an approximately correct amount to take.

In the first place, this is about the amount of the sums which Germany had to borrow for the actual conduct of the war, and as the indemnity was not afterwards appropriated to defray the war expenditure, and there were no other extraordinary resources, the loans must be nearly the measure of the outlay of the German Governments. So far as can be ascertained, the new loans and additions to the floating debt were:

North Germany—	
First issue of Treasury Bills	£5,000,000
First issue of Treasury Bonds	7,500,000
Second ditto ditto	7,500,000
Funded loan	15,000,000
	£35,000,000
Bavaria	5,000,000
Smaller German States	5,000,000
	£45,000,000
Prussian war treasure exhausted	4,500,000
Total	£49,500,000

This was all the money which it was necessary for Germany to provide during the progress of the war. To err on the safe side, however, we may put the amount at £60,000,000, to allow for arrears left over.[1]

The direct expenditure for the war thus cost Germany, in the first instance, about £60,000,000, against £164,000,000, which we have seen was the cost to France. Such is the difference made to a country, first, by being unprepared, and so having to spend more hastily; and second, by being the seat of war, when war is carried on in conformity with the rules which the Germans have followed. In any case, it is expensive to be the seat of war, but France was caught unprepared every way, and would have had to pay far more dearly than its opponent, even if there had been no indemnity to follow.

The other direct losses of Germany—viz., the losses of individuals—seem hardly worth considering. The only losses of the kind appear to have been the captures of German ships by French cruisers, but the captures were only eighty in number, and the total outlay thus occasioned, as well as for ships detained, appears to have been only £450,000.[2] The amount is absolutely insignificant compared with the figures with which we are dealing. Claims have also been made by German shipowners on account of ships lying idle, but they belong to the department of indirect losses, with which we have yet to deal.

Another direct loss which would also be sustained by the Germans is the difference between the real value of articles requisitioned by the Government in mobilising the army and the price which the Government pays for them. But there are no data for es-

[1] The actual outlay according to the latest German account is pu at rather more than £90,000,000, but this sum includes many indirect items, so that the above estimate is really near the mark. See "Preussischen Jahrbuch für 1875."

[2] Berlin correspondent of "The Times," June 3 1871.

timating this loss, which could not however be large.

There is one other item which we must discuss before leaving this part of our subject. We may fairly include as part of the direct cost of the war the capital of the new pensions which the losses of the war occasion. They are part of the pay of the soldiers, and are directly caused by the war, although they are only paid in subsequent years. We must charge as part of the direct cost therefore a capital sum sufficient to provide the pensions. No very exact amount can be stated for two reasons: (1) the annual amount of the additional pensions will probably not be ascertainable for a year or two; and (2) there are hardly any data for calculating the capital value. Still the item is worth mentioning. In the French Budget for 1872 the additional military pensions charged amount to £150,000, which at twenty years' purchase would represent a capital of £3,000,000, and it is not unlikely that before the accounts of the war are closed the amount will be about double, say £5,000,000 altogether. The cost to Germany will be at least as great, though no similar figure can be mentioned, as one of the uses of the French indemnity to the Germans has been the establishment for the first time of a military pension fund. It is impossible to say, then, what the cost of the pensions caused by the war will be. But as the war was not more murderous for Germany than France, but rather less murderous, and the scale of living has not been so high in Germany, we shall probably not be under the mark in estimating the cost of the war pensions to Germany at the same rate as the cost of the like pensions to France. We have thus an additional sum of £10,000,000 to add to the direct cost of the war—£5,000,000 to each country.

The whole account up to this point will stand:

DIRECT COST TO FRANCE.

War credits and expenses of re-equipment, etc.	£120,000,000	
Fines, requisitions, and destruction of property (less £4,000,000 reckoned in war credits)	44,000,000	
Capital value of war pensions	5,000,000	
		£169,000,000

DIRECT COST TO GERMANY.

War credits, etc., less requisitions levied in France	£60,000,000	
Capital value of war pensions . . .	5,000,000	
		65,000,000
Total Direct Expenditure		£234,000,000

Such was the direct cost of the war to both Governments, so far as we can ascertain it. The two countries would have been "out" of this sum, and no more, had they been able to carry on their war operations without a stoppage of industry and production, and by hiring soldiers from distant countries with which they had no other relations. Looked at in this way, as the Finance Minister of a despotic country might be disposed to view it, war cannot be considered a very expensive game. For this sum of £234,000,000 the Governments of two great nations carried on unremitting hostilities against each other, employing altogether two-and-a-half millions of men for a period of nearly eight months. That is, it cost them *both* nearly £30,000,000 a month. At this rate, war is cheap. The aggregate annual income of the people of the two countries is probably about £1,200,000,000, so that the direct cost of war at this rate for a twelvemonth would have been a little over a third of the national income. Both countries therefore, so far as mere expenditure on warlike operations is concerned, and if the expense were divided equally, could have gone on fighting for an indefinitely longer period without exhausting their material resources. This is a somewhat different view from the popular one about the expense of modern warfare, but there is no doubt about the facts, and the conclusion is in agreement with what might be expected from the strength of modern industry. It is the natural result of the introduction of machinery and the great accumulation of wealth, that great communities should be capable of extravagance for lengthened periods without approaching exhaustion, a feat which was hardly possible before the age of mechanical invention. Of course they would impoverish themselves in time, but the margin before exhaustion comes, comparing modern societies with the old, appears to have been increased.[1]

II.—The Indirect Expenses and Losses.

We now come to more difficult ground. So far we have had tolerable data before us—the figures of budgets and official reports and the public borrowings of the belligerent Governments. But when we come to the indirect expense of a war we have no such guide. We know that it is quite as real a matter—that in any business the loss which a man has to undergo in withdrawing capital from some other undertaking to embark in it is fairly reckoned as part of the cost of the new business. If he is making ten per cent. elsewhere, and makes fifteen in the new business, his net gain by the change is five per cent. If his new business is wholly profitless, he loses ten per cent. Still worse, if he abandons the idea of profit altogether and expends his capital in extravagance, he is poorer not only by the loss of income for a time, but by the whole capital he wastes. This last is the case of a nation engaged in war to a greater or less extent—especially

[1] The contributions to various charitable associations in relief of the wounded and other victims of the war are also a part of the direct cost; but compared with the other items here dealt with it would be of no moment to reckon them, even if exact data were procurable. But the relief societies were so numerous and scattered, and so large a part of the contributions was in kind, that there are practically no data for an estimate.

in war as now conducted by European nations, who abstract from industrial pursuits enormous masses of the civil population. The community not only takes to spending, but part of its former income ceases. The expenditure and loss of income make up the bill which its extravagance really costs. But this loss of income in the case of great communities is difficult to ascertain. How far industry is suspended, and how far the war is the cause of it, are both very difficult questions to answer. And there are more serious difficulties behind. In the present conditions of modern industry, a nation whose pursuits are disturbed cannot fall back exactly into the old groove. When it settles down again it may have to engage to some extent in less productive industries than those which were formerly open to it. The difference between the old and the new profit is not only difficult to ascertain, but it is impossible of course to state the loss in capital which is equivalent to the loss of annual profit. On these points therefore, in relation to the present war, we shall only offer the roughest possible estimate.

To take the case of France first. The main point is the loss of national income, and one measure of the loss, it is conceived, will be the falling off of the national revenue. In proportion to the losses of the taxpayer, he would be able to pay fewer taxes, so that the national revenue would probably suffer in the same degree as the aggregate income of the nation. And as the national revenue and the falling off it sustained in the years of war are both ascertainable amounts, while the aggregate income of the nation is an approximately calculable amount, it will be possible to state in this manner what the deficiency on the aggregate income may come to. The figure to be thus obtained will obviously be a very rough one. Many parts of the French national revenue would not fluctuate with the prosperity or adversity of the people. The direct taxes on land, for instance, are in the nature of fixed charges, not varying with the income of those who pay them, but collected almost to the full amount, irrespective of individual profits or losses. A bad year will no doubt cause an unusual amount of "*dégrèvements*" to relieve the very poor, but the bulk of the tax will be unaffected. Much of the same may be said of the other direct taxes, which are all fixed on arbitrary bases similar to the direct tax on land. On the other hand, other parts of the revenue might fall off to an amount much greater in proportion than the diminution of the aggregate income which was the cause of the failure. The attempt of individuals not to trench on their capital, but to square their expenditure with their diminished income, might cause such an economy of luxuries as very seriously to diminish the amounts raised from optional taxation—the taxation, that is, which people regulate for themselves by the consumption of taxable articles. The business of transfer may also be suspended to a much greater extent than the business of production, and so cause a disproportionate loss of revenue arising from charges on transactions. On the whole, however, when it is considered that as regards all moderate charges on articles of consumption a very slight reduction of the national revenue would imply very large economies on the part of the taxpayer, the tax being only a small part of the cost, and when it is also considered that the direct taxes which are not optional in their nature are only a fourth part of the State revenue of France, so that the fixed revenue, unaffected by the adverse fortune of the nation, is the least important—it may be assumed as most probable that the aggregate income of the people will have fallen off in excess of the proportion to which the national revenue has fallen off. To assume a loss of aggregate income in proportion only to the loss of national revenue will give us a minimum and not a maximum estimate.

Now what has been the loss of national revenue to France through the war? The French official estimates are as follows:

Loss of revenue in 1870	£11,400,000
Do. do. in 1871	13,480,000
Total	£24,880,000

Such is the calculated loss for a period of eighteen months, but two deductions must be made for our present purpose, as we are dealing only with the loss occasioned by the interruption of business through the war. We must deduct, in the first place, the loss occasioned by the Germans collecting the taxes instead of the French authorities, the amount so collected, as above stated, being £1,960,000. The taxes were in fact paid, though the French Government did not get them. And we must deduct in the same way the loss of revenue occasioned by the transfer of Alsace and Lorraine to Germany. This loss also was not caused by the deficiency of income of the French taxpayers. As the annual loss appears to be about £2,452,000,[1] the loss for eighteen months would be £3,676,000, which falls to be deducted along with the amount of the taxes actually levied by the Germans from the above total of £24,880,000. The net loss of revenue to France therefore due to the interruption of business, withdrawal of civilians from industrial pursuits, and the like, would be as follows:

[1] Annual loss of Revenue to France by transfer of Alsace and Lorraine to Germany [compiled from Budget of 1872].

Land tax	£219,000
Personal and furniture tax	74,000
Door and window tax	71,000
Patent tax (estimate)	114,000
Mainmast tax	18,000
Registration of stamp duties	619,000
Customs and salt duties	296,000
Miscellaneous indirect tax	840,000
Postal revenue	120,000
Produce of forest	80,000
Total	£2,452,000

Total loss of revenue in eighteen months as above .		£24,880,000
Deduct taxes levied by Germans . . .	£1,960,000	
„ loss of revenue by transfer of Alsace and Lorraine to Germany	3,676,000	
		5,636,000
Net loss by interruption of business, etc.		£19,244,000

This is at the rate of £12,800,000 per annum, and as the annual revenue of France before the war, as fixed in the Budget for 1871, was £75,200,000, the proportion of revenue lost by stoppage of industry is as nearly as possible 17 per cent.—the loss running for a period of eighteen months.

We have only, then, to apply this measure to the aggregate income of France for a similar period, to see what individual loss the war has occasioned. Various estimates have been given of that income, but taking the most moderate estimate of £600,000,000 yearly, the loss in eighteen months, at the rate of 17 per cent., would be £153,000,000.

To this ought perhaps to be added the probable loss of income in years subsequent to 1871, before the routine of industry is fully re-established; but this would be too hypothetical an inquiry, and belongs rather to the question as to what has been the permanent loss of capital to France through the war.

Is there any way, however, of testing whether the French people on the average would only lose a fifth of their income for eighteen months, including a period of nearly eight months when both war and insurrection had been over, and much of the ordinary avocations of the people had been resumed? Let us consider for a moment in detail how far French industry would be affected.

It may be considered as certain, to begin with, that agricultural operations would not be very much interfered with. To a certain extent the season of the war was favourable to an agricultural country. The summer was far advanced when it began, and the autumn was well over before the levies whose absence would have seriously hindered agriculture were called out. Peace was finally concluded again before the end of February, in time to let the greater part of the levies return for the labours of the spring and summer. In this way the harvest of 1870 was gathered in somehow, notwithstanding the outbreak of war, and the harvest of 1871 could not have been much diminished by the want of preliminary cultivation. Even in the occupied districts the harvest of 1870 would not be lost, nor would the preparations for the crops of 1871 be much interfered with. As regards the harvest of 1870, the change which was made by the invasion was that the German armies to a large extent reaped it instead of the French farmers, or it was destroyed by the operations of the war. But the losses of this sort have already been counted under the head of direct losses,[1] and ought not to be counted twice over. As regards the preparations for 1871, the occupied districts stand in much the same position as the unoccupied, peace having been concluded in time to let the bulk of the labours of the season be proceeded with, and the occupation in no way preventing the return of the farmers to their work. There is no reason to believe that even in the occupied districts there was any material suspension of agricultural industry beyond what took place in other parts of France.

How much, then, would the suspension come to even on an extreme calculation—on the basis, that is, of all labour being stopped in proportion to the withdrawal of agricultural labourers for the numerous levies that were raised? Agriculture is unlike manufacturing in this respect, that its existence from day to day does not depend on the freedom of credit and perfect freedom of communication. These things are in the end important, but they can be borne for months without

[1] See p. 7.

more than the most passing damage, if the farmer ultimately gets a market for what he does not consume himself, and the facilities of credit and free communication are again opened up. The loss, then, could hardly be greater than in proportion to the withdrawal of hands, and the withdrawal could hardly be more than about one-twelfth of the whole. The agricultural population of France is about three-fifths of the whole, or about 22,000,000, of whom about 5,400,000 would be adult males engaged in the actual work of production. Possibly we ought to include the estimate of a large amount for female labour and for the labour of grown-up children, but our case is quite strong enough as to the small effect which the withdrawal of the levies would have on agricultural industry if we take the usual supply of labour at only 5,400,000 hands. The total new levies for the war being about 800,000, the proportion from the agricultural districts would be 480,000, which is almost exactly one-twelfth of the above total of 5,400,000 labourers. Assuming, therefore, that the diminution of agricultural labours for one year was one-twelfth—which is a strong assumption, as the labourers were only away for eight months, and that not for the best part of the season—we may estimate very quickly the loss of income that would be occasioned. The "net annual value" of the rural property of France is £106,000,000,[1] which, according to the usual mode of reckoning, shows a production of three times that amount, or £318,000,000. One-twelfth of this sum would be £26,500,000, which would be the maximum loss of agricultural income—apart from the amounts paid in requisitions and fines—occasioned to France in the war of 1870-1871. For the reasons above stated, however, the loss, it is believed, could not be so much. It is no doubt true that in exceptional districts, to which the services of the Peasant Farmers' Seed-Fund were so useful, there was a great hindrance

[1] See Reports on Land Tenure in different countries in Europe, and Mr. Goschen's Report on Local Taxation.

to production in the want of seed, owing to the thoroughness of the Prussian perquisitions; but in the absence of all reports as to large areas of land being left uncultivated, we may conclude that this cause exerted an almost inappreciable influence in comparison with the extent of French agriculture. Except in isolated cases, the war left the French agriculturists wealthy enough to resume their pursuits, and purchase seed and stock—the requisitions in the invaded districts, £13,000,000, and the destruction of property, £5,600,000, being, after all, barely 6 per cent. of the agricultural production of the whole of France for one year, and barely 12 per cent. of the production of the invaded districts.

We may set down, then, about £26,500,000 as the maximum loss of agricultural income. Reckoning in the same way the manufacturing loss, viz., in proportion to the withdrawal of labour, or about one-twelfth of the total production, we should have to add to this sum about £23,500,000, making the total loss of income by this mode of reckoning £50,000,000.[1] But the loss of manufacturing income would of course be greater, manufactures being so much more sensitive than agriculture to the disturbance of invasion. Without credit and without the means of communication, manufacturing establishments must be closed. Neither purchases nor sales except to a limited amount are made with ready money, and even if they could be made, war and invasion would prevent the conveyance of raw material and manufactured articles to and from distant spots which is essential to the life of any large trade. No doubt there are many industries which will go on as usual, the dealing from day to day in the necessaries of life going on nearly to as great an extent as before, and generally all retail commerce, as was the case in

[1] We estimate the manufacturing production at £282,000,000, making up, with the above sum of £318,000,000 allowed for agricultural production, the total of £600,000,000, which we have taken as the aggregate income of the French people.

Paris during the siege, being more or less active. In the unoccupied districts, too, manufacturing enterprise would only be partially suspended, though it would, on the whole, be much less profitable than before; and the Germans, it is known, managed to prevent the complete suspension of business not only in Alsace, but in such advanced towns in their occupation as Rheims and Rouen. If we estimate that outside the invaded districts, including Paris, business was one-fourth suspended for eight months of war, and that where the invasion extended it was three-fourths suspended for the same period, the estimate would hardly seem to be the least under the reality. But this would only make the loss of manufacturing income about £93,000,000, viz.:

One-fourth of manufacturing income in unoccupied districts (£140,000,000 annually [1]) for eight months	£23,333,000
Three-fourths of manufacturing income in occupied districts (£140,000,000 annually [1]) for eight months	70,000,000
Total	£93,333,000

Adding this sum to the above total of £26,500,000 allowed for the loss of agricultural income, we obtain as the figure for the total loss £119,833,000, which is about £30,000,000 less than the sum we arrived at above by drawing what appears to us a legitimate inference from the diminution of national revenue. If we remember, however, that the suspension of manufacturing enterprise would continue for some months in 1871 after the war was over, and that in the present mode

[1] Practically about one-half of France in population was occupied or besieged by the German troops, and the districts thus dealt with included Paris, Rouen, Rheims, Nancy, and other important towns, Paris itself being by far the most important manufacturing city in France. We assume, then, that half the manufacturing production was in the occupied and half in the unoccupied districts.

of computation we have only been dealing with a period of eight months, whereas the former estimate applied to the whole of 1870 and 1871, it will be recognized that the results of the two methods of computation very nearly correspond. So far as we can judge, £150,000,000 would be about the mark.

There is one circumstance which may, perhaps, throw doubt on this conclusion, unless explained. The exports and imports of France have not diminished as we should expect them to do with the diminution of manufacturing production. The exports and imports of the last three years compare as follows:

IMPORTS FOR CONSUMPTION.

	1871.	1870.	1869.
	1000 frs.	1000 frs.	1000 frs.
Articles of food	983,677	720,844	693,828
Raw materials and natural productions	1,862,296	1,679,988	2,030,618
Manufactures	314,591	218,560	264,616
Other articles	232,685	161,918	164,009
Total	3,393,249	2,781,310	3,153,071

EXPORTS OF FRENCH PRODUCTIONS.

	1871.	1870.	1869.
Manufactures	1,620,911	1,562,429	1,756,320
Articles of food, raw materials, and natural productions	1,110,522	1,181,848	1,185,667
Other articles	134,180	115,850	132,954
Total . . .	2,865,613	2,860,127	3,074,941

These are not the figures of a trade which has diminished; it is rather an increasing trade. But the explanation is very simple. One is, that great internal losses would be likely to cause a large export for realization, while after the war was quite over the imports would at first increase largely, in order to replenish stores and warehouses and set many establishments going. Another explanation of the increased external trade is also to be found in the fact that two provinces between which and the rest of France there was formerly a most intimate home trade have, for the first time, become external; so that what was formerly home trade is now reckoned as foreign. In reality, the figures prove a falling-off of business, though the exact amount cannot be stated, and may not correspond exactly to the exact diminution of manufacturing production in France in the years of war.

So much for the loss of income sustained by Frenchmen during the war. But not only does the suspension of business by war and invasion cause a loss of present income to a community, it entails a permanent depreciation of producing power, that is, of the annual income which the community is capable of earning—on which some estimate ought also to be placed. It is certain that some such depreciation cannot but occur. The connections of great establishments are destroyed, the staff is broken up, many labourers have been killed or injured, the business which is resumed after a war, at any rate after so prolonged an interruption of its usual course as French commerce sustained, is never precisely the same as it was before the war. Of course any estimate of the present capital value of an annual loss of income of this kind must be very wide indeed. Fortunately there is one French tax which appears to supply data for such an estimate. We refer to the Trade Licence Tax, which applies a varying scale to nearly every class of merchants and traders, according to the size of the towns in which they reside and the nature of business they pursue. Any great convulsion in business diminishing the amount of its profits must seriously affect the tax: many traders will be declassed; others will be driven from business altogether and occupy the place of labourers or assistants to larger capitalists; there will be a great deal of migration, during which capital will be locked up, or at least will be less productive. There will also be a great deal of emigration which will have the same effect, even if the emigrants, as will probably happen, should ultimately return. All the changes will cause the licence tax to be less productive, though perhaps the diminution may not go quite so far in proportion as the diminution in the earning power of the community. The scale of the tax remaining the same, and most people refusing to change their business even if they make less out of it than before, the result will be that the tax will yield nearly the same as before in proportion to the numbers affected, but those who pay it may all be somewhat poorer. Insufficient as the test is, however, it is the only one we have got, and it is perhaps better than none. The way to apply it will be to calculate what the annual loss of the business income of France will be if it suffers in the same proportion as the licence tax, and then multiply the sum so obtained by the number of years' purchase we may consider the income to be worth.

According to the Budget of 1872, the loss on the "principal" of the licence tax due to the general effects of the war is between 3 and 4 per cent. The total deficiency, as compared with the estimate for 1871, which was made before the war, is £168,800, equal to 7 per cent. on a total yield of £2,462,000; but of this deficiency, about £80,000, or 3.3 per cent., is caused by the transfer of Alsace and Lorraine to Germany. There remains, therefore, only £88,000 which can be ascribed to the general effects of the war, and the percentage of this loss is about 3.7, or say 4 per cent. If this test is fairly applicable, then we may assume that France has lost about one twenty-fifth part of its earning power in business in consequence of the war—that is, one twenty-fifth part of the above annual sum of £280,000,000 which we have reckoned as the income of the French people, independently of their agriculture, or an annual loss of £11,200,000. How many years' purchase must we reckon to ascertain the equivalent capital value of this loss? This point must plainly be left a good deal to conjecture, but the equivalent, we should think, will be at the very least ten years' purchase, making the loss £112,000,000. The value of businesses reckoned by multiples of the annual income yielded varies indefinitely, and perhaps ten years' purchase would be too high an average in such a country as England, where profits are large in consequence of the large amounts which traders are able to borrow in addition to the capital they themselves embark; but in a country like France, where there is far less credit, and business capital, amount for amount, is consequently less profitable, ten years' purchase is probably rather too little than too much. At any rate, it does not appear extravagant to reckon that a war like last year, and the invasion which followed, besides the immediate loss of income and heavier taxes which they entailed, should have cost the business men of France the equivalent of £112,000,000, or £11,200,000 per annum. There must have been a large loss of some kind on this head, and we do not see how it can be reckoned at less.

Probably the agricultural income of France may have permanently suffered in the same way, but it can hardly have suffered much, being almost independent of the credit and connections which make the life of business. A long-enduring war would have injured agriculture greatly, especially the culture of the grape, through the loss of markets and the displacement by competing vine districts, but a single winter's war could have no such effect.

We have still one more head of indirect loss to consider, viz.: the loss of life and the invaliding of wounded and sick. But we must pass these over very slightly, as losses on which no pecuniary value can properly be placed. We subjoin a calculation of what the capital value of the lives affected by death or invaliding in the French Army may come to:

Estimate of money value of lives destroyed or injured in French Army:

30,000[1] killed	30,000
30,000[1] totally invalided	30,000
90,000,[1] about one-eighth invalided on the average	10,000
Complete lives destroyed (say)	70,000
Average earning power, £40 per annum	£40
Total annual loss	£2,800,000
Present value of annuity of £1 on single life at age of 25, and reckoning 5 per cent. (Carlisle Tables)	£15
Estimated capital value of lives lost or invalided	£42,000,000

The total is £42,000,000, and we doubt if the loss or injury of life in an economic sense could be more. Still the calculation must only be taken for what it is worth, an imperfect way of representing in money the material loss which is certainly occasioned by the destruction of human life. In addition we should probably reckon that the loss and injury of life among civilians produced a similar loss. In Paris alone it is reckoned that the additional deaths due to the war were as follows in 1870 and 1871:

Deaths in 1870	73,581
Ditto 1871	99,945
	173,526
Less average mortality of two years	90,000
Total due to war	83,526

There must have been great injury to life beyond this where the additional mortality is so large. Throughout

[1] According to these figures, our estimate of the total killed and wounded in the French armies is 150,000, but there are few official data, and we have been obliged to make the best estimate we can from scattered and contradictory notices in books on the campaign. The German losses, reckoned in the same way, were about 100,000.

the country and in the numerous besieged places there would be a similar loss of civilian life by privations, but considering that Paris was exceptionally tried, and that the above total of 83,000 would include the deaths of the soldiers in Paris, it would, perhaps, be unsafe to put the total deaths throughout France owing to the war at more than 200,000. And of these one-half would be aged, of hardly any economic value compared with the young, whose expectation of life is at its highest.[1] Taking the loss of civilian life, therefore, as the basis of the preceding calculation at 100,000 units, the present capital value would be £60,000,000, which will fall to be added to the above £42,000,000 of Army loss—in all £102,000,000. We repeat, however, that this calculation is only given *pour mémoire*, and to render a little more definite the conception of the losses which are involved in war. It should be remembered, besides, that part of the losses on this account—so far at least as they affect the surviving community—must have been reckoned under the previous head, there being nothing to distinguish the failure of the licence tax through the death or invaliding of the licencees from the failure which is due to more general causes. In any general sum of the expenses of the war it would be improper to include both items to the full amount if they could be exactly ascertained.

The indirect losses of the French, therefore, in the war, omitting any direct estimate for the value of lives lost or injured, may be summarized as follows:

1. Loss of income in 1870-71	£150,000,000
2. Loss of permanent business, equal to .	112,000,000
Total Indirect Loss (say)	£262,000,000

We come, then, to the German losses of a similar nature, which may be very shortly dealt with. The

[1] Since this was written the fact of an unusual mortality having been occasioned directly and indirectly by the war, has been confirmed by the Census Returns of 1872.

principal causes of the great loss which France has sustained did not affect Germany. These causes, as we have seen, were not so much the abstraction of labourers from their employments, as the suspension of business through invasion. The loss of life in Germany was, moreover, confined to the Army, the privations of civilians, at least, being of the most insignificant kind compared with French privations. The indirect loss of Germany may therefore be summed up in the loss by abstraction of labourers, equal to estimated loss of France as above, or about £50,000,000; the loss by deaths and invaliding of soldiers, which we mention *pour mémoire*, would be about two-thirds of the estimated loss of France as above, or about £30,000,000.

We do not think it would be of any use reckoning anything beyond this for the suspension of business in Germany. Business, in fact, went on pretty much as usual. Though the German ports were blockaded, the ports of Belgium and Holland were open, and Germany retained all its land communications unimpaired. Loss, therefore, could hardly arise except to a quite inappreciable extent, for which it would not be worth while to make allowance. There is the more reason for this, too, because it is more than doubtful whether the loss by the abstraction of labour is not over-estimated, the labour having been abstracted, as we have already explained, at the season least injurious to agricultural pursuits. So far as any loss of the kind could be traced in its effect on German revenues, we have no data to go upon, the receipts of the various Governments having gone on increasing as if there had been no war.[1]

We may end our inquiry into the indirect losses at

[1] Something should perhaps be added for the indirect manufacturing losses of Alsace and Lorraine, but business there was not nearly so long disturbed as in the non-ceded districts of France, and the above allowance for German indirect losses is believed to be liberal enough in any case to cover those of the newly-acquired province.

this point. No doubt other countries besides France and Germany were made to suffer—England especially; but the amount of the injury, even if not compensated by some indirect gains consequent on English manufactures temporarily or permanently displacing those of the belligerents, is lost in the enormous magnitude of the business over which the loss would be spread.

III.—General Summary of the Cost of the War.

Having thus gone through the various items of expense and loss consequent on the war, we may see what the whole amounts to. The totals are as follows:

France.		
Credits for carrying on war, re-equipment, and the like	£120,000,000	
Requisitions and fines levied by Germans and destruction of property in the war	44,000,000	
Capital value of war pensions	5,000,000	
Indirect losses, omitting estimate for loss of life	262,000,000	
Total for France		£431,000,000
Germany.		
Credits for carrying on war and for re-equipment	£60,000,000	
Capital value of war pensions	5,000,000	
Indirect losses, omitting estimate for loss of life	50,000,000	
Total for Germany		115,000,000
Grand total of cost of war		£546,000,000

At this rate war is not so very cheap as it appeared when we looked only at the direct expenditure. It cost the two belligerents in seven or eight months about half their gross income, and such figures imply a very large exhaustion of stored-up capital. Even at this rate, however, it would no doubt have taken a long time to exhaust the material resources of France and Germany.

IV.—The Permanent Loss of Capital.

Up to this point we have been discussing the mere cost of the war, without any reference to the funds out of which it had to be defrayed. As we have already explained, the two questions are entirely distinct in theory. A very costly war may result in little or no permanent loss of capital, the belligerent nations paying the expense entirely out of their income, and likewise saving out of their income enough capital to compensate those indirect causes of subsequent annual loss which we have discussed at so much length. On the other hand, a very cheap war may prove burdensome from the mode of dealing with its finance. A nation may go on living as usual, and the capital burden will then prove very heavy. What usually happens, in fact, is the submission by the generation which carries on a war to the *quasi*-necessity of bearing a large part of the cost. The Governments, to secure credit for borrowing, if for no other purpose, must go as far as they prudently can in imposing taxes. Individuals who suffer loss of income have often no capital which they can trench upon, and will they nill they, must adjust their expenditure to their income. Those who have capital will try every possible expedient to keep it from diminishing. It is in this way that war, as a rule, is so quickly recovered from. A large part of the cost figures only as so much privation of those who carry it on.

Going over the items constituting the above total of £546,000,000 *seriatim*, we believe it will be found that a very large part indeed is not a permanent loss of capital, but is exclusively a loss endured at the time by the various victims of the war. Taking first the French expenditure, the principal item which became a permanent loss appears to be the direct expenditure by the Government, amounting to £120,000,000. No part of the extra war expenditure either of 1870 or 1871 was provided out of revenue. As regards 1870, the case stands thus:

BUDGET OF 1870.

Amount of peace expenditure	£72,440,000
" war expenditure	62,840,000
Total expenditure	£135,280,000
Estimated receipts, exclusive of loans . .	61,040,000
Deficit	£74,240,000

The receipts were thus insufficient to meet the current peace expenditure, much less defray any portion of the war expenditure.

As regards 1871, the account will stand:

BUDGET OF 1871.

Rectified amount of peace expenditure .	£70,840,000
Amount of war expenditure	35,082,000
	£105,922,000
Estimated receipts, exclusive of loans . .	66,800,000
Deficit	£39,122,000

Here, again, the estimated receipts are insufficient for the current peace expenditure.

The whole war expenditure of the two years has thus been defrayed by borrowing, and constitutes a permanent burden on the country.

The second important item is the sum of £44,000,000 for fines and requisitions, but a large part of this amount, if not the whole, will probably be defrayed out of revenue. This would be the case with the French taxes levied by the Germans, and a large part of the requisitions, losses by fire and war, and the alleged plunder of the Germans, would be dealt with in a similar manner by the individuals concerned. They make claims for reimbursement against their Government, but in the meantime they have charged the expense to revenue, and not to capital. How much has gone to the one account and how much to the other it would be impossible to say, and to divide the amount equally between the two heads where there are absolutely no data will perhaps be the safest plan. On the other hand, the Parisian contributions of £12,000,000 have certainly been charged against capital. The whole item of £44,000,000 may therefore be distributed as follows:

Charged against Capital.		
Parisian contributions . .	£12,000,000	
One-half of remaining items	15,064,000	
		£27,064,000
Charged against Revenue.		
Taxes levied by Germans .	£1,960,000	
One-half of remaining items	15,064,000	
		17,024,000
Total as above		£44,088,000

The direct expenditure of Germany, £60,000,000, was also defrayed entirely by loans, or by contributions of the French indemnity, which were entirely supplied out of special loans raised by the French Government.

The remaining item of £10,000,000 which we have mentioned as the capital value of the new war pensions is also a capital charge.

We come, then, to the indirect expenditure. The loss of income through the suspension of business was substantially a charge on the income of individuals. Many people, as we have explained, had no capital to fall back upon, and the unwillingness of owners of capital to trench upon it is also quite intelligible. In fact, all accounts from France agree in the statement that nothing could exceed the desperate pinching of the people during the progress of the war. Some capital, however, must have been lost through this loss of income, in consequence of savings which would otherwise have taken place not having been made. All the usual savings would not be prevented, the pinching being most unequally distributed, but say two-thirds were prevented. We should then have a loss of capital due to this cause amounting to about £60,000,000, the annual savings of France being at least £60,000,000, if not more, so that the usual savings for eighteen months would be £90,000,000.

On the other hand, while Frenchmen individually may have pinched to the extent of the £150,000,000 which we have estimated as their loss of income, they increased the burdens of the State by not paying taxes enough to meet the usual peace expenditure. The difference on this head in 1870 was £11,000,000, and in 1871, £4,000,000—a total of £15,000,000 falling to be added to the amount of savings prevented. We must also deal in the same way with £4,000,000 of Paris revenue lost, making the total charge to capital £79,000,000.

The second item of indirect loss, amounting to £112,000,000, is also a charge on capital, representing a permanent deficiency of earning power.

As regards German indirect expenditure, it may be considered that in the circumstances it has nearly all been borne by income. £50,000,000 is not a very large deficiency, and would be easily covered by the privations of those concerned, while the saving of other classes in the actual circumstances of the war may have gone on as usual. We may divide the amount equally, however, between capital and revenue.

Summarizing the account just given, the whole war waste, exclusive of the value of destroyed or injured lives, will have been borne by capital and revenue as follows:

	Capital.	Revenue.
France.		
Direct war expenditure of France .	£120,000,000	—
Requisitions, fines, etc.	27,062,000	£17,022,000
War pensions of France	5,000,000	—
French loss of present income . .	79,000,000	71,000,000
Capital value of depreciation of French earning power	112,000,000	—
Germany.		
Direct war expenditure of Germany	60,000,000	—
German indirect losses	25,000,000	25,000,000
War pensions of Germany . . .	5,000,000	—
Total for France and Germany	£433,062,000	£113,022,000

Four-fifths of a total expenditure of £546,000,000 which we consider to be the expenditure, exclusive of lives destroyed, may thus be considered a capital charge upon the resources of the communities concerned. It is probably equal to about five years' savings of France and Germany combined.

The distribution is, of course, very unequal, the capital loss to France being £343,000,000, and to Germany only £90,000,000; and the revenue loss to France being £88,000,000 against £25,000,000 primarily paid by Germany. But this and other inequalities in distributing the burden, we reserve for further discussion.

We need state very briefly the conclusions from these facts. Even a loss of capital of £400,000,000 cannot be considered a very serious drain on the resources of two such countries as France and Germany. Four years' saving will very soon be made up, say in two or three years, for one-fourth of the loss consists of savings prevented during the period of the war, viz.:

French savings prevented	£79,000,000
German ,, ,, ...	25,000,000
Total	£104,000,000

so that there is only £300,000,000 of actually stored-up capital wasted, and requiring to be made good by subsequent thrift. In three years, then, the people of the two countries should be as well off as they were before the war, if no other circumstances had to be considered. The war would still have injured them and thrown them back. Although in three years' time they might have been as comfortable as they were before the war, they would not have been exactly as if the war had not happened, because the intermediate savings which now make good a past loss would wholly or in part have been added to the previous wealth. Probably at some early date they might have caught up their lost ground in the race by more energetic saving, so that there would have been little permanent loss of capital after all. Such saving would of course increase the amount of the losses of the war which would have been charged to the revenue of the existing generation, but the effect in diminishing the permanent loss of capital is all that we are now considering.

Nor could the loss of permanent capital be thought very severe if it had fallen on the two nations in the proportions originally defrayed by them. To Germany the loss would only have been £90,000,000, viz.:

£60,000,000	for direct expenses.
5,000,000	for war pensions.
25,000,000	for indirect expenses.
£90,000,000	in all,

—which is no very great amount, probably about one and a half years' savings. To France the loss would have been four times as great, viz.:

£120,000,000	direct Government expenses.
5,000,000	war pensions.
27,000,000	requisitions, etc.
79,000,000	present income charged to capital.
112,000,000	depreciation of earning power.
£343,000,000	

—or about one-half more than if the amount had been equally divided, and equal perhaps to five years' savings instead of three. France therefore might have been expected to take two years more to recover than if that equal division had taken place. That is to say, it would have been five years after the war instead of three before the lost ground was recovered. No doubt the means of saving would be diminished by the interest which must be paid on the lost capital, but the former rate of saving, as we have already explained, will, for other causes, be increased rather than diminished.

We have still, however, to look at the subject from another point of view. The arrangements at the peace have complicated the question by shifting the burden, and perhaps more than the burden, on to the shoulders of only one of the belligerents. What changes have thus been made in the effects of the war losses, both as respects the total charge, and as respects the permanent loss of capital which each has to bear?

V.—The Indemnity and Cession of Territory and their Results.

There are two ways in which the incidence of the burdens of the war was changed by the terms of the peace. One of these—the money indemnity—is very easily described. In addition to all their other burdens and losses, the French people were made to pay to Germany a sum of five milliards of francs, or two hundred millions sterling. Germany had so much less to pay, and France had so much more. And there are no qualifications or deductions to be made. The value of the Alsace and Lorraine Railways, amounting to £13,000,000, was indeed deducted, but only as between the Governments of France and Germany. As they belonged to a French company which had other lines in French territory, and had close connections with the French Government, Germany preferred to buy them, and instead of doing so by an actual payment in cash, deducted the value from the money indemnity it had to receive. But the French Government in turn had to come under obligations to the Railway Company for the amount. It bought the railways at a stipulated price, and transferred them to Germany at the price of £13,000,000, in place of paying Germany so much money. This was no real deduction from the total indemnity of £200,000,000 which was stipulated to be paid. Nor are any deductions, at least none worth speaking of, to be made on account of delay in the terms of payment. The stipulations of the Treaty are precise—£40,000,000 to be paid within a year, and the remaining £160,000,000 within three years after ratification, but of this latter amount £120,000,000 is to bear interest at 5 per cent. from the date of the Treaty till payment. Any deductions, therefore, to be made for delay in payment apply only to a sum of £80,000,000, and of this sum £40,000,000 was in any case to be paid within a year, while the guarantees for paying the remainder were so stringent that the French Government in fact took care to pay the whole £80,000,000 by the beginning of March in the present year [1872]. The haste of payment caused the French to pay a good deal on account of commissions to bankers and loss by exchange, and these are a set-off against any advantage gained by having to pay no interest from the 1st of March, 1871, to the time of payment. France has thus had to pay to Germany £200,000,000 net.

The other mode in which the incidence of the war losses and expenses was changed, and the burden shifted from one belligerent to the other, may require a little explanation. This was the cession of the greater part of Alsace and Lorraine to Germany, viz., the departments of Haut-Rhin, Bas-Rhin, Moselle, and parts of Meurthe and the Vosges. The territory in question was ceded without any deduction for the value of the public property it contained, or for the share of the

French debt estimated to belong to it, or for its estimated value as a source of revenue. The effect of this arrangement necessarily was to increase the burden of the charges of the French State on the diminished territory and people. The diminished France was also less able to bear any increase of debt and taxes. It may be said, perhaps, that France was additionally burdened by no deduction being made for the debt, but nothing more, as the other expenses of government ought to be proportioned to the smaller area; but this is a narrow way of looking at the burdens of a great Power. A change of one or two millions in its people either way leaves it in pretty much the same position as it was before as regards its international duties and dangers. It is still practically the same unit, and most of its expenditure must be determined without any reference to the increase or loss of territory. The cession of territory, therefore, is a real loss, and its acquisition a real gain, without any drawback in either case so far as the material resources and taxpaying powers are concerned. France lost and Germany gained in a most distinct and measurable degree by the transfer of the two provinces from the one to the other.

The loss, measured by population, is about the one-and-twentieth part of France. According to the census of 1866, the population then was 38,067,000, and the cession would reduce the number by 1,597,000. As the debt of France after the war is close upon £1,000,000,000, it would follow that the diminished France has, in fact, been burdened with an additional debt of about £50,000,000 beyond what it would have to bear if the provinces had not been ceded. And the total addition to its burdens would be more than double that, as the interest of the debt is only about half the annual State expenditure which the French people have to meet.

There appears to be a more exact way of looking at the matter, however, and that is by comparing the revenue-yielding power of the ceded provinces with that of the rest of France. The comparison is not difficult to arrive at. The State revenue of France before the war was as nearly as possible £75,000,000, of which, as we have seen, the amount yielded by Alsace and Lorraine was £2,400,000. The ceded provinces, therefore, were hardly equal in economic vigour to the one-and-twentieth part of France, and their share may be more fitly stated at the thirtieth part. Still the deduction of a thirtieth would represent a very considerable sum, and the share of the increased debt alone would be upwards of £33,000,000. Double that amount, as above, would make the French loss of capital by the cession £66,000,000. Perhaps the following will be the most accurate way of arriving at an estimate. The revenue ceded at twenty years' purchase —which is not an excessive estimate for a country which has to borrow at 5 per cent. and upwards— would represent a capital of £48,000,000, but as France has had to increase its revenue one-third, we may consider that Alsace and Lorraine could have paid at least one-third more, or £3,200,000, making the equivalent capital at twenty years' purchase £64,000,000. We may consider, therefore, the loss of Alsace and Lorraine to France as equivalent to a loss of £64,000,000. In the case of any ordinary cession, half of this sum would at least have been allowed as the share of the debt, and the province was at least worth half as much again.

Some small allowance ought perhaps to have been made for the diminished expense of collecting the revenue and the diminution of one or two other charges, but suppose a tenth to be allowed—and this would far more than cover the saving in collecting the revenue— the capital loss to France on account of the cession would still remain about £60,000,000. *Per contra*, however, we ought to have added as part of the French loss the value of national property in the two provinces. The public buildings, fortresses, and similar property represent very large sums, and we cannot be far wrong therefore in retaining £64,000,000 as the figure for the total loss.

Such, then, has been the result of the arrangements for the peace. Germany gets £264,000,000 to set against her outlay and losses, and France has £264,000,000 more to pay. To both countries the change makes an enormous difference in the final accounts of the war.

To begin with Germany, the curious fact will be that the war in a material sense has yielded a profit instead of a loss. Her losses, as we have seen, were only about £145,000,000 (viz., £60,000,000 direct outlay of Government, £5,000,000 for new pensions, £50,000,000 for loss of income and capital, and £30,000,000 for loss of life). The war having brought in £264,000,000, she is a gainer of the enormous amount of £119,000,000. This is putting her loss in the most extreme form. Omitting, however, the very exceptional item for loss of life, the losses and outlay of the surviving community can only be put at £115,000,000, and as they have got £264,000,000, the net gain by the war is £149,000,000, or, in round numbers, ONE HUNDRED AND FIFTY MILLIONS STERLING.

The result is still more striking if we consider only the permanent loss of capital. Germany, as we have seen, lost permanently, that is spent out of capital instead of out of revenue, only about £90,000,000. The above £264,000,000, however, is all capital, so that Germany begins the world again after the war with £174,000,000 to the good. Whatever justice or injustice there may have been in exacting an indemnity from France, there need be no disguising the fact that the indemnity not only makes good losses, but actually enriches Germany. It is about as much to the Germans as two years' arduous savings, if not more, and no such windfall, it may be safely said, ever fell to the lot of any community as the result of seven months' war. To be quite just, we must, of course, recognize that the gain by such a cession as Alsace and Lorraine is very apt to be lost to the nation, the Government taking care to spend the additional money it gets, and not remit the taxation of its subjects in proportion. Even the gain by the indemnity will be less than a similar accession of capital by industrial savings would be, because it will be received by the Government, and not by individuals. But after all deductions, no such money can come into any State without adding to the general means, and enriching every single member of the community. The prospect of such an indemnity more than justifies the eager expectation with which the Germans have discussed its payment.

What Germany has gained France has lost, and as regards France, the net result must be to swell its already gigantic losses to an enormous total. The whole cost primarily borne, excluding the doubtful estimate for the value of the lives lost or injured, was £431,000,000, viz.:

Direct expenses of Government	£120,000,000
Requisitions, fines, etc.	44,000,000
War pensions	5,000,000
Loss of income, 1870-71	150,000,000
Depreciation of French earning power . .	112,000,000
Total	£431,000,000

To which we must now add,—

For indemnity	£200,000,000	
For ceded territory . . .	64,000,000	
		£264,000,000
Total		£695,000,000

making in all the formidable sum of £695,000,000, or, in round numbers, SEVEN HUNDRED MILLIONS STERLING. This is of itself very nearly as much as the English National Debt, and very much more than the National Debt of France before the war. Excluding any direct estimate for lives lost and injured, this is the total loss strictly falling upon the surviving French community, and either borne by them out of their current income, or paid by capital on which they will have to suffer a loss of interest in future. The amount is truly enormous,—more than one year's aggregate income of the people, and six times as much as the entire annual revenue of the State, both for national and local purposes.

The permanent loss of capital is almost equally serious. The amount so lost, apart from the indemnity and cession of territory, was about £340,000,000, and the losses now being dealt with being entirely from capital, the total permanent loss of capital will amount to £600,000,000. While Germany therefore starts in the world about £174,000,000 richer by the war, France is rather more than £600,000,000 poorer. In this case there is no doubt about the effect of the loss of territory. Whether the Germans gain by it individually or not, it is certain that every Frenchman loses. The three millions of revenue which the ceded provinces could have been made to yield are missed in the French budgets, and their absence aggravates materially the difficulty of the search for new taxes—in other words, compels the French Government to impose indefinitely more disagreeable burdens on the diminished population than would otherwise have been required.

We can now obtain a comprehensive view of what the war has really cost the French. Divided among a population of 36,500,000, the total of £695,000,000 represents a sum of £19 per head, or, taking the average French family as four persons, a sum of £76 per family. This was the entire cost of the war payable out of revenue and capital, but nearly an eighth was paid out of revenue, and the remainder, £603,000,000, which is the burden upon capital, represents a sum of £16 10*s.* per head. The English National Debt at this moment is £26 per head, so that in one short war the French have lost three-fifths as much capital per head as the individual share of the English people in that debt which has hitherto been regarded as the most gigantic and oppressive burden upon the resources of a nation.

In comparison with the aggregate annual income of the French people, the loss is, roughly speaking, about one year's income, and estimating the annual savings at about £60,000,000, must be about ten times the amount of these savings. In ordinary circumstances, therefore, it would take nearly ten years for France to recover lost ground. Without the loss of territory and without an indemnity to pay, the French had lost as much as would probably have taken five years to recover, but the indemnity and the cession very nearly double the wound. For reasons already suggested, the period of recovery may, in fact, be less—will probably be very much less—but the natural effect of the loss is to put France about eight years behind in its industrial career.

The greater part of the capital loss, it should be understood, falls upon France collectively, that is, upon the French State. Of the above total of £603,000,000, only two items will finally be borne by individuals, viz.:

Current loss of income borne by individuals	£60,000,000 [1]
Other indirect losses	112,000,000
Total	£172,000,000

leaving £431,000,000 to become a charge upon the State. This sum is made up as follows:

Direct expenses of the war	£120,000,000
War pensions	5,000,000
Requisitions, etc.	27,000,000
Indemnity	200,000,000
Cession of territory	64,000,000
Loss of individual income in 1870-71 thrown on State by diminished payment of taxes .	15,000,000
Total	£431,000,000

[1] The aggregate loss of income was estimated above at £150,000,000, and the amount charged to capital was £79,000,000, viz., £60,000,000

And the charge upon the State may be increased, and that upon individuals diminished, should the State finally repay not only as much of the requisitions as we have assumed to be charged to capital in private accounts, but the whole amount. That the charge is in no way exaggerated will be readily seen, if we compare the actual cash transactions of the French Exchequer during the last few months with the obligations which are still impending, and if we also inquire into the amount of the annual burden which will now fall upon the State. The accounts of the Exchequer will stand:

In the budget of 1870 the deficiency of receipts, exclusive of loans, was	£74,240,000
In the budget of 1871 it was	39,122,000
The indemnity paid in 1871, deducting value of Alsace and Lorraine Railways, was . .	47,000,000
Total actually borrowed	£160,362,000

To this we must add obligations outstanding at end of 1871, and the capital value of annual charges incurred without actual borrowing, viz.:

Indemnity remaining due after 1871 (three and a half milliards)	£140,000,000
Value of Alsace and Lorraine Railways . .	13,000,000
New war pensions	5,000,000
Requisitions, etc.	27,000,000
Ceded territory	64,000,000
Amount of special budget for liquidating arrears of war	20,000,000
Total	£429,362,000

At 5 per cent. the amount would involve an additional annual burden of about £21,000,000, and we find that, in fact, if the charge is less, it is due to a

of individual savings prevented, and 19,000,000 charged to the State and to Paris by the payment of taxes being diminished, so that the revenue in 1870-71 was insufficient for the ordinary peace expenditure by £15,000,000.

species of forced borrowing from the Bank of France at less than the market rate of interest. The French Government affirms that its agreement with the Bank is no injustice to the shareholders, the monopoly of an extended note-issue enabling the Bank to lend cheaper, but if the monopoly is worth much to the Bank, it would have been worth much to the State, and the transaction is, in fact, a sale by the Government of a certain privilege for the difference between the rate of interest which it does pay and what it would have to pay borrowing at the market rate. The additions to the annual charge of the debt traceable to the war as shown in the budget of 1872 are as follows:

Interest on loan of £80,000,000 (in 1871) .	£5,556,000
" " 30,000,000 (in 1870) .	1,584,000
" " 10,000,000 (in 1870) .	600,000
" " from Bank	367,000
" payable to Eastern of France Railway for Alsace Railways	650,000
" payable to Germany on £120,000,000 of indemnity at 5 per cent. . . .	6,000,000
New military pensions	148,000
Total new debt charges in budget . .	£14,905,000

Add,

Alsace and Lorraine revenues lost	£3,200,000
Difference between interest paid to Bank and interest payable at 5 per cent.	2,633,000
Interest on requisitions, etc. (27,000,000) . .	1,350,000
Five per cent. interest on £20,000,000 for special budget to liquidate war-arrears . .	1,000,000
Total annual charge	£23,088,000

The whole charge before the war for "debt and dotations" was £22,300,000, so that it is no exaggeration to say the annual burden has been really doubled by the war and its consequences to France. The whole additional charge which yet appears in the budget is £14,900,000, but more than £3,000,000 must be added for loss of the revenues of Alsace and Lorraine, and even if we add nothing for the interest under-paid to the Bank, there are still two sums amounting together to over £2,000,000 in suspense, which the State must undertake to pay before it can fully discharge all the arrears of the war. If it does not pay the £27,000,000 for requisitions claimed—only a part of the total claim—the charge on individuals and local authorities will be increased, but it can in no way escape the burden of £20,000,000 for liquidating the arrears of the war.

The amount is of course an unprecedented addition to the annual burdens of a people by the events of one calamitous year. Taking it at £22,000,000, it amounts to 12*s.* 3*d.* per head annually upon each inhabitant of France, or about 49*s.* per family. It is nearly equal to the annual charge for interest on the National Debt of England, for though the whole annual charge which appears in our budgets is £27,000,000, yet the interest at 3 per cent. on £800,000,000—and we do not pay so much as 3 per cent. on the whole of it—is only £24,000,000, the difference between that amount and the actual charge being, in fact, an annual appropriation to repay the capital of the debt. In one year, then, France has added to her annual State burdens, besides the loss of individual capital, as much as the entire charge of our accumulated debt.

Whatever way we look at the matter, then, we cannot but be impressed by the enormous magnitude of the loss which France has sustained. The war itself was not so very costly if both nations had but divided equally the actual outlay of the Governments, and fought their battles on some debateable land without incurring the terrible losses of an invasion. But France was in fact invaded, had to bear the losses incidental to that state, had to pay, as the war went on, a large part of its invaders' costs, and in the end had to pay an indemnity and suffer a loss of territory which nearly doubled its losses. The loss of capital and the addition to the national debt are enormous, while several years must elapse before France, at the ordinary rate of progress, is even at the point of industrial prosperity which she had attained before the war.

A remark or two may be allowed on one or two points suggested by these facts. Will Germany, in fact, really gain much by the indemnity and additional territory in a material point of view? The capital is really a loss to France, and the Germans ought to gain, but will they really do so? If they do not, the transaction will be a net loss to the world, as well as a special loss to France. To some extent it must be so. The money is taken from individuals and goes into the hands of a Government, and this is a disadvantageous change. Even if the German Government uses the bulk of what it receives in paying off the national debts of Germany, so that the money comes back to individuals again, it will have been a long time *in transitu*—consequently, for a long time in a condition of impaired efficiency. The operation is, therefore, a net loss to the world, and Germany will be far from gaining all that France will lose. We need not add that if the German Government should devote the money to any extravagance—to some fancied Imperial necessity or caprice—the loss will be very serious indeed. The operation will have all the effect of a great loan for a pernicious purpose, and it will make no difference that the Government which borrows is not the Government which ultimately receives the money. So far as matters have yet gone, however, the indemnity appears to be fairly well used in an economic sense, though it is producing some effects which it is difficult to trace. The chief good uses are the establishment of a gold currency for Germany, the repayment of German debts, and as a result of these the reduction of German taxes. By all these operations the money which the German Government has got is being put to useful ends, though it cannot be said it is so useful as it would have been if it had never been transferred at all. Another purpose which the money has been made to serve is of a more doubtful kind. The German Government having large surplus funds in hand has become a lender on a great scale, and is the means of supplying German speculators and traders, and through them speculators and traders in England and throughout the world, with stores of cheap money. The money which Germany pours into the market competes with the ordinary loanable capital, and has prolonged the period of very cheap money which set in with 1867. Is the effect of this diversion of capital in the end to be good or bad? Probably it makes trade more prosperous for a time than it would otherwise be, so that one result of the French indemnity is to give a bonus to the trade of England, because England attracts the surplus money of the world, but it would be hazardous to say that an effect so artificially produced will in the end prove a benefit at all. Trade and speculation get to depend on the artificial stimulant, and the crash that may come on its withdrawal, of which there was a foretaste last autumn, may more than destroy all the unusual profits it has created.

The second point to be noticed is the probability of France recovering with unexpected speed. At its estimated past rate of saving we have been inclined to give it ten years to recover, and to save £60,000,000 effectually each year it must really save £20,000,000 more than it did before, for there is so much more taxation to pay. But all the chances are that the past rate of saving will be greatly increased. The anxiety of each individual in a nation which is habitually thrifty will assuredly be to make up for the storm which has passed over them by the most desperate industry and saving. They will seek in a year or two not only to recover lost ground, but to place themselves at the point of prosperity which they had looked forward to reach at a given period of their lives. It would not be at all surprising if the phenomenon to be witnessed in France for the next year or two were the multiplication of the national wealth by the doubling or trebling of the former savings of the people. A few years' savings of only £100,000,000 would go a long way to fill up the chasm which has been made in the national resources; and a single bountiful harvest at such a time would be greedily made use of to repair the waste which is still fresh in every one's remembrance. France is very far indeed from being exhausted, though taxes are now difficult to find. A revenue which has augmented a million annually for many years is sure to have immense elasticity. The existing taxes must soon provide for all needs, if only the fatal habit of deficits in time of peace is scrupulously shunned.

VI.—The Finance of the War and the Money Market.

Our *fourth* question was the effect of the war losses and expenses and the financial arrangements made to meet them on the money markets of the world. Hitherto we have been dealing only with the economic aspect of the war in its most general form—with the effect of losses and expenses which all belligerent communities are liable to feel, whether they possess the elaborate machinery of the modern money market or not. We have now to inquire how that machinery is affected or disturbed by war, and in what special way the last war operated and may still operate. Properly speaking this might have been a branch of the other parts of the inquiry, the losses or gains which arise to the world from war through its influence on the money market being an addition to or a set-off against all the other losses which are otherwise traceable to it, but it is conceived that it would have been inconvenient to deal with the subject in this manner. The losses or gains at the best would be quite incalculable, and the nature of war influences on "money" is in reality so intricate and important a topic as to justify separate treatment.

The common opinion—and in the usual case perhaps

the true opinion—about the effect of war on money is very simple. War, it is understood, makes money dear. It creates a new and heavy demand on the circulating capital of the world, and must enhance the value of that capital. But this opinion carries us a very little way in studying the effects of the last war. The phenomena we meet are various. First came a spasm of dear money just at the outbreak of the war; then a long period of cheap money, lasting all through the war and for some months after it; then another spasm of rather dear money, and again a prolonged period of cheapness. At present it would be hazardous to say that it now tends in any way to make money perceptibly dearer. It may be said that after minor fluctuations economic theory will come right in the end, but the circumstances are perhaps enough to raise a doubt of the universal applicability of the theory. It is plain that in a war like the last it will be more practical to understand the laws of variation from the usual result than to rest contented with the knowledge of what the usual result may be.

To understand the matter thoroughly, it is submitted, the money market must be looked at in two different aspects. There is first of all its singular liability to momentary and superficial disturbance. The money markets of the world are now so much interconnected as to make practically but one market, with London for the centre, and the organization of this central market is of the most delicate sort. It is so contrived, by means of a hierarchy of banks and discount houses centring in the Bank of England, that in ordinary times the money it contains is made to go as far as possible, but when anything goes wrong the strain is very severe. The complete abstraction of any considerable amount, though it may be small in comparison with the aggregate transactions of the market, may disturb largely the current relations of supply and demand, and its effect will be multiplied tenfold by the sensitiveness of all concerned and the precautions they are induced to take. The natural structure of the market is such that this liability to disturbance must always be great; but, as if to intensify the evil, the natural means by which a sudden demand could be tided over and alarm allayed has been artificially destroyed. The expansion of the note-issues of great banks, when there is a sudden demand for money and the credit of the note is not shaken, is the obvious method of meeting a sudden strain, but Peel's Act forbids the exercise of any such power in London by the bank which has the monopoly of issue. Now that the inelasticity of the Act has become familiar, each sudden disturbance is liable to be increased in severity by the knowledge of all concerned that the natural remedy for it cannot lawfully be used. The second aspect of the market is the more general and important one of steady and periodic change, according as the supply of circulating capital exceeds or falls short of the demands of borrowers in the market. We must make a broad distinction between these two different aspects of the market in studying the effects upon it of war or of any other cause which produces large financial operations.

As respects the first aspect of the market, we do not think there can be any doubt as to the probable effect of a great war. It can hardly fail to cause the most serious spasmodic disturbance and a short period of dear money. Many of its demands are likely to be of extreme urgency, and the precautions which its outbreak and some of its incidents necessitate on the part of all who have money engagements to meet are also likely to be extreme. There is something formidable in the very name of war. But the dear money thus produced is only temporary and occasional, unless perhaps the temporary panic should be converted into a prolonged convulsion, a possibility which may be sometimes very threatening.

The effect of war on the money market, looked at in its second aspect, does not appear to be so clear. No doubt war absorbs capital, and the natural tendency of such an absorption, whether resulting from war or any other extravagance, should be scarcity of capital, for which accordingly higher rates would be charged. But when we examine the matter carefully we find that the effect of the absorption of capital is one of circumstances and degree. Much will depend on the amount of the war requirements, and great as these often are, we should not forget the magnitude of the market out of which the supplies have to come. Though the market may be so delicate as to quiver to a sudden demand of insignificant amount compared with its total business, its real resources are enormous, and if time is only given the most extravagant expenditures may be supplied without a shock. For such a purpose, it may be repeated, all the markets are one. Even if France and Germany had been unable to launch their loans in London, they would still have supplied themselves from the common resources of the European markets. French and German securities would have been sold abroad that Frenchmen and Germans might subscribe to their own loans, and as regards any effect on the money market, this is almost an equivalent process to having a loan subscribed in London. The question of circumstances is even more important. According as the war comes at a period when the current savings of the chief industrial communities are small or great, its effects will be serious or the reverse. If savings are abundant, the expenditure may be met out of surpluses which it might otherwise be difficult to employ. What is perhaps still more important, there is one secondary effect of war which in the actual circumstances of modern industrial societies will always help to counteract the tendency to dearer money which is the direct consequence of the war expenditure itself. This secondary effect is the diffused apprehensiveness and limitation of enterprise which war on a great scale between two leading members of the society of nations invariably produces. As thus viewed, war provides the capital for its own sustenance by checking the employment of capital in other directions. It may be quite true, perhaps, that all the while the belligerent communities gradually get poorer, but this process appears to be really consistent after all with an easy money market. So long as capital is found for war by withdrawing it from other pursuits, the effect on the borrowing and lending markets will be *nil.* People will have less to borrow and lend, but the supply will be adjusted to the demand, and the rates will not be dearer. It would be the tendency of a prolonged war, of course, for the demand to outrun the process of diversion from other pursuits, but until that process is outrun, money will not grow dearer. The point is that war, to cause dear money, must not merely produce a great demand —it must produce a certain excess in the whole demand for capital, whatever causes may be operating at the time to increase the supply or to diminish other demands.

The phenomena of the war and its after-effects, up to the present date, suggest and confirm these views. And *first,* as to the influence of war in causing spasmodic disturbance. The first monetary spasm in the war, in July, 1870, was clearly due to the precautions forced upon people who had money engagements to meet. War was declared upon the 15th of July. On the 21st the Bank of England rate was raised from 3 to 3½ per cent.; on the 23rd, to 4; on the 28th, to 5; and on the 4th of August, to 6—the rate having thus been doubled in little more than a fortnight. All happened long before the great spending and borrowing on account of the war began, and the cause was notorious and palpable. As the "Economist"[1] at the time explained, we were "receiving securities from borrowers on the Continent, who think that money is more easily procured in London than elsewhere. These borrowers are mostly persons under heavy liabilities, and they send for cash in time of danger because they feel that at any

[1] "Economist," July 23rd, 1870.

moment they may be asked for cash themselves." At the same time, foreign bankers having bills on London sent them in for payment, and did not take fresh bills, the same end of providing themselves being thereby secured. The demand for gold was also increased in London by the Bank of France exercising its option of paying in silver. In other words, the crisis in London was intensified by the precautions of the Bank of France, which undoubtedly would have taken another form had not this been open to it. We see, then, in a moment, how war produces a spasm of dearness without any of the expenditure which will ultimately act on the market having even begun. Of course, the demand, once begun, was increased by the precautions of people at home, and so the effect was great and immediate. But a disturbance of this sort is very soon over. A week after the rate was at 6, it was reduced to $5\frac{1}{2}$; a week later, viz., on August 18th, it was reduced to $4\frac{1}{2}$; on August 25th, to 4; on September 1st, to $3\frac{1}{2}$; and finally, on September 15th, to 3 per cent., the Bank all through having followed the open market somewhat tardily, but the whole period, nevertheless, commencing on July 21st, and terminating on September 15th, having lasted less than two months. Taking it that the crisis was really over when the rate was reduced to $4\frac{1}{4}$ on August 18th, the disturbance had, in fact, only lasted a month.

The second disturbance was in no way more prolonged, and though it arose in a somewhat different way, was distinctly traceable to a cause characteristic of the war. The Germans in the autumn of 1871 were receiving payment of a large part of their war indemnity. Besides the fine of £8,000,000 on Paris stipulated in the armistice, and the other fines and taxes levied in the occupied districts of France subsequent to the peace preliminaries on 26th of February, 1871, estimated according to the table in the Appendix to amount to £450,000—

Viz.:	Contributions	£59,000
	Direct taxes	285,000
	Indirect taxes	106,000
		£450,000

besides likewise the sums paid by the French Government for the expense of the German army of occupation, which must have amounted at least to five or six millions more—the Germans in 1871 received altogether from France and on account of the indemnity alone the large sum of £47,000,000 *in cash or bills.* This amount was paid, with the exception of a sum of £5,000,000, between the 27th of June, when the £80,000,000 loan was subscribed and the first days of September, in the following form:[1]

Cash paid at Berlin	£316,000
Commercial bills	32,915,000
Notes of Bank of France	5,000,000
French gold	4,360,000
5-franc pieces	2,521,000
Bills of foreign banks	272,000
German money	1,831,000
Total	£47,215,000

A large part of the bills fell due in London, and the amount representing them had been transferred to the credit of the German Government by September, while other bills were to come due in November following. Accordingly, the German Government, having previously received large sums in cash which it had locked up, was an unusually large creditor of Lombard Street at the most difficult period of the year, and wanting gold for the purposes of a new German coinage, suddenly exercised its power. The effect was almost instantaneous. The gold in the Bank and the Reserve rapidly fell off, and the rate was as quickly raised, as the following table shows:

[1] Budget of 1872, Introduction, pp. xxviii.-xxix.

	BULLION.	RESERVE.	RATE OF DISCOUNT.
September 14 .	£24,159,000	£14,424,000	2 per cent.
,, 21 .	23,497,000	13,711,000	3 ,,
,, 28 .	21,090,000	11,077,000	4 ,,
October 5 . .	20,215,000	8,920,000	— ,,
,, 12 . .	19,173,000	8,064,900	5[1] ,,

The high rate in this case was maintained for five weeks—a longer period than in the crisis of July and August, 1870, but the Bank had only followed more tardily than before the movement in the open market. The spasm was in reality equally superficial and almost equally soon over. In this case it did not, as in the former one, arise from the acts of individuals acting in view of the war, and it may be said that it would not have occurred if the German Government had been careful to avoid it, but it is one of the incidents of such large operations that the market is exposed to the caprice or mistake of the operating Governments. Precisely the same consequence might have followed upon the acts of a Government in suddenly calling up or discounting the instalments of a large loan.

While we speak of such disturbances as superficial, it would be a mistake to underrate their consequences and dangers. The chief sufferers in 1870 and 1871 were bankers and the Stock Exchange, principally the latter, but no such disturbance can take place even on the Stock Exchange without much private loss and hardship to people who are not "speculators." It is easy to conceive besides, that crises thus beginning might have very wide effects, one crash leading to another all through the world of finance and trade, and there is no warrant that a future disturbance may not have such effects, though the conditions necessary for its development did not exist in 1870 or 1871.

The present war, therefore, has acted as we may usually expect wars to do, in the production of spasmodic disturbance. As regards the other mode in which

[1] The rate was really raised to 5 per cent. on October 7, five days before the usual weekly court, when the rate is changed.

war produces dear money—and that not temporarily, but for a long period—viz., by the absorption of capital—it will follow, from what we have said, that in the late war there have been counteracting circumstances. Speaking of the money markets of Europe generally, money has been cheap and not dear for a long period indeed, notwithstanding all the borrowing which the war has occasioned. In France, no doubt, the rate has been rather high, the Bank of France rate having risen to 6 per cent. at the commencement of the war, and been maintained at that figure till the 27th of February last, a period of rather more than eighteen months. But France is the only part of Europe where money has been dear, and the rate there cannot be considered very high, when it is considered that the brunt of all the borrowing we have described had to be borne originally by one country alone. It is doubtful, moreover, whether so high a rate could have been maintained in France so long but for the artificial nature of its currency and banking system, which have impeded the free influx of money from the adjacent markets. Had France been more *en rapport* with the rest of Europe it would have been more quickly relieved from sources so numerous as hardly to have felt the drain. Even with this exception, then, we are entitled to say that money has been cheap in Europe, notwithstanding the war, and France is daily becoming less and less an exception.

We should say, then, that in fact there were several circumstances present to an unexampled degree during the late war, which counteracted the usual tendency of wars to produce a period of permanently dear money. The war broke out, in the first place, at a time of the most unprecedented prosperity—at the very flow of a most prosperous tide, and before the usual following of high prices and inflation had come to check the profits. The money markets of Europe were therefore well prepared to meet the unusual demand. Whether they could have met it without sensibly dearer money had everything else gone on as usual may be doubted, but the war, in fact, diffused a most unusual amount of apprehensiveness, and if it did not prevent the continuance and expansion of ordinary trade, at least it checked numberless new ventures of a speculative kind. There is no doubt, however, that in France ordinary trade was checked to a large extent, that being, as we have seen, one of the main causes of the French indirect losses. Great as the loss thus caused was, one result must have been that the French Government would have fewer competitors in the home loan market for means to carry on its struggle. A third cause of the abundance of capital was the extended issues of paper money in France. It is doubtful whether the diminution of the demand for capital in France by the suspension of business would not have been counteracted by the new demand which would spring up in consequence of the old capital becoming of diminished effectiveness through the destruction of the machinery of credit; but if such a demand arose to any extent, it was in turn compensated by the large issues of paper. We shall not of course be understood to mean that capital was created by this process. What is true is that paper money economizes capital, and its issue has all the effect for the moment of an increase of capital, whatever bad results may afterwards ensue. In these four ways, then—the occurrence of the war at a prosperous period in Europe, the diffused apprehensiveness it produced, the suspension of trade in France, and the extension of the Bank of France note issue—the natural tendency of war to cause dear money by absorbing capital was counteracted, and perhaps more than counteracted. We have perhaps had cheaper money longer than we would otherwise have had, if there had been no war.

The effect in England has perhaps been greater than in the belligerent countries in this way, that besides all our own savings diverted from new enterprise by the diffused apprehensiveness of the time, the disposition has grown among foreign bankers and governments to accumulate spare money in London. London is the most convenient place for them to put their reserves, the war illustrated in a most powerful manner its special security, and one of the very steps by which the French Government made its borrowing easier—the issue of inconvertible paper—also tended to increase the exchange business of London, and consequently the foreign surpluses accumulated there. Paris had formerly been a rival of London as an exchange centre, but with inconvertible paper it could no longer compete. This has certainly been a cause of cheaper money. Had Paris and London continued to compete, more money would have been required by their aggregate business than is now required. The concentration of business in one centre only cannot but produce an economy of the instruments for carrying it on. The Paris money, moreover, is now used by a more efficient mechanism than it was used by in Paris, the agencies of the London money market being altogether superior. A certain amount of money has in this way been taken into a new channel where the same amount of money does more work than in the old channel. In every way, then, the foreign money goes farther than ever it did before.

Within the last three or four months there has been an additional counteracting circumstance. The German Government, instead of spending the money which is the usual destination of the proceeds of war loans, and instead of locking up the money as it did at one time, which had a still more disastrous effect than even extravagant expenditure, has taken to lending out a large part—how much is not known—of the funds which it has received. The aggregate loanable capital of the world is thus artificially increased by the finance arrangements in progress. Had the German Government employed all the surplus money to repay debt, the effect would have been less, because there is always a tendency for free circulating capital to become fixed.

By the process of lending out, however, the money is kept more in hand, and competes with the ordinary supply of loanable capital in the world.

How powerful all these counteracting influences must have been is shown by the large amount of the French and German borrowings since July, 1870. The Governments alone have borrowed:

Germany	£50,000,000	
less repaid	20,000,000	
		£30,000,000
France:		
1870 Imperial loan . .	£30,000,000	
1870 Morgan loan . .	10,000,000	
1871 loan	80,000,000	
From Bank of France .	60,000,000	
	180,000,000	
City of Paris loan	14,000,000	
		194,000,000
Total borrowed		£224,000,000

Money has not been cheap, therefore, because war did not require much spending and borrowing. Large sums have, in fact, been taken out of the market, though plainly not larger than could easily have been met out of the current savings of France, Germany, and England, if only new enterprise was sensibly checked.

Something else has been taken out of the money market by the private borrowings of French merchants and manufacturers, but probably no large amount. Such demands would necessarily be limited by the deficient credit of the sufferers. The chief way, again, in which these losses would be replaced would be by the sale of securities, and it is noticeable that many French securities are now cheaper than just at the close of the war; but this may partly be due to the diminution in apparent value of the property represented by these securities. In any case, it is clear that the sale of securities has not checked to any material extent a general rise in the value of such property on all the exchanges of Europe. As that rise is due to the competition of accumulated savings for investment, it is clear that the private borrowings of Frenchmen have not sensibly aggravated—any more than the public borrowings—the general demand for capital.

The war of 1870-71, therefore, so far as it has gone, though it has illustrated the usual tendency of wars to cause disturbance in the money market, has hardly illustrated their tendency to cause permanently dearer money by the destruction of capital. It has illustrated, on the contrary, the strength of the counteracting influences which sometimes exist. There is nothing in the facts, however, to prove that these counteracting influences are always likely to exist. War will always cause diffused apprehensiveness, and invasion will suspend trade, and probably extended issues of paper will produce for a moment a new economy of capital, but the coincidence of a period of great prosperity throughout the world is not always to be looked for. Nor is it likely that the money borrowed will be often lent out in consequence of its being borrowed by one Government and ultimately received by another. Such a very favourable conjuncture for cheap money during and after a war is not certain to occur again. As we have already remarked, too, the war was not prolonged enough to test what the destruction of capital would lead to, or the tendency of war to outrun the process of diverting capital from other employments, and so make it in excessive demand. All that can be said is, that in certain given circumstances a great European war, which involved spending and borrowing to the amount of over £200,000,000 in about a twelvemonth, did not produce dear money. In the circumstances described, and with the means which the society of nations now possesses, this scale of expenditure was not large enough for such an effect to be produced.

But the account is not yet over; France has not yet borrowed all she wants; Germany has not received all she is to get; we do not yet see how Germany will dispose of what she does get. What effects may we yet expect from the financial operations to be completed?

On one point we think—viz., the possibility of spasmodic disturbance—there can be very little doubt. The German Government is still the holder of large sums at call or at short notice. In addition to the £47,000,000 indemnity money it got last year, besides smaller sums, it has just got £26,000,000 more, and so far as is known it has spent only a part of the money, not more than about twenty or twenty-five millions, in repaying debt, and not more than ten millions besides in miscellaneous purposes. We do not reckon what it keeps for the new gold coinage, for the coins will not be issued without a full equivalent being received, so that their issue will not lessen its power like a real expense. Germany has thus about £40,000,000 still at its disposition, which it may use for any object or any caprice it pleases. The absolute disposition of so enormous an amount, is almost a new power for any Government to possess, and increases, we fear, the liability of the money market to accidents. A Government which has the instalments of a loan to receive has great command over the market, but the German Government is in a superior position, having lent out the money on its own terms, retaining a large part of it at call or very short notice, and having in any case the power of rediscounting, by which it could convert the whole—or far more than enough to disturb the money market—into cash at a moment's notice.

The German Government has moreover £120,000,000 still to receive, and the French Government must not only borrow that, but considerable amounts besides. Experience justifies us in believing that there is a liability to accident in these operations, however anxious the Governments concerned may be to avoid them. What the state of matters will be when the German Government has got the command of the whole, in addition to all its previous command of the market, we forbear to speculate. Even after paying off all the debts of Germany, except the railway loans, which are profitable investments—with this exception not more than £150,000,000—the German Government will have a large surplus, and it is not certain that it will pay off all the debts. It may prefer rather to lend out the funds, and have control of them, and so avoid the necessity of ever borrowing again. Even if it does pay off the debts, it will have annual accruing surpluses, by which it will still possess control over large amounts. There is thus no visible end to the possibility of catastrophic action on the part of the German Government on the money markets of Europe. Nothing short of a great war or revolution can change this disagreeable condition, under which monetary business must now be carried on.

As regards the other class of effects, it appears at first sight not improbable that the course of the market may be pretty much what it has hitherto been. The larger part of the actual borrowing is over, and surprising as this fact may seem, considering what the French losses have been, and that the borrowing of France has only been £194,000,000, it is not difficult of explanation. A great many of the losses, though real enough, do not affect the money market at all. The loss sustained, for instance, by the cession of Alsace and Lorraine requires no loan operation. It takes the shape of a new rent-charge upon the resources of France—for the retention of an old charge upon a diminished property has precisely the same kind of effect as the imposition of a new charge upon a property which is not diminished—but though the loss is a real one and will diminish in future the aggregate net income of Frenchmen, it has not the effect of the destruction of so much capital, which had to be taken out of the money markets where it was used. The same remark applies to the loss caused by the creation of new war pensions. The losses endured at the time and charged upon the annual income are also settled, and cannot now affect the money market. The individual loss of capital, and the loss represented by the depreciation of annual earning power, will also have a smaller effect than would be supposed from their apparent amount. So far as they consist of savings prevented, the world is poorer by a capital which would otherwise have existed; but the undertakings which the capital would have supported—that is, the demands upon the capital—have diminished too. The loss by depreciated earning-power would only be partially mitigated by loans, and it implies, moreover, the diminished credit of the borrowers, so that the *effective* demand on the aggregate capital of the world is far from being in proportion to the loss. The whole market is smaller, but the supply is adjusted to the demand. In this way, then, it happens that the larger part of the borrowing is over. The amount borrowed, even deducting what Germany has repaid, and not including private borrowings, has been £224,000,000, and, so far as can be seen, France will be clear, if it only borrows about £120,000,000 to pay off the indemnity, and £40,000,000 more to liquidate arrears. It is probable, too, that most of the private borrowings have already taken place, the earliest opportunity having been seized to restore establishments and resume business as completely as diminished means would permit.

It has also to be remembered that the greater part of the future borrowings will not be for purposes of expenditure, but only to transfer capital from one set of people to another. The money taken from the money market will be given to the German Government, and will not be spent, but used as capital. We have already shown that this will give the German Government very great power, but at present we have nothing to do with that point. It does not alter the fact that loans which are to be so used will not only not exhaust the resources of the money market, but by keeping in it funds which might otherwise have been sunk in some fixed form may even enlarge its resources. So far, then, there is some likelihood that the future finance operations of the war may help very little to cause dear money.

Another circumstance which points in the same direction is this. We shall continue in all probability to hold the private foreign money which comes to us in connection with our increased exchange business. France in any case could only get back its share in that business with difficulty, but the first condition of its even attempting to get it back—the restoration of a bullion basis for its currency—is not likely to be fulfilled for an indefinite time.

On the other hand, other circumstances which were very powerful during the last eighteen months have changed. There is now much less diffused apprehensiveness than there was. There is some apprehensiveness still, for foreign money partly comes to or remains in England for security, but the apprehensiveness is indefinitely less than when war was actually raging or only just concluded. The current savings of the world are also probably less than when the war of 1870 broke out or than they were during its continuance. We have now come to a period of high prices, and on all sides the complaint of manufacturers and traders is that their profits are very much less than they were. It may happen that even a smaller demand on account of the war than what has hitherto been so easily met may tell very much on the market. It may come into competition with other increasing demands, and hasten a period of dear money. The point is that the finance of the war is only one element out of many in determining the future of the money market, and while some of the special circumstances which have hitherto counteracted the natural tendency of war to turn the balance in favour of dear money are still in operation, some very important circumstances which acted in the same direction are changed.

Or the whole, we should be inclined to say that the

most important circumstances are changed. The most important single influence on money is undoubtedly the annual savings of England, and the savings have been diminished while the employment for new capital has increased. This change is the more likely to operate because the other special circumstances which have counteracted the tendency of war to make money dear—the increased supply of foreign money in London and the practice of the German Government to make loans—are likely to have been most powerful at first. The current demand gets adjusted to the new supply and other capital is displaced, and then the more permanent causes which govern the market return in nearly full force. The approach of a period of dear money may possibly have been retarded on the whole by the aggregate effects of the war, but the retarding influences are probably played out, and the future can hardly be the same as the past.

We must again repeat, however, that the possible action of the German Government is apparently the most important question for the future. Its power of spasmodic disturbance is obvious, and we may further point out that the more its practice of making loans has been discounted, so that the market has got to depend on this extraordinary supply, the greater its power will be. It may not only cause a spasmodic disturbance of unprecedented severity, but by withdrawing its supplies it may induce in a moment what may prove to be a prolonged change from cheap to dear money. It is not likely so to act, but its motives will be purely political, and no one can guess at all the circumstances and motives which from time to time may determine it to act.

VII.—Conclusions.

The principal conclusions arrived at in the preceding pages are the following:

First.—The direct expenditure in conducting the war amounted to TWO HUNDRED AND THIRTY-FOUR MILLIONS STERLING, of which the amount primarily spent by France was ONE HUNDRED AND SIXTY-NINE MILLIONS STERLING, and by Germany, SIXTY-FIVE MILLIONS STERLING. The items are:

Spent by France.

Extra war credits of French Government, including special budget of £20,000,000 for liquidating war arrears	£120,000,000	
Fines and requisitions levied in occupied districts; destruction of property, etc., less £4,000,000 voted by Government included in war credits	44,000,000	
Capital value of war pensions created	5,000,000	
		£169,000,000

Spent by Germany.

War credits, including maintenance of French prisoners, etc.	£60,000,000	
Capital value of war pensions created	5,000,000	
		65,000,000
Total Direct Expenditure		£234,000,000

The above includes every cash outlay in actually conducting the war by the respective belligerent Governments, and the loss of property occasioned to the inhabitants of the invaded districts.

Second.—The indirect losses occasioned by the war to the communities of France and Germany respectively, amounted to THREE HUNDRED AND TWELVE MILLIONS STERLING—viz., TWO HUNDRED AND SIXTY-TWO MILLIONS suffered by France, and FIFTY MILLIONS suffered by Germany. The items are:

SUFFERED BY FRANCE.

Estimated loss of income in 1870-71 by suspension of trade and abstraction of labourers from employment . .	£150,000,000	
Estimated loss of permanent business or depreciation of annual earning power	112,000,000	
		£262,000,000

SUFFERED BY GERMANY.

Estimated loss of income in 1870-71 by suspension of trade and abstraction of labourers from employment	50,000,000
Total	£312,000,000

This statement of indirect losses is of course an estimate. The basis as regards the loss of income is, in France, that the loss may be taken to have been in the same proportion to the aggregate income of the people as the loss of the State Revenue in 1870-71 was to the whole of that revenue; and in Germany, that the proportion of the annual income of the labourers withdrawn for war to the whole income of the people would be the maximum amount of the loss, as trade was very little interrupted. As regards the depreciation of annual earning power in France, the data for calculation are obtained by taking the per-centage of loss on the patent-licence tax the first year after the war, and reckoning that the annual loss of trade income would be in proportion. As the yield of taxes in Germany has not diminished, it is assumed that after-effects of the war of the kind which have been felt in France have not been felt in Germany.

THIRD.—The total cost and loss of the war thus reckoned is FIVE HUNDRED AND FORTY-SIX MILLIONS STERLING, the particulars being:

	France.	Germany.	Total.
Direct .	£169,000,000	£65,000,000	£234,000,000
Indirect .	262,000,000	50,000,000	312,000,000
Total .	£431,000,000	£115,000,000	£546,000,000

FOURTH.—No estimate is made in the above calculation for the loss of life or injury thereto in the war. It is believed that no proper estimate can be made of such losses, and so far as they are felt by the surviving community, they would be shown among the other items of indirect loss. A calculation is given, however, for what it is worth, showing that the loss and injury to life in France might be represented by a sum of £102,000,000, and in Germany by a sum of £30,000,000. The reason of the much larger figure for France compared with Germany is that Germany lost no civilian life, but in France, which suffered greatly by the siege of Paris and otherwise, this cause of loss accounts for sixty out of the above one hundred and two millions. The loss of soldiers' lives was also one-third greater on the French than on the German side, the total on that head alone being £42,000,000 against the German £30,000,000. These estimates, however, are only given *en passant*, and are not used in subsequent calculations respecting the war losses.

FIFTH.—The above losses have been principally defrayed out of capital—that is, have increased the indebtedness of the belligerent communities—but a considerable part has been dealt with at the time and paid out of revenue. The distribution of the items is as follows:

	Charged on Capital.	Charged on Revenue.
FRANCE.		
Direct war expenditure of France	£120,000,000	—
Requisitions, fines, etc.	27,062,000	£17,022,000
War pensions of France	5,000,000	—
French loss of present income	79,000,000	71,000,000
Capital value of depreciation of French earning power	112,000,000	—
GERMANY.		
Direct war expenditure of Germany	60,000,000	—
German indirect losses	25,000,000	25,000,000
War pensions of Germany	5,000,000	—
Total for France and Germany	£433,062,000	£113,022,000

Thus the amount charged to capital is FOUR HUNDRED AND THIRTY-THREE MILLIONS, and to revenue ONE HUNDRED AND THIRTEEN MILLIONS; the amount primarily charged to capital by France being £343,000,000, and to revenue £88,000,000, the corresponding charges primarily made by Germany being £90,000,000 and £25,000,000.

SIXTH.—The above losses are not considered very serious, compared with the aggregate income of the communities concerned. Estimating that aggregate for each at about £600,000,000 annually, the direct outlay is only about one-fourth of that income, the total cost—omitting any estimate for loss of life—about one-half, and the loss of permanent capital about one-third. Such losses should be easily recovered from, especially when it is recollected that £104,000,000, or one-fourth of the permanent loss of capital, does not represent any waste from accumulated stores, but merely an amount of annual savings prevented which would otherwise have been made. The waste from past accumulation is under three hundred and thirty millions sterling.

The cost, no doubt, had been unequally distributed even in the primary outlay—the primary loss of capital to France being £343,000,000 against £88,000,000 lost to Germany. Still, even as thus unequally distributed, the loss might have been quickly recovered from. But—

SEVENTH.—The changes made at the peace have immensely increased the burdens of France, and even made Germany a gainer. France has had to pay to Germany an indemnity of £200,000,000 in money without any deduction, and the cession of Alsace and Lorraine is equivalent to a transfer of £64,000,000. The loss of France has therefore been increased by £264,000,000, while the loss of Germany, as the indemnity is so much in excess of all the war had cost it, is turned into a gain.

Omitting any estimate for loss of life, GERMANY'S final account for the war will stand:

Indemnity and territory received	£264,000,000
Less total direct and indirect expenditure .	115,000,000
Net gain	£149,000,000

Looking only at the permanent loss of capital, however, the gain of Germany is greater, because part of the war cost was charged to revenue, and the indemnity comes in as capital. The capital account will stand:

Indemnity and territory received	£264,000,000
Spent out of capital	90,000,000
Net capital gain of Germany by the war .	£174,000,000

On the other hand, the final account of FRANCE will stand:

TOTAL COST OF WAR.

Direct expenditure	£169,000,000
Indirect "	262,000,000
	£431,000,000
Indemnity and cession of territory . . .	264,000,000
Total cost to France	£695,000,000

CAPITAL COST OF WAR.

Amount of first outlay charged to capital .	£343,000,000
Indemnity and cession of territory . . .	264,000,000
Net capital loss to France by the war	£607,000,000

The result is that while Germany gains ONE HUNDRED AND FIFTY MILLIONS on the whole, and ONE HUNDRED AND SEVENTY-FOUR MILLIONS in permanent capital, France loses nearly SEVEN HUNDRED MILLIONS on the whole, and rather more than SIX HUNDRED MILLIONS in permanent capital.

EIGHTH.—The magnitude of the loss to France is illustrated in various ways. The total of £700,000,000 represents the sum of £19 per head among a population of 36,500,000, or about £76 per family. The capital loss of £600,000,000 is £16 10*s.* per head, or £66 per family, the English National Debt being £26 per head: the French in a few months of war have lost three-fifths as much capital per head as the individual share of the English in their famous Debt. The total addition to the Debt of France is over £400,000,000, and the annual charge, allowing for the loss of Alsace and Lorraine revenues, and making a proper allowance for interest on the amount borrowed from the Bank of France, is virtually increased £23,000,000. This is about as much as the annual charge for interest on the English Debt.

NINTH.—The opinion is, however, expressed that France must recover quickly, though the new burden is equal to ten years' annual savings. The thrift of the people will be increased; an effort will be made individually to recover lost ground. A single bountiful harvest at such a time would go a long way to fill up the void created by these immense losses.

As regards Germany, a doubt is expressed whether the Germans will gain so much as France loses, the capital of the indemnity being transferred from individuals to the German Government, who cannot use it so profitably as individuals. It is doubted whether the practice of lending out large sums, though a preferable course to locking them up, will not in the end be injurious.

TENTH.—The financial operations incidental to these great losses and expenses seriously affect the money market. They have been a fruitful cause, in the first place, of spasmodic disturbance. The outbreak of war caused a monetary panic in July, 1870, by the anxiety of people who had money engagements to meet to provide against the chances of war, and there was another monetary crash in September, 1871, owing to the sudden withdrawal by the German Government of the money it had to receive. The war thus illustrates the tendency of wars in general to cause spasmodic disturbance in a market so delicately organized as that of London now is. And the liability to spasmodic disturbance continues, as the financial operations will not be complete till Germany receives £120,000,000, and France borrows £40,000,000 more for miscellaneous purposes. The German Government has also complete control of the market, in consequence of the large amount of its loans.

A second tendency of war is to make money permanently dearer by destroying capital. But the effect of this cause has hitherto been counteracted, although the actual finance has been on a large scale, by the prosperity of the period when war broke out, the diffused apprehensiveness it generated, the partial suspension of trade in France, the accumulation of foreign money in London, which has risen to increased importance as an exchange centre, and the practice of the German Government latterly to lend out large sums from what it received. It is conceived, however, that as we are now entering on a less prosperous period, the war demands, although of smaller amount, may be more felt, and will help to accelerate a period of dearer money. Some of the counteracting circumstances have exhausted their first effects, and the market is left to the operation of the usual permanent influences. The fact that we are coming to a less prosperous period is in this view the most important, and ensures that the financial operations to be completed will have a maximum effect.—[March, 1872.]

II.

THE DEPRECIATION OF GOLD SINCE 1848.

HAVING made a somewhat extended inquiry into the facts of the supply and distribution of gold since 1848,[1] we propose to comment directly on these facts in connection with the alleged depreciation of gold. Such an inquiry is probably not susceptible of any perfectly satisfactory conclusion. The common notion is that, as the supply of gold has enormously increased in the last quarter of a century, therefore there must have been a general rise in prices, and the sovereign will no longer go as far as formerly. And this easy belief has found a plausible confirmation in the conspicuous rise of prices, especially in a few conspicuous articles, which has just occurred. The very notion of a fall in the value of gold was likely to strike the imagination and produce belief; and the notion that a sovereign will not go as far as formerly is also one to which men are prone, although the real difficulty in a period when the scale of living is rising may be to make a sovereign go *farther* than it formerly did. But those who are acquainted with such inquiries will see at once that the common notion, though easily enough accounted for, is unconnected with any valid evidence. It is not a mere increase of supply which tends to cause a fall of value, but an increase of supply in excess of the demand. And supply and demand themselves are not mere accidents. In the long run supply is ultimately dependent on real causes operating on producers and merchants, and the effective demand

[1] This paper was written in 1872, as the sequel to a series of articles on the supply and distribution of gold from 1848 to date.

changes with every change of price. The inquiry, therefore, if exhaustively carried out, would be resolved into an inquiry into the whole causes affecting the supply and demand for gold. It is obvious again that a mere rise of prices even of a large number of articles in a particular year or years proves nothing. Rises of price are known to have proceeded in past times from many other causes besides additions to the supply of money. Before it can be asserted that gold has depreciated in consequence of the gold discoveries, the other causes of a rise of price must be excluded, and a general rise, covering a mass of retail as well as of wholesale articles, and extending over a long period, must be established. But evidence on such points is nearly impossible. Invention is continually at work, diminishing the cost of production, and even producing wholly new articles, so that a group of articles representing fairly the general stock of goods in the world at one time would not so represent the general stock at an earlier or later time. A general change of prices, therefore, between two points of time would not be easily proved, and the work is ten times more complicated when the comparison is made over long periods. In making the inquiry, therefore, we are far from hoping to arrive at any complete results. Instead of rushing at the popular conclusion or its opposite, we should be quite satisfied if the facts yield some results, however incomplete, on which dependence can be placed.

There are two ways in which the fact of depreciation, or non-depreciation, may be approximately tested. The *first* is to compare the prices of as large groups of articles as possible, impartially selected, to ascertain whether there is an average rise, comparing one long period with others. If there is such a rise, the presumption will be that there has been a depreciation of gold—that its value in relation to other commodities has diminished, no matter what the cause may have been. But the comparison, for the reasons already stated, will be incomplete. In consequence of the increasing complexity of production, a group of articles which fairly represented the world's stock ten or twenty years ago, is now an unfair representation, and it will be necessary to inquire, if possible, on which side the inaccuracy of the mode of comparison would produce error. The *second* test, for which the facts we have collected will be most useful, will be to see whether the gold money of the nations using it has increased in greater proportions than their population and trade. Other things being the same, it follows from a general rise of prices that a greater quantity of metal must be employed in circulation to do the same work as before. If other commodities are unchanged, and population and business are the same, then if a sovereign is reduced to the value of half-a-sovereign, double the number of sovereigns will be required to make the same payments. And any similar reduction of value must be accompanied by a similar increase of quantity. No doubt the qualification that other things must be the same is very important, but it appears to be not altogether impossible to ascertain whether the requirements of a community for a gold circulation in proportion to the population have or have not changed, so that if they have not we should be able to affirm that a general rise in prices must have involved an addition to the circulation disproportionate to the increase of population and of trade. The existence or non-existence of such an addition in a given case, when other elements of difficulty can be excluded, would be determinative of a general rise of prices. Both methods of inquiry are necessarily incomplete, and it will be interesting to see how far they corroborate or confirm each other.

I.

We have to inquire, *first*, then as to the fact of a general rise of prices, selecting as large a group of articles as possible. This part of the inquiry is almost done to our hand. Mr. Jevons, in the inquiry which he made in 1863, grouped together a large number of articles, whose prices he compared from year to year between 1851 and 1862 with the average of 1845-50, the last industrial cycle of expansion and depression which occurred before the gold discoveries; and a similar comparison of prices has been carried out in the Annual Commercial History of the "Economist." In both cases the superficial result brought out is undoubtedly a general rise of price. Mr. Jevons, amongst other things, compared 39 articles, both separately and in the following groups: "1, silver; 2-7, metals; 13, timber; 8-9, oils; 10-12, tallow; 16-18, cotton; 19-21, wool, etc.; 23-28, corn; 29-31, hay, etc.; 32-35, meat; 36-39, sugar, etc.; 14-15, dyes; 22, hemp omitted"; and the result of his inquiry was that the average ratio of prices each year, 1845-62 to the average prices of 1845-50, was as follows:

1845-40.		1851-60.		1861-62.	
1845	104.4	1851	92.4	1861	115.1
1846	105.4	1852	93.8	1862	113.4
1847	110.8	1853	111.3	Average	114.3
1848	94.1	1854	120.7		
1849	89.6	1855	117.6		
1850	92.1	1856	122.5		
Average	99.6	1857	128.8		
		1858	114.2		
		1859	116.0		
		1860	117.9		
		Average	113.52		

From these, and other figures of a like sort, Mr. Jevons drew the conclusion that the average prices of the first industrial cycle after 1850 were upwards of 10 per cent. above the average before 1850, each portion of the curve in the latter period being higher than the corresponding portion of the curve in the earlier period. Not only this, but the level of price in 1861 and 1862, when prices were at a minimum point of the new cycle then beginning, was 14 per cent. above the average of 1844-50. Hence the conclusion that there had been a general rise in prices, or, in other words, a depreciation of gold.

The history since 1862 is given in the Commercial History of the "Economist," but although the articles referred to are nearly the same,[1] the figures are not the average of each year, but the prices at the beginning of the year only.[2] They confirm, however, Mr. Jevons's figures previous to 1862, and show a great rise in price immediately afterwards, such as Mr. Jevons predicted. The rise is shown in the table we quote from, by an index number, forming the aggregate of the ratios of the articles to the average price of 1844-50; but besides the index number we subjoin the average ratio for all the articles in the form given by Mr. Jevons:

	Total Index No.	Average Ratio to Prices of 1844-50.	Average Ratio of Periods.
1845-50	2200	100	100
1851—Jan. 1	2293	104.2	114.2[3]
1853—July 1	2361	107.3	
1857— "	2996	136.2	
1858—Jan. 1	2612	118.7	
1861— "	2727	124.0	140.1
1862— "	2878	121.7	
1863— "	3492	158.7	
1864— "	3787	172.1	
1865— "	3575	162.5	
1866— "	3564	162.0	
1867— "	3024	137.4	
1868— "	2682	121.9	
1869— "	2666	121.1	
1870— "	2689	122.2	
1871— "	2590	117.7	
1872— "	2835	128.9	

[1] Viz.: Coffee, sugar, tea, tobacco, wheat, butcher's meat, cotton, raw silk, flax and hemp, sheep's wool, indigo, oils, timber, tallow, leather, copper, iron, lead, tin, cotton-wool; Pernambuco only—cotton-yarn, cotton-cloth.

[2] For the purpose of an inquiry like this, a set of prices at a given date in each year is practically almost as good as the average of the year. The object is to compare the average of one period of years with that of another period, and it is most improbable that in each year prices at the given date would vary materially from the average of the year owing to some abnormal cause.

[3] This figure is the average of the whole period deduced from Mr. Jevons's statistics.

Making every allowance for the difference in the data, the fact of a much greater increase of prices between 1861-70 than between 1851-60, as shown by Mr. Jevons, is apparent. We may take it as certain that in the first decade after 1850, prices generally rose upwards of 10 per cent. above the average of the preceding period, and that in the second decade there was a further rise, which cannot, however, be deduced from exactly the same data. The second set of figures gives apparently a higher series of ratios all through than the figures compiled on the method of Mr. Jevons, the excess being about 10 per cent. Deducting this excess from the above average of 140 per cent. in the decade 1861-70, we arrive at 130 as the probable ratio of the wholesale prices of that period to the period before 1850. According to this, the depreciation of gold had amounted, in two decades, to something like 30 per cent.

So far, therefore, a depreciation of gold is made out, but there are two important objections to the conclusions from the above figures. One relates to the extent of the depreciation which is due to the gold discoveries, and is, therefore, assumed to be more or less permanent. Textile fabrics, and the raw material of them, enter very largely into the table which is given in the Commercial History of the "Economist," the ratios for such articles comprising a third of the ratios included in the index number. But textile fabrics were the subject of a most exceptional rise of price in the years of the American War. Tobacco also rose in price from the same cause in the 1861-70 decade. The great rise between 1861 and 1870, therefore, was due largely to an exceptional cause, and the consequent depreciation of gold, on the average, was thus to some extent temporary.

The second objection to the figures is of a more general nature, and suggests an important qualification. The prices dealt with are wholesale prices, and mainly the prices of leading articles of raw material or of provisions. The prices of manufactured articles are almost wholly excluded, although the number and value of transactions in articles, after they leave the manufacturer's hands and are on their way to the consumer, probably far exceeds the number and value of similar transactions in the raw material. The distribution of a manufacture—say, woollen or silk fabrics—must, from the nature of the business, be a more complicated process than the growth and collection of the raw material for the purposes of manufacture. Omitting the prices of such articles, therefore, the tables omit the most important half of prices which require to be dealt with before a perfectly general rise can be ascertained. We admit, of course, that it would be quite impossible to compare the prices of an immense miscellany of manufactured articles, although a rough comparison can be made of the prices of a few raw materials, but the significance of the necessary omission ought not to be overlooked. As Mr. Jevons remarked in his volume, the whole tendency of industry since the gold discoveries has been towards the diminution of the cost of manufacturing and distribution—a circumstance which itself has increased the demand for the raw material. In omitting, therefore, the prices of manufactured articles, the effect has probably been to make the general rise of prices, which would argue a depreciation of gold, appear greater than it really has been, or even to exhibit the appearance of a general rise when no such rise had in fact occurred. That this is no mere quibble is shown very forcibly by some figures in the tables themselves. The Commercial History of the "Economist" happens to contain columns for the prices of cotton-cloth as well as for raw cotton, and the smaller rise of price in the manufacture compared with the rise of the raw material is very curious. We give the entire ratios:

	Cotton.	Cotton-cloth.
1845-50	100	100
1851—Jan. 1	86	118

	Cotton.	Cotton-cloth.
1853—July 1	86	107
1857— ,,	95	113
1858—Jan. 1	73	99
1861— ,,	86	125
1862— ,,	140	127
1863— ,,	314	222
1864— ,,	460	275
1865— ,,	363	252
1866— ,,	383	222
1867— ,,	227	178
1868— ,,	100	114
1869— ,,	155	131
1870— ,,	173	135
1871— ,,	118	118
,, —July 1	123	117
1872—Jan. 1	141	125

In some years, it will be observed, the rise in the raw material is indeed enormous, compared with the rise in the manufacture, and the difference goes to show that a table dealing mainly with raw materials would err on the side of showing a greater general rise than what had really occurred.

Another objection to the completeness of tables dealing with principal commodities only, and one indicating an error of the same sort, viz., an excess in the estimated rise of price, is supplied by Mr. Jevons's statements respecting "minor articles." To supplement his conclusions he made a table comprising, in addition to the 39 chief articles dealt with in his principal table, 79 minor articles, and worked out the rise of price in 1860-62 over the average of 1844-50. The result was that the 79 minor articles showed a much smaller per-centage of increase than the 39 chief articles. Mr. Jevons states:

"Doing this separately for the 39 chief and the 79 minor articles, I find that the prices of the former have, on an average, risen between 1845-50 and 1860-2 in the ratio of 100 to 116.2, which is equivalent to a depreciation of gold in the ratio of 100 to 86.0, or by 14.0 per cent. The minor commodities, however, give a somewhat different result. In taking the mean, I have treated those which are bracketed together in the last column as having the importance only of a single commodity, so that only the mean of the ratios bracketed entered into the general average. We thus find there are 64 independent minor articles, of which the prices have, on the averages, risen between 1845-50 and 1860-2 in the ratio 100 to 106.76, which would indicate a depreciation of gold in the ratio of 100 to 93.66, or by 6.34 per cent., not half the change shown by the chief commodities."

The conclusion would therefore be, that the more miscellaneous the comparison can be made the smaller would be the general rise shown. Coupling this with the omission of manufactured articles, we obtain sufficient grounds for thinking that the general rise of price exhibited in the above figures is the maximum and not the minimum average. Taking into account such changes in price as have been caused by the invention of the Bessemer process for making steel, we should be inclined to doubt whether it could be proved that the general purchasing power of the sovereign has much diminished since 1850. A table of the articles in which its power was likely most to be felt shows an average depreciation of about 30 per cent., but the real general depreciation, if any, must have been very much less.

It will have been noticed, perhaps, that we do not take into account at all the extraordinary rise of prices this year. That rise has been most sudden, and has undoubtedly raised almost every price except those of cotton and wool temporarily above the level of 1861-70. But we have yet to see, when this is absorbed in a group of years, what the average rise will prove to be. So far as can be judged, the present decade will *not* show any rise above the average level of 1861-70. It was a great point with Mr. Jevons, when he wrote in 1863, that the level of price then established, at the minimum point of an industrial cycle, was considerably above the level at the corresponding point in 1851. But it is evident from the above figures that prices in 1868-71, when they were again at a minimum point, had fallen back to the level of 1861-2. The probability is then that the curve will not rise higher, and we may assume that there has been no further depreciation of gold since 1862.[1]

II.

We have now to deal with the second test which we proposed to apply in considering the question of a depreciation of gold since 1848. The direct test of prices, as we pointed out, is in various ways defective. Even after making the best comparison possible between two industrial cycles, the question will remain whether the groups of articles selected for comparison in respect of prices are fairly representative of the whole stock of commodities. In point of fact, as we have since shown, there is reason to believe that the group of articles selected for comparison being mainly wholesale articles was likely to cause error on the side of showing an excessive rise of price, although the selection was as impartial as possible. At the same time it would be difficult, if not impossible, to compare anything but the prices of wholesale articles, retail commodities being too various and changing to permit of any such comparison. The object of our second test, then, is to supplement and correct the first. It may be assumed, we say, that other things being equal—that is, no change occurring in the conditions which make coin be used—the circulation of coin in a country will vary in exact proportion to the growth of population and industry. If the population has grown in a certain proportion without being, man for man, more

[1] This was the conclusion in 1872. Since that date the index numbers in the Commercial History of the "Economist," on the 1st of January in each year, have been:

1872	January 1	2835	1875	January 1	2778
1873	"	2947	1876	"	2711
1874	"	2891	1877	"	2715

When these are compared with the table on p. 79, the conclusion in the text is fully confirmed for the period subsequent to 1872.

industrious, the coinage remaining of the same value would increase in exactly that proportion. If the population had also become more industrious, so that, man for man, transactions and payments were increased, then, besides the increase of coinage in proportion to the population, there would be an increase in proportion to the accelerated activity of business, and hence too it would follow—this being the most important inference for our present purpose—that if the coinage depreciated in value it would increase in nominal amount in greater proportion than the increase of population and industry combined. The excess of such increase would be a measure of the depreciation which had occurred, and would corroborate or correct the inferences drawn directly from the rise of prices, which, for the reasons above given, must necessarily be incomplete.

The most important—perhaps the only important—country for which a comparison need be made is England. As the most developed country commercially at the time of the gold discoveries, English prices are more likely than almost any other to show the effect of a general depreciation of the measure of value. Is it possible, however, to make any real comparison of the growth of population, industry, and currency in England? The common notion is that it is not possible, the gradual perfection of the Clearing House arrangements having, it is supposed, economized currency in the interval since 1850. But a little consideration, we think, will show that there are really some data to go upon. In England there are in fact two standard currencies—the sovereigns, which are in the pockets of the people and are used as small change, and the Bank of England notes, which are used for large payments. The economy of the Clearing House arrangements, it is conceived, applies only to the latter currency. So far as the use of sovereigns is concerned, the necessities and habits of the people are unchanged. Deposit banking was quite as much developed in 1850, in proportion to the population, as it is now. What the Clearing House has accomplished is not anything which applies to the mass of the people in their use of sovereigns, but only something which applies to the arrangements among bankers themselves in which notes only are used. We may assume, then, that every increase of population and business since 1850 must have involved a proportionate expansion of the sovereign circulation, and that it is only an expansion beyond that proportion which can be considered as indicating a depreciation of gold.

What we have to compare, then, is the increase of population and industry in England since 1850 with the increase of the sovereign circulation. The increase of population is easily ascertained. As we showed in an article on the coinage,[1] the population of the United Kingdom increased between 1848 and 1871 from 28,000,000 to 32,000,000, or 14.3 per cent. In such a comparison, however, we ought to look at the narrower England. Scotland and Ireland do not use a gold currency, and the increase of the circulation of sovereigns in the United Kingdom is, therefore, practically an increase of the circulation in England proper. And the increase of population in England and Wales since 1850 has been very much greater than the average increase in the United Kingdom.

In 1871 the population was	22,704,000
In 1851 it was	17,927,000
Increase in 20 years . . . -	4,777,000

—which is at the rate of 26.6 per cent., or about 1.3 per cent. per annum.

Such has been the increase of population, and the increase of industry has been in much greater proportion. The annual income assessed to the income-tax increased in England between 1848 and 1868 as follows:

[1] See "Economist," June 29, 1872.

Amount in 1868	£365,366,000
Amount in 1848	229,868,000
Increase in 20 years . . .	£135,498,000

—which is at the rate of about 60 per cent., or 3 per cent. per annum. And this is probably the minimum increase of business. As we showed in the article above referred to, our staple industries have increased enormously. The production of coal, between 1856 and 1869 only, rose 60 per cent., and of iron 53 per cent., while the development of the export trade, as respects the quantities of all our manufactures, was truly prodigious. We are within the mark, then, in assuming as the basis of comparison with the increase in the coinage, that population since 1850 has increased at the rate of 1.3 per cent. per annum, and industry and wealth at the rate of about 3 per cent. per annum. The population is one-fourth more numerous than before 1850, and, man for man, their industry is nearly twice as productive as it was then. For these reasons their small change should have greatly increased, even without a depreciation of value; and if there has been depreciation, the increase should have been enormous.

But what has the increase been? Here we are beset by new difficulties. The amount of the circulation at any given time can only be approximately stated. It is conceived, however, that if a minimum amount at an early date can be compared with a maximum amount at a later date, the full expansion of the circulation will be more than accounted for, the proportion of increase being made to appear greater than it really has been. This will be a safe figure to compare with the increase of population and industry, so far at least that any inference of a depreciation of gold will be quite as strongly, if not more strongly, supported than the facts would fairly warrant.

The gross addition to the circulation since 1850 has been about £50,000,000. As we showed in our article of August 31st, the addition to the coinage since 1857, deducting light coin withdrawn, and the exports of English coin, has been £27,576,000; between 1848 and 1857 the total addition, as reckoned in Tooke's "History of Prices," was £22,000,000—the two sums making together almost exactly £50,000,000. But this is undoubtedly far in excess of the real addition. Mr. Jevons, in 1868, in his Paper on the Gold Coinage read before the Statistical Society, pointed out that there was an excess in the statement of the gold coinage upon a mere computation of the addition in the above manner, amounting to about £14,000,000. And he gave other reasons for believing that there was a much larger melting of coined money than was commonly supposed. Deducting a million more for sovereigns melted since 1868, we arrive at the sum of £15,000,000 as a moderate deduction from the above addition of £50,000,000 to the coinage since 1848, the real maximum addition to the minimum coinage before 1850, whatever we may take it to be, being thus only £35,000,000.

Now the coinage before 1850 could hardly be less than £60,000,000. There are no data for estimating the amount exactly, but the figure may be arrived at indirectly. Mr. Newmarch, for instance, estimated that the gold coinage in circulation in 1844 was £46,000,000, and allowing only £2,000,000 for subsequent additions, which has been the average for many years, this would bring the total in 1850 to the sum named. The actual new coinage in the interval was £27,000,000. Another mode of verification yields the same conclusion. Mr. Jevons, in 1868, ascertained that there were 44,000 sovereigns coined before 1850 out of every 100,000 then in circulation. This figure being then £80,000,000, the conclusion is that in 1868 there were still £35,000,000 of the coinage before 1850 in circulation. But meanwhile there had been withdrawn in light coin at least £10,000,000, and there would also be some withdrawals for export, besides losses through melting, wear and tear, and the like which would easily sum up to £15,000,000, the difference to be accounted for. There is a high probability, therefore, that the coinage at 1850 could not be much under £60,000,000, if at all under that amount.

The increase in the coinage has therefore been:

Amount in 1871 (minimum)	£95,000,000
Amount in 1850 (maximum)	60,000,000
Increase	£35,000,000

—which is at the rate of 58.3 per cent., or rather less than 3 per cent. per annum. Comparing this with the increase of population alone, which was 25 per cent. in 20 years, it would appear that there is an excess of 33 per cent. in the expansion of the circulation, which, according to this mode of verification, would be the limit of the depreciation of gold. As compared, however, with the increase of wealth and industry, there is no excess, the production of the staple raw materials of manufacture, coal and iron, having been at as great a rate between 1856 and 1869 alone, while the development of our export trade has been truly prodigious. We may safely say, then, that if there has been a great depreciation of gold since 1848—that is to say, anything over 10 or 15 per cent.—there has been no such expansion of the small change circulation as we should have expected to follow that depreciation. As a corroboration of the direct evidence from prices formerly given, to the effect that the rise of prices has been little more than 10 per cent., if any, the facts now brought out are clearly worth something, although it would be foolish to dogmatize on such points. The data are imperfect, but so far as they go they clearly point to a very limited depreciation of gold as the past consequence of the gold discoveries.

The question will arise on these facts whether the economists were right or wrong who predicted manifold economic changes as the result of the depreciation of gold following on the gold discoveries. The conclusion must be, we think, that so far as the facts have yet gone, the speculation indulged in was exaggerated. A depreciation of 10 or 15 per cent. in the measure of value spread over a quarter of a century is hardly of a kind to produce any social disruption. At the worst it is a 10 per cent. income tax, and though a 10 per cent. income tax would be all but intolerable when levied directly, experience has fully shown that a much heavier per-centage can be levied on communities indirectly without the victims being individually conscious of the process. This would be the modifying consideration in regard to fixed incomes, and, of course, as regards the other transactions of life, the change would be quite imperceptible. The fluctuations of prices in commerce are so large, that this gradual change diffused over a lengthened period would be wholly imperceptible, and would in no way alter the basis of contracts, or the effect of the continual adjustments of wages. In justice to the economists, however, it should be remembered—and the point is also important as a corrective of the popular ideas—that the condition of the expected depreciation has not been fulfilled. M. Chevalier's estimate of the probable annual production of gold was £35,000,000, and he thought it might be £42,000,000; Mr. MacCulloch's estimate was £39,000,000. As we have seen, however, the annual production has for many years been only about £20,000,000 per annum, which is very little in excess of M. Chevalier's estimate of the total annual consumption, viz., £17,850,000. The material fact of production having thus differed so materially from the hypothesis on which the theory of a great depreciation, amounting to 50 per cent., was built, it is not surprising at all that the economists were out in their estimate of the depreciation. But there could be no better illustration of the error of the popular habit of assuming, with little proof, a permanent rise of prices, and then assigning the gold discoveries as the cause, with the assured conviction that this is all done in accordance with economic authority. The calculations which have helped the growth of this popular conviction were not positive but hypothetical, and the subsequent facts having contradicted the hypothesis, the calculations fall to the ground.

III.

The last question to be discussed in connection with the gold statistics we have lately collected, is the probable course of the future movement and its effect on prices. The past effect, as we have seen, is of a moderate description, not exceeding about 10 per cent. in the central wholesale markets of the world, where the effect of any change in the value of gold is most easily distinguished from other causes in the fluctuations of prices. It is urged, however, on one side that the causes of the depreciation of gold are only beginning to operate, that future supplies coming upon an overstocked market will have an immense influence; and on the other side that there are rather signs of a falling off in production, and that, considering the growing demands of the world, an appreciation of the standard is more likely than any further decline in value. What light is thrown on these opposing views by the facts which we have been investigating?

At the outset, we may say we have no intention of making any distinct prophecy. What the actual demand of the future will be, and what will be the actual supply, and in what way any tendency to fluctuations in value will be corrected by a check to production on one side or a diminished demand on the other, are all questions on which there are perhaps no sufficient data in existence for a sure opinion. The experience of the past twenty years should moreover counsel the utmost modesty of prediction. No one in 1850 would have predicted that of the immense new supply of gold then coming into the world one-fifth would be absorbed by India and the East, and nearly two-fifths more by a single European country—viz., France, which would practically substitute a gold currency for a silver one. No one would have predicted, moreover, that the United States would substitute paper for gold. Yet all these facts were more or less essential in 1850 in calculating the ratio of the demand to the then future supply of gold. Any prediction of the future is equally liable to be upset by unexpected incidents. All we shall do, therefore, is to point out the relation of the current supply to the current demand, and on what side the probable great changes that will affect the value of gold are likely to be.

According to the figures which we published in our general article on "The Production and Movement of Gold since 1848,"[1] the current supply may be taken as £20,000,000. There may be some production besides in outlying countries, but this figure of £20,000,000 represents the amount which comes into the general bullion movement of the world. And this annual amount has also been a tolerably steady one for more than ten years. In the five years between 1852 and 1856 the annual production was as high as £29,000,000, and in the following five years the average was still as high as £25,000,000, but since 1862 the average has been £20,000,000, with £22,000,000 on one side and £19,000,000 on the other as the extremes of variation. The condition of production may, of course, change very quickly, but so steady a supply for a long period seems to argue that the industry is being carried on under stable conditions, and that about £20,000,000 may be relied on while the demand continues what it is.

The question of the current demand is a more intricate one. The whole history of the market in past times shows the powerful influence of extraordinary demands. But for the demand for India, and the demand for France, there would not have been sufficient

[1] See "Economist," Vol. XXX., p. 954.

outlets for all the new supplies of gold, aggravated as they were by the substitution of paper for gold in the United States. At the present moment, besides, the course of the market is likely to be governed as much as ever by extraordinary changes in the demand. Germany and Scandinavia are substituting a gold for a silver coinage on the one side, and France is substituting paper for gold, though its policy may change at any moment. The Indian demand, which was formerly so great, has also of late years fallen off, though it would be rash to assume that under no circumstances will it again revive.[1] But omitting the question of these great movements for a little, there appears to be an ascertainable current demand of no small magnitude. (1.) England absorbs on the average about £5,000,000 a-year—about £2,000,000 for coinage, and the remainder for the arts and other purposes. (2.) There is a demand of about £1,000,000 per annum for South America. Our exports to Brazil and other South American States in the ten years ending 1871 were almost exactly £10,000,000,[2] and this demand being for English sovereigns is apparently a steady demand. (3.) The annual consumption of Spain, Portugal, etc., appears to be about £800,000.[3] (4.) The annual absorption by India, though not so great as it was in 1862-66, appears still to exceed £4,000,000. In the five years ending 1871 the amount absorbed was £21,458,000, or over £4,000,000 annually, the extremes of variation being £2,283,000 on the one side, and £5,592,000 on the other.[4] Even before 1850, it must be remembered, India was an absorbent of gold to the extent of about a million and a half annually, and it is not surprising that its great growth during the last twenty years should enable it to increase its demands. (5.) There is a steady Australian demand of uncertain amount, but probably nearly equal to the annual minimum

[1] It has since revived to some extent.
[2] See Table XI., "Economist," p. 957, Vol. XXX. [3] *Ibid.*
[4] "Economist," Vol. XXX., p. 1430, Table II.

coinage of the Sydney mint, or about £1,200,000 a-year. All these demands are comparatively stable, and have practically existed for ten years without any traceable permanent change in the level of prices, no further rise or fall, as we have seen, having occurred since 1862. They sum up as follows:

(1.) English consumption	£5,000,000
(2.) South American ditto	1,000,000
(3.) Portugal, Spain, etc., ditto	800,000
(4.) Indian ditto	4,000,000
(5.) Australian ditto	1,200,000
Total current annual consumption	£12,000,000

The figure is perhaps not quite complete, as there are no doubt many other miscellaneous demands not easily traceable; but increase such demands as we may, the conclusion is plain that a current annual demand of £12,000,000 or thereabouts, would not take up a production of £20,000,000. If there were nothing else to be considered, the probability as regards gold movements of the next few years would be the accumulation of gold upon the commercial markets of the world, and a somewhat rapid inflation of prices, accompanied by a real and permanent change in the standard of value.

As we have seen, however, the extraordinary demands are most important in this question, and we have now to ask how far the annual excess of £8,000,000 in the current supply over the current demand will meet the extraordinary demands which seem in prospect. On this point we shall be inclined to say that there will not be enough for these extraordinary demands without a great increase of production during the next few years. The *first* known demand is very urgent and of great magnitude, viz., the demand for Germany. The Germans have decided to have a gold currency, and in round numbers this means that within the next few years Germany must obtain between

£60,000,000 and £80,000,000 of gold. Germany is very much in the economical condition of France, and is now a good deal more populous, but France in twenty years took up about £200,000,000 of gold. To assume that Germany will use up half the amount in half the time is no extravagant supposition, especially as the German Government to begin with has extraordinary means at command, and being richer now than France was in 1850, will require more at once than France then required. Last year, in fact, Germany, it is now known, coined about £21,000,000, and she proposes to coin £18,000,000 in the current year; and the scale of coinage is not above her needs, and will probably remain high for the next two or three years. In this single extraordinary demand, therefore, there is far more than enough to absorb the excess of current production over the ordinary current demand which we have above described. In addition, the known demands for the Scandinavian countries will absorb a good deal, though it is hardly worth reckoning them when so overwhelming a demand as that for Germany is impending.

The next great point as regards the future is the possibility of a resumption of specie payments by the two great "paper" countries—France and the United States—whose standard previous to inconvertible paper was practically gold. This resumption of specie payments will not cause so serious a demand as that for Germany, because gold in both instances has undoubtedly been hoarded, and will come out of its hiding-places as soon as it is once more legal tender. But the United States at least has grown immensely since 1868, when inconvertible paper was introduced, and the presumption is, that the old hoards would not be sufficient for the new work they would have to do. To resume specie payments the United States must begin by a considerable coinage, and some additional coinage will probably also be required for a similar purpose in France. Here, then, we have the elements of another extraordinary demand besides that for Germany during the next few years; and we do not think the contingency should be disregarded. The inappreciable premium on gold in France is itself an indication that the evil of inconvertible paper is being kept within bounds, and always keeps the probability of a resumption of specie payments within sight. And the financial and political authorities of France will both be equally desirous that specie payments should be resumed at the earliest possible moment. In the United States, again, there is a growing opinion in favour of specie payments, and though the gold premium there is a serious matter, as it is not in France, the United States has ever shown a boldness and thoroughness in expedients which is foreign to the usages of the old world, and the fact of a high premium on gold is, therefore, a less barrier to the resumption of specie payments in the United States than it would be anywhere else. If the public mind in America is once made up to have specie payments, a somewhat revolutionary and decided action is quite as likely as not.

Our conclusion, therefore, is that the better probability of the next few years is an excessive demand for gold compared with the current supply. We have a regular annual demand for £12,000,000 or upwards, leaving an excess of £8,000,000 for any extraordinary demands; but one known demand of this sort seems likely to take far more than this excess for several years to come, and there are heavy contingent demands which it is needful to keep in mind. What the result will be it would be needless to speculate. Compensation will, perhaps, be found in a greater economy of existing stocks and a reduction of current demands, as well as in a pressure to produce more, which may have some result. But if the extraordinary demands continue, and if little can be made of the last expedients suggested, we should rather expect within the next decade that gold will rise in value, instead of continuing the fall which was arrested in 1862—in other words, that the general range of prices is rather more likely to fall during the next ten years than it is to rise. We must again repeat, however, that the point is one on which we have no pretension to dogmatize.—[December, 1872.]

III.

THE LIQUIDATIONS OF 1873-76.

WHAT are the characteristic marks of the great depression of trade during the last three or four years? It is now ascertained that such depressions are periodical. They recur at tolerably regular intervals, following in the wake of equally regular periods of great prosperity in trade, when everybody makes profits or seems to make them. The alternation has no doubt its roots in human nature, which lends itself to an ebb and flow, an action and reaction, in affairs. The depressions, like the periods of prosperity coming before them, have also many features in common. Just as the prosperity is shown by the prevalence of good credit, an active money market, and a high range of prices for both securities and commodities, so the depression is marked by a low range of prices, heavy failures, bad credit, and consequently a sluggish money market. But each depression has likewise its own special features and incidents. The crisis in which it begins, or which it produces, indicates some special development of trade at the time, or some special disease in it—the favourite business of a country changing from time to time, and a constant tendency existing to go to an extreme with the momentary fashion. We propose, then, to inquire what are these special features in the recent depression; this proceeding being likely, it is obvious, to be more instructive than a mere examination and record of those features which most depressions have in common. There is an additional reason for this course. An impression prevails that the present stagnation of trade is unprecedented in intensity and duration, and that it is likely to be permanent. A similar impression has often been found to prevail at such times, and it will be interesting to inquire whether it is now, for once, well founded, or whether in reality the depression is not much less than those to which trade has often been subject, and is not as likely as any other to terminate in a new period of prosperity.

I.

Endeavouring to answer the question we have put, what we are first struck with, in a general survey of the last three or four years, is the universality of the depression. Almost every civilized country has been affected. The beginning was in 1873, with the great Vienna panic and crash in May of that year—a crash which was accompanied by immense agitation throughout Germany and in England, and the occurrence of incidents on almost every European Bourse which only stopped short of panic. Next came a great panic and crash in the autumn of 1873 in the United States, perhaps the greatest event of the kind to which that country, though it has had many great panics, has ever been subject. This was accompanied by a renewal of agitation in England, as well as generally on the Continent, as the rates of discount in November, 1873, significantly prove. At that date the minimum bank rate of discount was in London no less than nine per cent., the maximum being two and three per cent. higher; the minimum in Paris and Brussels was seven per cent.; in Berlin and Frankfort, five per cent.; Vienna, five per cent.; and Amsterdam six and a half per cent. The following year was comparatively quiet, but it was marked by great monetary disturbances in South America, and by a great fall in prices both at home, on the Continent, and in the United States. In 1875 came renewed disturbances in South America, a renewal of agitation in the United States and Germany, and then the Im Thurn, Aberdare, Collie, Sanderson, and other failures, constituting the commercial crisis of that year in England. This was in turn succeeded by a great collapse in foreign loans, which had been heralded and partly rehearsed in 1873, on the occasion of the bankruptcy of Spain, and of which the conspicuous incident now was the non-payment of the Turkish debt interest. To all these events succeeded renewed depression and stagnation in trade at home, as well as on the Continent, the crisis in Russia in 1876 being very marked, and the whole continuing till it seemed to have a fresh cause in the apprehension and actual outbreak of the present war. Thus the depression has been widespread and general, Italy, Spain, and France perhaps escaping with little hurt, but Austria, Germany, Russia, the United States, and the South American countries having all been in deep distress.

This universality, on a comparison with former periods of crisis, may be in fact apparent only, arising from the greatly increased facilities of observation at the present day. There never was a time, probably, since commerce was sufficiently advanced in more countries than one to admit of crises, in which the commercial misfortunes of one country did not react on countries with which it did business. At such periods as 1825, 1837-39, 1857-58, 1861-62, and 1866-68, it is undoubtedly the case that the crisis in England has been accompanied by more or less severe crises elsewhere—France, America, England, Holland, and the German towns on the Elbe, having shared each other's fortunes more or less during the whole period. Now the crisis is felt to be more extended, because we are immediately informed of the events in most distant places, because we see at once the association of failures at centres remote from each other, because we also see at once the effect in one place of the call upon it to render assistance at another disturbed centre of business. But it is also true that commercial relations are themselves far more extended than was the case before railways and telegraphs; that there are wide regions—in the United States, for instance—which could not have been the subject of crisis twenty or thirty years ago, because they were unpeopled; that such countries as Austria and Russia have lately shared more largely than before in industrial development; and that Germany has also advanced farther in the path which makes it possible for it to be the subject of a commercial crisis. There is consequently a real reason for the greater extension of the commercial depression of the last three years as compared with anything before witnessed, while it is equally true that steam and telegraphs, by facilitating communication, have destroyed the natural barriers between the different communities of the commercial world. The London money market appears to be the great equalizer of markets, because it receives the shock of every important business event throughout the world, and transmits the shock of what it feels to every other centre. But whatever the nature of the connection, it is certain that there is a connection between commercial crises in different parts of the world, and that the wider range of business increases the possible area of disaster when once disaster has set in.

II.

The next important characteristic of the depression, and, perhaps, the most important characteristic of all, appears to be that the conspicuous industry which has failed is that of the "exploitation" of new countries with little surplus capital, and whose business is mainly that of producing raw materials and food for export, by old countries which have large surplus capital, and are largely engaged in manufacturing; in other words, the investment in new countries by the capitalists of old countries. Much bad business is brought to light in every depression; but it is the peculiarity of the commercial cycle, as we have noticed, that there is a change from time to time in the favourite business, so that every period has its special trade development, and special trade disease. The favourite business for many years before 1873 had become that of foreign investment, and now the depression occurs where there was the greatest expansion. Direct evidence in such matters is difficult: it would hardly be possible to measure precisely the extent of the various descriptions of disaster which combine to make a crisis; but there are many facts and circumstances which can leave little doubt in the mind that the direct evidence, if it could be obtained, would wholly confirm the conclusion stated.

The order of events in the crisis affords of itself a very striking confirmation of the assumption. The difficulties commenced in the countries more or less farmed by the capital of England and other old countries; whose industries are nourished by public loans from England, and by the investment of private English capitalists within their territories, principally in the form of English iron and manufactures. The crisis in Austria, which was the first in the whole series, was a crisis in a country answering this description to some extent. To the United States, where the next great crash occurred, the description is still more applicable. The South American countries, whose prolonged suffering was the special feature of 1874, are almost a domain of England; and Russia, too, is largely "developed" by English capital. Some of these countries, especially Austria and Russia, have not been exclusively dependent on English capital. They have also benefited by the accumulation of capital in Holland, Belgium, and France, which had been drawn largely to Germany before 1873, through the French indemnity, and had overflowed thence into Austria and Russia; but the indemnity payments, though they helped to precipitate and aggravate the crisis in Austria, did not alter the power of that crisis to react on England. No doubt, in 1873, as already noticed, the collapse of the foreign loan financing had been foreshadowed; but the anticipatory events of that year were in themselves comparatively unimportant, so that down to 1875 what chiefly happened was a succession of monetary and commercial crises in countries dependent on England, but from which England by comparison escaped. In 1875 these crises were succeeded by a crisis in England itself of very great intensity, naturally leading to a renewal of crises and distress elsewhere, though not of actual panic, and the whole culminating in the financial disorders of the foreign loan collapses, which will probably form, in after years, the most conspicuous feature of the whole series of liquidations. There appears to have been a natural order, therefore, in the successive crises to which the countries dependent on England have been subjected, leading to a crisis in England itself, and finally to a financial as well as a commercial collapse.

We have next to adduce in evidence the fact of the great expansion of the business of investment in foreign countries previous to the depression. The great multiplication of foreign loans in the period is now familiar. Not to speak of Turkish and other loans, which were so largely mere borrowings to pay interest, there was a loan of £32,000,000 for Egypt, after there had been large loans in 1868 and 1870; Chili in the same time (1867-73) borrowed £5,250,000; Peru, £24,000,000; Brazil, £10,000,000; Russia, £77,000,000; and Hungary, £22,000,000—exclusive of minor borrowings by guaranteed companies and otherwise. These were the nominal amounts of the loans, and the real money or money's worth ever transmitted to those countries in respect of them must have been much less; but, making all deductions, they indicate an immense direct credit opened up in this country in favour of the States named. The minor borrowings we have referred to were equally important, if not more important, and, especially in the case of the United States, the aggregate of small loans for railways and other purposes was immense. All this direct borrowing likewise implied a great investment of capital privately in foreign countries. Merchants and traders were induced to set up establishments abroad to facilitate the business which the loans brought into existence, and accommodate the wants of emigrants to the new fields of industry. The result was a luxuriant industrial growth in the new countries by means of this vast direct and indirect credit which old countries were giving. Thus in the United States, immediately before 1873, the length of the whole railway system had been doubled in seven years; in Russia almost the entire system of 12,000 miles has been created since 1868; in Austria there had been an increase from 2,200 in 1865, to over 6,000 miles in 1873; and in South America, Brazil, the River Plate Republics, Chili, and Peru, had all been endowed with railways in a very few years—the loans for these countries above enumerated, and especially the above loan of £24,000,000 for Peru, being avowedly all for railways. And never was there a more rapid development of the foreign trade of the United Kingdom. The total import and export trade, which was £500,986,000 in 1867, had risen in 1873, or in six years only, to £682,292,000, or 36 per cent.; and the trade per head from £16 1*s.* 3*d.* to £21 4*s.* 9*d.*, or 32 per cent. The exports of British produce alone, to take the two extreme years, had risen from £179,678,000 in 1868 to £256,257,000 in 1872, or 42 per cent. in four years, the increase per head being in the same period from £5 17*s.* 4*d.* to £8 1*s.*, or 37 per cent. All this had followed a rapid rise in previous years; for the panic of 1866 was chiefly the collapse of a home company mania, and had not brought with it discredit of foreign loans, or a collapse of the business of lending to foreign countries. And in one or two trades the increase of business was even greater than the general increase. Thus the quantity of our iron and steel exports rose from 2,042,000 tons in 1868 to 3,383,000 tons in 1872, or 66 per cent. in four years; while there was simultaneously a rise of price which made the increase in values immense, not only in these, but in other articles where there was no such increase of quantity.

It is sometimes said that the burst of trade which culminated in 1872-3 was largely due to the extra demand for our manufactures created by the Franco-German War. This war checked manufacturing on the Continent for nearly a twelvemonth, besides causing a war demand for certain of our manufactures. But the comparison we have made is of a year when the war was long over, with a year quite before the war, while the most conspicuous instance of increase in our exports was in iron and steel, which was clearly in connection with increased railway construction abroad. The expansion of our foreign trade was thus manifestly in connection with the general expansion of our foreign investment business, and not the result of the accidental or temporary causes which have been assigned.

That there has been a most disproportionate stoppage of the foreign investment business, which would go far to account for the present depression, is also very obvious. I do not refer so much to the notorious stoppage of the issues of foreign loans, small and great: after every great crisis new issues of almost every kind come to a standstill, as frequent experience has shown. It was so after 1866, and has been so after similar years of crisis, although I doubt if foreign issues, as distinguished from home enterprises, have ever been so completely stopped as they are now. Quite apart from this, we have unmistakable evidence of the decline in foreign investment business in the financial and industrial embarrassments in new countries, of which, as I write, the great railway strikes in the United States furnish a new illustration. There has also been a diminution of singular magnitude in our export trade. That trade has frequently fallen off in times of general depression, but never to such an extent as has lately been witnessed. The diminution altogether in the exports of home produce and manufactures has been from £256,257,000 in 1872 to £200,639,000 in 1876, the change being partly due as usual, and perhaps rather more than usual, to a fall in price, but only partially to that cause. There has not since the free trade period been such a decline in our foreign trade, just as there had been no previous example of so great an expansion. The decline has also been mainly in the exports to such countries as the United States, which had been our great borrowers—the falling off to the United States alone being from £40,737,000 in 1872 to £16,834,000 in 1876, this latter figure being the lowest since 1864. It has also been mainly in such articles as iron and steel; the exports of which diminished from 3,383,000 tons and £35,996,000 in value in 1872, to 2,224,000 tons and £20,737,000 in value in 1876; while the exports to the United States alone fell from 975,000 tons in 1872 to only 160,000 tons in 1876. The recent diminution in our export trade is therefore not only unusual, but it is a diminution of the exports to new countries, and a diminution of those articles which we send abroad for the purpose of new works in such countries. So great a change in one great branch of our business would go far to account for the general depression now prevailing, which is thus once more traced to the failure of our foreign investments.

The embarrassments in the new countries were also connected with the excessive development of their capabilities which had been attempted. A very considerable amount of the railway and other speculation during the last few years, has been proved to have been wholly in anticipation of the wants of the world, the evidence of this being an over-production of raw materials and food, the characteristic products of the new countries. Of this over-production the most significant sign was the low price of wheat in 1875, notwithstanding the bad harvest of that year in several countries. There had previously been complaint of low prices in the United States—in 1873, for instance—and of inability to "keep back" crops. Similar complaints had also been received from Russia in 1874. Even in 1876 the price of wheat was slow in rising in the autumn, notwithstanding a generally bad harvest, and the extreme war rise the following spring was only maintained a few days. In other words, the assumption as regards wheat that new countries might be settled indefinitely has proved to be erroneous. The result of what appears to be excessive cultivation is an unremunerative price, which leaves merely agricultural communities in distress, and disturbs their whole system of industry. It has been the same with other raw materials, such as cotton, although perhaps not to the same extent. But in general the business of producing raw materials and food had been overdone, and the crises in Austria and the United States in 1873, followed as they have since been by the similar crises in South America and Russia, were evidence that the power to support the financing of the previous two or three years, which was based on the business of investment in new countries, had ceased.

The uglier features of the collapse of foreign loans also furnish evidence of the characteristic mark of the crisis with which we have been dealing. In addition to the issue of loans, which involved the investment of capital in a fixed form to an extravagant extent, so that immediate loss and ruin could not but ensue, there had taken place in a few years before 1872 frequent issues of loans for foreign countries so called, which were only disguises to plunder the public. We refer to the loans for Honduras, Paraguay, San Domingo, and Costa Rica, which were investigated by the Foreign Loans Committee, and to a numerous class of which these were perhaps the most flagrant specimens. These were simply issues by knots of speculators, usually on the plea that they were for some public work—to which a small portion of the money raised was perhaps, in fact, devoted—but really with the design, as carried out by those concerned, to pay themselves large sums in commissions and otherwise, so long as the public could be got to believe in such things by the payment of interest out of the funds they had themselves advanced. All this was very natural. The peculiarity of the time being the development of foreign countries by loans, it was only natural that the illegitimate financing of the time should also consist of so-called loans. As there had been bogus companies in the days of the company mania, so now there were bogus loans.

These are all circumstances tending to show how much the bad business brought to light in the recent depression was connected with the business of investment in new countries, and its accessories, which had previously just received so great an expansion. As we have already remarked, there was much bad business besides. In the set of failures connected with that of Messrs. Collie, what seemed to be shown especially was a peculiar disorder in the trade with India, the result, it is probable, of the undue investment of capital in that trade at a date as far back as the cotton mania in 1863 and 1864. But the bad business of foreign investment and financing has certainly been far the most prominent.

III.

A third distinguishing mark of the crisis appears to be the singular lightness of its effects on English industry and wages. As has been hinted already, such is not the common impression regarding it. On the contrary, the depression of trade is spoken of in common speech as something entirely unprecedented both in intensity and duration. But a careful examination must prove that, as far as matters have yet gone, the common impression is wrong, and the facts are entirely the other way.

The common impression appears to be due to a misinterpretation of two undoubted facts: first, the evident magnitude of the financial collapse in foreign loans, which has been productive of great social distress among the classes who have most ample opportunities of proclaiming their grievances; and next, the magnitude of the decline of the foreign trade of the country, which is identified with a decline in its whole trade. But it is easy to see that there is a misinterpretation. The magnitude of the financial collapse is, of course, very serious. The novelty of the deception of the public by bogus loans has increased the evil as compared with the evil of a company mania, while the opportunities of fraud were really more favourable to the conspirators than in the manufacture of bubble companies. A State loan sounds more respectable than a company issue. On the whole, the securities of States for a long period had also answered better than the shares of companies, and although also in former years many State loans had proved the source of loss to English investors—several South American States, Greece, Spain, and one or two States of the American Union, having all proved defaulters—yet there had been no flagrant instances of loans which were merely cloaks to let promoters and financiers have commissions. The agents and institutions connected with States also controlled larger resources than had been controlled by the financiers of companies. The inability of investors, therefore, to form a good judgement on the investments submitted to them, their disposition to rely on market price, and other extraneous or irrelevant circumstances, was never experimented on so widely, or with more unfortunate results. Hence the magnitude of the bad business and the ensuing collapse. In the loans for Turkey, Egypt, and Peru alone, the depreciation of securities within a year after the Turkish collapse amounted to about £150,000,000, while there is a total destruction or suspension of income from tainted securities exceeding £20,000,000 a-year. But, great as this collapse is, it has probably affected very little the accumulation or real wealth of the country. Many people feel themselves poorer than they were before, but the community as a whole is not really poorer by the pricking of all these bladders. A certain number of people are simply prevented from continuing any longer the process of living on their capital, for that was what they were doing when they were spending the so-called interest paid them, which was really only a return of what they had themselves advanced. But the whole of the so-called interest was not so spent, a great deal of it, as is the case with the interest of every description of investment, being reinvested, and in this way the collapse really changes nothing, except to let many people know that their accumulations were imaginary. The direct economic effect is consequently *nil*, although the social effects and individual disasters are of the most serious kind. The depression of trade attending a financial collapse ought not, therefore, to be measured by the seeming magnitude of the financial collapse itself, which last may be very great without the ordinary industry of a country being seriously checked.

As regards the second fact which is misinterpreted —viz., the decline of the foreign trade—the common impression only requires to be challenged to prove its unsoundness. We have probably a larger proportion of foreign trade than any other great nation. Our workmen and capitalists have gradually come to exchange a larger proportion of the products of their industry for foreign products than any other people. But even yet we are very far from exchanging more than a small part of what we produce. Our whole agriculture is for home consumption; our coal and iron mining, our cotton and wool spinning and weaving, our manufactures generally, are also mainly for home consumers. A decline in our foreign trade, therefore, is only a decline in a branch of our whole trade, and should by no means be identified with a general depression in business. The recent decline in the foreign trade, moreover, is almost entirely a decline in "optional" business. It is a decline in our exports of such articles as we have been in the habit of exporting as a means of investing our capital abroad. When we stop such exports, certain branches of home industry, which have been fitted to this peculiar trade, suffer; but the capital which would otherwise have been sent abroad, and the means of producing that capital, are not destroyed. In the course of time, if the taste for foreign investment does not revive, the capital and labour employed in making articles for export will be turned to the production of articles for consumption and investment at home. Instead of merely looking at the foreign trade, then, we should look at our aggregate trade in such times of depression, and not suffer our opinions to be distorted by one or two conspicuous facts.

Coming to the subject in this way, we do not see how it can be doubted that the recent depression, although it is very protracted, is as yet singularly light in degree. Our imports of the chief articles of popular consumption, to begin with, have not diminished, but increased. Indeed, one of the favourite complaints about the depression of trade is the old cry of the excess of imports over exports, which is certainly greater than usual, because our investments in new countries have ceased for a time, but which is the permanent characteristic of English trade. It is quite certain, however, that no country sends us any goods on credit; it is England which always gives credit in the trade of the world. Whatever increase of imports there may be, then, is a sign of real ability to pay for them, and *pro tanto* of the undiminished prosperity of the country. To the same effect, we have the fact of an *increase* of railway traffic year after year during the depression. The increase in 1874 and 1876, and again in 1877, has been small; but in 1875, the very year of the great commercial and financial collapse, it was considerable. Evidence in the same sense is also supplied by the non-increase of pauperism all through the depression, and by the steady augmentation of the national revenue, until the present year, and by the increase of the savings-bank deposits. The non-increase of pauperism is no doubt partly due to our improved administration, but no improvement of administration could have prevented such an increase of paupers and decline of revenue as followed the panics of 1847, 1857, and 1866, not to speak of the awful convulsions and distress which marked the depression of trade in still earlier periods. To any one who has even glanced at the economic history of England during the present century, the common talk now about the "unusual" depression of our trade appears simply ludicrous. The people who indulge in it have simply never thought of what depression of trade is. There has probably never been a great commercial crisis in England which caused so little suffering to the mass of the nation.

When we think of the matter a little, it seems reasonable enough also that the depression should be a mild one. Severe as the crisis has been, we were lucky enough to escape an actual panic, with the shock to credit and other lamentable incidents which a panic invariably produces. It is probable also that we were really befriended by the peculiar events in the money market in connection with the German coinage. The withdrawals of gold for Germany had the effect of anticipating the stringency in the money market which a period of great expansion ends in. The expansion was thus hindered from reaching the extreme it would otherwise have reached, and the reaction is less severe. Some good judges are of opinion that we have to thank yet another cause—the high normal wages of our workmen, and their independence of abundant harvests and cheap wheat, as compared with what was formerly the case, so that all our staple industries are steadier than they were. But I should doubt the effect of this cause without greater experience than we have yet had. Workmen will suffer, it is to be feared, in a way in which they have not lately suffered, if another time of expansion such as there was in 1872 should reach its full term, and industry be subjected to the strain of the inevitable reaction. But without this cause, the actual facts of the absence of a panic during all this depression, and of the successive stringencies in the money market which checked the exuberant growth of 1872 and 1873, appear quite sufficient to account for the comparative mildness of the effects of the depression we are witnessing.

IV.

The marks of the present depression which we have enumerated are thus its universality, its origin in the breaking down of the bad business of foreign investment, and its mildness in the United Kingdom as compared with former periods of depression. Is there anything in these peculiarities, or in any other circumstances of the depression, to lead us to anticipate that it will be unusually protracted or that its effects will be permanent? Is the depression, in other words, the beginning of anything unusual or unprecedented?

To put the questions thus explicitly is perhaps to answer them. Although there is much vague talk about existing depression—which is really based on an assumption that it is something utterly unheard of and must be lasting—it is not so easy to assert explicitly what is so confidently assumed. To suppose the permanence of almost any depression would, in fact, be to suppose a change in human nature itself. Universal dulness and poverty are, in fact, contradictions in terms, unless it is supposed that all people will voluntarily be idle when they have the strongest motives to work. Whatever awkwardness there may be in the distribution of labour and capital at certain times, the power to produce and the wish to consume ensure that with the means of production unimpaired—and there is no allegation that the means of production in the present case are impaired—production will go on and increase with the increase of population and with every species of chemical and mechanical improvement. It is thus morally certain that if at any time the industrial machine, as a whole, is partially disused and times are dull, a period of full employment and prosperity will return.

And short of the depression being permanent, its

effects will not, we think, be worse than usual, if indeed the worst is not already past. The disorder has been very general throughout the world, because, industrially, the world is getting to be more and more one country; but there is manifestly nothing in the extent of a depression to alter its character or the power of the communities affected to recover. So far as England is concerned, moreover, all that has happened is that a particular part of our trade—our exports of domestic produce and manufactures—is momentarily weak, just as in former times the home trade dependent on railway contractors or bubble companies was weak. Our new investments in a particular direction have failed, but that is all. There is clearly no reason in this for any prolonged stoppage or diminished use of the industrial machine for all the miscellaneous purposes of life, although it will only be by degrees that new outlets for our surplus capital can be found. All the reasons assigned to account for the lightness of the depression until now—the absence of panic, the fact that the collapse is so much a merely financial one, and the circumstance that the expansion previous to the depression was arrested in its natural development—are also reasons why it should not be more protracted than usual. Some new mischief may of course arise, but there is nothing on the face of the facts, according to all former experience, to lead us to expect an aggravation of the present evils.

Nor do the special causes sometimes assigned for expecting an unusual degree and continuance of depression appear to be entitled to much weight. The British workman, it is said, drives business away by his misconduct and his demands for excessive wages. Foreign nations are increasing their manufactures of the very articles of which England, till lately, had a monopoly. Every import of a foreign manufacture into England, at a time like this, gives occasion for a new exclamation that English industry is threatened. The changes are constantly rung upon such facts as the increased capacity of the United States for the production and manufacture of iron; the importation of certain descriptions of American cotton manufactures into England; the appearance of Belgian and German manufactures in our markets at a cheaper price than the articles can be made by ourselves. But those who use this language appear to fail altogether in measuring the extent of the mischief they point out. A great deal of the apparent competition of foreign manufactures is due to the search for a market which occurs in every time of depression, and which furnishes no sure indication whatever of any real change in the currents of trade. All we know for certain is that on the other side the complaints abroad of the competition of English manufactures are loudest at such a time, and that facts as to foreign competition, similar to those now alleged, have been brought forward in every time of depression for the last half century, without any serious permanent result on English trade being traceable. That trade, on the contrary, as, for example, after the year 1869, when a great noise was made about similar facts, always makes a more rapid advance than ever after each depression. No one can dispute, indeed, that English workmen are often foolish for their own interest, or that some English trades have diminished, and others may yet diminish or may become stationary, while foreign trades of the same kind increase. Still the question here is of the general prosperity, and it is easy to recognize the strength of the influences which are likely, and, we believe, are certain to limit the evils feared, as, in fact, they always have limited them. Our workmen do, in fact, succeed in getting higher wages, as a rule, than foreign workmen; they do not migrate, and pauperism does not, on an average of years, increase—all signs that manufacturing, as a whole, whatever may happen to particular trades, increases in England. It is because there is so much more profitable manufacturing here than elsewhere that our workmen can enforce the higher wages. As we certainly cannot expect that foreign countries should manufacture nothing at all, but must rather desire their manufacturing to increase, there is really nothing in all that is said of foreign competition to concern us in an inquiry as to the permanence of the present depression.

The fallacy in the use of these alleged facts as to foreign competition consists, indeed, very largely in the forgetfulness of other facts which are equally material: that our foreign trade itself is not everything to us, but is, after all, only a fraction of our whole business; that long before competition can diminish that trade materially it must produce a fall of wages, while wages abroad will rise if foreign trade increases; and that although foreign countries increase their manufactures, we are not necessarily ruined—probably we are greatly gainers. To take what seems as formidable a case of possible competition with us as any that is threatened—viz., the increase of the American iron and coal industries under natural conditions. It seems probable enough that in course of time these industries will be very largely developed in the United States. The people have natural aptitude and skill, and other advantages, and they may produce iron manufactures cheaper than they can buy them abroad. In time they may export them to other countries. But how is England necessarily the poorer for that, and how much? We may come to export a smaller quantity of our iron manufactures to the United States than in the years before 1872; but at most we shall only lose the *profit* on so much trade, not the whole value of what we sold to the United States, which was, in comparison with our whole trade, by no means a large sum. Nor shall we even lose the whole profit. We can only lose the difference of profit between what was derived from that trade and the return on the less profitable trade, into which a portion of our capital and labour are diverted. Possibly, also, the growth of the world may be such that the expansion of the American industry will not be exclusive of, but will be coincident with a similar expansion of our own—there may be room for both of us. In that case there would be no reduction of the profits on our own trade at all, although America had become an exporter of iron manufactures. *Ex hypothesi*, the increase of the American iron trade would also mean that America becomes richer, and consequently a better customer to the world generally for other things—thus causing an increase of the general prosperity in which, with our extended and various trade, we could not but participate. Worse things may thus happen to us than a natural extension of the American iron trade; and if it is extended by protection only, it can of course do us still less harm. There is something essentially unsound, therefore, in the continual references to the increase of manufacturing abroad. Our concern should rather be to have that manufacturing increase. To anticipate that the world outside England is to be merely agricultural or mining, is to anticipate the maintenance throughout the world of the least productive forms of applying human industry, and of low purchasing power among other countries. What mankind require for the greater efficiency of their labour is that the proportion of people employed in agriculture and mining should diminish, and more and more attention should be given to other forms of industry. How England should grow poorer as this transformation is being effected, it is difficult to imagine. It appears to be as clear as any proposition, that the general increase of production, leading to still greater varieties and subdivisions of manufacturing than those which now obtain, must benefit most of all the countries like England, which have got the start of others, and possess all the best manufacturing appliances.

We should fully expect then, when the liquidations which have been in progress are over, to see once more a great revival of prosperity. Still more, according to all former experience, the prosperity to come must be even greater than anything yet seen. Ever since

1844 there has been an ascending scale in the rate of our industrial advance. The years after 1848-49 were more prosperous than any before, but the prosperity of 1863-65 exceeded that of 1850-53 just as the prosperity of 1870-73 exceeded that of 1863-65. In like manner the next period of prosperity will probably exhibit a fuller development than 1870-73, and for a similar reason—viz., that the productive capacity of mankind in civilized nations, in proportion to their numbers, is annually increasiag—being capable of almost indefinite increase. More railways and more machinery, the improved knowledge of chemical and other arts, imply that one year with another, in proportion to their population, civilized communities can produce more real wealth than they did before. Depression comes at times, because mistakes have been made, and the wrong things are produced; but when the mistakes are corrected, or some new favourable influence operates, such as a good harvest, the tide flows again, industrial communities work up to their full power, and they are all richer than before. Possibly the workmen at a given place may take out their share of the increased production in the privilege of working fewer hours; but the prosperity is there, however it may be enjoyed. The great extension of railways throughout the world in anticipation of real wants, which was the mistake of the period of inflation, should, now that the mistake has been paid for, contribute to a more rapid advance of general prosperity than would take place if the world had fewer railways.

There has naturally been much talk during these liquidations of the commercial and financial dishonesty brought to light. At every such period there is an endless discussion of such matters, as if the worst evils of every crisis arose out of dishonest acts, and the practical questions were how such acts are to be prevented in future. But while recognizing the importance of such discussions in their own place, I doubt if they are as profitable and instructive as those who engage in them suppose. Improvement in morality is necessarily a slow process, and in so complex a world as that of modern business the efficacy of any external aids to prevent dishonest or quasi-dishonest practices, or an abuse of credit in some form or other, may be doubted. It would no doubt be important to discuss the immoralities disclosed during a period of crisis, provided a great deterioration of character had become manifest; but I should not look for a change of this sort in so short a time as that which elapses between different crises, and at any rate there was no such change manifest in the last crisis. There was nothing very novel in character after all in the Collie frauds, or in the financial swindling which has occurred. The Collie accommodation bills were no better and no worse than the accommodation bills in the leather trade discovered in 1857, or the similar discoveries in other crises. At times, when trade becomes unprosperous, it is inevitable that bills will deteriorate in quality through the desperate efforts of people to carry on after they have become insolvent. The point where insolvency is passed must be difficult to discern for many houses which depend on borrowed money, and which engage incessantly in large speculations. Probably before the fact of irretrievable insolvency is fairly recognized by a house like Collie's, and desperate expedients to avert bankruptcy increase in number and frequency, enormous mischief has been done, and enormous losses to the people who have trusted them are unavoidable. The chief practical lesson to be learnt from such failures is really a detail of practice—the revelation to our great joint-stock banks of a defect in their system which should be easily curable, and the cure of which would mitigate the effects of catastrophes like that of Messrs. Collie. The financing of foreign loans was also no better and no worse than the financing of companies, or the construction of contractors' railways in past times. There are reasons in the nature of times of prosperity for the creation of pinchbeck securities, and the details and particular form of security chosen are not of permanent interest. If the class of promoters is checked in one way, they will invent new methods and new fields of deception, still keeping within the wind of any laws that may be contrived. Since 1866 there have been few companies with large amounts of uncalled capital, the special evil of the pre-1866 period; but the activity formerly witnessed in this field has been equally injurious, as we all see now, in the field of foreign loans. The exposures of the Foreign Loans committee in 1875 have so effectually stopped these, that it has already become unnecessary to consider the particular recommendations they made. Probably promoters will now go into a totally different field, which I am disposed to think may be the creation of trusts or trust companies to "amalgamate" securities, and so distribute the risks. The principle seems fascinating: more than one of the numerous trusts now in existence have been fairly successful: we may accordingly expect an extension of the principle by which investors will be once more encouraged in the impossible experiment of making a high interest safely. But trust companies are really as dangerous as limited companies with much uncalled capital, or foreign loans, though in a different way. They amalgamate securities and distribute risks, it is true, but they add the great risk of a new set of intermediaries between the investor and his investment. In addition to his former risks, the latter, when he belongs to a trust, runs the risk of employing an adventurer or a thief to select and keep his securities. The danger is manifest. But if promoters do not go into trusts, or trusts do not "take," we may be certain they will try something else which will probably be found to answer, so great and so enduring is the infatuation of the public; and the mischief will be done before effectual warning can be given.—[1877.]

IV.

ON THE FALL OF PRICES OF COMMODITIES IN 1873-79.[1]

THERE is a general agreement that during the last few years there has been a heavy fall in prices. The fall in cotton and iron, and the various manufactures of cotton and iron, is notorious, and for the rest the losses in trade, in almost every description of business, have been such as to leave no doubt of a fall in price. It is usually a fall in price which cripples the weaker borrowers, and causes bad debts, and this makes a beginning of losses by which stronger borrowers are in turn crippled, farther falls in prices ensue, and more bad debts and losses are produced. When we see so many failures as are now declared, therefore, we may be quite sure that they are preceded and accompanied by a heavy fall in prices. But the question for statisticians in such a matter is not the fact of a general fall, but whether it can be measured and compared with other facts of a similar kind, and whether there is anything to show the fall to be of a more or less permanent character, and not merely a temporary fluctuation which will be corrected by an immediate rebound; in other words, whether the average of two or three years, including the present, will or will not exhibit a decline when a comparison is made with a date two or three years back. Looking at the matter in this more definite way, I have come to the conclusion that not only is there a decline of

[1] Read before the Statistical Society, 21st January, 1879. The tables referred to in the paper are not reprinted here, but will be found in the Statistical Society's "Journal" of March, 1879.

prices at the present time from the high level established a few years ago, but that this decline is more serious than the downward fluctuation of prices usually exhibited in dull times, and that it may be partly of a permanent character unless some great change in the conditions of business should occur at an early date. I think this can be shown without difficulty with the help of some well-known figures which have been published lately, and which I propose to analyze and sum up, after which I shall proceed to discuss the causes of this apparently serious decline in prices, and some of the probable consequences.

I.—The Extent of the Fall.

To take the matters in the rough first: we may see what the general fall of prices has been by which the popular impression has been created. For this purpose I have made use of tables of prices of certain leading wholesale commodities which I prepared for a series of articles commencing in 1874 and continued for several years. From these tables I have extracted the prices on the 1st of January, in each year, carrying them back for the sake of comparison to the 1st of January, 1873, which was the period, as we shall see, of maximum inflation during the late prosperous period, and bringing them down to the 1st of January of the present year. The result is seen in the first table of the appendix to this paper, which certainly gives the impression of a tremendous fall, continued as regards almost every article from the time the table begins. Thus Scotch pig iron, which is the first on the list, falls from 127*s.* to 107*s.* 6*d.* the following year, and then to 80*s.*, 64*s.* 3*d.*, 57*s.* 6*d.*, 51*s.* 6*d.*, and 43*s.*, the fall in the end amounting to no less than 66 per cent. of the original price. In Straits tin the fall is from £142 per ton in January, 1873, to £120 the following January, and then to £94, £82, £75 10*s.*, £66, and £61, the fall in the end amounting to 57 per cent. of the original price. To pass from the metals to the raw materials of the textile manufactures, we find the fall in cotton to be from 10*d.* per lb. in January, 1873, to $8\frac{1}{8}$*d.* in the following January, and then to $7\frac{1}{4}$*d.*, 7*d.*, $6\frac{7}{8}$*d.*, $6\frac{1}{2}$*d.*, and $5\frac{3}{8}$*d.*, the fall in the end amounting to 46 per cent. of the original price. In wool the fall is from £23 per pack in January, 1873, to £19 15*s.* in January, 1874, and then to £18 5*s.*, £17 10*s.*, £16 10*s.*, £15 10*s.*, and £13, the fall in the end amounting to 43 per cent. of the original price. The fall is not quite continuous in all cases. In wheat, for instance, although the fall in the end is from 55*s.* 11*d.* to 39*s.* 7*d.* per quarter, or equal to 29 per cent. of the original price, we find the price in January, 1874, to have been higher than in January, 1873, while in 1877 and 1878 the price was nearly as high as in 1873. But in a good many instances at least there is a continuous and steady decline, and in some instances of intermediate reaction, as in the case of sugar, the recovery appears to have been for a short period only. As regards sugar itself, the price of 22*s.* in January, 1877, stands out isolated among the years of low price on either side. Altogether there are sufficient instances of a continuous decline, and of other instances where the intermediate recovery was very brief, to justify us in speaking of the whole table as showing not only a heavy, but for the most part a continuous, fall in the prices of commodities, which commenced in January, 1874, and has lasted to the present time. Of course this must be on the assumption applicable to all such tables, that the articles are really representative of the wholesale markets. Short as the table is, however, I believe the articles are fairly selected, and they have at least this advantage, that they were selected in the beginning of 1874, with a view to recording current prices in a convenient and easily handled form, and have not been put together *ex post facto* for the purposes of the present paper.

To show how heavy the fall is, comparing simply

January, 1873, with January, 1879, I have made up the following table:

Prices of Leading Wholesale Commodities in January 1873 *and* 1879 *compared.*

		January, 1873.	January, 1879.	Fall in 1879.	
				Amount.	Proportion per Cent. on Price of 1873.
Scotch pig iron . . .	per ton	127*s.*	43*s.*	84*s.*	66
Coals	,,	30*s.*	19*s.*	11*s.*	37
Copper, Chili bars . .	,,	£91	£57	£34	37
Straits tin	,,	£142	£61	£81	57
Wheat, Gazette average .	per qr.	55*s.* 11*d.*	39*s.* 7*d.*	16*s.* 4*d.*	29
,, Red spring, at New York	per bshl.	$1.70	$1.10	$0.60[1]	35
Flour, town made .	per sack	47*s.* 6*d.*	37*s.*	10*s.* 6*d.*	22
,, New York price	per bshl.	$7.5	$3.70	$3.80[1]	51
Beef, inferior . . .	per 8 lbs.	3*s.* 10*d.*	2*s.* 10*d.*	1*s.*	26
,, prime, small . .	,,	5*s.* 3*d.*	4*s.* 9*d.*	6*d.*	10
Cotton, mid. upland .	per lb.	10*d.*	$5\frac{3}{8}$*d.*	$4\frac{5}{8}$*d.*	46
Wool	per pack	£23	£13	£10	43
Sugar, Manilla Musca	per cwt.	21*s.* 6*d.*	16*s.*	5*s.* 6*d.*	26
Coffee, Ceylon, good ord.	,,	80*s.*	65*s.*	15*s.*	19
Pepper, black, Malabar .	per lb.	7*d.*	$4\frac{1}{4}$*d.*	$2\frac{3}{4}$*d.*	39
Saltpetre, foreign .	per cwt.	29*s.*	19*s.*	10*s.*	34

A table like this speaks for itself, and fully justifies the popular impression of a great and general decline in the prices of commodities. I think it even strengthens the impression. We should hardly have suspected beforehand that prices of wholesale articles not selected with a view to make out a case, but impartially chosen years ago as representative of the markets, would exhibit a fall in the last six years, ranging from 66 per cent. in the most extreme, to 10 per cent. in the least extreme case, and ranging, with three exceptions only, between 26 and 66 per cent. So great a change would seem to make it probable both that unusual causes

[1] The fall in the latter of these two cases appears to have been affected by the appreciation of the paper money in the United States.

have been at work, and that unusual effects have been produced.

We come then to the question which we stated at the outset, viz., whether the *primâ facie* impression is correct, and the fall is anything more than what has happened before, in the change from a period of inflation to a period of depression. To help in a solution of this question, I have availed myself of a table which was drawn up and is continued annually in a well-known "Commercial History and Review," by a distinguished Member of this Society, whom it is not necessary for me to name. In this table (*see* Appendix Table II.) a certain value, 100, is assigned to each group of a considerable number of articles in respect of the average prices of these articles in the years 1845-50, the value of all of these together forming the index number 2200. The proportionate results in each year or period of years since the above date are then deduced, the sum of 100 being added to when the price has risen and subtracted from when the price has fallen, and the results for each year being added giving a new index number. The net result now is the following series of index numbers, the one for January of the present year being my own addition, and being subject of course to the correction of the author of the table when he continues his work:

Date.		Index Number.
1845-50	Average six years	2200
'57	1st July	2996
'58	1st January	2612
'65	"	3575
'66	"	3564
'67	"	3024
'68	"	2682
'69	"	2666
'70	"	2689
'71	"	2590
'72	"	2835
'73	"	2947
'74	"	2891
'75	"	2778

Date.		Index Number.
'76	1st January	2711
'77	"	2715
'78	"	2554
'79	"	*2227*[1]

According to this, comparing January, 1873, with the present time, we have a change in the index numbers from 2947 to 2227, which is equal to a fall of 24 per cent. on the average. It appears, however, that between 1865 and 1871 there was a still greater fall, the change in the index number between these dates being from 3575 to 2590, or equal to 27 per cent. Great as the fall in recent years has been, therefore, it would appear that on striking an average it is more than paralleled by what happened in the immediately preceding period of depression. The explanation, I believe, is that in 1865 the index number was excessively raised by an exceptional circumstance, the great rise in cotton and cotton goods owing to the American War; but, apart from this exceptional circumstance throwing out the comparison of the former period, the recent decline is greater than that which followed 1865. Without any such exceptional occurrence to raise prices at first, there is finally on the average, according to this table, a decline of 24 per cent. I may add, perhaps, though I should be most unwilling to criticise the construction of the table, that it seems to me to give an excessive weight to cotton and wool, and too little to the metals, while coal is altogether omitted. The result is that changes in the price of textile articles affect the table much more than they would affect a similar table into which the metals entered more largely. On the other hand, considering how textile articles enter into general consumption, the table may be more perfectly representative of general prices than if the index number were differently composed.

[1] The index number eventually published was 2202.

But while this table does not show that the recent decline of prices is without a parallel, it indicates another fact of no small importance for the present inquiry. This is, that the closing index number approaches most nearly of all to that of the average of 1845-50. That average is 2200, but in all the years named, including 1857 and 1858, and every year from 1865 inclusive, the lowest index number is higher than that for January, 1879. The lowest of the previous depressions following 1865 was 2590, but the figure now touched is 2227 only. Even therefore if the fall from the highest point of the previous inflation is now less than it was after 1865, we have still to consider that the inflation from which there is now a fall was not aggravated as that of 1865 was by a cotton famine, and that the descent is now to the lowest level of prices which appears to have been touched since 1850. In other words, we seem to have been getting back in our years of depression to the average prices of the period just before the Australian and Californian gold discoveries began to tell on the markets of the world. This does not mean of course that prices are getting back to that average; we seem yet to be a certain way from that point; only that in our years of depression we touch a point much more nearly approaching that average than we did in the years 1868 and 1869.

Passing from these figures, I come to certain tables which were prepared last summer by my friend Mr. Arthur Ellis, one of the young Members of this Society, and who has already been a credit to us. As a supplement to the "Statist" of 9th June last, he published a long essay on the "Money Value of Food and Raw Materials," in which he compared the prices of 1859, 1869, 1873, 1876, and the first quarter of 1878, using for that purpose a new species of index number, based upon the relative amounts of articles imported, with certain additions for articles produced at home. The principal results of this procedure are exhibited in two tables, which are reprinted in the Appendix (*see* Appendix III.), and of which we have the net effect in the following short table in the body of the article:

	Index Number.	Relative Cost in				
		1859.	1869. Standard.	1873.	1876.	1878, First Quarter.
Foods . .	53	49.780	53.000	60.230	56.010	60.550
Materials .	47	41.790	47.000	54.830	40.600	37.925
Aggregate, as above	100	91.570	100.000	115.060	96.610	98.475

In other words, taking 1869 as the standard, we find that in 1873 the average prices of food and raw materials according to this mode of computation had risen about 15 per cent., but in 1876 they had fallen rather more than 3 per cent. compared with 1869, and in the beginning of 1878 were $1\frac{1}{2}$ per cent. below the 1869 level. Considering the great fall of prices which has occurred since these tables were prepared, they may be considered to confirm fully what has been deduced from the above figures, that there has been a fall to a lower level during the present depression than what was established after the inflation of 1865. Even at the beginning of last year prices were lower than they had been in 1869, and there has been a great and general fall of prices since the beginning of last year.

A noteworthy point in this table is the circumstance that the fall is almost exclusively in raw materials. Since the table was prepared, however, there has been a great fall in articles of food, which are now at a low level of price like other things.

I have yet another set of figures, which you will perhaps allow me to refer to before I leave this question of the extent of the fall of prices in recent years. In a report which I have lately prepared for the Board of Trade, on the prices of our exports, copies of which are just being circulated, I have first of all shown in detail the prices of the various articles of our export trade, as deduced from the declared quantities and values in each year from 1861 to 1877, and I have then endeavoured to show the average rise or fall in price, taking 1861 as the basis, by the above method of an index number, using the actual proportions of the value of the exports of each article to the whole value exported in calculating the average rise or fall of price. The result, I find, is that in the under-mentioned years, assuming 73.1 as the index number, that being the proportion of the value of the enumerated articles of export to the whole export values, the following additions or deductions would fall to be made according to the average changes of prices as compared with 1861:

1865	+ 22.71
'73	+ 20.60
'68	+ 9.99
'75	+ 8.26
'76	+ 1.17
'77	− 2.04

Here, again, without allowing for the great fall of prices in 1878, we find an indication that prices are now at a much lower level than they were after the depression of 1865. In 1868 the index number is still 9.99 above the level of 1861, but in 1877 it is already 2.04 below that level, while in 1878 there has been a fall below 1877. Curiously enough also it would again appear that in 1865 prices rose to a higher level in a time of inflation than they have since touched. The fall now is from a lower height than the fall after 1865, though a much lower depth has been reached. Of course this table only deals with exports, but in that respect it is supplementary and confirmatory of the above tables of Mr. Ellis's as to food and raw materials, which are mainly based upon the imports.

The general effect of all these figures may now be summed up. *First*, it has been shown by a general table of prices at the beginning of each year, from 1873 to 1879 inclusive, that there has been a general and remarkable fall in the prices of wholesale commodities in the period, this fall having also been to a large extent continuous, and amounting in the end, with three exceptions only, to between 26 and 66 per cent. *Second,* it would appear from a comparison of prices by means of the index number in the "Commercial History and Review," that the average fall between 1873 and 1879 is 24 per cent., and that the level of price now established is lower than anything recorded since 1850 in the tables referred to, these tables comprising the years 1857 and 1858, and each year since 1865 inclusive; further, that although the fall between 1865 and 1871 appears greater by this index number than between 1873 and the present time, yet there is a special explanation of this, and there is reason to believe the present fall to be unusually great. *Third,* it has been shown by certain tables of Mr. Ellis's that as regard food and raw materials, prices at the beginning of 1878 were lower than in 1869, one of the years of depression following 1865, while prices are now considerably lower than at the beginning of 1878. *Fourth,* it has been shown as regards the prices of exports, that the average in 1877 was considerably lower than in 1868, while the fall to the present level was from a lower height in 1873 than the previous fall in 1868-70 from the height of 1865. Allowing for the further fall of prices in 1878, we are confirmed in the belief that prices are now unusually low, and that the facts shown by the first index number cited rather understate than overstate the change. In other words, it is ascertained, by the concurrent testimony of all the facts examined, that prices of commodities are unusually low, though one of the sets of the figures would seem to throw doubt on the idea that the fall from the height of an inflated period to the present depth is unusually great. The preponderance of evidence seems, however, to be that there is an unusual fall, although it began from a lower level than what had been established in the previous inflated period. I have not attempted, however, to measure exactly what the extra depreciation is, though I should be inclined to put it at between 10 and 20 per cent. below the prices of 1868-71. In these matters great exactness is impossible; without waiting to aim at great exactness, I have thought it would be useful to bring the rough facts together, pending the more elaborate efforts which I trust some of our Members—perhaps Mr. Jevons—may be induced to attempt.

II.—The Causes of the Fall.

To a certain extent there is no doubt or mystery about the causes of so general a fall of price. They are the same as the often recognized causes of similar downward movements. When trade is good a state of things is created in which a downward movement of prices is sooner or later inevitable. A great stimulus has been given to production in certain favourite industries; capital has been employed in creating new establishments, or in extending fixed works and plant; labourers have flocked into the trade, attracted by the high wages; at a point the demand is found to be below the supply, the prices of the manufactured article become unremunerative, and in time the raw material and labour employed in the trade are at a discount. The fall is precipitated moreover by the inability of speculative holders of stocks to hold on in face of falling markets. At each new stage of the decline new sales become necessary, till there is apparently no limit to the fall, just as before there seemed no limit to the rise. By sympathy almost all markets come to be affected, the low prices in one market attracting capital to it, and so weakening other markets, while speculators who are hit in one department of trade seek to cover their losses by sales of some commodity or stock which has not depreciated. This is the ordinary explanation of a general fall in prices; and the only feature in the late decline it would not explain would be the long continuation of that decline, and its renewal from time to time when many circumstances appeared to combine in favour of a new upward movement. This feature is, however, quite consistent with the usual course of a general fall of prices, though it has seldom, perhaps, been so prominently brought out as during the recent fall. In almost all markets there is constant action and reaction as well as the more general tidal movement which attracts attention when the course of prices for several years is looked at. It depends upon minor circumstances, we might almost say accidents, whether a given reaction will amount to a turn of the tide or not. If these minor circumstances are unfavourable for a time, the definite turn of prices upwards may be retarded, although the circumstances may be of a kind that when trade is stronger they would have little apparent effect. In this way it is quite possible, for instance, that the wars and rumours of wars during the last three years may have retarded the recovery in prices which is sure to come sooner or later, although trade is often brisk in time of war and amidst great political disquiet, as was the case for instance in 1870-71 during the Franco-German War. The great prolongation of the late decline, therefore, is not inconsistent with what we may expect at times when there is a general fall of prices.

We have something more to account for, however, than a general fall of prices, viz., the lower level which has been reached as compared with the last period of depression. This may be accounted for in part by the circumstance that the rise from which the present decline has taken place was not to so great a height as the rise which preceded the former decline; although a lower level has now been touched, the recent movement may be no greater; but even if we had not this explanation, or if it did not account for the entire descent which has taken place, there are not wanting special circumstances which go far to account for this great descent, as well as to account, if necessary, for that prolongation of the decline which has been referred to. Among these circumstances I would notice *first* the extremity of the discredit in recent years, and the piecemeal way in which the failures and disclosures causing the discredit have occurred. It is difficult in such matters to compare one time with another, and probably in every time of depression there is a feeling that things were never so bad before. I recollect perfectly well after the 1866 panic the languid and despairing feeling which pervaded the City for two or three years, when there was a prolonged reign of 2 per cent., and for a time discount houses were barely paying 10*s*. per cent. for deposits. A famous article was written at that time in the "Edinburgh Review," on the strike of capital, and people blamed Lord Clarendon for having made matters worse than they were ever known to be before by the explanatory circular he sent to our representatives abroad with reference to the 1866 panic. The Overend failure had also been unprecedented, and so people were satisfied that the depression was the worst. But in spite of the gloominess of affairs after 1866, it must be admitted, I think, that what came to light then was not so calculated to cause discredit as the revelations of the last three or four years. To that period belonged the Overend failure, the disclosures attending the break-up of a company mania of a not very extreme type, and some temporary difficulties of our great railway companies, whose debentures could not for a time be floated. Within the last four years, on the other hand, we have twice had commercial revelations of the most discreditable kind, viz., in 1875, when Messrs. Im Thurn and Co., Collie and Co., Sanderson and Co., and the Aberdare Iron Company all failed, besides many more, and next in the present year,[1] when we have had such firms as Messrs. Smith, Fleming, and Co., Messrs. Heugh, Balfour, and Co., and Messrs. James Morton and Co., all collapsing. Next, there has been perhaps the greatest

[1] *I.e.* 1878, when the paper was written, although it was not read till January, 1879.

financial collapse ever known, viz., that of foreign loans, which has not, so far as known, inflicted incurable wounds in the banking world as the commercial revelations have done, but which has dried up the channels of investment, and reproduced the strike of capital so strikingly written about ten years ago. Last of all, we have had banking disasters quite on the scale of 1866, including, perhaps, the most alarming, I might almost say bewildering, catastrophe ever known in banking annals, that of the City of Glasgow Bank. The spectacle of such colossal fraud, and of the danger run by investors in unlimited banks, seems calculated to create more distrust, and has, I believe, created more distrust, than the disaster of Overend's failure, great as that catastrophe was. Happily there has not been a panic during the last four or five years, although the City has more than once been on the verge of one; but, with this exception, the circumstances likely to cause discredit have altogether been stronger in the last few years than they were in and after 1866. Allowing then for the illusion which present evils are apt to create, there appears to me something in the extreme discredit of recent years to account for the fall of prices to a lower level than after 1866, although the real distress in trade may be no greater. The same result would have followed from the long continuance of discredit. If the disclosures which have been spread over three years had come all at once, say in 1875, perhaps we should have had in that year a greater panic than that of 1866, and the distress which is now being felt would have followed sooner, but the reaction might have come quicker, through the more effectual clearing of the air. It is at any rate all but certain that in 1875 itself there was a reaction upwards, which was greatly checked by the revelations of that year, although another cause co-operated, viz., a succession of bad harvests, which I shall presently mention; and again, last year there was a general feeling that improvement had set in, when the disturbance in the money market in the autumn, culminating in the Glasgow Bank failure, at once threw matters back. The gradual character of the failures and revelations has thus had something to do with the greatness of the fall in prices. When just sufficient time has been given for speculators to take heart, suddenly some new evil breaks out, and prices tumble, as if from an inflated level, from the lower level at which they had been fixed in the first effort at improvement.

The *second* cause I would notice as probably contributing to the severity of the fall is the bad harvests of the three years 1875, 1876, and 1877. It has long been an axiom of economists that nothing so powerfully conduces to depression in trade, and a consequent fall in prices, as a succession of bad harvests. One bad harvest among several good ones may not have much visible influence, but a succession of them is recognized as a potent cause of mischief. The usual explanation has been that the bad harvest, leading to a high price of bread, causes direct distress among the masses of consumers, that their purchases of staple manufactures fall off, that the people in the trades so affected also become poor, and so by a quick round all trades become impoverished. If a second bad harvest follows the first, and a third the second, these evil effects are aggravated, and affairs at last come to be very bad. In addition, in a country like England, which has to import more largely from abroad when its own harvests are deficient, the bad harvests tend to make the exchanges adverse, raise the value of money, diminish new investments, and so injure trade. Whatever the *modus operandi*, the bad times following on bad harvests have been too notorious for the connection to be overlooked. Now, perhaps, we are only beginning to appreciate how bad the harvests were in this country for the three years before 1878. The fact that the great rise in the price of wheat and bread which was formerly considered the worst effect of a bad harvest, and the most powerful cause of the succeeding depression, has not been observed in recent years, helped to blind business men to the actual deficiency. But the deficiency was most serious. The wheat harvest, to begin with, was undoubtedly most deficient. According to Mr. Caird, taking the average yield of the last thirty years to be 100, the yield of 1875, 1876, and 1877 was respectively:

1875	78
1876	76
1877	74

In other words, our wheat harvest was deficient by one-fourth as compared with the average, and much more of course as compared with a good year for three years running. The usual rise in wheat and bread has not followed, owing to the very fact that the home yield is now less important than the aggregate foreign importations, but other effects of a deficient harvest must have ensued. Nor was there any compensation, as there often is in England, in the yield of grass and root crops, but the reverse. Here we cannot measure the yield in the same way, but the diminution of the stock of cattle and sheep in the three years ending 1877 was most marked. In Great Britain the reduction in cattle was:

	Stock of Cattle.	Reduction on previous year.
1874	6,125,000	—
'75	6,013,000	112,000
'76	5,844,000	169,000
'77	5,698,000	146,000

—making a total reduction of 427,000 in a stock of 6,125,000, or about 7 per cent., in three years. In sheep the reduction was:

	Stock of Sheep.	Reduction on previous year.
1874	30,314,000	—
'75	29,167,000	1,147,000
'76	28,183,000	984,000
'77	28,161,000	22,000

—making a total reduction of 2,153,000 on a stock of 30,314,000, or 7 per cent., in three years, the reduction in this instance having been almost wholly in the first two years. Such a reduction clearly implies, I think, some difficulty in the farming and landowning industry owing to the diminished productiveness of the industry, although it may be in part explained by the gradual substitution of superior for inferior stock—the diminution in numbers being accompanied by an improvement in weight and quality—and in part by the substitution of permanent pasture for other crops, the permanent pasture giving a larger net but a smaller gross produce. These explanations do not cover the entire ground, and something is left which can be placed to no other account than the unproductiveness of the industry.

Now although these bad harvests have not produced the effect of raising the price of bread, which used formerly to cause so much distress and depression in trade and a fall in general prices, with the exception of bread, business men and economists have both, perhaps, overlooked what the result must be of such a succession of mishaps to the greatest single industry in the country. Mr. Caird estimates the average annual value of our crops at 260 millions, and if the gross produce has fallen off 10 per cent. for three years running, the cumulative effect on our home industry may have been very great. Instead of being able to save largely, farmers and the rural population may only have been able to save a little, and many, perhaps, have had to live on their capital, changes which would tend to weaken our whole internal trade, and diminish the fund for new investments. In actual fact, I believe it has been a characteristic of the money market since the spring of 1876, at which date the effect of the bad harvest of 1875 would begin to be felt, that the banks connected with the agricultural districts have been poorer than they were. Some have been obliged from time to time to draw upon their spare money in London, and generally they have not been transmitting to

London the usual large sums they have been able to send awaiting new investment. Another consequence of the bad harvest has undoubtedly been a less favourable foreign exchange, although it was only in 1878 that this unfavourable exchange culminated in anything like a serious stringency in the money market, and that stringency was much less than bad harvests had often led to in former times, owing mainly, I believe, to the plentifulness of floating capital throughout the world, which enabled us to attract with comparative ease what temporary money we required. Still there has been a stringency which would tend directly to check trade and lower prices a little, especially when trade was only barely convalescent, and which has indirectly checked trade a great deal by precipitating banking failures, and so causing much discredit.

It will be said, perhaps, that this unfavourable exchange was the result of the excess of imports and the wasting of our foreign capital, of which we have heard so much during the last few years. But so far as the excess of imports is due to a temporary deficiency of our harvest, I think it hardly proper language to describe the unfavourable exchange resulting as due to a waste of capital or to anything very mysterious, when it is the common and familiar, and also transitory effect of a common, familiar, and also transitory cause. Everybody allows that bad harvests make bad times, but unless bad harvests are to continue indefinitely, of which we have had no experience, this cause of mischief will soon be absent; undoubtedly it has helped to bring about the present extreme depression of prices.

A *third* cause which must be mentioned is the extraordinary demand for gold for the new coinage of Germany, and for the United States on its resumption of specie payments during the last few years. It is a little difficult to consider this point except in connection with the question of the supply of gold, and any variation in that supply which may have occurred, but what I desire to bring out is that apart from a permanent diminution of the supply, whether absolutely or in relation to the growing wants of the world, which would necessarily have a permanent effect on prices, extraordinary demands like those referred to would tend to produce a momentarily extreme fall. The reason is that a sudden pressure on the stock of the precious metals at a given period tends to disturb the money markets of the countries using them; makes money dear, or creates a steady apprehension that it may at any moment become dear; and so by weakening the speculation in commodities and making it really difficult for merchants and traders to hold the stocks they would otherwise hold, contracts business and assists a fall in prices. It is conceivable that after such a pressure the current supply of the metals may again be found sufficient to meet the current demands with prices raised to their former level; but while the pressure lasts prices are low.

Now the extraordinary demands of the last few years —I think I may say eight years, the German lock-up having commenced in 1871—have certainly been of a kind to produce some momentary effect, even on the assumption that the supply of gold, when the pressure is removed, remains sufficient for the wants of the world with prices at their former level. Altogether during the last six years Germany has coined 84 millions of gold, very little of this being re-coinage. The accumulation of gold in the United States, again, principally during the last two years, amounts to about 30 millions sterling,[1] the stock of gold in the country above what it had for several years previous having been increased by that amount. These two sums amount to 114 millions, and if we allow for other extraordinary demands, such as that for Holland, which has been substituting a gold for a silver money, and at the same

[1] The whole demand for the United States was ultimately much larger than this.

time make deductions for what Germany may have recoined, we may say in round numbers that the extraordinary demands for gold during the last eight years have amounted to 120 millions, or 15 millions a-year. As the annual production of gold eight years ago was estimated at from 20 to 22 millions only, and has since rather fallen off, as we shall presently see, it is quite plain that these extraordinary demands can have left very little for the ordinary wants—the wear and tear of coinage, losses, use in fine arts, and new coinage to correspond with the wants of populations increasing in numbers and wealth. My own calculation in 1872, in a series of articles which I then wrote,[1] was that for many years previous the average requirements of the gold-using countries, excluding both Germany and the United States, which were not then in the list, had been 12 millions annually But if you deduct 15 millions from 20 or 22 millions, you have much less than 12 millions left, and consequently the former state of things as regards prices could not have been maintained during these eight years. Now that the extraordinary demands are over, prices may recover, but the extraordinary demands must have contributed to the present adverse fluctuation.

These three causes then—the extreme and prolonged discredit, the bad harvests, and the extraordinary demands for gold—appear to me to have concurred in bringing prices of commodities to the lowest level which has been reached at any period for many years. That they would be sufficient to account for much of the effect which has been produced can hardly be disputed, and that they have existed is beyond all doubt.

The question is infallibly suggested, however, whether in addition there is not a subtler cause at work—an actual insufficiency of the current supply of gold for the current demands of gold-using countries. This is quite a separate question from the effect of the extra-

[1] See above, p. 75—"The Depreciation of Gold since 1848."

ordinary demands which have been described, and it seems to me most important that we should keep it separate. It is a subject infinitely more complex and difficult to treat, and one on which even the most skilled, I believe, would venture to give an opinion with far more diffidence than on the effect of the extraordinary demands themselves.

My own opinion is that some such cause may have been at work, though whether its effects would have been at all marked as yet, in the absence of the extraordinary demands, may be doubted. The main presumptions to this effect are—*first*, the undoubted falling off of the gold supplies during the last twenty years. I have reprinted in the Appendix (Table IV.) that portion of the table put in by Sir Hector Hay in his examination before the silver committee which relates to the production of gold, as containing, I believe, the most generally accepted estimate of what the gold production has been. The following is a summary of that Table in quinquennial periods, with the annual average for each period:

Estimated Production of Gold in the Years 1852-73, in Quinquennial Periods, with annual Averages for each Period.

Period.	Total Production.	Annual Average.
	£	£
1852-56	149,665,000	29,933,000
'57-61	123,165,000	24,633,000
'62-66	113,800,000	22,760,000
'67-71	108,765,000	21,753,000
'71-75 (4 years) .	76,800,000	19,200,000

The dwindling of the supply in this table is very marked, and naturally suggests that the effect on prices of the great gold discoveries may not have been continued much beyond 1861, while lately the difference is so great that, even apart from extraordinary demands for gold, that effect may have been reversed. The difference of an annual yield of from 25 to 30 millions between 1852 and 1861, and an annual yield of less than 20 millions at the present time, is palpable. Of course the question is not settled by this consideration. One of the effects of the great gold discoveries was to create new markets for gold itself. Under its bimetallic *régime* France replaced an enormous stock of silver by gold, and, becoming a gold-using country, absorbed the new supplies to an enormous extent. India again absorbed an immense sum, especially during the years of the cotton famine, when her credit abroad was so suddenly and so enormously augmented. Until 1866 it may be said that the market for gold was so affected by extraordinary demands that there was hardly time for prices to settle down into a normal state, and the full effect of the new supplies on gold-using countries alone was never fully tested. But it is at least obvious that the diminished supply could not now meet the extraordinary demands which were met by the supply of the earlier years, even if the ordinary demands have continued the same.

I should add that not only do the figures show an actual falling off of supply, but there is a probability of the supply being obtained at a greatly increased cost of production. The nineteen millions now produced are obtained with more effort than the thirty millions twenty years ago. This means that if prices were to tend upwards a check might be put upon the movement by a still farther falling off of the gold supply. It might not pay to work mines which are now profitable if prices all round, necessarily including wages as well as commodities, were to rise.

We come then to the question whether ordinary demands have continued the same, to which the answer must, of course, be that coincident with the gradually declining supply of gold there must have been an enormous increase of current demands. The increase of population in the gold-using countries alone must have been nearly 50 per cent. In the United Kingdom alone, the annual rate of increase has been for long nearly 1 per cent. per annum, 0.83 per cent. between 1861 and 1871, which gives 28 per cent. in thirty years, while in the Australian colonies the rate of increase is, of course, much greater. Suppose the world's annual supply of gold before 1848—say six millions sterling—was quite sufficient to maintain equilibrium then, which I doubt, the natural increment of population, assuming it to be no more wealthy and to use no more coin per head than the population before 1848, would make the present usual requirement from the gold-using communities in existence before 1848 or their descendants about 9 millions. But the wealth per head has increased enormously. In the paper I read last year on Recent Accumulations of Capital in the United Kingdom, the rate of increase in the ten years ending 1875 was estimated at 27 per cent., and this rate of increase being deduced from the actual rate of increase in the assessments to the income tax, is not subject to the doubts which may be entertained respecting the totals of the accumulations themselves. Whatever the figures may be at the beginning and end of the period, such has been the rate of increase. Not only then must the requirements of gold-using people be increased by 50 per cent., to allow for the natural increment of population, but another 50 per cent. must be added for the greater wealth per head. This would further raise the usual requirements according to the previous 1848 standard from the above sum of 9 millions, which allows for the increase of population only to 13½ millions. The same conclusion is reinforced by a consideration of the quantities of goods dealt with in our principal industries. The production of coal in 1846, as you will see by reference to Mr. Mundella's paper last year, was estimated in 1846 at 36,000,000 tons; in 1876 it was 133,000,000 tons; or about three times as much. Between 1854 and 1876, or little more than twenty years, the production was rather more than doubled. The production of pig iron again has increased between 1840 and 1876 from 1,396,000 to 6,556,000 tons, or about five times in less than forty years. The entries and clearances of ships in the foreign trade again have increased from 13,307,000 in 1848 to 51,531,000 tons in 1877, or nearly quadrupled. The imports of raw cotton again have increased from 6 million cwts. in 1848 to more than 12 million cwts. in 1877, or 100 per cent.; and although this seems less striking than some of the previous figures, it is to be noticed on the other side that the exports of cotton-piece goods have risen from 1,096,751,000 yards in 1848 to 3,838 millions in 1877, or nearly four times. But it would be needless to multiply instances. The peculiarity of the period has been the increase of mechanical invention and the constant augmentation of goods, so that the accumulation of capital above shown is even in less proportion than the increase of the movement in trade which the money in use has to move. It is a moderate calculation that if only the countries which used gold in 1848, including their colonies, were now using it, the requirements to correspond with the increased population and wealth would be at least three times what they were, assuming prices to remain in equilibrium.

Nor is this all. The extension of the area of gold-using countries since 1848, first, by the practical inclusion of France, and next, by the more recent inclusion of Germany and the United States, has no doubt added to the usual demands to an extent it is unnecessary to determine exactly, but at least by several millions. Thus while during the last thirty years the annual yield of gold has been falling away from its first superabundance, the current demands for the metal have certainly been growing with marvellous rapidity. If there was much need twenty years ago of new channels for the new gold supplies to prevent an enormous rise in prices, it is at least possible that more recently the increasing current demands have been sufficient to use up the diminishing annual supply. So far as we can judge, the point of junction of the two curves must have been at some date within the last ten years, though in such matters precision is of course impossible. In this view the fall of prices in the last ten years has been aggravated by a subtler cause than the extraordinary demands for gold which have existed. These demands have come upon a market which apparently had no surplus to spare. They have consequently been supplied very largely by a continued pressure upon existing stocks, till an adjustment has at length been made by a contraction of trade and a fall in values.

It may be said, perhaps, that the usual requirements of gold-using countries have been changed from what they were by the extension of the cheque and clearing-house system, by the diminished use of gold in the arts, and by similar means. Perhaps there is some diminished use of gold in the arts, but, of course, the only really important question in this matter is the use of gold in coinage, and I should doubt if any great economy in the use of gold has been established in the last thirty years. Excluding Germany and the United States, which have just been added to the number, the principal gold-using countries besides the United Kingdom and its colonies are France, Portugal, Egypt, and the South American countries, but it would be difficult to show, I think, that the cheque system or any other system of economizing money has been greatly extended in those countries in the period. In the United Kingdom again all the recognized expedients for economizing money—especially the cheque and clearing-house system—seem to have been fully operative thirty years ago as they are now. The United Kingdom was very fully "banked" before 1850, the growth of banks and banking business having since been no more than in proportion to the increasing wealth of the community.[1] The circumstances are such, however, that a considerable allowance may be made

[1] This is true substantially, notwithstanding the fact of a great increase of the number of bank *branches* in England in the last thirty or forty years.

for the introduction of economizing expedients, without altering the fact that the current gold requirements of the world have increased enormously since 1848, while the annual supplies which threatened an incalculable rise of prices have been dwindling away.

Let me add, that whatever doubt may be entertained as to the actual meeting of the two curves of demand and supply of gold during the last few years—apart from extraordinary demands—all the facts and circumstances seem to indicate that the meeting point must come very soon unless the supply of gold is increased, or economizing expedients introduced and extended. At the recent rate of progress the current demands may be expected to increase at least 20 per cent. every ten years, so that if 20 millions annually are now just sufficient for all purposes, not less than 24 millions will be required ten years hence. In another ten years the annual requirement will be more nearly 30 millions. If we start from a lower total now, say from 16 millions, all the same the figure of 20 millions will soon be exceeded. And this without leaving any margin for extraordinary demands, which experience seems to show are never wanting, so that, as in a budget, allowance should be made for the unforeseen as in some sense more certain than all that is exactly forecast. If the scarcity of gold has as yet contributed very little to our money troubles or the fall in prices, it must at least be about to have that effect if no great change comes. Whether such a change is likely to come in the shape of an increased gold supply it will be for geologists and mineralogists to judge, but it is not reassuring to see how little comes practically of the recent gold discoveries in India, and the re-discovery in Midian. Whether on the other hand change may come in the shape of economizing expedients will be a point of no little interest for bankers and all other business men, and for legislators. Considering the slowness with which such expedients become effective when they are first introduced, and the perfection to which they have been brought in countries like England where they are introduced, I feel great doubts whether much relief can come in this way. On the whole, I see no other outlet from the situation than in the gradual adjustment of prices to the relatively smaller and smaller supply of gold, which must result from the increasing numbers and wealth of the populations of gold-using countries.

III.—What the Fall explains, and its Consequences.

The fact of a fall of prices such as has been described explains a good many things, while the consequences of it, or, to speak more correctly, perhaps, of the more permanent of the causes which have contributed to it, must be far-reaching. There are one or two topics of importance in this connection on which I have a few brief remarks to offer.

First, we have a sufficient explanation in the fall of prices of much of the falling off in trade, especially our foreign trade, which is the occasion of so much alarmist writing. There is a constant assertion by some writers of two alleged facts, one, that our foreign trade is diminishing, the other, that foreign countries are gaining as we lose, from which the inference is that the decline of our trade is to be accounted for by the successful competition of foreigners. Indeed, it is sometimes said that the foreigner is taking the bread out of the mouths of our manufacturers and the men whom they employ. I have never seen this view supported by any careful examination of what the growth of the trade of foreign countries really is, or by a consideration of what goes on in our trade generally, and not merely in particular trades which may be affected here and there by the pressure of foreign competitors; but the question of the fall of prices appears to open up a new view. What if there is no falling off, or no material falling off, of our trade at all, so that all this writing about our decaying trade, and the gain of foreigners at our expense, is only so much writing in the air? It is clear that an average fall of 20 or 30 per cent. in prices must make all the difference in the world. We are not left to conjecture in the matter. The exports of British and Irish produce show a falling off in total value between 1873 and 1877 of about 22 per cent.

The exports in 1873 were . . .	£255,165,000
" '77 " . . .	198,893,000
Reduction	£56,272,000

which is almost exactly in the proportion stated. But we have already seen that while the index number of 73.1 falls to be increased in 1873, when a comparison is made with 1861 prices, by the sum of 20.60, the index number falls to be decreased in 1877 by 2.04, so that there has been an average fall of price between 1873 and 1877 of more than 20 per cent.[1] There is nothing in the figures then to imply that the quantities of the articles exported in 1877 were less than in 1873. To throw farther light on the point, I extract from the report to the Board of Trade already referred to, a table in which the prices of the articles of export enumerated in the statistical abstract, according to their declared values in 1873, have been applied to the quantities exported in 1877. The result is, that while the aggregate declared value of these enumerated articles in 1877 was £147,801,000, their aggregate value at the prices of 1873 would have been £191,530,000, which is within a million of the aggregate value of the exports of the same articles in 1873. There are variations in the quantities of the articles, some increasing, and others diminishing between 1873 and 1877, but the upshot is that if the prices of 1873 had been maintained all round in 1877, the returns as far as the enumerated articles are concerned, and presumably as regards the remaining articles of trade where the entries

[1] And exclusive, of course, of the additional fall in 1878.

are mostly by value only, would have exhibited no decline at all.

It cannot be maintained of course that a fall of values only is immaterial. Profits depend on price, and this is an especially important consideration in the foreign export trade as regards articles exclusively or mainly of British origin, and where a large part of the value is not constituted by the cost of the raw material previously imported. Our trade may consequently be less profitable, though the quantity we turn out has not diminished. But other countries must suffer by the fall in price exactly as we do ourselves, and the question here is not of the profitableness of the trade at a given time, but of its extent; and as to this the impression that our foreign trade has diminished to any material extent during the last few years may be pronounced to be absolutely without foundation. Regarding profit, moreover, I may be allowed to say in passing, a good deal might be urged in favour of a time like this being really the most profitable in the end, notwithstanding all the complaints of depression. Much of the prosperity of years like 1873 is in reality hollow, and much of the dullness of dull times is due to the fact that people are forced to acknowledge themselves not so rich as they thought. But this is perhaps taking us away from the matter in hand, which is that of the volume of our trade only.

To be quite fair, it must be acknowledged that holding our own in such matters is not all that is necessary. If business is to be in a real equilibrium, there should be a steady increase in it *pari passu* with the increase of population. There has been some real check then to the growth of our foreign trade during the last five or six years. But on the other hand, we must remember that previous to 1873 there was a marvellously rapid growth, much above the annual average. All things considered, it is yet too soon to complain of the check of the last five years as indicating the beginning of a permanent retrogression.

The *second* point I shall advert to is the possible connection between the appreciation of gold and the depreciation of silver. It is an obvious enough suggestion that as silver in the markets of gold-using countries is only a commodity, it will probably sympathize with any general movement in the prices of commodities. Indeed, it has been urged by the Calcutta Government that it is not silver which has changed, but gold. Silver prices, they say, have not perceptibly risen in the Indian markets, although gold has risen. Without going into detail on this subject, which would take up a whole paper by itself, and which we may safely leave to Mr. Bourne when he comes to read his paper on the silver question, I may be allowed to remark that very likely gold and silver have *both* changed. One or two of the causes we have described as likely to produce a general fall in prices—the prolonged discredit and the bad harvests—have been as applicable to silver-using as to gold-using countries, and have surely been applicable to India and China, with their tremendous famines and much rottenness in their foreign trade. It was therefore possible that silver prices should have fallen like gold prices, and the relation between the two metals have been left unchanged; if silver prices have been stationary, or have not fallen so much as gold prices, then, as we cannot be sure how much the scarcity of gold has aggravated the fall of prices here, it is difficult to argue from the fall of silver in relation to gold that the difference between them arises from an appreciation of gold only. There may have been depreciation of silver as well, even if of a temporary kind only; the events of the last few years relating to silver—especially the sudden sales of the stocks of German silver, and the stoppage of silver coinage by the Latin union—being calculated to have that effect. The wonder, perhaps, rather is that silver has not depreciated still more. Possibly the stock in use in the silver countries is so large that great additions can be easily absorbed; but the change has yet to be tested, we must remember, by a period of good business and naturally rising prices in the silver-using countries. So far as it goes, however, the depreciation of silver in relation to gold, whatever changes may have occurred in silver itself in relation to other commodities, is not inconsistent with the supposed change in gold in relation to such commodities.

A *third* point to notice is the connection between a great fall in the prices of commodities and a fall in wages. The two things are inseparably connected. First, in certain trades—and this connection has been specially shown of late years in the iron trade—the gross price of the articles produced is so much diminished, that if the cost of labour is unaltered the labourer will be receiving an enormously increased share of what is produced. Say an article formerly selling for £20, the cost for labour being one-fourth or £5, falls in price to £10, then the £5 given to the labourer would be 50 per cent. of the selling price. It is incredible that so great a change could occur without the labourer being affected, and there have been even greater changes in the iron and coal trades. But, *second*, in almost all trades, especially those in which the cost of labour constitutes a large part of the cost of production, there is necessarily some connection, in the long run, between the money rate of wages and the prices of the usual articles of the labourer's consumption, according to his standard of living. It would take us out of our way to enter into a controversy here about the wages fund, but it is quite plain that the real wages paid by the capitalist to the labourer consist mostly of commodities; if money wages remain the same while commodities fall in price, there is an increase of real wages. In some way or other, then, an adjustment of money wages to reduced prices becomes inevitable. In miscellaneous industries this may be effected by the constant action of individual interests when changes of employment occur; by the steady substitution of superior for inferior workmen; by the transfers of business enabling wages of clerks and others to be revised; and by similar means. In more conspicuous trades, where large groups of men are employed, there are notices of reduction on a large scale as well as these minor instruments of effecting a reduction. But nominal reduction must come somehow, unless there is to be a real rise in wages. The visible opportunity of employers is of course the scarcity of employment and the disorganization of industry which attend a great fall of prices; but employers would obviously be unable to continue paying for any length of time really increased wages. There is no Fortunatus's purse which would not quickly be exhausted in such an attempt.

There is another subject of, perhaps, greater complexity which seems to be suggested. If a general downward movement of prices, due to a comparative scarcity of gold, has begun, are we not on the eve of a reversal of the changes which commenced with the Australian and Californian discoveries—changes so admirably described in Mr. Jevons's well-known book? These changes were substantially a gradual lightening of debts for the benefit of the debtor class, and to the immediate loss of annuitants and capitalists, however much the latter might be compensated in the end by an increase in the nominal income of their land, houses, and other securities. Now we may witness a gradual increase of the burden of debts to the loss of debtors, and for the immediate advantage of creditors, although, in the end, the latter may lose by the relatively diminished nominal income of their securities, following the adjustment of all prices to the new circumstances. There can be no doubt that some such general effect as this must follow, if it should, in fact, turn out that a serious appreciation of gold has set in, and the circumstances of its production and the use of economizing expedients do not change. In the end the effect in contracting trade is looked forward to with some apprehension by many of our best authorities.

I do not propose to dispute this conclusion here. It

would land us in an almost endless controversy if we were to discuss whether a constant influx of new money, leading to a prolonged rise in prices, does more good or harm in the long run, than a constant failure of new supplies to meet current demands leading to a prolonged fall in prices. A great deal, I imagine, could be said on both sides; the rebound from excessive inflation more than compensating perhaps all its alleged benefits, and the additional fall in prices due to a gradual scarcity of gold being as nothing when compared with the falls which take place from time to time owing to the simple failure of credit. But while avoiding this discussion, I may at least point out that the most serious effects of this incipient gold scarcity will probably be gradual, just as the effect of the discoveries in causing a rise of prices has been much more gradual and confined within narrower limits than economists were in the habit of anticipating. Particularly at the present moment the depression may have gone so far that the accumulating stocks of the precious metals will be sufficient for a good while to support a considerable expansion of trade—that it will only be later on, as prices tend to get back to the former level, that the real pressure of the scarcity will be felt. A year or two's ease in the money market following the events of last year will however be no proof at all that the causes above described have not been operative and will not again be operative.

IV.—Concluding Observations.

In bringing this long paper to a close, I have only one or two practical observations to offer. The "moral" of much that has been said is clearly this—that if possible the scarcity of gold which has contributed to the present fall of prices, and may have farther serious effects in future, should, if possible, be mitigated, and should at any rate not be aggravated, by legislative action. I have expressed great scepticism as to whether, in fact, seeing how slow men's habits are to change, any mitigation is probable in the shape of expedients for economizing money. But it must be recognized that if bodies of men were amenable to reason in currency questions, and there was really a widely-felt belief of serious mischief impending from a gold scarcity, some economizing expedients could be tried. To give only one illustration: I suppose few things are more unlikely than that £1 notes, or notes for less than £5, will again be reintroduced in England, but the introduction of such notes alone, with all suitable arrangements for their convertibility, would certainly go far to neutralize even such another extraordinary demand as that for the German coinage. The German demand for gold would itself have been much smaller than it was, but for the banking reform which accompanied the coinage, and part of which reform was the abolition of notes of small denominations. The United States' pressure for gold during the last few months would also have been far more serious than it has been, if the Government of that country had complicated its resumption arrangements by the abandonment of all greenbacks of from 5 to 25 dollars, and the prohibition of bank notes for such amounts. There seems a possibility of gaining something then by reintroducing £1 notes if the present gold scarcity should continue. I hope I shall not be understood as advocating such a change, or as being insensible to the weight of many practical objections which could be urged against it if it were immediately proposed. I am only mentioning it as a possible expedient for economizing money, and there are no doubt others. As regards small notes, however, it would seem that at least any change by countries which still retain them in the direction of their further abolition, leading to a greater demand for the precious metal, ought to be deprecated. Still more we ought to deprecate any change in silver-using countries in the direction of substituting gold for any part of the silver in use. It would be nothing short of calamitous to business if another demand for gold like the recent demands for Germany and the United States were now to spring up. Even a much less demand would prove rather a serious affair before a very long time elapsed.

V.

RECENT CHANGES IN PRICES AND INCOMES COMPARED.[1]

CONTENTS: Preliminary—The Appreciation of Gold—The Degree and Character of the Appreciation—The Appreciation or Depreciation of Silver—Characters of Appreciation and Depreciation at different Periods—The Causes of Appreciation and Depreciation—The Redistribution of Wealth—The Future Course of Prices.

Preliminary.

ALMOST ten years ago I read a paper to the Society on "The Fall of Prices of Commodities since 1873,"[2] in which the suggestion was made that we were probably then in presence of, or about to be in the presence of, the phenomenon known to economists as appreciation of money, *i.e.*, as our money is gold, appreciation of gold. The subject has since been widely discussed as a branch of the great bimetallic controversy, but I have not myself engaged in it except to reiterate the original suggestion in a paper on "Trade Depression and Low Prices" in 1885, and to discuss generally some aspects of the theory of the relation of the quantity of money to prices. It may now be permitted to me to return to the topic, and to explain more fully than I have hitherto thought of doing the extent and nature of the appreciation which was only a little more than apprehended when I wrote in 1879, and some of the problems that arise for discussion in connection with it. In doing so I hope to be excused if the bearings or alleged bearings of the discussion on the bimetallic controversy are avoided.

[1] Read before the Royal Statistical Society, 18th December, 1888. For Appendices see Statistical Society's "Journal."

[2] See Statistical Society's "Journal," March, 1879, and preceding essay.

Mr. Bagehot said in his "Lombard Street" that he proposed to keep clear in that book of the Bank Charter Act, because if he spoke on that subject nobody would heed what he said on any other. It would be much the same now with bimetallism: if that topic were to be touched upon, the main topic would be forgotten. It is of the utmost importance, however, that the question of the appreciation of money at the present time should be discussed for its own sake as a question of fact merely, and as a purely statistical rather than an economic question; a practical currency controversy interposed only confuses issues of the utmost consequence.

There is the more reason to keep clear of all controversy because it may be hoped that much of the discussion which has gone on will be shown to be verbal only, or to arise from mutual misunderstanding of terms. The leading facts are not really in dispute, and the only question is how to arrange and name them and use them in other discussions. When the phrase is properly limited and defined, the appreciation of gold of late years will be found to be in reality universally admitted, although in words opposed and controverted by many. Limitation and correct definition will enable us also to explain in what sense and to what degree, if any, silver has depreciated.

It will be convenient to begin with a few explanations and definitions.

First it is convenient to employ the phrases appreciation of money and depreciation of money in a strict study of the subject, and when the expressions are used scientifically, as the mere equivalents of the fall or rise of the prices of those articles or groups of articles with which money is compared. In other words, in this sense appreciation of gold would be only another phrase for a rise in the purchasing power of gold—depreciation for a fall in that purchasing power.

The phrases have no doubt been used as bearing a different meaning, though a meaning, it is to be feared, not very clearly defined, and I should not pledge myself that there is no passage in my own writings, though I trust I have generally been careful, which does not seem to read into the phrases a larger meaning than what is here expressed, but the convenience of strict definition, if it can be adhered to, is self evident. It agrees best, moreover, with the original literary use of the expression, purchasing power of money, and if the phrases did not exist in this sense, it would be absolutely necessary to invent phrases that could be so used.

It will be observed, moreover—and this is most important—that the phrases are themselves incomplete. To make them intelligible we must always understand or sub-understand some definite thing or things with which the money is compared. Instead of the general phrases, appreciation or depreciation of gold, appreciation or depreciation of silver, appreciation or depreciation of money of any kind, we ought to say in each case, appreciation or rise in the purchasing power of gold measured by wheat, or pig iron, or copper, or a certain group of articles arranged in a way so as to show a mean or average; and so on: whether we speak of gold or silver, or any other kind of money, always there must be something definite said or understood.

It may be convenient to assume afterwards that what is true of the measurement of gold or silver, or any sort of money, by one article or a group of articles, would be true if an average of all articles could be constructed; but always the scientific language which is exactly true is definite enough, and a clear line should be drawn between what is exactly known and what is inferred.

Confusion has arisen because a convenient shorthand phrase has come to be used dissociated from its primary uses, and its necessary limitations have been forgotten. The origin of inquiries as to changes in the purchasing power of money, was largely historical. What a historian sometimes wants is to be able to say that a certain payment two or three centuries ago represents so much in the money of a different time, usually the present. But all that has ever been proposed, or is necessary, for such purposes, is to measure the money by certain other articles, and give an approximate answer more or less complete. What the measure should be, for what purposes it can be used, and so on, are later questions, but the idea of an external measure of money of some kind is necessarily involved in any references to changes in its purchasing power. When we speak scientifically we must say the purchasing power of money over certain definite things, although popularly our idea may be the purchasing power of money over things in general, or the bulk of things.

The next preliminary point is that in dealing with the appreciation or depreciation of money, the nature of the economic movement in the country where the appreciation or depreciation takes place, or in two or more countries which may be compared, ought to be carefully considered. The signs of appreciation or depreciation are not the same in any two cases unless the economic movement is the same.

Thus in a stationary community, which goes on from year to year with the same population, producing and consuming the same things, and neither advancing nor going back, appreciation or depreciation of money, should it take place from any cause, would probably have uniform effects. The fall or rise of prices would extend to all commodities equally, and to wages and incomes also. A rise would entail a proportionate increase of wages and incomes; a fall a proportionate decrease. Nothing would be easier apparently than to ascertain appreciation or depreciation in such a community.

Of course, however, there is no such ideal community. In actual life the disturbance of money alone would probably disturb a great deal besides.

The case of an absolutely retrograding community, which is no doubt a very rare one, would supply somewhat different signs. It is quite conceivable that in such a community there might be a depreciation of money measured by commodities or large groups of them, and yet there would be no apparent increase of wages or incomes, because, the community retrograding, there is less of real things to divide, and there being in fact as much income expressed in money to go round as before, the loss to the community by its retrogression might be measured by the percentage rise of prices. Superficial observers would, however, be apt to say that because there is no rise of wages or incomes there is no depreciation of money, although there is unquestionably depreciation when commodities are the measure.

Retrogression is a rare case, but advance is not so rare, and we must consider carefully what may be the signs of appreciation or depreciation in an advancing community as distinguished from a stationary community.

Three kinds of appreciation and depreciation—six cases in all, if not seven—may apparently be distinguished plainly in such a community:

1. As regards appreciation there may be a case of falling prices of commodities coupled with stationary incomes and wages. In this case the fall of prices might be the measure of the increase of the return to the industry of the community, assuming that the labour employed in services improves generally as does the labour employed in the production of commodities. Still measured by commodities there may be an appreciation of money, although the diminution of wages and incomes which accompanies some forms of appreciation of money is absent.

2. There may be a case of less wages and incomes per head, in which case the fall of prices would be greater than in the first case, and the *difference* between it and the fall in wages and incomes might represent the advance in the return to the industry of the community. But the only distinction between the first and second instances is clearly the degree of appreciation. There can be no warrant for saying that in an

advancing community appreciation as it has been here defined may not take place without an actual diminution of wages and incomes.

3. There may be a case of not only less wages and incomes per head, but an absolute diminution of the aggregate of all individual incomes, notwithstanding an increase of population. In this last case the fall of prices and diminution of wages and incomes per head would be more severe than in the second case, where the diminution per head might not be so great as to prevent altogether the growth of the aggregate of individual incomes. Still this extreme form of the appreciation of money must not be looked for in every instance.

4. As regards depreciation again, there may be a case of stationary prices of commodities coupled with increasing wages and incomes per head. The increase in the latter case might correspond with the increase of the return to the industry of the community.

The important point to understand is that there may be a case of what may properly be described as depreciation of money where prices do not rise, just as there may be a case of appreciation where incomes and wages do not fall. Measured by incomes, though not by the prices of commodities, there may unquestionably in such a case be depreciation.

5. Depreciation may go so far that there is a rise of wages and incomes more than in proportion to the increase of the return to the industry of the community, in which case the improvement in the latter might be measured by the *difference* between the rise in the prices of commodities and the rise in wages and incomes.

6. Depreciation may go so far that there is absolute inflation in all prices along with a continued cheapening of production. In this last case along with the rise in commodities there would be an enormous rise in wages and incomes. But there may well be depreciation rightly called such without this extreme.

There is also as already hinted a seventh case, which may be described as intermediate between the mildest types of appreciation and depreciation above specified, a case namely in which, on the one hand, prices fall a little, showing appreciation measured by commodities, *pro tanto*, and on the other hand wages and incomes rise a little, showing depreciation measured by incomes *pro tanto*. Such a case may in fact occur in an advancing community, however it may be described.

It is expedient to put the cases thus generally, in order to understand in what class in each country respectively we are to put the appreciation of gold or depreciation of silver at the present time. There is nothing but confusion possible so long as people argue that because wages have not fallen lately there is no appreciation of gold, or because prices have not risen in silver countries, or have even fallen a little, therefore there is nothing which can properly be described as depreciation of silver in those countries. The economic movement of the country concerned, and the degree of the appreciation or depreciation of money, according to the measure of the money employed, are first to be understood. It will be found also, I believe, that one of the puzzles of the matter is strictly connected with this point. The figures of appreciation of gold, measured by commodities, in European countries, have not been balanced by signs of depreciation of silver in silver-using non-European countries. If the economic movement in India has been different from that in England, if an increase of the return to industry has been absent there, or has been at a different rate, may it not be somewhat difficult to state what are the proper signs of depreciation in India to be looked for?

A short preliminary explanation may be useful on yet another point.

A rise or fall between two dates in the purchasing power of money—an appreciation or depreciation of money—in itself implies a contraction or expansion of money. There is relative contraction or expansion, and this is true on any view of the relation of money to prices. Whether the quantity of money in use is the cause or the effect of a given state of prices, or partly the one and partly the other, a low range of prices means less employment for money than there would otherwise be, and a high range of prices means more employment. Consequently when prices change from high to low or from low to high, there must be in the former case contraction, and in the latter expansion of money. Absolutely there may or may not be less or more money at the latter date compared than at the starting, the absolute amounts being dependent on many causes, such as change in people's habits and the like, but relatively there must always be contraction or expansion.

In connection with this last point yet another explanation may be made. Whatever the thing used to measure the purchasing power of money may be, it must be treated while so used as an absolute measure, and when we do so, it becomes necessary to treat the rise or fall in gold as due to a change of demand for, or change of supply of gold, leaving out all consideration of changes in the measure itself. This is done every day when money is the measure; we neglect any changes in money itself, and treat only of demand and supply of the things measured. For those purposes where money in turn becomes the thing measured, and a commodity or group of commodities or the bulk of commodities becomes the measure, it is equally necessary to consider all the changes as arising from the demand or supply of the thing measured, *i.e.*, money.

The question is largely one of language, and the two processes, viz., using money and commodities alternately as measures one of the other, are not inconsistent. The one variable is simply put against the other the better to understand the phenomena according to the special object in view. There is also a clear distinction between the cases where money is the measure, and those where another measure is sought. Money has become money because it changes least in short periods. For short periods therefore, and for comparing one commodity with another, in those periods, money is the common measure; any changes in it may practically be disregarded. But for longer periods, as already pointed out, the convenience of a different measure is felt. When we desire to know what the real wealth of a previous generation was compared with the present, some of the things which make wealth are found to be a better measure than money. Money then seems to change more from generation to generation than any other commodity almost compared with the average of the mass. But there would be no occasion for using a measure for money at all, unless the changes in the money were of such a kind that for the purpose in hand the changes in the measure used could be neglected.

The Appreciation of Gold.

Passing from these preliminary points, I begin by referring back to my former papers, and asking whether the suggestion there thrown out has since been confirmed by the facts, and in what sense there has been appreciation of gold in recent years.

Two things were stated with regard to the connection between the low prices of 1879, and the contraction of gold which had taken place in the years following 1873. The first was that the events in the money market consequent on the gold withdrawals for Germany, and for the resumption of specie payments in the United States, had contributed to the fall of prices by acting on the discount market, and assisting an oscillation from a credit to a discredit range of prices. This was an obvious and palpable fact of the time, but I laid no great stress on it. Oscillations in the money market and prices incidental to the ebb and flow of credit are familiar phenomena, and it could not be said in 1879 that the oscillation towards discredit was so very much more than usual, that apart from other circumstances the low prices should have been deemed remarkable. The second suggestion, however, was that although it was then early to speculate, there was reason to apprehend we were in the presence of, or about to be in the presence of, the phenomenon known to economists as appreciation of money. I did not define the terms, assuming them to be sufficiently understood by those interested, but the meaning, I believe, was clear enough. Appreciation or depreciation of money being phenomena only to be measured at long intervals, for it is only at such intervals that it becomes expedient to make commodities a measure, and so to measure money, what I had in my mind was to suggest that the course of prices in the immediately following years would probably deserve attention; that when time had passed for another cycle of credit and discredit, it would clearly be seen whether prices had fallen to a permanently lower level than in the period before 1873, in which case there would be no question as to an "appreciation of money" having occurred. The reasons for that opinion, in which to a large extent there was only a repetition of what I had said so long ago as 1872, appeared also to be overwhelmingly strong. There was visibly a strong "pull" upon gold, which was passing out of circulation in England instead of passing into it, as in the twenty years before 1873. The production was obviously diminishing; there was also to all appearance an increase of the cost of producing gold, which pointed in the same direction of an increase of its purchasing power. All this was said with the least possible amount of theorizing. The quantity of money in supply and the demands upon it were certainly assumed to have some connection with prices, the theory of the connection having never before been disputed to my knowledge, but I did nothing more than point out that if the world was about to witness an appreciation of gold—a rise in its purchasing power measured by commodities, and ascertained after long intervals, so as to allow for minor oscillations and to permit of the use of the fact for the comparisons to which it is adapted—then there were sufficient facts in the supply of and demand for gold to account for the appreciation.

If the test of prophecy be the event, there was never surely a better forecast. The fall of prices in such a general way as to amount to what is known as a rise in the purchasing power of gold is generally, I might almost say universally, admitted. There is much assertion in some quarters that there is no appreciation of gold, but the assertion is made by those who attach a meaning, or think they attach a meaning, to the words which I confess I am unable to make out and express in my own language, and there can at any rate be no doubt that, as the phrase is here limited and defined, we have for some years been in the presence of the phenomenon known as appreciation of money. Measured by any commodity or group of commodities usually taken as the measure for such a purpose, gold is undoubtedly possessed of more purchasing power than was the case fifteen or twenty years ago, and this high purchasing power has been continued over a long enough period to allow for all minor oscillations.

It would be slaying the slain to recapitulate all the facts as to the fall of prices; but as the question was first distinctly raised at our meetings, and the record may be convenient, we may refer briefly to the evidence adduced in 1879, and see how the tables look when continued to the present date, and what additional evidence has been worked up.

Let me first refer to the short table with which the paper in 1879 began, and which was made use of, it will be remembered, as an extraneous table which had been commenced several years before for another purpose, and which, though short, seems to me to contain a great deal:

A.—*Prices of Leading Wholesale Commodities in January*, 1873, 1879, 1883, *and* 1885, *and December*, 1888, *compared.*

		1873.	1879.	1883.	1885.	1888.
Scotch pig iron . . .	per ton	127*s.*	43*s.*	47*s.* 8*d.*	41*s.* 9*d.*	41*s.* 11*d.*
Coals	,,	30*s.*	19*s.*	17*s.* 6*d.*	18*s.*	17*s.* 9*d.*
Copper, Chili bars . .	,,	£91	£57	£65	£48½	£78
Straits tin	,,	£142	£61	£93	£77½	£101½
Wheat, Gazette average	per qr.	55*s.* 11*d.*	39*s.* 7*d.*	40*s.* 4*d.*	34*s.* 11*d.*	31*s.* 9*d.*
,, red spring, at New York . .	per bshl.	$1.70	$1.10	$1.18	91*c.*	106½*c.*[1]
Flour, town made . .	per sack.	47*s.* 6*d.*	37*s.*	38*s.*	32*s.*	33*s.*
,, New York price	per brl.	$7.5	$3.70	$4.30	$3.25	$3.60
Beef, inferior . . .	per 8 lbs.	3*s.* 10*d.*	2*s.* 10*d.*	4*s.* 4*d.*	4*s.*	2*s.* 8*d.*
,, prime small . .	,,	5*s.* 3*d.*	4*s.* 9*d.*	6*s.*	5*s.* 4*d.*	4*s.* 2*d.*
Cotton, middling upland	per lb.	10*d.*	5⅜*d.*	5 11/16*d.*	6*d.*	5 7/16*d.*
Wool	per pack.	£23	£13	£11	£11	£11
Sugar, Manilla muscavado	per cwt.	21*s.* 6*d.*	16*s.*	16*s.* 6*d.*	10*s.*	13*s.* 3*d.*[2]
Coffee, Ceylon, good red	,,	80*s.*	65*s.*	78*s.* 6*d.*	71*s.*	91*s.*[3]
Pepper, black Malabar	per lb.	7*d.*	4¼*d.*	5¾*d.*	8*d.*	7⅝*d.*
Saltpetre, foreign . .	per cwt.	29*s.*	19*s.*	19*s.*	15*s.* 3*d.*	16*s.* 6*d.*

The advantage of this table is that it leaves off at a point when trade is good, and there has been a good deal of inflation in different quarters, but although some prices are higher now than in 1885, they are still in very few cases higher than in 1883, while they are far below the level of 1873, and a good deal below the level of 1879; the latter, it must be remembered, being a year of depression, while the present is a year of expansion. The fact of continuously low prices for the bulk of staple articles is accordingly established by this short table, and this is what is meant by an appreciation of gold measured by commodities. There may be no appreciation, using the words in some sense not clearly defined; but that if we measure by the mean or average

[1] Corner.

[2] In 1888 this is the quotation of Brown West Indian. I have been unable to find a quotation for "Manilla Muscavado" in the usual price list; but the price of Brown West Indian in 1885 was nearly the same as that here given for Manilla Muscavado.

[3] This is Ceylon Plan. Mid., as I do not find the old quality quoted in the lists before me. The price taken in 1885 was rather higher than Ceylon Plan. Mid. at that time, but the difference was not material, and I have now taken the top price instead of the mean price.

of the articles named there is a rise in the purchasing power of gold is self evident. The phrase is only a synonym for the fall of prices. There can be no dispute about the fact.

To the same effect are the conclusions from the index numbers, of which there has been so much talk of late years—the "Economist" index number, Mr. Sauerbeck's number, Dr. Soetbeer's number, and the Board of Trade index number, the latter based on the average prices of imports and exports. These numbers are so well known that I may simply copy a few extracts from the records and place them side by side, along with similar extracts for the price of silver, leaving them to tell their own tale. The table, of course, could be easily enlarged:

B.—*Comparison of the Index Numbers of the "Economist," Mr. Sauerbeck, Board of Trade Import and Export Prices, Dr. Soetbeer, and an American Index Number.*

		Average Years, 1868-77.	Average Years, 1878-87	Decrease in Second Period.	
				Amount.	Per Cent.
I. "Economist"		2750	2300	450	16½
II. Sauerbeck		100	79	21	21
III. Soetbeer [1]		129	120	9	8
IV. American [2]		113	93	20	18
V. Board of Trade import and export prices	Exports [3]	85.7	59.9	25.8	30
	Imports [3]	85.6	71.7	13.9	16
VI. Silver (Sauerbeck)		100	82	18	18

Thus, whichever of these measures be adopted, we

[1] 1866-75 and 1876-85.

[2] 1866-70 and 1876-80. The American figures are not later than 1880. See Appendix III., appendix to first report of Royal Commission on Trade Depression.

[3] Figures of 1873 and 1883. These figures not being calculated for every year, it is not possible to give an average of a ten-yearly period; but the results would be much the same comparing any other years at ten years' interval.

are equally led to the conclusion that, measured by staple articles, no matter how we select them, gold is found to have increased its purchasing power; and the increase has lasted over a long enough period to allow for minor fluctuations, and to show a change which can be made use of for such comparisons as a rise or fall in the purchasing power of money is adapted to illustrate.

In my evidence before the Royal Commission on Gold and Silver, I said a great deal about index numbers, and how they can be used, to which I may be permitted to refer here, as well as to the papers on the "Prices of Imports and Exports," laid before Parliament. Let me only say here, for the purpose of continuing the logical thread of the argument, that an index number, apart from the details of its construction, is a very simple matter. It is nothing more than a device to enable a mean or average to be struck of the prices of a great number of articles, the mean being the result of an addition of the prices of all the articles named divided by the number, and the average being arrived at after weighting the prices selected according to an estimate, on a subjective or objective basis, of their relative importance. The estimate in the case of the prices of imports and exports with which I have myself dealt, is on an objective basis, that of the relative importance of each import to the whole imports, and of each export to the whole exports. Formally the latter process gets rid of the only good theoretical objection ever made to the use of index numbers as a means of averaging a group of prices, the objection, viz., that all articles, important or unimportant, are treated alike; but I may state that practically, as the result of Mr. Edgeworth's mathematical investigations for the monetary committee of the British Association, of which several of us are members, the ordinary index numbers, which are exposed to the theoretical objections stated, yield much the same results as the formally more correct indexes. The reason is, that having been selected almost at random as it were from among staple articles which happened to be quoted in wholesale price lists, the articles in general have moved in sympathy, so that one selection yields much the same results as any other. This is what theory would lead us to expect, but in fact Mr. Edgeworth has tried and compared the different index numbers not only with each other, but with a new number based on a different objective basis, and for practical purposes there is not much to choose between them.

All this is important when we proceed to the next step, which is to infer from the appreciation of gold measured by the commodities or groups stated, the probable appreciation if we had for measure a still greater number of articles, or in fact all articles. This is a matter of inference; but when in fact the different groups include from 50 to 90 per cent. of the chief commodities in use or consumed, or good types of these commodities, it would require very strong suggestions as to an opposite movement in the smaller number of articles which cannot be brought to the test to overbalance the conclusion to which the index numbers point. There are facts which would lead us to presume that the fall of prices in the excluded articles has been even greater in proportion than in the case of the articles included; but without laying stress on this, the proportion excluded is so small that we may have confidence in the general conclusion from the actual measure. Thus it is a mere matter of arithmetical statement that, measured by any of the groups named, the purchasing power of gold has increased of late years; it is a matter of practical certainty, though there can be no arithmetical proof formally complete, that measured by things in general gold has appreciated—its purchasing power has risen.

There is also corroborative evidence of a very strong kind in favour of the same conclusion in various sets of facts as to values, which are referred to in the essay already referred to, published in 1885. These are the facts as to the growth of import and export values compared with the growth of quantities, the facts as to income tax valuations, and the like. The facts on these heads are now notorious. The logic of the use of them is that they show effects in a mass, and thus get rid of any objections based on the possible peculiarities of some prices, though these are also got rid of, as we have seen, in a different way. Thus as regards imports and exports, if we are entitled to assume from the growth of quantities a certain growth of business, then if the growth of import and export values is at a different rate, the inference clearly is that the money expression of the individual things has changed. Hence only can it be that the mass of values is lower. The same with income tax valuations, as I pointed out in my paper at the British Association last year,[1] and as I shall have occasion to point out again in a book on the "Accumulations of Capital in Recent Years," which will continue the paper read before the Society in January, 1878, and which is all but ready for publication.[2] If the produce of land commands a less money price than before, rent falls and the capital value falls; if houses are built of less costly materials, object for object, their capital value and rent are also lower than they would otherwise be. It is quite easy to calculate, given the increase of population, and assuming a certain growth in real wealth per head, what difference is made in the figures by the change in the money expression, which can only be ascribed to a fall in the money value of average things.

Now with regard to a comparison of the growth of imports and exports in quantities and values, the facts are very clear. To bring this out has been one of the objects of the various reports to the Board of Trade which I have made in the "Prices of Imports and Exports," and it was obviously a point of various tables which were laid before the Royal Commission on Trade Depression. It is unnecessary to go into an elaborate

[1] See *postea*, "Recent Rate of Material Progress in England."

[2] See "The Growth of Capital" (George Bell and Sons).

comparison here. Let me only condense from the latter tables the following short table, comparing the growth of the money values of imports and exports per head with the growth of the entries of shipping per head:

C.—*Average Imports per Head and Total Imports and Exports per Head of the Population of the United Kingdom in the Undermentioned Quinquennial Periods; with the Entries of Shipping per Head in the same Periods; also showing Percentage Increases or Decreases.*

[Extracted from First Report of Trade Depression Commission, p. 127, etc., and continued.]

	Imports per Head.				Imports and Exports per Head.				Entries of Shipping per head.	
	Amount.			Increase or Decrease per Cent. on Previous Period.	Amount.			Increase or Decrease per Cent. on Previous Period.	Amount.	Increase per Cent. on Previous Period.
	£	s.	d.		£	s.	d.		Tons.	
1855-59.	6	0	3	—	10	19	2	—	0.38	—
'60-64.	8	1	4	34	14	4	3	30	0.45	18
'65-69.	9	8	2	17	16	19	1	19	0.53	18
'70-74.	10	17	2	15	19	19	3	18	0.65	23
'75-79.	11	3	5	3	18	16	6	− 6	0.75	15
'80-84.	11	11	0	3	20	0	1	+ 6	0.86	15
'85-87.	9	16	9	− 19	17	15	10	− 11	0.86	—

Thus while, in the earlier quinquennial periods, the increase in values is more than the increase of shipping, although the latter is very great, the increase in values practically stops short about 1874, or amounts to very little after that; while the increase in shipping goes on at a very rapid rate, if not quite at so rapid a rate as formerly. There is much other evidence, if we go into details, of a rapid growth of our foreign trade, judging by quantities only, while values do not increase, for which those interested may be referred to the tables mentioned.

With regard to income tax and other property valuations, it will be enough to call attention to the failure of their growth as compared with the growth in the immediately preceding period, in the simplest manner. The following short table is extracted from the tables produced by Sir Algernon West to the Trade Depression Commission:

D.—*Statement of Gross Amount of Profits Assessed to Income Tax per Head in Undermentioned Quinquennial Periods.*

[Appendix to First Report of Trade Depression Commission, p. 212.]

		£
1865-69.	Annual average per head . . .	14.0
'70-74.	" . . .	15.6
'75-79.	" . . .	17.4
'80-84.	" . . .	17.2

Allowing for the notorious increase in production per head shown by other statistics, such as the entries of shipping and the like, such a failure of money values to respond surely confirms the impression, derived from the above figures of fall of prices shown by index numbers and otherwise, as to the rise in the purchasing power of money being quite general. Whatever doubts may be raised as to the generality of the fall, when we look at prices merely, however grouped, there seems to be no room for them when we look at such mass observations as those of the growth of import and export values and valuations of property compared with the growth of things.

The evidence is not necessary for the purpose of proving the point, but the same divergence between the growth of quantities is noticeable in the statistics of import and export values, and statistics of property valuations, in foreign countries. The tables put in by myself before the Royal Commission on Trade Depression fully show this; and reference may also be made to a statement on this head by Sir Louis Mallet, in a note of his to the Report of the Gold and Silver Commission.

It hardly seems necessary to mention the point specially, but so much has been said quite properly as to retail prices not following necessarily to the full extent wholesale prices, and as to the danger, therefore, of relying too exclusively on the latter, that it may be useful to point out the bearing of these mass figures on the question of how far wholesale prices are to be trusted as a measure of gold, because they may be assumed to be representative of prices of commodities in general. It seems to be plain that if retail prices did not follow wholesale prices more closely than would be thought likely at first sight, results like what is here shown in the mass would not appear. A little reflection will also show, I think, that retail prices can hardly fail to follow wholesale prices closely. So far as the difference between them and wholesale prices is made up by cost of distribution, there appears to be no small reason to believe, first, that the real cost of distribution, as well as the real cost of production, has lately diminished; and next that, at most, the mere cost of distribution is only a fraction, 20 or 30 per cent. at most, of the final cost of articles, so that, even if no economies are effected in distribution in a given period, the fall in wholesale prices must still drag with it substantially the fall of retail prices. Some retail prices may not fall nominally, as they embody largely labour expended on the wholesale article; but this phenomenon belongs in part to the phenomenon of a non-diminution of wages while prices fall, which may be the characteristic of some cases of appreciating money, and which is a characteristic of the present case, as we shall presently discuss. Thus the point of retail prices was a proper one to raise, and there is something in it, but there is nothing to prevent us forming the conclusion that the increase of the purchasing power of money of late years, indicated by the measure of wholesale commodities, is, in fact, quite general. We do not need to include all commodities, each properly weighted, to arrive at this conclusion.

The Degree and Character of the Appreciation.

The rise in the purchasing power of gold measured by commodities being established, it remains for consideration to which of the types described in our preliminary remarks this appreciation belongs? Is it an appreciation in which the income per head of the community, and the earnings per head of the wage-earners, diminish? Is it an appreciation in which the aggregate income of the whole community diminishes? Or is it a case where incomes remain stationary although commodities fall?

I assume the community to be itself one of the advancing type, as in fact all the communities which are gold-using undoubtedly are. Tried by the test of things produced, all these communities have lately been advancing in population and wealth, however difficult it may be to measure what the percentage of advance is. Appreciation of money in their case must accordingly conform to one of the three types stated: (1) a fall of prices along with stationary incomes; (2) a fall along with diminishing incomes per head; (3) a fall along with a diminution of the aggregate money income of the community. To which category does the appreciation belong?

The facts here are most difficult of measurement, owing to the want of records of wages in a tolerably complete statistical form. Records of wages for a purpose like the present ought to show the aggregate earnings of the wage-earning part of the community, from which, with a knowledge of the population, the amount per head can be deduced. With such records at short intervals, the result we now wish to arrive at would appear at once, not as a matter of inference, but as a statement of fact. But no such records are in existence. Instead there are only records of isolated rates of wages, not "weighted" in any way, with apparent changes in opposite directions from time to time, so that it becomes most difficult to deduce what the general movement is. Fortunately for us, however, there is in England at any rate a record of a large part of the income of the nation which may be considered tolerably complete, and which may help, along with careful study of such wages records as exist, to show what the conclusion on the point before us must be.

The records referred to are those of the income tax, which have already been quoted for another purpose, but which may again be used with greater detail for the somewhat novel question now raised. Here there is an account of a large part of the gross income of the nation from time to time, largely, though not exclusively, the earnings or profits of capital. Assuming the recipients of this income not to change greatly from year to year in proportion to the general population, though we cannot count their numbers, then we may infer that the income per head diminishes or increases as we find that the annual amount divided by the numbers of the general population diminishes or increases. We can also see directly whether in the aggregate this portion of the national income diminishes or increases.

Looking at the income tax income then we find that the figures for the last twenty years, ending 1886, and beyond this we need not go, are as follows:

Income Tax Income in the undermentioned Years.

[In millions.]

	£		£
1867	424	1877	570
'68	430	'78	578
'69	435	'79	578
'70	445	'80	577
'71	466	'81	585
'72	482	'82	601
'73	514	'83	613
'74	549	'84	628
'75	571	'85	631
'76	579	'86	630
Annual average	492	Annual average	599
" per head	15*l*. 10*s*.	" per head	17*l*.
" of 1875-76,	17*l*. 8*s*. 6*d*.	" of 1885-86,	17*l*. 5*s*.

This shows a material increase even in the amount per head comparing ten years' period with a ten years' period. It will not fail to be observed, however, that while in the first ten years' period, the increase from the beginning to the end of the period is very great, the reverse is the case in the second ten years' period, the income having increased little all through. The average in the first ten years' period is thus the average of years of rapid growth; the second of an almost stationary period. Comparing the two last years of each period only the income per head is found to have even slightly diminished.

Unless therefore there has been something different in the progress of non-income tax incomes from what has taken place in income tax incomes, the inference would be that the appreciation of gold measured by commodities of late years is an appreciation which has not extended, or has yet extended very little, to the diminution of incomes per head, much less to a diminution of the aggregate of individual incomes; in other words it must be an appreciation of a comparatively mild type.

So far as I can judge, also, what we do know of wages points in the same direction. I shall mention the facts and circumstances which seem to point in this direction, and refer to and explain any opposing facts which seem to point in the opposite direction.

First then there is a general impression that wages have not declined at all, or at least have declined very little. Popular impressions count for very little as a rule when they can be brought to the test of figures; but if there had been at all a general and heavy fall of wages, a fall at all approaching the fall in the prices of commodities, it is an event which must have made a great deal of noise. I remember Mr. Jevons, who was present when I read my paper in 1879, remarking to me as we left the meeting that he looked forward with some foreboding to an appreciation of money, anticipating, as we all did then, that wages would follow suit to the fall of prices, and not adverting to the possibility of a considerable fall of prices without incomes per head declining. That there have not been strikes and lock-outs on an extensive scale, such as Mr. Jevons anticipated, is evidence *pro tanto* that the general and severe fall in wages he rather looked forward to, and many more of us also looked forward to, has not in fact occurred.

As a farther proof of there being no great fall in wages, I may perhaps remind you of Mr. Goschen's puzzle on this very head when he delivered his address on appreciation of gold at the Bankers' Institute in 1883. He could not then account for wages and incomes keeping up and prices declining. Since 1883 certainly there has been no material decline of wages, and the puzzle would remain unless upon the hypothesis now put forward of an increase of real wealth, which is represented by the same money income as before, but to which the fall of prices ensures that the same income will go farther than it did.

I have still more important evidence to adduce, however, as to the generality of the impression that there has been no general fall in wages of late years corresponding to the fall of commodities. Looking over the bulky volumes of the Trade Depression Commission, we find that one of the questions put to chambers of commerce and other mercantile bodies, and to workmen's associations, bore on this very point. They were asked to say in 1885 whether wages were then less on the average than they had been in the previous twenty years. This was not precisely the question we should have liked to put for the present purpose, but allowing for the fact that the average would include the inflated years of 1872-76, the answer that wages were not then under the average of the previous twenty, or very little under the average, if at all general, would seem to show that there can have been no material fall in money wages of late from the average of the ten years 1867-76, which is the starting point of the comparison of the fall of prices. The answers however are most conclusive on the point. I have extracted them one and all, except one or two detailed tables which I deal with specially; and I have placed these answers in the appendix. They speak for themselves. They seem to be absolute proof that there could have been no great and general fall in wages of late years.

There is moreover statistical evidence of the general maintenance of wages in the leading industries of the country. In the last report on Trades Unions, by Mr. Burnett, the labour correspondent of the Board of Trade, there will be found a series of tables, including among other particulars the standard rates of wages for a long period of years in various trades there mentioned.[1] From this I extract the following particulars:

E.—*Comparison of Wages Rates published in the Second Report of the Labour Correspondent of the Board of Trade on Trades Unions.*

			Normal, 1866-76.	Maximum, 1873-74.	Latest.
1. Engineers	(p. 31)	per week	22*s.* to 36*s.*	26*s.* to 36*s.*	26*s.* to 38*s.*
2. Amalgamated Society of Carpenters and Joiners	(" 33)	"	20*s.* to 37*s.* 8*d.*	21*s.* to 42*s.* 4*d.*	20*s.* to 42*s.* 4½*d.*
3. Steam Engine Makers . .	(" 35)	"	24*s.* to 36*s.*	26*s.* to 36*s.*	26*s.* to 38*s.*
4. Iron Founders	(" 37)	"	26*s.* 3*d.*	26*s.* 6*d.*	24*s.*
5. United Kingdom Pattern Makers	(" 45)	"	[33*s.* in 1885]	—	31*s.* 7½*d.*
6. Operative Bricklayers (summer)	(" ")	"	20*s.* to 39*s.* 9*d.*	24*s.* to 45*s.* 5*d.*	24*s.* to 42*s.* 4½*d.*
7. Iron Moulders of Scotland .	(" 47)	per hour	7¼*d.*	7⅝*d.*	7*d.*
8. Compositors (time only) .	(" 49)	per week	33*s.*	36*s.*	36*s.*
9. Journeyman Bookbinders .	(" 51)	"	32*s.*	32*s.*	32*s.*
10. Associated Blacksmiths .	(" 53)	"	25*s.*	27*s.*	28*s.*
11. Alliance Cabinet Makers .	(" 55)	per hour	7*d.* to 8½*d.*	8½*d.*	8½*d.* to 9*d.*
12. Operative Stonemasons (summer)	(" 59)	per week	20*s.* to 37*s.* 2*d.*	18*s.* to 40*s.* 0½*d.*	20*s.* to 40*s.*
13. Glass Bottlemakers of Yorkshire	(" 65)	"	33*s.*	36*s.*	30*s.*
14. Northumberland Miners[2] .	(" 69)				
Stonemen		per day	4*s.*	7*s.* 5*d.*	4*s.* 8*d.*
Onsetters		"	5*s.*	7*s.* 9*d.*	4*s.* 4*d.*
Banksmen		"	5*s.*	7*s.* 8*d.*	4*s.* 3½*d.*
Putters		"	3*s.* 1½*d.*	5*s.* 1½*d.*	2*s.* 9½*d.*
15. Kent and Sussex Labourers	(" 71)	per week	13*s.*	15*s.*	12*s.* 6*d.*
16. Pressmen	(" 75)	"	not stated	36*s.*	36*s.*
17. Zincworkers	(" 77)	"	36*s.* to 39*s.*	36*s.* to 39*s.*	36*s.* to 39*s.*
18. Coopers (Leith and Edinburgh)	(" 81)	"	23*s.* to 25*s.*	27*s.*	27*s.*
19. United Operative Bricklayers (summer) . .	(" 83)	"	23*s.* to 30*s.*	27*s.* to 33*s.*	27*s.* to 36*s.*
20. Perseverance Society of Carpenters and Joiners	(" 85)	per hour	not stated	9*d.*	9*d.*
21. Operative Plasterers . . .	(" 87)	"	"	6*d.* to 9*d.*	6*d.* to 9*d.*
22. Co-operative Smiths . . .	(" 89)	per week	25*s.*	33*s.*	30*s.*
23. Plumbers	(" 91)	per hour	not stated	8*d.*	8*d.*
24. Durham Colliery Enginemen	(" 121)	per day	"	5*s.* 11*d.*	4*s.* 4*d.*

[1] "Report on Trades Unions, C-5505, Sess. 1888," pp. 134 *et seq.*

[2] A great number of rates are given. I select a few only as specimens.

E.—*Comparison of Wages Rates, etc.—continued.*

		Normal, 1866-76.	Maximum, 1873-74.	Latest.
25. Carpenters and Joiners Scotland [1]				
Aberdeen	(p. 143) per hour	4½*d*.	7*d*.	6*d*.
Bishopsbriggs . . .	(„ „) „	6½*d*.	9*d*.	7½*d*.
Coatbridge	(„ „) „	6*d*.	8*d*.	6½*d*.
Dundee	(„ „) „	6*d*.	8*d*.	7*d*.
Edinburgh	(„ „) „	6½*d*.	8½*d*.	7*d*.
Glasgow	(„ „) „	6½*d*.	9*d*.	7½*d*.
Johnstone	(„ „) „	5*d*.	7*d*.	6½*d*.
Nairn	(„ „) „	4½*d*.	6*d*.	5*d*.
Stirling	(„ „) „	5½*d*.	8*d*.	6*d*.
26. Friendly Ironfounders . .	(„ 147) per week	26*s*. 3*d*.	26*s*. 3*d*.	24*s*.

It would be most desirable to have more details of this sort, but the indication is certainly not that of greatly declining wages of late years when period is compared with period. There are some cases of decline, but on the whole the normal wages of ten or fifteen years ago are maintained. The cases where the decline takes place are mainly in the coal and iron trades, where there was special inflation in 1872-76, and also agricultural labour, where there was also some inflation about the same date; but even in these cases the decline below the average wage as it stood before the inflated years, or even below an average for a long period, including the inflated years, is not very marked. Of course a few exceptions would not alter the general conclusion. Incessant changes are going on in the conditions of different trades and their relations to others. The average wage may be maintained throughout the labouring community, notwithstanding these special declines.

To the same effect are various tables which can be extracted from the bulky volumes of the Trade Depression Commission. I begin with two or three tables put in by Mr. Lord, the President of the Manchester Chamber of Commerce, the last being a summary of longer tables whose construction does not appear logically correct, but which contain data, as far as I can judge, pointing to the conclusion arrived at, although

[1] About 86 places given. About one place in ten picked out.

the process by which it is actually arrived at may not appear strictly and logically correct. These tables are as follows:

F.—*Wages in Lancashire Mills given by Mr. Lord, President of the Manchester Chamber of Commerce.*

[Appendix, Part I., to 2nd Report of Royal Commission on Trade Depression (p. 377).]

M.—*Cotton Spinning and Weaving.*

Numbers Employed.	Description.	Average Weekly Earnings. 1850. £	s.	d.	1860. £	s.	d.	1870. £	s.	d.	1877. £	s.	d.	1883. £	s.	d.
10	Strippers and grinders	0	11	0	0	14	0	0	17	0	1	1	0	0	19	0
16	Rovers	0	7	6	0	11	0	0	11	6	0	19	6	0	18	0
52	Minders	0	18	0	0	18	0	1	2	0	1	10	0	1	9	0
60	Winders	0	8	6	0	9	0	0	11	6	0	14	0	0	12	6
330	Weavers	0	8	2	0	14	9	0	15	6	0	16	0	0	15	0
2	Mechanics	1	1	0	1	4	0	1	6	0	1	10	0	1	10	0
10	Overlookers and tacklers	1	1	0	1	5	0	1	10	0	1	14	0	1	13	0

At the above rates the weekly wages of operatives working a mill of 1,000 looms with requisite spinning, viz.:

	£	s.	d.
480 persons, amounted in 1850 to . .	231	3	0
And in 1883 to	403	16	0
Increase . .	£172	13	0

= 74.69 per cent.
Increase in 1883 over 1850.

In 1850 the great majority of weavers had only two looms each; now they average about three looms each.

N.—*Cotton Spinning and Weaving, Medium Quality.*

Numbers Employed.	Descriptions.	Male or Female.	Average Weekly Earnings. 1850.	1860.	1870.	1877.	1883.
			£ s. d.	£ s. d.	£ s. d.	£ s. d.	£ s. d.
10	Strippers and grinders .	M.	0 10 6	0 13 0	0 16 0	0 19 0	1 1 0
16	Rovers	F.	0 7 6	0 11 0	0 14 0	0 17 0	0 18 0
50	Throstle spinners . .	F.	0 7 6	0 10 0	0 13 0	0 15 0	0 15 0
25	Minders	M.	0 16 0	0 18 0	1 0 0 to 1 2 0	1 5 0 to 1 8 0	1 5 0 to 1 8 0
60	Winders	F.	0 7 0	0 8 0	0 11 0	0 16 0	0 16 0
350	Weavers	M. & F.	0 11 2½	0 14 6	0 17 0	0 18 0	0 19 8½
2	Mechanics	M.	1 3 6	1 5 0	1 7 0	1 8 0	1 12 0
10	Overlookers and tacklers	M.	1 2 0	1 5 0	1 10 0	1 14 0 to 1 16 0	1 16 0 to 1 18 0
1	Stonemason	M.	1 0 0	1 3 0	1 8 0	1 10 0	1 10 0
2	Labourers	M.	0 12 0	0 15 0	1 0 0	1 2 0	1 2 0

At the above rates the weekly wages of operatives working a mill of 1,000 looms with requisite spinning, viz.:

	£	s.	d.
526 persons, amounted in 1850 to . . .	282	13	11
And in 1883 to	513	16	5
Increase . .	£231	2	6

= 81.75 per cent.
Increase in 1883 over 1850.

In 1850 each weaver tented on the average 2.74 looms.
„ '83 „ „ 3.88 „

G.—*Summary of Tables showing Increase of Wages given in several Trades in Lancashire, given in by Mr. Lord, President of the Manchester Chamber of Commerce.*

[Appendix to First Report of Royal Commission on Trade Depression, p. 99.]

Descriptions.	Percentage Increase in Wages Earned in the undernoted Years on those Earned in 1850.			
	1860.	1870.	1877.	1883.
Cotton spinning and weaving, medium	16.85	43.59	64.47	74.72
,, fine	Unchanged	9.68	30.21	16.27
,, and weaving, fine, Bolton	,,	15.13	37.72	35.16
,, No. 150 weft . . .	No returns			37.00
Bleaching	33.06	31.40	56.60	50.00
Calico printing	8.00	25.00	50.00	50.00
Shipping warehouse	15.46	25.77	31.44	35.05
Mechanical engineering	Unchanged	2.42	12.73	10.30
Coal mining	22.78	24.64	55.64	43.53
Building	10.12	23.11	48.21	39.76
Average advance	11.70	22.30	43.00	39.18
	9 trades	9 trades	9 trades	10 trades
Iron manufacture, decrease	8.71	11.98	10.16	14.88

(*Signed*) GEORGE LORD,
President.

Manchester Chamber of Commerce,
May, 1883.

Thus it seems to be demonstrated that in the leading industries of Lancashire, comparing a date two or three years ago—since which there has been no fall in wages—with a middle period in the wages course between 1865 and 1875, there is not only not a fall in wages, but even a rise. The details in M and N fully show this, and give the necessary strength to the above summary of more detailed tables, which it would occupy too much space to quote.

To the same effect is a record of wages paid at Newcastle in the chemical trade, laid by Mr. Allhusen before the Commission, and which happens to be in a very convenient form for showing the facts.

H.—*Record of Wages Paid at the Newcastle Chemical Works from 1840 to end of 1885.*

[Statement of Mr. Allhusen. Appendix to Third Report of Royal Commission on Trade Depression, p. 307.]

Record of Wages Paid at the Newcastle Chemical Works from 1840 to end of 1885.

Years.	Blacksmiths.		Millwrights.		Bricklayers.		Joiners.		Labourers.
	Per week.		Per week.		Per week.		Per week.		Per week.
	s.	*d.*	*s.*	*d.*	*s.*	*d.*	*s.*	*d.*	
1840	20	0	21	0	20	0	18	0	12*s.* to 13*s.*
'50	22	0	23	0	22	0	20	0	14*s.*
'55	24	0	25	0	24	0	22	0	14*s.* to 15*s.*
'60	26	0	27	0	29	0	24	0	16*s.* ,, 18*s.*
'72	28	0	30	0	22	0[1]	28	0	20*s.*
'73	32	0	32	0	32	0	32	0	20*s.* to 22*s.*
'74	32	0	32	0	32	0	32	0	22*s.* ,, 24*s.*
'75	32	0	32	0	36	0	36	0	20*s.* ,, 22*s.*
'76	32	0	32	0	36	0	36	0	22*s.* ,, 24*s.*
'77	30	6	30	6	34	0	34	0	20*s.* to 22*s.* 6*d.*
'78	28	0	28	0	30	0	30	0	18*s.*
'79	26	0	26	0	28	0	28	0	17*s.*
'80	27	6	27	6	29	6	27	6	18*s.*
'81	30	0	30	0	29	6	29	6	18*s.*
'82	30	0	30	0	29	6	29	6	18*s.*
'83	31	6	31	6	29	6	29	6	18*s.*
'84	31	6	31	6	29	6	29	6	18*s.*
'85	27	6	28	6	28	0	28	0	18*s.*

Note.—Up to year 1871 a week's work consisted of 61 hours; from that period, 54 hours.

[1] *Sic* in original; but ought not the figure perhaps to be 32*s.*?

To the same effect is a similar table put in by Sir I. Lowthian Bell as to coal mining, though here the short period of inflation in 1873-74 is very distinctly marked, and the normal rates of wages before and after that date are in this case not distinctly marked:

I.—*Earnings of Coal Hewers in Durham.*

[Statement of Sir I. Lowthian Bell. Appendix, Part I. to II. Report of Royal Commission on Trade Depression, p. 341.]

Year.	Weight of Coal Worked.	Daily Earnings.		Year.	Weight of Coal Worked.	Daily Earnings.	
	cwts.	*s.*	*d.*		cwts.	*s.*	*d.*
1871	83.87	4	5.67	1878	90.00	5	0.55
'72	76.03	5	7.40	'79	74.63	4	4.42
'73	71.96	8	3.54	'80	91.96	4	3.73
'74	70.80	6	10.65	'81	94.79	4	10.20
'75	70.14	5	9.13	'82	107.74	5	2.57
'76	78.64	5	10.16	'83	107.21	5	3.53
'77	86.96	5	3.9	'84	106.96	5	1.27

Putting all the evidence together, there seems little doubt that in staple trades wages have been maintained, or nearly so, as compared with the average of 1867-77. There are exceptions, but not sufficient to obscure what the general movement has been.

To be quite fair it may be useful to conclude this review with a table of agricultural labourers' wages, in which, as already referred to in connection with the figures from the Trades Union Report, there is apparently a decline, at any rate from the high level of 1872-76. The table in question was put in before the Royal Commission on Trade Depression by Mr. Druce, who had been one of the Assistant Commissioners of the Royal Commission on Agriculture some years before, and is as follows:

Rate of Money Wages of Ordinary Agricultural Labourers, 1870-71 *and* 1880-81. *Statement of Mr. S. B. L. Druce.*
[Appendix to 3rd Report of Royal Commission on Trade Depression, p. 296.]

APPENDIX A.—II.

K.—*Statement put in by Mr. S. B. L. Druce.* (See Question 9, 153.)

Name of County.	1870-71. Per week.	1880-81. Per week.
Beds	10*s.* to 11*s.*	12*s.* to 13*s.*
Berks	10*s.*	11*s.* ,, 13*s.*
Bucks [1]	11*s.* to 13*s.*	13*s.* to 14*s.*, winter 14*s.* to 15*s.*, summer
Cambs [2]	10*s.* ,, 12*s.*	12*s.* to 13*s.*
Chester	12*s.* ,, 15*s.*	No general return
Cornwall	11*s.*	14*s.* to 15*s.*
Cumberland	15*s.* or 9*s.* [3]	18*s.*
Derby	14*s.*	15*s.* to 18*s.*
Devon	8*s.* 6*d.* to 12*s.*	11*s.* ,, 15*s.*
Dorset	8*s.* 6*d.* to 11*s.* 6*d.*	10*s.* ,, 12*s.*
Durham	15*s.* to 17*s.*	17*s.* 6*d.* to 18*s.*
Essex	10*s.* ,, 12*s.*	12*s.* to 13*s.*
Gloster	9*s.* 6*d.* to 12*s.*	12*s.* ,, 15*s.*
Hants	10*s.* to 11*s.*	11*s.* ,, 13*s.*
Hereford	9*s.* to 10*s.*	12*s.* ,, 14*s.*
Herts	10*s.* 9*d.* to 11*s.* 3*d.*	12*s.* ,, 15*s.*
Hunts	11*s.*	12*s.*
Kent (extra Metropolitan)	13*s.* to 15*s.*	15*s.* to 18*s.*
Lancaster	15*s.* or 7*s.* [3]	17*s.* ,, 18*s.*
Leicester	12*s.* to 14*s.*	11*s.* to 12*s.* ordinary districts 14*s.* ,, 15*s.* ironstone ,,
Lincoln	13*s.* 6*d.*	13*s.* 6*d.* to 15*s.*
Middlesex	No return	15*s.* to 16*s.*
Monmouth	11*s.* to 16*s.* 6*d.*	12*s.*
Norfolk	10*s.*	12*s.* to 13*s.*
Northampton	11*s.* to 12*s.*	13*s.* ,, 14*s.*
Northumberland	15*s.* ,, 18*s.*	15*s.* ,, 18*s.*
Notts	12*s.* ,, 14*s.*	13*s.* to 15*s.* ordinary 18*s.* to 20*s.* colliery district
Oxon [1]	10*s.* ,, 13*s.*	11*s.* to 15*s.* 6*d.*
Rutland	12*s.*	No return
Salop	10*s.* to 12*s.*	12*s.* to 14*s.*
Somerset	10*s.* ,, 11*s.*	11*s.* ,, 15*s.*
Stafford	13*s.*	12*s.* ,, 15*s.*
Suffolk	10*s.* to 12*s.*	12*s.* ,, 13*s.*
Surrey (extra Metropolitan)	13*s.* ,, 14*s.*	14*s.* ,, 16*s.*
Sussex	11*s.* ,, 13*s.*	12*s.* ,, 15*s.*
Warwick	11*s.* ,, 12*s.*	12*s.* ,, 16*s.*
Westmoreland	14*s.* ,, 17*s.*	18*s.*
Wilts	9*s.* 6*d.* to 11*s.*	11*s.* to 13*s.*
Worcester	10*s.* to 12*s.*	13*s.* 6*d.*
Yorks (E. R.)	No return	15*s.*
,, (N. R.)	12*s.* to 15*s.*	16*s.* to 17*s.*
,, (W. R.)	13*s.* 6*d.* to 17*s.*	15*s.* ,, 18*s.*

[1] Extracted from the Report of the Commissioners on the Employment of Women and Children in Agriculture, 1867-68.
[2] For quarter ended Michaelmas, 1869 (harvest money not included).
[3] The latter with board and lodging.

From this it is evident that the fall in agricultural wages recently which has undoubtedly taken place, can hardly have been very great from the normal average of 1867-77, as marked by the wages of 1870-71 included in the above table, but must have been from the high level of 1880-81, to which they had risen in the interval. This is evidently the case, in fact, if we look at the figures for agricultural labour in the above Trades' Union Table E. Even agricultural labour cannot be said to have sustained a material fall from the high average of 1867-77, though there is a distinct decline from the maximum of those years.

While revising the proofs of this paper, I have had the advantage of receiving a copy of Major Craigie's most valuable paper on the Agricultural Labour Bill read at the Farmer's Club on the 10th instant. Major Craigie's conclusion is that at the present time, as compared with ten years ago, the drop in that part of the labourer's wage paid in money is from 18 to 20 per cent. in the east, and in the rest of England about 12 per cent. He adds that as the numbers of labourers are about $\frac{5}{7}$ths of the whole in the latter districts, perhaps a drop of 14 per cent. will represent the loss of wages over the farmed surface of England. But this is comparing the present time with the high level ten years ago, and the average drop would of course be less comparing ten years' period with ten years' period. Major Craigie at the same time gives most interesting tables showing the real improvement in the labourer's position notwithstanding the fall in money wages, which confirms in the strongest way the present argument that the appreciation is a case of appreciation measured by commodities in an advancing community, so that money incomes, though just maintained, or not quite maintained, go further than they did before.

It would be needless to multiply figures. The common impression as to wages having been maintained, while the prices of commodities have fallen, is not only confirmed by the proof above given as to income tax incomes having been maintained, and by the statements of numerous observers with special means of knowing, but by actual tables of wages statistics derived from a variety of sources, and all telling the same tale. The appreciation of money, therefore, as far as England is concerned, is an appreciation unaccompanied by any serious general decline in average incomes and wages per head, much less by any decline in the aggregate national income.

It should be added, however, that the maintenance of individual incomes at the former average level has at most been barely accomplished, and no more. The appreciation has very nearly, if not quite, been one of the second type, viz.: where not only prices of commodities fall, but where average incomes expressed in money decline.

It is not necessary for confirmation's sake to go abroad, but it may be useful to do so, while the facts cannot but throw light on the further question, which is a most interesting one, as to the area of the appreciation.

As regards Germany, I have only to refer to Dr. Soetbeer's "Materialien," from which I extract and place in the Appendix certain particulars as to wages and incomes. Dr. Soetbeer uses these very particulars to disprove the assertion that gold has appreciated, but this is with reference to the peculiar meaning or no meaning of the word which has been productive of so much confusion in all these discussions. We are at liberty to use the same particulars to demonstrate the character and degree of the appreciation as we have limited and defined the phrase.

With regard to Belgium the figures are contained in a blue book issued last session,[1] compiled from an inquiry into the wages and condition of the working classes, which has just been made by the Belgian Government. From this blue book I have compiled

[1] See C-5269, Sess. 1888.

and put in the Appendix one or two short tables. The figures certainly show a fall in the iron and coal trades, but not a general fall at the present time as compared with the average of 1867-77. I desire to refer especially to the table in which the wages are directly compared with the quantities purchaseable at the average prices of the years in question. This is the most direct way of course of putting the rise in real wages. Whatever the intermediate changes in money have been, and although they are no higher at the end than the beginning, their purchasing power has been immensely increased.

Similar particulars for France yield the same conclusion, the difficulty here being to show any general decline. I do not make any extracts, however, and may content myself with a reference to the elaborate particulars at p. 132 *et seq.*, Appendix, Part II., Second Report of the Royal Commission on Trade Depression.

Similar particulars for Italy are to be found in the Report of the Royal Commission on Trade Depression. To corroborate them I extract and put in the Appendix an extract from a report by Mr. Kennedy, lately Secretary of Legation at Rome, which appears to be conclusive on the point.

Thus the phenomenon of falling prices of commodities and stationary or, at least, not greatly declining incomes and wages, appears to be very general in gold-using countries. It does not follow that the result should be the same in every country. We cannot assume the rate of advance in material progress to be the same in each, or that the margin between the average prices of commodities and the average income should widen in the same way. But although the same result precisely is not to be looked for, if we could measure with the necessary degree of fineness, we cannot but assume that the communities of all the countries named are progressing to some extent, and that consequently, if commodities fall and incomes remain stationary in one, the same results should appear in the other with only minor divergencies. When we find, therefore, that everywhere in Europe at least, wages and incomes remain stationary, or at least fall much less than the average prices of commodities, we cannot but conclude that the type of appreciation is everywhere the same, and that we are in the presence of a phenomenon which extends over a wide area—that phenomenon being an undoubted rise in the purchasing power of money measured by commodities, but this rise being unaccompanied by any corresponding diminution of wages and incomes which would not unnaturally be looked for, but which reflection shows need not take place in advancing communities when prices fall.

The Appreciation or Depreciation of Silver.

The appreciation of gold measured by average commodities being thus established, and the appreciation being of a type in which, as the communities affected are advancing at the same time in material wealth, there is no diminution, or at any rate no great diminution, of average incomes, the question arises, what are the similar facts respecting silver?

Of course, as regards the relation of silver to commodities, there can be no question. In each case, whatever fall in the gold prices of commodities is shown, would either be less or more than the fall in the gold price of silver by an exact percentage. There is no room for theorizing. It is a case of exact measurement, with this difference only, that silver and gold can be measured against each other with more exactness than any other commodity against one or the other.

It would seem to follow also that on the whole, if we avoid extreme years, the average fall in commodities measured by gold rather exceeds the average fall in silver measured by gold. In other words, instead of speaking of the depreciation of silver, though that is a correct enough phrase when we measure it by gold, we should be quite justified in speaking of the appreciation of silver when we measure it by the average of commodities in the way above described.

This is true when we measure silver in gold-using countries, but what is true there, a little reflection will show, must also be true in silver-using countries. In these days of quick communication it must be assumed that every improvement is for the benefit of consumers generally in the long run, though there may be important exceptions for a time when a backward country is first brought into contact with the rest of the world, and all its produce obtains an enhancement of value. Still the latter cases are exceptions, and it may be taken for granted that a rise or fall in prices in one locality, if at all general, is accompanied by a similar rise or fall throughout the world. I assume then that silver has appreciated a little, measured by commodities, in those countries at least which, like India, are in close and intimate intercourse with the civilized world. If necessary the exact correspondence between Indian and European prices could be shown, but it does not seem worth while to labour the point.

But to what type does the appreciation of silver conform in India? Clearly, if the community of India had been advancing as European communities, and especially the community of the United Kingdom, have been advancing, there would be a material difference in the growth of incomes in India and England respectively. Silver prices having fallen very little compared with gold prices, then, in an advancing community using silver, money wages and incomes ought to have risen in order that wages and incomes may maintain the same relation to commodities that they do in advancing gold countries, where, as we have seen, wages and incomes remain stationary while prices fall. The one change would be the exact counterpart of the other. But, so far as I have been able to learn, no such increase in Indian wages and incomes has, in fact, taken place. On this head I can only accept the statements of Indian authorities, and Mr. Barbour, who is in the best position to be an authority, is quite explicit on the point. In his evidence before the Royal Commission on Gold and Silver, he was asked by the Chairman (Question 1,162) whether, with respect to labour, the value of silver had decreased in India, and he replied:

"I think that the wages of labour have risen in large towns, and along the railways, and in places where large manufactures have been started, and especially the wages of skilled labour. As regards the great mass of the people, I do not think there has been much change; and very often the labourer is paid in kind [paid by produce], so that one could not say that the money wages had risen or fallen. I have made some inquiries as to the cost of carrying the mails by runners. I applied to the head of the post office, who obtained from the auditor of the post office accounts a statement of the wages paid to what are called postal runners, and I found very little change in the rates. I will put in a paper giving those rates: it goes back for a considerable number of years. There is a rise in the rates up to, I think, about 1870 or so, and since that there has been very little change—a slight tendency to rise." —"First Report of Gold and Silver Commission," Question 1,162, p. 60.

Nothing more need be said, but I may add that I am led to believe from conversation with residents in India who are shrewd observers, that the authorities are right. There has been no general or material rise in wages and incomes in India in the last ten or fifteen years. What I believe has occurred is a rise of wages in the large cities of India and in some districts near the gold mines, not sufficient to affect greatly the general average. The conclusion consequently is not that the facts as to appreciation of gold in Europe measured by commodities, and as to a less appreciation of silver in India measured by commodities, implying a depreciation of silver measured by gold, are out of harmony, but that

India, as a community, has not of late been advancing as European communities have advanced. Hence the absence in India of many of the usual phenomena of depreciation of money, though some of them must have accompanied an increase of wages and incomes in India, such as would undoubtedly have taken place of late if India had been an advancing community, although the silver prices of commodities had fallen a little.

I make these observations with some diffidence, and in the absence of fuller information, which is much to be desired, as to prices and wages in India. It would be most interesting to know, on its own merits, how much the people of India have been gaining in material wealth of late years. It appears somewhat remote to bring in the relations between gold and silver prices and gold and silver wages as having a bearing on this point, but with good statistics the topic should be in no way remote.

Similar statements, it may be noticed, are made by consuls of the United Kingdom in silver-using countries, in reply to the wages query of the Royal Commission on Trade Depression contained in the circular sent to H.M.'s representatives abroad by that body. From Mexico, from China, from Japan, or at least from many places in these countries, and from other countries also, the report is that there has been no noticeable rise of wages for twenty years, or since 1870. From Russia and Austria, which are paper countries, but with little discount on the paper compared with silver, there is much the same reply.

The inference as to the slow growth of silver-using communities as compared with that of gold-using communities is a specially important one, as we shall afterwards see. It bears upon the question of the future demand for gold compared with that of silver. For the present purpose, however, I am using it merely to show the nature and extent of the depreciation of silver. It can hardly be spoken of anywhere as a depreciation at all, even when the measure is the income per head of a community, and there is obviously no depreciation, but appreciation only, when the measure is that of the average of commodities.

At this point we may notice what was adverted to in the opening remarks with reference to the puzzle caused by there being no phenomena of depreciation of silver in India answering exactly to its depreciation measured by gold in Europe. Clearly the correspondence cannot be exact, because the economic movement in India and in Europe is not the same. The difference accounts, especially, I think, for that most curious puzzle of all, which seems so insoluble, viz., the slowness with which wages adjust themselves in England and India to the changed ratio between gold and silver, so that the Indian producer who has no more wages to pay, while his produce commands relatively more silver than the produce of the English producer commands of gold, in comparison with what was formerly the case, appears to have a permanent advantage over the English competitor. Clearly if real wages are rising in England generally more than they are in India, wages here may not apparently be adjusted to this specific change, because along with the apparent adjustment required another change has to be adjusted, viz., the increase in real wages. Thus the English producer appears to be more and more handicapped by his Indian competitors, because he cannot get money wages down. If, however, there had been no fall of prices and no fall in silver, this difficulty would have been the same, only it would have taken the form of *rising* wages here with prices stationary, instead of the form of stationary wages and falling prices. Always the real changes must have been the same. The change, however, implies no insuperable difficulty in the English competition maintaining itself. Real wages increase because the work done is better generally, and though there may be momentary difficulties in special trades, always this improvement in work will tell.

The facts as thus described also appear to account

for the extent of the recent flow of silver to the East, on which there appears to be some misconception, and on which I may be allowed to say something, as the name of a revered authority, Mr. Bagehot, whom I am specially bound to defend, has been brought into question. Mr. Bagehot, it is said, when the depreciation of silver measured by gold began, discouraged a panic feeling by predicting a great export of silver to the East, and a continual demand for silver as it fell in value, so that unlimited depreciation was not in prospect. The event, it is said, has belied his prediction, and shows that his appeals against panic were not well founded.

I remember no conversation with Mr. Bagehot having the purport stated, and I was in close communication with him till he died. What he was always speaking of was a sudden depreciation of silver such as took place in 1876, when the market fell away suddenly to 3*s.* 11*d.*, and of this he predicted that it would speedily right itself by stimulating exports of goods from India, and so creating a demand for silver for export to India. In this Mr. Bagehot was undoubtedly right. Indian trade was stimulated, and there was a large export of silver from Europe to India immediately after Mr. Bagehot made his statement as to what was going to happen, while the price of silver recovered to over 4*s.* 6*d.*, and only fell very gradually after that for a good many years until, in 1886, another fall occurred such as Mr. Bagehot wrote of in 1876. Mr. Bagehot by no means predicted that silver would go back to its ancient level, nor was any such idea in his mind. He was the last man in the world to discount the future or to take very long views.

Since Mr. Bagehot died, however, the circumstances relating to both silver and gold have very greatly changed, and I am tolerably confident that he never said anything to imply a belief that the stimulus to Indian trade, which he anticipated from a momentary great drop in silver, would be permanent and continuous in totally different circumstances. The new circumstances are what economists would recognize as rather an appreciation than depreciation of silver, and this aspect of the fall in silver was certainly not so visible before 1877, when Mr. Bagehot died, as it has since become.

I have further to point out that the flow of silver to India of late years has in fact been on a considerable scale. Since 1877 the influx into India in tens of rupees has been:

Net Imports of Silver into India by Sea in the undermentioned Years.

[In thousands of tens of rupees.]

Year ended 31st March.	Imports.	Exports.	Net Imports.
1874	4,143	1,648	2,495
'75	6,052	1,410	4,642
'76	3,464	1,909	1,555
'77	9,992	2,793	7,199
'78	15,776	1,100	14,676
'79	5,594	1,623	3,971
'80	9,605	1,735	7,870
'81	5,316	1,423	3,893
'82	6,466	1,087	5,379
'83	8,358	878	7,480
'84	7,408	1,003	6,405
'85	9,110	1,864	7,246
'86	12,386	780	11,606
'87	8,220	1,064	7,156
'88	—	—	9,219

And I maintain these are large figures. They would hardly have taken place unless there had been some increase of wages and incomes in India, though, as we have seen, there is no large general increase of such wages and incomes. India remains a consumer of silver on a large scale. No doubt for many years, owing to the great advance in prices and wages which took place in India between 1850 and 1870, India was a consumer on a still larger scale, just as England was a large consumer of gold for monetary purposes in the same years; but while in the last fifteen years England has ceased to be a consumer of gold, India remains a large consumer of silver. The difference arises in part, I believe, from the fact that, while gold has appreciated greatly, measured by commodities, and gold incomes have not increased, silver has appreciated only a little, measured by commodities, and silver incomes, though silver-using communities have not advanced as gold-using communities have done, have nevertheless advanced a little.

I have to apologize for this digression as to the flow of silver to the East, but my excuse must be the expediency of showing that all the facts, when rightly understood, are in harmony. The flow of silver to India should be in strict relation with the degree and nature of depreciation in its money and the economic progress of its inhabitants.

Characters of Appreciation and Depreciation at Different Periods.

Making the broad distinction we have made between the course of prices and incomes, it may be useful to look at what happened in previous periods of appreciation or depreciation, and see how they may be characterized with reference to this distinction. A good deal of light seems to be thrown on the subject by so doing. Much doubt is removed as to when there has been appreciation or depreciation.

We may take first the period following the Australian and Californian gold discoveries. Mr. Jevons showed for this period an appreciation of money, measured by staple commodities in England, amounting to about 15 per cent. As you are aware, however, the statement was not universally accepted as representing the change in prices of commodities generally; and still retaining the confused idea as to appreciation being something absolute and independent, which is so difficult to get rid of, economists argued that Mr. Jevons had not made out his case. I have been told myself that because I agreed that the limit of the depreciation measured by commodities in the twenty years after 1850 was a very narrow one, I must admit that the subject is extremely difficult, and we may equally conclude now that appreciation is not established with any certainty! When we bring in the question of incomes, however, the character of the period which Mr. Jevons described is placed beyond all question. If the margin of the rise in the prices of commodities was a narrow one, the rise in incomes and wages was immense. As to income tax incomes, the facts are notorious. The income tax income per head of the people of the United Kingdom, which was about £11 just before 1850, amounted about 1875 to over £17. There is reason to believe moreover that the growth of working class incomes corresponded, on which head I may be allowed to refer to the papers on the "Progress of the Working Classes" which I read to the Society in 1883 and 1885.[1] The case between 1850 and 1870 therefore was one in which there was a moderate depreciation of gold measured by commodities, but as the community was advancing in real wealth at the same time the improvement in its condition was indicated by the larger growth in incomes than in the prices of commodities. Scientifically stated then, there was unquestionably depreciation between 1850 and 1870; the depreciation being that characteristic of an advancing community, when prices of commodities rise a little, and incomes rise a great deal.

Looking at the matter broadly the difference between that period and the later period since 1873 may simply be described as being that while the increase in real wealth in the two periods was much the same, the community received the benefit in the former period in the form of a great rise in money incomes accompanied by

[1] See Statistical Society's "Journal," 1883 and 1885, and for the first of these essays *postea*.

a much less rise in commodities, and in the latter they have received the benefit in the form of stationary and almost slightly declining incomes, accompanied by a great fall in the prices of commodities. The facts are all in harmony. The substantial result to the community, apart from the redistribution of wealth involved, is the same in both periods, but the money expressions and the changes in these money expressions are different.

Going back a little further, again, it is easy to see that the period between the early part of the century and the eve of the gold discoveries of 1848-50 was one of great likeness to the present period since 1873. In both there was the same steady fall of general prices, a fall which has long been recognized, in spite of the unwillingness of many economists, such as Tooke, to speak of it as a rise in the purchasing power of money. Now we must add that there is a farther likeness in the circumstance that between the early part of the century and 1845 average money incomes increased very little. Nothing is more remarkable than the small advance of income tax incomes between the date when the income tax was left off in 1815 and its renewal in 1843, there being in fact no advance, or barely any advance, allowing for the increase of population. It is equally on record, though there are no exact statistics, that money wages during the same period were with difficulty maintained. Hence the general likeness between the period 1815-45 and the present time. Appreciation of money shows itself in both periods in much the same way, and is of much the same type, though I am inclined to think that the advance in real wealth before 1845 was not so great as it has since been.

Going back still further, it will be found that towards the close of last century, and during the early part of the present century, there was a remarkable rise of prices, and an equally remarkable, if not more remarkable, rise of incomes, indicating that, on the whole, the community was then advancing. In thus speaking, I leave out, of course, that part of the rise of prices and incomes which answered to the depreciation of paper. Apart from this element, there was a great rise in prices and incomes in the last quarter of last century and the beginning of the present century, though rather more in incomes than in prices. The data are too scattered to enable us to speak with much exactness, and it would take us too far at present to go into historical investigations; but that there was at the time spoken of depreciation of money, measured by commodities, such as we had between 1850 and 1870, is undoubted, and there was at least sufficient advance of incomes to raise a question whether the whole change was not of the same type, though the *degree* of advance in real wealth was not nearly so marked as in the period 1850-70.

It is not proposed to go back any farther at present; but enough has perhaps been said to show how fruitful such investigations may be made when the relations between prices and incomes are kept steadily in view, and how necessary it is to allow for the economic movement in a community in studying the signs of appreciation or depreciation of money. The apparent inconsistencies between a fall of prices and no fall of wages, or no corresponding fall, and *vice versâ*, are all to be reconciled. When this is done there can be no sort of doubt as to the changes in the purchasing power of money at different times in the last hundred years.

Equally when we turn to another field the utility of the comparison is shown. In India, as we have seen, since about 1873, there is notably no depreciation of silver measured by commodities; there is perhaps a slight appreciation. There appears also to be a slight increase of incomes, though not much. Just before 1870, however, there was unquestionably depreciation of silver in India, marked by a rise of both prices and incomes, and a little more in incomes than in prices. In India the real progress in both periods has been less than in Western Europe, but the facts again are all in conformity. As the community advances, though somewhat slowly, depreciation of money measured by commodities is accompanied by a greater increase in money incomes than in the prices of commodities. On the other hand a stationary value or slight appreciation of money measured by commodities is accompanied by stationary or only slightly rising incomes.

This characterization of the various sorts of appreciation and depreciation may be used generally in comparing different countries at different times. The fact of appreciation or depreciation of money is one which must be frequently kept in view in economic comparisons, and the nature and degree of appreciation or depreciation must equally be considered. A study of the economic movement in the chief countries of the world, and in different provinces of the same countries for the last century, if not longer, comparing prices and incomes all through, could not but be most instructive.

A useful explanation with regard to the employment of certain phrases in economic discussions appears likewise to be suggested. We often hear of certain things, such as war, causing high prices, and other things, such as abundant harvests, causing low prices; and the high prices are spoken of as "dearness," and the low prices as "cheapness." But when the expressions are analyzed it will be found that the "dearness" and "cheapness" can have really nothing to do with money prices; that real "dearness," that is a high price in relation to income, and real "cheapness," that is a low price in relation to income, are intended; while it is farther obvious from what has been said here that "dearness" and "cheapness" in this sense may co-exist or come about with any conceivable range of money prices or any conceivable change in that range. Things may become cheap in this sense when money prices rise and dear when money prices fall—not perhaps in a short period, and especially as regards a particular article, money then being the most stable measure, but certainly as regards an average of articles in those long periods when it is found convenient to invent measures for money itself. Much confusion has arisen from the neglect of this distinction. The common notion that war prices are high money prices, which is so inveterate, although it is absolutely disproved by experience as well as by theory, is an instance. Perhaps—to give an illustration from present controversies—the question whether abundance of commodities or scarcity of money causes a given appreciation of money, which we shall presently have to notice, would never have become a question at all, if it had been clearly recognized from the first that the effect of abundance of commodities properly belongs to a question of real cheapness, where the ratio of the commodities to incomes is involved, and that the effect of scarcity of money properly belongs to a question as to the range of money prices only where the ratio of commodities to money is involved, so that there is no antagonism between the two causes as they are not related to the same class of effects.

The Causes of Appreciation and Depreciation.

What are the causes of the changes in money with which we have been dealing? I approach this topic with great diffidence. The changes have been rung, as you are aware, on the antagonism, or supposed antagonism, which has just been mentioned, between the influence of abundant commodities and the influence of scarce money on prices. It has become extremely difficult for a modest student like myself to strike in with a few appeasing words, and show that there is a great deal to be said on the subject which does not touch on the conflict at all, and that the conflict itself is more about words than things.

I would begin by saying that there is, necessarily, ambiguity in asking generally what are the causes of the appreciation of gold or depreciation of silver? There is liability to misunderstanding, as we have seen, in the fact that there may be appreciations and depreciations of quite different types, and what is true of one may not be true of another; but in addition causes are hardly to be treated in this general way when we are dealing with economic phenomena, or indeed with any scientific phenomena. We should hardly ask what are the causes of the sun rising in the east, without limiting the question in some way so as to show what facts are assumed, and where the point as to the rising in the east comes in. In the same way we must limit and define the inquiry as to the causes of appreciation and depreciation of money at one time as compared with another.

I have to begin then by drawing attention to what is stated in the preliminary remarks, to the effect that there must be a sense in which the ascription of every case of appreciation of money to a contraction of money, and every case of depreciation to an expansion, must be true. There must be *relative* contraction and expansion whatever the absolute changes may be; and as there is an incessant action and reaction in all economic phenomena, this means that contraction of money may always be taken as the cause of an increase of the purchasing power of money, in the sense that such an increase necessarily *implies* contraction as compared with what would otherwise be. We may infer the one fact from the other, which is the important point for us, without troubling our heads very much about metaphysical ideas of cause.

Using the words contraction and expansion in this sense, however, a very different view would be taken of the causes and order of the phenomena from what would be taken by anyone attaching a totally different meaning to contraction and expansion, and overlooking the relative nature of the expressions as thus used. Both disputants might be right, but then they would not be talking of the same things.

According to this view, then, as already explained, it becomes convenient, to say the least of it, to treat all the changes, whether in the demand for or supply of money or the demand for or supply of commodities as changes in the circumstances of money, although in discussions where money itself is treated as the measure the same circumstances may be spoken of as changes in the circumstances of the things which money measures. Everything turns on the point of view. Thus, a general and continued fall of prices being proved, and commodities being taken as the measure of money, the circumstances imply a contraction of money as compared with the time just before. Whatever the real changes may have been, and whatever may be the ultimate causes of one thing exchanging at a particular ratio for another, for the purpose of the special inquiry, where money is being measured, the changes must be spoken of as changes in money, and as the purchasing power of money is increased, there is contraction of money.

It would only vary the language a little to substitute for the phrase contraction of money increased cost of production, just as it would be to substitute in the opposite case lowered cost of production, in both cases relatively to commodities. Relative contraction and expansion of money may either be conceived of as causes or effects of changes in the ratio of exchange with commodities; if we conceive of them as effects we should speak of the relative change of cost of production as the cause; but the result is the same so far. It is the circumstances of money we must view as having changed.

It appears to be possible, however, to go farther, and to point out that by comparison, if we attend carefully to the terms of the comparison, we can say positively that the recent change from a high to a low level of prices is due to a change in money, of the nature or in the direction of absolute contraction.

If we look at the matter dynamically, what we find is that over a long period of years the circumstances affecting the two factors in the ratio between money and commodities, viz., money on one side and commodities on the other side, so varied from moment to moment at one time that the ratio remained steady, and so varied at another time that the ratio changed. If at the moment of transition from the steady to the changing ratio it is found that the circumstances of the one factor have not altered dynamically, but that the progress remains what it was before, then it is a proper conclusion that the circumstances of the other factor have altered dynamically, and that the change in the ratio is to be ascribed to the change in that other factor.

This description applies exactly to what went on between commodities on the one side and money on the other from 1850 to 1873, and the change which occurred about the latter year. Before 1873 for rather more than twenty years the circumstances of commodities and of money, supply on one side and demand on the other, were undoubtedly in a state of constant flux, but the movement was such in both cases, the changes so kept pace with each other, that the ratio remained unchanged, or if anything gold fell and commodities rose. About 1873 there was an alteration, but according to the best observation the movement in commodities continued what it had been, the quantity increasing at as great a rate as in the period just before, but not at a greater rate. The inference seems conclusive therefore that after 1873 the alteration in the economic movement was in money, and to this must be ascribed the change of prices which has occurred.

It is only an additional confirmation of this view that actual changes in the movement in money in a direction likely to lead to a fall of prices can be referred to. The argument, on the assumption that the movement in commodities has been correctly described, would be complete, even if we knew less about the changes in money than we do. Whatever may be the qualities or conditions which make money exchange at a particular ratio for a group of commodities, then the changes in those conditions from day to day which made money remain steady in price towards commodities or to fall a little before 1873, must have undergone an alteration in their course about 1873. The effect being different, and the course of commodities being the same after 1873 as before that date, it must have been the course of money that changed.

The actual facts that we find as regard changes in the movement of money before and after 1873 are most striking.

In the fourteen years ending 1871, which was the last year before me when I wrote the paper in 1872 already referred to, the net imports of gold into England, the excess of the imports over the exports amounted to no less a sum than £67,776,000, viz.:

Excess of Imports of Gold into the United Kingdom over Exports.

	£
1858	10,226,000
'59	4,217,000
'60	3,057,000
'61	926,000
'62	3,892,000
'63	3,840,000
'64	3,621,000
'65	5,993,000
'66	10,768,000
'67	7,911,000
'68	4,428,000
'69	5,297,000
'70	8,793,000
'71	921,000
Total . . .	£67,776,000

This is an average of about £5,000,000 per annum or nearly so. In the following sixteen years, however, there has been hardly any excess, as the following statement shows:

Excess of Imports of Gold into the United Kingdom over Exports, 1872-87.

	Excess of Imports.	Excess of Exports.
	£	£
1872	—	1,280,000
'73	1,540,000	—
'74	7,439,000	—
'75	4,493,000	—
'76	6,960,000	—
'77	—	4,932,000
'78	5,902,000	—
'79	—	4,210,000
'80	—	2,374,000
'81	—	5,536,000
'82	2,353,000	—
'83	665,000	—
'84	—	1,269,000
'85	1,446,000	—
'86	—	391,000
'87	632,000	—
Total	31,430,000	19,992,000
Deduct excess of exports	19,992,000	—
Net Total	11,438,000	—

Allowing for the increase of population, the excess of imports in the second period, to correspond to the excess in the first period, should have been very nearly £80,000,000; actually it has only been £11,438,000.

Whatever evidence there may be about the quantities of gold in the world and in the banks or Government treasuries of other countries, the difference in the amount available or required for the United Kingdom is enormous. As the United Kingdom, it may be added, is and has been practically the only free market, working on the same basis all through, the figures are worth all the others. In the one period then we get nearly £70,000,000. In the other period, when in the same proportion we might have expected nearly £80,000,000, we got about £11,000,000 only. It is clearly impossible to contend there has been no change in the movement of gold, comparing the one period with the other.

If we looked at coinage or other details, the result would be the same. The stock of gold in England available for money has not been added to of late years as it was in the period just before. The stock with the additions has had to do more work, and it has only been able to do so because prices have fallen, and incomes have not risen, whereas from 1850 to 1873, when gold was going so largely into England, not only did prices rise a little but incomes a great deal.[1]

Of course, however, the special point of view has always to be considered. The comparison is of movements in two periods, and the change in ratio is ascribed to an arrest of the movement in one of the factors which is apparently established beyond all question.

To put the matter into more popular language, we might perhaps say that the stationary or rather rising prices of commodities between 1850 and 1873, although commodities were increasing as much as they have done since 1873, were maintained by continual additions to the stock and efficiency of money. Since 1873 the movement of additions to the stock which was a very pronounced one has been arrested, if there has not been an actual withdrawal from or diminution of stock uncompensated by an increase in the efficiency of money. Consequently the fall of prices since 1873 is explained by the check to the previous movement, when the matter is looked at dynamically and the periods are compared.

The utility of this mode of comparison is also obvious, and it was simply by using it that it was possible to anticipate fifteen and then ten years ago the actual

[1] The comparison would be still more striking, I believe, if we could compare the excess of imports of gold from 1850 downwards. But there are no official statistics of gold imports before 1858.

course which prices have since followed. In my paper in 1872 on "The Depreciation of Gold since 1848,"[1] this was exactly the method followed. The real progress of the community at a certain rate was assumed, and then as it appeared probable that the amount of new gold available for an increase of business could not be the same as before, but was likely rather to diminish, the conclusion was that the course of prices would be different from what it had been. The common opinion then was different. It was freely said that as there was so much gold about, there was enough for every purpose, and prices would rise farther. But the method of dynamic comparison, as the event has proved, made a true forecast possible. Again in 1879 it was always the dynamic comparison that was in view. Two passages may be extracted from the paper of 1879 which put the view plainly. First, speaking of the past, I said:

"The peculiarity of the period has been the increase of mechanical invention and the constant augmentation of goods, so that the accumulation of capital above shown is even in less proportion than the increase of the movement in trade which the money in use has to move. It is a moderate calculation that if only the countries which used gold in 1848, including their colonies, were now using it, the requirements to correspond with the increased population and wealth would be at least three times what they were, assuming prices to remain in equilibrium."[2]

Next as regards the future:

"Let me add that whatever doubt may be entertained as to the actual meeting of the two curves of demand and supply of gold during the last few years apart from extraordinary demands—all the facts and circumstances seem to indicate that the meeting point must come very soon unless the supply of gold is increased or economizing expedients introduced and extended. . . .

[1] See *supra*, pp. 75-97.

[2] *Supra*, p. 144.

Whether such a change is likely to come in the shape of an increased gold supply it will be for geologists and mineralogists to judge, but it is not reassuring to see how little comes practically of the recent gold discoveries in India and the re-discovery in Midian. Whether on the other hand change may come in the shape of economizing expedients will be a point of no little interest for bankers and all other business men, and for legislators. Considering the slowness with which such expedients become effective when they are first introduced, and the perfection to which they have been brought in countries like England where they are introduced, I feel great doubts whether much relief can come in this way. On the whole, I see no other outlet from the situation than in the gradual adjustment of prices to the relatively smaller and smaller supply of gold, which must result from the increasing numbers and wealth of the population of gold-using countries."[1]

I spoke to much the same effect in a few words following on Mr. Goschen's address to the Bankers' Institute in 1883. "If it is found," I said, "that the annual supply of gold, now that the transition period may be considered over, is not sufficient to maintain things in what we may call an equilibrium, that there is a constant increase in population and in the resources of mankind from time to time going on, and the supply of new money is not quite equal to keep things at an equilibrium, then we may have a long-continued fall of prices from generation to generation, and this will probably have very great effects as time goes on. We may perhaps have what may be called a permanent transition period, as far as I can see."

Thus the idea of a dynamic equilibrium has always been in my mind as the basis of any comparison between period and period, and I must maintain it, especially after the event, to be a useful method of comparison. In any case you must define your idea of an equi-

[1] See *supra*, pp. 146-147.

librium at starting, or you can have no clear notion of the facts at all.

It would perhaps be possible to leave the discussion at this point. If the dynamic comparison here made is useful, partly for forecasting the future course of prices, and partly for explaining generally the relations of money, commodities, and incomes to each other when prices change, then it is a comparison which ought to be made, whatever else is done or omitted. It carries us a long way in the investigation. So much is said, however, about other comparisons, especially about the abundance of commodities causing the fall of prices and not the contraction of money, that at the risk of burdening myself with controversy I propose to add a short criticism on this discussion.

Clearly the suggestion already made that the two causes are not on the same plane—abundance of commodities properly belonging to a question of real cheapness, while scarcity of money belongs to a question of money prices only—covers the whole ground. But the point need not be pressed. The argument from the abundance of commodities may be demonstrated to be faulty in other ways.

The question immediately arises, looking at the whole course of the discussion, whether those who insist so much on the increasing abundance of commodities as excluding any idea of the contraction of gold are not really attempting the impossible, viz., to measure two variables, one against the other, without a third common measure by which to try them. We know, however, so little of the ultimate facts which regulate the ratio of exchange between particular commodities, that it would be useless to determine, except in a comparative and limited manner, what are the facts which change at a given time, and how one commodity may exchange for less than before, although it may be produced in smaller quantity; another for more than before, although it may be produced in greater abundance; and although it may be true generally in theory that increase of supply means a lower rate of exchange for the article supplied, and a less supply a higher rate of exchange. The concrete facts are in truth infinitely difficult to follow out, and no one should attempt to do so without limiting his quest in some way.

When, therefore, abundance of commodities is pitted against scarcity of money in the way that is sometimes done, I confess my inability to follow the discussion at all. I seek in vain for the exact terms of the comparison —the definition of the equilibrium which is the starting point of the comparison, and a description of the changes as from this equilibrium. The whole discussion is bewildering to a degree.

I would say, however, though it is not quite safe to speak in the absence of all clear definitions by the disputants themselves, that the contention that the recent change in prices or in the purchasing power of gold is to be ascribed rather to the increasing abundance of commodities than to any contraction of money, is obviously, as far as it has any reason at all, based upon an attempt at a totally different comparison from the one which we have now made. For the purpose of this comparison the quantities of commodities and money, or the conditions of their production, or whatever determines the ratio between them, are assumed to be in a state of rest just before the change in prices occurs —a statical and not a dynamical equilibrium is assumed; —and as it is found that commodities go on increasing, and there is no actual diminution of money from that point or very little, the subsequent change in prices is ascribed to the change in commodities. But whatever may be thought of the validity and usefulness of such a comparison, what I have to submit is that it is obviously, and by the terms of it, a totally different comparison from what is attempted when the two periods are looked at dynamically and a dynamic comparison attempted.

The difference between the two comparisons can be

illustrated very simply by diagrams, which show at a glance that those who argue for abundance of commodities as causing the recent fall of prices, start from an assumed equilibrium of rest at the date when the fall began, while the comparison which asserts a change in money is really a dynamic comparison. (See p. 214.)

The first diagram, it will be seen, shows commodities and money both increasing from 1850 to 1873, and the ratio between them remaining steady; there was in truth a moderate rise of prices, but it would complicate the diagram to show this; after 1873 commodities went on increasing as before, but there was a check to the increase of money, and hence the fall of prices is ascribed to this check to the increase of money. This was the change that took place in 1873 or thereabouts. The recent fall of prices, therefore, in a dynamic comparison, is clearly due to a change in money.

The second diagram, on the other hand, starts from 1873 only, assumes a state of rest as at that date, and thence as commodities increase, while money does not, the fall in prices after that date is ascribed to the increase of commodities. It is the increase of commodities which causes a change from the assumed state of rest. But this second diagram is only a copy of the second half of the first, and deals with the same facts, only presenting them in a different way, and without comparison with the previous period, which is the essential point of the comparison in the first diagram.

The two comparisons, it is plain, are fundamentally different, and to argue as if they were the same must cause endless confusion.

My own opinion is that a statical comparison, besides being much more difficult than those who attempt it imagine, is not of much use when you do make it. The economic world is in incessant movement, and the comparison required for any purpose is almost always dynamic. You have to compare movement with movement if you want to find out what is changing, not state with state. In any case also the movement is much

DIAGRAMS

ILLUSTRATING DIFFERENT COMPARISONS AS TO THE CAUSES OF THE RECENT FALL IN PRICES.

FIRST DIAGRAM.

CHANGE IN MONEY VIEWED AS CAUSE OF CHANGE.

DYNAMIC COMPARISON.

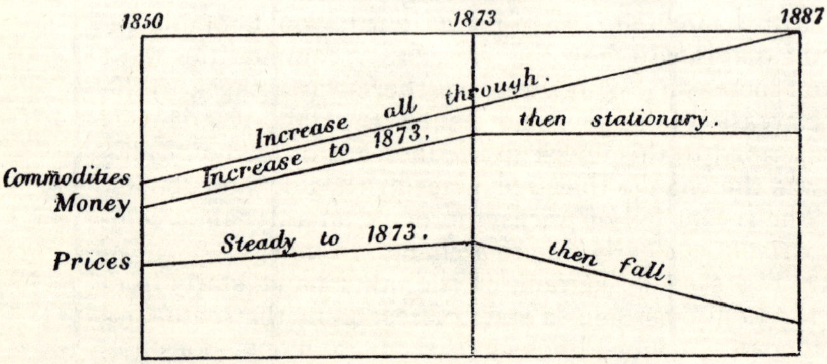

SECOND DIAGRAM.

CHANGE IN COMMODITIES VIEWED AS CAUSE OF CHANGE.

STATIC COMPARISON.

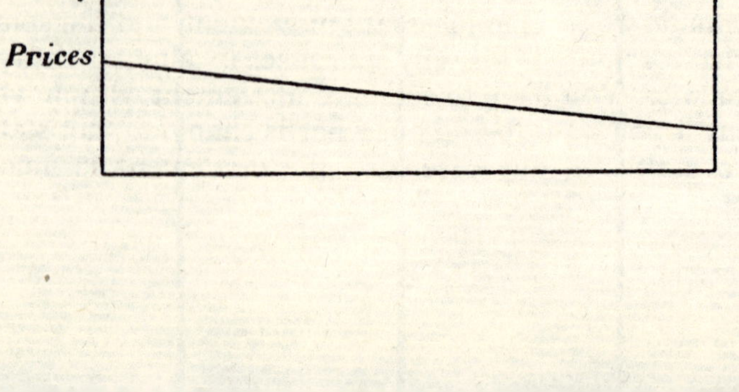

more easily compared. You may not be able to tell all the causes of a given economic condition so as to compare it with another economic condition and its causes; but if you can take two economic conditions succeeding each other, and point out a difference in the movement of one of two factors which must have contributed to the conditions, you have something definite and palpable to rely on.

Those who dwell on the abundance of commodities rely on the great authority of Tooke, and much of their writing is in fact a reminiscence of Tooke. I may be allowed a word therefore regarding Tooke's place in the literature of these discussions. To my mind he is completely superseded by Jevons. With all his industry and knowledge of business—and there is no more acute or fruitful author to study—Tooke never seems to have got into his mind the notion that the causes of changes in prices which he dealt with were not all on the same plane, and that most of what he said about good crops and the rest of it causing a fall in prices could be admitted without bringing into question the notion that looking at the whole history from another point of view the average changes from generation to generation could be described as changes in the value of money. He had no good idea besides of the logical or scientific value of an index number, such as his successor, Mr. Newmarch, found himself compelled to adopt in his continuation of the "History of Prices." Mr. Jevons has changed all that. By demonstrating how an index number can be used on an extensive scale, he has in fact demonstrated that in point of fact changes in average prices from generation to generation can be traced, *i.e.*, changes in the average purchasing power of money; and most of Tooke therefore, as far as questions like the present are concerned, goes by the board. In theory, however, Tooke never denied that there might be changes in the supply and demand for money adequate to cause great changes in prices. Where he failed was in recognizing the special character of the problem, and the inapplicability of most of the points he raised—as to good harvests and the like accounting for changes in particular commodities—in a discussion in which from the necessity of the case the average of commodities is itself the measure, and the question is not of real cheapness or dearness, but of money prices only. After Jevons, Tooke is really out of date, and nothing is more curious than to see how in the recent discussions disputant after disputant seems unable to follow Jevons, and prefers to go back to an order of ideas which is entirely superseded.

As showing farther the difficulty of the method of a statical comparison in this very matter, I may refer to the excellent mathematical work of Dr. Kral, with a preface by Dr. von Neumann-Spallart, in which an attempt is made to prove that the change from a high to a low level of prices is due to a change in commodities and not in money. It is evident from this book that if a solution could be found for this question, starting from a statical equilibrium, the most difficult mathematics would be necessary, whereas when a dynamic comparison is attempted, the result stands out with striking distinctness, and there is no difficulty.

I have only to add that for the purpose of forecasting the future it is absolutely necessary we should look at the matter dynamically. We cannot trace out all the causes which produce a given ratio between prices and commodities. We can see, however, that the movement in one or two important factors of that ratio is in a certain direction, by which an equilibrium of a certain kind is established. It is easy to predict that a continuance of the movement in the leading factors must lead to one kind of result, and an alteration in that movement to a different result.

The Redistribution of Wealth.

The consequences of an appreciation of money would demand a chapter to themselves, but though unable to treat the subject fully in the present paper, I am unwilling to pass over it altogether, as it must be referred to when we come to draw conclusions as to the future prospect.

These consequences are usually dealt with in two divisions: 1. The effect of appreciation in checking industry and so retarding the increase of wealth; and 2. The social and other effects of appreciation in redistributing wealth. The former of these branches need not, however, detain us. I do not consider it really important. Industry goes on with any sort of currency provided it does not change in short periods. It is hard to say whether abundant money causing inflation is better or worse in the end in its effect on production than a contraction of money which causes appreciation. What I have to say on these points moreover is said elsewhere. I shall only deal then with the effects of appreciation, and of course in this connection appreciation of the special character above described, in redistributing wealth.

It is obvious beyond all question that these effects may be important. Measured by a certain standard, the average of commodities, the weight of all permanent burdens is increased as compared with what would have been the case if there had been no appreciation. People in paying annuities or old debts have to give sovereigns which each represent a greater quantity of commodities, a greater quantity of the results of human energy, than it would have represented if there had been no appreciation. It may be quite true that on the average the individual in paying a debt, as his average income is not less, only uses the same proportion of that income or the capital represented by it to discharge the debt, and in this sense there is superficially no increase of the burden on the average in the case supposed; but it is hardly to be assumed, I think, that the increase of production is an increase without additional effort—it is the effort rather of a human unit who is always becoming on the average a stronger producer—and in admitting consequently that the same proportion of a larger production is required to pay larger debts, it remains true that there is an increase of burden, although it happens to be borne by stronger producers. It is at any rate quite clear that the benefit of an increase of production is distributed differently when money appreciates measured by commodities than when it does not appreciate. The debtors pay more than they would otherwise pay, and the creditors receive more.

The matter is thus not unimportant to the two large classes of people who make up the community. Appreciation is a most serious matter to those who have debts to pay. It prevents them gaining by the development of industry as they would otherwise gain. There may be compensations in different directions, as by the lowering of the rate of interest which seems to take place as the result of appreciation, but on the whole the balance is against the debtor, as compared with what it would be if there were no appreciation.

On a large scale this applies to transactions between nations. A creditor nation is able to draw more from its tributaries, who have to pay it in the appreciating money, than it would otherwise be able to draw. To pay the same debt they must send to their creditors 30, 50, perhaps 100 per cent. more produce than they would otherwise have to send. There is no doubt that in this sense the weight of the gold debt of a debtor-country like India or the United States has enormously increased of late years. The resources in both cases may have grown even more largely than the burden, but there is nevertheless an increase of the burden itself.

All this is treating the question with regard to the average effect. It is still more important to remember, however, that the average may be made up of a great variety of cases, and in fact there is no doubt the redistribution described spells ruin to individuals and classes. Although average production is increased, there are large masses of property where there is no increase, or little increase, where the fall of prices therefore means a diminution of the gross money return, and where, consequently, the property being mortgaged, the margin of the mortgagor is swept away. This has now become a familiar matter to most people in connection with the depression in land-owning, but the landlord only exemplifies an extreme case of a general mischief. He owns very often only the margin of a margin. The rent itself is the margin of profit remaining after the expenses of cultivation and the farmer's profit have been deducted from the gross produce, these expenses not being reducible, at any rate at once, with the fall in prices. Of this margin again the nominal owner only gets a remainder, and he would often be a loser, even if the rent represented the same proportion of the gross produce as before, because being less in money the whole of it is swept away by the charges and debenture interest so that there is no remainder. In this way landowners who seemed to have so safe a position have been ruined by the score. But this case is the case *mutatis mutandis* of every ordinary shareholder in a company who has debenture holders and holders of preference shares in front of him. Margins are everywhere endangered. On the other hand the owners of the preferences so long as they are safe are paid much more than they would have been paid if there had been no appreciation. They belong to the creditor class, and gain where the others lose.

All this, let me repeat, is involved in the appreciation of money measured by commodities, even though incomes as a rule do not diminish. The mischiefs are no doubt less than if there was a still greater fall of prices, accompanied by a serious diminution of incomes on the average. But they are mischiefs as far as they go. No doubt one reason they have been less felt than would otherwise have been the case is that many people are both debtors and creditors. They not only own land, perhaps, but they own Government and the like stocks, where they are preferred creditors, and where they gain consequently by the appreciation of money. But there are sufficient cases of marginal owners whose margins have been swept away to make the social effects of the redistribution of wealth involved in the appreciation of money measured by commodities very widely felt.

At the same time, it should be recognized that in some cases the appreciation, though it means apparently a redistribution of wealth, does not really involve that mischief; it only anticipates what would otherwise happen. For instance, in giving more to a wage receiver or salaried servant, whose nominal income is unchanged, it may still only place him in the position in which a gradual rise in the scale of living would have placed him. If real wealth had been increasing without a corresponding fall of prices, or rise in the purchasing power of money, then wages and salaries must infallibly have risen. In these cases, although redistribution of wealth seems involved in the appreciation, there is no real redistribution involved; there is a general increase, in which all incomes participate on the average.

The appreciation in any case is not one to be regarded with a panic feeling except in special cases. Especially as regards national debts, which are not themselves increasing in amount, the increase of burden need not be very formidable, for two reasons: 1. The reason already mentioned, that the income per head in the case supposed does not diminish, so that the charge per head cannot be more than it was before; and 2. The fact that population in an advancing community is always increasing, so that if the debt does increase, the burden on each individual taxpayer must diminish from period to period by the increase of their numbers. The taxpayer does not gain as he would gain if there were no appreciation of money; but the case must not be spoken of as that of a debt growing and swamping the debtor. There is a third reason, viz., the reduction of interest which seems to be a consequence of the appreciation of money; but as this involves disputable matter, I do not insist upon it, although in the case of our own national debt the reduction of interest by conversion, as we all know, has been most serious. It is obvious practically that there are many national debts where the appreciation of money, for the reasons stated, and also because the debt is so small, does not lead to such an increase of burden as to be serious. It does not follow, of course, that all communities and all national debts are in the same case. Where debts increase fast, and where, in addition, as in the case of France, there is no rapid increase of population, the problems involved in the appreciation of money may at any time become serious. I should look for troublous times, for instance, both for some of our Australasian colonies and for a country like the Argentine Republic, even if the appreciation does not grow more serious than it has been. That the pile of debts has to be paid, principal and interest, in appreciating money, even if individual money incomes do not diminish, is a most serious consideration. The increase of the wealth of such borrowers ought to be enormous to enable them to bear safely the debts they are incurring.

The Future Course of Prices.

What is to be the movement of prices in the future? Of course no one would attempt prophecy in such a matter. We can only assume the continuance of certain conditions which seem more or less probable, and infer from past experience what the result will be. In 1872 this method of proceeding enabled me to anticipate as highly probable the fall of prices which has since in fact occurred. What are the data now for an anticipation regarding the future?

On this head then I am bound to say all the evidence seems to me to point to a continuance of the appreciation. So far as can be judged, there is no end to the progress of invention or improvement in industrial qualities among gold-using communities. The increase of the numbers of such communities, especially

English-speaking communities, also goes on at a very rapid rate. The conditions therefore are generally so far the same as they were in 1872. There are no special demands for gold ahead such as were then in view, first of all for Germany, and more recently for the United States; but, *per contra*, the area of ordinary use has been enormously enlarged. France and England before 1872 were almost the only gold-using countries, the United States at that moment, though gold was its principal metallic money in use, being on a paper basis; but since 1872 Germany, the United States, and Italy, among the leading countries of the world, have all become gold-using. The increase of population among some of these new additions to the gold-using area has also been remarkable, while the increase in England goes on at as great a rate as before, and the increase among the minor gold-using countries, such as the Australian colonies, the Cape, and Brazil has also been remarkable. It has to be considered again that the transition from a silver to a gold standard among wealthy nations is a secular phenomenon, and that we may fairly expect the gold-using area to increase as one nation after another becomes richer. First England about two centuries ago went over to gold; more recently, rather more than fifty years ago, the United States went over to gold with the help of a bimetallic law, but really with the deliberate intention to get gold; still more recently, France took to gold, refusing to part with it after having once got it, and suspending the coinage of silver when silver threatened to become the principal money in use, and therefore the standard, just as England, for similar reasons, suspended the coinage of silver in 1798; still more recently Germany, and then Italy, not to speak of minor countries, have become gold-using. It is impossible to suppose that this favour to gold is accidental, or that the movement to adopt it will not extend to other countries as they grow richer. We who are gold-using may think it highly desirable that other nations should favour silver more than they do, but the tendency to go over to gold must be recognized as a fact. At this very moment two of the countries to whom a silver money might be thought most useful when they resume specie payments, viz., Russia and Austria, do in fact keep large bullion reserves in gold, this being especially noticeable in the case of Russia; while the intention to have a basis in gold is further marked in the case of Austria by the fact that silver is at a discount compared with the paper, and gold only at a premium. I should anticipate, therefore, as most likely an extension, and not a contraction, of the gold-using area in the coming years. There is also a natural reason of great weight for the preference. As peoples become richer the mere weight of silver makes it inconvenient for all concerned to handle it to the necessary amounts if it is used at all in the daily transactions of life. Gold becomes a *quasi* necessity and not merely a luxury, and this necessity increases rather than diminishes not only among communities which are not gold-using, but even among those which are already on a gold basis. With regard again to the use of gold in the arts, we cannot but expect the demand of the richer nations as they grow richer to increase. It is now very considerable, amounting at a low computation to two-thirds of the annual production, and is most likely to increase.

All these facts point to a continued pressure upon gold, against which the only compensation would be a more extended use of economizing expedients. Such economizing expedients will in fact, as I believe, mitigate and modify the demand for gold, but the question is to what extent? and just as I believed in 1872 that they would not do so to the extent of preventing a fall of prices, should the supply of gold not increase, so I do not believe now that they will have a mitigating effect to any serious extent. The question then becomes, what is to be the supply of gold? A great deal is said about the Transvaal and other sources of supply, and if there should be an enormous development of gold mining the tendency towards a rise in the purchasing power of gold would no doubt be checked or reversed. But it would take a very large development indeed to produce any result of the kind, perhaps an addition of 10 or 20 millions to the annual supply, while the demand itself will of course increase with a diminished cost of producing gold as compared with other things. The better probability seems therefore to be that the increase of the purchasing power of gold will continue from the present time. If it does not increase, there must be a very large increase of the supply.

Will silver participate in the fall along with other commodities? Here the better probability seems also to be that the tendencies rather are towards an increase of the divergence between gold and silver which has been going on for centuries, in consequence, as I believe, of the growing wealth of nations making them turn to gold one after another as they find or make opportunity. The silver-using nations are nations with much smaller individual incomes than gold-using nations; they are not so progressive; while if they do progress they are apt to resort to gold more and more, partly as a supplement to, and partly as a substitute for, silver as they come to have a variety of dealings and transactions in which gold is more useful than silver. At the same time nothing is more remarkable than the continued increase of the supply of silver, which is produced geologically as yet under different conditions from gold, and is more susceptible of almost unlimited development. The difference between gold and silver geologically was well expressed by M. Leon Faucher forty years ago, when people were excited by the gold discoveries, and his remarks have since been confirmed by the subsequent great development of silver mining. M. Faucher says:

"It is not without some show of reason that mythology, transporting the analogy of the physical into the moral world, made the age of silver succeed that of gold. Historically, in fact, the discovery of and the working of gold preceded that of silver. Gold is almost always found either pure or mixed with silver. In searching the beds of rivers and streams it has been obtained by the mere process of washing. This work is within the reach of the rudest state of society. It appears like a treasure spread over the surface of the earth, under the very feet of the first occupier of the soil. Silver, on the contrary, is embedded in rocks of primitive formation, and is seldom found near the surface of the earth; its extraction requires a combination of science, machinery, and capital. It is the work of a state of civilization already far advanced, and firmly established. . . . Not only did the value of money and of the precious metals increase in the long dark night of the middle ages, but the relative value between silver and gold which had been established by the progress of industry again changed. Gold preserved its value the longest; its supply was fed by the washings of the golden sands, a fit occupation for the knowledge and tastes of an ignorant people. The working of the silver mines, on the other hand, being a work befitting a civilized and scientific people, was naturally interrupted, and languished during a period of spoliation and endless warfare. Hence, as we may suppose, even the scarcity, both relative and absolute, of silver; the comparison with gold remained at 11 and 12 to 1 from the ninth to the middle of the sixteenth century. It required the excessive and sudden abundance springing from the working of the mines of Potosi and Peru, and of Zacatecas in Mexico, to reduce the proportion to 14 and 15, the average rate at which it remained in Europe until the end of last century.[1]

There is a strong drift of things therefore towards appreciation of gold, and relative depreciation of silver, though not as yet an actual depreciation of silver mea-

[1] Leon Faucher, "Remarks on the Production of the Precious Metals." Translated by Thomson Hankey, jun. London, 1852.

sured by commodities. If this drift goes on, the divergence between the two metals will increase and not diminish. This impression will be confirmed, I think, when the ratio between the two metals is looked at historically. I extract the following short table from Soetbeer, adding the figures subsequent to 1680 as of common knowledge:

Ratio of Silver to Gold from 1500 *to the present time.*

Years.	Ratio Silver to Gold.	Years.	Ratio Silver to Gold.
1501-20	10.75 : 1	1641-60	14.50 : 1
'21-40	11.25 : 1	'61-80	15.00 : 1
'41-60	11.30 : 1		
'61-80	11.50 : 1	1800	$15\frac{1}{2}$: 1
'81-1600	11.80 : 1	1800-50	$15\frac{3}{4}$: 1
1601-20	12.25 : 1	'50-70	15.40 : 1
21-40	14.00 : 1	Present time	22.00 : 1

The steady dwindling of the ratio of silver to gold over the whole period is manifest, and perhaps it may be lawful to mention, without incurring the charge of bringing in the bimetallic controversy, that the great nations of the world, with the single exception of England after 1680, before which a considerable part of the fall took place, were bimetallic almost the whole time. The movement has thus been steadily towards a decline of silver in reference to gold. Of course the change in the last few years has been most unusually sudden and severe, but there was, it will be observed, a very serious change, indeed, in the early part of the seventeenth century, and it may be suggested that the whole economic movement in modern times is quicker than it was formerly, while the run upon gold has been fostered by the unusual supply which came on the market from 1850 onwards, and the increase of supply in the case of silver, from the sheer weight of it, produces no such effect, if it does not produce the opposite effect.

I regard all this movement and have described it as a natural movement. This would hardly be the place to discuss the bimetallic theory if we were inclined to do so, but certainly it may be allowed, even by bimetallists, I think, that the tendencies to divergence between gold and silver are strong enough to require a very powerful controlling influence to keep a constant ratio between them, if they are to be controlled at all, which I do not believe to be possible. In fact, but for the accidental gold discoveries of 1848-50, and the previous discoveries in Russia, the increasing divergence between gold and silver which was manifested before that time would have long previously produced a fall of silver in relation to gold like that we now witness. Such a fall was in fact anticipated by economic experts before 1850. The events of 1848-50 suspended the economic development. To all appearance it is again in full course. The probabilities appear to point to a further heavy fall of silver in the next ten or twenty years, the reason at bottom being the run upon gold and the short supply of it, though the steady increase of the production of silver, and the comparatively limited natural area of its use, also count.[1]

Is there anything to be done by Governments to mitigate the appreciation of gold or provide against its effects, is a question which will naturally arise. The anticipation I ventured to indulge in in 1879 to the effect that we should infallibly have such topics as the issue of £1 notes brought up for discussion has certainly been more than fulfilled. To find a Royal Commission recommending the issue, not merely of £1 notes but of 10*s.* notes, and these based on silver, is certainly a sign of increased readiness to discuss currency innovations. But the only suggestion I would make is of a statistical kind. All these difficulties seem to me to suggest the expediency of further

[1] This has been fully confirmed by the actual course of silver prices since 1888. [1903.]

scientific study by those interested of the theory and practice of index numbers, which supply a means for providing for deferred payments by substituting a different currency for money, as is done by the corn averages for tithe and by corn rents generally. If we cannot invent a money that will itself be stable over generations, may it not be possible to devise a substitute by which the deferred payments will themselves change with the changing value measured by some other standard, and in that way the redistribution of wealth will in some degree be lessened?

This last suggestion can hardly be expected to be a very popular one at present, while as yet index numbers are hardly known to the public. It is remote enough from any practical issues. But in any case, it may be hoped, studies like what we have been engaged in to-night will not be in vain apart from practical issues. Knowledge is always useful, and a clear insight into what is going on and what is fairly to be anticipated may both prevent panic and enable business people to make sensible arrangements in their provisions for the future which otherwise they would not think of. In documents charging estates, for instance, lawyers might have been able to save their clients much embarrassment by charging a *percentage* of net rental only, or a sum to be varied by another measure, as the tithe is varied, instead of a fixed and unchangeable sum in money. Generally in a time of appreciating money business men must consider carefully the effect of engagements to pay money at distant dates. Many mischiefs might have been avoided if all concerned had realized ten or fifteen years ago what was likely to happen in money, and good will now be done if possibilities are kept steadily in view.

NOTE (1903).—The anticipations as to the likelihood of a farther appreciation of gold were not realized in consequence of the South African, Westralian, and North American gold discoveries, but enormous as these discoveries have been, there is as yet little sign of another great depreciation of gold.

VI.

MR. GLADSTONE'S WORK IN FINANCE.[1]

THERE is a universal agreement of opinion that Mr. Gladstone's strength is finance. Those who dispute his capacity in other respects allow that figures steady him, and his achievements in this field have been the principal boast of his admirers. Until lately, indeed, it might be said, there was little else to boast of; Mr. Gladstone's career had been otherwise mainly interesting as a psychological study, exhibiting the process by which a peculiar mind, starting with a false appreciation of the tendencies of the time, and imbued with notions of a theological cast, has gradually harmonized itself with these tendencies, and discarded theological conceptions in the domain of politics. Because, then, Mr. Gladstone is so prominent, and his repute is so largely due to success in one department of politics, an inquiry into what his work here has been, without embracing his whole career, may be more than justified. This would be the case altogether apart from his recent accession to the premiership. No doubt the past history of any premier, the predilections he has manifested, and his success, or supposed success, in a particular department, are likely to throw light on his future policy. But it is enough to know that Mr. Gladstone, as a prominent party leader, is mainly praised for his finance—has his achievements here put forward as a main reason for supporting him. This fact alone proves that the work is considered of a vitally important character, intimately concerned with the business of politicians in the present time. By studying Mr. Glad-

[1] Written in 1868.

stone's finance we are likely to get light on some of the most important problems which our public men have to solve—unless it should prove, what we find is not the case, that great achievements in finance, of the kind so much praised, are no longer possible. It will be said, perhaps, that the subject is familiar enough—Mr. Gladstone and his financial deeds have been in all the papers these many years. But common as is the talk of Mr. Gladstone's finance, it may be doubted how far it is really known. A generation has grown up which knows not Mr. Gladstone directly, or the work that he has done—to whom his great budgets are matters of history quite as much as the Reform Bill of 1832, or the dreary politics which preceded it from 1815 downwards. There are plenty of men among us who have lived through the whole period, but the last events are almost as unknown as the first to those who were at school during the Crimean War, or have graduated since 1860, but who will henceforth have their share in the politics of the future. On this account it may be useful to resume questions and arguments which may to some be stale and commonplace, and mark out the outlines of a period from which the present has been developed. Perhaps those who are older may not wholly lose by looking broadly at the past. A deliberate retrospect may remove or modify the partial impressions of the hour—may show what was essential and permanent, what are probably, therefore, the strongest influences in the times which are beginning.

The talk is of finance, but the fact which meets us at the threshold is the secondary place of what passes by that name in the financial record of this country during recent years—that is to say, since 1842. The ordinary understanding of a financier's duty—and usually the correct understanding—is, that he is to find ways and means for expenditure, and maintain the credit of his Government. With the expenditure itself it is not supposed he has much to do, except that having to furnish the means he is expected to criticise it closely, and reduce the bill if he can. What he must know is the way to borrow cheaply, or to raise a revenue with the minimum of resistance. The unpardonable sin is not the infliction or maintenance of bad taxes, but the failure to find the money. The history of States, as a rule, has shown Governments spending up to the limit of their means, the limit of what could be screwed out of their subjects; and books on taxation bear curious witness to the anxiety of the problem—how to find a new instrument of raising the wind. There is nothing, says Adam Smith, which governments have been so ready to borrow of each other as a new tax. The most important financial exploits on record have likewise been those of financiers, such as the younger Pitt, in the conduct of a great war. To keep the stream of expenditure flowing, without totally exhausting the nation, and to devise a new expedient with every fresh strain on the national resources, were the tasks that had procured most renown. But the problems of recent years have been of a different order—a different exercise of ingenuity has been required. The conditions have wholly changed. The experiment of free trade, so much recommended as it was in order to improve the revenue, had other relations as important, or more important, to the general welfare of the country. Whether the experiment was worth trying for the good of the country, and how to find the means of trying it, became the financier's questions. But the necessity of looking so much more to the general welfare of the country is not the only change. What must besides be taken into account is the marvellous and unprecedented increase of the national wealth in the course of a very few years—an increase which apparently has not yet approached a permanent check. The aggregate income of the nation has probably been doubled within the last thirty years; the taxable income of the country must have increased in much greater proportion. To maintain in such circumstances an equilibrium between State income and expenditure became so easy a task that, if that were all, a financier might fold his hands. But the overflow of means beyond all former precedent, as soon as it began to be felt, could not but impose new duties. Among these a financier of the old school would hardly have thought of aught else but the wholesale reduction of taxation, and the improvement of the national credit by the diminution of debt, or the accumulation of a "reserve"—the steps which are suggested at the close of a great war, when the diminution of the demands on the Exchequer produces a similar abundance. But much else was to be thought of. The signal growth of wealth, if it had preceded, instead of succeeding, the commencement of free-trade legislation, should itself have suggested the revisal of a scheme of taxation handed down from other times. Happening as it did, it furnished another reason for carrying on the work begun, for making the revision complete, and thus enlarging the cause which had assisted so much in producing this very effect. All the reasons for continuing the experiment were reinforced by the initial success. Whether at the time the idea of that success was not much exaggerated is not now in question. In other circumstances commerce and industry might not have flourished as they actually did after free-trade measures; there might have been an advance to prosperity, although not the same brilliant prosperity, without any such measures at all. Still the proofs are abundant that this new legislation had been a large part of the battle. Before 1842 the condition of the country was alarming, in a way we cannot easily imagine. Successive deficits in the revenue were but a feeble index to the complaints of suffering which arose from every quarter. The country was standing still, with a vast gulf between the rich and the poor, and political discontent assuming the most threatening forms. The visible beginning of a change was the free-trade experiment—the abolition of the burdens which those concerned at the time felt to be hindering their business. If other forces, such as railways and steamships, came into play, and intensified the apparent effect, it is still true that there was an effect to be intensified, and that politicians had some excuse if they ascribed, perhaps, more than its fair share of the cause to what their own hands had wrought. It could not be a question, at least, that the work should be carried on which had assisted so beneficial an end—one of the effects being the supply of more means with which to carry it on. What remained for financiers to consider was the order of the subsequent steps, and how far the process should be carried.

The change suggested another problem of equal importance—the assistance to be given by finance in ameliorating the condition of the masses of the community. The whole tendency of the time is to bring this problem directly before statesmen and Parliaments; but the new increase of wealth, by raising the masses a little, by putting them on a better vantage-ground, by opening out for them new and unexpected vistas, has perhaps been more effectual than any other single cause. The conception of a vast manufacturing community, well fed, and housed, and clothed, living in comfort—what would even have been thought affluence only a century ago—was hardly thought possible till people witnessed the growth of such a community almost before their eyes. But once made a possible, almost an actual, fact, the expediency of consulting this people's welfare, of giving them more chances, of making life richer and more enjoyable for them, became much less problematical than it had seemed even to very good men. Statesmen came under new obligations, and the idea forced on financiers, almost unconsciously, was that, instead of benefiting the masses merely by undoing still further an antique legislation, they could also add to their means by reducing the taxes which pressed on them. To distribute the accumulated wealth of the country more evenly, to cause it to be shared more and more largely by the mass—especially those who are just struggling out of the borders of pauperism—are objects of paramount importance, which might be worth, if need were, the weighting of the balance of taxation in favour of the poor. Whether their condition could not yet more be improved by the appropriation of the new wealth to the development for the general interest of the "monopolies of civilization"—whether financiers should not be prepared to find means for this sort of expenditure —is equally a question which presses. To urge this earnestly may appear to some to be devotion to a not very high aim, but not to those who know what "wealth" for the poor means. Command of the means of enjoyment is, in truth, the beginning of civilization. The roughest navvies may gain little by the sudden possession of high wages, but the second generation of a highly-paid labouring class develops new tastes and gifts. Recent history has furnished too many illustrations of the fact to make it any longer doubtful. The increase of wealth in the possession of the mass of the community is therefore an aim of first importance. If a financier can accomplish it by reducing taxation, or by other means in his power, all his energies should be bent to the task.

What share, then, had Mr. Gladstone in the financial tasks of the period? in what direction will his future influence be bent? are the questions we have to answer. Glancing backwards, it is not difficult to see that all the problems stated have been solved, or many steps made towards solving them; and, whatever the criticism of detail, the respective merits of the financiers of the time can almost be measured by the bulk of their contributions to the work. Tried in this manner, Mr. Gladstone's contributions are confessedly the largest of the whole twenty-six years since 1842. All that is characteristic in the last sixteen is exclusively his. There have been other Chancellors of the Exchequer—Sir George Lewis, Mr. Disraeli, and Mr. Ward Hunt —but, as fortune or management would have it, they have contributed almost nothing among them to the work of the period. Mr. Disraeli's insignificant contribution in the budget of 1867 is literally almost the only thing which Mr. Gladstone cannot claim. It is obvious, too, that a very large share of the work has been got into these sixteen years. Of the four great stages into which the whole period may be divided, two at least are included in the later time. To Sir Robert Peel belongs the first step in 1842, and the second step in 1845; but the stages of 1853 and 1860 were marked with equal distinctness, and were hardly of less importance. To take the test of the amount of taxation reduced, it appears that, in the years 1842-52, the balance of remission was £7,000,000, while in 1853-66 the balance is £13,000,000. This, too, was in spite of the fact that the expenditure in the former period was only between £50,000,000 and £52,000,000; whereas in the latter period it has been between £65,000,000 and £70,000,000. The proportionate merit of Mr. Gladstone is not so great as the figures show, because all our figures are now bigger, and the taxes reduced would not have been so productive, when they came to be reduced, but for Sir Robert Peel. They are proof, nevertheless, that a great deal was done; and when the details are looked at, the conclusion is not less unfavourable. To the first period necessarily belongs the redress of the worst evils in the old system—the abolition of export duties, of import duties on the raw material of manufacture, and of certain oppressive excise duties, such as that on glass; above all, the destruction of the corn laws, with the reduction of duties on other articles of food. Still, how incomplete the work would have been without Mr. Gladstone's contribution. There were no export duties left for him to touch, but every other feature of Sir Robert Peel's work is found in his. The abolition of the excise on soap and on paper released two home industries of the first magnitude, and were quite as important measures in that kind as the repeal of the duty on glass. Mr. Gladstone, again, first reduced yet further the customs duties on articles of food, and finally abolished every duty of that kind, with the single exception of the shilling duty on corn. Sir Robert Peel, besides, only began the total abolition of duties, his main steps being merely to make reductions. Mr. Gladstone has swept the tariff clear, leaving only certain charges on great articles of consumption, with supporting duties on a few articles besides.

This is a fair account, so far, of the difference between the two periods—without any design, it may be added, to disparage the work of the first period for the sake of eulogizing Mr. Gladstone. The measures of 1842 and 1845 have the merit of novelty, which, in a matter of this kind, far outweighs every other. They broke the spell of the old system, and gave the country, as it were, life from the dead: any fresh additions to that life are hardly to be compared. Still it is also just to see how large the additions were. Their full effect is hardly perceived, because they came in the midst of abounding prosperity; yet without them the new era would show fewer signs of an economic revolution. The occasional fits of languor would probably have been far more severe. Mr. Gladstone's share, however, appears the more important, if we consider that the later problems were almost exclusively his. They were all raised, more or less, in the earlier period. Even then the success of free trade had suggested the continuance of the work; Mr. Gladstone was only one of many on whom the experiment made a deep impression. Even then the idea of relieving the burden of taxation so as to ameliorate directly the lot of the masses by taking less out of their pockets, as well as by lightening the springs of industry, had come into view. But the main work in that period before 1853 still was the relief of industry—the continuance of the free-trade experiment through its earlier stages. Mr. Gladstone, on the contrary, had to pursue the task through all the later and less obvious stages; while, as he completed the task, the relief of the tax-paying masses came directly in his path. His work, on the whole, was one of greater complexity; and where the indications were less sure, the personal merit of success was proportionately greater. Mistake in development was more easy than at the first start, when things were so bad that you could hardly shake off anything without doing infinite good. By the necessity of the case, too, he has had rather less popular support. He has not had the popular clamour to carry him through, which made some of the steps so easy to Sir Robert Peel after the first had been taken. He has been compelled to create an artificial intelligence, an artificial agitation, to supply the place of feelings his predecessor had at command. Add only one more difference. The one lever with which Sir Robert Peel wrought was the income tax, to replace the revenue sacrificed until the natural process of recovery. Mr. Gladstone has devised more than one subsidiary aid, like the extension of the succession duty to real and settled property, and the increase of the spirit duties—processes which leave in his favour, as we have stated, the balance of remitted taxes, but which made a good deal easier the various steps in his progress. Of the same order of work, in a financial view, is the vigorous warfare he has waged from the beginning to the end of his career against the growth of expenditure—a warfare not required in the same degree before the Crimean time.

Little more need be said, perhaps, to show the extent of Mr. Gladstone's share in the finance of the period. But the fact that his period required so much management may need some explanation. It may not be plain at first sight that the questions were very difficult. There is a popular impression that the progressive increase in the revenue is the whole secret—when financiers have surpluses to give away, it is thought they cannot go far wrong. To remove the impression, let us watch what the history has been, how little would have turned the scale.

In 1853 it was far from certain whether the mere work of relieving industry would be carried any further. The country already was feeling itself more prosperous, and although various taxes, such as the advertisement duty, were the subject of agitation, although the general sentiment was in this direction, yet there was no such strong body of opinion as would have forced things in the direction which Mr. Gladstone selected. On the other hand, there were various powerful circumstances tending to an opposite course. Thanks to its own demerits, and perhaps also to the ingenuity with which public men, not excepting Mr. Gladstone, had committed themselves to its condemnation, the income tax was almost as good as doomed. The work bargained for when it was imposed had long since been performed, and the first thing desired was to be free of the burden. Proposals to renew it were unpopular; and just before, a committee which had been appointed to consider its reconstruction had been unable to agree, while collecting a mass of evidence to prove its inequalities. At the same time, all the interests which had been deprived of protection were clamorous. The agricultural interest especially was eagerly demanding the transfer of local charges to the Consolidated Fund, and would have welcomed, above all things, a reduction of the malt tax as a concession to its claims. A popular proposal talked of was a re-adjustment of the house tax, which had been substituted for the window duty, so as to make it fall on a lower class of houses. Thus it was quite possible in the circumstances of that time that, but for good guidance, these interests would have been heard above everything—that the income tax would have been sacrificed gradually, without securing any more relief to trade (excepting the trade in malt), and that in a house duty the lower middle classes and the working classes would have had imposed on them a drawback on the reduction of the tea duty, which was the only boon suggested for their benefit. All the while, too, though this could not be foreseen, the national expenditure was destined to rise to an unwonted height, partly in a great war, partly in the military excitement which that war nursed into new life all over Europe. Had no decisive remissions been made in 1853, had not the way to do so been discovered notwithstanding every obstacle, it is altogether doubtful when they would have been made—what agitations and controversies would have been necessary to effect them when the country, in the actual course of events, was pushing on to new conquests.

That the remissions took place—to the extent in money of more than £5,000,000—may be held in these circumstances to show that the financier who had the management of them had a true insight into the situation. The impression is more than confirmed by an examination of the budget of 1853. The budget was a surprise to the Chancellor's contemporaries; but looked at closely, it rests upon the firm discernment of two points which ought to have been as clear to every one as they were to him, but were not, in fact, so clear. The first is the great value of the work of having set trade free. In their very prosperity people had forgotten it, so that the willingness to pay the price of the income tax had died out. Mr. Gladstone only urged that what was good in 1842 and 1845 must be good in 1853, though the sharpness of the stimulus in the earlier years no longer existed. Such a position suggested as a natural corollary the continuance of the income tax for the sake of further remissions—the great point at which Mr. Gladstone aimed. Although expenditure had not increased in the ten years as it afterwards did, it had still increased so far that the abolition of the income tax was not so easily manageable as it was calculated it would have been. Its reduction could only take place gradually; and it was easy to argue that as the tax must at any rate remain, they might as well keep it at a higher amount than was absolutely necessary, and associate it with further remissions. This was the vital point of the budget, and made the subsidiary points more easy to handle, though, looking upon the whole as a piece of persuasion, hardly anything was unimportant. The controversy about the inequalities of the income tax was especially placed in an entirely new light. These inequalities were to be no worse than they had been, and as the practical difficulties in the way of its reconstruction were endless, and it was still to be only temporary and to do for the country the old work, there were good practical reasons for enduring it somewhat longer. It was, perhaps, more effective to remind people that, after all, those who were most hardly dealt with by the tax, who would have cause to grumble most, had really been direct gainers in money by the new legislation, as well as by the general improvement of the national industry. This was the Minister's justification for extending the tax to incomes under £150, by which its amount and effectiveness would be increased. The argument was special and narrow, but it reminded people in the most telling way of the nature of the new *régime*, and taught them not to calculate too nicely the price they were called on to pay. The idea of calling in new aids to help in the work—mainly, the extension of the succession duty to real and settled property—was even more exclusively Mr. Gladstone's. A like proposal had not been made since the days of Mr. Pitt. Though it has not realized what was expected at the time, it has gradually become profitable, and has yielded assistance in the task of remission which is not to be despised. It was like the discovery of a national estate, which had been appropriated to their own use by the individuals of a favoured class, and it secured to the country for all purposes a source of revenue peculiarly unobjectionable. By directing attention to new sources of income, Mr. Gladstone undoubtedly solved the problem of meeting the high expenditure of the years that were to come, without stopping the work of reform. Without such aids we should, perhaps, have been paying to this day a shilling income tax, without the remissions which were contained in the latest budgets of the series.

The features of personal effort in the next great stage, that of 1860-66, are perhaps more difficult to make out. The start would seem to have been made amid the loud din of party wrangling about comparatively small points—objections to proceeding in the way of free trade by means of treaties; clamour about Coventry distress; and the woes of paper-makers subjected to foreign competition, while foreign nations were allowed to maintain their export duties on rags, so denying them perfectly free access to the raw material. It may well seem, in the midst of such wrangling, that there was no real controversy, and no real difficulty—that only some minor points of procedure had to be adjusted, so that no one financier could claim any particular credit. The perplexities of 1853, it is plain, had likewise come to an end. The agricultural and other interests were less clamorous, having survived the deluge, and found themselves more prosperous than before. The inequalities of the income tax were less talked about, either because of the circumstance so well known to economists, that taxes, the longer they continue, tend to adjust themselves; or because, being richer, people felt less the pinching of the tax. But the situation, when looked at, discloses great difficulties, which made the selection of the right path hardly a bit more easy than it had been in 1853. The danger caused by public indifference to the work of reform was now very marked. They were disposed to approve and acclaim another characteristic budget, but their hearts were not so set upon it as to compel Ministers to introduce such budgets, or make an Opposition forbearing and careful. Perhaps they thought themselves, in their prosperity, almost sure of such work. But the great danger of all, which threatened an indefinite postponement of the whole work, was undoubtedly the growth of expenditure. Between 1853 and 1860 the annual charge for the supply services had actually increased by the sum of £14,000,000—had increased, as Mr. Gladstone explained, at the rate of 58 per cent., while the wealth of the country had only increased at the rate of $16\frac{1}{2}$ per cent. And there was no repugnance in the public mind towards almost any expenditure: that the country was rich, and could afford what it really wanted, was the new formula coming into vogue.

With such a condition of things, then, in 1860, the budgets of finance ministers were not likely, as a matter of course, to be progressive. The temptation must have been strong, with Palmerston in power, to let things slide. People would have been quite satisfied with a little effort to reduce the income tax and the war duties on tea and sugar, which had not yet been repealed, and there end. Here, then, was Mr. Gladstone's personal mark upon the time. He would not have it that the work should stop; but in spite of high expenditure, and the indifference of popular feeling, proposed changes of the very greatest magnitude—in fact, proposed almost at once to finish the work of the period. To carry out the French Treaty was itself a large work, involving the sacrifice of a considerable revenue by the lowering of the wine duties, but to add on to it the repeal of the paper duty, and of all duties on articles of food, except the shilling duty on corn, and the clearing away from the tariff of all the small burdens, was to show a new sense of the importance of the task. Mr. Gladstone, in short, was not satisfied with a small effort, but desired a remission which people would perceive, which would tell on commerce and industry. That he was right in his aim will surely not be doubted after the event; nor should it be doubted that by thus presenting the question, by showing the possibility of a great achievement, he created a new interest in the work which would not have been felt in piecemeal reductions. Good judges say that the French Treaty was enough; that the inauguration of free trade on the Continent was sufficient to mark a single great budget; and there was probably ample work, in passing it, in explaining how the treaty might yet be a free-trade one, although in form more suited to the days of protection—a topic, by the way, with which Mr. Gladstone had long before been familiarized when Sir Robert Peel's Government was vainly negotiating a very similar treaty.

But, judging by the event, it is difficult not to feel that the larger the work, the more beneficial it was likely to be in proportion, and that the excitement of interest required the very strongest stimulants. Perhaps in no other way could the income tax have been maintained at a high figure, or a vantage-ground obtained for fighting expenditure, which last is perhaps the cardinal feature of Mr. Gladstone's latest policy. As it happened, his failure in this warfare made it very convenient, financially, that his repeal of the paper duty was checked for a year by the action of the House of Lords; but any further failure would have been disastrous, and the following series of budgets would have been utterly impossible. The figures have lately been discussed *ad nauseam*, but it is not possible to go outside the fact, that but for the reduction of expenditure from £69,502,000 in 1860, and £72,792,000 in 1861, to £65,914,000 in 1866, the whole process of that time —the gradual diminution of the income tax and tea duties, and smaller reliefs to industry, the clearing off of the remnants of the great work—must have come to an end. In the latter years, it seems plain, Mr. Gladstone was preparing another great *coup*: the income tax was left at the manageable rate of 4*d.* in the pound, while the revenue for the year 1866-67 showed a surplus of about £2,700,000 on an expenditure of £66,780,000. Had the same management continued, the year 1867 might well have been the era of another great budget, in which the alternative would have been, more distinctly than at any period since 1842, the laying of the income tax on the shelf—but this time a light income tax—or the continuance, if there was room for it, of the work of invigorating the industry of the country, and ameliorating the lot of its masses. This was the fruit of keeping expenditure down, whatever damage, in the shape of insecurity or inefficient services, may have been the consequence. In a financial view the success was complete enough, and it was got by following a path which was far from patent.

Mr. Gladstone, in another way, has shown in this later period his discernment of what is required by proposing to tax the charities—a measure which, in addition to its other merits, would have added to the fund by which the general work of remission might be carried on. He failed to carry it as he had carried the succession duty on real property in 1853. The attempt, nevertheless, proved how strenuously he was fighting for the sake of those measures of finance by which the country has prospered so much.

It hardly comes within my plan to criticise in detail Mr. Gladstone's qualities as a financier; but before glancing at the work of the future, and the probable direction of his influence, it may be useful to look at him personally, and point out in one or two important particulars his strength and his weakness. What is the main secret of his splendid success? As far as reputation goes, I believe the impression is that even in finance, what has made him successful and popular is his oratorical power. People look to his budget speeches, remember their startling effects, have been moved by stirring speeches and comparisons to take an interest in subjects which, as usually treated, are repugnant. But for his oratorical art, it is hardly to be questioned, he would not have created that artificial intelligence which was essential to success. Looking back on the whole series of his speeches, however, it is not this power which strikes the reader most. One is sure to find, indeed, not a few faults in taste, and very often a defective exposition. In his last budget speech, for instance, an impressive statement as to the danger of a load of debt, and our duty to discharge it before the exhaustion of the coal-fields, is merely the preface to a scheme on the paltriest scale by which this duty was to be discharged. Defects of this kind are apt to spoil the appreciation of harangues which can hardly be understood without a feeling of the whole circumstances, not afterwards easy to supply. But what begins to be clear is something not so obvious to those who listened to the speeches at the time—who had almost forgotten one before they heard another. This is the continuity of the orator's own mind, his firm grasp of certain leading ideas of which every new speech is only an application. We see this conspicuously in his notion about checking expenditure. There is hardly one of his great financial efforts in which he does not recur to the theme—his whole financial theory being plainly coloured with a passion against the waste of money, with which experience has taught him to identify almost any Government expenditure. The cry, he has lately said, is always for more efficiency; but he had found that when any money was granted, the cry was as loud as ever. Perhaps more conspicuous still is his impression of the power of free trade. The salient fact he got hold of from the first was the multiplication of the means of employment by taking off artificial restrictions. Long before his first great budget, while he was at the Board of Trade under Sir Robert Peel's Government, we find him making numerous proposals, of which this was the theme; as, for instance, in a remarkable speech on abolishing the prohibition of the export of machinery. Even in defending the corn laws he assumes that the prospect of increased employment for the people is an irrefragable reason for their abolition—only they must beware of giving too great a shock to old arrangements, and suddenly throwing people out of work. The changes are rung on these phrases almost to the last. The invigoration of trade and commerce, the lightening of the springs of industry, are much in his mind even when proposing the reduction of tea duties, by which money would be put directly into the pockets of the poor. If Mr. Gladstone has changed his financial opinions at all, it is on such a matter as the income tax. It has been a gradual or cyclical change. As the experiment proceeded, he has come to appreciate more and more its merits as an engine of fiscal reform, though, perhaps, also, the circumstances have changed—the increased expenditure upsetting all the calculations by which the tax would have been temporary, and yet every existing benefit secured. Change of this kind is plainly not inconsistent with the utmost firmness and continuity which characterize a sure-judging mind. To this quality I would attribute in the highest degree Mr. Gladstone's success. The power to persuade others was a valuable gift, but in scientific questions—and finance is scientific, or it is nothing—it is essential to be right in fact. Mr. Gladstone understood at a very early period, and in all its thoroughness, the meaning of the work to be done, and hence the steadiness of his aim.

At the same time, in other matters besides the income tax, he has not been insensible to the teaching of events. He did not anticipate the overflow of prosperity which has marked the time. Free-trade measures, it should not be forgotten, were rather promoted at first to keep England from decaying altogether. But as the prosperity advanced, he has continued to enlarge on the duty and necessity of ameliorating the lot of the masses—of keeping this, likewise, as an aim constantly to be cherished. That this sure-judging mind is commonplace and average in its sympathies, always looking at the things as they can be presented to a popular audience, such as Parliament really is, narrows its range of action very much, but that is only saying that the defect is inherent in the very qualities by which the success has been gained.

Were this the only great quality in Mr. Gladstone as a financier, there would be some cause to wonder at the excuse he has given for applying to his finance the epithets, adventurous and crotchety. It is a remarkable alliance with love of subtlety and detail, and with abounding activity and energy, which has introduced into Gladstonian budgets those brilliant devices from which common people are apt to revolt. But Mr. Gladstone, with all his foundation of commonplaceness and steady popular judgment, would yet have been very little in finance without his love of detail and wonderful knowledge of expedients. To a very large extent this only means that he has the enthusiasm of his occupation. People succeed in nothing unless they give their days and nights to it, and Mr. Gladstone has given to finance the sweat and toil of many years of his life. By dint of much study he has acquired a genuine love of the niceties of the malt tax credits, the alcoholic test in the wine duties, the effect of an extra Sunday in a year diminishing, and an extra day in leap year increasing, the amount of revenue, and the infinitely complex problems which are bound up with sugar. He had a real intellectual pleasure in inventing and explaining that intricate operation B in the Terminable Annuities Bill of three years ago. The singularity is, that people rather like in him an exposition of minute detail which hardly another financier could make tolerable. The net result is, that he is what may be termed *rusé* in finance—never without resource at any crisis. The abundance of expedients, and his audacity, have damaged him in the past, but would hardly have done so if full justice had been done to the solid qualities in which, after all, they had their root.

Mr. Gladstone, nevertheless, has committed many financial sins. Trying so many ingenious schemes, he could not but fail in some; as he failed with the plan for converting the debt, and so reducing the interest, in his budget of 1853, and as he failed on a smaller scale with the stamp on shipping forms, which he expected to parallel his successful penny stamp on receipts. Perhaps, too, he owes to the want of pliancy in his nature a certain capacity of provoking and stimulating opposition. The proposal to tax the charities in 1863 was pushed on with too much haste and vehemence; not even Mr. Gladstone could bring all the world to see at once the force of that logic by which the conclusion in his own mind was slowly built up. On one occasion, too—in 1860—his haste and vehemence led him to make arrangements which would have landed him in a huge deficit, and possibly damaged irretrievably his financial repute. The primary duty of financiers, though it has been dwarfed by other considerations, cannot wholly sink into abeyance, and a great gulf between expenditure and income would not have been forgiven. In fairness, however, it must be allowed, Mr. Gladstone was at least conscious of the risk, and was only more passionately bent than others on the remissions he was effecting. As we could hardly have had the work done at all without him, the error is comparatively venial. It is, perhaps, a graver fault that on the question of expenditure his teaching and preaching have been too one-sided. He has taken a somewhat narrow view, with the obstinacy of his nature, and harped upon that—very effectively, no doubt, but not with the effect a fuller exposition would have had. It is not the whole truth about expenditure that it is to be discussed as a natural evil, which financiers must league themselves with such allies as they can get to keep under. Nor can any certain measure of expenditure be found in a comparison between one period and another. In addition to what he has done, beyond pointing out the importance of a nation setting a scale for itself, and comparing always the price it pays in taxation with what it gets in money spent, Mr. Gladstone would have done well to examine directly the services to which the money is applied. The exposure of inefficiency and waste, of the multitude of useless objects which are sought after, would have been worth a great many speeches in the air, which left behind a vague doubt whether there was not something right on the other side—whether, with all its inconveniences, the high expenditure had not some excuse. Direct teaching by the highest financial authorities on the principles of military and naval expenditure is really a good deal required; and Mr. Gladstone, if some critics are right, might only too easily have shown how all the efficiency talked of, or even more real efficiency, might have been gained at less cost.

Imperfect as this survey has been, it may not be impossible to derive from it some clue to the future.

The general features of the situation, it will be evident, are substantially the same. If we have no longer to do with the extension of a free-trade policy, our revenue being derived from no protective duties, and our tariff being so contrived as to yield a large revenue with the least possible injury to trade, and the least trouble to the taxpayer, we have still the main condition of all—the rapid increase in the national wealth and the elasticity of the revenue. The present temporary arrest of our progress—if, indeed, there has been any real arrest—does not alter the general set of the current, which begins once more to flow in the old direction. We may fairly count on the revival of prosperity for an indefinite period to come, just because labour grows daily more intelligent and effective, and mechanical agencies are continually multiplied. A financier may safely count on a return to nearly the old average of £1,750,000 increase in the year. Such a fact must furnish ever-new opportunities of great budgets, and would have furnished an opportunity two years since had there been any one to seize it, or had the country not been occupied with other matters. The opportunity may at once be made by reducing expenditure to the level at which it stood when that opportunity arose, and trusting to the immediate revival of the revenue. But without any such effort—by merely keeping things as they are, or reducing a very little—any Government may easily have the chance of continuing the work. Is it worth continuing? or are there any counter-schemes to make the finance of the new period altogether novel?

Looking at the past, there is hardly a doubt as to what the action of financiers should be, or as to the line of action Mr. Gladstone would recommend. There is still much in a financier's power towards ameliorating the lot of the masses. The duty on corn, the taxes on locomotion, not a few of the stamp duties, the fire insurance tax, the tea and sugar duties, are all burdens whose abolition would benefit the country, and for the most part put money directly into the pockets of the poor.[1] So long as taxes of this kind remain, and the wealth of the country grows as it has done, it will be the business of financiers to give people the benefit of the facts. That taxation may rapidly be made much less burdensome than it is should be the guide of their action. The objection may be urged that people would really gain more by a more judicious expenditure—as on education and other things which are now starved. But sudden expenditure on a large scale, even for the best of objects, is not likely to be productive—is not likely in this country to be tried; so that finance ministers may remain at ease notwithstanding this contingency. They need not apprehend any expense to swamp their budgets if there is any decent management, procuring for the country all the real benefit it can gain. The most extravagant could hardly pretend that the new things wanted will cost the country an increasing amount of nearly £2,000,000 a year, which would be necessary to keep pace with the increasing growth of revenue. Others, however, will say that attention should exclusively be given, for a long time to come, to the diminution of the debt. But this purpose ought surely to be compatible with very large remissions of taxation, as it was, in point of fact, during Mr. Gladstone's last period. To divide the work would be a very fair arrangement, applying equal sums to the remission of taxation and the reduction of debt—an arrangement which has this advantage, that every diminution of the debt lessens the annual charge, and so increases the surpluses that future Chancellors of the Exchequer may expect to give away. How much may be done in this direction is perhaps not well understood. But two facts may set it in a proper light. One is that

[1] The taxes here referred to were almost all abolished a few years after 1869, tea being the principal exception. The reimposition of the corn and sugar duties in late years and the repeal of the corn duty after existing for one year only need not be more than mentioned in this place.

during the last fifty years the capital of the debt has been reduced by £100,000,000. During the next fifty, if we only have a similar period of broken peace, we should, if we do as well as the last two generations, reduce the debt by £300,000,000. Our taxable income is three times greater than it was in 1815, and we should be capable of thrice the effort. The other fact is, what might have been during the last sixteen years if the growth of expenditure had been checked with firmer hand. Long before this the free breakfast-table, which Mr. Bright has imagined, might have been enjoyed, and the capital of the debt still farther reduced. If we choose to stand still, and devote all our surpluses with accumulations to paying off debt, we might accomplish as much in the next ten as we have done in the last fifty years. Of course, all this must be written barring accidents, but it proves the measure of the nation's ability; and, much as may be allowed beforehand for accidents, it is hardly wise to forget a high aim altogether, merely because an undefined worst may happen. The facts show, however, that even a great disaster—a war on the largest scale—might occur without arresting for a long time the work of financial reform. It is surely, then, the more allowable to look forward to a better future for our masses, for better conditions of existence so far as the State can make them better, than these now enjoy. Not only might there be a free breakfast-table, but, better still, it should be possible in a very near future to make England a free port, except for spirits and tobacco, without entertaining any grand scheme of direct taxation. Of course so much will not be done without raising the question of equalizing taxation upon the various classes of the community—a question which the working classes will *not* lose by having raised; but if it is possible to do so much, the worst difficulties of the question may be evaded. With the income tax at a vanishing point, if not quite abolished, the richest classes could hardly complain of others gaining rather more than they do by the wholesale remissions of taxation which common prosperity has made possible.

Of course the financial work of the next few years will include much more than this. The succession duty may be further extended, the charities taxed, and many more expedients tried. There are points without number for financial ingenuity, and in a Government of his own, Mr. Gladstone may be expected to aid with all the suggestions his experience and study have furnished. Above all is the question of extending the principle which has been called in to sanction the purchase of the telegraphs. Here, too, much might be said to show how well disposed Mr. Gladstone will be to venture farther in this direction—to acquire the railway monopoly, and work it for the benefit of the whole community.[1] This will be the introduction of some novelty in finance, as the State may lose or gain, financially, by the experiment, though the community can only gain; but it does not seriously affect the prospect of direct financial benefit through the continuance of the work of reform in its recent groove.—[1869.]

[1] How far the country has ever been from any measure like the purchase of the railways by the State, which was at one time so popular, need not now be pointed out. I should not myself be so decidedly in favour of such a scheme as I once was, but the present state of the railway question is as unsatisfactory as it ever was, and either purchase or an analogous measure must be held to be still on the cards. I leave the sentence in the text as I wrote it as an indication of opinion at the time. Of course no reference is made to Mr. Gladstone's work as Chancellor of the Exchequer at later periods when he was also Prime Minister, long after the date when this essay was written. But there was nothing special in the later finance, in comparison with what was accomplished in the earlier period.

VII.

TAXES ON LAND.[1]

A CURIOUS and instructive collision has just occurred between a bold and comprehensive project in the application of political economy, and one of those traditional cries in English politics which originate in some class interest, or in circumstances quite different from those which now exist, and yet colour strangely the discussion of practical reforms. I refer to the proposals of the Land Tenure Reform Association on the one side, and the agitation against local rates, or rather against the burdens on land, on the other. There could not be a wider divergence of ideas and aims than what is here discovered. The Association addresses itself directly to one of the gravest questions which can come before an old and crowded community—the question, namely, how the ownership and occupation of its narrow area should be regulated. It challenges the complete applicability here of the rule of absolute ownership which is found expedient as regards other property, and proposes, among other restrictions, that individuals who are allowed to have exclusive possession of any part of the national soil should be specially taxed. In this way, it is argued, the whole community may benefit in some degree from the competition which is inevitable when a large population is crowded into narrow room. The proposal has at least the merit of coming down from philosophy to practice, and raises in a suitable manner a question of the first importance in a democratic society, where the political power is in

[1] Written in 1871.

the hands of masses who are not the possessors of the soil. The opposing cry—that the possessors of land, or that land itself, are already unjustly burdened—is of a very different kind. It has long occupied a principal place in the party politics of England, though perhaps it was never louder or more persistent than it is now. But it is based upon no great principle. Apparently it began when all taxation was heavy, and when the possessors of land, from their political influence, had a peculiar power of making themselves heard; and it has descended to our own day, partly from habit and partly from keen self-interest, the promised gain to a class from any material change being, as we shall see, very great. But whatever its history, it springs evidently from the lowest practical side of politics—the exact opposite of the rival agitation. In discussing, as I now propose to do, the question on which this collision of opinion occurs, it will probably be useful to keep in mind the contrast which is here presented. Some good may be done by bringing scientific principles to bear on the traditional cry against rates, and by confronting the philosophical principles of Mr. Mill, and of the Association whose programme he expounds, with the practical facts and difficulties of English finance.

I.

It will be convenient to examine, first, the traditional cry. While a good deal has been said and written on the economic theory by which the proposals of the Association are supported, the means of reducing it to practice have only been discussed in the most general terms. If we begin with a question in the practice of English taxation in this matter, we shall obtain a near view of the field to which the theory must be applied. On the other hand, the indigenous discussion, as it may be termed, is most confused; and progress will be difficult till the confusion is cleared up.

The confusion is at the very beginning. It is difficult

to get an exact statement of the grievance of which so much is made. The common mode of speech is something like this:—that land, or real property, has to bear more burdens, in proportion to its value, than any other kind of property. Lord Salisbury, Sir Massey Lopes, and a hundred others, have rung the changes on this theme during the last few months; and I have read not a few laborious estimates of the personal property in the country, and the burdens upon it, got up for comparison with the more accurately ascertained facts as to real property and its burdens. But what is meant by real property bearing burdens is found on examination to be far from clear. The case is sometimes argued as if the burdens were in the nature of an income tax upon the owners of property, and the rate of the tax is contrasted with the rate which falls on incomes from personal property, or on incomes which are not from property at all; but at other times there is evidently some vague notion that property, as such, should be equally taxed, and that the rule is broken in the case of land. Confused as the statement is, we must take it as it comes, and inquire into the principles it assumes.

Whichever alternative we take, it must strike every student of finance that the principle laid down does not make out the case, even if the facts are as supposed. In either case it is a misapplication of the real doctrine of equality in taxation which political economy lays down. Taking the first alternative, that it is the owners of real property who pay a larger income tax than others, it is no doubt true that each taxpayer should contribute according to his ability; but it would not follow that a special income tax on a certain class would offend against the maxim. If this were so our present income tax would be grossly unjust, for the masses of incomes are exempt. Theoretically, however, it is obviously quite possible that to produce the final result it may be necessary to tax some sort of incomes exclusively, or more than any other sort. Say, for instance, in a country where a large part of the taxation is raised by duties on articles of general consumption, and is therefore borne by the masses of the people, and another large part by an income tax which in conjunction with the other taxes falls with peculiar weight on the lower middle class—clearly, in such a community there might be some reason for a third set of taxes designed to fall on the classes more or less exempt from the other two branches of taxation. And if these classes possessed almost exclusively some special kind of property, a tax on that property, supposing it could be made to fall on its owners, would be the very thing to redress an existing inequality. I am only supposing a hypothetical case; but it is enough to show that inequality of burdens on different kinds of property is no part of the theory of taxation.

If we take the other alternative, which makes no assumption that taxes upon a particular sort of property fall upon the incomes of the owners, the theory of the grievance will even appear absurd. How can it be supposed that there is any principle of political economy, when one sort of property is taxed, requiring all property to be taxed alike? *Ex hypothesi*, the ultimate incidence of the tax is not upon the owners of it, and before deciding to tax all property equally it would be necessary for a legislator both to weigh the immediate effects of his measures and the object he wishes to arrive at. In point of fact, the considerations which induce a legislator to impose or retain special taxes on property will induce him to tax some kinds and let others be exempt. As with taxes on the profits of a particular trade, with which a tax on property may be classed, his object will either be to impose some charge on the general consumer, in which case the tax will fall to be dealt with as one of the many taxes on consumption, or he will select some trade in which the limitation of the area of profit—the tax not being charged to the consumer—will produce the minimum of inconvenience to the whole community. The particular tax will not be unjust *per se*, but its injustice will be determined by the nature of its ultimate incidence, and the extent of its hindrance to business as compared with other taxes. Such considerations have hardly been touched on by those who complain of unequal taxes on property, but they are essential to the question when the so-called burdens on property are not of the nature of an income tax upon its owners.

What has been said may be enough to prove the great imperfections in the statement of the grievance under discussion. It may be useful to note, however, that in the actual circumstances of England, on the principles suggested, there is a violent presumption in favour of existing taxes on property or profits. They are not likely to be objectionable on any of the grounds suggested. The reason is that they are the last of a heavy burden of a similar kind, and the fact that they are the last is so far a proof that they have been distributed—that if the persons who pay them suffered at one time, they have long since been compensated. Any long-continuing tax on profits tends to adjust itself, but in the case of England during the last thirty years the adjustment has been favoured by the remarkable growth of the country under the stimulus of the removal of other taxes. The limitation of the profit area caused by the tax has been more than made up by the general progress. Unless, then, there is some overwhelming objection, or some greater good to the whole community would result, such as comes, for instance, from a larger reduction of Customs duties, it would even be inequitable to remove these old taxes. To do so would be simply to make a present of a capital sum to the followers of some particular industry or the owners of some particular property. They have already shared to the full in the general prosperity of the community caused by the lightening of taxation, and now they would obtain in addition the capital value of the tax which they do not really pay, since its burden has been transferred.

There can be no objection, besides, to special taxes on real property, on the ground of their hindrance to trade. Land-owning is so simple a business, that it is divorced from the very notion of trade, and considered a special occupation for trustees and widows and orphans. So simple a business can hardly be checked by a few plain conditions. The objection of hindrance to trade is also compensated by the consideration that the business itself is in the nature of a monopoly. The abolition of brewers' licences was objected to for this among other reasons, that the business had become practically a monopoly in a few hands; to abolish the licences would have been to put money in the pockets of a few without any real chance of its reaching the public. The passenger duty on railways is defended for a similar reason. The duty, it is said, is only a way by which the State reserves to itself the share of a monopoly. This may be wrong as regards railways, but the principle of the reasoning is obviously sound. Now land-owning is, beyond all other callings, in the nature of a monopoly. The whole quantity in a particular country cannot be increased, and there are besides hundreds of specially favoured spots. As regards land, therefore, that condition exists in the highest degree of force, which makes it probable that any abolition of a tax on profits would not benefit the community.

We are thus a long way from the proposition so confidently assumed, that all property should be taxed alike. There are many questions affecting the regulation of special taxes on property of a very different order. We may look, then, at the particular taxes which form the gravamen of the complaint, and see what portion, if any, offend against the true principle of equality in taxation, by pressing unduly on some classes of income, and which of them, on other grounds, are liable to objection.

The maximum taxation which can form the subject of this inquiry appears to be, from Mr. Goschen's recent report:

Stamp duties on deeds	£1,033,000
Probate and succession duties	715,000
Land tax	1,082,000
House tax	1,062,000
Rates	16,783,000
Total . . .	£20,675,000

Besides these there is the income-tax, which the owners of real property pay like all others; but this is not an exceptional impost on income, and the only question here is of exceptional burdens.

The total of taxation affecting real property looks very formidable. In fact, it is nearly one-third of the entire taxation of the country, imperial and local, and amounts to a charge of about 3*s.* per pound on the estimated annual value of the property in the country.[1] But the moment we examine the items, we find how little reason there is to suppose that the burden is of the nature of an income tax on the owners of real property, or that any part is of such a nature as to raise an overwhelming objection against it.

1. The stamp duties on deeds may very well be left out. The heaviest of them is a half per cent. *ad valorem* charge on the sale of property, a charge which is borne by many kinds of other property as well; and even a half per cent. charge is a hardly perceptible tax. It is sunk in charges of much greater magnitude, which always take place at sales. In any case, the incidence of stamp duties is so peculiar, that it cannot be said to affect a class so much as individuals of a class, and these unevenly amongst each other, in comparison with the amount of the duties. Where they are not defensible as a minute charge on transactions, like the receipt and cheque stamps, as I think they may perhaps be now in the case of real property, though it was not always so, there would be a case for their reduction, so as to make them minute enough for the purpose. In that case they would cease to be taxes which could

[1] Viz., £143,000,000.

be set off against others in a question of comparative taxation. It would be a mistake, however, in the meantime, to make their existence a ground for interfering with some other impost.

2. The probate and succession duties appear to me also to be a tax *sui generis*, with which no others properly come into comparison. I have to discuss them afterwards; but the distinguishing peculiarity is apparent. They are charges upon a very special extension of the ordinary rights of property, its bequest or descent after death—an extension which necessitates the direct intervention of the State; and as such, the burden which they constitute cannot properly be weighed with burdens of a different nature. If it is discussed as a charge upon a particular description of property, the difficulty at once arises that it is most unequal and severe. Some owners escape with hardly a charge, while others, who own no more, have much to pay. The only plea by which it can be defended, therefore, is that the Acts in respect of which it is levied—the authorizations given by the State to the transmission of property from the dead to the living—furnish occasion for a wholly exceptional charge. In any case, so far as the probate and succession duties are a tax upon real property generally, it will not be denied that they are more moderate than the corresponding imposts upon other property and its owners.

3. The land tax, which is next on the list, should equally cause but little controversy. It is persistently claimed as a burden upon land or landowners; but this will not bear scrutiny when we inquire out of whose income the tax is paid, or what way it causes pressure, so that its reduction or abolition would be a benefit to the community. As a fixed charge upon land for generations, it is now past all controversy a rent-charge. In many instances it has long since been redeemed, the property having subsequently changed hands; in others, inheritors of property have acquired it under the burden, and have calculated their income minus the tax, while

purchasers, in buying, invariably allow for it. To reduce it now would be to present the landowners of England with a capital sum of nearly £30,000,000. Their estates, relieved of the burden, would become at once so much more valuable, and if they did not sell, they would pocket an additional income which they never inherited or paid for.

There remain the house duty and the rates—still a formidable amount, if they are considered to fall on the incomes of real property owners, or as forming an objectionable tax on profits, notwithstanding that the burden is shifted to the consumer. We may class them shortly as rates, the only difference being that the house duty is a fixed rate limited to certain descriptions of property, whereas the rates apply more or less to all real property, though in fluctuating proportions. But what is the incidence of these rates? Are they, in the first place, an income tax on the owners of real property? There is one very short answer to this question. If they were an income tax there is none more outrageously unjust. Most properties, we are told, are incumbered, often heavily incumbered, and the residuary owner, as we may call him, the man who would benefit by a reduction of the rates, has often but a barren interest. Measuring the rates with his income from the property, they might be ten or fifteen shillings in the pound. Is it possible to believe that the owners of real property are subjected to any such income tax? The inequality in itself suggests that the incidence of the tax is different—that the burden is on the property and not on the individuals who have incomes from it.

The question remains, however, whether the rates are on other grounds objectionable. And here it should be noticed that it is by no means unanimously admitted that they are burdens on the profits of land-owning at all. A large party maintains that to no inconsiderable extent they really are passed on to the consumers—in the country districts, farmers, who pass it on as a deduction from their farming profits; and in towns, the class of occupiers, who both pay it and ultimately bear it. But granting that this transference does not take place to any material extent—a view, I am willing to admit, which I am disposed to agree with—granting that in consequence the whole or most of the charge falls on the profits of owners, are the circumstances such that they have any cause for complaint? The answer is that in the lowest view the business is one which has increased enormously, stimulated by other changes in taxation, and that being a monopoly, as land-owning confessedly is, the magnitude of the charge, even if it has been an increasing one, makes nothing against its propriety. Look only for a moment at what the increase of business has been. In 1815 the annual value of real property—in other words, the annual return of the business—was £53,000,000; in 1853 it was £85,000,000; in 1868 it was £143,000,000.[1] At the same time the rates have barely doubled in the last thirty years, and have not doubled if we take an earlier date for comparison.[2]

The improvement it may be said has arisen through the investment of capital, but this statement cuts two ways. If it means anything at all, it would mean that the charge upon the profits of the business checks investment, but nothing of the sort is alleged. The fact that investment has continued is thus a proof that the burden, whatever it is, has still left a large enough margin of profit to induce a resort to this species of business. It is certain, however, that a large part of the improvement is due to the increasing value of advantageous sites, an unearned increase of value such as Mr. Mill speaks of, and therefore a kind of profit which the State may restrict with least harm. The increase of the annual value of house property in the country

[1] In 1884 it was £193,000,000, and in 1901-2, the latest year before me, £238,000,000.

[2] Rates increased from £20,000,000 to £31,000,000 between 1868 and 1883. In the latest year, 1900-1, they were (England and Wales only) £43,000,000.

since 1815 has been £54,000,000, or 356 per cent., although the population has barely doubled. If we estimate that only a fifth of this amount is for extra ground rents—that is, rentals in excess of the value of the area occupied for agricultural purposes—we shall probably be far under the mark. And this is not the only unearned increase of value. Against the large amount of rates therefore is to be set an unearned increase of value which altogether will be of equal amount, and double, perhaps treble, what the increase of rates has been.

Nor does the case as to profit end here. The increase of rental value does not measure the actual increase of profit with which the rating-charge should be compared. It is probably the case that as respects the bulk of property in area, the increase of rental measures the whole increase of value; but there is one kind of property, that in the suburbs of large towns not taken up for building, extending in the case of London in all directions but the east over an area of about eighty miles diameter, where the increase of rental is no measure at all of the increased value. The position of the property is in effect discounted, and it is no exaggeration to say that its real selling value is now double what it would have been ten or fifteen years ago upon the same rental. It would be useless to put any figure estimate upon this increase of value, but it must be remembered as a set-off against "increasing" rates.

The question might well be left upon these broad facts, and these general principles stated, but there are other facts about the rates which affect the question of the business profits on which they are a charge. When we look into them we discover that the increase has been far from uniform geographically, or in respect of the class of property affected. The increase has in fact been confined to that class of property in which the investment of capital has taken place to the largest extent, while as respects the remainder of the property, there has either been a diminution of the burden or no material increase. The inference is, that while the rates where they have increased have not checked investment, there is an immense mass of property which has augmented in value without any proportionate charge upon its profits. The facts speak for themselves. First of all, of the above sum of £16,783,000 of rates proper,[1] there are upwards of £4,000,000 of comparatively recent rates which not only form a charge upon the property in which the investment of capital has taken place, but were mainly intended for the improvement of that property. The remainder, £12,689,000, is very little more in amount than similar rates have been during the present century, and the rate per pound is less.

In 1817	the rates were	£10,000,000,	or per £	3*s*. 10¾*d*.
1826	,,	9,500,000,	,,	3*s*. 8*d*.
1841	,,	8,000,000,	,,	2*s*. 7*d*.
1852	,,	8,700,000,	,,	2*s*. 7*d*.
1868	,,	12,689,000,	,,	2*s*. 6¼*d*.

Thus, as respects a large part of the real property in the country, it is incorrect, strictly speaking, to talk of the increase of rates.[2]

The second fact is, that at a time when real property was different in its constituents from what it is now, there was an enormous diminution of the burden, precedent to the subsequent rise in proportion to the value.

In 1826—	The rates were	£9,500,000
	House duty	1,182,000
	Window duty	1,167,000
		£11,849,000
In 1843—	The rates were	£8,000,000
	House duty	Nil.
	Window duty	1,436,000
		£9,436,000

[1] This is for England and Wales only.

[2] This is still true, although rates (for England and Wales only) are

showing an actual diminution of about £2,500,000, representing a capital sum of about £75,000,000 in the charges upon the property then existing—a burden which has never since been reimposed, as the rates, including house duty, have only risen in proportion with the augmentation of rent. The relief to the old property has been permanent.

It is thus evident, that while so much has been heard of the increase of rates, the actual fact is entirely different. The increase, such as it was, has been limited in extent, and conceals an actual diminution in the amounts levied upon part of the property which has since never been made good. To complete the statement, we need only ask ourselves what the effect would be of any such reduction of rates as the principles of the anti-rate agitators point to. Consequences are very often a test of principles, the logical result proving the groundlessness of the plea. And this appears to be the case in the present matter. Grant that certain rates[1] are thrown on the Consolidated Fund, as the most eager reasoners of the party contend, or that they are reduced one half, which would be the effect of throwing them rateably on all the schedules of the income tax, what would be the result? It is not difficult to see that in the former case some people would have £11,000,000 a-year, and in the latter case £5,500,000 a-year more than they had before. Possibly it would not all go to the so-called owners of property, for the occupiers would gain where they are dealt with on tenant-right principles; but it may be treated practically as a bonus to owners, and, as such, it is of magnificent dimensions. In the one case, at thirty years' purchase only, it represents a capital of £330,000,000, and in the other of half that amount—all to be transferred to a single class by a few lines in

now about £43,000,000 annually, as above stated (see note, p. 262). The bulk of the increase has been in improvement rates.

[1] Viz., poor and police rates, amounting to about £11,000,000. [£18,000,000 in England and Wales in 1900-1.]

an Act of Parliament! To state such a result is to make the argument absurd. Unless it is to be contended that the State keeps out of the pockets of the class some £300,000,000 which they ought to have now, there is no call to give the money. And if the State inflicts such a wrong, the sooner it pays back what it has exacted, with interest, the better.

II.

Having thus examined the case against existing burdens on land, I turn to the second part of my subject—the claims urged by the Land Tenure Reform Association for securing to the State a share of the unearned increase of value. The inquiry, however, should have prepared the way for looking at the question from the Association's point of view. It has been seen that upon the general theory of taxation special burdens on this particular description of property are not unreasonable, that they are not without analogy in taxes upon trade profits, which no one thinks of altering on the ground that "other property" escapes the burden, or that they are a special income tax on the people in the trade. It has also been shown that, if taxes on profits are justifiable in any case, the circumstances of land-owning are such as to reduce the hardship of the owners to a minimum when their profits are taxed. The business is a monopoly, and simple in the highest degree, and nowhere else can be found more favouring conditions for a tax upon profits. We are thus prepared for the inquiry, whether so peculiar a business could not be made to bear a larger burden; and for the theory of the Association, that while it is only on grounds of expediency the State permits individual property in land at all, there is no reason of expediency against its limiting that right of individual property by a large reservation in its own favour. If there is any reason in this theory at all, the facts stated will have suggested the magnitude of the value in which the State may claim a share. The augmenting value, on which it is urged the State would have had the first claim under a proper financial system, must have amounted, in the last thirty years, to hundreds of millions sterling.

Now in theory, so far as I can see, there is absolutely nothing to be urged, and nothing has, in fact, been urged, against the principle of the Association. The soil of the nation *is* primarily the property of the whole nation—the common inheritance of all, regarding which the State, according to its lights, cannot help laying down rules from time to time for the common advantage. There is no other final authority, and if the action of that authority is to be limited by so-called rights, if on cause shown it may not destine the whole land, or any part of it, to any use it pleases, then we have this anomaly—that the most vital necessity of national existence is to be held, not under the direction of the State, but subject to some arbitrary limitations in favour of individuals or classes, based on a superstition of right. In point of fact, as well as theory, no such limitation has ever been admitted by English law. Year after year the national Parliament exercises in innumerable cases the right of diverting some part of the "common inheritance" from one use to another. If it so acts in part and detail, it has clearly a right to take a wider range and exercise its discretion upon the whole or a large part of the soil of the country. The only question would be whether the particular regulations or uses proposed to it are wise.

And whatever regulations may be objected to, it seems to me that, assuming private property in land to be retained as the rule, the imposition of special charges on it, which will be in the nature of mining royalties, or a reserved rent-charge, or like the casualties under feudal tenures, will be about as innocent a way of limiting the privilege, interfering as little as possible with the individual enjoyment as could well be desired. It leaves untouched the right of exclusive possession, which is the main thing coveted, and merely keeps to the State a charge, which exactly resembles many other charges by which the privilege of absolute possession is limited. Of course the mode of the reservation will be an important matter; but theoretically there is no reason against reserving something.

It may be added that the more progressive a community, the more likely it is that any proper reservation will be little felt as a burden. By the hypothesis, it is in such communities that competition will cause an immense unearned increase of rent and of capital value. There will be a large margin for ground rents of every description, and the State ground rent will be no more felt than the others. So free from hardship will the charge in fact be, that just as the commuted tithe rent-charge and the land tax are no longer felt as burdens by the present possessors of land, the whole charge of the State, when it is carefully studied, will be acknowledged as equally light.

But what form should the charge of the State assume, and how much in the present condition of things, as respects property, business, and population, should the State endeavour to obtain? Clearly, if the phenomena of the last thirty years are about to be repeated—and there is a reasonable chance that they will be, for there is no sign of check to the growth of population or the increase of machinery and inventions—it is much to be wished that a better system should, if possible, be at work than has hitherto existed for securing to the nation a portion of the augmenting value of its soil. The problem, however, is excessively difficult, and I doubt very much whether Mr. Mill's own suggestion, which must be first considered, will be found, as a general measure, to answer the purpose. It is in effect a proposal to go straight to the end in view—that the State should inquire at prescribed intervals what is the augmenting rental of land, and make a charge upon the owners of some definite portion of that augmentation. If there is no increase of rental due to general causes, there will be no increase of tax, and owners who object will have the opportunity of surrendering their estate on what Mr. Mill's enemies must admit will be full compensation. One objection to this proposal is that it is almost wholly novel in European countries, at least where the art of taxation has been most carefully studied, and is least of all fitted for a country in the circumstances of England. Mr. Mill has apparently in view the ideal of the *foncier* taxes on the Continent, in which the process is for the State at a certain date to impose a lump charge on the whole land of the country in proportion to its estimated value, and then apportion this charge among the various localities and parts of soil in the country, by a carefully arranged *cadastre.* But there is nothing more tedious in fact than the completion of a *cadastre*, or unequal when it is completed. Even in France, which has set the example in these *foncier* taxes, the new *cadastre*, which was commenced forty years ago, was only completed the other day, and while it was being put into operation the value of the whole land subject to it was changing. It is hardly possible to imagine that even if in England we could give that attention to the nice adjustment of competing qualities of land or property which could alone make the basis of French direct taxes endurable, we should be content to await the slow development of a pretentiously perfect, but really imperfect, *cadastre* for a period of forty years. It is a still more fatal objection that such taxes do not appear to draw. It is officially estimated in France that the annual value of real property has increased since 1821 from £64,000,000 to £160,000,000, which is quite comparable with the increase in England. But while the rates have risen in England from about £10,000,000 to £17,000,000, the special land tax of France has only risen from £11,720,000 to £12,280,000, including the additional hundredths imposed for local purposes, as well as the "principal" of the tax. The special tax of England is thus more elastic and effective than the special tax of France, which is proposed as a model. Besides, if these objections could be got over, if it could be shown that an improved *cadastre* is easily possible, and is capable of frequent renewal, there would remain the objection that such a tax, so imposed, might interfere with the enjoyment of private property in an inexpedient manner. It would be very difficult to reassure individuals against the operations of the tax assessors. Every few years they would foresee a demand of an indefinite amount, depending on many points of taste and opinion, and they would only have the alternative of paying or surrendering their property to the State. Careful as Mr. Mill is to suggest safeguards, the essential nature of the transaction would be such as to destroy confidence in the continuity of private right in some particular plot of land. The apprehensions might in the main be unfounded, but their existence would be a public calamity, unless the theory is admitted that the abolition of private property would be beneficial, which in some localities it might be.

Turning from this suggestion, I think there is much to be said in favour of our present special taxes on land, imperfect as we have shown them to be. They have permitted the growth of an immense mass of value in the hands of individuals only, and at a very recent date there was a sudden reduction of the burden, by which a small class received a considerable gain. But with all their imperfections they have the merit of elasticity. They are set apart for the discharge of certain branches of expenditure; and, without fluctuating so widely as to disturb property rights, they may be increased materially, and so reserve for the State some portion, however insignificant it may be, of the augmenting value of property. This is no small merit, especially when compared with the model of the continental land taxes, which have no such capacity of expansion. It is an additional convenience that, as the branches of expenditure which are thrown specially on this property are local, local administration and local taxation can be associated. In this view rates are, in fact, a happy English invention, by which different and unconnected advantages are obtained in a rough practical fashion, and as it is a familiar system we have another obvious reason for trying to make the most of it. Could not something more be made of it? It will be of some use perhaps if the discussion of the principles on which the burden is imposed makes it clear that no injustice is now committed—that the support of a certain burden of expenditure is a condition of the enjoyment of the property which the State may properly impose. Every one knows the condition beforehand, and as it is quite a calculable one, notwithstanding the loud talk of the increase of rates, and the addition of new rates, there is no inexpediency in it as a too heavy restriction on the enjoyment of private property in land. But the discussion, I think, may do more, and justify the imposition of new charges which are convenient for local administration. As the tendency of the functions of local government is to increase, and the additional expense has not yet proved commensurate with the increase of the value of property, we have a security in the recognition of this principle, both of the reservation to the State of a part of that value—though, I fear, a most inadequate part—and for the safety of private property against any great disturbance. If I might venture to make a suggestion, there is one new charge which escapes notice, and which might very properly be treated as a branch of local expenditure: the army for home defence ought to be locally maintained. For many reasons it is important that a good deal of local management and self-government should be associated with the organization of our militia and volunteers, and the charges might very properly fall on the rates. This would not only relieve the Imperial army estimates of a heterogeneous charge, but by really associating localities with the work, would contribute much to the strength and vitality of our home system of defence. There is another way in which something more could be made of the present system. Under the haphazard methods and want of principle which have hitherto prevailed the local rates have gradually been relieved of a large portion of the burden which properly falls upon them. On one pretext or another, the Imperial Exchequer has been drawn on for "grants," amounting annually in England to a million and a quarter, by which the growth of the local burden has been retarded—or, in other words, the individual landowner has been permitted to retain a larger share than otherwise he would retain of the augmenting value of land. Good reasons, I think, have been furnished for putting a stop to this system, if rates continue to be the form of our especial tax. The proper course would now be to institute a mode of discontinuing the grants by degrees, according to a defined scale, and so reimpose on property a burden which it has escaped.[1]

But while the system of rates is preserved and amended, as the principal agency for securing to the State a share in the national soil, there is another mode in which it seems to me a smaller advantage of the same sort may be gained, equally without disturbing the security of private property in land. I have already referred to the probate and succession duties, pointing out the confusion of thought which leads to the share of them derived from land being added in with taxes of different kinds, so as to present a large total of burdens on land. But the *rationale* of these taxes is so important a part of the art of taxation that, even apart from the suggestion I intend making, I may be excused from returning to the subject and showing how the special nature of these taxes makes it improper to classify them with the burdens on property.

Their distinguishing feature, as has been already said, is that they are a charge for a special intervention of the State—for the authority it gives to the transmission of property from the dead to the living. It is

[1] The system, alas, has been much extended in recent years. [1903.]

common to consider the bequest and descent of property as mere extensions of the right of private property, but they are not so historically or practically. The reasons which make private property expedient during life do not apply with the same force to the transmission of it at death. It would be difficult to conceive of a large society existing without absolute ownership in the fruits of individual industry, but so long as people are secure in what they earn themselves a very severe strain may be put on the rules for disposing of it at death without endangering the existence of society. Instead of the absolute right of bequest and the unincumbered descent of property to individuals when there is no bequest, being an ordinance of nature as of natural right, they are in fact very peculiarly the creations of the State, and have been modified in all civilized countries to suit its varying policy. For these reasons a special tax on successions has an undoubted justification. The State being their author, and having, strictly speaking, the power and right to absorb them altogether, a power which it would be infinitely less inexpedient to exercise than would be its similar power in regard to private property—the special tax becomes virtually a charge for a concession which the State grants, and which it might conceivably withhold, or at least very seriously curtail. Viewed in any other light, it appears to me wholly indefensible, for though it would no doubt fall on the payer at a convenient time for payment, its pressure on individuals would be most unequal, and it would thus offend against a cardinal maxim of taxation.

Regarding it as a charge upon a concession however, we may recognize in the State a capacity for varying it which would not exist in the case of an ordinary tax. It may take into account, in adjusting the so-called tax, the whole policy of the law of succession and bequest, and the nature of the property itself. The principles to guide it seem hardly to admit of discussion. The tax must not be so severe as to check accumulation, or be severely felt, so as to cause individual suffering even when accumulation is not checked. Subject to these restrictions the State should simply take by a succession duty what it can. It follows that its charge should be most moderate where the transmission resembles most a continuance of the enjoyment of private property, or is the transmission of property which the deceased person has acquired by his own industry, and in acquiring which he may be supposed to have been influenced by the prospect of regulating the succession; and should be most severe in the contrary case, where the transmission is to strangers, or where the property has been inherited. Unless these points are kept in mind the State will not be able to levy so large an amount as would otherwise be possible for it. To make the charge uniform would simply be to limit it to the minimum possible in those cases where the succession of the dependents of a deceased person, whose income dies with them, gives the tax the appearance of a charge not upon inheritance, but impoverishment. It would be quite consistent with the principle of the tax, however, to look at the composition of the property bequeathed; to say that as the possession of a certain kind of property over which the State had primary rights was keenly competed for, one condition of its enjoyment should be a special liability to taxes on successions. No person could complain, for there are abundant modes of investment besides land, and those who wished to have an unrestricted privilege of bequest could invest in other property. Even a charge of five per cent., however, would probably present no inducement to people to keep away from land. It is very seldom that an entire fortune is thus invested (it would be sheer folly so to invest it), and the total charge on the succession, though it is five per cent. on a portion of it, might not be much higher than it is. I need not add that if there is any reason in this view of succession duties, the singular arrangement by which land now pays least of all is more than indefensible; it is a gross neglect of the State to secure a due to which it is most fairly entitled. The arrangement is another instance of the perversity of discussions about the incidence of taxes according to the historical method in England. An illogical mode of comparison has not only enabled the owners of land to secure for themselves an augmenting value in which the State might well have had a larger share, but has enabled a class which enjoys a valuable monopoly to escape payment on its successions of the charges which other classes of the community, enjoying no monopoly, have to bear.

After all, it may well be doubted whether by any process that would not be worse that the disease, anything but a small fraction of the augmenting value of land will ever be secured for the State. At the past rate of increase, the real property of England, which is now worth about £150,000,000 a year, will be worth £250,000,000 in another thirty years. And a large part of this additional £100,000,000, perhaps the half of it or more, will not be owing to any investment of capital in improvements, but to increasing monopoly value. At the past rate of increase, however, our rates will be under £30,000,000, so that, at the outside, there will not be an additional burden of £15,000,000 to set against an additional value of £100,000,000, while much of that additional burden will also have fallen, not on the property generally, but on the profits of the improvements. There is little hope of touching this immense augmentation. But this is hardly a result to be rejoiced over by the defenders of private property in land. If they were wise in their generation it should be their aim to show that the present system, besides any indirect advantages to the community it may have, is also directly beneficial to the State, because it provides a large fund for the support of national charges. Looking forward to the great increase of value which is inevitable, they should rather, of all others, be anxious to secure a large appropriation to the State, as some compensation to the masses for the privilege of exclusive possession which they enjoy. The divorce of the people of England from the soil would be more, and not less, defensible than it is if it could be shown that private property in it was so regulated as to relieve the general taxpayer of his burdens.—[1871.]

VIII.

THE TAXATION AND REPRESENTATION OF IRELAND.[1]

THE House of Commons was occupied on Monday and Tuesday with two subjects which are not at first sight connected, but between which a real connection of some interest may in our opinion be established. We refer to the debate on Monday on the alleged disproportionate taxation of Ireland, and to the debate on Tuesday on Mr. Trevelyan's motion as to the electoral system as far as the question of redistributing seats is concerned. These two debates suggest to us that whatever difficulties there may be about a redistribution of seats within each particular division of the United Kingdom, there can be little question of the expediency of a redistribution of seats between these divisions themselves. The Irish members complain that Ireland is unduly taxed, but England and Scotland may complain that Ireland is unduly represented, and use in support of their complaint the very arguments as to taxation in Ireland which Irish members employ to prove that Ireland should pay less to the Imperial Exchequer. There ought clearly to be some proportion between the representation of different communities in a common Parliament and the wealth and population of these communities; there is an unstable political equilibrium wherever the poorer and weaker communities have a disproportionate share in dictating the general policy, and so voting the burdens which their richer and stronger associates have to bear; and as

[1] Written and published as an article of the "Economist" in 1876.

Ireland now has, and has always had, a larger representation in the Imperial Parliament than the proportion of the taxes it paid would give it, the argument that it should pay a still less proportion implies that it should also be less represented. Until lately this argument was partly counterbalanced by the large proportion of the population of Ireland to that of Great Britain, but year by year the claim of Ireland on this ground has become weaker, till now it has no existence.

The facts can be stated very shortly. Ireland sends to the Imperial Parliament 105 members out of 658, or almost exactly 16 per cent., as compared with 553 members, or 84 per cent., representing Great Britain. As regards taxation, therefore, assuming an exact proportion between it and representation, Ireland would not be unjustly burdened if it contributed 16 per cent. of the Imperial revenue. But its contributions in 1874-5, the last year mentioned in the return obtained by Mr. Mitchell-Henry for the purpose of the debate, were only in the proportion of 10.6 per cent. Of a total of £74,986,397, which was the revenue of 1874-5, Great Britain and Ireland contributed as follows:

	£	Per Cent. of Total.
Great Britain	67,016,346	89.4
Ireland	7,970,051	10.6
Total	74,986,397	100.0

The inhabitants of Great Britain may surely ask with some fairness that there shall be no complaints of Irish taxation until Ireland pays taxes in some more exact proportion to the number of representatives it has—that is, 16 per cent., instead of 10.6 per cent., of the total Imperial revenue. If it did so its contribution would have been in 1874-5, not £7,970,000, but £11,998,000, or 50 per cent. more.

We fear it would be hopeless to tax Ireland in proportion to its present representation, but the inequality could be redressed by reducing the representation. In that case Ireland would only elect 10.6 per cent. of the members of Parliament, instead of 16 per cent., or 70 members instead of 105. And matters would be still worse for Ireland in this respect if the Irish members had their way, and Irish taxation were reduced as they say it should be. Great Britain, we are told, would pay £200,000,000 if it were taxed as Ireland is. In other words, Great Britain is affirmed to be twenty-five times richer than Ireland. But if representation were to be adjusted accordingly, Ireland would only elect 1-25th of the members of the Imperial Parliament, or 26 instead of 105. As far as it goes, this argument for diminished taxation is also an argument for enormously diminished representation.

We come then to the facts as to the relative population of Ireland and Great Britain, on which the claim of Ireland to a larger representation than one in proportion to the share of taxes it pays may be based. At the time of the Union, and for many years after, it was certainly intelligible that the magnitude of the population of Ireland should be a set-off to its poverty in a question of representation in a common Parliament with Great Britain. In 1821, which is the first year for which we have good data, the population of Great Britain and Ireland were respectively:

	Numbers.	Per Cent. of Total.
Great Britain	14,391,631	67.9
Ireland	6,801,827	32.1
Total . . .	21,193,458	100.0

In other words, Ireland was about a third of the United Kingdom as respects population, and in consequence its claim to have a larger share of representation than the proportion of its wealth and taxation to that of Great Britain would have given it had some foundation. Ireland with such relative numbers, whatever their condition, was a large unit to which much less than a sixth of the representation could not reasonably have been assigned. And this proportion continued during the two following census periods. In 1831 and 1841 the proportions of Great Britain and Ireland in the total population of the United Kingdom were:

		Great Britain.		Ireland.	
Year.	Total Population.	Numbers.	Per Cent. of Total.	Numbers.	Per Cent. of Total.
1831	24,306,719	16,531,318	68.1	7,767,401	31.9
1841	26,916,991	18,720,394	69.6	8,196,597	30.4

But since 1841 a great change has taken place. The following twenty years were the period of the Irish exodus, and although of late the population of Ireland has remained stationary, or has only diminished very slowly, the stationariness has been coincident with a rapid increase in the population of Great Britain, which is constantly altering the proportion. The effect is seen if we compare the population for the last three census years, and also for 1875. The figures are:

Population of Ireland and Great Britain compared at various Dates since 1851.

		Great Britain.		Ireland.	
Year.	Total Population.	Numbers.	Per Cent. of Total.	Numbers.	Per Cent. of Total.
1851[1]	27,435,000	20,883,000	76.2	6,552,000	23.8
1861	28,974,362	23,185,947	80.0	5,788,415	20.0
1871	31,513,442	26,126,734	82.9	5,386,708	17.1
1875	32,737,405	27,439,673	83.9	5,297,732	16.1

Thus the proportion of the population of Ireland, which was thirty per cent. of that of the United Kingdom as late as 1841, had fallen in 1851 to 23.8 per cent., and in 1871 to 17.1 per cent. only, while since the latter year it has gradually come to be still lower, or 16.1 per cent. It is thus quite manifest that Ireland has lost the claim it once had, on the score of its great population, to a larger share of representation than its wealth and taxation would give it. If existing taxation

[1] Part estimated for Scotland.

were to be the test, the argument for reducing the representation of Ireland in the Imperial Parliament from 105 members to 70, which is the proportion existing taxation would give it, as we have above seen, and for proportionally raising the representation of Great Britain, would now be irresistible.

We are not using these arguments in a controversial spirit, and as a *tu quoque* to the Irish members in their demand for lessened taxation. The excessive representation of Ireland in the Imperial Parliament is a substantial mischief to the whole United Kingdom. It gives undue influence to one of the elements in the Union the least in harmony with those which really preponderate, and consequently impedes and thwarts the naturally stronger forces of the nation in their development. On Ireland itself the effect is most pernicious, because the scale of Irish affairs is artificially altered from the natural one. Because Ireland has such tremendous power to force its affairs on Imperial notice, the Irish people are encouraged in the belief that their local affairs really compare in importance with those of Great Britain, whereas Ireland is now only a fragment, and relatively a diminishing fragment, of the State in which it is absorbed, and whose fortunes more and more it must inevitably share. Even for obtaining attention to peculiar legislation for Ireland a smaller number of representatives would be better than the present, because their weakness on the one hand would tend to unite them and give them strength for all reasonable ends, while diminishing on the other hand the natural distrust of Ireland and Irish members in Great Britain, which is certainly stimulated at present by the artificial weight of the Irish vote. We are not much in favour of electoral changes so soon after the Reform Act of 1867, but a reduction of the Irish representation, and an increase of that of Great Britain, constitute a question apart which should be dealt with at no distant date. [1903. Not yet dealt with!]

IX.

THE USE OF IMPORT AND EXPORT STATISTICS.[1]

I.—Introductory.

WE must all agree in this place, I think, that there is cause both for encouragement and discouragement to us as regards the prospects of the study in which we are engaged in the very extensive use of statistics which some recent controversies have occasioned. I refer particularly to the balance of trade controversy, and the controversy between fair trade and free trade which made so much noise last autumn, but which has rather subsided of late, as questions of the kind are apt to do when trade itself is improving. In these controversies, which have run very much into each other, the fair traders having made use of the alleged balance of trade being against this country to support their arguments, the appeal has been very largely to statistics. Literary journals and magazines, which rather dread figures as a rule, have admitted them into their columns on a liberal scale, including even tables in the rough, as we should here consider them. But while this appeal to statistics is cause for satisfaction to us, the actual handling of the subjects of our study has been such, I think, as to prove how little it has really advanced, not merely amongst the multitude only, but amongst the classes who are most carefully and highly cultivated. There has been a great hash of figures, indicating that those who use them

[1] Read before the Statistical Society, March 21, 1882. The Tables in the Appendix referred to in the course of the paper will be found in the "Journal of the Statistical Society" for June, 1882.

have hardly the rudiments of statistical ideas, whether true or false. In journals of the highest standing there are the wildest blunders of the schoolboy order. Thus in the "Quarterly Review" of July last, a writer states and argues upon the statement: "It is estimated that about a million of acres of land have gone out of cultivation during the last ten years."[1] The fact, of course, is that there is not a year in the last ten in which the cultivated area of the United Kingdom has not increased, the total increase being nearly two million acres. The same writer also makes a great mess of the very figures of imports and exports with which I propose to deal specially to-night. He makes the excess of imports into the United Kingdon in 1879 £170,595,983, and in 1880 £187,179,530, and in the first five months of 1881 £78,782,396, having obviously omitted in all cases the re-exports of foreign and colonial merchandise, by which these figures would be reduced by 60 million pounds a year or upwards, while he quotes as his authority the *quarterly* returns of the Board of Trade, which issues no quarterly returns relating to imports and exports, but only monthly and annual returns.[2] Similarly a writer in the "Nineteenth Century" for August last, Sir Edward Sullivan, compares the property assessed to the legacy and succession duties in England with the property assessed to similar duties in France, which has no such duties at all, but which has only probate duties, which are levied like ours on the gross amount of the estates of deceased persons, without deduction for debts, whereas our legacy and succession duties are imposed on the net amounts of property.[3] Similarly he speaks elsewhere of the "commerce" of the world having increased 36 per cent. in

[1] "Quarterly Review," July, 1881, p. 282.

[2] *Ibid.*, July, 1881, p. 288. It is just possible that the writer may refer to a quarterly account published at intervals in the monthly Board of Trade returns, but his allusion is so vague as to indicate that he has little idea what the publications are.

[3] "Nineteenth Century," August, 1881, p. 173.

ten years, and English commerce so much less,[1] the actual fact being of course that there is no figure in existence which can be spoken of as representing the commerce of the world; while the writer probably meant the foreign commerce, and yet excluded from his comparison one of the most important parts of English fcreign commerce, viz., the shipping. Our satisfaction therefore at seeing so frequent an appeal to statistics must be considerably qualified by the nature of the appeal. It is evidently still quite possible for essays to find admission to journals of high standing like the "Nineteenth Century" and the "Quarterly Review," in which the writers not only make mistakes, but mistakes of an elementary and substantial character, as if in discussing chemistry a writer were to confound oxygen with hydrogen, or as if in discussing geometry he were to confound an isosceles with a right-angled triangle. Writers who were capable of making such mistakes in chemistry and geometry, however cultivated in other respects, would either not find admission to the pages of the "Nineteenth Century" or the "Quarterly Review," or their mistakes would be corrected by the editors; but the popular standard for statistics is evidently as yet not so strict as it is for other scientific studies. Any man, it seems to be thought, can handle figures, and writers who are otherwise competent are not afraid to touch them as they would be afraid to touch chemistry, or geometry, or botany, or geology, or almost any science one could name. That our special study should be so little advanced, although there is a dim idea in the public mind of the utility of statistics, must surely be a matter for concern to a Society which has been established for nearly fifty years for the express purpose of diffusing right ideas and information. We have still, it is plain, a great work before us to perform.[2]

[1] "Nineteenth Century," August, 1881, p. 172.

[2] How many fresh illustrations have been furnished by the recent fiscal controversy.

It is in this view that the present paper, which is mainly directed to the method of statistics, has been written. The object is to show how great may be the errors in using the comparatively well-known figures of imports and exports, unless proper caution is exercised, and how difficult it is to elicit true conclusions on the questions respecting the balance of trade and free trade *v.* protection, which have lately been discussed. Statistics, I need hardly say in this company, are almost always difficult. No table almost can be used without qualification and discretion. The moment we perceive that figures are used without qualifications and without anxiety to appreciate them in their right meaning, and to support no greater conclusion than they can be made to bear, we may be sure there is something wrong. My object will have been gained if the remarks I have to make, and the discussion they elicit, help to popularize what are really truisms within these walls, but which ought also to be truisms outside, if statistics held the place they ought to do among politicians and public men.

II.—General Remarks on Import and Export Figures.

In dealing with the causes of error in handling import and export statistics, it would of course be superfluous for me to do more than mention such questions of method as are common to them and all other statistics. In using them, as in other statistics, it is of course necessary to see that in comparing different years or different countries the data are substantially of the same nature. I shall have to notice some special difficulties of this sort in regard to imports and exports which I am aware of; but I am only at first noticing the principle as a well-known one. It is also necessary in comparing one period with another, so as to draw out a curve of progress or retrogression, to ascertain whether the figures of single years or of less periods can safely be used, or whether, as is more likely to be the case, the mean or average of groups of years ought to be used. For some purposes, as we know from statistics of crime, population, and the like, five, and even ten years' periods are by no means too long to be considered, and common sense will tell us that for many purposes this will also be the case with trade statistics, trade having ups and downs, if nothing else has, whatever *régime* it may be subject to, and the statistician's first business being to eliminate the errors which may be due to such ups and downs. A large discourse might be written even on these points, which are habitually neglected by popular writers who use statistics, and by persons of more authority. A question, for instance, was put by Mr. McIver last session,[1] to the President of the Board of Trade, the whole point of which was that our exports to France had diminished from 33 million to 28 million pounds in ten years, while our imports had increased from 30 million to 42 million pounds in the same period, and the explanation being that the apparent decrease in the one case and increase in the other corresponded only to temporary facts of trade, because the year 1871, owing to the Franco-German war, was of a wholly exceptional character as regards the trade between France and England. Another elementary difficulty is in the use of percentages, especially those of increase or decrease, nothing being more necessary than a cautious use of such percentages, and, especially when comparisons are made, a use of them only with reference to amounts as well as percentages. In the beginning of things percentages may be large, as we all know, but the real growth may be largest where the percentage is least, in consequence of the greater amount at which the percentage is calculated. We are all familiar here also with M. Quetelet's illustration of the enormous mortality of a particular street, in which nearly all the inhabitants died, and where the area was really too small to yield any good

[1] "Times," June 14, 1881.

average. Some of the arguments of the "Nineteenth Century," already referred to as to the percentages of the growth of the commerce of different countries, are really as illogical. But elementary as this paper is intended to be, I may perhaps be excused from going into such extreme commonplaces, which relate not merely to imports and exports, but to all statistics. When these matters are properly attended to, enough remains to be considered as regards imports and exports which may well demand the utmost caution.

The *first* point to be considered, as in all statistics, is the degree of accuracy obtained in the original data. The figures of imports and exports are sometimes used, and we are all of us too apt to use them, as if they were figures in accounts, giving rise to no question respecting the nature of the data; as if every particle of commodities and every pound of value sent out or brought into a country, and to and from what countries they were sent or brought, were recorded with perfect accuracy; and as if too the accounts of all countries, and of each country at different times, were made up on the same principles, and could be trusted to the same degree. Those who know anything of statistical compilation, and even those who do not know, if they only consider for a moment the necessary conditions, will perceive at once that no impression could be more unfounded. In all statistical inquiries the nature of the data is a necessary question, and there are great varieties in the possible degree of accuracy, while the same data may be sufficient for one purpose and not for another. Thus a census like that of the United Kingdom, made on the same day for the whole kingdom, by a staff of enumerators collecting individual returns from all householders, yields results which are absolutely trustworthy to a most infinitesimal fraction as regards the numbers of the people, as regards the sexes, as regards the conjugal condition, that is, whether married or not, and—with some exceptions perhaps—as regards the numbers at each age. The population of small localities on the day of the census may also be considered to be stated as regards all these details with practically complete accuracy. But when we come to such details as the occupations of the people, which involve inherent difficulties of statement by those who have to make the returns, and of classification by those who compile, we are plainly on more treacherous ground. Especially with the smaller occupations, and in comparisons between different localities, it would become necessary for inquirers to use the figures with judgment and discretion, and to bring to their aid a study of the instructions to the enumerators, and information from local or special sources. In using the population figures again for deducing birth, marriage, and death-rates, the fact that the population returned is only the population on a given day, and that there are many localities in which the population on other days of the year would be less or more, has to be considered; while the special birth, marriage, and death-rates themselves, that is the rates as compared with the population at particular ages, would be still more liable to error. There are methods for eliminating errors known to statistical experts by which the data can be used, but the methods must be employed if any good result is to be obtained. To give another illustration from matters within my own department—the emigration statistics. As far as numbers are concerned, these statistics are complete—we have practically a complete record of passengers leaving the country for places out of Europe, and returning to it from places out of Europe. Making the assumption, as I believe we may do, that the balance of the resident population is unaffected by people coming and going from and to European ports,—the excess of "imports" from such places, if I may adapt a well-known expression to this subject, being practically all exported to places out of Europe,—the emigration and immigration statistics become perfectly trustworthy as to numbers. I think also the distinctions made as to the nationality and sex of the emigrants, and the conjugal condition, with the numbers of children, are fairly to be trusted. But when we get to the "occupations" I am not so sure. We have nothing to trust to but the description given by the emigrants themselves, as reported by officers who are busy with other work; and I confess I should not like to found important inferences on minute changes in the numbers from year to year of so-called joiners, or painters, or farmers, or even "labourers." It would be impossible to use the figures for such details to any good purpose without much discretion and a wide knowledge of local facts determining the emigration. To take yet another illustration —again from my own department. While the total entries and clearances of ships at ports in the United Kingdom in the foreign trade may be held to be completely accurate, there is an undoubted defect in the statistics of particular ports, owing to the practice which has been established of only returning a vessel as entered and cleared at one port, though it may really enter and clear at more than one. By the present practice the total of the port accounts agrees with that of the United Kingdom, and I believe the trade of the ports generally is relatively fairly accurate, but the practice nevertheless might obviously lead to difficulty and wrong inferences in special cases. The nature of the data is thus an all-important matter.

Now, as to the nature of the data in import and export statistics, we have the advantage of a paper in our own "Journal," which Mr. Bourne read to us in 1871, and which will be found the first in his volume, "Trade, Population, and Food." A more useful paper, I think, was never laid before the Society, and I shall do little more than refer to it. Those interested will find a full account in it of how the data are obtained, and the means used to check them, with some critical observations on the main point I am now suggesting—the degree of accuracy of the data. There are many points in the paper and in the whole subject which in my official position I should hardly feel at liberty to discuss, but the main points are indisputable. The data, both as to quantities and values, with the countries of origin or destination, are derived from the declarations of importers in the case of imports, and of shippers in the case of exports, subject to a certain check by the customs' officers, and there is a margin of error to be allowed for in these declarations. Mr. Bourne, as regards quantities only, compares the declarations in the case of dutiable goods imported with the actual weights or measurements subsequently made by the customs' officers, and points out a variation between the two ranging from 0.21 per cent. in the case of cocoa, to 5.70 per cent. in the case of tobacco, and averaging for all the articles 1.50 per cent. According to this, the declarations actually made, and which are the basis of all the statistics, are subject to such variations. They are no doubt checked by the customs' officers and corrected for the annual statement of trade, so that the limit of error is farther reduced, but in the case of non-dutiable goods some limit of error must remain. These are the facts as regards quantities only. As regards values, what Mr. Bourne points out as regards the imports is especially important:

"The present system has great disadvantages, arising from the want of knowledge on the part of the importers, the indifference of many who pass the entries, and the impossibility of the department exercising a valid check. It is well known that a very large proportion of the goods sent to this country are on consignment, and not on purchase, in which case there is no invoice or statement of prices. In these cases the consignee is very much in ignorance of their quality or price, and therefore unable to fix a proper value until they have been examined and sampled. Where, again, as is very frequently done, the entry is made by a mere agent, who may gather the description of the goods from the ship's report, and estimate the weight from the nature of the packages; there is no guide at all to the value. In other instances there is great indisposition to let the true value be known. Supposing, as is constantly the case, wine to be brought from Hamburg in casks, branded with the mark of the best Spanish vintages, it is very improbable that, however vile the stuff may be, it will be valued at less than the price of good sherry. The greatest vigilance, therefore, is necessary to guard against the most erroneous values, but the department can only interfere in extreme cases, for it is unable to discover or question any but very extravagant departures from the average. The law has given it the power of calling for invoices or other proof, which is frequently done, and fines are often inflicted for wilful or careless departures from the truth. The only real security, however, is in exciting an interest amongst those who have to declare the value. When once it is understood that these and other particulars are of real importance, there is, in importers generally, too much good feeling and desire to do what is right, to permit of other than the best information it is in their power to give being placed at the disposal of the authorities. There seems, however, no way of providing for the very numerous cases in which the consignee is ignorant of the value, or the agent who puts in the entry is without instructions to guide him."

So far as I can judge, the check on values in the case of exports must be even more difficult of application than it is in the case of imports.

We have thus two facts before us: first, a possibility of error in the original declarations as to quantity, which are found to vary from the actual quantities on a considerable average of articles as much as 1.50 per cent., and in extreme cases nearly 6 per cent., and which cannot be completely controlled by the officers compiling the statistics; and next, a farther possibility of error in the declarations of values, owing to the want of interest in the merchants or agents making them. I need hardly say here, that errors arising in this way are not likely to affect the returns as a whole as much as they may affect special articles; that in the absence of special motives for making wrong declarations in one direction, the errors made through indifference or carelessness by thousands of people are likely to compensate each other in so vast a field as that of the imports and exports; and that the comparison between two or three years coming together, in which there is no great change of system, might be fairly trustworthy as to the progress or retrogression shown, even allowing for a larger margin of error than it is necessary to allow for in the original data. But the more detailed the use which is made of the statistics, the more necessary it is to keep in mind that there is a margin of error.

Another point has also to be considered. We may

know pretty well where we are in comparing two or three years at the present time; but the farther we go back the less is our knowledge as to the way the business was done formerly, and as to the increased or diminished accuracy of the data from that time. This last fact we know is especially important as to the imports, for there was a very considerable change of system in 1870, which Mr. Bourne fully describes in the paper already referred to. One of the principal changes was in the mode of ascertaining the values, which previously to that date, from 1854 downwards, had been computed according to a plan introduced by Mr. James Wilson, but which have since been declared by the merchants as already explained. We cannot be quite sure, I think, that the computed values before 1870 are on all fours with the declared values since; the presumption would be that they are not. On this head I can most heartily re-echo the complaint made by Mr. Bourne in the paper already cited, that the old plan was not maintained in conjunction with the new for several years. His assertion that the change of system produced in many articles of import an apparently great divergence between the values of 1871 and former years, is a most serious one, and should warn us all to use a great deal of caution in carrying our comparisons of import values farther back than 1870.

Farther, whatever dependence may be placed on the returns of the total imports and exports of particular articles, and of the aggregate imports and exports, a fresh difficulty arises in making the data complete as regards particular countries traded with. Formerly it was a very general practice to consider imports as coming from the country they had last left, although they might only have been in transit through that country; and exports as being despatched to the country they would first arrive at, although they might only be going there in transit. The attempt has been made in recent years to show the countries of ultimate origin and destination, but it is impossible to suppose that this attempt has been completely successful. Where there is a through bill of lading, merchants can easily declare the country of origin or destination as appearing in that document, but such documents themselves do not always disclose the exact facts on this head. I have again to refer to Mr. Bourne's statements in the paper already referred to, but I may add one or two obvious facts, which you can all test. It is beyond question that there is an appreciable amount of trade between this country and Switzerland. We import Swiss clocks and watches, and we send there cotton and other yarns to be made up, besides other articles. But Switzerland does not even figure as a separate country in our returns. Our trade therewith figures as part of the trade with France, Belgium, Holland, and perhaps Italy. Another of these facts is, that in recent years a great deal of the raw sugar we imported was of Austrian origin, but the bulk of it figured in our returns as an import from Germany. Apart then from the above question as to the data themselves, there is a special source of error in the accounts of the trade with particular countries. It must not be supposed that all the so-called trade with France, or Belgium, or Holland, or the United States, is really our trade with those countries. Large deductions or additions may have to be made in a thorough study of the subject.

I have spoken mainly of the import and export statistics of the United Kingdom, but *mutatis mutandis* the same remarks apply to the data of imports and exports in every country. Governments which have a voluminous tariff are probably more careful about the imports than we are, verifying values and quantities in a way we do not attempt; such Governments are probably also very careful in verifying the quantities and values of articles exported on which there is a drawback; but they are none of them likely to be more careful than we are about exports where there is no drawback, and none, we believe, are in fact more careful, while their extra care as to imports is no doubt balanced in most cases, in countries like the United States for instance, by the ingenuity and resource of the smuggler. No foreign country, therefore, any more than England, has import and export statistics which can be used as absolutely accurate in the sense commonly assumed. The remarks already made as to the possibility of useful comparisons, the nearer the years compared are together, and the danger of not allowing for changes of system, also apply to foreign countries as well as our own. On this latter head it happens to be possible to give one or two good illustrations from the experience of foreign countries. My first illustration is from the experience of the United States. Mr. Wells, the special commissioner of revenue of the United States in 1867-69, in one of his well-known reports, that for 1869, after stating at one place that he assumes the sums chargeable to smuggling and undervaluation of imports to be counterbalanced by the undervaluation of exports, goes on to say in a footnote: "If we confine ourselves to the comparison of the values given to imports and exports respectively, in previous years, this may be considered a reasonable estimate; but for the last fiscal year it is certainly not the case. Under the present organization of the bureau of statistics, the values given to the exports of the country have been scrutinized and verified to such an extent as to leave but little doubt that the statement for last year is substantially accurate and complete. The fraudulent undervaluation of imports, however, it is not within the power of such an agency to prevent."[1]

A statement like this discloses the existence of a very serious pitfall for us, when we carry our comparisons of United States trade farther back than 1869. It may throw some light perhaps on such questions as the excess of exports from the United States in recent years, which may after all be largely due to the insufficient record of the imports. As regards compari-

[1] Report of Mr. Wells for 1869, pp. xxix to xxxi.

sons before 1869, it is immediately suggested that the apparently slow increase of United States trade between 1860 and 1870 may in part be apparent only, being due to the imperfection of records, and especially to a check on the record of imports through the introduction of the war tariff between the two dates.

The second illustration I shall give is from the last number of the foreign statistical abstract, in which it is noticed that the Austrian Statistical Bureau has lately begun to substitute real for official values, and tables are given showing side by side for four years these official and real values. The subject is of so much interest that I propose, for the sake of reference in our "Journal," to extract the tables. They will be found in the Appendix (Table I.). The following is a summary of the totals:

[Values in £1,000 sterling—000's omitted.]

	Imports.		Exports.	
	Official Values.	Real Values.	Official Values.	Real Values.
	£	£	£	£
1875	55,255	54,927	50,447	55,086
'76	51,807	53,428	50,857	59,523
'77	54,666	55,526	55,060	66,660
'78	59,672	55,210	59,970	65,469

The discrepancies in the two values are perhaps not very serious in the case of the imports, except for the year 1878, but in the case of the exports they are serious all through, the "real" being 5 millions to 11 millions more than the "official," and the proportion of the discrepancy being from 10 to 20 per cent. In the case of special articles, it will be observed, on referring to the tables, that the discrepancies are still more serious, and that the very first article on the list—animals (except horses)—is a good instance of extreme differences. In the imports of this article the "real" are in almost all cases about twice the "official" values, and in the exports they are about four times the "official" values.

I have a third illustration to give you, derived from French experience. In 1870 the French statistical authorities began to give the countries of origin and destination. It is impossible, therefore, in France to continue from the French accounts any real comparison of French trade with certain foreign countries from a period before 1870. The change of practice throws out all comparisons, and throws out especially any comparison of French trade with England, England being a country of transit to and from France.

The conclusion surely is that in regard to imports and exports, as with most other statistics, comparison with distant periods is not the easy matter it seems. The changes in the data from time to time interpose certain difficulties in the way of comparisons, which must be recognized and met. Besides these foreign instances, I have already given a recent illustration from the change in our own statistics so late as 1870, but the instances might be increased indefinitely. As regards our own statistics especially, the imports were affected by a change from official to computed values in 1854, already referred to, involving quite as serious consequences as those just mentioned in the case of Austria. At a still earlier date also there was a change from official to declared values in the case of the exports, involving large discrepancies.

There is yet another question as regards these data which I must notice before passing on to the next point. The "values" so called when ascertained, whether official, computed, or declared, or in whatever way yet devised they are ascertained, are not identical with the values realized by merchants. They do not profess to be so when they are official or computed values, but even when they are declared by the merchants themselves, they are still different things from the values which the merchant realizes. A merchant who declares a particular quantity and value at the time of import may be himself misled. A cargo of wool or grain when it comes to be delivered may turn out less or more than invoiced or estimated by a slight percentage, and the cargo when sold may realize less or more per lb. or cwt.; consequently may realize less or more in the aggregate than the value in the merchant's declaration. Errors in the estimate of quantities may possibly tend to compensate each other in accounts on a large scale, and such errors are also liable to check by the customs authorities, but the difference between the declared and realized values must remain and will not be so surely compensated. We must always consider, then, when we deal with these declared or other values, that they are not necessarily the same as the realized values, but are only the best substitute we can obtain for them, and we must not use them as if they were accurate to a fraction. When an argument is used in which that accuracy must be assumed in order to make it of any value, we may be sure that the argument is bad, and the person who uses it does not know the necessary limitations of statistics.

A *second* cause of difficulty in the data—operating more especially when comparisons are made between the imports and exports of different countries—is to be found in the difference of methods by which the data are obtained. I am referring now especially to the values. The nature of the difficulty has already been glanced at in reference to the changes of system in a particular country itself, but the systems used are still so various in different countries, that the fact requires to be incessantly remembered in any comparisons. The most important foreign countries have none of them adopted our practice of declaring values, which, as regards imports even here, is comparatively recent. In France the values of both imports and exports are computed according to tables of prices established by a commission of values; in Austria values are partly computed and partly official; in other countries there are still official values, modified in part as to imports, where there are *ad valorem* duties, by the declarations of the importers. There is the greatest variety of system. Not only then do the statistics of imports and exports in all countries vary from the values actually realized by the merchants, to which they ought to approximate, but they probably vary in different ways and degrees from the true standard, so that a comparison of the figures of two different countries ought to be made with great caution.[1] One fact alone will show what is meant. The tendency of our own method is at least to indicate very quickly any great change in the level of prices which may occur. The statistics being made from declarations of value, checked by the daily use of price lists, changes in price act instantaneously, even in the returns as they are issued month by month. But it is not so in France. The monthly returns of quantities are there valued according to the last table established by the commission of values. They do not show quickly, therefore, any change in the level of price. In years when prices are falling they do not fall off as the English monthly returns do, and in years when prices are rising they do not increase so quickly. Again, in countries where official values are used, the variations will depend on quantities far more than on values, and the changes from year to year will consequently be different from those of a country which has declared or computed values. In comparing two countries together, or several countries with each other, or one country with all others or with a group, the

[1] How great the difference is, any one who chooses may find out by comparing the exports from England to France, say, as they appear in the English official returns of exports, with the imports into France from England as they appear in the French official returns of imports. See also return of the trade between England and France, according to the official statistics of the respective countries (No. 405, Sess. 1881), in which other difficulties in the comparison of the returns of the two countries are pointed out.

differences arising from the original differences of data must be remembered. We must always beware of pushing any conclusions too far.

I need hardly say how much this conclusion strikes at a good deal of reasoning lately about the comparative growth of English foreign trade, and the foreign trade of other countries. A country with official values in a time of falling prices would show steady progress, where a country with declared values, as in the United Kingdom, would show a falling off, although in both countries the real movement might be much the same.

A *third* point to be considered, in using import and export statistics, is the periodical variations in price to which commodities are liable. As regards particular articles variations in price do not matter so much if quantities are also given. In showing the progress of wheat exports from the United States, for instance, it would be expedient to use the record of quantities and not of values. But when articles come to be grouped, values must be used, as they must also be used in showing aggregate trade, and here variations in prices are most important. A low range of values in a particular year will make the aggregate smaller than it would otherwise be, and a high range of values would increase it; and clearly this cause of variation must be allowed for. How it is to be allowed for may be a difficult problem, but the difficulty cannot safely be ignored. When it is considered that the range of difference in the aggregate values of the exports of the United Kingdom, owing to difference of price only, amounted to 30 per cent. between 1873 and 1879, we can easily perceive that no comparison between the two years which omits to take note of the different levels of price, can be of any value. This consideration, by the way, disposes altogether of the fair trade argument, which assumes a decline of the English export trade between 1873 and 1879, corresponding to the decline of value only.

This difference of price may also be most material

in comparing the relative progress of the foreign trade of two different countries. The articles of one country may be affected more by a change in the level of values than the articles of another. If the exports of cotton manufactures, for instance, constitute a larger part of the export trade of the United Kingdom than they do of the export trade of France, and the price of cotton manufactures has declined greatly, it would be reasonable, other things being equal, to look for a greater apparent reduction in English than in French exports, although perhaps, as the decline may have been mainly due to a decline in the price of the raw material contained in the exports, the falling off in the real exports of France, *i.e.*, the exports of what is strictly the production of the country, may be greater than the falling off in the real exports of England. In other words, not only is the comparison of the trade of the same country in different years not simple but difficult, owing to this question of price, but a comparison of the progress of two foreign countries may be still more complicated by the same cause of variation.

A *fourth* difficulty in using the statistics of imports and exports, so as to show normal progress or retrogression, arises from the disturbing influence of great economic events. A great war, for instance, between two countries, may destroy the foreign trade of one or the other, or both—stimulate certain parts of the foreign trades of third countries, necessitate large loans, which may in turn stimulate the foreign exports of the third countries trading, and in general act as a cause of great disturbance to the foreign trade of their neighbours as well as themselves. Such an event, again, as the gold discoveries of California and Australia, disturbs the normal course of trade by causing an immense migration and colonization. The Lancashire cotton famine, itself one of the secondary consequences of the American civil war, disturbed the trade of the civilized world for probably fifteen years. It stimulated the growth of cotton in countries like India, Egypt, and Brazil; led to a great export of capital to those countries for their farther development; induced a great movement of the precious metals, which in turn stimulated trade in various ways; and finally, as the stimulant was withdrawn, and the cotton trade returned nearly to the old channels in which it ran before 1860, contributed to such incidents as the failure of Alexander Collie in 1875 and the City of Glasgow Bank in 1878, the rottenness disclosed by these failures having been largely due to the excessive investment of capital in the eastern trade in the times of the cotton famine. The abnormal swelling of trade at one time, in consequence of the disturbance of this great event, and its abnormal diminution at another time, when the stimulus is withdrawn, have all to be allowed for of course in extracting the real lessons as to trade progress or the reverse from import and export statistics. The payment of the German indemnity in 1871-73 may be noted as another disturbing event, tending to swell for a time the export trade of France and the countries which lent to France. But it would be needless to enumerate all such causes. Suffice it to note that the history of the last forty years alone comprises the Irish famine, and the exodus to America which followed, the gold discoveries, the Crimean war, the Franco-Austrian war, the American civil war, the Lancashire cotton famine, the Austro-German war of 1866, the Franco-German war of 1870-1, the Franco-German indemnity, the introduction of gold and demonetization of silver in Germany, the resumption of specie payments in gold in the United States, and last of all, an unusual run of bad seasons for agriculture in England between 1875 and 1879 inclusive. What a complicated business it must really be to extract from the records of imports and exports of the period any conclusion as to their normal progress, or as to the effect of differences in the economic *régime* of different countries in promoting their foreign trade or general welfare, especially when differences in the volume of imports and exports due to differences of price and changes in the mode of obtaining the returns may also have to be allowed for.

A *fifth* cause of difficulty in appreciating the figures of imports and exports, especially for comparative purposes, arises from the different character intrinsically of the foreign trade of different countries. Admitting that quantities and values are stated in precisely the same way, the figures do not mean the same thing to each country. There are at least two important differences possible, which I shall notice, viz., the differing degrees in which the trade may be one of transit only, and the different amounts of the carrying trade of different countries, as to which there is no precise record of values, yet the outlay on which, by a shipping country, may be as much an "export" as the export of grain from a grain-growing country like the United States, which happens to be exactly recorded.

As regards the degrees in which the foreign trade of different countries may be one of transit only, I think the differences are really most signal. Some of these differences are on the surface. England has on the face of the account a large transit trade, the re-exports, as they are called, being a very large item. Belgium affords a still more striking illustration of a large transit trade. But there may be further differences of a vital character which are not on the surface. Any foreign articles once admitted into consumption in a country, and re-made up in any way, and sometimes with little or nothing done to them, are treated, when exported, as exports of native produce and manufactures. You will actually find tea, coffee, and raw cotton among the exports of domestic produce from France. The result is that the exports, so-called, of domestic produce and manufactures from a country which manufactures largely, are, in part, in the strictest sense of the word, re-exports. The raw material previously imported goes out in a different guise, but it is still the same raw material. To compare the exports of native produce of such a country with those of a country which does not import raw material to be re-exported in a manufactured form, we ought clearly to deduct from the exports the value of the previously imported raw material which they contain. The explanation specially applies to a country like England, which is a manufacturing country more than any other, as compared with countries like the United States, which re-export in a manufactured form very little of what they import. If a correction were made, probably it would appear that our exports of domestic produce, exclusive of our carrying trade, though nominally larger than those of any other country, are not really much larger than some, and are perhaps, in some cases, exceeded. The United States, for instance, exported in 1879-80 about 170 million pounds' worth of domestic produce and manufactures, hardly any raw material previously imported being included, for the manufactures altogether are only a few million pounds. The United Kingdom, on the other hand, exported nominally, in 1880, 223 million pounds; but from this sum a large deduction must be made for the value of the previously imported raw material contained in it, perhaps about 60 million pounds; deducting this, the real export of British produce would be only 163 million pounds, as compared with 170 million pounds from the United States. Our exports per head would still be larger than those of the latter country, and a special difference is made by the shipping, which again brings up our total, but the figures may serve to illustrate how different the real may be from the apparent facts. When the real magnitude of the export trade of different countries is compared so as to show their dependence on foreign countries for markets, the point of view here referred to is not to be lost sight of.

A similar rectification is also necessary as regards the imports, in any comparison at least of what is imported for final consumption with the exports of native produce. In some countries the whole imports, less the re-exports, may be treated as imports for final consumption; in the United Kingdom, to arrive at a comparable figure, we must deduct the value of the previously imported raw material contained in the manufactures exported, this raw material being merely the block to which British capital and labour are applied. Applying these considerations to the case of England and other countries, we find that our imports for final consumption are still by far the largest, but the interval between us and other countries is considerably reduced. Our gross imports last year in round figures were 410 million pounds, but deducting

	£
For re-exports	65 mlns.
„ raw material previously imported included in manufactures exported	60 „
Total	125 „

we arrive at a sum of 285 million pounds only as the net imports for final consumption in the country. This is a very different figure, though large, from the gross total of 410 million pounds.[1] It shows that our dependency on foreign countries for supplies, or for a market for our own produce, is really much less than is sometimes supposed. We are no doubt dependent on them for the "blocks" with which we work in making for export, and this is an important fact by itself, while the fact of so much foreign produce going through our hands, though we do not ourselves consume it, has its value in the proper place; but our dependency in these respects is a different thing from our requiring foreign markets where we may sell what we produce, in order to buy what we finally consume. In this respect foreign countries are more nearly on an equality with us than is sometimes supposed.

[1] This last figure, it may be explained, is itself, strictly speaking, too small, not including the transhipment trade and bullion, which ought, I think, to be included, and which would bring the total up to 450 million pounds; the imports for final consumption being, however, as stated in the text, only about 285 million pounds.

Another important conclusion is to be drawn from this consideration. The exports of a manufacturing country may be nominally affected by a change in the value of the previously imported raw material, although there is no real change in the native produce exported, or when the real change may be the opposite of the nominal one. Say that a fourth of the exports consists of previously imported raw material, then a decline of 50 per cent. in the value of the raw material would produce a decline of 12½ per cent. in the aggregate exports, which would be entirely nominal. If at such a time the exports were apparently stationary, the real fact would be that they had increased 12½ per cent., or rather about 17 per cent., allowing that the increase really takes place on three-fourths only of the nominal total. The influence of changes of price has already been referred to generally, but the special influence of this factor on the exports of manufacturing countries appears also worthy of attention. It is by no means an immaterial point. The apparent falling off in the exports of British produce and manufactures between 1873 and 1879 is to be accounted for largely by a reduction merely in the price of the raw cotton—the block to which our industry was applied—contained in the manufactures.[1] To talk of the decline between 1873 and 1879 without taking note of such facts would clearly be to mistake show for substance. No wonder figures are so often said to be capable of proving anything, when pitfalls like these, which have seldom even been referred to in past discussions, are in the way.

With regard to shipping, the facts may be more simply stated. A country with a large carrying trade may export little in the shape of commodities, and yet be to all intents and purposes a considerable exporter. Its outlay in wages and provisions for ships' crews, in equipping and repairing ships, in insurance and renewals, and the profits it earns, are all parts of its ex-

[1] See Report on Prices of Imports and Exports, C-3079, Sess. 1881.

port as much as if the export were embodied and stored up in a commodity. In any complete account of the foreign trade, therefore, the carrying done by carrying countries, with analogous charges, ought to be included; otherwise no proper comparison is possible with countries which have a small shipowning business. The so-called foreign trade in the one case is the whole foreign trade, in the other it is only part of the whole.

I shall have to make use of this principle afterwards in dealing with the question of the balance of trade; but it is enough to state it, I hope, to prove its reasonableness. To put the point in a concrete shape, the import and export statistics of a shipowning country like England do not show its foreign trade, as the imports and exports show the foreign trade of the United States, which has only a very small shipowning business.

That all these questions are substantial and not formal may be shown by a single example of how much our view of the foreign trade of the United States as compared with that of England would be altered by taking account of them. See, it is said, how much of American goods the United Kingdom imports, and how little of British goods America imports. This difference, I confess, would not, in my opinion, be at all material if the real facts were the same as the apparent ones. Trade is well known to be very often triangular; we may buy from America, and send goods elsewhere on American account, though not directly to America. But the statement is itself untrue if we examine the facts carefully. No doubt we record an import of 107 million pounds from the United States, and only record a return of 38 million pounds, showing an excess of imports over our exports amounting to 69 million pounds, which it is supposed the Americans prevent us by their tariff from sending to them. But people forget first that our trade is largely one of transit both directly and indirectly through our manufactures. Among the articles we import from the United States there was £31,784,000 worth of raw cotton alone in 1880, of which directly as a re-export, and indirectly through our manufactures, we would send away at least four-fifths or 26 million pounds. Why should we expect the United States to take goods directly from us for this amount? Surely the countries which ultimately get the raw cotton directly or indirectly are the countries which should pay, and they may do so in part directly as well as through our agency, our only share being a commission on the whole transaction. The second fact is that we export to America in the form of carrying goods on American account, and this item probably amounts at the present time to 16 million pounds a year. These two sums together—what we send away elsewhere of raw cotton alone among articles we have imported from America, and what we export to America in the shape of doing carrying work for her—go a long way towards extinguishing the apparent balance against us on the import and export account. They amount together to 42 million pounds, thus reducing the apparent balance from 69 million pounds to 27 million pounds. This is a much smaller sum than might at first be expected from the bare record of so-called imports and exports, and shows how short a way the latter figures carry us by themselves. As already stated, it is of no consequence whether there is an exact balance or not, but the actual facts should be well understood, and they cannot be understood without appreciating the totally different character of the foreign trade of the two countries.

The above, let me add, are not the only points of difficulty in the study and use of import and export statistics which ought to be considered. I have not attempted to make an exhaustive catalogue. I have simply noticed a few points which have lately been brought under my notice as material or which recent controversies have suggested. They are enough to show, however, that there is no royal road to this branch of learning any more than to other branches. There is a great deal in the study, and patience and labour are required of all who would enter into the field. That there are yet more difficulties will be apparent when we come to the special applications of these statistics which I have thought it would be useful to investigate, viz., their bearing on the question of the balance of trade or balance of indebtedness between countries, and their bearing on the points in dispute in the fair-trade controversy. We can show not only by a statement of principles, but by the actual steps necessary in applying the statistics, how much consideration is required in the application of figures which appear very simple, and how difficult it is to arrive at correct views. To prevent misunderstanding let me only add that, while pointing out the difficulties of the study, I am saying nothing to imply any doubt of conclusions which are arrived at after a sufficient study of all the facts. There are conclusions in all studies which it is hard for the unlearned to follow, but they are none the less certain to those who care to learn.

III.—Balance of Trade and Balance of Indebtedness. The Generality of the Excess of Imports.

The first special question I propose to discuss is the application of the import and export statistics to the problem of the balance of trade, and the connected problem of the balance of indebtedness of a country; the case I propose more particularly to investigate being that of the United Kingdom. Importance has come to be attached to the question in this way. The imports into the United Kingdom, as recorded, have in late years shown a great excess over the exports from the United Kingdom, as recorded. By many this excess is treated as a trade balance against this country, and without much ado there is also an assumption that the country is running into debt. We are buying, it is thought, more than we can pay for, and we can only pay by an export of securities. The conclusion itself seems so extravagant to any one who watches the constant issues of foreign securities on the London Stock Exchange, or the constant lending by private capitalists to foreign countries, which hardly ever ceases, that for one I have never thought it worth while to discuss it. A statement was actually brought me on one occasion showing that the country had become indebted to foreigners in twenty years to the extent of 1,000 million pounds, which had never been paid, and which was all represented by bills the non-payment of which would bring about, some day, a financial collapse. The writer was plainly unaware that the whole amount of bills current at one time in the country, in both home and foreign trade, was under 1,000 million pounds, that the amount has not been increasing lately, and that the foreign bills are only about a third or fourth part; and I think also he was unaware that in the foreign trade it is English capitalists who give credit to foreign nations, and not foreign capitalists who give credit to England. Still the statements as to the excess of imports have acquired a certain amount of currency, and we may see how far they are really countenanced by import and export statistics.

The general statement of the difficulties of the inquiry already made has somewhat cleared the ground. We are prepared to see at the very threshold that the imports and exports themselves are not exact to a fraction. There may be an error in the data of 1 or 2 per cent., and the values may also differ from the values realized by merchants. Suppose there is a difference of 2 per cent. only, and that it acts on imports and exports in opposite directions, increasing the former and diminishing the latter, we have a difference at once of about 15 million pounds in the so-called excess of imports. Our imports, bullion and transhipment included, amounting to nearly 450 million pounds; our exports, bullion and transhipment also included, to over 300 million pounds, on all of which 2 per cent. comes to the sum of 15 million pounds, as stated. The balance of probabilities is perhaps against any variation of such great magnitude from the amounts actually realized by merchants, while the variation may be in the opposite direction, tending to swell the excess of imports; but the great effect of what is really a slight percentage should warn us against reasoning too finely. Even the apparent amount by which the recorded imports exceed the recorded exports may be subject to great reduction.

The variations in the level of prices from year to year are also most material in such a question. A sudden rise or fall of 5 per cent. in the average price of the exports beyond the corresponding rise or fall in the average price of the imports, would alter momentarily the excess of imports to a most material extent, without implying any real changes in the general conditions of our trade. Similarly, any of the great disturbing economic events referred to, two of which have at least affected business during the last few years, viz., the resumption of specie payments in America, and the bad harvests in western Europe, might largely alter for a moment the balance of trade. Last, and more important, the fact of our being a ship-owning country, and doing other duties in connection with the foreign trade of the world, causes what is really a large export of the produce of our capital and labour in an unrecorded form, and there can be no commencement even of a discussion of the facts without a proper allowance for this export; while the trade balance itself, when properly ascertained, is no more than one item in the general account of international transactions, especially when the country concerned is a country like the United Kingdom, having investments abroad in endless number and variety. We see at once from these considerations that even to ascertain the exact excess of apparent imports over apparent exports is no easy matter; that this excess is different from the real excess in the case of a country like the United Kingdom, which has a large ship-owning business; and that the excess when ascertained is only one item in an international account. We are far enough already from the rough-and-ready handling which the excess of imports receives from writers in the "Quarterly Review" and the like authorities.

Grappling now with the subject more directly, what I have first to suggest, in accordance with a sound maxim of statistical investigation, is an inquiry how far the excess of imports is a new or not a general fact. There is little use in discussing it at all until we look about us. The question of the generality of the fact is very soon settled. An excess of imports is a very common thing indeed. I have only to refer you to the Appendix No. II. on the point. In this I have had taken out for a late year in each case, usually 1878 or 1879, the imports and exports of every country in the world: there is hardly an exception, I think. The result is that in forty-five instances there is an excess of imports, and in forty-two instances an excess of exports. I say nothing at present of amounts in each case: it is possible that the United Kingdom is specially unfortunate on account of the magnitude of the case. It is clear, however, that the mere fact of excess of imports is a very general one in the experience of nations. We do not stand alone.

Another general fact which appears is that, taken altogether, the column of imports is in excess of the column of exports. The totals are:

	£	
Imports	1,768	mlns.
Exports	1,606	"
Excess of Imports	162	"

This fact is surely very significant. It is the same goods substantially which are dealt with in both cases, the fact that it is not the same year which is dealt with in all cases making no sensible difference when so many countries are dealt with and the years are selected without any bias. But although it is the same goods that are dealt with, they are represented in the one column as 162 million pounds more than in the other column. This of itself suggests, I think, a natural reason for an excess of imports. A difference like this can only be due to a common cause, and that cause obviously is the cost of conveyance; the imports, being mostly or often valued at the place of arrival, include the cost of conveyance; the exports, being valued at the place of departure, do not include that cost. Hence the difference between the two columns. In so general an account, putting all the countries of the world together, I can suggest no other cause of difference. Of course, after what I have already said, you will not expect me to put forward the figure as absolutely exact. We know too little of the methods followed in more than eighty countries to be sure that the values are comparable one with another. Still the resulting difference, being in accordance with reasonable expectation, is evidently to be relied upon as a fact, though we cannot state a figure which pretends to any exactness.

It follows also that, as there is and must be an excess of imports in the aggregate, some particular countries are entitled to the excess. These must also be the carrying countries. Freight must be the chief matter; but the difference cannot be wholly freight, as the figures include goods which have passed from country to country by land, though not a large amount in proportion, as well as goods which have passed by sea. There are also other charges on the conveyance of goods besides the freight paid to ship-owners, and all must be included in the difference here stated, or the true figure which it approximately represents. Still, whoever carries, in proportion to what he does carry, or rather in proportion to the outlay he contributes for the carrying and the profit he thereby earns, must be entitled to a corresponding amount of imports. If the account were exact, and there were no other cause for an excess of imports or exports in particular cases, the table would show not only what the excess of imports was in the aggregate, but what were the carrying nations and how much each received. The table, however, does not show this. No doubt the countries with an excess of imports are largely carrying nations: the United Kingdom, Norway, Denmark, Germany, Holland, France, Italy; but there are other countries with an excess of imports, while in some cases, perhaps, the excess is not so large as that to which the share of the country concerned in the carrying trade would apparently entitle it. This suggests obviously that besides the cause which produces an excess of imports in the aggregate, the excess varies in the case of particular countries, or becomes even an excess of exports, owing to another cause. That cause I have to suggest is that countries are either borrowing or lending in their international transactions, or that some are receiving while others are paying interest. The result is that if we add the excesses of imports on the one side and put against them the excesses of the exports on the other, the aggregate excesses of imports are found to be 286 millions, and the aggregate excesses of exports 124 millions, the difference being the net excess of imports already stated. The excesses of exports in certain cases, amounting to 124 millions, would also imply that in the international transactions of the world, unless the figure should be modified by including the bullion, as we ought to do for this purpose, but which I have found it impossible to do in all cases, a sum of that amount was passed as the balance of the various loan and interest transactions of the world. The total amounts lent and the total amounts paid for interest may both have been larger, and there is nothing to indicate the amounts; but of the fact of a balance having to be passed there can be no question. While we conclude then, from the general fact of an excess of imports, that it corresponds to the cost of conveyance in international trade, it is quite possible that the countries entitled to share in it may show a smaller excess than they would otherwise do through their lending to foreign countries, or may show a larger excess through their receiving interest or borrowing on balance; while, on the contrary, non-carrying nations may show a small excess of exports, or even an excess of imports, in consequence of the balance of their other transactions. The figures in the case of each country are no guide to the state of its general account with other nations.

It is to be observed, however, that there is a geographical distribution to some extent of the countries having an excess of imports or of exports respectively. The nations in the tables are classified geographically, with a cross division for the British empire and for the rest of the world; and the result is, that while Europe shows an enormous excess of imports, viz.:

	£
United Kingdom and Malta . . .	112 mlns.
Other countries of Europe	142 „
Total	254 „

the other quarters of the world show on the whole an excess of exports, viz.:

	Excess of	
	Imports.	Exports.
	Mlns. £	Mlns. £
Africa—		
British empire	4	—
Other countries	—	4
Asia—		
British empire	—	19
Other countries	—	2
Australasia—		
British empire	6	—
Other countries	—	—
America and West Indies—		
British empire	1	—
Other countries	—	78
	11	103
Deduct	—	11
Excess of exports . . .	—	92

The figures at least suggest, I think, that it is the old countries—the homes of capital—which have to receive interest, and the new countries—principally the United States—which have to pay it. Certainly no inference can be drawn to the effect that it is the countries with an excess of exports which are the most prosperous, the list comprising Peru and other South American States, which have lately been passing through the most serious calamities. The most singular fact disclosed by the table is perhaps the excess of imports in the case of the Australian colonies; but this is partly to be accounted for, I believe, by the fact of the continuous lending of this country to Australasia, which has been going on for many years past. Its natural place would have been with America and the new countries generally. The facts as to the Cape Colony give rise to a similar remark.

I shall have to return to the figures shortly in reference to the question of the charges for conveyance to which the United Kingdom is entitled; but I pass on to remark that as the fact of an excess of imports is general, it is also by no means new, either in the case of the United Kingdom or of the world generally. With regard to the United Kingdom, the fact is tolerably well known; but to make this paper complete, I have included in the Appendix (Table III.) a statement of what the excess has been since 1854. The annexed (see p. 316) is a summary of this table in three years' periods:

Excess of Imports, and Proportion to Total Imports and Exports, including Bullion and Specie, 1854-80.

	Total Imports and Exports.[1]	Excess of Imports.	
		Amounts.[1]	Per Cent. of Imports and Exports
	Mln. £'s	Mln. £'s	
1854-56	330	37	11.2
'57-59	386	31	8.0
'60-62	432	53	12.3
'63-65	523	60	11.5
'66-68	566	67	11.8
'69-71	617	61	10.0
'72-74	732	61	8.3
'75-77	713	121	17.0
'78-80	690	119	17.2

Thus we have always had an excess of imports into this country. Of late years it has been larger in amount and in proportion to the imports and exports recorded than formerly, but the only novelty to be inquired into is clearly the increase of the excess: (1) whether it is apparent or real—a most important inquiry, as the mode of valuing the imports, we have seen, was changed in 1870, and in 1871 there is a sudden and remarkable increase in the imports, and a still more remarkable increase in the re-exports; and (2) whether there are any circumstances to account for a real increase of the excess of imports, such as an unusual diminution of our current lending to foreign countries, or an unusual increase of ship-owning business making our unrecorded exports unusually large. At present I do no more than suggest these answers, the main point to be considered being that the excess of imports, and that on a very large scale in proportion to our whole foreign trade, is itself no novelty.

The excess of imports, as I have stated, is also no novelty in the aggregate trade of the world. On this head I have to quote the figures given by Dr. von Neumann-Spallart,[2] to whom I am indebted for some of the figures in the second table of the Appendix, viz.:

[1] Averages of three years.

[2] Uebersichten der Weltwirthschaft, von Dr. F. X. von Neumann-Spallart. Jahrgang 1880. Stuttgart. 1881. P. 360.

Imports and Exports of the World.

[In millions sterling, converting the mark at 20 per £.]

	Imports.	Exports.	Excess of Imports.
	£	£	£
1867-68 . . .	1,165	1,045	120
'69-70 . . .	1,266	1,100	166
'72-73 . . .	1,554	1,334	220
'74-75 . . .	1,450	1,289	161
'76	1,493	1,296	197
'78	1,508	1,359	149
'79	1,571	1,355	216

Thus an excess of imports in the aggregate trade of the world is a permanent fact. There is nothing new in it. There is also some proportion between the aggregate trade and the excess of imports. The more trade there is the more charges for conveyance, though the progression is of course not quite constant, and the figures themselves are of course somewhat incomplete, which makes it difficult to exhibit a regular progress from year to year.[1]

IV.—Subject continued: how the Excess of Imports into the United Kingdom is to be accounted for.

Having thus brought out the facts of the generality and want of novelty in the excess of imports, and having suggested as a necessary cause of it the cost of conveyance between countries which must always exist, and as a contributing cause the settlements of international accounts through the remittance of loans or interest on money previously borrowed, I propose now to inquire more particularly with reference to the

[1] It will be observed that the annual amounts here are in no case so large as the annual amount in Table II. of the Appendix. Some of the figures in the latter table, however, are for a year later than 1879, and the figures I have used also include the bullion and specie as much as possible, which are not included, apparently, in Dr. Spallart's figures.

United Kingdom how the excess is to be accounted for.

How much, to begin with, is annually due to us as a ship-owning and carrying nation? As we have seen, there is no reason why the actual excess of imports, in the case of a ship-owning nation, should correspond to the sum it earns in the carrying trade; the actual excess may be less or more than that sum; but the sum is nevertheless an item in the account just as much as the so-called exports on the one side or the imports on the other. I have to call attention to the words ship-owning and carrying. According to the definition already given, the question is, what is the amount of our contribution to the carrying of the world's goods? and though it is mainly a ship-owner's question, it is not wholly so.[1]

Replying to this question, I propose to take the facts as to ship-owning first, and to use first in a general view of the subject the excess of imports already shown in the aggregate trade of the world. Assuming this excess of 162 million pounds to represent approximately the cost of conveyance, how much of it should fall to the share of the United Kingdom? I have to suggest first of all, for reasons to be given afterwards, that about 32 million pounds of the amount, or rather less than 2 per cent. on the aggregate trade, represent

[1] The following propositions appear to cover the various cases of an excess of imports or exports arising in connection with carrying operations:

1. A non-carrying nation, in the absence of borrowing or lending, ought to show in its accounts an equality between imports at the place of arrival, and exports at the place of departure.

2. A nation carrying half its foreign trade ought to have an excess of imports equal to the cost of carrying the goods one way; and so in proportion for whatever its contribution to carrying may be.

3. A nation carrying its whole foreign trade will have an excess of imports equal to the cost of carrying the goods both ways.

4. A nation carrying for others is entitled, in addition, to an excess of imports equal to the freight earned, less any expenses incurred abroad. Any nation contributing to carriage will also have something to receive.

miscellaneous charges and commissions, which all form part of the cost of conveyance, and of which the English share may be put at one-half, or 16 million pounds. Deducting this 32 million pounds, the sum of 130 million pounds is left as the amount due for freight. How much should fall to the share of England? It would also be natural in reply to compare the mercantile tonnage of England with the tonnage of the rest of the world, and divide the 130 million pounds between them in proportion. For all practical purposes England's proportion may be put at something like 55 per cent.,[1] and assuming this proportion, the division would be as follows:

	Per Cent.	Proportion.
		Mlns. £
United Kingdom	55	71½
Other countries	45	58½
Total	—	130

[1] This is a rough deduction from the tables in the return, "Progress of British Merchant Shipping," No. 125, Sess. 1881. The calculation (for 1879) in millions of tons is:

	Sailing.	Steam.		Total.	Per Cent. of Total.
		Amount.	Equivalent in Sailing tons.		
Tonnage of—					
United Kingdom . . .	4.0	2.5	10.0	14.0	50
Rest of British empire .	2.0	0.2	0.8	2.8	9
	6.0	2.7	10.8	16.8	59
Foreign countries . . .	7.2	1.1	4.4	11.6	41
Total	13.2	3.8	15.2	28.4	100

Thus the proportion of ships belonging to the United Kingdom alone is 50 per cent., and allowing a certain proportion of colonial ships to be owned in the United Kingdom, the figure of 55 per cent. in the text seems near the mark. Since 1879 our proportion has largely increased.

The sum of 71 millions sterling is certainly enormous. Still, the figures, whatever they may be worth, are not cooked in any way I have simply taken the excess of imports as I have found it, and made a proper deduction as I think, so as to leave only what is due to freight, and I have then merely divided this freight between England and other countries in proportion to their tonnage. As regards the actual amount of this freight, it cannot be called extravagant. On the total imports of the world, as shown in Table II. of the Appendix, it amounts to a charge of 7½ per cent. only, and on the total tonnage of the world, sailing and steam together, it would show a gross earning of no more than £8 per ton.

As regards the division between England and other countries, it would perhaps be necessary to make a correction for the amount of outlay by English ships in foreign ports, in excess of the outlay by foreign ships in English ports; but the outlay of this sort, I believe, from a consideration of the other outlays in earning freight, cannot exceed about a sixth part of the total earnings. Deducting a sixth from the above sum of 71½ millions would leave about 60 millions as the sum due to the United Kingdom for freight. This would be our share of the 130 millions.

Adding together the 60 millions for freight and the 16 millions for miscellaneous charges and commissions, we arrive at a total of 76 millions, as the share of the above 162 millions, for cost of international conveyance annually due to the United Kingdom at the present time.

These figures are, of course, too uncertain to be relied upon by themselves, but they are not without corroboration. I have first to refer to various authorities who have dealt especially with the amounts of freight earned in the direct trade of the United Kingdom. Mr. Bourne, in a paper read before the Society, and printed No. 3 of the volume already referred to, was one of the first to grapple with the problem. His method, I believe, was incomplete, but some of his statements were most interesting. One of them (p. 63) is to the effect that 11 per cent. on the value of our imports would be a fair average allowance for freight. The imports are now, roughly speaking, over 400 millions a year, on which 11 per cent. would be 44 millions, and of this 44 millions the English share, dividing the sum in the proportion of the entries of English and foreign ships—70 per cent. to 30 per cent. —would be very nearly 31 millions. Similarly Mr. Bourne gives the freight on exports as 20*s.* per ton for sailing vessels, and 30*s.* per ton for steamers, at which rates in 1880, the clearances of British sailing vessels being 3,182,000 tons, and of steamers 15,685,000 tons, the freight on exports in British bottoms would be nearly 27 millions. The total for imports and exports is 58 millions. Adding a sum for freights earned by British ships in the indirect trade, which must be enormous, and again making a deduction for outlays in foreign ports, we should still, on this showing, get well on to the figure of 60 millions, if not beyond it.

I must, of course, allow that Mr. Bourne was writing several years ago, and freights are a variable item; but I do not believe that one year with another they have fallen permanently below the level of price he quoted. Some freights have fallen, but not the run of freights to any material extent. There has been, in truth, no large margin for a fall in freights, the cost of working being itself from 70 to 90 per cent. of the income, and the absolute outlay per ton, though it tends to diminish with the increasing size of vessels, not having diminished very greatly from the time Mr. Bourne wrote.

Mr. Newmarch again, in a paper read to this Society in 1878,[1] proposes to deduct 5 per cent. from the imports and add 10 per cent. to the exports for all charges of conveyance. These amounts on our present trade would come to about 50 millions. Mr. Newmarch does

[1] Statistical Society's "Journal," vol. xli., pp. 218-220.

not indicate what he thinks the other charges as distinguished from freight would be, and does not enter into the question of outlays in foreign ports or of work done by British vessels for foreign countries. The sum of 50 millions, which he actually arrives at for the direct trade of the United Kingdom alone, appears to corroborate the notion that the sum of 60 millions for the whole earnings of our mercantile fleet, less all outlays abroad, is not wide of the mark.

In the same paper Mr. Newmarch quotes a letter of Mr. McKay, of Liverpool, who estimates the freights earned in British bottoms at 30*s.* per ton for imports and 20*s.* per ton for exports.[1] These rates on the tonnage of 1880, converting the net registered tons into gross tons in the proportion of two-thirds to 1, would give:

	£
Imports	37 mlns.
Exports	27 „
Total	64 „

Again, there is no mention of any outlays abroad, but the figures amply support those already stated. The sum these authorities deal with, it must always be remembered, is for the direct trade of the United Kingdom alone; and the figure of 60 millions already given represents our whole earnings from freight, less actual outlays abroad in earning it.

Quite lately I have obtained a calculation from a ship-owning friend (whom I shall call A, as I have many other facts from ship-owners, whose names I am not at liberty to mention, and to whom I shall assign the letters of the alphabet) with reference to average freights at the present time. His calculation is that on the weights of goods actually imported and exported in the American trade, freights come to about 27*s.* 6*d.*

[1] I am unable to identify the tonnage actually quoted by Mr. McKay.

and 20*s*. respectively. It is not quite clear what these weights are, or whether they would be represented by the tonnages entered and cleared; but assuming the latter to be the case, and converting the net registered tons into gross tons, as is done above, and assuming also that the American trade is a good average of the whole foreign trade, as I believe we may do, we get the following figures:

	£
Imports	34 mlns.
Exports	27 „
Total	61 „

This is substantially the same figure as that arrived at on Mr. McKay's calculation.[1] It manifestly supports the conclusion that 60 millions at least is earned by our shipping, after deducting all outlays abroad, in the direct and indirect trades.

I propose now, however, to deal more directly with the matter. The tonnage of the British mercantile fleet being known, how much per ton, according to direct evidence, does the sailing ship and the steamer earn on the average, and how much ought to be the deduction for outlay abroad? I have many figures on this head to submit to you, and I must crave your patience on account of the very great importance of the subject.

I have first to call your attention to Appendix No. IV., in which there are certain tables extracted from the "Statist" newspaper of 26th November last [1881]. These tables summarize the accounts of our principal joint-stock shipping companies in a form which was partly of my own suggestion, with a view to the present paper, though the tables themselves are not my own

[1] It is hardly worth while cumbering the paper with the details, but I have made a calculation of the actual weights of goods imported and exported, and these charges for freights would bring out a sum on such weights of 50 million pounds. I have also to call attention, on this head, to Appendix X., showing the amount of weights carried in our direct foreign trade, as far as weights can be stated.

work, but the work of a gentleman already well known to many of you, Mr. Wynnard Hooper, whose analysis, I think, does him great credit. The points in this statement to which I desire to call attention are these:

a. The capital value of the fleets of eight companies, including some of the largest and best, but also including one or two of a second class, comes out on the average at £16 13*s.* per ton gross, which is not less than about £25 per ton net, taking the net as two-thirds of the gross, and the real proportion being less. The range of value is from £13 2*s.* to £18 12*s.* per ton gross, or from £19 13*s.* to £27 16*s.* per net registered ton. These are much lower values in all cases, I believe, than the ships could be built for. They are not extreme values.

b. The gross income of six of the above companies, representing fairly well the average of the nine, works out at £14 12*s.* per ton gross, or about £22 per net registered ton. This is a percentage on the value of about 88 per cent. The percentage on the value in each case is:

	Per Cent.
Peninsular and Oriental . .	91
Pacific Steam	92
Royal Mail	70
Cunard	100
General Steam	84
Mercantile Steamship . . .	59

Thus the lowest value per net registered ton is about £20 and the lowest proportion of gross earnings about 60 per cent.

c. The proportion of expenditure to gross income works out as follows:

	Per Cent.
Peninsular and Oriental . .	92.4
Pacific Steam	92.6
Royal Mail	99.3
Cunard	83.9
General Steam	91.1
Mercantile Steamship . .	87.7

The average of the six is about 91 per cent., and the lowest is about 84 per cent. As the gross earnings are a large percentage of the value, so the gross outlay is also a large percentage of the gross earnings.

The outlay per ton gross amounts to £13 7*s.* on the average of the six companies, equal to about £20 per net registered ton. The value being £25, this shows an average outlay in proportion to the value of 80 per cent.

d. In the case of three of the principal companies practically little more than half the gross earnings are from freights, but they earn from freights alone £2,116,000, or about £8 per gross ton, equal to about £12 per net registered ton. In any case a part of their income from passengers, probably the larger part, being for the conveyance of foreigners, or of persons travelling on foreign account, has the same effect on the international account as a charge for conveyance of goods. It is a debit to foreign nations, and a credit to the ship-owner in this country.

e. The average expenditure per ton is stated under several heads for each of the three principal companies, and is in all very nearly alike, the mean being as follows:

	Per Ton Gross.		Per Ton Register.	
	£	*s.*	£	*s.*
Coal	2	12	3	18
Pay of Crews	1	10	2	5
Provisions	1	8	2	2
Repairs and Renewals	1	12	2	8
Insurance and depreciation . .	2	2	3	3
Other expenses	4	8	6	12
	13	12	20	8

I postpone drawing any deductions from the figures, as I have other figures to give, but I may note before passing that the figures as to the eight companies comprise 442,000 tons gross of shipping; the figures as to six, 400,000 tons; and the figures as to three, 278,000 tons. A considerable part of the steam mercantile fleet is thus represented.

I have next to direct attention to the series of statements respecting different classes of ships in Appendix No. V. The statement B is exactly parallel, it will be observed, to the statements above quoted, relating to the leading companies which publish their accounts, with the differences that only the outlay is stated, and that the outlay abroad is distinguished from the outlay at home. The general result is that on a somewhat higher valuation, the steamers being valued at £20 per ton gross, or £31 per ton net register, the outlay is also about 65 to 70 per cent. of the value, or £21.88 per registered ton in the one case and £20.34 in the other case. The amount spent per ton on wages, coal, and other items is less than in the case of the companies which publish their accounts, but the total outlay is swollen by a large charge for depreciation.

With regard to the distribution of the expenses between this country and abroad, the point to note seems to be that the total abroad in the one case is £7.70 per ton and in the other £7.60 per ton, or about 35 per cent. of the total outlay. The amount is chiefly for port expenses and Suez Canal expenses.

The next statement, C, also relates to a steamer, but of a different class from the above, the value being £19 only per net registered ton, and the gross outlay £14 3*s.* per ton. The wages are again much lower than in the case of the first-class steamers, but the outlay for coal is as much as £5 per ton.

The next statement, D, is also a steamer—a cargo boat—the actual value not being stated, but apparently belonging to a class which is valued at £25 per ton. Here the outlay is £14 13*s.* 7*d.* per ton, and the wages are as much as £2 17*s.* 6*d.* per ton.

E. Is another steamer, a plain cargo boat, valued at £25 per ton, with an annual outlay of £11 2*s*. per ton, including only £1 10*s*. per ton for wages.

F. Is another cargo boat, value about £22 per ton. Here the gross earnings are stated, and amount to about £17 per ton, nearly 80 per cent. of the value. Of the £17 per ton earned, the outlay abroad is £7 per ton, or between a half and a third.

G. Contains an account of four steamers in the Mediterranean trade valued at £15 per gross ton, or £22 net, whose average outlay amounts to about £10 16*s*. per ton gross, equal to about £16 per ton net. The results are in fact much the same as for F, though the payments abroad do not appear so large.

H. Is a record of four steamers engaged in the coasting trade or short voyages. Their average value is also about £15 per gross ton, or £22 per ton net, and the average outlay is about £10 10*s*. per gross ton, or £15 15*s*. per net ton.

The next records, I, K, and L, all relate to sailing ships: I shows an outlay of £5 17*s*. per net registered ton; K an outlay of £6 1*s*. 8*d*.; and L, which gives an average of no fewer than fifty vessels engaged in miscellaneous trades, an average outlay of about £5 6*s*. per net registered ton. The values in I and K are £15 and £14 respectively, and in L about £9 10*s*. per ton. In the case of L the statement is accompanied by a private note, indicating that the profit is about £1 16*s*. per ton, that is, about one-third of the outlay. This would make the gross earnings over £7 per ton; and as the outlay abroad is £1 10*s*. per ton, the gross earnings receivable at home would be about £5 10*s*. per ton.

Combining all the information from the various sources, what it seems to point to in the case of steamers is first a gross outlay, ranging from about £11 or £12 up to £20 and even more per net registered ton, this gross outlay being also about 80 or 90 per cent. of the income, which would thus range from about £15 to

£22 per ton. In no case, apparently, not even that of the lowest collier, can the gross income be put at less than about £15 per ton. The subjoined table brings out this clearly:

	Gross Income where Stated, per Ton.	Outlay per Ton.	
		Amount.	Per Cent. of Income.
	£	£ s. d.	
Six Steamers in "Statist"	22	20 0 0	88
Statement B	—	21 0 0	—
" C	—	14 3 0	—
" D	—	14 13 7	—
" E	—	11 2 0	—
" F	17	12 0 0	70
" G	—	16 0 0	—
" H	—	15 15 0	—

Thus, in any case where the income is mentioned at all, even in the case of an ordinary steamer spending no more than £12 per ton, there is no lower sum mentioned than £17 per ton. Assuming that in all the other cases the percentage of expenses is also high, and not less than 80 per cent. of the income, we should have an income in all, except the lowest class, amounting to about £16 to £18 per ton and upwards.

I shall propose then to place the earnings of our steam fleet on home account, inclusive of the earnings from passengers, at not less than £15 per ton, which would allow for expenditure in foreign ports. This on the tonnage registered at the end of 1880, viz., 2,723,000 tons, would come to about 41 million pounds.

With regard to the sailing vessels, the problem seems more simple. The average earnings may be put at not less than £7 per ton, the outlay being £5 6*s*. per ton. The sum of £7 per ton on a fleet of 3,851,000 tons comes to about 27 million pounds, from which about £1 10*s*. per ton, or say 6 million pounds, would fall to be deducted for outlay in foreign ports, leaving about

21 million pounds as earned on home account. The two sums together amount to 62 million pounds, which is not far from the sum of 60 million pounds already arrived at. A certain deduction would of course have to be made from this calculation for the earnings of the fleet engaged purely in coasting, but not sufficient, I think, to alter the round figure of 60 million pounds.

As a rough calculation, I would suggest that £5 per ton from sailing ships, and £15 per ton from steamers, will give us an approximate figure for the foreign earnings of our mercantile fleet, making all corrections for outlays abroad. If there is any over-estimate, there would be a set-off to some extent in the outlay on foreign vessels in our own ports.

My own impression is that the figure is under and not over the mark. The above account deals only with vessels on the register of the United Kingdom, and known to be employed in the foreign trade. There are many vessels, as already hinted, on colonial registers, or which have been lost sight of, which are really British owned, and which bring an income to British owners. We may be sure that there are considerable sums beyond what has been stated to be brought to account.

It will serve to make clear to us what all this trade means, besides confirming the conclusion as to the income derived from it to the United Kingdom, if we further inquire what the share of the gross earnings which comes to us is composed of. What are the principal items? The information in the Appendices IV. and V. bears a good deal on this point, and may be confirmed in various ways.

The principal items are clearly—wages, victualling, insurance, repairs, renewals and depreciation, and profit. I have to submit the following table, deduced from the accounts annexed, always premising that the figures show only what is earned for the United Kingdom:

	Per Ton.			Total for Tonnage of United Kingdom.
				Mlns.
Sailing Vessels—	£	s.	d.	£
Wages	1	1	0	4
Victualling	0	11	0	2
Insurance, 7½ per cent. on mean value of £10 per ton . . .	0	15	0	3
Repairs, renewal, and depreciation, 12½ per cent. on mean value of £10 per ton . . .	1	5	0	5
Profit, 12½ per cent.	1	5	0	5
Total	—			19
Steamers—				
Wages	2	0	0	5½
Provisions	1	10	0	4½
Insurance, 7½ per cent. on mean value of £25 per ton . . .	1	17	6	5
Repairs, renewals, and depreciation, 15 per cent. on mean value of £25 per ton . . .	3	15	0	10
Profit, 12½ per cent.	3	2	6	8½
Total	—			33½

Summary.

	Sailing Vessels.	Steamers.	Totals.
	Mlns. £	Mlns. £	Mlns. £
Wages	4	5½	9½
Provisions	2	4½	6½
Insurance	3	5	8
Repairs, etc.	5	10	15
Profit	5	8½	13½
	19	33½	52½
Add port expenses at home, including harbour and light dues, commissions, etc.			8½
,, coals shipped in steamers from United Kingdom .			2
Total			63

Here again little is included for the outlay on foreign vessels in English ports, while no deduction is made for the earnings of our fleet engaged in the coasting trade. Making all allowances, the figure of 60 million pounds as our foreign earnings in connection with shipping is submitted as near the mark.

The question arises whether the figures are *vraisemblable*, and it is immediately suggested as regards wages that we have a check. The number of persons employed in our mercantile fleet in 1880, not including masters, was 193,000. Dividing 9½ million pounds by this sum we get at an average money wage of £50 per per man. I do not consider this a very high average, allowing for the fact that it includes the pay of masters, and officers of every grade, engineers, stokers, and others, all receiving more than the ordinary A.B. wages, which are not less than £2 10*s*. or £3 per month.[1] The averages for sailing vessels and steamers would work out at about £40 per man for sailing vessels, and rather less than £70 per man for steamers, which of course include a much larger proportion of highly skilled labour.[2]

With regard to victualling, I think I need do no more than refer you to the paper of Mr. Bourne, already cited, in which he gives the estimate of 6 million pounds for victualling and stores for the year 1879—that is, victualling and stores put on board ships from the United Kingdom. As I understand Mr. Bourne's mode of doing the sum, this would include victuals and stores put on board foreign ships also, whereas this item in the above account only includes British ships; but the item in any case is not a large one.

[1] See return, "Progress of Merchant Shipping for 1880."

[2] It will obviously be suggested that two deductions should be made, one for the wages of the fleet engaged in coasting, the other for wages paid abroad; but the deductions on these heads would, I believe, be immaterial, while I have sought to allow for minor corrections like these by the moderation of the estimates. In 1881, wages generally advanced above the figures here dealt with about £6 per head, or nearly £1,500,000 in all.

The other items of insurance, repairs, renewals and depreciation, and profit require less remark. They amount altogether to 35 per cent. on the value of our shipping, which I assume to be about 40 million pounds for sailing vessels, and about 70 million pounds for steamers, in the year 1880. With regard to insurance, however, it may be pointed out that the annual replacements required by wrecks to vessels of the United Kingdom—I speak of total losses only—amount to about

150,000	tons,	sailing vessels
230,000	,,	steamers
380,000	,,	total

annually. The cost of building these vessels, at £15 per ton for sailing vessels, and £30 per ton for steamers, would be about 9 million pounds, or more than the 8 millions put down for insurance. I am inclined to think that this estimate in particular is under the mark, but I leave the figure as it stands, in case it should be thought by some that there is an over-estimate for repairs and depreciation. This last is a high estimate, though I consider it fully justified by the figures before me, shipping property ageing rapidly. With regard to the profit, in putting it at 12½ per cent., I have kept a good deal below what more than one ship-owner owns to, but the rate is undoubtedly a good deal more than that paid by the high-class steam shipping companies whose accounts are published. There is reason to believe, however, that the latter are among the least remunerative of vessels. With regard to port expenses at home, the broad facts are that harbour, pilotage, and light dues alone would account for nearly three-fourths of the amount here stated, and only a small part would fall on the coasting fleet. The final item of coal put on board steamers at home is rendered necessary in this calculation by the exclusion from the other items of any payments abroad, which are included in the general accounts above dealt with.[1]

There is a concurrence of testimony, therefore, to the effect that an enormous sum accrues annually to the United Kingdom in connection with its shipping business, and that the sum of 60 million pouuds is not far from the mark. First, in examining the imports and exports of the whole world, we find a difference between them which must represent the cost of conveyance, and analyzing and dividing this amount among the principal ship-owning nations, we get a figure of about 60 million pounds as due annually to the United Kingdom for freight alone. Second, according to various testimonies—Mr. Bourne, Mr. Newmarch, Mr. McKay and others—there is known to be a large sum annually accruing in connection with the direct trade of the United Kingdom alone, a sum of 40 to 50 millions sterling, and this sum, making due allowance for what comes to us from the shipping in the indirect trade, again points to the probability of a large sum being due to us which cannot be less than about 60 million pounds. Third, the direct evidence of the accounts of numerous steamers and sailing ships points to a gross earning of this amount, if not more, deducting all outlays abroad. Last of all, there is additional confirmation in the analysis of the different items of the expenses of our fleet, and the comparison of these items with other sources of information, such as, for wages—the number of men employed, for victualling and stores—the independent inquiry of Mr. Bourne, for insurance—the sums actually spent in replacing wrecks, for profit—the actual admissions of ship-owners themselves, and the accounts of leading companies, and

[1] There ought to be some further correction, perhaps, as regards the latter figures in respect of the earnings of our mercantile fleet engaged in the coasting trade, already referred to, but that portion, as already stated, is comparatively small, while these last calculations do not include anything for the earnings or profit of British-owned ships not on the register of the United Kingdom.

or such items as port expenses—the amounts actually paid for harbour and light dues. I must again repeat, however, my impression that probably a much larger sum is really due to us, in consequence both of the moderation of the estimates and the circumstance of a large number of vessels not on the register of the United Kingdom being in fact owned in the United Kingdom. It is not necessary, however, for the special purpose of this paper to name an exact figure. I shall be content if I have made clear that the business of ship-owning is really enormous, and that if we would make any use at all of the import and export figures in the question of the balance of trade, we must dwell on the invisible export which takes place by means of our shipping. The discussion on the subject ought to include a formal treatment of the question of how much our shipping earns.

The inquiry does not end here. I have already drawn attention to the point that the ship-owner is not the only person concerned in the cost of conveyance, of which the aggregate excess of imports in the imports and exports of the world is composed. There are other commissions and charges, of which I have suggested that the English share amounts at least to 16 million pounds—perhaps 20 million pounds would be nearer the mark. The latter sum is only 2½ per cent. on the total of our imports and exports—about 800 million pounds; and when I point out that insurance cannot be estimated at less than 15*s.* per cent., and bankers' commission, bill stamps, and minor charges 5*s.* per cent., leaving only 1½ per cent. for all other charges, the estimate must be held to be moderate. Mr. McKay, in the letter already referred to, makes the commission and charges amount to more than double this sum, and quotes the case of a Manchester shipment, in which the insurance and other charges came to 4 per cent. I confess I am afraid of too big figures, and have tried to keep well within the mark. The sum of 20 million pounds, added to the 60 million pounds due to us for freight, make a total of 80 million pounds, which is really, to use a phrase which I have tried to make familiar, an invisible export. In using the import and export statistics for the question of the balance of trade, we have to credit ourselves, in addition to our recorded exports, with a sum of at least this amount.

Such figures, if accepted, without any further correction for interest receivable for investments abroad, would serve of themselves to revolutionize the conception of the international balance between this country and other nations, which would be suggested by the bare consideration of the import and export figures. In the last few years the excess of imports, as we have seen, has been about 120 million pounds (see *supra*, p. 315), but a deduction from this sum of 80 million pounds would reduce the amount to 40 million pounds, without any correction whatever for other international transactions, such as the receipt of interest upon our foreign investments. Even apart from such a correction, then, the excess of imports is almost accounted for. A nominal difference of about 40 million pounds, subject to the qualifications already stated, is practically much the same thing as no difference at all. As we have seen, we cannot be sure to within 15 or 20 million pounds of the totals of our imports and exports and the balance shown by them, while there is also a very great probability that the sum of 80 million pounds, which I have assumed to be annually earned by the country in connection with its shipping, and other charges in connection with the conveyance of goods from country to country, is a good deal under the mark. When we establish, therefore, that 40 million pounds is a maximum sum for the apparent excess of imports, we establish that there is nothing in such a figure by itself to give us any concern about the nation living on its capital. An excess of that amount might easily be balanced by an excess in the opposite direction in other years; we must expect so great a trade as that of the United Kingdom to exhibit oscillations of this magnitude. If it is to be proved that the nation is living on its capital to any extent at all, it must be shown *aliunde*, from the operations of the stock exchanges and otherwise, that the nation is borrowing abroad, or is bringing home its capital.

The figures suggest another correction of the first impression of the import and export figures. The excess of imports being itself no novelty, and the only thing new being the sudden increase in recent years, the question is naturally suggested whether there is any change in the invisible items of our export which would help to account for such an increase. On this head I need hardly say that nothing has been more remarkable during the last twenty years than the wonderful progress of our shipping, both in absolute amount and in relation to the rest of the world. The figures as to the United Kingdom are:

Tonnage of Sailing and Steam Vessels belonging to the United Kingdom.

[In thousands of tons.]

	Sailing.	Steam.		Total in Sailing Tons.	Increase Per Cent. in Five Periods..
		Amount.	Equivalent in Sailing Tons.		
				Tons.	
1840	2,637	87	348	2,985	—
'50	3,336	168	672	4,008	30
'60	4,134	452	1,808	5,942	50
'70	4,506	1,111	4,444	8,950	50
'80	3,799	2,720	10,880	14,679	64

The business is thus a rapidly increasing one. Twenty years ago the mercantile fleet of the United Kingdom was capable of performing the work of about two-fifths only of the present mercantile fleet. Assuming the earnings to be in much the same proportion, the sum accruing to the United Kingdom in connection with its shipping would be about 27 million pounds only twenty years ago, as compared with 60 million pounds now. Even as compared with a period ten years ago, since which our mercantile fleet has increased 65 per cent., such an increase would imply that the earnings ten years ago were only about 35 million pounds, as compared with 60 million pounds now, a difference of 25 million pounds, by which our invisible exports, in connection with the shipping alone, have increased in the ten years. Not only then is the excess of imports no new fact, but the increase of it in recent years is obviously to be largely accounted for by the increase of our shipping business.[1]

The increase of our shipping has been going on quite steadily all through the recent years of depression. You had the figures before you at your last meeting in Mr. Glover's very able paper; but for convenience of reference I have included in the Appendix (No. VI.) a statement of the progress of our mercantile fleet in each year since 1854, from which date we are able to compare it with the excess of imports, adding a note of the estimated earnings for the United Kingdom on the basis already established. This shows a progressive increase from about 24 million pounds in 1854 to over 60 million pounds at the present time. It will be said perhaps that rates of freight have been diminishing, which is perhaps true to a certain extent; but such a reduction is allowed for in the mode of calculation adopted, the earning power of steamers being stated at three times only that of sailing ships, whereas their effectiveness is as 4 to 1. The reduction of freights cannot have been very great all round, though it may be large on some descriptions of cargo. The expenses, owing to the rise of wages, notwithstanding the great economy of iron as compared with wood, and the economy of labour by means of large vessels and the

[1] See also on this head Appendix X., already referred to, showing the great increase in recent years of weights carried in the direct foreign trade of the United Kingdom, where weights are stated or can be calculated.

substitution of steam for sailing, still remain very large, both per ton per annum and per voyage.

The other charges for conveyance accruing to a country like the United Kingdom must also have increased greatly during the last twenty years. The charge of 2½ per cent. on the foreign trade of twenty years ago would have been under 10 million pounds, as compared with 20 million pounds now.

These corrections will best be shown in a short table, for which I have made use of the figures in Table III., already summarized (see *supra*, p. 315):

Excess of Imports as shown in Appendix III., and Summarized above (supra, p. 169), Corrected by Deducting (1) the Charges for Gross Earnings of Shipping as shown in Appendix VI.; and (2) the charge of 2½ per Cent. for Commissions, Insurance, etc., on the Total Amount of the Direct Trade of the United Kingdom.

[In millions of pounds.]

	Total Imports and Exports.	Apparent Excess of Imports.	Charges to be Deducted.			Corrected Excess.
			Freight, etc.	Commission, Insurance, etc.	Total.	
	£	£	£	£	£	£
1854-56	330	37	24	8	32	5
'57-59	386	31	27	10	37	(–) 6
'60-62	432	53	28	11	39	14
'63-65	523	60	34	13	47	13
'66-68	566	67	37	14	51	16
'69-71	617	61	39	15	54	7
'72-74	732	61	46	18	64	(–) 3
'75-77	713	121	51	18	69	52
'78-80	690	119	58	17	75	44

This table needs no comment. The figures are not presented as exact, but they show approximately the difference between the real and the apparent excess, and one of the reasons for the apparent excess increasing in recent years. There remains, of course, the more general question of the balance of indebtedness between nations, all the points yet dealt with, the imports and exports themselves, and the sum accruing to the United Kingdom for the gross earnings of its mercantile fleet and for other charges of conveyance being only items in a more general account. On this head, however, I may be permitted not to enlarge. It is notorious that a large sum is due to this country annually for its investments abroad; we belong, as has been seen, to a geographical group which has probably such interest to receive. The usual estimate has been about 50 million pounds to 60 million pounds a year; but since these estimates were made our investments abroad have increased enormously, the public issues on foreign account of the last six years alone, *i.e.*, since the foreign loan collapse of 1875 on the London Stock Exchange, having been about 210 million pounds, this figure not including, moreover, some very large issues, in which the London Stock Exchange was interested, but where the issue was abroad. (See Appendix VII.) I am disposed to think also, from a consideration of the enormous investment of capital in the movement of goods in our ships, and in the conduct of our trade in foreign countries themselves, that this private capital has never been sufficiently estimated, and that our investments of capital abroad at the present time are not less than 1,500 million pounds sterling, on which interest at only 5 per cent. would be 75 million pounds per annum, at 6 per cent. 90 million pounds per annum, and at 7 per cent. 105 million pounds per annum. Whatever sum we take, looking at the small magnitude of the excess of imports which remains after proper corrections for the charges of the cost of conveyance, there can be no question that in recent years, large as the apparent excess of imports has been, this country has been continuing to invest capital abroad—from 40 million pounds to 60 million pounds per annum, if not more. But for this lending, the excess of imports would have been still greater than it has been.

I do not propose to go farther into this question of the balance of indebtedness in its international transactions for the United Kingdom. To complete it would require an elaborate investigation of the magnitude of private investments, while such points as the expenditure of British citizens abroad, and the expenditure by foreigners in this country, and the minor movements of international capital in connection with exchange operations, would all require to be considered. To treat this subject properly would require a paper by itself almost as long as the one now before you, which is already of ample dimensions. I shall be quite content if I have established to your satisfaction (1) that the question to be investigated is not that of the diminution, but of the increase, of our investments abroad—that there is really no question at all of the nation bringing home capital or living on its capital in recent years; and (2) that, whatever may be our conclusion on this point, the import and export figures themselves are only a small part of the question, and that the use of these figures by some writers as if they were the whole is only to be excused, if it is excusable, on the score of ignorance of the nature of statistics and the necessary conditions of dealing with them.

V.—Subject continued: the Excess of Imports or Exports in France and the United States. Conclusion.

Mutatis mutandis, all these points have to be considered of course in dealing with foreign nations. I shall only consider two, the United States and France. The United States is the country which has perhaps the largest excess of exports. In the last six years, including bullion, that excess has been 37 million pounds annually. (See Appendix VIII.) The United States is practically a country whose exports, apart from the question of interest on borrowed money, ought to balance its imports, its foreign shipping being quite insignificant, earning for it probably, according to the above calculation of £5 per ton for sailing ships, about 6 million pounds a year only. How then is the excess of exports to be accounted for? What economic circumstances or conditions does it imply? I have to suggest two things: (1) the expenditure by United States citizens travelling abroad less the expenditure of foreigners travelling in the United States; (2) the interest payable to foreigners on account of foreign capital invested in the United States. The former cannot be less, I believe, than 10 million to 15 million pounds, the annual migration of Americans to Europe being 20,000 to 30,000 in addition to an American colony of several thousands almost constantly resident in Europe, and the latter cannot be less than 30 million pounds; total 40 million pounds. Even if the latter ought to be a smaller figure, we should still have to consider the margin of error in the United States figures, especially those for the imports, on account of the undervaluations and smuggling, so that the apparent excess of exports would be more than the real excess, because of the imports being undervalued. There is certainly nothing in the excess of exports to indicate unusual prosperity, whether present or prospective. The recent increase of the exports, and of the excess of exports, is also to be accounted for by the fact that in the last twenty years American foreign shipping has been diminishing in proportion to its total trade. That trade twenty years ago was 135 million pounds only, the tonnage of American shipping in the foreign trade being over 2½ million tons, which, at the rate of £5 per ton, would entitle it to a gross income of 12½ million pounds a year. Now the trade is 347 million pounds, and the earnings from the shipping must be about 6 million pounds only. There is ample reason, therefore, for the excess of imports in the American trade ceasing, and an excess of exports beginning, apart from the farther obvious explanation that America borrowed large sums abroad during the civil war and afterwards, the interest of which has now to be paid. It seems a nice question whether America of late years has been reducing its indebtedness abroad, but there is nothing, at least in the import and export figures, corrected as they ought to be, to indicate such a reduction. I am only concerned, however, at present, with pointing out the nature of the inquiry which must be made.[1]

As regards France, the account stands as follows for the last twenty years (see Appendix IX.):

[In thousands of pounds.]

	Excess of			Excess of	
	Imports.	Exports.		Imports.	Exports.
	£	£		£	£
1860 . . .	—	13	'71 . .	19	—
'61 . . .	14	—	'72 . .	—	8
'62 . . .	—	3	'73 . .	—	7
'63 . . .	—	14	'74 . .	$20\frac{1}{2}$	—
'64 . . .	—	17	'75 . .	$12\frac{1}{2}$	—
'65 . . .	—	15	'76 . .	$40\frac{1}{2}$	—
'66 . . .	1.5	—	'77 . .	$29\frac{1}{2}$	—
'67 . . .	27	—	'78 . .	53	—
'68 . . .	34	—	'79 . .	48	—
'69 . . .	15	—	'80 . .	53	—
'70 . . .	$7\frac{1}{2}$	—			

Here the excess of imports is less marked than it is in the case of the United Kingdom, and there has been a smaller increase in the excess in recent years compared with six or seven years ago. The explanation, no doubt, is that French shipping is comparatively

[1] See also an Essay on the Foreign Trade of the United States ("Essays in Finance," 2nd Series, ed. 1886). I may add too a fact, of which I was not aware when I wrote this paper, that the system in America is to value the imports not at the port of arrival, but as at the place from which the goods were sent. The value in America therefore does not include the cost of conveyance, and the proportion of the exports is accordingly higher than it would otherwise be as compared with a country like England, where the value of the imports does include the cost of conveyance.

small, being 932,000 tons, and has increased very little in recent years, the only change being that since 1860 about 200,000 tons of steam shipping have been substituted for as many tons sailing, the total rather diminishing. The total gross earnings for France, at the same rate as for England, can only be about 6 million pounds, and the increase in twenty years little over 2 million pounds. At the same time, leaving out our shipping, the excess is as great in proportion for France as for the United Kingdom. There can be little question that France has increased its investments abroad, notwithstanding the payment of the indemnity, while it must derive a large income annually from the expenditure of foreigners travelling or residing in France, French citizens by comparison going very little abroad. It would be interesting for France as for England to trace the growth of its foreign investments in recent years, but the problem of stating its balance is neither so large as that for England nor so complicated in various ways. The figures, however, when rightly considered, are in apparent accordance with the economic circumstances of the country, while they teach nothing as to comparative prosperity or the reverse.

The broad conclusion is that the importance attached in some of the recent discussions to the excess of imports in any country, and to the increase of that excess in this country in recent years, and contrariwise to the excess of exports in the case of other countries, and to the increase of that excess, is wholly mistaken. There is nothing in the facts either way to indicate special circumstances of prosperity or adversity, or that one nation is living on its foreign capital, and another increasing its foreign capital or diminishing its indebtedness abroad. The facts when investigated throw a great deal of light on the industrial circumstances of different countries, but until investigated and compared with other facts they are entirely without meaning. In other words, import and export figures require delicate and careful handling for any such inquiry as the account of indebtedness between nations. *Quod erat demonstrandum.*

VI.—Import and Export Statistics and the Protectionist Controversy.

The second special inquiry I have proposed is the way to use import and export figures in the controversy between free traders and protectionists. How do the statistics assist?

In answering this question, we must be struck by the fact that there can hardly be any statistics available to settle directly the cardinal question between free trade and protection, viz., which *régime* favours most the general prosperity of a people, morally as well as materially. No such question can be treated practically from a material point of view alone; political and moral considerations must come in. I could quite understand a free trader admitting a protectionist system to be the best materially, and a protectionist admitting the free trade system to be the best materially, and yet each on moral and political grounds preferring the less advantageous system in a material view. But how difficult to trace out all the effects of an economic *régime* in the moral and political sphere! Even materially, however, there can hardly be adequate statistics. To make any statistical comparison at all possible between different *régimes*, it would be necessary either to find two countries practically alike in their economic and industrial circumstances, and in the character of their people, subject them to the opposite *régimes*, and then ascertain and compare their relative material progress; or to find a particular country subjected at different periods to the two opposite *régimes* without any other differences, and then compare the different results, if any such are appreciable. Experience does not supply us with such cases. No two communities are sufficiently alike to be comparable in strict logic. The slightest differences in the race or moral condition of the two communities which are to outward appearance much the same, might make a great deal of difference in their material progress. If the two are subjected to different economic *régimes*, how are we to tell whether the inferior progress of the one materially—even when we are sure about the inferiority—is due to the *régime*, and not to other differences in the character of the communities, which we cannot so well appreciate? The same with a community at different periods of its own history. How can we tell that there is no moral difference of a serious kind to affect the economic progress of the community between one period and another? External economic circumstances are, besides, incessantly changing, and may affect two communities apparently of much the same character and position quite differently. If it were possible to institute many pairs of comparisons and exhibit a uniform result in all, it might be safe to infer that it was the *régime* which did make the difference, no other uniform cause of difference being assignable; but this condition of course it is impossible to fulfil.

Quite lately an interesting attempt has been made by Mr. Baden-Powell[1] to show that the *régime* does make all the difference in the case of two communities which he compares—New South Wales and Victoria, the former free-trading and the latter protectionist; but directly, I fear, the comparison proves nothing. In strict logic one comparison is not enough. There must be many comparisons. It may be doubted, moreover, as regards this particular case, whether the two communities compared were really in sufficiently like circumstances at starting to make the comparison really valuable; while it is not shown that no other circumstances besides the economic ones may have helped to make the difference since; nor is it shown that the difference of the *régime* itself was so great as to justify us in calling the one colony free-trading and the other

[1] "Fortnightly Review," March, 1882.

protectionist. But granting the apparent likeness of the two cases in all except the one point, what I have to urge is that one comparison proves nothing in strict logic, and at best does no more than raise a presumption to be confirmed or set aside by farther inquiry.

There would be a farther difficulty in making such an inquiry statistically, in the facility with which the visible consequences of an inferior *régime* may be masked by an increase of industry on the part of the suffering community to make up the loss. The community, rather than lose in the return to its labour, might labour more energetically, and so the outward result would be as before—the production, consumption, and saving might remain what they were. It is even conceivable that the community suffering most might apparently gain, in consequence of a greater development of industry and energy than what is absolutely necessary to supply the loss. In any case, I am quite ready to believe that the visible difference, as between free trade and protection, if the protection is not extreme, may often not be so great as to be traceable by statistics. Suppose the protected industries in a country giving protection to be one-tenth of the whole, or the industries which might be protected in a free-trading community, but which are left free, to be also one-tenth, which is a large proportion, and that the loss arising to the community by the diversion of capital and labour from more profitable to less profitable employments is 10 per cent. on the production of this one-tenth of the people; then the loss to the whole community—the difference it makes—is only 1 per cent. of the total production. Even if the diversion should cause a waste of 25 per cent. in the protected industries in the one case, and the unprotected industries in the other case, the difference to the whole community would still be only $2\frac{1}{2}$ per cent. Such small margins, it is obvious, may be lost sight of among other things, and easily made up by a little more industry on the part of those who suffer. They may also affect still less the growth of wealth, through the community bearing what loss there may be out of its income and accumulating wealth as rapidly as before. There is an inherent difficulty, then, of a very formidable kind, in showing by statistics that any given economic *régime* is more favourable to the material welfare of a community than another. Unless the differences are extreme and marked, it seems hardly possible that there can be much difference in the results, of which statistics can take note, whether a community is free-trading or protectionist.

Such being the case as regards statistics generally, it is hardly necessary to add that import and export statistics alone cannot give much help. They are even irrelevant to the question to be answered. It is quite conceivable that a country may be very prosperous without foreign trade at all, or with very little foreign trade, or that for special reasons the foreign trade of the least progressing country as a whole may be making greater progress than the foreign trade of a more progressing country. Were the British Empire, for instance, to form one customs union, the foreign trade of that union would probably be less than the foreign trade of the United Kingdom alone is now, and its growth or decline would be less important in proportion to the whole business of the empire than the growth or decline of the foreign trade of the mother country is now to the mother country itself. The progress of the foreign trade of different countries is thus no index at all of their relative progress materially. Even therefore if you could reduce the so-called imports and exports of different countries to common denominators, and make all proper allowances for changes of prices and the like disturbing influences, which I have already shown to be most difficult, you would be no nearer than you were before to proving that the country whose foreign trade increases fastest is the most prosperous materially. There is a more serious difficulty still. Foreign trade is trade between nations, and the foreign trade of a country which has an inferior *régime* may consequently increase as much in amount, and perhaps infinitely more in proportion, than the foreign trade of a country with a superior *régime*. The trade of the inferior may be with the superior, and the two will increase *pari passu*, though the impetus may be given by the superior and not by the inferior. We may see this very clearly if we put the hypothetical case of two countries, the one free-trading and the other protectionist, trading exclusively with each other, that is, having no other foreign trade, with a third country doing no trade itself but carrying for the two others. Clearly, the foreign trade of the free-trading and protectionist countries must exactly balance. Their imports and exports will be exactly alike. Whether, to give a practical illustration, the foreign trade of the United States with the United Kingdom has been the result of the impetus of the former or the latter will, I think, hardly be open to question. It is the United Kingdom which by its purchases has stimulated the foreign trade of the United States, small as that trade is compared with our own. In any case, these considerations show sufficiently that the increase of foreign trade proves nothing by itself as regards the relative material prosperity of different countries. The circumstances affecting foreign trade, besides the differences of *régime*, are innumerable; and above all, it is a necessity that countries with different *régimes* should trade with each other, so that the greater prosperity of free trade countries may cause the foreign trade of protectionist countries to advance more rapidly than that of their own.

But while statistics are thus not available in giving a distinct yes or no to the cardinal question between free trade and protection, it does not follow that they are of no use at all. Rightly used and handled they may contribute materially to the solution of the points at issue. I have to suggest various ways in which they may be so used.

First. The proposition, if accepted, that statistics are not available to prove directly the superiority of one *régime* to another in promoting material prosperity, appears to be entirely on the free trade side of the argument. It is the protectionist on whom the onus of proof lies. He affirms that if the State interferes with trade and does certain things, the greater material prosperity of a country will ensue. He is bound therefore to furnish proof that the State ought to interfere, and interfere in the way indicated. The free trader, on the other hand, need not prove anything at all. He simply wishes to let things alone unless it can be shown that something should be done; the whole onus of proof is on his opponent. When it appears, therefore, that statistics cannot be appealed to in the direct issue between free trade and protection; that statistics can hardly be got to indicate in any way the superiority of one *régime* to another; this is as much as to say that the protectionist is not helped by statistics. One great branch of argument is cut away from him. Logically then the unsuitability of statistics, owing to their necessary imperfections, for solving the direct issue between free trade and protection, is a material fact. In pointing out that they are unsuitable we do a great deal to destroy the protectionist case.

It may be asked, then, how it is that the protectionist appeals so much to statistics—that he talks of the greater increase of prosperity in protectionist countries, of the greater increase relatively of the foreign trade of protectionist countries, of special industries promoted by protection, and so forth? The reply is that very often the facts appealed to are themselves misunderstood, being, as we have seen, very difficult to read, while their logical treatment is a difficult matter. I notice in all these discussions that the statement of the major premiss is avoided. The protectionists do not make clear to themselves what they wish to prove. They show, for instance, that the United States is prosperous; but that is not what they have to prove. What they have to prove is that it is more prosperous than it would have been under a free trade *régime*, a statement in which statistics cannot help them. They assert, again, that the foreign trade of protectionist countries increases faster than that of free-trading countries; but what they have really got to prove is not only that it increases faster than that of other countries, but that it increases faster than it would have done under free trade, and that this more rapid increase is itself an index of greater growth of material prosperity generally than would have otherwise taken place. The proof again that special industries have been ostered by protection is *nihil ad rem*. What has to be proved is that the industry of the country as a whole has prospered, which is a very different thing. Without discussing, then, the whole case between free trade and protection, we are entitled, as a scientific body, to point out that the call which protection makes on statistics is one which cannot be answered. The protectionist seeks an affirmative answer to a question which statistics cannot answer affirmatively or negatively.

We may perhaps go farther, and say that as the protectionist relies so much on statistics, and has nothing else to rely on,—his argument is always an appeal from theory to facts—then there can be no argument for protection. This appears, in fact, to be the logical position of the controversy.

VII.—Subject continued: the negative use of Import and Export Statistics.

Second. While statistics can be of no use to the protectionist, they may be of use to the free trader, negatively, by affording presumptive conclusions that the anticipations of the protectionist are unfounded. The protectionist, in arguing that a country will be better off under protection than under free trade, implies and assumes that the condition under free trade will not be satisfactory, that this is the reason for not letting things alone. If, then, it can be shown that, taking countries as they stand, the condition of things is tolerably satisfactory under free trade, the difficulty of the protectionist would be enormously increased. The reverse, as we have seen, would prove nothing against free trade logically, but if free trade, on the average, appears to do as well, or better than protection, the protectionist is clearly out of court. His only appeal is to statistics, which could not by any possibility help him; but if the answer they give, as far as it goes, makes against him, he is hopelessly in the wrong.

Looking at economic statistics generally in this way, it is plain that free trade nations, and especially the United Kingdom, have nothing to complain of. The fact of the United Kingdom having made great strides in material prosperity since the free trade period is undeniable, and is not really denied by protectionists. Of late, they say, owing to foreign tariffs and other causes, the results are less satisfactory, and they shake their heads ominously about the future, but the advance in the past, I apprehend, is not denied. If it is desired, I think there are ample materials in our "Journal" to prove the contrary, so that a mere passing reference may be sufficient for me to-night. The satisfactory result may not be wholly due to free trade, and no free trader ever said that it was; Mr. Newmarch's repudiation of any such idea, in his paper read in 1878, was most emphatic; but it has been consistent with free trade, and it is upon protectionists to prove that the result with protection would have been better.

We are concerned to-night, however, with import and export statistics specially, and on this narrower field I may perhaps be allowed to refer to one or two facts which appear to raise an insuperable presumption against protection. I should not think of going into the history of our foreign trade exhaustively, the subject having been treated so fully by Mr. Newmarch in 1878, and our special business to-night being with the method of statistics; but without exhaustive treatment a few broad facts can be made to stand out clearly enough. Before pointing them out, however, I must again call attention to the remark already made, to the effect that the progress of foreign trade is not necessarily an index of the progress of material prosperity in a country generally. It may or may not be so. But conceding it to be an index, the facts of our experience are not such as to encourage a protectionist to appeal to them. Our progress has been astonishing. The protectionist may imagine, or say he imagines, that under protection we would have done better, but surely he cannot deny that under free trade we have done well.

The first facts to be mentioned are those relating to the movements of shipping. Of these you had a very full account at the last meeting, and I have said a good deal to-night about the growth of our shipping business as a separate business; but I wish now to speak of those movements as an indication of the growth of imports and exports. To some extent they are a better indication than the figures of imports and exports themselves. The latter may fluctuate, as we have seen, owing to changes of price; but if increased quantities of goods are carried, whatever nominal sums they may be entered at, you must have more ships. It is quite true, of course, that shipping may increase disproportionately to the trade through the articles handled being more largely of a bulky and less valuable nature than before; but this is a point which can easily be inquired into. The entries and clearances of shipping, then, in the foreign trade of the United Kingdom during the last forty years have progressed as follows:

	Tons.	Increase on Previous Ten Years.	
		Amount.	Per Cent.
1840 . . .	9,440,000	—	—
'50 . . .	14,505,000	5,065,000	53.4
'60 . . .	24,689,000	10,184,000	70.2
'70 . . .	36,640,000	11,951,000	48.6
'80 . . .	58,736,000	22,096,000	60.4

And the increase from first to last, between 1840 and 1880, covering the whole free trade period, is no less than 49,296,000 tons, and 525 per cent. To be quite fair, even in dealing with protectionists, it may be admitted that the increased use of steamers which do a calling trade may have caused some increase of entries and clearances without an increase of goods carried to correspond; but the self-interest of ship-owners may of course be trusted to fill up their vessels as much as possible. Comparing the figures with the increase of population in the interval, it appears that while the entries and clearances in 1840 were 0.36 ton for each unit of the population, in 1880 they were 1.73 tons for each unit of the population, an increase of 381 per cent.

We may give some idea of these figures in another way. The entries and clearances of shipping in the foreign trade of almost all foreign countries put together, excluding British colonies, may be taken as 140 million tons.[1] The increase of our entries and clearances, therefore, since 1840 is equal to one-third of the whole existing business of all foreign countries put together. Assuming imports and exports, therefore, to have increased in the same proportion, we may say broadly that the increase of the foreign trade of the United Kingdom since 1840 is equal to one-third of the whole foreign trade of the world, not comprised within the British Empire. The increase, moreover, is equal to about $1\frac{2}{3}$ tons for each individual of the United Kingdom, or five-sixths of a ton of goods conveyed each way. If a growth of foreign trade like this does not please protectionists, what sort of trade is it which will satisfy them?

We come then to the suggestion that the goods have changed in character. They are said to be more bulky than they were. This is especially the case, we may be told, with the exports, where the increase is chiefly in coal and pig iron, in raw materials. But this does not prove that the real values involved have not risen in

[1] See Statistical Abstract for Foreign Countries.

proportion. On the contrary, it is probable that, value for value, an export of so much coal or pig iron implies a much larger employment for labour and capital within the country than an export of so much cotton manufactures. The whole value in these cases is an export of the produce of British capital and labour; whereas, in the case of cotton manufactures, four-fifths or two-thirds of the value may be a re-export. In other words, 10 million pounds worth of coal exported may mean an export of as much produce of British capital and labour as 50 million pounds worth of cotton manufactures. Not only so: the fact that equal values of coal or pig iron exported means more employment for shipping than values of cotton manufactures implies, as the shipping is mostly British, that there is an immense indirect employment for capital and labour in connection with the shipments. We may assume then that the increase in the movements of shipping is a very good index of the increase in the imports and exports themselves.

We may look, however, at the actual facts of a few chief articles, always remembering the circumstances pointed out by Mr. Newmarch in the paper already referred to, that the part of our foreign trade which has most conspicuously increased is the miscellaneous trade. Take first the exports of cotton yarn and piece goods. The progress we find is shown as follows:

	Cotton Yarn.			Cotton Piece Goods.		
	Total.	Increase on Previous Ten Years.		Total.	Increase on Previous Ten Years.	
		Amount.	Per Cent.		Amount.	Per Cent.
	Mln. lbs.			Mln. yds.		
1840.	118.5	—	—	790	—	—
'50.	131.4	12.9	11	1,358	567	72
'60.	197·3	65.9	50	2,776	1,418	104
'70.	186.0	(−) 11.3	(−) 6	3,267	491	17½
'80.	215·5	29.5	16	4,496	1,229	38

Note.—Percentage increase between 1840 and 1880: cotton yarn, 84 per cent., and cotton piece goods, 468 per cent.

On the same plan I make up the following short tables:

Exports of Iron and Steel.

	Tons.	Increase on Previous Ten Years.	
		Amount.	Per Cent.
	Mlns.		
1840	0.3	—	—
'50	0.8	0.5	167
'60	1.4	0.6	75
'70	2.8	1.4	100
'80	3.8	1.0	36

Note.—Percentage increase between 1840 and 1880 equal to 1,167 per cent.

Exports of Hardware and Cutlery.

	Value.	Increase on Previous Ten Years.	
		Amount.	Per Cent.
	Mln. £'s.		
1840	1.3	—	—
'50	2.6	1.3	100
'60	3.8	1.2	46
'70	3.8	—	—
'80	3.5	(−) 3	(−) 8

Note.—Percentage increase between 1840 and 1880 equal to 169 per cent.

Exports of Machinery.

	Values.	Increase on Previous Ten Years.	
		Amount.	Per Cent.
	Mln. £'s.		
1840	0.6	—	—
'50	1.0	0.4	67
'60	3.8	2.8	280
'70	5.3	1.5	40
'80	9.3	4.0	75

Note.—Percentage increase between 1840 and 1880 equal to 1,483 per cent.

Exports of Coal.

	Tons.	Increase on Previous Ten Years.	
		Amount.	Per Cent.
	Mlns.		
1840	1.6	—	—
'50	3.4	1.8	112
'60	7.3	3.9	115
'70	11.7	4.4	60
'80	18.7	7.0	60

Note.—Percentage increase between 1840 and 1880 equal to 1,070 per cent.

These tables of course are not, and do not pretend to be, exhaustive as regards foreign trade, while if they were exhaustive, many questions would be suggested as to the precise character of the increase, the countries with which it takes place, and other particulars. Comparing these exports, however, with the above stated facts as to shipping, they serve to show what a gigantic growth we are dealing with. It is difficult to imagine what foreign trade there can be which increases more rapidly. I have omitted giving any quantities for the imports, for the practical reason that the quantities of our importations are less in dispute, but they are easily enough accessible to all concerned.

The facts as to quantities being thus clear, we are able to use the facts as to values. The whole exports of British and Irish produce between 1840 and 1880, according to the declared values, have been:

	Total.	Increase on Previous Ten Years.	
		Amount.	Per Cent.
	Mln. £'s.	£	
1840 . . .	51.3	—	—
'50 . . .	71.4	20.1	40
'60 . . .	135.9	64.5	90
'70 . . .	199.6	63.7	47
'80 . . .	223.1	23.5	12

and the increase between 1840 and 1880 is 335 per cent. There are some points in detail to be observed upon, but the progress generally is evidently as remarkable as that of entries and clearances of shipping and the quantities of the principal articles of export, and, taken in conjunction with these facts, gives fair ground for supposing that the whole foreign export trade in quantities, as well as values, has increased in about the same degree.

Dealing with values alone, as regards the imports, we get the following comparison:

	Total.	Increase on Previous Decade.	
		Amount.	Per Cent.
	Mln. £'s.		
1854[1] . . .	143.5	—	—
'60 . . .	210.5	67.0	50
'70 . . .	303.2	92.7	44
'80 . . .	411.2	108.0	36

and the increase since 1855 is 186 per cent. Thus both in imports and exports there has been an enormous increase for the United Kingdom during the free trade period—an increase which has been demonstrated to be as great in quantities as in values in the case of the exports, and which is presumably so in the case of the imports, though it would encumber this paper too much to go into detail. As regards imports at least, there can be no question of its having continued to the latest date. There is no apparent falling off in the last few years to account for.

Clearly, then, in these figures the protectionist has a very difficult argument. If our foreign trade had progressed less, the onus of proof would still have been on the protectionist to show that under another *régime*

[1] In the case of the imports, there are no computed or declared values before 1854.

it would have progressed more; logically, figures showing a less progress would not have helped his argument a bit. But the figures being what they are, he has to prove that protection would have had a better result, and promises better in future. He must

> "Gild refined gold, and paint the lily."

Thus, negatively, the statistics of foreign trade are useful. The prosperity of the last forty years may not be owing to free trade, but it has been consistent with free trade, and protectionists must look elsewhere than in our import and export statistics for any argument against free trade policy.

There are one or two points, however, which are likely to be cavilled at, though the figures themselves will help to supply an explanation. There is apparently a little support given by some of the figures to the contention that in recent years foreign trade has ceased to progress quite as rapidly as it did at an earlier period. The increase in the export values is only 12 per cent. in the last decade, as compared with 47 per cent. in the previous decade, 90 per cent. between 1850 and 1860, and 40 per cent. between 1840 and 1850. There is a similar diminution in the quantities of the principal articles exported, though not in all; while in one decade at least, viz., between 1850 and 1860, the proportionate growth of the movements of shipping was a little greater than it has been since. A little consideration will show, however, I believe, that while there were probably real causes between 1850 and 1860 for a greater proportionate increase of our foreign trade than there has been since—such causes as the great growth of railways between 1840 and 1850, which came really into use between 1850 and 1860, the gold discoveries, and the great colonization which went on in the latter decade—yet the diminution in the rate of increase lately is much less than it appears to be. The period between 1850 and 1860 was the one in which the first effect of the gold discoveries, which beyond question raised prices considerably, was experienced. In the period since 1870 there has been a general decline in prices, aggravated, specially as regards our own exports, by a special decline in cotton. Keeping in mind then the important element of price, we see reason at once for looking more to the quantities and to the movements of shipping than to the values only. The figures, in fact, corroborate what has already been stated in the first part of this paper as to the importance of price. Unless we allow for this element, we shall be bewildered by the figures.

The point is perhaps worth even more minute consideration. Comparing the percentages of increase of the values of the exports and of the movements of shipping, we get the following results:

	Increase of Shipping Movements.	Increase of Export Values.
	Per cent.	Per cent.
1840-50	53.4	40
'50-60	70.2	90
'60-70	48.6	47
'70-80	60.4	12
1840-80	525.0	335

Thus between 1840 and 1850, before the gold discoveries had caused prices to rise, and when they were probably tending to decline, the increase of shipping was rather more than the increase of export values; in the following decade, when prices were undoubtedly rising, the increase of export values is more than the increase of shipping movements; in the third decade, viz., between 1860 and 1870, when prices were probably stationary, the rate of growth is about even in the two cases; in the last decade, when the level of price has probably declined considerably, the rate of growth of shipping remains much the same as in the previous decades, but the rate of growth of the export values shows a diminution. To my mind the suggestion of this table as to a fall of prices between 1870 and 1880 is most direct, and such questions of price, I am satisfied, will require to be more and more considered. We have not had import and export figures on a tolerably satisfactory basis for many years to deal with, and we are only beginning to find out the difficulties of using them when long periods are compared. Meanwhile the practical conclusion appears beyond question.

I have to suggest, moreover, what has already been stated in the previous part of the paper as to the increase of our shipping business as a means of accounting for the non-increase of our apparent exports. It is because our invisible exports have been increasing so enormously, that there is less increase of the visible. But it is the same thing of course whether we export the produce of our capital and labour stored up in goods, or in the shape of repairs to ships, or new ships built to replace old ones, which carry the foreign goods of the world. In any way that we take the figures, there has obviously been an enormous growth of our foreign trade since the free trade period, continued to the most recent date. What the protectionist has to prove is that protection would probably have done better or so well.

It would be impossible to go through the imports and exports of foreign countries in detail, to show how they also raise a presumption against the protectionist. Looking at the difficulties of analyzing the data themselves, and allowing for special circumstances which may have affected the foreign trade of different countries, the difficulty of inquiring what the facts are as regards foreign countries, and of finding suitable pairs of free trading and protectionist countries for comparison, would in truth be insuperable. To mention only some of the difficulties which occurred to me in endeavouring to form a group of protected European countries, I may state that the fact already mentioned as to the recent change from official to real values in Austria throws out all comparisons as regards that country; and that for Russia comparisons are equally thrown out by the recent depreciation of the rouble and rise in nominal prices, which unduly swell the figures of the foreign trade, while a reduction of the rouble to specie value in each year would be open to some exceptions. For Germany, again, we have statistics for ten years only, too short to be of any value. This leaves no other country than France among the great European States as to which a special inquiry would seem worth while, and even as regards France we have also to remember that the separation of Alsace and Lorraine ten years ago was a special cause of increase in the foreign trade, what was home trade in France becoming in fact foreign.

In the absence of any general grouping, then, I shall refer specially to two foreign countries only—the United States and France—the former a protectionist country, which became in the period under review more protectionist than at the beginning, and the latter a protectionist country, which became less protectionist. Is there anything on the face of the figures of either country to suggest such a progress in their foreign trade, assuming that trade to be a good index of material prosperity, as to imply that protection is a specially advantageous *régime*?

With regard to the United States, making a table in much the same form as that for the United Kingdom, but including specie, the general figures are:[1]

[1] I make use here of the figures in the Essay already referred to on the Foreign Trade of the United States.

Foreign Trade of the United States.

[In millions of pounds.]

	Imports.			Exports.		
	Amount.	Increase on previous Period.		Amount.	Increase on previous Period.	
		Increase.	Per Cent.		Increase.	Per Cent.
	£			£		
1840 .	21	—	—	26	—	—
'50 .	36	15	72	30	4	16
'60 .	72	36	100	80	50	165
'70 .	92	20	28	90	10	12½
'80 .	152	60	65	170	80	89

And the increase in the imports for the whole period is nearly 700 per cent., and in the exports between 500 and 600 per cent. In *proportion*, therefore, there is a greater rate of progress in protectionist America than in free trade England, though, if we take the whole period, not so much greater an increase as to raise any presumption in favour of protection as being more likely to develop the foreign trade. I need hardly say, however, that in such a question the mere proportion of increase is not the proper test. The amounts are also material, and it cannot fail to be observed that the United States being a larger unit than the United Kingdom, had at the beginning, and still has, a smaller foreign trade. The whole imports are, in fact, 150 million pounds only at present, as compared with 400 million pounds and upwards into the United Kingdom; and the whole exports are 170 million pounds, as compared with 223 million pounds of domestic produce exported from the United Kingdom; the latter figure, besides, as already explained, not including the invisible export in the shape of outlay for earning freight. The increase in imports again between 1840 and 1880 is 130 million pounds, as compared with an increase of 268 million pounds into the United Kingdom since 1854 only; while the increase of the exports between 1840 and 1880 is 144 million pounds, as compared with 171 million pounds in the case of the United Kingdom, again remembering in the latter case that our invisible exports have increased so much, and are not reckoned in this calculation.

These figures, then, rather suggest, if anything, the superiority of a free trading to a protectionist *régime*. They are something for the protectionist to get over if he appeals to progress in imports and exports as a proof of the superiority of protection. No doubt in any complete discussion we should have to analyze minutely what the foreign trade in each case is composed of; while it would be fair to allow, I think, that the United States, from its geographical extent and the ancient development of its manufactures—for the eastern States are as much an old country as England—may have a smaller foreign trade in proportion than another country of less extent with large manufactures, or another country of large extent without manufactures. It is an empire within a ring fence, and the foreign trade of the British Empire, if that empire were made a customs union, would, as already stated, be less than the foreign trade of the United Kingdom now is, and certainly much less in proportion to the home trade. Still all these nice considerations are out of place in the mouths of protectionists, who have dwelt lately on the wonderful progress of the American foreign trade. The figures, in the way they use them, turn against themselves.

Coming to the French figures, I have to submit a similar table, beginning, however, in 1850 only, as there are only official values in 1840:

General Imports into France, and Exports of Domestic Produce.

[In millions.]

	Imports.			Exports.		
	Amount.	Increase on previous Period.	Per Cent.	Amount.	Increase on previous Period.	Per Cent.
	£	£		£	£	
1850.	45	—	—	43	—	—
'60.	106	61	135	91	48	109
'70.	140	34	33	112	21	22
'80.	245	105	75	139	27	22

Here again the rate of growth is apparently as great as that of the United Kingdom, though an exact comparison is impossible, as we cannot go back to 1840. The amount of trade and amount of growth, however, are, like those of the United States, much smaller than the amount and growth of our own trade, although France, like the United States, is a larger unit. In the imports the growth is 200 million pounds between 1850 and 1880, as compared with 286 million pounds in the United Kingdom, between 1854 and 1880, and in the exports it is 96 million pounds between 1850 and 1880, as compared with 151 million pounds in the same period in the United Kingdom. There is nothing then in the French figures to make a case for the protectionist, while there is ground for claiming that between 1860 and 1880 France had made considerable steps in the direction of free trade, so that whatever progress had been made might be ascribed to free trade, and not to protection. There is no need, however, to press this point. France may be taken as a protectionist country. There is surely nothing in the figures to raise any doubt of our free trade *régime*, always remembering, besides, our own invisible exports.

It is interesting to note, in passing, the great augmentation of French trade between 1850 and 1860, a sign of the rise of prices I have already suggested in connection with the English figures for the same period. In France, however, the augmentation may partly be due to the more intimate connection which then took place between France and its neighbours on the different land frontiers, which must have been a powerful special cause, I believe, for the development of foreign trade among inter-continental countries.

To bring these figures to a point, it may be useful to look at a calculation per head of the population in each case:

Imports and Exports per Head of the Population in England, France, and the United States compared.

	United Kingdom.			United States.			France.		
	£	s.	d.	£	s.	d.	£	s.	d.
Imports—									
1840 . . .		—		1	5	2		—	
'50 . . .	5	3	2[1]	1	10	9	1	5	0
'60 . . .	7	7	0	2	6	1	2	17	4
'70 . . .	9	14	4	2	8	0	3	15	8
'80 . . .	11	18	7	3	0	9	6	12	5
Exports—									
1840 . . .	1	18	9	1	11	1		—	
'50 . . .	2	11	10	1	6	2	1	3	11
'60 . . .	4	14	7	2	10	11	2	9	2
'70 . . .	6	7	11	2	6	11	3	0	6
'80 . . .	6	9	5	3	8	1	3	15	2

Thus our imports are still about four times per head those of the United States, and twice per head those of France, and our exports are about twice those of either country, not counting, what I must always insist on, our invisible exports. The increase of our imports per head since 1850 is also double the whole of the present imports per head into the United States, and about equal to the present imports per head into France, and the increase of our exports since the same

[1] Year 1854.

date is between 25 and 50 per cent. more than the total exports per head in either case.[1]

We may conclude, then, that not only has England made satisfactory progress in its foreign business under free trade, but the most prominent foreign countries have advanced less under protection. The onus of proof thus laid on the protectionist to show that we would have done better than we have done under protection, or that we shall do better in future with protection, appears to me overwhelming. There is no bearing up against it. Thus statistics, though they cannot logically prove the affirmative in the direct issue between free trade and protection, from the difficulty of finding exactly parallel cases and eliminating other causes, may be used to prove negatively that there is nothing in the apparent facts to help the protectionist. The presumptions are altogether against the latter.

VIII.—Subject continued: other uses of Import and Export Statistics. Conclusion.

A *third* way in which statistics may be used in the argument is to show that protection does certain particular things which are obviously of an injurious tendency, while there is and can be no proof that the advantages of protection counterbalance these evils; and on the other hand that free trade effects certain ends which are obviously beneficial, which are *additive* to the welfare of a community, without any drawbacks. Facts of this nature corroborate the general theory of free trade, though they do not demonstrate completely and logically by themselves that the one *régime* is better than the other.

We may examine what a few of these facts are.

[1] For later figures as to English, French, and American foreign trade, I may refer to the Tables I laid before the Royal Commission on Trade Depression, and to the recent Board of Trade Blue-book Cd 1761, Sess. 1903.

Peoples adapt themselves quickly to any *régime*, and when a particular *régime* has been long established, it is difficult to see what its permanent effects are; but when changes are made, the nature of the influence may be perceived, and it is from such transition periods we get evidence for or against the one *régime* or the other.

To go back a long way, let me refer you to a comparatively old book, Sir Henry Parnell's "Financial Reform," published in 1832. At pages 37-39 *et seq.* of the book, this author gives numerous instances of the effect of high duties in checking consumption—that is, in diverting trade and imposing various hardships on the community. He refers to tea, tobacco, wine, spirits, and other articles, in which an increase of taxes produced no more or little more revenue; and I shall quote as a specimen what he says of flint and plate glass:

"In 1813 the duties on flint and plate glass were doubled. In four years to 1813, the average annual quantity made for home consumption was 66,500 cwts. In the four years following 1813, the annual average quantity was only 30,000 cwts. The duties on all other kinds of glass were doubled in the same year. The revenue received in the four years preceding 1813 was, on an average, £340,000; that received in the three years following 1813 was, on an average, £395,000, so that the doubling of the duties, instead of producing £340,000, produced only £55,000."

In the opposite sense Sir Henry Parnell then refers to numerous remissions of high duties which produced increase of revenue, and I shall again only mention the case of flint glass, in which a reduction of duty, in 1825, from 98*s.* to 56*s.* per cwt., was followed by an increase of consumption from 30,000 to 47,000 cwts. annually. Sir Henry Parnell adds:

"The Committee of Finance state, in their fourth report on the revenue and expenditure, that if the revenue had fallen off in the five years from 1825 to

1828 [*sic*] in the same proportion that taxes had been reduced, the diminution of it would have been 9 million pounds; but that, owing to increased consumption, it had only fallen off about one-third of that sum."

No doubt Sir Henry Parnell is speaking of high taxes generally, but the greater includes the less, and high tariffs of a protective character must have exactly the same or a worse effect in diverting industry and diminishing consumption as high taxes of a non-protective character. It is the tendency of the system which is exhibited in such instances as those given by Sir Henry Parnell. The book I refer to is comparatively forgotten nowadays, but it was famous once, and those who look into it will find it to deserve its reputation.

Another case of the effect of the large remission of duties at the period of transition is supplied by the experience of what occurred in this country in the first two years after the introduction of the free trade tariff of 1842. Historically this experience had a great deal to do with the practically unanimous conversion of the country to free trade principles, but the striking nature of the facts statistically is still worth repeating. They are recorded for us in a little book of Mr. Gladstone's, not, I fear, very well known, entitled "Remarks upon Recent Commercial Legislation," published in 1845.[1] It would be hopeless for me to attempt to give a condensed account of this book, to which I can but refer you; but among the principal points I note, (1) that the calculated money loss of the reductions of the tariff in 1842-44 was £5,142,000, and that other duties were repealed or reduced, involving a money loss of £1,162,000, making together a sum of £6,304,000, and that the free surplus of the income tax over and above what was required to supply actual deficiency was only £2,621,000. This was all that was really required, as the event proved, to balance remissions of taxation amounting to £6,304,000 (pp. 12 and 13). (2) The

[1] London: John Murray, 1845. Third edition.

mean estimated loss from remissions of duties on raw material mainly was £1,452,000, and the actual loss in the first year after the tariff Act was about this sum; but this first year was a year of great depression, and the actual loss in the second year was £1,133,000 only, showing a recovery in that year of £325,000 on a total of about 3 millions only (pp. 27 and 28). (3) The net loss of revenue from a great remission of the timber duties, while it was greater in the first year by £114,000 than Sir Robert Peel had estimated, was less in the second year than he had estimated by no less a sum than £193,000, showing a great recovery in the trade (pp. 36 and 37); and (4) the predictions of injury to our manufactures and other industries by exposing them to foreign competition—there was quite as much talk of foreign competition then as there is now—were ludicrously falsified in the case of cork-cutting, candle-making, vinegar-making, and other industries (pp. 49 *et seq.*). In all these matters a free trade tariff had apparently done what it was expected to do, and had contributed to swell the volume of national trade. As I have said, I am by no means condensing the volume, which is itself in a highly condensed form, but only pointing it out as a mine of information on the proposition that the change from a protective to a free trade *régime* appears to stimulate trade, from which we infer that the stimulus continues to operate afterwards, though it becomes impossible, from change of circumstances, to compare in a strictly logical manner a free-trading and a protectionist *régime*.

A third source of information to which reference cannot be too often made is Mr. Wells's valuable reports as commissioner of internal revenue in the United States. These are so well known that I may refer to them very briefly only. We hear a great deal of the growth of certain manufactures in the United States which have been protected, but these reports show clearly the reverse of the medal—the injury to other industries incidental to these changes. Thus the first report for 1866 dwells largely on the injury to the woollen manufacture by the protective tariff on wool designed to protect the growth of raw wool. Then in the report for 1869 we have many such statements as this about boots and shoes, viz., that the export value declined from 1,329,000 dollars in 1863 to 682,000 in 1867, and 475,000 dollars in 1869. Lastly, there is the well-known story of the decline in the American shipping trade, and the great increase in the amount of the foreign trade of the United States itself, carried on in foreign ships. Mr. Wells gives a table at p. 30 of the report for 1867, showing even then the preponderance of foreign vessels in the carrying trade of the United States, and calculating the amount which the United States has to pay to foreigners in consequence, the opposite of the calculations I have submitted to you to-night as to what this country has to receive. These are all instances of loss arising through protectionist measures, and they should be remembered, as being undoubtedly in operation as a check to industry, though we cannot well see the effects from day to day, when a country has adapted itself to a protectionist *régime*. What they prove is, that protection does not add to the industry of a country, but that it only *diverts* the industry at a great expense at the time and presumably at a continuous expense. The loss is certain and the gain entirely problematical, however much it may be proved that certain special industries have been fostered by protection.

As there are many later figures about American shipping since the date of Mr. Wells's report in 1869, and there is still a vague impression that it was the "Alabama" which diverted shipping business from the United States, I may be allowed to notice briefly these later figures, and see how far the impression as to the "Alabama" is confirmed. The first set of figures shows the increasing preponderance of foreign vessels in the American carrying trade. For the years ended 30th June, 1871-80, we get the following figures:

Table showing American Imports and Exports Carried in American and Foreign Vessels respectively.

[In millions of dollars.]

	Exports of Domestic Produce.	Imports.	Total.
In American Vessels—			
1871.	181	163	344
'72.	161	177	338
'73.	163	174	337
'74.	166	176	342
'75.	145	158	303
'76.	160	143	303
'77.	156	151	307
'78.	159	146	305
'79.	122	144	266
'80.	109	164	273
In Foreign Vessels—			
1871.	376	363	739
'72.	381	445	826
'73.	478	472	950
'74.	521	405	926
'75.	493	382	877
'76.	480	321	801
'77.	515	329	844
'78.	557	307	864
'79.	588	310	898
'80.	719	579	1,298

A table like this speaks for itself. While the amount of American trade carried in foreign vessels increases in ten years from 739 million to 1,298 million dollars, or more than 70 per cent., the amount carried in American diminishes from 344 to 273 million dollars. The American share, which is nearly half the foreign at the beginning of the period, is at the close just about a fifth of the foreign.

The second set of figures relates to American ship-building. I give the figures for twenty years, covering the whole of the "Alabama" period. They are as follows:

Tonnage of Vessels Annually Built in the United States in the Years 1860-80.

[In thousands of tons.]

Year.	Thousand Tons.	Year.	Thousand Tons.
1860	213	1871	273
'61	233	'72	209
'62	175	'73	359
'63	310	'74	432
'64	415	'75	297
'65	383	'76	203
'66	336	'77	176
'67	303	'78	235
'68	285	'79	193
'69	275	'80	157
'70	276		

What this table shows, I think, is, that American ship-building did not fall off till after the war. From 1863, the third year of the war, down to and inclusive of 1871, the ship-building is larger than in 1860 and 1861, and not much short, I may state, of the figures in the previous decade, which was one of great prosperity in American shipping. As late again as 1873 and 1874 the building is considerable. I think we may infer from this that down to a very recent period even American ship-building and ship-owning had a sufficient basis for its development, if that development had not been checked by external causes. The effects of the "Alabama" would in fact have been very speedily recovered from but for other causes. Probably, indeed, the operation of the civil war was not so unfavourable as it seemed. If ship-building for private individuals was checked, there was a great demand for Government ships, and miscellaneous vessels of all kinds, and at the close of the war there was nothing to prevent American ship-builders and ship-owners from recovering some of the ground they had lost. It may perhaps be doubted whether even with a free trade tariff in America the results would not have been the same as they have been. There were natural causes, I believe, operating in favour of the extension of the industry in British hands. But that the American tariff made impossible the extension of American ship-building, which would otherwise have been difficult only, is beyond doubt.

Last of all, coming to more recent times, the experience of the high tariff in Germany may be referred to as proving that those particular evils happen which free traders predict from such a tariff as Germany has established, viz., a high price of food, the deterioration of the position of the labourer, and a general *malaise*. On this head I need do no more than mention the well-known paper containing extracts from reports of the German Chambers of Commerce respecting the new tariff and its effects, lately presented to Parliament by the Board of Trade.[1] The reports summarized in that paper do not contain many figures, but the statements are distinctly quantitative, and when a sufficient time has elapsed we shall no doubt have the statistics.

Thus in many ways statistics can be used to show that the tendencies of free trade and protection are what they are said by free traders to be—the former *additive* to the material prosperity of a country, the latter *subtractive*, in some of their effects at least, so that no proof can be given of their being on balance beneficial. The quantity of evidence of this sort is overwhelming—I have only given a few instances. If we keep in mind the exact logical value of this evidence, it is destructive, I believe, of the protectionist case, as far as the appeal to statistics is concerned. In the absence of direct comparisons between free trade and protectionist *régimes*, which is a circumstance entirely against the protectionist, all the indirect evidence of tendencies exhibited at transition periods is in favour of the free trader.

A *fourth* way in which statistics may help in this controversy is by demonstrating the confusion of ideas

[1] See C. 3111. Session 1882.

which one always finds to be of the essence of a fair trade argument. The difficulty in dealing with these arguments is the difficulty of understanding them only, of trying to form a conception of what is in the mind of your opponent. We are told at one time that our foreign trade is falling off enormously, the alleged proof being that the exports of domestic produce have declined in value; while the obvious fact, apart from statistics, is the preponderance of English foreign trade in the business of the world, so that if the figures apparently showed the contrary, that would be no reason for arriving at a conclusion with which other facts would not fit in, but a reason only for studying and inquiring into the figures themselves, and seeing what they really meant, when properly rectified. We are told at another time that imports of manufactured articles into the United Kingdom are increasing, leading to the decay of manufacturing at home; the fact being, as distinguished from what some statistics may show or appear to show, that there never was more manufacturing than there is in England at the present time, of which the obvious proof is the rapid increase of the population in recent years, and the fact that pauperism has been stationary or declining. If any statistics therefore appear to show the contrary, that is only a reason for studying the statistics with all the collateral aids possible, not for blindly rushing at a conclusion with which nothing else will agree. Similarly we have had the excess of imports in a country dealt with as a proof that the country is running into debt; the excess of exports of other countries used as a proof that they are prosperous, these countries being also assumed not only to be protectionist, but to owe their great exports to protection, and so forth; the real facts as to whether one country is running into debt and another gaining not being otherwise inquired into. The peculiarity of most such ideas is, that even if true they do not help the protectionist argument, which is of such a kind, as we have seen, that it cannot be helped by statistics; but the so-called arguments and statements are themselves misleading and unintelligible. Now one supreme use of the study of statistics, including import and export statistics, which is our special subject to-night, is to clear up all this confusion; to introduce true ideas where there are strictly no ideas at all—no picture of what is really going on in the world; and in this way to purge the mind of any tendencies to protectionist heresy. The mind capable of thinking about economic questions from a statistical point of view, and forming a true picture of the facts of the business world, would not, I maintain, be liable to the influence of protectionist ideas. It is not among leading business men in the City, or men conversant with great business affairs anywhere, with the single exception perhaps of Prince Bismarck, that you find these confused notions, which are the congenial soil of protectionist heresy.

How statistics help in these matters has already been set forth, I hope, to some extent, by the discussion of the excess of imports controversy, and by reference to many special points. But a few more remarks may be permitted to illustrate the extreme confusion of ideas which require to be cleared up. To come back to the excess of imports controversy; even if the excess of imports meant what it is assumed to mean, it would not help the protectionist, but the real facts are wholly different from the apparent ones, and any true study of the subject gives quite a different idea of the business activity of England from the careless one. Our exports of British produce being nominally 223 million pounds, of which about 60 million pounds is raw material previously imported, the real export of the produce of British capital and labour shown in the so-called exports is thus about 160 million pounds only. We have found, however, on investigating the facts, that our unrecorded exports, in the shape of freights carried and other charges on the conveyance of goods, apart altogether from interest on investments abroad, amount to about 80 million pounds—about half the real amount of our recorded exports of British produce—so that without having some view of these unrecorded exports, we have no true idea of English trade. Without taking the unrecorded figures into account, we should err in our appreciation of the actual fact of England's business activity by 30 per cent. or more. It is not that the statistics—the figures themselves—are wrong. They merely require study and careful interpretation to get at the facts which underlie the statistics.

Another illustration of how the true study of statistics clears up false conceptions is supplied by the confutation of many historical arguments which have recently been used by fair traders. Not long ago an evening journal of the very highest literary reputation admitted into its columns a series of letters comparing the relative progress of English trade at different dates during the last two centuries, in which not the slightest reference was made to the fact that we have no good statistics of aggregate imports before 1854, and no declared values of exports before 1820, so that all comparisons before these dates, or between facts before and facts after these dates, are most difficult. The true study of statistics of course shows the necessary limitations of any such comparisons. I do not say it would be quite impossible to go back farther to some good purpose. It is quite likely that a careful student, with a good record of prices in his hand, willing to take the trouble to compare this record with the official valuations from time to time, and to attend to the relative magnitude of the chief articles of trade, might arrive at results which would throw a great deal of light on the economic history of the last two centuries. But for the present the confused notion that our recent progress under free trade has been less than in former periods before free trade, which was the conclusion or apparent conclusion of the remarkable letters I have referred to, must be dismissed as a mere wild notion which cannot be known to have any relation to actual facts. The range of our genuine knowledge in these matters is much more limited than such discussions assume.

Another illustration of how true ideas may be substituted for false is supplied by the discussion in Sir T. Farrer's recent pamphlet issued by the Cobden Club, on "Free Trade *v.* Fair Trade." A great deal of this pamphlet is taken up with the refutation of the idea that our trade with the colonies is specially beneficial, or tends to increase more than our trade with foreign countries. For myself, I cannot see how the idea which Sir T. Farrer refutes tends to support the protectionist argument. It rather seems to prove that as the colonies are less protectionist than foreign countries, their relative free trade is only a sign that if they were more free trading the better for us. But Sir T. Farrer's demonstration that there are "colonies" and "colonies," and that there have been great fluctuations in the amount of trade and its proportion to our whole trade which we have done with them in different periods, is conclusive as to there being nothing in the protectionist notion of the special value of colonial trade. Perhaps I may add that a reference to one of the tables which I have given to you to-night, viz., that showing the issues of public loans and companies on the London Stock Exchange on foreign account in the last six years, throws some light on the momentarily greater development of our trade with the colonies as compared with our trade with foreign countries. This list comprises a very large proportion of colonial issues, a much larger proportion than the previous six years, before the foreign loans collapse, would have shown. The truth is, I should say, our exports to the colonies lately have kept on increasing because their credit was never impaired, while our exports to many foreign countries fell off because we ceased to lend to them. At any rate the point seems worth investigating before drawing absolute conclusions.

Yet one more remark on this head. Sir T. Farrer shows conclusively enough that colonies are of different sorts, and they are not to be grouped together, nor are all foreign countries to be grouped together. This reminds me of a different grouping of countries, which some of you may remember, by a gentleman, Mr. Ernest Seyd, who was one of us, and for whom we all had the highest respect, though few of us agreed with his conclusions or methods. Mr. Seyd grouped countries into those having the gold standard, and those having the silver standard, and found, or believed he had found, that it was with countries having the gold standard our trade had progressed most, while with countries having the silver standard it had tended to decline. I do not know whether if Mr. Seyd had lived and observed the very last advance in the trade with India he would have adhered to his view, but his division was at least quite as logical as the division into colonies and foreign countries which has lately been made.

The conclusion is that such rough groupings and the facts apparently shown are not to be relied upon, and do not yield true ideas in a statistical view. The inquirer in this as in other matters must try many methods, and must not conclude that the apparent look of the figures corresponds to facts. A true history of the recent course of the foreign trade of the principal nations of the world would lay stress upon many things besides the division of nations into British colonies and foreign countries, or into gold standard and silver standard countries. The progress of invention; the growth of shipping in one country, and its decline in another; the settlement of new countries, and the like facts, would all have a place, and perhaps a larger place, than the points which protectionists and fair traders, or enthusiasts like Mr. Seyd, who concentrate their attention on one subject only, take up. I need not, however, multiply illustrations, especially as the whole course of the argument to-night has been to substitute, as I hope, true ideas for false ones, on many points.

In various ways, then, we conclude that a use can be made of statistics of imports and exports in the discussion between free traders and protectionists. The fact that such statistics cannot be used in the direct argument as to which *régime* is most favourable to material progress is against the protectionist, who calls for Government interference, and must thus prove his case, while the free trader is passive. The statistics at the same time supply ample proof *primâ facie* that there is nothing in the apparent figures of imports and exports to supply a case against free trade. Next, they can also be used to prove that at the period of transition from one *régime* to another, the tendency of free trade measures is to add to the prosperity of a country, while no such tendency can be proved of protectionist measures. Finally, they help to prove the utter confusion of ideas which is found to be the most fitting soil for the growth of the protectionist idea itself. Without then making more of statistics than can really be made of them, we can affirm that they are most useful in these controversies. They are, however, useful in proportion only as we observe their necessary limitations. If the example of protectionists is imitated by free traders, and the first figures that come to hand are shied at opponents on the principle that any stick is good enough to beat a dog with, I am not sure that figures will help the free trader much. The public will simply be puzzled, and induced more than ever to believe that there is nothing at all in statistics.

IX.—Conclusion.

I have now to return to the point from which I started. My complaint at the beginning was of the wrong use of statistics, and the neglect of the conditions upon which alone they can be rightly used. If I have made out a case at all, it is that even import and export figures, which are so familiar to many, cannot be handled with facility; that there is a world of knowledge to be learnt concerning them; and that in all directions sound and diligent study must precede any good use of them; but that if there is such a study of statistics, useful and valuable conclusions can be arrived at with certainty. My suggestion, then, would be that there is need, not only for the members of this Society to redouble their exertions in the way of diffusing a knowledge of statistical methods, but for some improvements in our system of education, in which there is hardly any visible place given to statistics. There are many chairs of political economy in this country, but no chair of statistics that I know of, and very few, if any, of the political economy chairs, where the teaching of statistics forms part of the course. Some remedy surely ought to be applied to this defect. As regards political economy, it is quite certain that any study of that science in its applications is impossible without statistics. A theoretical teacher may trace out tendencies or forces on paper, but in the real world quantities must be dealt with; and in the measurement of tendencies or forces statistics are absolutely needed. It is easy to prove theoretically, for instance, that a protectionist tariff does harm, but it is a different thing in the real world to give any notion of how much harm is done, and when the protection is slight in proportion to the whole business of a country to measure the effect at all. How to deal with such questions is the problem for the economist who is also a statistician, and they are much more difficult and complex than those belonging to theoretical or deductive political economy. The time has come then, it seems to me, when the public have a right to expect that in our universities statistics should have some recognized place as well as political economy. If the facts of the business world, as it is constituted at present, were taught statistically, and some notion given of the sources of information and of how they could be rightly used, much of the recent discussion between free traders and protectionists would probably have been saved:

most educated men would have seen at once when propositions were stated which were incapable of statistical proof, and when figures were used without any study or appreciation of the facts underlying them. The protectionist or fair trader would have been summarily laughed out of court, instead of being supposed for a time to have had so much of a case that party politicians on one side thought fit to give him some encouragement, and party politicians on the other side were a little apprehensive of the result. The study of statistics should undoubtedly form a necessary part of liberal education, especially of those who aspire to be politicians or public men.

NOTE.—In 1899 I read a paper at the Statistical Society on "The Excess of Imports," in which the figures on that part of the subject are continued and a new estimate is made of the earnings of our shipping fleet. The paper will be found in the "Journal" of the Statistical Society for March, 1899. See also the recent Board of Trade Bluebook in connection with the fiscal controversy, C d 1761.

X.

THE PROGRESS OF THE WORKING CLASSES IN THE LAST HALF CENTURY.[1]

IN assembling for the labours of another session, our first duty, as it was a year ago, is to commemorate the heavy loss which the Society has sustained by death. On the last occasion the names before us were those of Mr. Newmarch and Mr. Jevons, identified for many years with our work, and intimately known to many of us. On the present occasion the loss to be recorded is of another co-worker equally distinguished, though in a different way, and perhaps possessing a more exclusively statistical reputation—Dr. Farr. The "Journal" of the Society already contains a record of our sense of loss, but a few words more may surely be permitted here—in memory of one who was present year after year, not only at our inaugural meetings, but at almost all the ordinary meetings as well: who, throughout a long career, contributed numerous and valuable papers to our discussions, the interval between his first and last paper read at our meetings being over thirty years; who in the fulness of time, and certainly not before he deserved the distinction, presided over us for the usual period; and who, in fact, deserves credit as one of the makers and promoters of this Society, and of the study which we cultivate, in the most literal sense of the words. It is a very great loss we have sustained. Happily in Dr. Farr's case we have not to lament the premature shortening of days which we had to lament in referring to the loss of Mr. Newmarch and Mr. Jevons. Dr. Farr had reached

[1] Inaugural address as President of the Statistical Society. Delivered 20th November, 1883.

the limit of a tolerably long life, and, till within a very few years of the close, had been able to take an active part in the studies to which he was devoted. There are at least two remarkable monuments of his later labours, the special report to the Registrar-General on the mortality of the 1861-71 decade, which was completed only seven or eight years ago, and his paper on the mode of estimating the value of stocks having a deferred dividend, read at one of our meetings in King's College in the year 1876, after Dr. Farr had served his term as President of the Society. We can only lament Dr. Farr's loss, therefore, as the common lot of humanity, and though we could have wished a longer life and greater service, we may rejoice that the life was not incomplete, and that Dr. Farr had time to perfect his best work. What he has left is a noble monument of industry and ingenuity, full of example to all of us who have devoted time and strength to statistics, and he is certain to be honoured, we may be sure, by future generations even more than he has been by the present. To have organized, as he did, the official records of vital statistics on a model which has been widely followed not only here but abroad, and which has done much even already to promote the health and welfare of mankind, by revealing and making evident to all some main causes of disease and mortality, is a great work for one man to have done. Politicians and members of Parliament, who are ready enough to use whatever figures come to hand as implements of political warfare, but who seldom study them, may not have been able to recognize the work as the public did; but the work remains, and we, at any rate, as members of the Statistical Society, are all proud of it.

I am sorry to have to add that after this address was prepared, the announcement appeared in the newspapers of the death of Lord Overstone, who was also one of the founders of this Society, and one of its most active promoters in its earlier years, and who was President in the years 1851-53. Lord Overstone has long survived the limit of the active period of life, and as we have been reminded within the last day or two, the public have very largely forgotten the services which he rendered; but in this Society there is enough knowledge and enough interest in the economic pursuits to which Lord Overstone devoted himself, for many of us here really to possess some acquaintance with what he accomplished.

There can be no doubt that in the evidence which he gave before several Committees of the House of Commons, and in the opinions which he expressed privately to Cabinet ministers and public men on economic and more especially financial matters, upon which he was frequently consulted, Lord Overstone was able to render eminent services to the country. As a preacher of the doctrine of "hard money" he did much to settle the basis of the national currency in a difficult time, and that in a way which has left no room for change, and which has thus done not a little to steady the business of the country. There is no doubt also that it was in his capacity as a statistician very largely that he was able to render these services. He was pre-eminently one of those men who were extremely practical and careful about the facts upon which they gave their opinions. We may thus claim Lord Overstone as one of our distinguished members. I may add that of the original members of the Society there are now very few surviving. We have others surviving, as I shall notice presently, who were members almost from the beginning, but I am speaking now literally of our formal beginning. Amongst those who will be known to you, I think, Mr. Heywood and Mr. Edwin Chadwick are to be mentioned as among the very distinguished members who were at the foundation of the Society, and who still survive to take an interest in our labours.

The mention of the names of Lord Overstone and Dr. Farr carries us back naturally enough to the origin of the Society. We are carried back to the same date by an impending event which now casts its shadow before—our approaching jubilee, which we may hope will be worthily celebrated. It is of good augury, I trust, that we commence our fiftieth session with the election of no fewer than fifty-eight new members. It seems fairly probable now that when we complete our fiftieth year we shall have the round number of one thousand members—a wonderful improvement upon the small number of fifty years ago. On such an occasion I believe the subject on which I propose to address you to-night will be not unsuitable—a review of the official statistics bearing on the progress of the working classes—the masses of the nation—in the last half century. If you go back to the early records of the Society, you will find that one of the leading objects of its founders was to obtain means by which to study the very question I have selected. Happily we have still with us, in addition to those I have named as original members, one or two honoured members associated with the early history of the Society—Dr. Guy and Sir Rawson Rawson—who will bear me out in what I have stated. I may remind you, moreover, that one of the founders of the Society was Mr. Porter, of the Board of Trade, whose special study for years was much the same, as his well-known book, "The Progress of the Nation," bears witness; and that in one of the earliest publications of the Society, a volume preceding the regular issue of the "Journal," he has left a most interesting account of what he hoped might be effected by means of statistics in studying the subject I have put before you, or the more general subject of the "Progress of the Nation." In asking you, therefore, to look for a little at what statistics tell us of the progress of the great masses of the nation, I feel that I am selecting a subject which is connected with the special history of the Society. That it happens for the moment to be attracting a considerable amount of popular attention in connection with sensational politics and sociology, with agitations for land nationalization and collectivism among pretended representatives of the working classes, is an additional reason for our not neglecting this question; but it is a question to which the Society has a primary claim, and which the authors of the agitations I have referred to would have done well to study from the statistical point of view.

There are two or three ways in which statistics may throw light on such a question as I have put forward. The first and most direct is to see what records there are of the money earnings of the masses now and fifty years ago, ascertain whether they have increased or diminished, and then compare them with the rise or fall in the prices of the chief articles which the masses consume. Even such records would not give a complete answer. It is conceivable, for instance, that while earning more money, and being able to spend it to more advantage, the working classes might be no better off than formerly. There may be masses, as there are individuals, who do not know how to spend. The question of means, however, will carry us some distance on the road to our object. We shall know that the masses must be better off, unless they have deteriorated in the art of spending, a subject of separate inquiry.

In investigating such records, however, we have to recognize that the ideal mode of answering the question is not yet possible. That mode would be to draw up an account of the aggregate annual earnings of the working classes for a period about fifty years ago, and a similar account of the aggregate annual earnings of the same classes at the present time, and then compare the average per head and per family at the different dates. Having thus ascertained the increase or diminution in the amount per head at the different dates, it would be comparatively easy, though not in itself quite so easy a matter as it seems, to ascertain how much less or how much more the increased or diminished sum would buy of the chief articles of the workman's consumption. But no such account that I know of has been drawn up, except for a date about fifteen or sixteen years ago, when Mr. Dudley Baxter and Professor Leone Levi both drew up statements of enormous value as to aggregate earnings, statements which it would now be most desirable to compare with similar statements for the present time, if we could have them, and which will be simply invaluable to future generations. In the absence of such statements, all that can be done is to compare what appear to be the average wages of large groups of the working classes. If it is found that the changes in the money wages of such groups are in the same direction, or almost all in the same direction, then there would be sufficient reason for believing that similar changes had occurred throughout the entire mass. It would be in the highest degree improbable that precisely those changes which could not be traced were in the opposite direction. The difficulty in the way is that in a period of fifty years in a country like England the character of the work itself changes. The people who have the same names at different times are not necessarily doing the same work. Some forms of work pass wholly away and wholly new forms come into existence. Making all allowances, however, and selecting the best comparative cases possible, some useful conclusion seems obtainable.

What I propose to do first and mainly, as regards this point, is to make use of an independent official record which we have to thank Mr. Porter for commencing. I mean the record of wages, which has been maintained for many years in the miscellaneous statistics of the United Kingdom, and which was previously commenced and carried on in the volumes of Revenue and Population Tables which Mr. Porter introduced at the Board of Trade about fifty years ago. It is curious on looking back through these volumes to find how difficult it is to get a continuous record. The wages in one volume are for certain districts and trades; in a subsequent volume for different districts and trades;

the descriptive classifications of the workers are also constantly changing. Picking my way through the figures, however, I have to submit the following particulars of changes in money wages, between a period forty to fifty years ago—it is not possible to get the same year in all cases to start from—and a period about two years ago, which may be taken as the present time. This comparison leaves out of account the length of hours of work, which is a material point I shall notice presently.

Comparison of Wages Fifty Years ago and at Present Time.

[From "Miscellaneous Statistics of the United Kingdom," and Porter's "Progress of the Nation."]

Occupation.	Place.	Wages Fifty Years ago, per Week.	Wages Present Times, per Week.	Increase or Decrease.	
				Amount.	Per Cent.
Carpenters	Manchester	24/-	34/-	10/- (+)	42
"	Glasgow	14/-	26/-	12/- (+)	85
Bricklayers	Manchester [1]	24/-	36/-	12/- (+)	50
"	Glasgow	15/-	27/-	12/- (+)	80
Masons	Manchester [1]	24/-	29/10	5/10 (+)	24
"	Glasgow	14/-	23/8	9/8 (+)	69
Miners	Staffordshire	2/8 [2]	4/- [2]	1/4 (+)	50
Pattern weavers . .	Huddersfield	16/-	25/-	9/- (+)	55
Wool scourers . . .	"	17/-	22/-	5/- (+)	30
Mule spinners . . .	"	25/6	30/-	4/6 (+)	20
Weavers	"	12/-	26/-	14/- (+)	115
Warpers and beamers	"	17/-	27/-	10/- (+)	58
Winders and reelers .	"	6/-	11/-	5/- (+)	83
Weavers (men) . .	Bradford	8/3	20/6	12/3 (+)	150
Reeling and warping.	"	7/9	15/6	7/9 (+)	100
Spinning (children) .	"	4/5	11/6	7/1 (+)	160

Thus in all cases where I have found it possible from the apparent similarity of the work to make a comparison there is an enormous apparent rise in money wages ranging from 20 and in most cases from 50 to 100 per cent., and in one or two instances more than 100 per cent.[3] This understates, I believe, the real

[1] 1825. [2] Wages per day.

[3] The mean of the percentages of increase is over 70.

extent of the change. Thus, builders' wages are given at the earlier date as so much weekly, whereas in the later returns a distinction is made between summer and winter wages, the hours of labour being less in winter, and as the wages are so much per hour, the week's wages being also less, so that it has been possible to strike a mean for the later period, while it does not appear that anything more is meant at the early period than the usual weekly wage, which would be the summer wage. Without making this point, however, it is obvious that in all cases there is a very great rise.

Before passing from this point, there is another and continuous official record I would refer to. Unfortunately it does not go back for much more than thirty years. Still, as far as it goes, the evidence is in the same direction. I refer to the return of merchant seamen's wages annually issued by the Board of Trade, in what is known as the Progress of Merchant Shipping Return. From this Return may be derived the following comparison of seamen's wages:

Comparison of Seamen's Money Wages per Month at 1850 *and the Present Time.*

[From the "Progress of Merchant Shipping Return."]

	1850.	Present Time.	Increase.	
	Sailing.	Steam.	Amount.	Per Cent.
Bristol	45/-	75/-	30/-	66
Glasgow	45/-	70/-	25/-	55
Liverpool (1) . .	50/-	67/6	16/6	33
,, (2) . .	50/-	85/-	35/-	70
,, (3) . .	45/-	60/-	15/-	33
,, (4) . .	40/-	50/-	10/-	25
,, (5) . .	42/6	60/-	17/6	40
London (1) . .	45/-	75/-	30/-	66
,, (2) . .	50/-	77/6	27/6	55
,, (3) . .	45/-	65/-	20/-	45
,, (4) . .	45/-	70/-	25/-	55
,, (5) . .	40/-	67/6	27/6	69
,, (6) . .	40/-	67/6	27/6	69

Here again there is an enormous rise in money wages. This return is specially subject to the observation that money wages are only part of the wages of seamen, but I assume it is not open to dispute, that with the improvement in our shipping there has been an improvement in the food and lodging of the sailor, quite equal to the improvement in his money wage.

This question of seamen's wages, however, well illustrates the difficulty of the whole subject. Ships are not now navigated by able seamen so much as by engineers and stokers. It would seem that as a class the new men all round are paid better than the able seamen, but I should not press this point; it might well be the case that steam ships as a whole could be worked by an inferior class of labourers as compared with sailing-ships, and yet the fact that inferior labour is sufficient for this special trade would be quite consistent with the fact that the whole conditions of modern labour require more skill than the conditions fifty years ago, so that there is more labour relatively at the higher rates than used to be the case.

The comparison, except for seamen's wages, where it has only been possible to go back for about thirty years, is made between a period about fifty years ago and the present time only. It would have complicated the figures too much to introduce intermediate dates. I may state, however, that I have not been inattentive to this point, and that if we had commenced about twenty to twenty-five years ago, we should also have been able to show a very great improvement since that time, while at that date also, as compared with an earlier period, a great improvement would have been apparent. A careful and exhaustive investigation of the records of wages I have referred to, in comparison with the numbers employed in different occupations, as shown by the census reports, would in fact repay the student who has time to make it; and I trust the investigation will yet be made.

The records do not include anything relating to the

agricultural labourer, but from independent sources—I would refer especially to the Reports of the recent Royal Agricultural Commission—we may perceive how universal the rise in the wages of agricultural labourers has been, and how universal at any rate is the complaint that more money is paid for less work. Sir James Caird, in his "Landed Interest" (p. 65), put the rise at 60 per cent. as compared with the period just before the Repeal of the Corn Laws, and there is much other evidence to the same effect. The rise in the remuneration of labour in Ireland in the last forty years is also one of the facts which have been conspicuously brought before the public of late. In no other way is it possible to account for the stationariness of rents in Ireland for a long period, notwithstanding the great rise in the prices of the cattle and dairy products which Ireland produces, and which, it has been contended, would have justified a rise of rents. The farmer and the labourer together have in fact had all the benefit of the rise in agricultural prices.

The next point to which attention must be drawn is the shortening of the hours of labour which has taken place. While the money wages have increased, as we have seen, the hours of labour have diminished. It is difficult to estimate what the extent of this diminution has been, but collecting one or two scattered notices I should be inclined to say very nearly 20 per cent. There has been at least this reduction in the textile, engineering, and house-building trades. The workman gets from 50 to 100 per cent. more money, for 20 per cent. less work; in round figures, he has gained from 70 to 120 per cent. in fifty years in money return. It is just possible of course that the workman may do as much or nearly as much in the shorter period as he did in his longer hours. Still there is the positive gain in his being less time at his task, which many of the classes still tugging lengthily day by day at the oar would appreciate. The workman may have been wise or unwise in setting much store by shorter hours in bettering himself, but the shortening of the hours of labour is undoubtedly to be counted to the good as well as the larger money return he obtains.

We come then to the question of what the changes have been in the prices of the chief articles of the workman's consumption. It is important, to begin with, that, as regards prices of commodities generally, there seems to be little doubt things are much the same as they were forty or fifty years ago. This is the general effect of the inquiries which have been made first as to the depreciation of gold consequent on the Australian and Californian gold discoveries, and next as to the appreciation of gold which has taken place within the last twenty years, consequent on the new demands for gold which have arisen, and the falling off in the supply as compared with the period between 1850 and 1860. It would burden us too much to go into these inquiries on an occasion like the present, and therefore I only take the broad result. This is that while there was a moderate rise of prices all round between the years 1847-50, just before the new gold came on the market, and the year 1862, when Mr. Jevons published his celebrated essay, a rise not exceeding about 20 per cent., yet within the last twenty years this rise has disappeared, and prices are back to the level, or nearly to the level, of 1847-50. The conclusion is that, taking things in the mass, the sovereign goes as far as it did forty or fifty years ago, while there are many new things in existence at a low price which could not then have been bought at all. If, in the interval, the average money earnings of the working classes have risen between 50 and 100 per cent., there must have been an enormous change for the better in the means of the working man, unless by some wonderful accident it has happened that his special articles have changed in a different way from the general run of prices.

But looking to special articles, we find that on balance prices are lower and not higher. Take wheat.

It is notorious that wheat, the staff of life, has been lower on the average of late years than it was before the free trade era. Even our fair trade friends, who find it so difficult to see very plain things, were forced to allow, in that wonderful manifesto which was published in the "Times" some weeks back, that wheat is about 5*s.* a quarter cheaper on the average than it was. The facts, however, deserve still more careful statement to enable us to realize the state of things fifty years ago and at the present time. The fair trade statement, if I remember rightly, showed an average fall of 5*s.* in the price of wheat, comparing the whole period since the Repeal of the Corn Laws with a long period before. This may have been right or wrong for the purpose in hand, but for our present purpose, which is to compare the present period with that of half a century ago, it is important to note that it is mainly within the last ten years the steadily low price of wheat has been established. Comparing the ten years before 1846 with the last ten years, what we find is that while the average price of wheat in 1837-46 was 58*s.* 7*d.*, it was 48*s.* 9*d.* only in the last ten years—a reduction not of 5*s.* merely, but 10*s.* The truth is, the Repeal of the Corn Laws was not followed by an *immediate* decline of wheat on the average. The failure of the potato crop, the Crimean War, and the depreciation of gold, all contributed to maintain the price, notwithstanding free trade, down to 1862. Since then steadily lower prices have ruled; and when we compare the present time with a half century ago, or any earlier part of the century, these facts should be remembered.

There is a still more important consideration. Averages are very good for certain purposes, but we all know in this place that a good deal sometimes turns upon the composition of the average,—upon whether it is made up of great extremes, or whether the individual elements depart very little from the average. This is specially an important matter in a question of the price of food. The average of a necessary of life over a long period of years may be moderate, but if in some years the actual price is double what it is in other years, the fact of the average will in no way save from starvation at certain periods the workman who may have a difficulty in making both ends meet in the best of times. What we find then is that fifty years ago the extremes were disastrous compared with what they are at the present time. In 1836 we find wheat touching 36*s.*; in 1838, 1839, 1840, and in 1841, we find it touching 78*s.* 4*d.*, 81*s.* 6*d.*, 72*s.* 10*d.*, and 76*s.* 1*d.*; in all cases double the price of the lowest year, and nearly double the "average" of the decade; and in 1847 the price of 102*s.* 5*d.*, or three times the price of the lowest period, is touched. If we go back earlier we find still more startling extremes. We have such figures as 106*s.* 5*d.* in 1810; 126*s.* 6*d.* in 1812; 109*s.* 9*d.* in 1813, and 96*s.* 11*d.* in 1817; these figures being not merely the extremes touched, but the actual averages for the whole year. No doubt in the early part of the century the over-issue of inconvertible paper accounts for part of the nominal prices, but it accounts for a very small part. What we have to consider then is, that fifty years ago the working man with wages, on the average, about half, or not much more than half what they are now, had at times to contend with a fluctuation in the price of bread which implied sheer starvation. Periodic starvation was, in fact, the condition of the masses of working men throughout the kingdom fifty years ago, and the references to the subject in the economic literature of the time are most instructive. M. Quetelet, in his well-known great book, points to the obvious connection between the high price of bread following the bad harvest of 1816, and the excessive rate of mortality which followed. To this day you will find tables in the Registrar-General's returns which descend from a time when a distinct connection between these high prices of bread and excessive rates of mortality was traced. But within the last twenty years what do we find? Wheat has not been, on the average, for a whole year so high as 70*s.*, the highest averages for any year being 64*s.* 5*d.* in 1867, and 63*s.* 9*d.* in 1868; while the highest average of the last ten years alone is 58*s.* 8*d.* in 1873; that is, only about 10*s.* above the average of the whole period. In the twenty years, moreover, the highest price touched at any period was just over 70*s.*, viz., 70*s.* 5*d.*, in 1867, and 74*s.* 7*d.* in 1868; while in the last ten years the figure of 70*s.* was not even touched, the nearest approach to it being 68*s.* 9*d.* in 1877. Thus of late years there has been a steadily low price, which must have been an immense boon to the masses, and especially to the poorest. The rise of money wages has been such, I believe, that working men for the most part could have contended with extreme fluctuations in the price of bread better than they did fifty years ago. But they have not had the fluctuations to contend with.

It would be useless to go through other articles with the same detail. Wheat had quite a special importance fifty years ago, and the fact that it no longer has the same importance—that we have ceased to think of it as people did fifty years ago—is itself significant. Still, taking one or two other articles, we find, on the whole, a decline:

Prices of Various Articles about Fifty Years ago and at Present Time.

	1839-40.		Present Time.	
	s.	*d.*	*s.*	*d.*
Sugar . . . . per cwt.	68	8[1]	21	9[2]
Cotton cloth exported . . per yard	0	$5\frac{3}{8}$	0	$3\frac{1}{4}$

[1] Porter's "Progress of the Nation," p. 543. In the paper as read to the Society I gave the price without the duty, but including the duty the price was what is now given here. The average price with the duty of the ten years ending 1840 was 58*s.* 4*d.*

[2] Average price of raw sugar imported.

Prices of Various Articles—continued.

		1840.		1882.	
		s.	*d.*	*s.*	*d.*
Inferior beasts	per 8 lbs.	3	1	4	3¾
Second class	,,	3	6	4	9¾
Third ,, ...	,,	3	11¾	5	7½
Inferior sheep	,,	3	5	5	7
Second class	,,	3	10¼	6	1¼
Large hogs	,,	4	3½	4	6

I should have liked a longer list of articles, but the difficulty of comparison is very serious. It may be stated broadly, however, that while sugar and such articles have declined largely in price, and while clothing is also cheaper, the only article interesting the workman much which has increased in price is meat, the increase here being considerable. The "only" it may be supposed covers a great deal. The truth is, however, that meat fifty years ago was not an article of the workman's diet as it has since become. He had little more concern with its price than with the price of diamonds. The kind of meat which was mainly accessible to the workman fifty years ago, viz., bacon, has not, it will be seen, increased sensibly in price.

Only one question remains. Various commodities, it may be admitted, have fallen in price, but house rent, it is said, has gone up. We have heard a good deal lately of the high prices of rooms in the slums. When we take things in the mass, however, we find that however much some workmen may suffer, house rent in the aggregate cannot have gone up in a way to neutralize to any serious extent the great rise in the money wages of the workman. It appears that in 1834, when the house duty, which had existed up to that date, was abolished, the annual value of dwelling houses charged to duty was £12,603,000, the duty being levied on all houses above £10 rental in Great Britain. In 1881-82 the annual value of dwelling houses charged to duty, the duty being levied on houses above £20 only, was £39,845,000, while the value of the houses between £10 and £20 was £17,040,000, making a total of £56,885,000, or between four and five times the total of fifty years ago. Population, however, in Great Britain has increased from about 16½ millions in 1831, to nearly 30 millions in 1881, or nearly 100 per cent. Allowing for this, the increase in value would be about 32 million pounds, on a total of about 25 million pounds, which may be considered the increased rent which householders above £10 have to pay—the increase being about 130 per cent. Assuming that houses under £10 have increased in proportion, it may be considered that house rents are now 1½ times more than they were fifty years ago. In other words, a workman who paid £3 a year fifty years ago, would now pay £7 10*s.* Even, however, if rent were a fourth part of the workman's earnings fifty years ago, he would still be much better off at the present time than he was. His whole wages have doubled, while the prices of no part of his necessary consumption, except rent, as we have seen, have increased—on the contrary, they have rather diminished. Say then that the rent, which was a fourth part of his expenditure, has increased 1½ times, while his whole wage has doubled, the account, on a wage of 20*s.* fifty years ago, and 40*s.* now, would stand:

	Fifty Years ago.		Present Time.	
	s.	*d.*	*s.*	*d.*
Wage	20	0	40	0
Deduct for rent	5	0	12	6
Balance for other purposes .	15	0	27	6

—showing still an enormous improvement in the workman's condition.

It may be pointed out, however, that houses are undoubtedly of the better value all round than they were fifty years ago. More rent is paid because more capital is in the houses, and they are better houses. It appears also that fifty years ago there were far more exemptions than there are now, rural dwellings particularly being favoured as regards exemption. The increase of rent for the same accommodation, there is consequently reason to believe, has not been nearly so great as these figures would appear to show. It has further to be considered that the whole annual value of the dwelling houses under £10 even now is £17,885,000 only, the number of houses being 3,124,000. This must be a very small proportion of the aggregate earnings of those portions of the working classes who live in houses under £10 rent, and even adding to it the value of all the houses up to £20, which would bring up the total to £34,925,000, the proportion would still be very small. On the five million families at least of the working classes in Great Britain, the sum would come to about £7 per family, which is not the main portion of an average working man's expenditure.[1]

We return then to the conclusion that the increase of the money wages of the working man in the last fifty years corresponds to a real gain. While his wages have advanced, most articles he consumes have rather diminished in price, the change in wheat being especially remarkable, and significant of a complete revolution in the condition of the masses. The increased price in the case of one or two articles—particularly

[1] It may be convenient to note here that the figures as to dwelling houses which I have made use of are those relating to the Inhabited House Duty. The figures as to houses in the income tax returns include shops and factories as well as dwelling houses, and are not available in a question of house rent. I have also omitted the question of rates. The rates per pound, however, have not increased as compared with what they were formerly, and it would make no material difference if they were to be included. The workman's payment for rates and rent together cannot have increased more than is here stated for rent.

meat and house rent—is insufficient to neutralize the general advantages which the workman has gained. Meat formerly was a very small part of his consumption, and allowing to house rent a much larger share of his expenditure than it actually bore, the increase in amount would still leave the workman out of his increased wage a larger margin than he had before for miscellaneous expenditure. There is reason to believe also that the houses are better, and that the increased house rent is merely the higher price for a superior article which the workman can afford.

It has to be added to all this that while the cost of government has been greatly diminished to the working man, he gets more from the government expenditure than he formerly did. It would not do to count things twice over, and as the benefit to the working man of diminished taxes has already been allowed for in the lower prices of wheat and sugar, we need say nothing more on this head. But few people seem to be aware how, simultaneously with this reduction of the cost of government, there has been an increase of the expenditure of the government for miscellaneous civil purposes, of all of which the workman gets the benefit. It may be stated broadly that nearly 15 million pounds of the expenditure of the central government for education, for the post office, for inspection of factories, and for the miscellaneous purposes of civil government, is entirely new as compared with fifty years ago. So far as the expenditure is beneficial, the masses get something they did not get before at all. It is the same even more markedly with local government. In Great Britain, the annual outlay is now about 60 million pounds, as compared with 20 million pounds fifty years ago. This 20 million pounds was mainly for poor relief and other old burdens. Now the poor relief and other old burdens are much the same, but the total is swollen by a vast expenditure for sanitary, educational, and similar purposes, of all of which the masses of the population get the benefit. To a great deal of this expenditure we may attach the highest value. It does not give bread or clothing to the working man, but it all helps to make life sweeter and better, and to open out careers even to the poorest. The value of the free library, for instance, in a large city, is simply incalculable. All this outlay the workman has now the benefit of as he had not fifty years ago. To repeat the words I have already used, he pays less taxes, and he gets more—much more—from the Government.[1]

[1] With regard to this question of prices, I have been favoured since the delivery of this address with the copy of a letter, dated 11th June, 1881, addressed by Mr. Charles Hawkins, of 27, Savile Row, to the editor of the "Daily News" on the cost *per patient* of the expenditure of St. George's Hospital in 1830 and 1880. The facts stated confirm in an interesting way what is here said as to the cost of articles of the workman's consumption fifty years ago and at the present time. Mr. Hawkins, who was at one time one of the treasurers of the hospital, and therefore speaks with authority, gives the following table and notes:

"Although each patient costs now 1*s.* 1*d.* less than in 1830, there have been great alterations in the different items of expenditure, viz.:

	Cost per Patient.			
	1830.		1880.	
	s.	*d.*	*s.*	*d.*
Meat	18	4	22	2
Bread and flour	10	7	4	1
Wine and spirits	0	10	3	3
Malt liquor	5	5	2	6
Milk	6	2	5	11
Tea and grocery	3	10	3	5
Drugs	16	5	7	11
Coals and wood	10	6	3	10
Laundry	2	10	4	10
Instruments and surgical appliances	1	9	5	2
Staff;—officers, servants, nurses	20	3	34	3

"Had wheat cost in 1880 what it did in 1830, £1,884 must have been spent in bread and flour instead of £738. The cost of port wine in 1830 was £72 per pipe; in 1880 £45. In 1830 many of the patients provided themselves with tea and sugar. Under the head 'Drugs' is included the cost of leeches; in 1846, 14,800 leeches were used, at a cost of £143; in 1880 only 425, costing £1 16*s*. In 1833 another hospital, treating double the number of patients, used 48,900 leeches, but in 1880 only 250.

"These items show the great advantage of the reduction of price in

As already anticipated, however, the conclusion thus arrived at only carries us part of the way. Assuming it to have been shown that the masses have more money than they had fifty years ago, and that the prices of the chief articles they consume are cheaper rather than dearer, the question remains whether the condition of the masses has in fact been improved. This can only be shown indirectly by statistics of different kinds, which justify conclusions as to the condition of the people to whom they apply. To such statistics I propose now to draw your attention for a moment. I need hardly say that any evidence they contain as to the condition of the people having actually improved corroborates what has been already said as to their having had the means of improvement in their hands. The evidence is cumulative, a point of material importance in all such inquiries.

The first and the most important statistics on this head are those relating to the length of life among the masses of the nation. Do the people live longer than they did? Here I need not detain you. A very effective answer was supplied last session by Mr. Humphreys, in his able paper on "The Recent Decline in the English Death Rate."[1] Mr. Humphreys there showed conclusively that the decline in the death-rate in the last five years, 1876-80, as compared with the rates on which Dr. Farr's English Life Table was based—rates obtained in the years 1838-54—amounted to from 28 to 32 per cent. in males at each quinquennium of the twenty years 5-25, and in females at each quinquennium from 5-35 to between 24 and 35 per cent.; and that the effect of this decline in the death-rate is to raise the mean duration of life among males from 39.9 to 41.9

some articles of diet, and the great extra expenditure now necessary for the treatment of hospital patients, depending on the greater call for additional 'staff,' more especially for nursing, and an altered mode of treatment of accidents and operations, as also the greater amount of stimulants now exhibited, etc."

[1] See Statistical Society's "Journal," vol. xlvi., p. 195, etc.

years, a gain of 2 years in the average duration of life, and among females from 41.9 to 45.3 years, a gain of nearly $3\frac{1}{2}$ years in the average duration of life. Mr. Humphreys also showed that by far the larger proportion of the increased duration of human life in England is lived at useful ages, and not at the dependent ages of either childhood or old age. This little statement is absolutely conclusive on the subject; but we are apt to overlook how much the figures mean. No such change could take place without a great increase in the vitality of the people. Not only have fewer died, but the masses who have lived must have been healthier, and have suffered less from sickness than they did. Though no statistics are available on this point, we must assume that like causes produce like effects; and if the weaker, who would otherwise have died, have been able to survive, the strong must also have been better than they would otherwise have been. From the nature of the figures, also, the improvement must have been among the masses, and not among a select class whose figures throw up the average. The figures to be affected relate to such large masses of population, that so great a change in the average could not have occurred if only a small percentage of the population had improved in health.

I should like also to point out that the improvement in health actually recorded obviously relates to a transition stage. Many of the improvements in the condition of the working classes have only taken place quite recently. They have not, therefore, affected all through their existence any but the youngest lives. When the improvements have been in existence for a longer period, so that the lives of all who are living must have been affected from birth by the changed conditions, we may infer that even a greater gain in the mean duration of life will be shown. As it is, the gain is enormous. Whether it is due to better and more abundant food and clothing, to better sanitation, to better knowledge of medicine, or to these and other causes combined, the improvement has beyond all question taken place.

The next figures I shall refer to are those well-known ones relating to the consumption of the articles which the masses consume. I copy merely the figures in the Statistical Abstract for the years 1840 and 1881:

Quantities of the Principal Imported and Excisable Articles retained for Home Consumption, per Head of the Total Population of the United Kingdom.

		1840.	1881.
Bacon and hams	lbs.	0.01	13.93
Butter	,,	1.05	6.36
Cheese	,,	0.92	5.77
Currants and raisins	,,	1.45	4.34
Eggs	No.	3.63	21.65
Potatoes	lbs.	0.01	12.85
Rice	,,	0.90	16.32
Cocoa	,,	0.08	0.31
Coffee	,,	1.08	0.89
Corn, wheat, and wheat flour	,,	42.47	216.92
Raw sugar	,,	15.20	58.92
Refined sugar	,,	nil	8.44
Tea	,,	1.22	4.58
Tobacco	,,	0.86	1.41
Wine	galls.	0.25	0.45
Spirits	,,	0.97	1.08
Malt	bshls.	1.59	1.91 [1]

This wonderful table may speak for itself. It is an obvious criticism that many of the articles are also articles of home production, so that the increase does not show the real increase of the consumption of the whole population per head. Assuming a stationary production at home, the increased consumption per head cannot be so much as is here stated for the imported article only. There are other articles, however, such as rice, tea, sugar, coffee, tobacco, spirits, wine

[1] Year 1878.

and malt, which are either wholly imported, or where we have the excisable figures as well, and they all—with the one exception of coffee—tell a clear tale. The increase in tea and sugar appears especially significant, the consumption per head now being four times in round figures what it was forty years ago. There could be no better evidence of diffused material well-being among the masses. The articles are not such that the increased consumption by the rich could have made much difference. It is the consumption emphatically of the mass which is here in question.

As regards the articles imported, which are also articles of home production, it has, moreover, to be noted that in several of them, bacon and hams, cheese and butter, the increase is practically from nothing to a very respectable figure. The import of bacon and hams alone is itself nearly equal to the estimated consumption among the working classes fifty years ago, who consumed no other meat.

The only other figures I shall mention are those relating to education, pauperism, crime, and savings banks. But I need not detain you here. The figures are so well known that I must almost apologize for repeating them. I only insert them to round off the statement.

As to education, we have practically only figures going back thirty years. In 1851, in England, the children in average attendance at schools aided by parliamentary grants numbered 239,000, and in Scotland 32,000; in 1881 the figures were 2,863,000 and 410,000. If anything is to be allowed at all in favour of parliamentary grants as raising the character of education, such a change of numbers is most significant. The children of the masses are, in fact, now obtaining a good education all round, while fifty years ago the masses had either no education at all or a comparatively poor one. Dropping statistics for the moment, I should like to give my own testimony to an observed fact of social life—that there is nothing so striking or so satisfactory to those who can carry their memories back nearly forty years, as to observe the superiority of the education of the masses at the present time to what it was then. I suppose the most advanced common education forty or fifty years ago was in Scotland, but the superiority of the common school system there at the present day to what it was forty years ago is immense. If Scotland has gained so much, what must it have been in England, where there was no national system fifty years ago at all? Thus at the present day not only do we get all children into schools, or nearly all, but the education for the increased numbers is better than that which the fortunate few alone obtained before.

Next as to crime, the facts to note are that rather more than forty years ago, with a population little more than half what it is now, the number of criminal offenders committed for trial (1839) was 54,000: in England alone 24,000. Now the corresponding figures are, United Kingdom 22,000, and England 15,000; fewer criminals by a great deal in a much larger population. Of course the figures are open to the observation that changes in legislation providing for the summary trial of offences that formerly went to the assizes may have had some effect. But the figures show so great and gradual a change, that there is ample margin for the results of legislative changes, without altering the inference that there is less serious crime now in the population than there was fifty years ago. Thus an improvement as regards crime corresponds to the better education and well-being of the masses.

Next as regards pauperism; here again the figures are so imperfect that we cannot go back quite fifty years. It is matter of history, however, that pauperism was nearly breaking down the country half a century ago. The expenditure on poor relief early in the century and down to 1830-31 was nearly as great at times as it is now. With half the population in the country that there now is, the burden of the poor was the same. Since 1849, however, we have continuous figures, and from these we know that, with a constantly increasing population, there is an absolute decline in the amount of pauperism. The earliest and latest figures are:

Paupers in Receipt of Relief in the undermentioned Years at given Dates.

	1849.	1881.
England	934,000	803,000
Scotland	122,000[1]	102,000
Ireland	620,000	109,000
United Kingdom .	1,676,000	1,014,000

Thus in each of the three divisions of the United Kingdom there is a material decline, and most of all in Ireland, the magnitude of the decline there being no doubt due to the fact that the figures are for a period just after the great famine. But how remote we seem to be from those days of famine!

Last of all we come to the figures of savings banks. A fifty years' comparison gives the following results for the whole kingdom:

	1831.	1881.
Number of depositors .	429,000	4,140,000
Amount of deposits .	£13,719,000	£80,334,000
„ per depositor .	£32	£19

An increase of tenfold in the number of depositors, and of fivefold and more in the amounts of deposits! It seems obvious from these figures that the habit and means of saving have become widely diffused in these fifty years. The change is of course in part due to a mere change in the facilities offered for obtaining de-

[1] 1859.

posits; but allowing ample margin for the effect of increased facilities, we have still before us evidence of more saving among the masses.

There is yet one other set of statistics I should like to notice in this connection, those relating to the progress of industrial and provident co-operative societies in England and Wales. These I abstract from the special appendix to the "Co-operative Wholesale Society's Annual Almanac and Diary" for the present year (pp. 81 and 82). Unfortunately the figures only go back to 1862, but the growth up to 1862 appears to have been very small. Now, however, most material advance is shown:

	1862.	1881.
Number of members .	90,000	525,000
Capital—	£	£
Share	428,000	5,881,000
Loan	55,000	1,267,000
Sales	2,333,000	20,901,000
Net profit	165,000	1,617,000

Such figures are still small compared with what we should like to see them, but they at least indicate progress among the working classes, and not retrogression or standing still.

To conclude this part of the evidence, we find undoubtedly that in longer life, in increased consumption of the chief commodities they use, in better education, in greater freedom from crime and pauperism, and in increased savings, the masses of the people are better, immensely better, than they were fifty years ago. This is quite consistent with the fact, which we all lament, that there is a residuum still unimproved, but apparently a smaller residuum both in proportion to the population and absolutely, than was the case fifty years ago; and with the fact that the improvement, measured even by a low ideal, is far too small. No one can contemplate the condition of the masses of the people without desiring something like a revolution for the better. Still, the fact of progress in the last fifty years—progress which is really enormous when a comparison is made with the former state of things—must be recognized. Discontent with the present must not make us forget that things have been so much worse.

But the question is raised: Have the working classes gained in proportion with others by the development of material wealth during the last fifty years? The question is not one which would natually excite much interest among those who would answer the primary question as to whether the working classes have gained or not, as I have done, in the affirmative. Where all are getting on, it does not seem very practical in those who are getting on slowly to grudge the quicker advance of others. Usually those who put the question have some vague idea that the capitalist classes, as they are called, secure for themselves all the benefits of the modern advance in wealth; the rich, it is said, are becoming richer, and the poor are becoming poorer. It will be convenient then to examine the additional question specifically. If the answer agrees with what has already been advanced, then, as nobody doubts that material wealth has increased, all will be forced to admit that the working classes have had a fair share.

At first sight it would appear that the enormous figures of the increase of capital, which belong, it is assumed, to the capitalist classes, are inconsistent with the notion of the non-capitalist classes having had a fair share. In the paper which I read to the Society four years ago, on "The Recent Accumulations of Capital in the United Kingdom," the conclusion at which I arrived was that in the ten years, 1865-75, there had been an increase of 40 per cent. in the capital of the nation, and 27 per cent. in the amount of capital per head, that is, allowing for the increase of population.

Going back to 1843, which is as far as we can go back with the income tax returns, we also find that since then the gross assessment, allowing for the income from Ireland not then included in the returns, has increased from 280 million pounds to 577 million pounds, or more than 100 per cent. in less than fifty years. Assuming capital to have increased in proportion, it is not to be wondered at that the impression of a group of people called the capitalist classes getting richer and richer, while the mass remain poor or become poorer, should be entertained. Allowing for the increase of population, the growth of capital and income-tax income is really much smaller than the growth of the money income of the working classes, which we have found to be something like 50 to 100 per cent. and more per head in fifty years, but the impression to the contrary undoubtedly exists, and is very natural.

The error is partly in supposing that the capitalist classes remain the same in number. This is not the case; and I have two pieces of statistics to refer to which seem to show that the capitalist classes are far from stationary, and that they receive recruits from period to period—in other words, that wealth, in certain directions, is becoming more diffused, although it may not be diffusing itself as we should wish.

The first evidence I refer to is that of the Probate Duty returns. Through the kindness of the Commissioners of Inland Revenue, I am able to put before you a statement of the number of probates granted in 1881, and of the amounts of property "proved," with which we may compare similar figures published by Mr. Porter in his "Progress of the Nation" for 1838. I am sorry to say Mr. Porter's figures for 1838 are far more detailed than those I am able to give; a more minute comparison would be most instructive; but I was unfortunately too late in applying to the Commissioners of Inland Revenue for the details, which I found they were most willing to give. However, the statement they supplied to me, and the comparison which can thus be made, seem most instructive. They are as follows:

Statement of Number of Probates granted in 1882, *with Amounts of Property Proved, and Average per Probate* [*from figures supplied by the Commissioners of Inland Revenue*]; *and Comparison with a similar Statement for* 1838 [*from Porter's "Progress of the Nation," pp.* 600 *et seq.*].

	Number of Probates.		Amount of Property.		Amount of Property per Estate.	
	1882.	1838.	1882.	1838.	1882.	1838.
			£	£	£	£
England . . .	45,555	21,900	118,120,961	47,604,755	2,600	2,170
Scotland . . .	5,221	1,272	13,695,314	2,817,260	2,600	2,200
Ireland	4,583	2,196	8,544,579	4,465,240	1,900	2,000
United Kingdom	55,359	25,368	140,360,854	54,887,255	2,500	2,160

Thus, in spite of the enormous increase of property passing at death, amounting to over 150 per cent., which is more than the increase in the income-tax income, the amount of property per estate has not sensibly increased. The increase of the number of estates is more than double, and greater therefore than the increase of population, but the increase of capital per head of the capitalist classes in England only 19 per cent., and in the United Kingdom only 15 per cent. Curiously enough, I may state, it is hardly correct to speak of the capitalist classes as holding this property, as the figures include a small percentage of insolvent estates; but allowing all the property to belong to the capitalist classes, still we have the fact that those classes are themselves increasing. They may be only a minority of the nation, though I think a considerable minority, as 55,000 estates passing in a year represent from 1,500,000 to 2,000,000 persons as possessing property subject to probate duty; and these figures, it must be remembered, do not include real property at all. Still, small or large as the minority may be, the fact we have before us is that in the last fifty years it has been an increasing minority, and a minority increasing at a greater rate than the increase of general population. Wealth, to a certain extent, is more diffused than it was.

If I had been able to obtain more details, it would have been possible to specify the different sizes of estates and the different percentages of increase, from which it would not only have appeared whether the owners of personal property were increasing in number, but whether the very rich were adding to their wealth more than the moderately rich, or *vice versâ*. But it is something to know at least that there are more owners. I trust the Commissioners of Inland Revenue will see their way in their next report to give more details on this very interesting point.[1]

Before passing on I should like to add a caution which may not be necessary in this room, but which may be needed outside. All such figures must be taken with a good deal of qualification, owing to variations of detail in the method of levying the duty at different times, variations in the character of the administration, and the like causes. I notice, for instance, an unusually remarkable increase both in the number of owners and amount of property passing in Scotland; this last fact, I believe, having already given rise to the statement that there has been something unexampled in the increase of personal property in Scotland. The explanation appears to be, however, that the increase of property in Scotland is, to some extent, only apparent, being due partly, for instance, to the fact that by Scotch

[1] It appears that the increase in the number of probates for less than £1,000 is from 18,490 to 41,278, or about 120 per cent., the average value per probate being much the same; while the increase of the number of probates for more than £1,000 is from 6,878 to 12,629, or over 80 per cent., and the average value per probate has increased from £7,150 to £9,200.

law mortgages are real property, whereas in England they are personal property, so that it was necessary, in the course of administering the tax, to pass a special law enabling the Commissioners of Inland Revenue to bring Scotch mortgages into the category of personal property.[1] This is only one illustration of the caution with which such figures must be used. Taking them in the lump, and not pressing comparisons between the three divisions of the United Kingdom, or any other points of detail which might be dangerous, we appear to be safe in the main conclusion that the number of owners of personal property liable to probate duty has increased in the last fifty years more than the increase of population, and that on the average these owners are only about 15 per cent. richer than they were, while the individual income of the working classes has increased from 50 to 100 per cent.

The next piece of statistics I have to refer to is the number of separate assessments in that part of Schedule D known as Part I., viz., Trades and Professions, which excludes public companies and their sources of income, where there is no reason to believe that the number of separate assessments corresponds in any way to the number of individual incomes. Even in Part I. there can be no exact correspondence, as partnerships make only one return; but in comparing distant periods, it seems not unfair to assume that the increase or decrease of assessments would correspond to the increase or decrease of individual incomes. This must be the case, unless we assume that in the interval material differences were likely to arise from the changes in the number of partnerships to which individuals belonged, or from partnerships as a rule comprising a greater or less number of individuals. Using the figures with all these qualifications, we get the following comparison:

[1] See "Special Report of Commissioners of Inland Revenue," 1870, vol. i., p. 99. The law on this and other points was altered by 23 & 24 Vict. cap. 80.

Number of Persons at different Amounts of Income charged under Schedule D in 1843 and 1879-80 compared [in England].[1]

	1843.	1879-80.
£ 150 and under £ 200	39,366	130,101
200 " 300	28,370	88,445
300 " 400	13,429	39,896
400 " 500	6,781	16,501
500 " 600	4,780	11,317
600 " 700	2,672	6,894
700 " 800	1,874	4,054
800 " 900	1,442	3,595
900 " 1,000	894	1,396
1,000 " 2,000	4,228	10,352
2,000 " 3,000	1,235	3,131
3,000 " 4,000	526	1,430
4,000 " 5,000	339	758
5,000 " 10,000	493	1,439
10,000 " 50,000	200	785
50,000 and upwards	8	68
Total	106,637	320,162

Here the increase in all classes, from the lowest to the highest, is between two and three times, or rather more than three times, with the exception of the highest class of all, where the numbers, however, are quite inconsiderable. Again a proof, I think, of the greater diffusion of wealth so far as the assessment of income to income tax under Schedule D may be taken as a sign of the person assessed having wealth of some kind, which I fear is not always the case. If the owners of this income, at least of the smaller incomes, are to be considered as not among the capitalists, but among the working classes—a very arguable proposition—then the increase of the number of incomes from £150 up to say £1,000 a year is a sign of the increased earnings of working classes, which are not usually thought of by that name. The increase in this instance is out of all proportion to the increase of population.

[1] The figures for 1843 cannot be given for either Scotland or Ireland.

In giving these figures I have omitted the incomes under £150. There is quite a want of satisfactory data for any comparison, I think, except as regards incomes actually subject to assessment, and the data at the beginning of the period are specially incomplete.

Whichever way we look at the figures, therefore, we have this result, that while the increase of personal property per head of the capitalist class, according to the probate returns, is comparatively small, being only about 15 per cent., yet there is an increase of the number of people receiving good incomes from trades and professions out of all proportion to the increase of population. We cannot but infer from this that the number of the moderately rich is increasing, and that there is little foundation for the assertion that the rich are becoming richer. All the facts agree. The working classes have had large additions to their means; capital has increased in about equal ratio; but the increase of capital per head of the capitalist classes is by no means so great as the increase of working-class incomes.

I should wish further to point out, however, that it is a mistake to speak of the income in the various schedules to the income tax as the income of a few, or exclusively of classes which can be called capitalist or rich. A suspicion of this has already been raised by the facts as to trades and professions. Let me just mention this one little fact in addition. Out of £190,000,000 assessed under Schedule A in 1881-82, the sum of £11,359,000 was exempted from duty as being the income of people whose whole income from all sources was under £150 a year. If we could get at the fact as to how the shares of public companies are held, and as to the immense variety of interests in lands and houses, we should have ample confirmation of what has already appeared from the probate duty figures, that there is a huge minority interested in property in the United Kingdom, great numbers of whom would not be spoken of as the capitalist classes.

To test the question as to whether there has been

any disproportionate increase of capital, and of the income from it, in yet another way, I have endeavoured to make an analysis of the income tax returns themselves, distinguishing in them what appears to be the income of idle capital from income which is derived not so much from the capital itself as from the labour bestowed in using the capital. Only the roughest estimate can be made, and the data, when we go back to 1843, are even more incomplete than they are now; but I have endeavoured as far as possible to give everything to capital that ought to be given, and not to err on the side of assigning it too small a share. The whole of Schedule A is thus assigned to capital, although it is well known that not even in Schedule A is the income obtained without exertion and care, and some risk of loss, which are entitled to remuneration. In Schedule D also I have allowed that all the income from public companies and foreign investments is from idle capital, although here the vigilance necessary, and the risk attendant on the business, are really most serious, and part of the so-called profit is not really interest on idle capital at all, but strictly the remuneration of labour. I have also rather exaggerated than depreciated the estimate for capital employed in trades and professions, my estimate being rather more than that of Mr. Dudley Baxter in his famous paper on the National Income. With these explanations I submit the accompanying estimate of the share of capital in the income-tax income at different dates (see p. 416).

This estimate may be summarized as follows:

Summary of Analysis of Income-Tax Income in undermentioned Years.

[In millions of pounds.]

Year.	From Capital.	From Salaries, etc.	Total.
	£	£	£
1843	$188\frac{1}{2}$	$93\frac{1}{2}$	282
1862	$252\frac{1}{2}$	$107\frac{1}{2}$	360
1881	407	177	584

Analysis of the Income Tax Returns for the undermentioned Years, showing the Estimated Income from Capital on the one side, and the Estimated Income from Wages of Superintendence and Salaries on the other side.

[In millions of pounds, 000,000's omitted, *i.e.*, 10=£10,000,000.]

	1881.		1862.		1843.	
	From Capital.	From Salaries, etc.	From Capital.	From Salaries, etc.	From Capital.	From Salaries, etc.
Schedule A—						
Land, tithes, etc., exclusive of houses . .	70,	nil	60,	nil	57,	nil
Messuages, etc. .	117,	nil	62,	nil	41,	nil
Schedule B—						
Occupation of land	25,[1]	44,	22½,	38½,	20,	36,
Schedule C . . .	40,	nil	29,	nil	29,	nil
„ D (Part I.)	64,[2]	100,[2]	32,	49,	29½,	46½,
„ „ („ II.)	91,	nil	47,	nil	12,	nil
„ E . . .	nil	33,	nil	20,	nil	11,
	407,	177,	252½,	107½,	188½,	93½,

NOTE.—In the estimate for 1843 the figures assigned to Schedule A are only those of lands and tithes and houses to correspond with the existing Schedule A: and the figures of Schedule D include mines, quarries, railways, etc., now in Schedule D. An estimate is also made of the totals for Ireland, based on the returns of 1834, the total gross income under all the schedules thus estimated being about 30 million pounds.

---

[1] Interest on 500 millions of capital in 1881 at 5 per cent. In my paper on accumulations of capital, I estimated agricultural capital at a larger sum than this; but since then there has been some loss of agricultural capital, and if a larger sum were taken, the rate of interest used in the calculation for the present purpose should be less.

[2] Estimating that the income here is worth four years' purchase, and that it may be capitalized at that rate; and then allowing that this capital earns 10 per cent., the rest being wages of superintendence or salaries.

Thus a very large part of the increase of the income-tax income in the last forty years is not an increase of the income from capital at all in any proper sense of the word. On the contrary, the increase in the income from capital is only about two-thirds of the total increase. This increase is, moreover, at a less rate than the increase of the capital itself, as appearing from the Probate Duty returns,[1] a point which deserves special notice. The conclusion therefore is, that the working classes have not been losing in the last fifty years through the fruits of their labour being increasingly appropriated to capital. On the contrary, the income from capital has at least no more than kept pace with the increase of capital itself, while the increase of capital per head, as we have seen, is very little; so that it may be doubted whether the income of the individual capitalist from capital has on the average increased at all. If the return to capital had doubled, as the wages of the working classes appear to have doubled, the aggregate income of the capitalist classes returned to the income tax would now be 800 instead of 400 millions. In other words, it would not be far short of the mark to say that almost the whole of the great material improvement of the last fifty years has gone to the masses. The share of capital is a very small one. And what has not gone to the workmen, so called, has gone to remunerate people who are really workmen also, the persons whose incomes are returned under Schedule D as from "Trades and Professions." The capitalist as such gets a low interest for his money, and the aggregate return to capital is not a third part of the aggregate income of the country, which may be put at not less than 1,200 millions, and is, I should estimate, not much more than a fourth part.

It will be interesting, I think, to present these conclusions in the form of an account. We have not, as I have already said, an exact statement of aggregate

[1] These returns, however, it should always be remembered, do not include real property.

earnings, either at the beginning or at the end of the period; but assuming the aggregate income of the people as about 1,200 millions now, and that the wages of working men are, per head, twice what they were, the aggregates in 1843 and at the present time would compare as follows:

Progress of National Income.

[In millions of pounds.]

	Income in 1843.	Income at Present Time.	Increase.	
			Amount.	Per Cent.
	£	£	£	
Capitalist classes from capital	190	400	210	110
Working income in income-tax returns	90	180	90	100
Working income not in income-tax returns	235	620	385	160
	515	1,200	685	130

Progress of National Capital Paying Probate Duty.

	1838.	Present Time.	Increase.	
			Amount.	Per Cent.
	£	£	£	
Amount of capital	55 mlns.	140 mlns.	85 mlns.	155
,, per estate	2,200	2,500	300	14

NOTE.—Increase of working income per head 100 per cent.

From this it appears that the increase of what is known as working-class income in the aggregate is greater than that of any other class, being 160 per cent., while the return to capital and the return to what are called the capitalist classes, whether it is from capital proper or, as I maintain, a return only in the nature of wages, has only increased about 100 per cent., although capital itself has increased over 150 per cent. At the same time the capitalist classes themselves have greatly increased in number, so that the amount of capital possessed among them per head has only increased 15 per cent., notwithstanding the great increase in capital itself, and the average income per head can have hardly increased at all. On the other hand, as the masses of the nation, taking the United Kingdom altogether, have only increased about 30 per cent. since 1843, when these income tax figures begin, while their aggregate incomes have increased 160 per cent., it is explained how these incomes have gained, individually, about 100 per cent. as against hardly any increase at all in the incomes of what are called the capitalist classes, on the average. Thus the rich have become more numerous, but not richer individually; the "poor" are, to some smaller extent, fewer; and those who remain "poor" are, individually, twice as well off on the average as they were fifty years ago. The "poor" have thus had almost all the benefit of the great material advance of the last fifty years.

We may now conclude this long inquiry. It has been shown directly, I believe, that, while the individual incomes of the working classes have largely increased, the prices of the main articles of their consumption have rather declined; and the inference as to their being much better off which would be drawn from these facts is fully supported by statistics showing a decline in the rate of mortality, an increase of the consumption of articles in general use, an improvement in general education, a diminution of crime and pauperism, a vast increase of the number of depositors in savings banks, and other evidences of general well-being.

Finally, the increase of the return to capital has not been in any way in proportion, the yield on the same amount of capital being less than it was, and the capital itself being more diffused, while the remuneration of labour has enormously increased. The facts are what we should have expected from the conditions of production in recent years. Inventions having been multiplied, and production having been increasingly efficient, while capital has been accumulated rapidly, it is the wage receivers who must have the benefit. The competition of capital keeps profits down to the lowest point, and workmen consequently get for themselves nearly the whole product of the aggregate industry of the country. It is interesting, nevertheless, to find that the facts correspond with what theory should lead us to anticipate.

The moral is a very obvious one. Whatever may be said as to the ideal perfection or imperfection of the present economic *régime*, the fact of so great an advance having been possible for the masses of the people in the last half-century is encouraging. It is something to know that whether a better *régime* is conceivable or not, human nature being what it is now (and I am one of those who think that the *régime* is the best, the general result of a vast community living as the British nation does, with all the means of healthy life and civilization at command, being little short of a marvel if we only consider for a moment what vices of anarchy and misrule in society have had to be rooted out to make this marvel); still, whether best or not, it is something to know that vast improvement has been possible with this *régime*. Surely the lesson is that the nation ought to go on improving on the same lines, relaxing none of the efforts which have been so successful. Steady progress in the direction maintained for the last fifty years must soon make the English people vastly superior to what they are now.

I should like to add just one or two remarks bearing on questions of the moment, and as to the desirability or possibility of a change of *régime* now so much discussed, which the figures I have brought before you suggest. One is, that apart from all objections of principle to schemes of confiscating capital,—land nationalization, or collectivism, or whatever they may be called,

—the masses could not hope to have much to divide by any such schemes. Taking the income from capital at 400 million pounds, we must not suppose that the whole of that would be divisible among the masses if capital were confiscated. What the capitalist classes spend is a very different thing from what they make. The annual savings of the country now exceed 200 million pounds, being made as a rule, though not exclusively, by the capitalist classes. If then the 400 million pounds were to be confiscated, one of two things would happen: either the savings would not be made, in which case the condition of the working classes would soon deteriorate, for everything depends upon the steady increase of capital; or the savings would be made, in which case the spending power of the masses would not be so very much increased. The difference would be that they would be owners of the capital, but the income would itself remain untouched. The system under which large capitals are in a few hands may, in fact, have its good side in this, that the Jay Goulds, Vanderbilts, and Rothschilds cannot spend their income. The consequent accumulation of capital is, in fact, one of the reasons why the reward for labour is so high, and the masses get nearly all the benefit of the great increase of production. The other remark I have to make is that if the object really aimed at by those who talk of land nationalization and the like is carried out, the people who will suffer are those who receive large wages. To effect what they intend, the agitators must not merely seize on the property of a few, they must confiscate what are as much earnings as those of a mechanic or a labourer, and the wages of the most skilled mechanics and artisans themselves. The agitation is, in fact, to level down, to diminish the reward of labourers who receive a large wage because they can do the work the community requires, the proof being that in a market without favour they get the wage, and to increase the reward of other labourers beyond what in the same free market the community would freely give them. Whether the production would be continued at all if there were any success in these attempts, common sense will tell us. Those who have done some hard work in the world will, I am sure, agree with me that it is only done by virtue of the most powerful stimulants. Take away the rewards, and even the best would probably not give themselves up to doing what the community wants and now pays them for doing, but they would give themselves up either to idleness or to doing something else. The war of the land nationalizer and Socialist is then not so much with the capitalist as with the workman, and the importance of this fact should not be lost sight of.

[NOTE.—This essay is reprinted as it stood originally, for the general reasons stated in the preface to the present volumes, though it is specially tempting to give later figures in this case, prices having become lower and wages having risen in the last twenty years. I would refer all interested to the recent Board of Trade Blue-book (C. d. 1761) mentioned in notes to previous essays, and to the Report on Wholesale and Retail Prices, No. 321, Sess. 1903.]

XI.

FOREIGN COMPETITION.[1]

A PHENOMENON is being repeated at the present time which is often witnessed in times of depression of trade. The cry is raised that trade is being destroyed by foreign competition. Every bale of goods or ton of ironwork which comes from a foreign country into England "at a lower price than the same articles could be produced at home" is made the text of a discourse on the decline of English manufacturing. The multiplication abroad of manufactories of those articles which we produce for export is made the text of similar discourses. "See," it is said, "how some nations which were formerly our customers are manufacturing for themselves, and how other nations are going to the shops of rivals like the United States, France, and Germany, who are gaining upon us every day in the race." There is an essential fallacy in the whole argument, for the alleged facts, even if they were true, would not prove that foreign competition causes our manufacturing industry to decline, although it may be coincident with that decline. It is notorious, indeed, that everywhere abroad, and not least in Germany and the United States, manufacturing industry is depressed as much as it is here, so that our agitators really mean that English manufacturing causes that of Germany to fall off and German manufacturing that of England, whereas the natural inference would be that a common effect must have a common cause, and that it is something else than competition which makes foreign and

[1] Written in 1877.

English manufacturing be simultaneously depressed. But, apart from direct arguments as to the causes of the present depression in trade, we think it may be useful to inquire into the meaning of the words so freely employed. What would happen if English manufacturing were "declining" to any material extent and foreign manufacturing beginning to take its place? What would be the loss of income or transfer of labour and capital involved? If people were accustomed to measure their words in such discussions, or realize to themselves what they mean, a good deal of loose talk would be prevented, and a juster and more practical view formed of the economic incidents of the hour.

To take first the question of our foreign export trade. How much of the national income is really derived from that trade? To judge by the common language of the agitators we refer to, England would be nothing without its exports to foreign nations. Almost our whole trade and industry, it seems to be thought, would be at an end; an extensive emigration would be necessary; we should be a ruined nation. But, apart from questions as to the mutual conveniences of our exchanges with foreign nations, from whom we get much we cannot produce at home, and to whom we also send much they cannot produce at all, and much they cannot produce so easily as what they send us—conveniences which are such that the total extinction of our foreign export trade is inconceivable—we believe it may be affirmed that the possible loss of income from the entire loss of our foreign trade would be a most measurable and by no means a fatal injury. It may be calculated that the earnings of the people of the United Kingdom approximate at the present moment £1,200,000,000 sterling a year, if they do not exceed that amount. Mr. Dudley Baxter, in his well-known book on the "National Income," published in 1868, computed that in the previous year the aggregate income of the people was £814,000,000, and there is ample reason to believe both that he was fairly accurate and careful in his calculations, into which the element of conjecture enters comparatively little, and that since he wrote the numbers, wealth, and resources of the people have increased at a wonderful rate. In these estimates there is one central fact about which there is no dispute—the amount of income assessed to income tax; and we know that income has increased over 40 per cent. in the last ten years of which we have an account. In the year ended the 5th of April, 1865, the gross amount of annual value assessed to income tax was £396,000,000 sterling, and in 1875 the corresponding amount was £571,000,000. This is an increase of very nearly 44 per cent. in ten years, and shows with what rapid strides the country has progressed. In 1865, again, the amount charged to income tax, as distinguished from the gross annual value, was £349,000,000 sterling, while in 1875 the corresponding figure is £498,000,000 sterling, the increase being at the rate of 43 per cent. Taking into account the increase of exemptions and abatements from the income tax, which has been a characteristic of our recent finance, we can well believe that the real increase of net income must have been more, and must have exceeded the proportionate increase of gross income. That the net incomes chargeable to income tax, if the exemptions were the same now as in 1865, would considerably exceed £500,000,000 there can be no doubt; and altogether, allowing as well for the incomes under Schedule D which escape assessment through incomplete returns, we can hardly err in placing the net incomes of the income-tax-paying classes at somewhere about £600,000,000 sterling. But the income thus arrived at does not include the large incomes in the aggregate of the wages-receiving classes, or the incomes of many in the upper and middle classes which are under the income-tax limits; and this remainder can hardly be taken as less than another £600,000,000. What with the increase of population and the great rise of wages which has occurred since 1867, there is no reason to believe that the proportion of the aggregate income of the country to what pays income tax is less now than it was when Mr. Dudley Baxter wrote, and this proportion would give about £1,200,000,000 sterling as the aggregate. There is thus some sanction beyond mere conjecture for putting the aggregate income of the country at the latter figure.

Now, to come to our present question—How much of this income is derived from our foreign exports? We perceive at once that instead of these exports being our main business, it may be doubted if they contribute more than an eighth or so much to the total. Last year, which we take to be a more normal year for prices than such years as 1872 and 1873, when our exports seemed so much augmented, we exported goods of British and Irish produce to the value of £200,000,000 sterling. But this amount was not in reality exclusively British and Irish produce. It included the value of an immense amount of raw material imported from abroad which we had worked up—where we had added to, but had not created the whole value. It included, for instance, in cotton yarn and piece goods, about 970,000,000 lbs. of raw material, worth, say, £25,000,000 at the average price of the cotton imported in the same year. It included, again, in woollen yarn and manufactures, about 140,000,000 lbs. or more of raw material, worth, say, £10,000,000 at the average price of the wool imported in the same year. Altogether, deducting for the value of raw material in these exports which had previously been obtained from abroad, we doubt if we can estimate the probable maximum amount of the net income directly derived from our exports as more than £140,000,000. In addition, there are, no doubt, indirect benefits in the connection between our trade and shipping interests which are difficult to estimate, but no large sum important for such an inquiry as the present would fall to be added in that way to the amount. Comparing, then, £140,000,000 with £1,200,000,000, it is at once seen that the labour and capital engaged in foreign manufacturing is only a fraction of our whole industry. England might still be a great and prosperous country —not so great and prosperous as it is now, but still great and prosperous—even if the whole of that fraction were to be at once swept away. But even if we were to lose our entire foreign custom, the whole of the income from what we send to foreigners would not be lost. The machines and tools used in manufacturing and the labourers would remain, and some use could be made of them. Only the difference between what would be earned in that use and what we now get from abroad in return would be lost. The precise net loss would be difficult to state; but it would be something much less than £140,000,000, and perhaps not a tenth or a twelfth of the aggregate income of £1,200,000,000. It is evident that no such loss would be fatal to a great country. It would make us no worse, probably, than the reimposition of the taxes which have been remitted during the last twenty years, and would be a less calamity, in proportion, than the economic losses of the Franco-German War to France, which was much less fitted beforehand than we are to stand such a calamity. Probably it could all be made up by the community sacrificing only a portion of that additional leisure which it has acquired during the last thirty years, in addition to the increase of money wages and profits.

But there is, of course, no question of losing our whole foreign custom at one fell swoop. What people have in their minds is that we are threatened with the loss of a considerable part of our export trade. They should be asked, then, to define what they mean by a considerable part. Is it a half, a fourth, a fifth, or what? Of course, as we reduce the amount, the ridiculous smallness of it, compared with our whole industry, becomes apparent. The loss of a fifth of our foreign export trade would only be the loss at most of a fortieth or fiftieth part of our whole income, which a very little additional industry would make good. Looking at the matter in this way, besides, there is one conspicuous illustration that a considerable breach in the foreign trade is not fatal to our whole industry. In 1863-65 England suffered from the cotton famine, which came upon us quite suddenly. But, saddening and distressing as the results of that famine were, the distress was merely local; the country, as a whole, prospered, and probably the distress in Lancashire would have been less but for the common expectation of a more rapid turning of the tide than what actually occurred. The diversion of labour and capital to other pursuits was retarded by the belief that the loss of trade was only to be temporary.

On the other hand, while our foreign export trade is small in proportion to our gigantic industry as a whole, it is large enough to make it a very difficult matter for any foreign competitors to displace us materially. The capital sunk in producing annually £140,000,000 of value must be immense—at least several hundred millions. But even £100,000,000 would not be easily found in the whole civilized world outside of England for the erection of new works to compete with our manufactories. The annual accumulations of France are computed at £60,000,000 a year, and of Germany at £40,000,000; and the accumulations of the United States must also be very large. But the accumulations are not free savings, to be directed into any enterprise. They are largely used in building houses, in furniture, in improving land under the direction of its owners, and in other ways, so that it is only a small surplus which is annually available for new enterprise. We see, therefore, what an effort of imagination is required when the displacement of England as a manufacturer for export is talked of. Even if she could be displaced at once from her whole export trade, the loss would be much less than is sometimes thought; but the amount of capital required to displace us even partially is so great that it must take many years for our competitors to accumulate any such amount. The displacement of labour, we believe, would be an equally serious matter; for workmen are not made in a day, and many more skilled workmen must be trained abroad if they are to undertake any serious part of the labour which is now performed in England. There is even a more serious difficulty, we believe, in the way of quickly-increased foreign competition. It is the complexity, variety, and minute subdivision necessary in great manufacturing enterprise which make displacement almost inconceivable. No workshop is complete in itself; we doubt if any manufacturing town is complete; England is one vast workshop, fitted with complete appliances of every sort, with a capability of turning on great force in any given direction, unexampled and not even approached elsewhere. But, apart from this complexity, we are content to call attention to the mere amount of the capital involved in any question of a material transfer of our foreign export trade.

We come, then, to the question of our home trade. Foreign nations, we are told, are not only going to do without us and cease altogether to be our customers; they are to send goods here and cut up our home manufactures. But our remarks in the last paragraph apply with tenfold force to the question of such a foreign invasion. If foreign nations are likely to find it difficult to procure capital which would enable them to take away a material part of our foreign export trade, how are they to find capital to make any impression on our vast manufacturing industry for home consumers? Here it is a question, not of hundreds, but of thousands of millions of capital, and of a transfer of labour which fairly takes one's breath away. In this respect foreign nations would have to begin at the beginning. Of our whole imports in 1876, amounting to £375,000,000, little more than £40,000,000 were of manufactured goods, and these included a great deal which we could hardly make for ourselves at home, even if our workmen were not otherwise employed; while the manufacturing in them, representing wages and profits—*i.e.*, exclusive of the value of raw material, which we should have to buy in any case—would only be a part of the total.[1] How are foreign nations to add seriously to this relatively insignificant sum, at least within any reasonable limit of time to which we can look forward? If they are to displace any considerable part of our home trade, the work must be one of generations, and it is not to be lightly associated with a few isolated augmentations of imports of Belgian iron or American cotton goods.

We trust we shall not be misunderstood. We have not a word to say against efforts to keep the public informed of the prices of foreign manufactures and the nature of their competition with our own manufactures at points where there is competition. There is enough indolence and routine and mismanagement even in English manufacturing to make it desirable in every way to have the stimulus of foreign competition applied. But when the decline and ruin of our whole manufacturing, or even any material part of it, are talked of, people should know what they mean. If they did know, they would not, as sensible men, confuse their minds with notions which are just as sensible and relevant, and no more, as the familiar illustration of Tenterden Steeple being the cause of Goodwin Sands. Harm is done in the end by all such confusion of ideas, including the harm in the present case of distracting attention from the obvious causes of the depression of our foreign trade.—[1877.]

[1] There are larger figures now (1903), but the so-called manufactures imported from abroad are still for the most part raw materials of our own industries, which have increased enormously since 1877, and are still increasing.

XII.

THE ECONOMIC VALUE OF IRELAND TO GREAT BRITAIN.[1]

THAT one of the roots of mischief in Ireland is economic everybody agrees. The curse of Ireland is its poverty. The hunger for land which is so unintelligible to English feeling is at the bottom of outrages of every kind, and is played upon by political agitators. It is not, however, generally understood how the weakness of Ireland affects the whole aspect of the Irish political difficulty.

I have thought it worth while, therefore, when the notion of splitting partnership is in the air, to bring together some notes as to the economic position of Ireland, relatively to Great Britain, from the point of view of a statesman in Great Britain looking at the suggested proposal to part company as a mere matter of business—as he would look, in fact, at the analogous suggestion of union with a State which was seeking partnership with us. The statesman, of course, must weigh moral and political considerations as well as economic, and the various questions involved are necessarily intermixed; but it is expedient nevertheless to separate the economic from the other elements. We shall know better what we are doing or going to do in Ireland if the business loss or gain is clear.

The first point to notice in such a question is population. The people of Ireland are rather less than five millions, as compared with nearly thirty-one and a half millions in Great Britain. If Great Britain were to be

[1] From the "Nineteenth Century" of March, 1886.

offered a partnership of about five millions of people of equal character and resources to those of Great Britain themselves, the addition to the strength of the empire would be as five to thirty-one and a half. The population thus to be added would constitute in the new State somewhat less than a seventh of the whole. Equally the deduction of a people of this magnitude from the existing Union would be the deduction of rather less than a seventh.

A change of this description would be a very considerable one. But, apart from what it might lead to, it cannot be described as in itself formidable. With the loss of a seventh, the United Kingdom would be as great a Power as it was in 1870, and in fact a much greater Power, because the remaining six-sevenths are richer and stronger individually than the population of 1870. Their condition in the interval has enormously improved.

Of course, if by any arrangement the splitting of partnership were only to be partial—if we retained Ulster, while permitting to the rest of Ireland more or less complete separation—the deduction from the United Kingdom would be materially less. The disaffected parts of Ireland are not more than three-fifths of the whole, or three millions. In losing the three millions we should only lose one-twelfth of our numbers, or less than the growth of our population every decade.

Looking at the matter historically, we must come to the conclusion that the problem of disaffection in Ireland is mitigated in its intensity by the changes of population which have occurred. Down to about 1845, from the beginning of the century, the people of Ireland were about half those of Great Britain—about a third of the whole population of the United Kingdom. The population of the disaffected parts of Ireland was also nearly three-fourths of the whole of that country, and consequently about a fourth of that of the United Kingdom. The change from such proportions to those of about one-seventh for the proportion of Ireland itself to the United Kingdom, and one-twelfth for the proportion of the disaffected parts of Ireland, requires no comment. Disaffection in Ireland is obviously not what it was in relation to the United Kingdom as a whole.

I have called attention to this point for some years past as necessarily altering our entire conception of the Irish difficulty. It is dealt with in "Essays in Finance" (first series), in an essay on the "Taxation and Representation of Ireland," which was first published in 1876,[1] and I have introduced the same topic in two essays in the second series of "Essays in Finance"—viz., an essay on the Utility of Common Statistics,[2] and another on Some General Uses of Statistical Knowledge. I doubt if the full force of this consideration is properly appreciated even yet. Relatively Ireland is still losing ground most rapidly, not so much because Irish population diminishes, as because that of Great Britain increases. We grow a new people in Great Britain equal to the whole disaffected part of Ireland at the present time every ten years. In a few generations, at this rate, Ireland must become relatively to Great Britain very little more than a somewhat larger Isle of Man or Channel Islands. To let Ireland split partnership would differ in no way in kind, and comparatively little in degree, as far as business is concerned, from letting the Isle of Man remain a separate State.

The second point is even more important. The people of Ireland are not equal in industrial character and resources to those of the United Kingdom. They are very far from being equal. Great Britain, in adding to itself an Ireland, would add a community having only a twentieth part of the income of the United Kingdom; the United Kingdom, in losing an Ireland, would only lose a small percentage of its strength.

It is very difficult, of course, dealing with questions of the aggregate income of different communities; but,

[1] See *supra*, p. 277. [2] See *postea*, vol. ii., p. 1.

practically, we need have little doubt of the proportions stated.

In the assessments to the income tax the proportion of Ireland is as 1 to 17—viz., United Kingdom (including Ireland), £629,000,000 sterling; Ireland, £37,000,000 sterling. This is more than five per cent., but not very much more. And there is reason to believe that Ireland is more strictly valued than Great Britain, and that it is over-valued.

At any rate, when it comes to be a question of the whole aggregate income of the different communities, there can be little doubt that other sources of income, outside of the income tax, are larger relatively in Great Britain than in Ireland. In dealing with the subject lately in "Further Notes on the Progress of the Working Classes," I put down the whole income of Great Britain as about £1,200,000,000, and that of Ireland alone as just over £70,000,000. But I have a strong feeling that in these figures, which were based very much on what Mr. Dudley Baxter and Mr. Leone Levi had done, I gave too little to Great Britain, if not too much to Ireland.

With regard to Ireland specially, it is easy to see that the income cannot be very large. The chief industry is agriculture, which employs in round figures about sixty per cent. of the population. Out of 1,290,000 males of twenty years and upwards, with specified occupations, according to the census of 1881, no fewer than 757,000 were engaged in agriculture, which is just under sixty per cent. Among the remainder, there were no fewer than 115,000 called "mechanics or labourers," among whom, I suspect, would be many partly or largely engaged in agriculture. The proportion of sixty per cent. may, however, be taken. In other words, three millions of people in Ireland depend on agriculture directly—the breadwinners of the family are engaged in that occupation. And this means that, all told, the average income of these three millions, including those who receive rent, as well as farmers and labourers, is not more than about £13 or £14 per head. The gross produce of the crops of Ireland, according to the latest returns, is about £33,000,000 only, from five million acres, of which about £10,000,000 are from cereal crops, £10,000,000 from potatoes, and the remainder mainly from hay and green crops, which latter, of course, along with a large part of the cereal crops themselves, are not in their final form when thus valued. Making a deduction from the £33,000,000 on this account, and making an estimate for the value of cattle, sheep, and pigs sold, and for dairy produce, the gross produce of pasture-land being, of course, much less than that of cereal or other crops, it seems impossible to arrive at a larger figure than about forty to forty-five millions as the value of the agricultural produce of Ireland, deducting seed, manures, and expenses of that nature. On this forty to forty-five millions, three millions of people have to live, which gives about £14 per head; or less than £60 for a family of four persons.

Deducting the total rent of just under £10,000,000 according to the income-tax returns, with practically no deduction from the numbers of people on the other side, we should leave about £11 per head only for farmers and labourers and their families. And if we take the rent at a less figure, as I believe we ought to do—say at about eight millions sterling only—we should still make the income of the Irish agricultural classes, farmers and labourers together, only £12 per head; or under £50 for a family of four persons. Comparing this with England, it would appear that the tenant-farmers and labourers of Ireland are not so well off as the average of the English agricultural labourers, which implies that very many must be far below that level.

On this basis, also, we may calculate the aggregate income of Ireland. Assuming the income per head of the rest of the people of Ireland to be one-half equal to the income per head of those engaged in agriculture, and the other half fifty per cent. more, we should still arrive at a figure of less than eighty millions only as the total aggregate income of the whole people of Ireland.

In this way, according to estimates of income generally, the proportion of Ireland to the United Kingdom also comes out as one to seventeen, the same as from income-tax assessments only.

Another test of resources would be the relative capital of Great Britain and Ireland. I have to refer to Irish capital later on, and estimate it at £400,000,000, or thereabouts. There can be no exact estimates in such matters; but the total capital of the United Kingdom ten years ago I ventured to estimate at not less than £8,500,000,000, and, calculating on a similar basis now, it cannot be less, I think, than £9,600,000,000. In other words, Irish capital is only a twenty-fourth part of that of the United Kingdom. And, whatever doubt there may be about the figures, which are necessarily very wide, and which assume that a nation can be valued as a going business concern, it is at least certain that no emendation would sensibly alter the proportions. An addition to Irish capital and a deduction from English capital that would both be large would leave the proportions much the same.

It is easy to see, then, how little the gain of an Ireland would add to the resources of Great Britain, or the loss of it would deduct from those resources. The taxable income of Ireland must bear a still smaller proportion to the taxable income of Great Britain than does its gross income or capital to the gross income or capital of Great Britain. The taxable income is the income remaining after allowance for the minimum necessary to maintain a population upon a given standard of living. In this sense, giving the people of Great Britain an average of £12 per head as the minimum, they have a taxable income of about £800,000,000 sterling annually.[1] On the same scale, five millions of people in Ireland would absorb sixty out of, say,

[1] Thirty-two millions, multiplied by 12, is 384 millions, deducting which from 1,200 millions leaves rather more than 800 millions.

seventy-five millions gross income, leaving a taxable income of £15,000,000 sterling only. Even allowing that the standard in Ireland is necessarily lower, the taxable income would not be much increased. As a partner with so rich a State as Great Britain, Ireland must therefore be considered strictly as entirely insignificant. It hardly counts one way or the other.

Of course the practical taxable income of Great Britain is not so much as £800,000,000. The State could not levy £800,000,000, or anything like that sum, without reducing many classes in the scale of living. There would be a revolution if any such levy were attempted. But, limiting the £800,000,000 as we may, there would still be a vast amount to compare with the taxable income of Ireland, where the practical taxable income must be very small indeed.

Here again, as with regard to population itself, it is quite true that Ireland is becoming less and less important to Great Britain. At the beginning of the century there was some excuse for an expectation that was never fulfilled—that Ireland would participate in the burdens of the United Kingdom to the extent of two-seventeenths. With a third of the population of the United Kingdom, Ireland, it was calculated, might contribute rather less than one-eighth to joint objects. This was allowing that even then Ireland, man for man, was not half as rich as Great Britain, which seemed an extreme calculation, as both countries were then mainly agricultural, and Ireland had quite a third of the cultivated area. Now there is no question that Ireland's resources in proportion, instead of being two to seventeen, are less than one to seventeen. Its numbers are relatively to Great Britain not half what they were, and the distance between the average incomes per head of the two communities continues very great. The taxable income and capital of Great Britain have increased enormously, and those of Ireland hardly at all.

To put the matter shortly, and in the roundest

figures—there can, of course, be no exact figures of income and capital—Ireland in population has sunk from one-third to less than one-seventh; in gross income, from two-seventeenths to less than one-seventeenth; in capital, from a proportion that was material to about one-twenty-fourth only; in taxable resources, from a proportion that was also material, being perhaps about one-tenth, to a proportion that is almost inappreciable —the proportion of only one to fifty. In resources, Ireland has no doubt increased absolutely. The Irish people are much better off individually, partly because there are fewer people than there were fifty years ago, but with much the same resources; but as a community in relation to Great Britain there is an immense decline.

The relative decrease of the disaffected part of Ireland only is quite as remarkable. From being about one-tenth of the United Kingdom in resources, it has become about one-fortieth or less. As regards taxable income, the proportion of the whole of Ireland to the United Kingdom being only about one to fifty, that of the disaffected part of Ireland only must be about one to a hundred!

How small the proportion of Ireland is will also be impressed on us more if we consider for a moment the economic relations of Great Britain with other British dependencies. Compared with Ireland, our interests in India, where we have invested over £200,000,000, and in Australia, where we have invested over £100,000,000, are enormous. And our trade with India figures up as £66,000,000 annually, and with Australia as £55,000,000 annually, as compared with a trade of about £40,000,000 with Ireland, imports and exports together. The Indian and Australian trades also give more employment to our shipping in proportion than that of Ireland does. And neither India nor Australia imposes on us any direct charge for government, such as we shall find Ireland does, to constitute a deduction from the profit we derive, as a community, from the connection.

As regards this question of resources, it will be interesting to go farther and to look at the matter a little more closely. Great Britain and Ireland have been in close partnership for over eighty years. How does the account stand as regards government and people? Has Ireland been a help or the reverse?

It is obvious, to begin with, that Ireland has not helped as the framers of the Union expected. According to the Act of Union, Ireland was expected to contribute to the joint expenditure of Great Britain and Ireland in the proportion of two-seventeenths. In point of fact, Ireland could not do so under the strain of the enormous outlay at the beginning of the century. Under that arrangement between 1800 and 1815 Irish debt increased rapidly—viz., from £24,000,000 to £128,000,000—although Irish taxation was enormously increased, viz., from three and a half to nearly seven millions. In 1816, the amalgamation of the exchequers and indiscriminate taxation were recommended, because it was quite impossible for Ireland to bear two-seventeenths of the joint burdens.

Actually at the present moment Ireland is no gain to the exchequer of Great Britain. The facts are as follows: Ireland's gross contributions from Customs, Excise, and Inland Revenue generally are put down in Thom's Almanac as about £7,700,000; but of course no such account shows exactly what Ireland's proper contribution is. Duties are paid in Ireland on spirits consumed in England, and duties are paid in England on tobacco and tea consumed in Ireland. An exact account is impossible. It seems to be believed, however, according to the return No. 36, session 1884, that, after corrections are made on this head, about £6,700,000 represents the contributions of Ireland to imperial purposes, exclusive of Post Office, etc., the contributions of Great Britain being nearly ten times that amount. In other words, Ireland, while constituting only about a twentieth part of the United Kingdom in resources, nevertheless pays a tenth or eleventh of the taxes. Ireland ought to pay about £3,500,000 and it pays nearly £7,000,000. To the extent of the difference Great Britain is better off in the partnership than could have been expected beforehand.

This is only a part of the account. When we look at the other side—viz., the disposal of the taxes—we shall see that Great Britain does not gain so much as would appear from the revenue side only. But I ought to explain in passing that it is not surprising, considering the nature of our imperial taxes, that Ireland should contribute more than its proper share, although the taxes are not merely indiscrimate, but Ireland is really exempted from some of them. The reason is that imperial taxes fall so much on the common luxuries of the poor—on spirits, tobacco, and tea. Nearly the whole cost of the first two articles to the consumer is a tax, and the *ad valorem* tax on tea is also very high. The poor, if they are to have these common luxuries at all, must contribute disproportionately to the exchequer. Ireland as a poor country is disproportionately taxed, although the taxes of the United Kingdom are technically indiscriminate.

Turning to the other side of the account, what we find is that the Imperial Government has, first, to garrison Ireland to a degree unnecessary in Great Britain; and, second, to pay disproportionately for the local government of Ireland. If the home troops were to be stationed in Ireland in proportion to the population, the troops in Ireland would be about 12,000 only; if in proportion to resources, about 5,000 only. Actually Ireland has at least 24,000 troops, sometimes more,[1] an excess on the first basis of 12,000 troops, and on the second basis of nearly 20,000. At £150 per man, which is the cost of the British standing army, we thus spend in Ireland on the first basis £1,800,000 which we might save; and on the second basis nearly £3,000,000.

[1] In 1884 the numbers were 24,400, out of a total of 90,000 at home.

Next, the Imperial Government spends a certain amount of money on the internal administration of different parts of the United Kingdom—the Civil Service expenditure. Altogether it spends in this way the sums shown in the following table (the particulars being extracted from the last finance and revenue accounts):

Statement of Charges on Imperial Revenues for Local Administration in Great Britain and Ireland compared. From the Finance and Revenue Accounts, 1884-85.

[In thousands of pounds—000's omitted.]

	Total.	Great Britain.	Ireland.
	£	£	£
Pensions for judicial services. pp. 52-60 .	127	103	24
Salaries and allowances, pp. 63-65 . . .	84[1]	42	42
Courts of Justice salaries, pp. 66-79 . .	506	392	114
Civil Service, Class I.—Public Works and Buildings (less spent abroad)	1,662	1,457	205
Civil Service, Class II. (Civil Departments)	2,397	2,109[2]	288
" Class III. (Law and Justice)	6,341	4,101	2,239
" Class IV. (Education) . .	5,135	4,368	767
" Class VI. (Non-effective) . .	1,193	1,078	115
Total	17,445	13,650	3,794

In addition there have been numerous grants of loans to Ireland in the last forty years which have never been repaid.

It is easy to see that, on any hypothesis, the Imperial Government spends on Ireland more than its proper share, whether measured by its resources, its population, or its actual contributions to imperial revenues. Out of a sum of £17,500,000 spent out of imperial revenues for the internal administration of Great

[1] Including salary of Lord-Lieutenant and Queen's Colleges. I have only included salaries and allowances special to Great Britain and Ireland.

[2] Ireland gets the benefit of part of this sum.

Britain and Ireland, it obtains very nearly a fourth. The following compares what Ireland would be entitled to on these different hypotheses with what it actually receives out of this sum of £17,500,000:

	—	Sum due to Ireland from Imperial Revenues.	Sum actually received by Ireland.	Excess of actual Receipts.
	Proportion.	£	£	£
Proportion to resources .	$\frac{1}{20}$th	872,000	3,800,000	2,928,000
„ population	$\frac{1}{7}$th	2,492,000	3,800,000	1,308,000
„ contributions	$\frac{1}{10}$th	1,744,000	3,800,000	2,056,000

In any case Ireland gets more than is due to it, assuming in the last two cases that a contribution according to population or on the present scale is just. In these two ways, then, partly through excessive military expenditure, and partly through excessive civil expenditure, Great Britain spends upon Ireland a disproportionate sum. Taking the resources as a measure, the account would balance as follows:

	£	£
Overspent for British troops in Ireland .	3,000,000	
„ local administration . .	2,928,000	
		5,928,000
Deduct excess of receipts from Ireland in proportion to its resources . .		3,200,000
Deficit		2,728,000

The English Government is thus a loser by Ireland to the extent of about £2,750,000 per annum, although it receives from Ireland over £3,000,000 more revenue than Ireland, on any fair computation, ought to pay. If Ireland only paid a fair contribution for imperial purposes, we should be out of pocket by this £3,200,000 more, or nearly £6,000,000. Actually, it is beyond question, we lose as a government nearly £3,000,000, while taxing Ireland over £3,000,000 more than it ought to be taxed.

Of course it may be said that we do not lose by the army expenditure; that the troops being in Ireland are available, to a certain extent, for the miscellaneous purposes of the United Kingdom. Unfortunately, it is beyond question that the troops are not available. The extra 12,000 or 20,000 troops that are in Ireland, beyond what is necessary to garrison it in proportion to Great Britain, are lost to us for imperial purposes. The expenditure is pure waste.

So much for the balance of the account as far as the Government is concerned. The question remains as to the account of the community as a whole.

English capital, it may be said, is invested in Ireland, and there is a large profit to the community, if not to the Government. I am sorry to say I can find little foundation for this impression. There is some profit, but not a large profit.

The whole capital of Ireland must be inconsiderable —probably not over £400,000,000—the principal items being:

	£
Value of land (£160,000,000) and houses (£40,000,000)	200,000,000
Tenants' capital	80,000,000
Railways	36,000,000
Furniture of houses and other movable property	20,000,000
Other capital (say)	60,000,000
Total	400,000,000

What banking capital there is I include in other capital, as part of it at least is no doubt invested by loan or otherwise in agriculture, railways, etc., and it ought not to be counted twice over. The £400,000,000 is probably over the mark.

And most of this capital must be held locally. The trading and farming capital is so held. The banking capital is so held; out of the £400,000,000 of resources of the Irish banks, capital and deposits together, the share owned by English people must be very small, for the deposits are necessarily those of the locality, and Irish bank shares, I know, are held locally. Part of these resources finds its way to London, and is invested in London. Irish railway shares are also, for the most part, held in Ireland. There remains only the real property, which is said to be mortgaged largely to English insurance companies, and so on. But English insurance companies only hold a little over £70,000,000 of mortgages altogether, and I should doubt if a fifth part of these mortgages are in Ireland. The mortgages there, all told, can hardly exceed £50,000,000, of which only a part would be held in England. There are, of course, the landlords who reside in England. *Per contra*, however, residents in Ireland hold English securities, not inconsiderably, I believe, in proportion to the resources of Ireland, and this holding, putting the two communities against each other, is a set-off to Irish securities held in England.

Ireland, as a field for English capital, does not seem, therefore, to count for much. But, if we allow that even a sum equal to a fourth part of the *nominal* agricultural rent of Ireland, which appears to be under £10,000,000, finds its way to England on balance in the shape of mortgage interest, etc., deducting what is received in Ireland on similar account from Great Britain, the English community as a whole, Government and people together, would still have very little out of Ireland. The gain to the community, whatever it is, would be balanced, *pro tanto*, by the deficit on Government account. If Ireland were only to be taxed according to its resources, there would be a very large deficit.

It is quite clear, it may be added, that, as compared with the enormous capital and income from capital which the community of Great Britain enjoys, the share due to the Irish connection, even if the whole nominal rental of Ireland were to be remitted to Great Britain, would be inconsiderable. Our income from capital is over £400,000,000 annually, to which a contribution of £10,000,000 would not be very material. What has been said above as to the superior importance to us of India and Australia has a bearing on this point. There are many parts of the world which are more important, economically, to Great Britain than Ireland is.

Next, it may be said, we gain by the trade of Ireland. Ireland is a good customer of Great Britain, and we get conveniently from Ireland much of what we require. It will follow, however, from what has been said, that, as the income of Ireland altogether is about £75,000,000, only, the trade with Ireland must be limited (1) by the surplus which Ireland can afford to export out of that sum, and (2) by the proportion of that surplus which Ireland can afford to spend on the produce and manufactures of Great Britain.

The total exportable surplus of Ireland cannot be very large. The exports and export value of cattle, sheep, and pigs, valuing them at about the average given by "Thom" for Irish live stock in general in 1884[1] are as follows (average of three years 1881-83):

		Value per head.	
Cattle	630,000	£12	£7,560,000
Sheep	530,000	£2 3s.	£1,220,000
Pigs	450,000	£3	£1,350,000
Total			£10,130,000

And the export of butter and cheese, allowing that the produce available for export from each milch cow is about £4 per head, would not be more than about £6,000,000.

Adding these two sums together, the total agricultural exports of Ireland would be about £16,000,000

[1] Thom's Almanac for 1885, pp. 692-694.

only; of course at lower prices the exports would be less.

In addition, there are the exports of the linen manufacture, the Belfast shipbuilding trade, the spirits and porter of Dublin and Belfast, the produce of Irish fisheries, and other miscellaneous productions, amounting in all, I should say, to about other £5,000,000—total £21,000,000. The calculation is necessarily very rough.

The imports on the other side would more than balance, I think, but they are largely of articles which are not the produce and manufactures of England. Grain of different kinds is a principal item. There are no returns of imports now, but in 1874 they amounted from foreign countries only, principally grain and flour, to £10,000,000. At recent prices the same quantity of imports would of course be of less value.

Ireland in addition takes sugar, tea, and other articles of tropical produce, principally imported from Great Britain, probably to the amount of £5,000,000, giving a much smaller quantity of tea and sugar per head than is consumed in the United Kingdom generally.

Adding these two amounts together, the total is £15,000,000, and the difference between this sum and the total required to balance the estimated exports only amounts to £6,000,000. Ireland probably imports somewhat more; the particulars I cannot give, except for coal, of which Ireland imports 3,000,000 tons, worth, say, including freight, rather more than £2,000,000. The other articles which Ireland must import, including textiles, would necessarily contain a large amount of raw material. Altogether, it may be doubted whether Ireland is a customer for British labour to the extent of more than a few millions per annum.

When it is considered that even complete separation need not involve loss of trade, and partial separation, by which I mean any tolerably comprehensive scheme of local self-government, would not involve loss of trade at all, except through Ireland falling into anarchy, it cannot be said that the risk to our trade is a very serious element in the question of the loss or gain which the separation of Ireland, and *à fortiori* a mere alteration of the form of the political connection, would involve.

I have been looking at the question exclusively from the British point of view. The view presented, when looked at from an Irish standpoint, is somewhat different. The precise interest of Ireland in the connection requires a little explanation.

1. On the direct Government account, Ireland would probably gain by separation or by a revisal of present arrangements. It would have about £7,000,000 of revenue to dispose of, which it now contributes to the Imperial exchequer, and out of the difference between this sum and the sum of £3,800,000 it gets back from the Imperial Treasury for internal administration, it would have to defray its army and navy, if any, its share of the Imperial debt, and any expenses of that sort. Assuming economy in spending for the purposes on which the £3,800,000 is now spent, Ireland might get on very well, the scale of expenditure all round being lower than in Great Britain. For less than a million a year Ireland could have a very tolerable force to maintain internal order; its share of the imperial debt, proportioning that share to its resources, would not cost more than £1,500,000 per annum; there would remain over £4,000,000 for all the miscellaneous purposes of internal administration, which is more than what is now spent. Ireland would thus gain by the severance; while Great Britain, which loses now, although extracting over three millions more from Ireland than its proper share of taxation, would decidedly gain. Both sides would gain, assuming no political danger to arise, because the present government of Ireland by England involves very serious waste.

2. Ireland would lose indirectly by the withdrawal of English troops. English army expenditure in Ire-

land now recoups a part of the loss inflicted on Ireland by disproportionate taxation.

3. Separation, if it should bring about an interruption of trade between Ireland and Great Britain, would be disastrous to Ireland. The £20,000,000 which Ireland exports find almost their sole market in Great Britain. If more capital is to be invested in Ireland, the capital must come from England. In this respect Great Britain is indispensable to Ireland.

On balance the direct advantages to Ireland from complete or partial separation are apparently so little that they cannot compensate the danger involved in anything like complete separation. Of course in isolation and hostility to Great Britain, Ireland would be lost. It is utterly without resources to maintain such an attitude. On the other hand, the advantage to Ireland of a partial separation, involving a settlement of the direct accounts, and leaving to it all the advantage of forming part of the United Kingdom, would be enormous.

I have thus answered the question with which I started, or nearly so. The conclusion is that Great Britain has not much to lose in dissolving partnership, while Ireland has.

The only point I have left untouched is the question of the indirect political danger in separation and the loss it may involve. This is almost too remote a speculation for such an inquiry as I have been making. It is obvious, however, still keeping strictly to the economic question, that the sum of £2,750,000, the amount of the deficit we now incur on account of Ireland, would go some way towards the expense of extra military and naval preparation which the presence of a hostile Ireland near us might involve. I should like further to ask the question why a State like Ireland beside us, if completely separate, should add sensibly to the dangers we incur from States like Belgium and Holland, which are just about as populous and much richer, and almost equally near. The question is one of military strategy; but, without being dogmatic, I would suggest that the experience of past times, when France tried to use Ireland against us, does not wholly apply. In past times Ireland was useful positively to Great Britain, because of the relative magnitude of its resources in both men and wealth. The loss of it would have been a great loss to Great Britain in the life-and-death struggles in which it was engaged. Further, Ireland hostile might in former times have been a real danger to England for two reasons—the first, its relative magnitude, already referred to; and next, the necessity or convenience, in the days of sailing-ships, of using as the basis of hostile operations against a State which was to be reached by sea a place near to that State, so that a Power like France might have gained something by "enveloping" Great Britain. Now all the circumstances have changed. Ireland is so poor in resources that the loss of it positively would hardly count. Even as a recruiting ground it is no longer required, because a State like Great Britain with 31½ millions of men, not to speak of its colonial reserves, can have as many men for soldiering as its finances can afford out of its own numbers. Negatively also we can keep military possession of Ireland much more easily than was formerly the case; it is an easier task than it was in proportion to our resources; and just because it is easier, it is less worth the while of an opponent to seek to overcome us through Ireland. In these days of steam also a great Power meaning to attack us could do so as easily, or nearly as easily, from Antwerp or Hamburg or Havre, or even Cadiz, as from Dublin or Belfast; to attempt to reach us through Ireland would not be worth while. To guard against accidents, it is prudent and best for both countries that we should keep military hold of Ireland; but it would seem to be conceivable that Ireland, even if disposed to be hostile, would not "count" when separate, if we were only to put forth our strength. If we lose command of the sea, we shall be liable to be assailed directly by a military Power; if we keep the command, Ireland will not count.

There is less need, however, to discuss a point like the last, because there is no question, under any scheme of local self-government or Home Rule that I have seen, of permitting to Irish local authorities an army or a navy. Many of those who are in favour of Home Rule appear to admit as a possibility that the Irish local authorities may attempt illegally and covertly to raise a military force. But the cost of guarding against such a risk, which is the economic aspect of the question, ought not to be very material. Would it conceivably be necessary to keep more troops in Ireland than we now do? I consider myself precluded from fully discussing the latter question. It involves those moral and political considerations from which I have endeavoured to disentangle the economic problem. But it would seem just at least to notice, economically, that Ireland, even if separate, would have overwhelming motives to be on good terms with Great Britain.

I propose to leave the question of the economic value of Ireland to Great Britain at this point. As I have stated at the beginning, and as I have just been repeating, there are moral and political considerations to be taken into account after the economic aspect of the question has been studied. For historical reasons, for the sake of the connection between Ulster specially and Great Britain, for the sake of a minority who have been encouraged to trust to English law administered by an English Parliament, neither separation nor any form of Home Rule for Ireland may be desirable or possible. To discuss all these matters would take me into regions which, for many reasons, even if I desired to do so, I must avoid. I may venture to express the hope, however, that the facts I have stated are of a tendency to mitigate apprehensions which are generally entertained. If Ireland in a business view hardly counts in a question of force against Great Britain, we can afford to arrange its destinies and its relations to Great Britain in any way that may be politically found expedient. Having practically omnipotent power, we should discuss with reasonable coolness how Ireland is to be governed.

I shall only, then, permit myself one or two remarks appearing to verge on politics, because they arise directly out of a consideration of the economic and business aspects of the Irish problem.

The first of these remarks is that all claim of Ireland to be represented in Parliament, if it really contributes nothing material to the strength of the empire when properly taxed, is taken away. At present it is unprofitable to us, because, though it is overtaxed, the circumstances are such that it absorbs the surplus taxation. If it were to be taxed properly, and the present system of government were to continue, it would be still more unprofitable. It appears, then, to be an intolerable anomaly that such a State should be represented in the Imperial Parliament, helping to vote the taxes which another community pays, and meddling in all the affairs of that community. The anomaly might be endurable if the representatives returned happened to be friendly or to be sensible of deriving advantage from the imperial connection. But to admit into the Imperial Parliament representatives of a State which can be no contributory to imperial needs; which could not bear the strain of an imperial emergency; which requires for its own internal administration all the taxable income it can spare, and which, moreover, sends representatives avowedly hostile, with no other mission than to make imperial government impossible, is nothing less than the *reductio ad absurdum* of Parliamentary government. The affairs of an empire like that of England cannot possibly go on upon such conditions. The enormous reduction or absolute extinction of the Irish representation in the Imperial Parliament, with or without terms of Home Rule for Ireland, is a measure on which both parties in Great Britain might justifiably unite.

Another remark I have to make is with reference to a certain scheme which appeared in the "Statist" newspaper, and which became known as "Economist's" plan of settling the Land and Home Rule questions in Ireland. There is no reason why I should not assume responsibility for a suggestion which I was encouraged to ventilate, when I first put it forward in conversation, by official and political friends, although for obvious reasons I am most anxious to keep out of political controversy, and could take no part, either in my own name or anonymously, in the incessant discussions of the last few months. What I should like to point out is that the idea of buying out Irish landlords at the expense of the imperial exchequer, and of handing over a rent-charge to Irish local authorities in lieu of the present imperial payments for the internal administration of Ireland, is closely related to the view of Ireland's economic position which I have set forth in this paper. It is all based on the notion that Ireland is a comparatively small State which has gained a footing in the imperial system of Great Britain to which it is not entitled, and for which, therefore, another system, excluding Irish representatives wholly, or nearly so, from the Imperial Parliament, must be devised. If Irish local authorities can be set up amicably, and with the consent of Ireland's representatives, so much the better; if no such authorities can be set up, then it will be necessary still to exclude hostile Irish representatives from the Imperial Parliament, and set up local authorities of a non-popular kind. As far as I can see, there is no getting out from between the horns of this dilemma. In either case a settlement of the land question seems expedient, in order to give the new authorities a chance, and in order to disentangle the imperial and Irish exchequers. No merely Irish authorities could buy out the landlords, because they would not have credit enough. If the exchequers are not disentangled, the Irish people would have the apparent grievance of being taxed without representation, whereas in some form or other they could be represented in local councils. It is, therefore, expedient at the same time at once to buy out Irish landlords effectively, which can be done by the imperial exchequer, and to give the new local authorities a revenue which they could collect and administer themselves, and which would be the *equivalent* of the contributions to the imperial exchequer they would continue to make under existing taxes, deducting a certain fixed proportion as due from them for the imperial protection. Subject to the condition that the Imperial Parliament imposed no new taxes on Ireland, which it is not worth while doing, there would be no injustice in such an arrangement, and the Irish people could not then say they were taxed without representation. But the existing intolerable anomaly would be got rid of, and Great Britain would cease to be governed in a large degree by a hostile faction coming from a country which contributes nothing to imperial strength.

I desire, likewise, to call special attention to the fact which has come out incidentally that Ireland is overtaxed in comparison with Great Britain. It contributes twice its proper share, if not more, to the imperial exchequer. The taxation in one view is not reprehensible; it is levied in the shape of indirect taxes, mainly on spirits and tobacco. The Irish masses could untax themselves by the simple expedient of consuming less spirits and tobacco. This is the easy view which has often been acted upon when the subject has come up in the Imperial Parliament. Long ago, in 1864, when there was a Committee on Irish Taxation, Mr. Lowe embarrassed an able witness, Mr. E. Senior, a Poor-law Inspector in Ireland and well acquainted with Irish poverty, by putting this very point (see No. 513, Session 1864). But it is not the right view. How much of the expenditure of the Irish people on spirits and tobacco is really wasteful is not certainly known. People who have so little taxable income have at any rate a claim to have the money thus taken from them by the Government applied for their special benefit. At present, nearly the whole taxable income of the Irish people is, in fact, absorbed by the State. The taxable income being about £15,000,000 only, the Imperial Government, as we have seen, takes nearly £7,000,000, and the local taxes are over £3,000,000 more, or about £10,000,000 in all. So large a proportion of taxation to taxable income would be a serious fact for any country, and there can be little accumulation in Ireland under such conditions. Considerations like these, which are so material, have, however, made no impression in the Imperial Parliament hitherto, and that this has been the case is one reason, among many others, why on this side of St. George's Channel we should speak with some modesty of the Imperial Parliament being capable of dealing with Irish affairs. Here is certainly a matter on which, with no intention to be unjust, with an apparent willingness to be more than fair to Ireland, as is shown by the exemption of Ireland specially from certain taxes, we have nevertheless acted unjustly and to the injury of Ireland. I may commend Mr. Senior's evidence on this head, in the Blue Book of 1864 already referred to, to those who care to study the subject. Surely the whole blunder clearly suggests the expediency of devising some form of government for Ireland, under which the special needs and circumstances of the country and people would receive more and better attention than they do under present arrangements, although the attention which they do get disturbs and disorganizes the management of Imperial affairs themselves.

[This essay was originally prepared for a discussion at the Political Economy Club early in 1886, when the agitation about Home Rule was at its height. At this distance of time I may be allowed to explain, what I could hardly have said at the time, owing to my position in the Civil Service, that I was not, and have never been, a Home Ruler in the sense of favouring a *separate* Parliament and executive for Ireland. The question of the relative overtaxation of Ireland has since been much discussed, and formed the subject of inquiry by a Royal Commission presided over by Mr. Childers, before which I gave evidence as to the resources of Ireland, though not as to taxation, which was officially done by Treasury experts. The subject of late years has lost its practical interest, in consequence of Government grants to compensate for Irish overtaxation, which have been accepted by Irish representatives as such compensation. This arrangement for meeting the grievance does not commend itself to me, and I opposed it in my evidence to Mr. Childers's Commission; but the matter is obviously in a different position from what it was when this paper was written.]

END OF VOL. I.

CHISWICK PRESS: PRINTED BY CHARLES WHITTINGHAM AND CO.
TOOKS COURT, CHANCERY LANE, LONDON.